CONTENTS

Editor
Guy Thomas
guy.thomas@dhpub.co.uk

Consultant Editor
Richard West

Art Director
Julie Bentley

Advertisement Manager
Jay Jones
jay.jones@dhpub.co.uk

Advertisement Production
Nik Harber

Publishers
David Hall Publishing Ltd,
Nene House, Sopwith Way,
Daventry, Northamptonshire
NN11 8AE.

Copyright David Hall Publishing
Ltd. Published in 2023

This guide is produced by
the team which brings you
Stamp Magazine

www.stampmagazine.co.uk

REFERENCE
How to use this book 5
Guide to printers 6
Guide to watermarks 7

MARKET PRICES
Queen Victoria issues (1840–1901) 11
King Edward VII issues (1901–1911) 22
King George V issues (1911–1936) 24
King Edward VIII issues (1936) 28
King George VI issues (1937–51) 29
Queen Elizabeth II pre-decimal (1952–1970) 32
Queen Elizabeth II Machins (1967–2022) 48
Queen Elizabeth II decimal (1971–2023) 80
King Charles III issues (2023) 234
Regional issues (1948–71) 238
Country definitives (1958–2022) 240
Stitched or stapled booklets (1904–1976) 258
Folded booklets (1976–2000) 266
Retail booklets (1987–2000) 276
Self-adhesive booklets (1993–2023) 282
Christmas booklets (1978–2023) 290
Greetings booklets (1989–1998) 293
Prestige stamp books (1969–2023) 294
Business sheets (1998–2023) 306
Officials (1840–1904) 308
Postage dues (1914–94) 310
Post & Go stamps (2008–2023) 314
Frama labels (1984–1985) 325
Smilers and collector's sheets (2000–2023) 326
Commemorative sheets (2008–2018) 334
Presentation packs (1960–2023) 338
Yearbooks and year packs (1967–2023) 351

THE PURPOSE OF THIS BOOK
The objective of this guide is to give collectors accurate market values of Great Britain stamps: the selling prices of most dealers, as opposed to the inflated prices quoted by some catalogues. The publisher of *British Stamp Market Values* is not a dealer and is not affiliated to any dealer.

BRITISH STAMP MARKET VALUES 2024 3

Alliance
AUCTIONS

PO BOX 12305 BISHOPS STORTFORD HERTS CM23 9 JW
☎ 01279 758854 • info @allianceauctions.com

Regular monthly auctions postal and online with easylive You can bid for a flat £3 with them or send bids direct to us free Up to a 1000 or so lots of world stamps, covers, box lots etc also a few coins and postcards

Vendors lots gladly accepted at commission of just 12%

John Auld

TRUSTED FOR OVER FORTY YEARS

HOW TO USE THIS BOOK

The prices we quote and the abbreviations we use

This guide offers independent price information about all Great Britain stamps issued from 1840 to date, based on the typical selling prices of reliable dealers rather than on the prices quoted in most reference catalogues.

The publisher of *British Stamp Market Values* is not affiliated to any dealer, but we consult a number of specialist dealers and collectors when deliberating over prices.

ABBREVIATIONS
The following abbreviations are used throughout this guide:
Des: designer
Perf: perforation
Wmk: watermark

PRICES
■ Prices may be quoted in one, two or three columns; the meaning of each column is stated at the beginning of the section.

■ Used prices quoted are for fine examples with full perforations or reasonable margins as applicable, and with either a light duplex cancellation (pre-1880) or a clear steel datestamp (post-1880).

■ Unused prices assume stamps are se-tenant, in cases where they were available as such.

■ As modern special issues are usually sold only in complete sets, prices might not be quoted for individual stamps.

EXPERTS WE CONSULTED OVER PRICING

BB STAMPS
PO Box 6267, Newbury, Berkshire, RG14 9NZ
Run by Brian Bayford, BB Stamps deals in GB stamps from Queen Victoria to Wildings.

MARK BLOXHAM
PO Box 204, Morpeth NE61 9AA
Mark Bloxham is a specialist in classic British stamps at the top end of the market.

DAUWALDERS
42 Fisherton Street, Salisbury, Wiltshire SP2 7RB
Run by Paul Dauwalder, this firm has been a leading GB and Commonwealth dealer since 1958.

IAN HARVEY
Member of the RPSL Expert Committee
Ian Harvey is a specialist collector of booklets from Edward VII to Elizabeth II.

RICHARD WEST
Stamp Magazine editor-at-large
Richard West is a Past President of the National Philatelic Society.

SIMON HEELEY
PO Box 7352, Kingswinford, West Midlands DY6 6AZ
Simon Heeley is an experienced dealer in modern GB and a specialist in Machin definitives.

STAMP PRINTERS

A brief guide to who printed what, and when

A relatively small number of security printers has dominated the production of British stamps since 1840. Here are their details.

PERKINS BACON 1840–1879
American inventor Jacob Perkins developed intaglio printing, and his son-in-law Joshua Bacon joined him in business in London.
First issue: 1840 1d black
Last issue: 1870–79 1½d rose-red

SOMERSET HOUSE 1847–1926
The Stamp Office at Somerset House in London had been printing revenue stamps since 1694, and was familiar with embossing technique required for the first high-value postage stamps.
First issue: 1847–54 1/- green
Last issue: 1924–26 definitive series

DE LA RUE 1855 to date
Guernseyman Thomas De La Rue came to prominence by offering surface-printing, which was ideal for stamps requiring perforation.
First issue: 1855–57 4d carmine

HARRISON & SONS 1911–1998
After initially printing by typography, this firm became synonymous with the photogravure technique from 1934 and remained the dominant printer of British stamps for many years. It was taken over by De La Rue in 1997.
First issue: 1911–13 definitive series
Last issue: 1998 The Queen's Beasts set

WATERLOW & SONS 1913–1955
There were two different Waterlow firms until 1920, after a family feud. The business was taken over by De La Rue in 1960.
First issue: 1913 'Seahorses' high-value series
Last issue: 1955 'Castles' high-value series

BRADBURY WILKINSON 1918–1973
A producer of colonial stamps since 1875, this firm was owned by the American Banknote Company from 1903 and was acquired by De La Rue in 1986.
First issue: 1918–19 'Seahorses' high-value series
Last issue: 1973 Parliamentary Conference set

ENSCHEDÉ 1979 to date
The Dutch company founded in 1703 became a back-up for Harrisons because of its capability of printing by photogravure.
First issue: 1979 8p red definitive

WADDINGTONS 1980–1981
This firm produced stamps under its own name only briefly, before acquiring House of Questa.
First issue: 1980 4p greenish-blue definitive
Last issue: 1981 4p and 20p definitives

HOUSE OF QUESTA 1980–2003
Initially independent, the company was owned by Waddingtons from 1984, MDC from 1996 and De La Rue from 2002.
First issue: 1980 75p black definitive
Last issue: 2003 Extreme Endeavours set

WALSALL/ISP 1989 to date
The company initially promoted itself as an expert in self-adhesive printing, but has also printed gummed issues by litho and gravure. Stamps were produced under the International Security Printers name from 2013.
First issue: 1989 14p and 19p definitives (booklet)

CARTOR/ISP 2005 to date
This French company known for litho production and special printing techniques has been part of the Walsall/ISP group since 2004, and the entire group took its name in 2022.
First issue: 2004 customised Smilers sheets

WATERMARKS

GUIDE TO WATERMARKS

Identify the watermarks referred to in the price listings

Watermarked paper was used to print most British stamps from 1840 until the later 1960s, as a security measure to make forgery difficult

BRITISH STAMP MARKET VALUES 2024 **7**

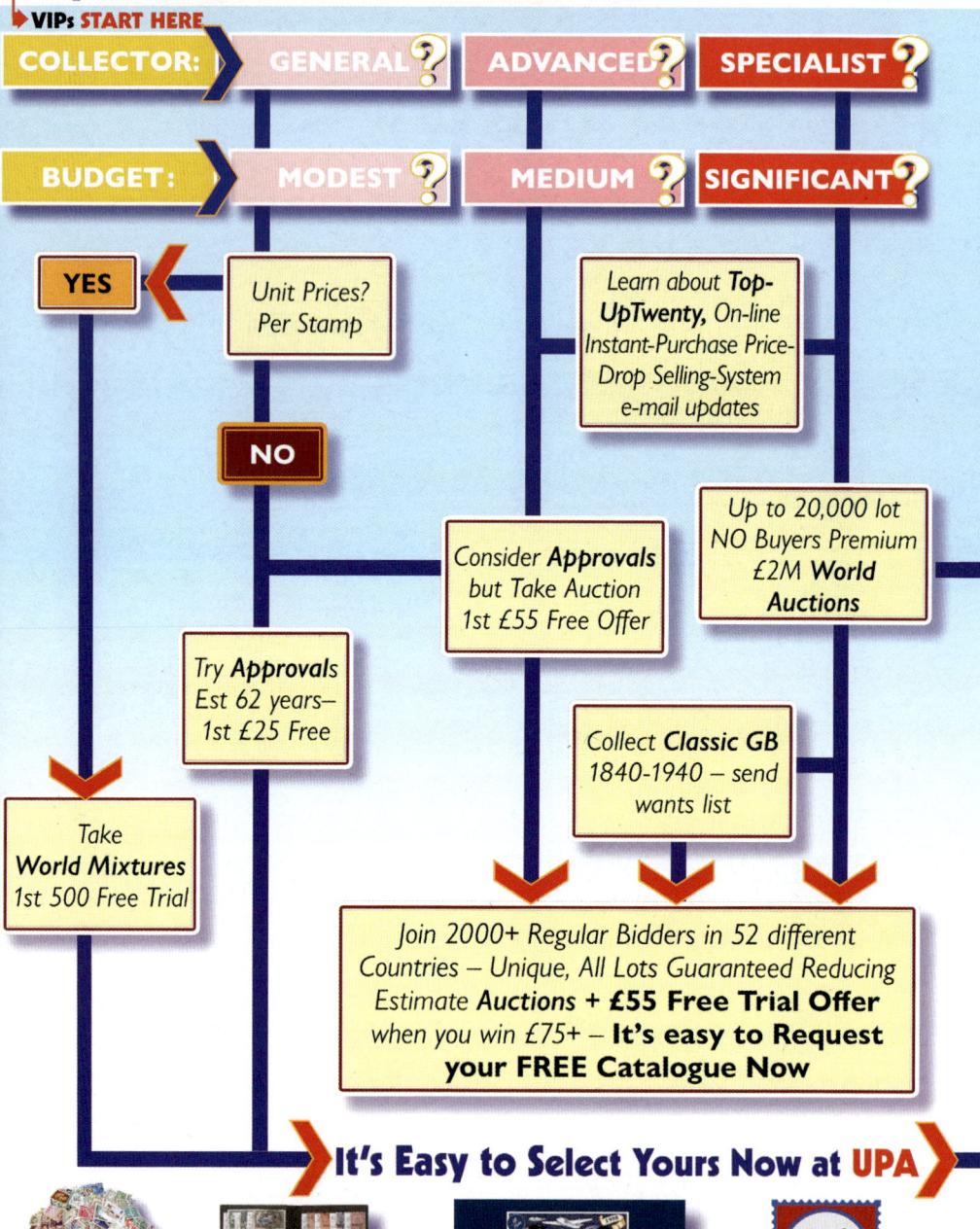

Sometimes Collectors Get a Raw Deal
Determine how You wish to be treated Here ...

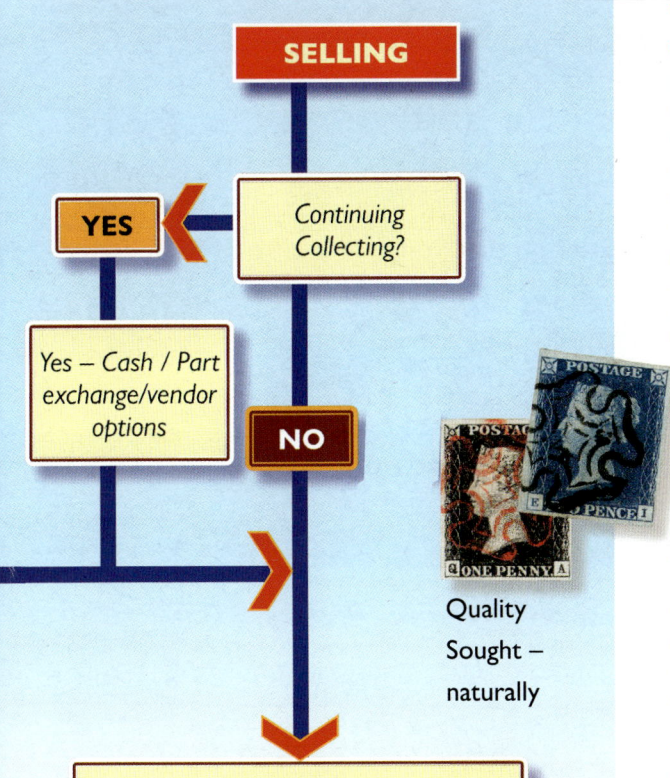

'money spent in the wrong way soon mounts up ...'

Successful and enjoyable collecting depends upon understanding the relationship of your budget to your interest.

Offers and services can be confusing can't they, and money spent in the wrong way soon mounts up.

In philately, sometimes it is hard to decide which way to go. Your passion may exceed your resource, so just what may be best for you?

Often, it is not what you collect but how you collect

This is the reason why my team and I have devised this quick and easy philatelic route-map QUIZ which does not ask you what you collect – but helps you to determine by your answers just which type of collecting service may best suit you ...

Presently you may find few philatelic companies other than UPA which can offer you integrated philatelic selling systems, but obviously once you determine which philatelic services best suit your collecting interest – you may have a clearer idea of which way is best to go – depending upon your levels of specialism and philatelic budget, of course

Check out our Philatelic QUIZ right now and see for yourself. To select your choice, visit our website or call my team

Dedicated to De-mystifying Philately

Andrew McGavin,
Veteran Philatelic Auctioneer
Philatelic Expert & Author
Managing Director Universal Philatelic Auctions (UPA)

Visit: www.UPAstampauctions.co.uk

Fax: 01451 861297 ~ info@upastampauctions.co.uk ~ T: 01451 861111
Participate in this Philatelic Route-Map to Enjoyable Collecting.
Find UPA also on-line at www.top-uptwenty.co.uk
New Instant-Purchase Price-Drop Selling-System

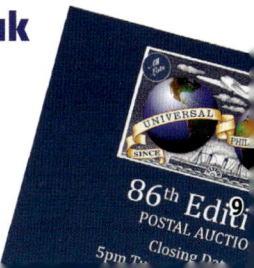

If you share our interest or are considering collecting GB Used Abroad you will benefit from our list which also includes rare items

PHONE, WRITE OR EMAIL TODAY...

ERIC PAUL LTD
P.O. BOX 44 MARPLE CHESHIRE ENGLAND SK6 7EE

TEL: +44(0)161 427 2101 FAX: +44(0)161 427 6386
EMAIL : info@ericpaul.co.uk   WEB SITE : www.ericpaul.co.uk

Members: PTS   M&DPTA   GBPS   ADPS

The directors have asked us to point out that the images in this advert bear no resemblance to them... yet!

QUEEN VICTORIA

QUEEN VICTORIA

For this reign prices are given for lightly mounted unused (left) and fine used (right). The exception is for the 1840–1841 issues, where fine used prices are subdivided into stamps with four margins (centre) and three margins (right).

Take care when buying unmounted mint because there are known cases of regumming.

LINE–ENGRAVED ISSUES

1d black

2d blue

■ **1840, May 8. Twopenny Blue**
Engraved by Charles and Frederick Heath. Printed in recess by Perkins, Bacon. Wmk: Small Crown. Imperforate. Letters in lower corners only.

2d blue	£32,000	£550	£140
2d deep full blue	£36,000	£650	£170
2d pale blue	£36,000	£600	£150
Plate 1	£30,000	£550	£140
Plate 2	£40,000	£650	£170
Wmk Inverted	£60,000	£5,000	£2,800
Red Maltese cross cancel (Plate 1)	–	£600	£150
Red Maltese cross cancel (Plate 2)	–	£1,100	£225
Black Maltese cross cancel	–	£550	£140
Blue Maltese cross cancel	–	£6,000	£1,250
Magenta Maltese cross cancel	–	£4,000	£850
Ruby Maltese cross cancel	–	£2,000	£500
Number in cross (1–12)	–	£11,000	£3,000
Penny Post cancel only	–	£5,000	£1,200
Town datestamp only	–	£3,750	£800
1844 cancel	–	£1,250	£250

■ **1840, May 6. Penny Black**
Engraved by Charles and Frederick Heath. Printed in recess by Perkins, Bacon. Wmk: Small Crown. Imperforate. Letters in lower corners only.

1d black	£11,000	£250	78.00
1d intense black	£15,000	£275	90.00
1d grey black	£14,000	£275	90.00
Plate 1a	£14,000	£300	90.00
Plate 1b	£11,000	£225	80.00
Plate 2	£11,000	£225	80.00
Plate 3	£14,000	£250	85.00
Plate 4	£11,000	£225	80.00
Plate 5	£11,000	£225	80.00
Plate 6	£11,000	£225	80.00
Plate 7	£12,000	£275	90.00
Plate 8	£14,000	£300	95.00
Plate 9	£14,000	£350	£125
Plate 10	£24,000	£600	£175
Plate 11	£16,000	£4,000	£750
Wmk inverted	£32,000	£2,200	£600
Bleute paper	£15,000	£500	£150
Red Maltese cross cancel	–	£250	90.00
Black Maltese cross cancel	–	£225	78.00
Blue Maltese cross cancel	–	£8,000	£2,000
Magenta Maltese cross cancel	–	£2,200	£400
Ruby Maltese cross cancel	–	£750	£225
Violet Maltese cross cancel	–	£12,000	£3,000
Number in cross (1–12)	–	£10,000	£3,000
Penny Post cancel only	–	£2,600	£600
Town datestamp only	–	£2,750	£600
1844 cancel	–	£1,000	£200

1d red

■ **1841, February 10. Penny Red**
Engraved by Charles and Frederick Heath. Printed in recess by Perkins, Bacon. Wmk: Small Crown. Imperforate. Letters in lower corners only.

1d red brown	£300	10.00	3.00
1d deep red brown	£550	15.00	4.00
1d orange brown	£1,200	£120	12.00
1d lake red	£3,500	£550	£100

BRITISH STAMP MARKET VALUES 2024

QUEEN VICTORIA

Plate 1b	£18,000	£300	40.00
Plate 2	£19,000	£225	25.00
Plate 5	£6,000	£175	20.00
Plate 8	£8,000	90.00	20.00
Plate 9	£4,000	90.00	20.00
Plate 10	£2,000	90.00	20.00
Plate 11	£4,000	75.00	15.00
Wmk inverted	£4,000	£325	£150
Lavender paper	£1,000	£150	40.00
Red Maltese cross cancellation	–	£3,850	£875
Black Maltese cross cancellation	–	40.00	6.00
Blue Maltese cross cancellation	–	£375	75.00
Green Maltese cross cancellation	–	£8,000	£1,000
Violet Maltese cross cancellation	–	£9,000	£1,500
Number in cross (1–12)	–	£110	30.00
Penny Post cancellation only	–	£700	£125
Black town datestamp only	–	£300	95.00
Blue town datestamp only	–	£1,200	£275
Green town datestamp only	–	£2,750	£650
Black 1844 cancellation	–	9.00	3.00
Blue 1844 cancellation	–	£125	25.00
Green 1844 cancellation	–	£1,250	£250
Red 1844 cancellation	–	£12,000	£3,000
Violet 1844 cancellation	–	£2,500	£600
B blank error	–	£40,000	£18,000

1d rose-red

2d blue

■ 1854
Designs as above. Wmk: Small Crown. Perf: 16.
1d red-brown (February 1854)	£250	12.00
2d blue (March 1, 1854)	£2,200	60.00

■ 1855
Designs as above. Wmk: Small Crown. Perf: 14.
1d red-brown (January 1855)	£450	45.00
2d blue (March 4, 1855)	£7,000	£160

■ 1855
Designs as above. Wmk: Large Crown. Perf: 16.
1d red-brown (May 15, 1855)	£900	65.00
2d blue (July 20, 1855)	£10,000	£230

■ 1855
Designs as above. Wmk: Large Crown. Perf: 14.
1d red-brown (August 18, 1855)	£160	8.00
2d blue (July 20, 1855)	£1,600	30.00

2d blue

■ 1841, March 13. Twopenny Blue
Engraved by Charles and Frederick Heath. Printed in recess by Perkins, Bacon. Wmk: Small Crown. Imperforate. Letters in lower corners only. Horizontal white lines added to design.

2d blue	£3,000	50.00	12.00
2d pale blue	£3,200	55.00	12.00
2d deep full blue	£4,000	70.00	15.00
2d violet (lavender paper)	£22,000	£950	£175
Plate 3	£3,000	60.00	12.00
Plate 4	£3,500	50.00	12.00
Wmk inverted	£7,500	£450	£125
Black Maltese cross cancel	–	£150	22.50
Blue Maltese cross cancel	–	£3,000	£400
Number in cross (1–12)	–	£500	£120
Black town datestamp only	–	£1,000	£275
Blue town datestamp only	–	£4,000	£700
Black 1844 cancel	–	50.00	12.00
Blue 1844 cancel	–	£500	£100
Green 1844 cancel	–	£3,500	£750
Red 1844 cancel	–	£17,500	£3,500

1d rose-red

2d blue

■ 1858–1879
Designs as above. Wmk: Large Crown. Perf: 14. Letters in all four corners. Plate number included in design.
1d rose-red (April 1, 1864)

Plate 71	40.00	2.00
Plate 72	40.00	2.50
Plate 73	40.00	2.00
Plate 74	40.00	1.50
Plate 76	40.00	1.50
Plate 77	–	–
Plate 78	45.00	1.50
Plate 79	25.00	1.50
Plate 80	30.00	1.50
Plate 81	35.00	1.50

QUEEN VICTORIA

Plate 82	£110	2.75	Plate 144	75.00	16.00
Plate 83	£160	6.00	Plate 145	23.00	1.75
Plate 84	40.00	1.60	Plate 146	25.00	4.50
Plate 85	27.00	1.60	Plate 147	30.00	2.00
Plate 86	35.00	2.75	Plate 148	25.00	2.00
Plate 87	22.00	1.50	Plate 149	25.00	4.50
Plate 88	£200	7.00	Plate 150	15.00	1.50
Plate 89	30.00	1.50	Plate 151	40.00	7.50
Plate 90	25.00	1.50	Plate 152	40.00	4.00
Plate 91	35.00	4.50	Plate 153	90.00	7.00
Plate 92	21.00	1.50	Plate 154	30.00	1.50
Plate 93	30.00	1.50	Plate 155	30.00	1.75
Plate 94	28.00	4.00	Plate 156	35.00	1.50
Plate 95	25.00	1.50	Plate 157	30.00	1.50
Plate 96	28.00	1.50	Plate 158	23.00	1.50
Plate 97	25.00	2.50	Plate 159	23.00	1.50
Plate 98	30.00	4.50	Plate 160	23.00	1.50
Plate 99	35.00	4.00	Plate 161	40.00	5.00
Plate 100	40.00	1.50	Plate 162	30.00	5.00
Plate 101	40.00	7.50	Plate 163	30.00	2.00
Plate 102	28.00	1.50	Plate 164	30.00	2.00
Plate 103	30.00	2.75	Plate 165	35.00	1.50
Plate 104	£100	4.00	Plate 166	35.00	4.50
Plate 105	£120	5.50	Plate 167	35.00	1.50
Plate 106	35.00	1.50	Plate 168	30.00	6.00
Plate 107	45.00	5.00	Plate 169	30.00	6.00
Plate 108	70.00	1.75	Plate 170	21.00	1.50
Plate 109	65.00	2.50	Plate 171	15.00	1.50
Plate 110	40.00	7.50	Plate 172	23.00	1.50
Plate 111	36.00	1.75	Plate 173	48.00	6.50
Plate 112	50.00	1.70	Plate 174	23.00	1.50
Plate 113	30.00	9.00	Plate 175	40.00	2.50
Plate 114	£240	9.00	Plate 176	40.00	1.75
Plate 115	85.00	1.75	Plate 177	32.00	1.50
Plate 116	60.00	7.50	Plate 178	40.00	2.50
Plate 117	28.00	1.50	Plate 179	30.00	1.75
Plate 118	30.00	1.50	Plate 180	40.00	4.00
Plate 119	28.00	1.50	Plate 181	36.00	1.50
Plate 120	15.00	1.50	Plate 182	75.00	4.00
Plate 121	25.00	8.00	Plate 183	35.00	2.00
Plate 122	15.00	1.50	Plate 184	23.00	1.75
Plate 123	25.00	1.50	Plate 185	30.00	2.00
Plate 124	22.00	1.50	Plate 186	35.00	1.75
Plate 125	25.00	1.50	Plate 187	30.00	1.50
Plate 127	35.00	1.75	Plate 188	50.00	7.50
Plate 129	25.00	6.50	Plate 189	50.00	5.50
Plate 130	35.00	1.75	Plate 190	30.00	4.50
Plate 131	45.00	12.00	Plate 191	23.00	5.50
Plate 132	£300	18.00	Plate 192	30.00	1.50
Plate 133	£105	7.50	Plate 193	23.00	1.50
Plate 134	18.00	1.50	Plate 194	30.00	6.50
Plate 135	70.00	22.00	Plate 195	30.00	6.50
Plate 136	65.00	17.00	Plate 196	30.00	4.00
Plate 137	22.00	1.75	Plate 197	35.00	7.00
Plate 138	15.00	1.50	Plate 198	32.00	4.50
Plate 139	40.00	12.50	Plate 199	35.00	4.50
Plate 140	16.00	1.50	Plate 200	40.00	2.00
Plate 141	£100	7.00	Plate 201	23.00	4.00
Plate 142	50.00	22.00	Plate 202	40.00	6.50
Plate 143	40.00	12.00	Plate 203	23.00	13.00

BRITISH STAMP MARKET VALUES 2024

QUEEN VICTORIA

Plate 204	35.00	1.75
Plate 205	35.00	2.25
Plate 206	35.00	7.00
Plate 207	40.00	7.00
Plate 208	35.00	12.50
Plate 209	30.00	8.00
Plate 210	45.00	10.00
Plate 211	50.00	18.00
Plate 212	40.00	10.00
Plate 213	40.00	10.00
Plate 214	45.00	15.00
Plate 215	45.00	15.00
Plate 216	50.00	15.00
Plate 217	50.00	6.00
Plate 218	45.00	7.00
Plate 219	£100	58.00
Plate 220	32.00	6.00
Plate 221	50.00	15.00
Plate 222	60.00	30.00
Plate 223	75.00	50.00
Plate 224	£110	45.00
Plate 225	£2,900	£650
2d blue (July 1858)		
Plate 7	£1,200	40.00
Plate 8	£1,200	25.00
Plate 9	£250	8.00
Plate 12	£1,800	£100
Plate 13	£260	15.00
Plate 14	£340	16.00
Plate 15	£320	16.00

½d rose-red (October 1, 1870)		
Plate 1	£180	50.00
Plate 3	£120	25.00
Plate 4	£100	18.00
Plate 5	75.00	10.00
Plate 6	80.00	10.00
Plate 8	£225	60.00
Plate 9	£5,000	£600
Plate 10	85.00	10.00
Plate 11	80.00	10.00
Plate 12	80.00	10.00
Plate 13	80.00	10.00
Plate 14	80.00	10.00
Plate 15	£115	24.00
Plate 19	£140	28.00
Plate 20	£200	50.00
1½d rose-red (October 1, 1870)		
Plate 1	£450	48.00
Plate 3	£275	32.00

EMBOSSED ISSUES

½d rose-red

1½d rose-red

6d lilac

10d brown

1/- green

■ 1847–1854. High values
Die engraved at the Royal Mint by William Wyon. Printed using the embossed process at Somerset House. Wmk: VR (6d), or unwatermarked (10d, 1/–). Imperforate.

6d lilac (March 1, 1854)	£17,000	£525
10d brown (November 6, 1848)	£8,500	£775
1/– green (September 11, 1847)	£20,000	£550

(*These stamps are priced cut square; examples cut to shape are worth considerably less.)

■ 1870–1879
Printed in recess by Perkins, Bacon. Wmk: Half Penny extending over three stamps (½d) or Large Crown (1½d). Perf: 14. Letters in all four corners. Plate number included in design, except plate 1 of the 1½d value.

Great Britain
1840 – 1952

Fine Stamps and Postal History

Visit our website to view hundreds of fine GB items:

www.andrewglajer.co.uk

Andrew G Lajer Ltd
sales@andrewglajer.co.uk / T: +44 (0) 1189 344151
The Old Post Office, Davis Way, Hurst, Reading, Berkshire, RG10 0TR

QUEEN VICTORIA

SURFACE-PRINTED ISSUES

Most issues from 1862–64 to 1880–83 have the plate number incorporated into their design. Many can be found with wing margins, where the vertical gutters between panes were perforated by way of a single row of holes down the centre.

■ 1856
Surface-printed by De La Rue. Wmk: Emblems. Perf: 14. No corner letters.

6d lilac (October 21, 1856)	£775	68.00
1/– green (November 1, 1856)	£2,200	£160

4d carmine

3d carmine

4d red

■ 1855–1857
Surface-printed by De La Rue. Wmk: Small Garter (1855), Medium Garter (1856) or Large Garter (1857). Perf: 14. No corner letters.

4d carmine (July 31, 1855)	£8,000	£275
4d carmine (February 25, 1856)	£9,000	£325
4d rose (January, 1857)	£1,600	55.00

6d lilac

6d lilac

9d bistre

1/– green

1/– green

■ 1862–1864
Surface-printed by De La Rue. Wmk: Large Garter (4d), Emblems (3d, 6d, 9d, 1/–). Perf: 14. Small corner letters.

3d carmine (May 1, 1862)	£1,800	£225
4d red (January 15, 1862)	£875	55.00
6d lilac (December 1, 1862)	£1,600	50.00
9d bistre (January 15, 1862)	£4,000	£280
1/– green (December 1, 1862)	£2,200	£150

16 BRITISH STAMP MARKET VALUES 2024

QUEEN VICTORIA

3d carmine   4d vermilion   6d lilac (without hyphen)   2/- blue

6d lilac (with hyphen)   9d bistre

10d brown   1/- green

■ 1865–1867
Surface-printed by De La Rue. Wmk: Large Garter (4d) or Emblems (3d, 6d, 9d, 10d, 1/-). Perf: 14. Large corner letters.

3d carmine (March 1, 1865)
Plate 4	£1,000	£125

4d vermilion (July 4, 1865)
Plate 7	£500	65.00
Plate 8	£400	40.00
Plate 9	£400	40.00
Plate 10	£475	85.00
Plate 11	£400	40.00
Plate 12	£400	40.00
Plate 13	£400	40.00
Plate 14	£440	60.00

6d lilac (April 1, 1865)
Plate 5	£650	55.00
Plate 6	£2,200	£100

9d bistre (December 1, 1865)
Plate 4	£4,000	£360

10d brown (November 11, 1867)
Plate 1	–	£55,000

1/- green (February 1, 1865)
Plate 4	£2,000	£125

(*Mint examples of the 9d exist from a perforated imprimatur sheet from plate 5.)

■ 1867–1880
Surface-printed by De La Rue. Perf: 14. Wmk: Spray of Rose. Designs as above except 6d and 2/-.

3d red (July 12, 1867)
Plate 4	£1,100	£125
Plate 5	£375	35.00
Plate 6	£400	35.00
Plate 7	£500	35.00
Plate 8	£400	35.00
Plate 9	£400	35.00
Plate 10	£550	75.00

6d lilac (June 21, 1867)
Plate 6, with hyphen	£1,400	55.00
Plate 8, without hyphen	£600	55.00
Plate 9, without hyphen	£500	55.00
Plate 10, without hyphen	–	£32,000

9d bistre (October 3, 1867)
Plate 4	£1,300	£200

10d brown (July 1, 1867)
Plate 1	£1,900	£225
Plate 2	£50,000	£16,000

1/- green (July 13, 1867)
Plate 4	£675	40.00
Plate 5	£500	25.00
Plate 6	£700	25.00
Plate 7	£750	45.00

2/- blue (July 1, 1867)
Plate 1	£2,100	£140

2/- brown (February 27, 1880)
Plate 1	£27,000	£4,000

6d grey

■ 1872–1873
Surface-printed by De La Rue. Perf: 14. Wmk: Spray of Rose.

6d brown (April 12, 1872)
Plate 11	£450	35.00
Plate 12	£2,400	£160

6d grey (April 24, 1873)
Plate 12	£1,100	£130

BRITISH STAMP MARKET VALUES 2024

QUEEN VICTORIA

5/– red

10/– grey–green

2½d mauve

3d red

£1 brown

4d green

6d grey

8d orange

1/– green

£5 orange

3d on 3d lilac

6d on 6d lilac

■ **1867–1883. High values**
Surface-printed by De La Rue.

Wmk: Maltese Cross. Perf: 15
5/– red (July 1, 1867)
Plate 1	£4,500	£450
Plate 2	£7,000	£550

10/– grey-green (September 26, 1878)
Plate 1	£45,000	£2,500

£1 brown (September 26, 1878)
Plate 1	£70,000	£4,000

Wmk: Large Anchor. Perf: 14
5/– red (November 25, 1882)
Plate 4	£25,000	£1,950

10/– grey-green (February, 1883)
Plate 1	£100,000	£4,000

£1 brown (December, 1882)
Plate 1	£120,000	£6,500

£5 orange (March 21, 1882)
Plate 1	£12,000	£4,500

■ **1873–1883**
Surface-printed by De La Rue. Perf: 14.

Wmk: Small Anchor
2½d mauve (July 1, 1875)
Plate 1	£385	55.00
Plate 2	£385	55.00
Plate 3	£600	80.00

Wmk: Orb
2½d mauve (May 16, 1876)
Plate 3	£750	75.00
Plate 4	£350	35.00
Plate 5	£350	35.00

QUEEN VICTORIA

Plate 6	£350	35.00
Plate 7	£350	35.00
Plate 8	£350	35.00
Plate 9	£350	35.00
Plate 10	£375	40.00
Plate 11	£350	35.00
Plate 12	£350	35.00
Plate 13	£350	35.00
Plate 14	£350	35.00
Plate 15	£350	35.00
Plate 16	£350	35.00
Plate 17	£1,050	£190

2½d blue (February 5, 1880)

Plate 17	£325	40.00
Plate 18	£350	22.50
Plate 19	£325	22.50
Plate 20	£350	22.50

Wmk: Spray of Rose
3d red (July 5, 1873)

Plate 11	£300	30.00
Plate 12	£325	30.00
Plate 14	£375	30.00
Plate 15	£300	30.00
Plate 16	£300	30.00
Plate 17	£325	30.00
Plate 18	£325	30.00
Plate 19	£300	30.00
Plate 20	£300	55.00

6d buff (March 15, 1873)

Plate 13	–	£22,000

6d grey (March 31, 1874)

Plate 13	£300	40.00
Plate 14	£300	40.00
Plate 15	£300	40.00
Plate 16	£300	40.00
Plate 17	£525	90.00

1/– green (September 1, 1873)

Plate 8	£700	80.00
Plate 9	£700	80.00
Plate 10	£700	90.00
Plate 11	£700	80.00
Plate 12	£475	65.00
Plate 13	£475	65.00
Plate 14	–	£28,000

1/– brown (October 14, 1880)

Plate 13	£4,000	£400

Wmk: Large Garter
4d vermilion (March 1, 1876)

Plate 15	£2,000	£300
Plate 16	–	£24,000

4d green (March 12, 1877)

Plate 15	£825	£180
Plate 16	£775	£170
Plate 17	–	£14,000

4d brown (August 15, 1880)

Plate 17	£2,250	£325

8d orange (September 11, 1876)

Plate 1	£900	£175

Wmk: Imperial Crown
2½d blue (March 23, 1881)

Plate 21	£350	18.00
Plate 22	£325	18.00
Plate 23	£325	14.00

3d red (February 1881)

Plate 20	£500	90.00
Plate 21	£380	55.00

3d (in red) **on 3d** lilac (January 1, 1883)

Plate 21	£400	80.00

4d brown (December 9, 1880)

Plate 17	£300	38.00
Plate 18	£300	38.00

6d grey (January 1, 1881)

Plate 17	£350	45.00
Plate 18	£310	45.00

6d (in red) **on 6d** lilac (January 1, 1883)

Plate 18	£425	80.00

1/– brown (May 29, 1881)

Plate 13	£525	90.00
Plate 14	£425	90.00

½d green

1d Venetian red

1½d Venetian red

2d red

5d indigo

■ **1880–1881**
Surface-printed by De La Rue. Perf: 14. Wmk: Imperial Crown.

½d green (October 14, 1880)	35.00	6.00
1d Venetian red (January 1, 1880)	18.00	3.00
1½d Venetian red (October 14, 1880)	£140	30.00
2d red (December 8, 1880)	£180	60.00
5d indigo (March 15, 1881)	£600	65.00

QUEEN VICTORIA

1d lilac

■ 1881–1901
Surface-printed by De La Rue. Perf: 14. Wmk: Imperial Crown.

Die I. 14 white dots in each corner
1d lilac (July 12, 1881)   £200   15.00

Die II. 16 white dots in each corner
1d lilac (December 12, 1881)   1.75   0.75

2/6 lilac   5/- red

10/- blue

£1 green

■ 1883–1891. High values
Surface-printed by De La Rue. Perf: 14.

Wmk: Large Anchor
2/6 lilac (July 2, 1883)   £350   70.00
5/- red (April 1, 1884)   £700   £110
10/- blue (April 1, 1884)   £1,800   £300

Wmk: Imperial Crown
£1 brown (April 1, 1884)   £26,000   £2,500
£1 green (January 27, 1891)   £3,000   £700

Wmk: Orb
£1 brown (February 1, 1888)   £55,000   £4,000

½d blue   1½d lilac, 5d green

3d lilac, 1/- green   4d green

6d green, 2d lilac   9d green, 2½d lilac

■ 1883–84. 'Lilac & Green' series
Surface-printed by De La Rue. Perf: 14. Wmk: Imperial Crown (sideways on 2d, 2½d, 6d, 9d).

½d blue (April 1, 1884)	14.00	3.50
1½d lilac (April 1, 1884)	80.00	23.00
2d lilac (April 1, 1884)	£140	40.00
2½d lilac (April 1, 1884)	57.50	5.00
3d lilac (April 1, 1884)	£135	38.00
4d green (April 1, 1884)	£325	£100
5d green (April 1, 1884)	£325	£100
6d green (April 1, 1884)	£300	£110
9d green (August 1, 1883)	£725	£300
1/- green (April 1, 1884)	£775	£150

QUEEN VICTORIA

½d orange

1½d purple and green

6d purple on red

9d violet and blue

2d green and red

2½d purple on blue

10d purple and red

1/– green

3d purple on yellow

4d green and brown

4½d green and red

5d purple and blue

■ **1887–92. 'Jubilee' series**
Surface-printed by De La Rue. Perf: 14. Wmk: Imperial Crown.

Wmk upright

½d orange (January 1, 1887)	1.20	0.50
½d green (April 17, 1900)	1.40	0.60
1½d purple and green (January 1, 1887)	10.00	2.00
2d green and red (January 1, 1887)	18.00	8.00
2½d purple, blue paper (January 1, 1887)	14.00	0.75
3d purple, yellow paper (January 1, 1887)	18.00	1.50
4d green and brown (January 1, 1887)	22.00	7.00
4½d green and red (September 15, 1892)	7.00	25.00
5d purple and blue (January 1, 1887)	26.00	5.00
6d purple, red paper (January 1, 1887)	20.00	5.00
9d violet and blue (January 1, 1887)	45.00	25.00
10d purple and red (January 1, 1887)	40.00	24.00
1/– green (January 1, 1887)	£150	40.00
1/– green and red (July 11, 1900)	45.00	70.00
Set	£400	£200

Wmk inverted

½d orange	60.00	60.00
½d green	60.00	60.00
1½d purple and green	£1,400	£400
2d green and red	£1,400	£400
2½d purple, blue paper	£3,500	£1,200
4d green and brown	£1,400	£500
5d purple and blue	£15,000	£1,200
6d purple, red paper	£8,000	£1,500
9d violet and blue	£8,000	£1,800
10d purple and red	£8,000	£2,700
1/– green	£1,600	£800
1/– green and red	£1,700	£900

BRITISH STAMP MARKET VALUES 2024

KING EDWARD VII

KING EDWARD VII

For this reign, most stamps are priced in three columns: unmounted mint (left), mounted mint (centre) and fine used (right). However, booklet panes are priced for mounted mint only.

De La Rue printings are generally cleaner, with good centring and neat perforations. Harrison and Somerset House printings are coarser, with poor centring and ragged perfs.

A vast range of shades exists, the details of these being beyond the scope of this publication.

6d purple

7d grey

½d yellow-green

1d scarlet

9d purple and blue

10d purple and red

1½d purple and green

2d green and red

1/- green and red

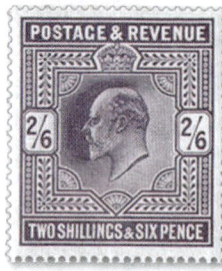

2/6 lilac

2½d blue

3d purple on yellow

5/- red

10/- blue

4d orange

5d purple and blue

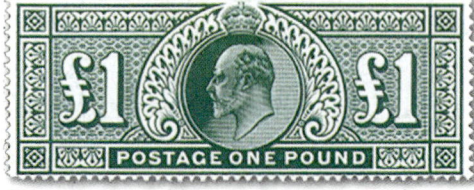

£1 green

22 BRITISH STAMP MARKET VALUES 2024

KING EDWARD VII

■ **1902–10**
Surface-printed by De La Rue. Wmk: Imperial Crown (½d to 1/-), Large Anchor (2/6, 5/-, 10/-), Three Imperial Crowns (£1). Perf: 14.

½d blue-green (Jan 1, 1902)	2.00	1.00	0.70
½d yellow-green (Nov 26, 1904)	2.00	1.00	0.70
Wmk inverted	20.00	12.00	12.00
1d scarlet (Jan 1, 1902)	1.75	1.00	0.50
Wmk inverted	7.00	5.00	6.00
1½d purple and green (Jan 1, 1902)	60.00	30.00	10.00
on chalky paper	60.00	30.00	10.00
2d green and red (Mar 25, 1902)	70.00	30.00	10.00
on chalky paper	60.00	28.00	12.00
2½d blue (Jan 1, 1902)	25.00	12.00	3.00
3d purple on yellow (Jan 1, 1902)	70.00	30.00	7.00
on chalky paper	60.00	30.00	10.00
4d green and brown (Jan 1, 1902)	95.00	40.00	18.00
on chalky paper	65.00	30.00	15.00
4d orange (Nov 1, 1909)	32.00	15.00	10.00
5d purple and blue (May 14, 1902)	90.00	40.00	15.00
on chalky paper	85.00	45.00	15.00
Wmk inverted	£6,500	£4,000	£3,000
6d purple (Jan 1, 1902)	60.00	28.00	14.00
on chalky paper	60.00	30.00	14.00
7d grey (May 4, 1910)	10.00	7.00	16.00
9d purple and blue (Jan 1, 1902)	£170	70.00	40.00
on chalky paper	£155	60.00	40.00
10d purple and red (Jul 3, 1902)	£210	60.00	40.00
on chalky paper	£175	55.00	40.00
1/- green and red (Mar 24, 1902)	£165	60.00	20.00
on chalky paper	£165	60.00	24.00
2/6 lilac (Apr 5, 1902)	£450	£200	75.00
on chalky paper	£450	£300	90.00
Wmk inverted	£7,500	£4,000	£2,500
5/- red (Apr 5, 1902)	£700	£280	£120
10/- blue (Apr 5, 1902)	£1,800	£525	£350
£1 green (Jun 16, 1902)	£2,800	£1,200	£600

Booklet panes	*Wmk Upright*	*Inverted*
Pane of five ½d with label showing St Andrew's Cross	£500	£500
Pane of six ½d	55.00	90.00
Pane of six 1d	40.00	70.00

■ **1910**
Surface-printed by De La Rue. Wmk: Imperial Crown. Perf: 14. Prepared for use but not issued. One example is known used.
2d Tyrian plum £115,000 –

■ **1911–13**
Designs as 1902–10 series.

Surface-printed by Harrison. Wmk: Imperial Crown. Perf: 14

½d yellow-green (May 3, 1911)	3.50	2.00	1.30
Wmk inverted	60.00	40.00	40.00
1d red (May 3, 1911)	10.00	6.00	8.00
Wmk inverted	60.00	40.00	40.00
2½d blue (Jul 10, 1911)	£100	45.00	18.00
Wmk inverted	£1,800	£1,000	£1,000
3d purple (Sep 12, 1911) on yellow paper	£200	£150	£200
4d orange (Jul 13, 1911)	£130	60.00	45.00

Booklet panes	*Wmk Upright*	*Inverted*
Pane of five ½d with label showing St Andrew's Cross	£1,100	£1,100
Pane of six ½d	80.00	£110
Pane of six 1d	70.00	90.00

Surface-printed by Somerset House. Wmk: Imperial Crown (½d to 1/-), Large Anchor (2/6, 5/-, 10/-), or Three Imperial Crowns (£1). Perf: 14

1½d purple and green (Jul 13, 1911)	50.00	25.00	12.00
2d green and red (Mar 11, 1912)	46.00	24.00	11.00
5d purple and blue (Aug 7, 1911)	50.00	28.00	11.00
6d purple (Oct 31, 1911)	50.00	26.00	14.00
chalky paper	50.00	28.00	60.00
7d grey (Aug 1, 1912)	20.00	12.00	15.00
9d purple and blue (Jul 24, 1911)	£105	65.00	40.00
10d purple and red (Oct 9, 1911)	£140	75.00	45.00
1/- green and red (Jul 17, 1911)	£115	58.00	25.00
Wmk inverted	£250	£150	–
2/6 purple (Sep 27, 1911)	£450	£190	85.00
5/- red (Feb 29, 1912)	£700	£280	£120
10/- blue (Jan 14, 1912)	£1,800	£600	£400
£1 green (Sep 3, 1911)	£2,800	£1,200	£700

Surface-printed by Harrison. Wmk: Imperial Crown. Perf: 15x14

½d green (Oct 30, 1911)	50.00	30.00	30.00
1d red (Oct 5, 1911)	32.00	16.00	8.50
2½d blue (Oct 14, 1911)	45.00	21.00	7.00
3d purple on yellow (Sep 22, 1911)	55.00	30.00	13.00
4d orange (Nov 22, 1911)	48.00	26.00	10.00

2d Tyrian plum

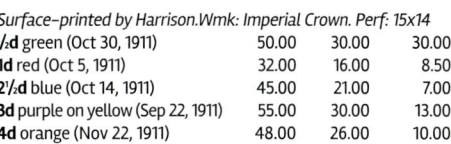

KING GEORGE V

KING GEORGE V

For this reign, the stamps are priced in three columns: unmounted mint (left), mounted unused (centre) and fine used (right).

Stamps are found in a wide range of shades, details of which are beyond the scope of this guide.

½d green

1d red

■ 1911–1912
Des: Bertram Mackennal and George Eve. Portrait based on photograph by W. & D. Downey. Die engraved by J. A. C. Harrison. Printed in typography by Harrison. Perf: 15x14.

Wmk: Imperial Crown. Issued in sheets and booklets

½d green (Jun 22, 1911)	7.50	3.50	2.00
Wmk inverted	15.00	7.50	3.50
1d red (Jun 22, 1911)	6.50	3.00	1.50
Wmk inverted	12.50	7.00	3.00

(*These stamps also exist with Wmk sideways and printed in error with perf: 14.)

Booklet panes	Wmk Upright	Inverted
Pane of six ½d	80.00	£120
Pane of six 1d	75.00	£110

Wmk: Simple Royal Cypher GVR. Issued only in booklets

½d green (Sep 28, 1912)	80.00	30.00	28.00
Wmk inverted	80.00	30.00	28.00
1d green (Sep 28, 1912)	35.00	16.00	18.00
Wmk inverted	35.00	16.00	18.00

Booklet panes	Wmk Upright	Inverted
Pane of six ½d	£550	£550
Pane of six 1d	£250	£240

■ 1912
Designs as above, except that the King's hair is lighter on the ½d and the lion is shaded on the 1d. Printed in typography by Harrison. Perf: 15x14.

Wmk: Imperial Crown

½d green (Jan 1, 1912)	8.50	4.50	1.00
Wmk inverted	£1,400	£800	£500
1d red (Jan 1, 1912)	5.00	2.00	0.80
Wmk inverted	£450	£350	£250

Wmk: Simple Royal Cypher GVR

½d green (Aug 1912)	8.00	4.00	1.25
Wmk inverted	£500	£300	£200
1d red (Aug 1912)	7.00	3.50	1.00
Wmk inverted	22.00	14.00	12.00

Wmk: Multiple Royal Cypher GVR

½d green (Oct 1912)	12.00	7.00	9.00
Wmk inverted	15.00	12.00	12.50
Wmk sideways	–	–	£3,250
1d red (Sep 1912)	15.00	9.00	4.50
Wmk inverted	20.00	15.00	16.00
Wmk sideways	£220	£150	£160

½d green, 1½d brown   1d red, 2½d blue

2d orange, 3d violet, 4d green   5d brown, 6d purple, 7d green, 8d black

9d black, 9d green, 10d blue, 1/- brown

■ 1912–1924
Des: Bertram Mackennal and George Eve. Die engraved by J. A. C. Harrison. Printed in typography by Harrison (all values except 6d) and Somerset House (all values except 1d). Perf: 15x14.

KING GEORGE V

Wmk: Simple Royal Cypher GVR

½d green (Jan 16, 1913)	1.00	0.40	0.40
Wmk inverted	4.00	2.25	1.10
1d red (Oct 8, 1912)	1.00	0.40	0.40
Wmk inverted	4.00	2.25	0.90
1½d brown (Oct 15, 1912)	3.50	2.00	0.80
Wmk inverted	8.00	4.00	1.60
2d orange (Aug 20, 1912)	3.50	1.75	0.60
Wmk inverted	20.00	10.00	8.50
2½d blue (Oct 18, 1912)	16.00	8.00	2.25
Wmk inverted	£110	75.00	75.00
3d violet (Oct 9, 1912)	8.00	3.75	1.00
Wmk inverted	£160	95.00	95.00
4d green (Jan 15, 1913)	16.00	7.00	1.50
Wmk inverted	40.00	25.00	25.00
5d brown (Jun 30, 1913)	20.00	8.00	4.00
Wmk inverted	£1,100	£700	£700
6d purple (Aug 1, 1913)			
chalk-surfaced paper	18.00	8.00	2.00
Wmk inverted	85.00	50.00	50.00
7d green (Aug 1, 1913)	28.00	11.00	7.50
Wmk inverted	80.00	50.00	50.00
8d black (Aug 1, 1913)			
yellow paper	42.00	20.00	11.00
Wmk inverted	£180	£110	£110
9d black (Jun 30, 1913)	20.00	10.00	3.75
Wmk inverted	£200	£125	£125
9d green (Sep 1922)	£200	75.00	24.00
Wmk inverted	£1,200	£800	£750
10d blue (Aug 1, 1913)	32.00	15.00	18.00
Wmk inverted	£3,750	£2,500	£1,800
1/– brown (Aug 1, 1913)	28.00	13.00	1.80
Wmk inverted	£300	£250	£200

Booklet panes		Wmk Upright	Inverted
Pane of six ½d		35.00	45.00
Pane of six 1d		35.00	45.00
Pane of six 1½d		60.00	75.00
Pane of four 1½d with two advert labels		£750	£750
Pane of six 2d		80.00	£130

Wmk: Multiple Royal Cypher GVR

½d green (Aug 1913)	£160	£100	95.00
Wmk inverted	£800	£450	£450
1d red (Aug 1913)	£350	£225	£180
Wmk inverted	£1,500	£1,000	£1,000

■ **1924–1926**
Designs as above, but printed by typography by Waterlow (all values except 6d), Harrison (all values) or Somerset House (1½d, 6d), Wmk: Multiple Crowns and block GVR.

½d green (Feb 1924)	0.60	0.30	0.20
Wmk inverted	5.00	2.50	1.00
Wmk sideways	11.00	5.50	4.50
1d red (Feb 1924)	0.85	0.35	0.20
Wmk inverted	5.00	2.50	1.25
Wmk sideways	26.00	15.00	16.00
1½d brown (Feb 1924)	0.90	0.40	0.20
Wmk inverted	2.50	1.25	1.00
Wmk sideways	14.00	7.00	4.50
2d orange (Sep 1924)	2.00	0.85	0.70
Wmk inverted	60.00	40.00	40.00
Wmk sideways	£175	60.00	65.00
2½d blue (Oct 1924)	7.50	4.00	1.10
Wmk inverted	125.00	70.00	50.00
3d violet (Oct 1924)	11.00	5.00	1.00
Wmk inverted	125.00	70.00	50.00
4d green (Nov 1924)	18.00	7.00	1.40
Wmk inverted	£200	£110	75.00
5d brown (Nov 1924)	30.00	12.00	2.00
Wmk inverted	£140	95.00	80.00
6d purple (Sep 1924)	3.80	1.50	0.50
chalky paper	15.00	9.00	1.75
ordinary paper, Wmk inverted	£120	70.00	60.00
chalky paper, Wmk inverted	80.00	60.00	40.00
9d green (Dec 1924)	20.00	7.00	2.50
Wmk inverted	£120	75.00	70.00
10d blue (Nov 1924)	65.00	28.00	22.00
Wmk inverted	£3,500	£2,200	£1,600
1/– brown (Oct 1924)	35.00	16.00	1.40
Wmk inverted	£550	£400	£260

Booklet panes		Wmk Upright	Inverted
Pane of six ½d		35.00	45.00
Pane of six 1d		35.00	45.00
Pane of six 1½d		60.00	75.00
Pane of four 1½d with two advert labels	£125		£125

(*A wide range of advertising labels exists.)

2/6 brown

■ **1913–1934. High values. 'Seahorses'**
Des: Bertram Mackennal. Dies engraved by J.A.C. Harrison. Wmk: Simple Royal Cypher GVR. Perf: 11x12.

Printed in recess by Waterlow. White gum. 22mm high

2/6 brown (Jun 30, 1913)	£600	£175	£100
5/– red (Jun 30, 1913)	£1,000	£325	£175
10/– blue (Aug 1, 1913)	£1,900	£700	£300
£1 green (Aug 1, 1913)	£4,000	£2,250	£1,100

Printed in recess by De La Rue. Yellowish gum. 22mm high

2/6 brown (Oct 1915)	£500	£200	£100
5/– red (Sep 1915)	£900	£280	£190
10/– blue (Dec 1915)	£3,500	£2,000	£600

KING GEORGE V

Printed in recess by Bradbury Wilkinson. White gum. 22.5mm–23mm high.

2/6 brown (Dec 1918)	£225	75.00	32.00
5/– red (Jan 1919)	£325	£150	45.00
10/– blue (Jan 1919)	£600	£300	£100

Printed in recess by Waterlow. Die re-engraved so that the background to the portrait consists of horizontal and diagonal lines.

2/6 brown (Oct 16, 1934)	£130	60.00	12.00
5/– red (Oct 16, 1934)	£350	£120	45.00
10/– blue (Oct 16, 1934)	£500	£300	50.00

1½d brown

2½d blue

1d red, 1½d brown (1924 issue)

1d red, 1½d brown (1925 issue)

£1 black

■ 1924–1925. British Empire Exhibition

Des: Harold Nelson. Printed in recess by Waterlow. Wmk: Multiple Crowns and block GVR. Perf: 14.

Set (April 23, 1924)	18.00	8.00	8.00
Set (May 9, 1925)	45.00	30.00	30.00
First day cover (1924)	–	–	£375
First day cover (1925)	–	–	£1,700

■ 1929, May 10. Postal Union Congress

Des: F. W. Farleigh (½d, 2½d), Ernest Linzell (1d, 1½d), Harold Nelson (£1). Printed in typography by Waterlow (½d to 2½d) or in recess by Bradbury, Wilkinson (£1). Wmk: Multiple Crowns and block GVR (½d to 2½d), or Large Crown and script GVR (£1). Perf: 15x14 (½d to 2½d), or 12 (£1).

½d green	1.50	0.50	0.45
Wmk inverted	20.00	11.00	8.00
Wmk sideways	70.00	25.00	25.00
1d red	2.50	1.50	1.00
Wmk inverted	25.00	13.00	14.00
Wmk sideways	90.00	60.00	60.00
1½d brown	2.00	1.25	0.80
Wmk inverted	12.00	6.00	4.50
Wmk sideways	65.00	20.00	20.00
2½d blue	16.00	7.00	5.00
Wmk inverted	£3,500	£2,000	£1,000
Set	20.00	9.00	6.75
First day cover	–	–	£450
£1 black	£1,000	£550	£550
First day cover	–	–	£12,000

Booklet panes	*Wmk Upright*	*Inverted*
Pane of six ½d	40.00	£120
Pane of six **1d**	45.00	£200
Pane of six **1½d**	30.00	90.00
Pane of four **1½d** with two advert labels	£250	£280

½d green

1d red

KING GEORGE V

½d green, 1½d brown   1d red, 2½d blue

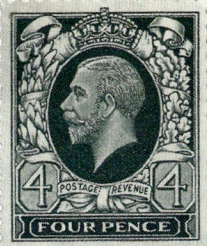

2d orange, 3d violet, 4d green   5d brown

9d deep green, 10d blue, 1/– brown

1934–1936
Designs as 1912-24 and 1924-26 issues, but with dark shading behind the portrait. Printed in photogravure by Harrison. Wmk: Multiple Crowns and block GVR. Perf: 15x14.

½d green (Nov 19, 1934)	0.25	0.10	0.15
Wmk inverted	15.00	7.00	3.00
Wmk sideways	9.00	6.00	3.00
1d red-brown (Sep 24, 1934)	0.25	0.20	0.15
Wmk inverted	15.00	7.00	2.50
Wmk sideways	22.00	11.00	14.00
1½d brown (Aug 20, 1934)	0.20	0.15	0.10
Wmk inverted	2.50	1.25	0.60
Wmk sideways	10.00	6.00	2.50
2d orange (Jan 19, 1935)	0.60	0.35	0.40
Wmk sideways	£175	70.00	65.00
2½d blue (Mar 18, 1935)	1.40	0.90	0.75
3d violet (Mar 18, 1935)	1.80	1.00	0.75
4d grey–green (Dec 2, 1935)	2.50	1.40	0.75
5d brown (Feb 17, 1936)	9.00	5.00	2.50
9d deep green (Dec 2, 1935)	16.00	7.00	2.25
10d blue (Feb 24, 1936)	25.00	11.00	9.00
1/– brown (Feb 24, 1936)	32.00	12.00	0.75

Booklet panes		Wmk Upright	Inverted
Pane of six ½d		60.00	£100
Pane of six 1d		60.00	£150
Pane of six 1½d		20.00	25.00
Pane of four 1½d with two advert labels		75.00	75.00

½d green, 1d red, 1½d brown, 2½d blue

1935, May 7. Silver Jubilee
Des: Barnett Freedman. Printed in photogravure by Harrison. Wmk: Multiple Crowns and block GVR. Perf: 15x14.

½d green	0.80	0.40	0.30
Wmk inverted	11.00	6.00	6.00
1d red	1.40	0.70	0.70
Wmk inverted	11.00	6.00	6.00
1½d brown	1.25	0.50	0.40
Wmk inverted	2.00	1.00	0.90
2½d blue	3.00	2.00	4.00
2½d Prussian blue	£17,000	£13,000	£15,000
Set (excluding Prussian blue)	6.00	3.25	4.75
First day cover	–	–	80.00
Pictorial cover	–	–	£800

Booklet panes	Wmk Upright	Inverted
Pane of four ½d	30.00	60.00
Pane of four 1d	30.00	60.00
Pane of four 1½d	15.00	20.00

KING EDWARD VIII

KING EDWARD VIII

For this reign stamps are priced in two columns: unmounted mint (left) and fine used (right). The exception is booklet panes, which are priced only for unmounted mint with good perforations.

½d, 1d, 1½d, 2½d

1936. Accession

Des: Hubert Brown, adapted by Harrison. Portrait by Hugh Cecil. Printed in photogravure by Harrison. Wmk: Multiple Crown and E8R. Perf: 15x14.

½d green (September, 1, 1936)	0.15	0.10
Wmk inverted	6.00	2.50
1d red (September 14, 1936)	0.20	0.20
Wmk inverted	5.00	2.25
1½d brown (September 1, 1936)	0.20	0.10
Wmk inverted	0.75	0.80
2½d blue (September 1, 1936)	0.20	0.30
Set	0.50	0.50

Booklet panes	Wmk Upright	Inverted
Pane of six ½d	15.00	42.00
Pane of six 1d	15.00	42.00
Pane of two 1½d	10.00	10.00
Pane of four 1½d with two advert labels	£110	£100
Pane of six 1½d	8.00	14.00

Stamp Magazine is Britain's best for GB collectors

Every issue includes:
- Analysis of all Royal Mail issues
- Latest British and world news
- Regular features on GB themes
- Hard-hitting opinion columns
- Exhibition, auction and fair dates

Available from newsagents, or visit www.stampmagazine.co.uk

KING GEORGE VI

For this reign, prices are priced in two columns: unmounted mint (left) and fine used (right). The exception is booklet panes, which are priced only for unmounted mint with good perforations.

½d, 1d, 1½d, 2d, 2½d, 3d

4d, 5d, 6d

7d, 8d, 9d, 10d, 11d, 1/–

1937–51. Definitives
Des: Edmund Dulac and Eric Gill (½d to 6d), Edmund Dulac (7d to 1/–). Printed in photogravure by Harrison. Wmk: Multiple Crown and GVIR. Perf: 15x14.

Original colours

½d green (May 10, 1937)	0.15	0.10
Wmk inverted	7.00	0.50
Wmk sideways	0.25	0.30
1d red (May 10, 1937)	0.15	0.10
Wmk inverted	30.00	2.50
Wmk sideways	15.00	5.00
1½d red-brown (July 30, 1937)	0.15	0.15
Wmk inverted	9.00	1.00
Wmk sideways	1.00	0.50
2d orange (January 31, 1938)	0.50	0.35
Wmk inverted	36.00	2.50
Wmk sideways	36.00	20.00
2½d blue (May 10, 1937)	0.25	1.00
Wmk inverted	32.00	3.00
Wmk sideways	50.00	25.00
3d violet (January 31, 1938)	1.50	0.60
4d green (November 21, 1938)	1.75	0.20
5d brown (November 21, 1938)	2.00	0.30
6d purple (January 30, 1939)	1.00	0.15
7d emerald (February 27, 1939)	3.50	0.50
8d carmine (February 27, 1939)	5.00	0.50
9d deep green (May 1, 1939)	4.00	0.50
10d blue (May 1, 1939)	3.00	0.50
11d brown–purple (December 29, 1947)	1.75	1.00
1/– brown (May 1, 1939)	4.00	0.15
Set	24.00	4.00

Booklet panes

	Wmk Upright	Inverted
Pane of two ½d	60.00	60.00
Pane of six ½d	30.00	60.00
Pane of two 1d	60.00	60.00
Pane of six 1d	30.00	£170
Pane of two 1½d	20.00	30.00
Pane of four 1½d with two advert labels (*)	£120	£120
Pane of six 1½d	30.00	60.00
Pane of six 2d	£120	£300
Pane of six 2½d	£120	£250
		Wmk Sideways
Pane of four ½d	–	70.00
Pane of four 1d	–	£110

(*15 different combinations of advertising labels exist. Prices quoted are for the cheapest; scarcer panes can fetch up to twice as much.)

Paler colours

½d pale green (September 1, 1941)	0.15	0.10
Wmk inverted	3.00	0.40
1d pale red (August 11, 1941)	0.20	0.10
Wmk sideways	3.00	3.00
1½d pale red-brown (September 28, 1942)	0.50	0.35
2d pale orange (October 6, 1941)	0.50	0.25
Wmk inverted	3.00	0.40
Wmk sideways	10.00	8.00
2½d pale blue (July 21, 1941)	0.15	0.10
Wmk inverted	1.00	0.50
Wmk sideways	7.00	6.00
3d pale violet (November 3, 1941)	1.00	0.25
Set	1.50	1.00

Booklet panes

	Wmk Upright	Inverted
Pane of two ½d	9.00	–
Pane of six ½d	20.00	30.00
Pane of two 1d	25.00	–
Pane of two 1½d	9.00	–
Pane of six 2d	20.00	30.00
Pane of six 2½d pale blue	10.00	15.00

Changed colours

½d pale orange (May 3, 1951)	0.10	0.20
Wmk inverted	0.20	0.30
1d pale blue (May 3, 1951)	0.10	0.10
Wmk inverted	2.25	1.00
Wmk sideways	0.20	0.40

KING GEORGE VI

1½d pale green (May 3, 1951)	0.25	0.20
Wmk inverted	2.75	2.00
Wmk sideways	1.25	1.50
2d pale red-brown (May 3, 1951)	0.25	0.25
Wmk inverted	4.00	3.50
Wmk sideways	0.75	0.75
2½d pale red (May 3, 1951)	0.15	0.15
Wmk inverted	1.00	0.50
Wmk sideways	0.60	0.85
4d pale blue (October 2, 1950)	1.00	0.65
Set	1.50	1.10

Booklet panes	Wmk Upright	Inverted
Pane of two ½d	10.00	–
Pane of four ½d	10.00	10.00
Pane of six ½d	6.00	6.00
Pane of two 1d	10.00	–
Pane of three 1d with three labels ('Minimum Inland Printed Paper Rate 1½d')	25.00	25.00
Pane of three 1d with three labels ('Shorthand In One Week')	35.00	35.00
Pane of four 1d	10.00	20.00
Pane of six 1d	20.00	25.00
Pane of two 1½d	10.00	–
Pane of four 1½d	10.00	15.00
Pane of six 1½d	20.00	25.00
Pane of six 2d	20.00	60.00
Pane of six 2½d	6.00	8.00

1½d

■ **1937, May 13. Coronation**
Des: Edmund Dulac. Printed in photogravure by Harrison. Wmk: Multiple Crown and GVIR. Perf: 15x14.

1½d	0.25	0.15
First day cover	–	3.00
Pictorial cover	–	20.00

2/6, 5/–

10/–, £1

■ **1939–1948. High values**
Des: Edmund Dulac (2/6, 5/–), George Bellew (10/–, £1). Printed in recess by Waterlow. Wmk: Single Crown and GV1R. Perf: 14.

2/6 brown (September 4, 1939)	70.00	5.00
2/6 green (March 9, 1942)	9.00	0.50
5/– red (August 21, 1939)	18.00	1.25
10/– dark blue (October 30, 1939)	£220	17.00
10/– ultramarine (November 30, 1942)	30.00	3.50
£1 brown (October 1, 1948)	18.00	12.00
Set	£280	40.00

½d green, 1d red,
1½d brown,
2d orange,
2½d blue, 3d violet

■ **1940, May 6. Centenary of the First Adhesive Postage Stamps**
Des: H. L. Palmer. Printed in photogravure by Harrison. Wmk: Multiple Crown and GVIR. Perf: 14½ x 14.

Set	4.00	3.50
First day cover	–	7.50
Pictorial cover	–	35.00

Farming, homes, industry, transport (2½d)
Dove of peace (3d)

■ **1946, June 11. Peace & Reconstruction**
Des: H. L. Palmer (2½d), Reynolds Stone (3d). Printed in photogravure by Harrison. Wmk: Multiple Crown and GVIR. Perf: 15x14.

Set	0.20	0.25
First day cover	–	9.00
Pictorial cover	–	55.00

KING GEORGE VI

2½d

£1

Two hemispheres (2½d)
UPU monument (3d)
Globe and compass (6d)
Globe and posthorn (1/-)

■ **1949, October 10. 75th Anniversary of the Universal Postal Union**
Des: Mary Adshead (2½d), Percy Metcalfe (3d). Hugo Fleury (6d), George Bellew (1/-). Printed in photogravure by Harrison. Wmk: Multiple Crown and GVIR. Perf: 15x14.

Set	1.50	1.25
First day cover	–	9.50
Pictorial cover	–	47.00

H.M.S. Victory (2/6)
White Cliffs of Dover (5/-)
St. George and the Dragon (10/-)
Royal Coat of Arms (£1)

■ **1951, May 3. High values**
Des: Mary Adshead (2/6, 5/-), Percy Metcalfe (10/-, £1). Printed in recess by Waterlow. Wmk: Single Crown and GVIR. Perf: 11x12.

Set	65.00	15.00

■ **1948, April 26. Royal Silver Wedding**
Des: George Knipe (2½d) and Joan Hassall (£1), from photographs by Dorothy Wilding. Printed in photogravure by Harrison. Wmk: Multiple Crown and GVIR. Perf: 15x14 (2½d), 14 x 15 (£1).

Set	27.00	25.00
First day cover	–	50.00
Pictorial cover	–	£425

■ **1948, May 10. Liberation of the Channel Islands**
Although this set was also placed on sale at eight post offices in Great Britain, it is listed under Regional Issues.

Globe surrounded by a laurel wreath (2½d)
Globe with Olympic rings (3d)
Olympic rings (6d)
Victory and Olympic rings (1/-)

■ **1948, July 29. Olympic Games**
Des: Percy Metcalfe (2½d), Abram Games (3d), Stanley Scott (6d) and Edmund Dulac (1/-). Printed in photogravure by Harrison. Wmk: Multiple Crown and GVIR. Perf: 15x14.

Set	7.00	6.00
First day cover	–	8.00
Pictorial cover	–	35.00

Commerce and prosperity (2½d)
Festival symbol (4d)

■ **1951, May 3. Festival of Britain**
Des: Edmund Dulac (2½d), Abram Games (4d). Printed in photogravure by Harrison. Wmk: Multiple Crown and GVIR. Perf: 15x14.

Set	0.35	0.40
First day cover	–	3.00
Pictorial cover	–	17.00

QUEEN ELIZABETH II PRE-DECIMAL

QUEEN ELIZABETH II PRE-DECIMALS

In this section, prices are priced in two columns: unmounted mint (left) and fine used (right). The exception is booklet panes, which are priced only for unmounted mint with good perforations.

Except where otherwise stated, all the stamps have the same technical details: Printed in photogravure by Harrison. Perf: 15x14 (definitives), 15x14 (special issues with a horizontal design) or 14x15 (special issues with a vertical design).

½d, 1d, 1½d, 2d

2½d, 3d

4d, 4½d

5d, 6d, 7d

8d, 9d, 10d, 11d

1/–, 1/6

1/3

■ **1952–1967. Wilding definitives**
Des: Enid Marx (½d, 1d, 1½d, 2d), Michael Farrar-Bell (2½d, 3d, 4d, 4½d), George Knipe (5d, 6d, 7d), Mary Adshead (8d, 9d, 10d, 11d), Edmund Dulac (1/–, 1/3, 1/6); portrait by Dorothy Wilding Studios. On the 2½d value the top line of the diadem was initially broken (Type I), but this was later corrected (Type II).

Wmk: Multiple Tudor Crown and E2R

½d orange (August 31, 1953)	0.10	0.10
Wmk inverted	0.15	0.40
1d blue (August 31, 1953)	0.15	0.10
Wmk inverted	4.50	2.50
1½d green (December 5, 1952)	0.10	0.10
Wmk inverted	0.35	0.30
Wmk sideways	0.35	0.30
2d deep brown (August 31, 1953)	0.20	0.15
Wmk inverted	20.00	12.00
Wmk sideways	0.75	0.50
2½d carmine (type 1) (December 5, 1952)	0.15	0.10
Wmk inverted (type 2)	0.40	0.30
Wmk sideways (type 1)	3.50	4.00
3d violet (January 18, 1954)	1.00	0.20
4d blue (November 2, 1953)	1.00	0.70
5d brown (July 6, 1953)	4.00	2.50
6d purple (January 18, 1954)	3.00	0.75
7d pale green (January 18, 1954)	8.00	2.00
8d magenta (July 6, 1953)	5.00	0.75
9d myrtle-green (February 8, 1954)	14.00	1.50
10d blue (February 8, 1954)	12.00	1.50
11d brown-red (February 8, 1954)	30.00	10.00
1/– bistre (July 6, 1953)	1.00	0.50
1/3 deep green (November 2, 1953)	3.00	1.50
1/6 grey-blue (November 2, 1953)	12.00	1.25
Set	55.00	20.00
Set Wmk inverted	20.00	15.00
Set Wmk sideways	6.00	6.00
First day covers (set of 6)	–	£140
Pictorial cover	–	£600

Booklet panes	*Wmk Upright*	*Inverted*
Pane of two ½d	2.00	–
Pane of four ½d	4.00	4.00
Pane of six ½d	2.00	4.00
Pane of two 1d	2.00	–
Pane of four 1d	3.00	25.00
Pane of three 1d with three labels reading: MINIMUM INLAND PRINTED PAPER RATE 1½d	£300	£300
Pane of three 1d with three labels reading: PLEASE POST EARLY IN THE DAY	40.00	40.00
Pane of three 1d with three labels reading: PACK YOUR PARCELS SECURELY/ADDRESS YOUR LETTERS CORRECTLY/POST EARLY IN THE DAY	40.00	40.00
Pane of six 1d	8.00	30.00
Pane of two 1½d	2.00	–
Pane of four 1½d	4.00	4.00
Pane of six 1½d	2.00	4.00
Pane of six 2d	27.00	£160
Pane of six 2½d	3.50	3.50

Wmk: St. Edward's Crown and E2R

½d orange (August 1955)	0.15	0.10
Wmk inverted	0.20	0.20
1d blue (September 19, 1955)	0.20	0.10
Wmk inverted	0.50	0.50

PRE-DECIMAL QUEEN ELIZABETH II

1½d green (August 1955)	0.15	0.10
Wmk inverted	0.30	0.20
Wmk sideways	0.20	0.25
2d deep brown (September 6, 1955)	0.25	0.30
Wmk inverted	7.00	5.00
Wmk sideways	0.50	0.50
2d brown (October 17, 1956)	0.25	0.10
Wmk inverted	5.00	4.00
Wmk sideways	5.00	3.00
2½d carmine (type 1) (September 28, 1955)	0.25	0.15
Wmk inverted	0.75	1.00
Wmk sideways	0.75	1.00
2½d carmine (type 2) (September 1955)	0.30	0.60
Wmk inverted	0.30	0.30
3d violet (July 17, 1956)	0.25	0.20
Wmk inverted	1.75	1.50
Wmk sideways	12.00	7.50
4d blue (November 14, 1955)	1.50	2.00
5d brown (September 21, 1955)	5.00	3.00
6d purple (December 20, 1955)	3.50	1.00
6d deep purple (May 8, 1958)	3.00	1.00
7d pale green (April 23, 1956)	30.00	7.00
8d magenta (December 21, 1955)	4.00	1.25
9d myrtle-green (December 15, 1955)	12.00	2.00
10d blue (September 22, 1955)	10.00	2.00
11d brown-red (October 28, 1955)	0.50	1.25
1/– bistre (November 3, 1955)	6.50	0.50
1/3 deep green (March 27, 1956)	14.00	1.00
1/6 grey-blue (March 27, 1956)	20.00	0.75
Set	100.00	25.00
Set (Wmk inverted)	14.00	7.00
Set (Wmk sideways)	14.00	9.00

Booklet panes	Wmk Upright	Inverted
Pane of two ½d	3.00	–
Pane of four ½d	4.00	4.00
Pane of six ½d	2.00	3.50
Pane of two 1d	3.50	–
Pane of three 1d with three labels reading: PACK YOUR PARCELS SECURELY/ ADDRESS YOUR LETTERS CORRECTLY/ POST EARLY IN THE DAY	30.00	35.00
Pane of four 1d	4.00	4.00
Pane of six 1d	2.50	3.00
Pane of two 1½d	3.50	–
Pane of four 1½d	4.00	4.00
Pane of six 1½d	2.00	2.00
Pane of six 2d deep brown	13.00	65.00
Pane of six 2d brown	8.00	22.50
Pane of six 2½d	3.00	3.00
Pane of four 3d	10.00	15.00
Pane of six 3d	6.00	20.00

Wmk: Multiple St. Edward's Crown

½d orange (November 25, 1958)	0.10	0.10
chalky paper (July 15, 1963)	2.00	2.50
Wmk inverted	0.30	0.10
chalky paper and Wmk inverted	4.50	4.50
Wmk sideways	0.25	0.15
1d blue (November 1958)	0.10	0.10
Wmk inverted	0.30	0.30
Wmk sideways	0.75	0.75
1½d green (December 1958)	0.15	0.15
Wmk inverted	2.50	0.90
Wmk sideways	7.50	6.00
2d brown (December 4, 1958)	0.10	0.10
Wmk inverted	75.00	45.00
Wmk sideways	0.50	0.40
2½d carmine (type 1) (October 4, 1961)	0.10	0.40
Wmk inverted	0.30	0.30
2½d carmine (type 2) (November 1958)	0.35	0.20
chalky paper (July 15, 1963)	0.30	0.25
Wmk inverted	3.50	2.50
chalky paper & Wmk inverted	0.40	0.40
Wmk sideways	0.60	0.60
3d violet (November 1958)	0.15	0.10
Wmk inverted	0.65	0.65
Wmk sideways	1.00	1.00
4d blue (October 29, 1958)	0.50	0.25
4d deep blue (April 28, 1965)	0.20	0.10
Wmk inverted	2.00	2.00
Wmk sideways	1.00	1.00
4½d red-brown (February 9, 1959)	0.15	0.15
5d brown (November 10, 1958)	0.20	0.10
6d deep purple (December 23, 1958)	0.25	0.10
7d pale green (November 26, 1958)	0.50	0.20
8d magenta (February 24, 1960)	0.35	0.10
9d myrtle-green (March 24, 1959)	0.35	0.20
10d blue (November 18, 1958)	0.75	0.25
1/– bistre (October 30, 1958)	0.35	0.25
1/3 deep green (June 17, 1959)	0.35	0.15
1/6 grey-blue (December 16, 1958)	3.00	0.15
Set	6.00	4.00
Set (Wmk inverted)	80.00	50.00
Set (Wmk sideways)	11.50	11.00

Booklet panes	Wmk Upright	Inverted
Pane of three ½d and one 2½d (chalky paper)	8.00	8.00
Pane of four ½d	2.50	2.50
Pane of six ½d	1.25	2.00
Pane of four 1d	2.50	2.50
Pane of six 1d	1.50	2.50
Pane of four 1½d	2.50	2.50
Pane of six 1½d	5.00	6.00
Pane of six 2d	40.00	£500
Pane of four 2½d (chalky paper)	1.00	1.00
Pane of six 2½d	3.00	15.00
Pane of four 3d	2.00	2.00
Pane of six 3d	1.50	1.50
Pane of six 4d deep blue	1.50	1.50
		Wmk Sideways
Pane of two ½d se-tenant with two 2½d (type 2)		1.00
Pane of four ½d		2.00
Pane of two 1d se-tenant with two 3d to left		5.00
Pane of two 1d se-tenant with two 3d to right		5.00
Pane of four 1d		3.00
Pane of four 1½d		25.00
Pane of four 3d		2.00
Pane of four 4d		2.00

QUEEN ELIZABETH II PRE-DECIMAL

■ Wilding definitives, graphite-lined issue
Designs as above, but with black graphite lines on the back. All values have two vertical lines, except for the 2d which has just one line, on the right as viewed from the back.

Wmk: St. Edward's Crown and E2R upright

½d orange (November 19, 1957)	0.20	0.20
1d blue (November 19, 1957)	0.20	0.20
1½d green (November 19, 1957)	1.25	0.50
2d brown (November 19, 1957)	1.00	1.25
2½d carmine (type 2) (November 19, 1957)	4.50	3.50
3d violet (November 19, 1957)	0.75	0.50
Set	6.75	5.50
First day cover	–	75.00

Wmk: Multiple St. Edward's Crown

½d orange (June 15, 1959)	5.00	5.00
Wmk inverted	1.00	1.25
1d blue (December 18, 1958)	1.00	1.00
Wmk inverted	1.00	0.75
1½d green (August 4, 1959)	60.00	50.00
Wmk inverted	20.00	20.00
2d brown (December 4, 1958)	4.75	2.50
2½d carmine (type 2) (June 9, 1959)	6.00	6.00
Wmk inverted	35.00	30.00
3d violet (November 24, 1958)	0.60	0.45
Wmk inverted	0.55	0.40
4d blue (April 29, 1959)	3.25	3.25
4½d red-brown (June 3, 1959)	3.50	2.25
Set	70.00	55.00
Set (Wmk inverted)	60.00	50.00

Booklet panes	Wmk Upright	Inverted
Pane of six ½d	20.00	12.00
Pane of six 1d	7.50	7.00
Pane of six 1½d	£500	£125
Pane of six 2½d	30.00	£300
Pane of six 3d	4.00	4.00

■ Wilding definitives, phosphor-graphite issue
Designs as above, but with phosphor bands on the front in addition to the graphite lines on the back. All values have two bands, except for the 2d which has just one band to the left.

Wmk: St. Edward's Crown and E2R upright

½d orange (November 18, 1959)	3.00	3.00
1d blue (November 18, 1959)	9.00	9.00
1½d green (November 18, 1959)	2.50	3.00
2d brown (November 18, 1959)	£100	£100

Wmk: Multiple St. Edwards Crown

2d brown (November 18, 1959)	4.00	3.00
2½d carmine (type 2) (November 18, 1959)	10.00	10.00
3d violet (November 18, 1959)	14.00	7.50
4d blue (November 18, 1959)	8.00	5.00
4½d red-brown (November 18, 1959)	25.00	20.00
Set	50.00	40.00
First day cover	–	75.00

■ Wilding definitives, phosphor issue
Designs as above, but without graphite lines. All values have two phosphor bands, except where stated. Released on June 22, 1960 except where stated. Wmk: Multiple St. Edward's Crown.

½d orange	0.15	0.15
Wmk inverted	1.00	1.00
Wmk sideways	12.50	12.50
1d blue	0.10	0.10
Wmk inverted	0.35	0.30
Wmk sideways	0.75	0.75
1½d green	0.12	0.20
Wmk inverted	20.00	18.00
Wmk sideways	12.00	12.00
2d brown (one band)	14.00	12.00
2d brown (October 4, 1961)	0.20	0.10
Wmk sideways	0.30	0.25
2½d carmine (type 2)	0.20	0.20
Wmk inverted	£160	£140
2½d carmine (type 2, one band)	1.50	0.50
Wmk inverted	35.00	30.00
2½d carmine (type 1, one band)	40.00	35.00
3d violet	0.50	0.35
Wmk inverted	0.80	0.50
Wmk sideways	1.25	0.55
3d violet (April 29, 1965) (one band at left)	0.30	0.40
Wmk inverted	60.00	60.00
Wmk sideways	5.00	5.00
3d violet (one band at right)	0.30	0.40
Wmk inverted	6.00	6.50
Wmk sideways	5.00	5.00
se-tenant pair	0.60	1.50
se-tenant pair with Wmk inverted	65.00	65.00
se-tenant pair with Wmk sideways	8.00	10.00
3d violet (December 8, 1966) (one band)	0.25	0.25
Wmk inverted	3.00	3.50
Wmk sideways	0.40	0.50
4d blue	2.75	3.25
4d deep blue (April 28, 1965)	0.15	0.25
Wmk inverted	0.25	0.20
Wmk sideways	0.75	0.75
4½d red-brown (September 13, 1961)	0.15	0.25
5d brown (June 9, 1967)	0.20	0.25
6d deep purple (June 27, 1960)	0.20	–
7d pale green (February 15, 1967)	0.20	0.25
8d magenta (June 28, 1967)	0.20	0.25
9d myrtle green (December 29, 1966)	0.50	0.25
10d blue (December 30, 1966)	0.50	0.40
1/– bistre (June 28, 1967)	0.40	0.20
1/3 deep green	1.00	1.00
1/6 grey-blue (December 12, 1966)	2.00	2.00
Set	4.50	5.00
Set (Wmk inverted)	£180	£170
Set (Wmk sideways)	27.00	27.00

PRE-DECIMAL QUEEN ELIZABETH II

Booklet panes	Wmk Upright	Inverted
Pane of six ½d	3.00	4.00
Pane of six 1d	2.00	2.00
Pane of six 1½d	8.00	£120
Pane of six 2½d (type 2, two bands)	80.00	£1,100
Pane of six 2½d (type 2, one band)	22.00	£220
Pane of six 3d (two bands)	5.00	5.00
Pane of six 3d (one band at left or right)	20.00	£130
Pane of six 3d (one centre band)	4.00	15.00
Pane of six 4d	2.00	3.00
		Wmk sideways
Pane of four ½d		35.00
Pane of two 1d, two 3d (two bands)	–	3.00
Pane of two 1d, two 3d (one band, left)	–	11.00
Pane of two 1d, two 3d (one band, right)	–	11.00
Pane of four 1d	–	5.00
Pane of four 1½d	–	50.00
Pane of four 3d (two bands)	–	5.00
Pane of four 4d	–	1.00

Crowns and orb (2½d)
Rose, daffodil, thistle and shamrock (4d)
Coronation robe (1/3)
Crowns and cypher (1/6)

■ 1953, June 3. Coronation
Des: Edgar Fuller (2½d), Michael Goaman (4d), Edmund Dulac (1/3), Michael Farrar–Bell (1/6). Wmk: Tudor Crown and E2R.

Set	14.00	15.00
First day cover	–	30.00

(*The 1/3 design was reissued with a face value of £1 in the 2000 Her Majesty's Stamps miniature sheet and the 2003 A Perfect Coronation prestige stamp book.)

Carrickfergus Castle (2/6)
Caernarvon Castle (5/–)
Edinburgh Castle (10/–)
Windsor Castle (£1)

■ 1955–1968. Castle high value definitives
Des: Lynton Lamb. Printed in recess. Perf: 11x12.

Wmk: St. Edward's Crown and E2R. Printed by Waterlow

2/6 brown (September 23, 1955)	14.00	2.00
5/– carmine (September 23, 1955)	30.00	3.00
10/– blue (September 1, 1955)	60.00	10.00
£1 black (September 1, 1955)	85.00	20.00
Set	£160	30.00
First day cover	–	£300
Pictorial cover	–	£850

Wmk: St. Edward's Crown and E2R. Printed by De La Rue

2/6 (July 17, 1958)	28.00	3.50
5/– (April 30, 1958)	55.00	8.00
10/– (April 25, 1958)	£175	14.00
£1 (April 28, 1958)	£215	37.50
Set	£450	48.00

(*The top perforation tooth of each side of stamps from the De La Rue printing is narrower than on the Waterlow printing.)

Wmk: Multiple St. Edward's Crown. Printed by De La Rue

2/6 (July 22, 1959)	5.00	0.50
5/– (June 15, 1959)	20.00	1.00
10/– (July 21, 1959)	25.00	2.75
£1 (June 23, 1959)	55.00	7.00
Set	90.00	10.00

Wmk: Multiple St. Edward's Crown. Printed by Bradbury Wilkinson

2/6 (July 1, 1963)	0.40	0.15
5/– (September 3, 1963)	0.60	0.40
10/– (October 16, 1963)	2.00	2.50
£1 (November 14, 1963)	7.00	4.00
Set	9.00	7.00

(*The Queen's diadem is more detailed on the Bradbury Wilkinson printing than on the De La Rue printing.)

Wmk: Multiple St. Edward's Crown. Printed by Bradbury Wilkinson on chalky paper

2/6 (May 30, 1968)	0.50	0.75

No Wmk. Printed by Bradbury Wilkinson

2/6 (July 1, 1968)	0.30	0.40
5/– (April 10, 1968)	1.00	0.75
10/– (April 10, 1968)	4.00	3.00
£1 (December 4, 1967)	7.00	3.50
Set	10.50	7.00

Scouting badge (2½d)
Flying swallows (4d)
Globe within compass (1/3)

■ 1957, August 1. World Scout Jubilee Jamboree
Des: Mary Adshead (2½d), Pat Keely (4d), William Brown (1/3). Wmk: St Edward's Crown and E2R.

Set	3.75	4.00
First day cover	–	22.00

(*These stamps were also issued in coils.)

QUEEN ELIZABETH II PRE–DECIMAL

Wilding design with added inscription (4d)

■ **1957, September 12. Inter-Parliamentary Union Conference**
Des: Frank Langfield. Wmk: St. Edward's Crown and E2R.
4d	0.80	1.20
First day cover	–	82.00

Welsh dragon holding ribbon (3d)
Games emblem on banner (6d)
Welsh dragon holding laurel wreath (1/3)

■ **1958, July 18. British Empire & Commonwealth Games**
Des: Reynolds Stone (3d), William Brown (6d), Pat Keely (1/3).
Wmk: St. Edward's Crown and E2R.
Set	1.50	2.50
First day cover	–	60.00

1660 postboy on horseback (3d)
1660 posthorn and crown (1/3)

■ **1960, July 7. 300th Anniversary of General Letter Office**
Des: Reynolds Stone (3d), Faith Jaques (1/3). Wmk: Multiple St. Edward's Crown.
Set	2.00	2.50
First day cover	–	35.00

Europa emblem (6d, 1/6)

■ **1960, September 19. First Anniversary of CEPT**
Des: Pentti Rahikainen and Reynolds Stone. Wmk: Multiple St. Edward's Crown.
Set	6.25	6.50
First day cover	–	27.00

Thrift plant (2½d)
Squirrel and tree (3d)
Thrift plant (1/6)

■ **1961, August 28. Post Office Savings Bank Centenary**
Des: Peter Gauld (2½d), Michael Goaman (3d, 1/6). Wmk: Multiple St. Edward's Crown.
Printed on a Timson machine
Set	1.75	2.50
First day cover	–	38.00

Printed on a Thrissell machine (2½d, 3d only)
Pair	2.00	2.00

(*The portrait on the 2½d is greyer from the Thrissell machine, and that on the 3d is much clearer on the Timson printing.)

CEPT emblem (2d)
Doves and emblem (4d)
Doves and emblem (10d)

■ **1961, September 18. CEPT Conference**
Des: Michael Goaman and Theo Kurperschoek. Wmk: Multiple St. Edward's Crown.
Set	1.00	1.50
First day cover	–	4.00

PRE-DECIMAL QUEEN ELIZABETH II

Roof of Westminster Hall (6d)
Palace of Westminster (1/3)

■ **1961, September 23. Commonwealth Parliamentary Conference**
Des: Faith Jaques. Wmk: Multiple St. Edward's Crown.

Set	1.75	2.50
First day cover	–	20.00

Boxes bearing arrows (2½d)
Arrows over the British Isles (3d)
Joining arrows (1/3)

■ **1962, November 14. National Productivity Year**
Des: David Gentleman. Wmk: Multiple St. Edward's Crown, inverted on 2½d and 3d values.
Non-phosphor issue

Set	1.75	2.00
First day cover	–	25.00

Phosphor issue (one band on 2½d, three bands on 3d, 1/3)

Set	13.00	14.00
First day cover	–	£100

Ears of wheat (2½d)
Three children (1/3)

■ **1963, March 21. Freedom From Hunger**
Des: Michael Goaman. Wmk: Multiple St. Edward's Crown, inverted on both values.
Non-phosphor issue

Set	1.25	1.50
First day cover	–	16.00

Phosphor issue (one band on 2½d, three bands on 1/3)

Set	14.00	14.00
First day cover	–	32.00

Centenary of the 1863 Paris Postal Conference (6d)

■ **1963, May 7. Paris Postal Conference Centenary**
Des: Reynolds Stone. Wmk: Multiple St. Edward's Crown, inverted.
Non-phosphor issue

6d	0.30	0.80
First day cover	–	8.00

Phosphor issue (three bands)

6d	3.75	4.00
First day cover	–	30.00

Bee on flowers (3d)
Selection of wildlife (4½d)

■ **1963, May 16. National Nature Week**
Des: Stanley Scott (3d), Michael Goaman (4½d). Wmk: Multiple St. Edward's Crown.
Non-phosphor issue

Set	0.50	1.00
First day cover	–	12.00

Phosphor issue (three bands)

Set	2.00	2.00
First day cover	–	34.00

Helicopter over lifeboat (2½d)
19th-century lifeboat (4d)
Lifeboatmen (1/6)

■ **1963, May 31. International Lifeboat Conference**
Des: David Gentlemen. Wmk: Multiple St. Edward's Crown.
Non-phosphor issue

Set	1.75	2.00
First day cover	–	17.00

Phosphor issue (one band on 2½d, three bands on 4d, 1/6)

Set	21.00	22.00
First day cover	–	37.00

QUEEN ELIZABETH II PRE-DECIMAL

Red Cross (3d, 1/3, 1/6 with different borders)

■ **1963, August 15. Red Cross Centenary Congress**
Des: Harold Bartram. Wmk: Multiple St. Edward's Crown.
Non-phosphor issue
Set	2.75	3.00
First day cover	–	20.00

Phosphor issue (three bands)
Set	32.00	35.00
First day cover	–	60.00

Cable over globe (1/6)

■ **1963, December 3. Opening of Compac Cable**
Des: Peter Gauld. Wmk: Multiple St. Edward's Crown.
Non-phosphor issue
1/6	1.25	1.50
First day cover	–	15.00

Phosphor issue (three bands)
1/6	8.00	8.00
First day cover	–	35.00

A Midsummer Night's Dream: Puck and Bottom (3d)
Twelfth Night: Feste (6d)
Romeo and Juliet (1/3)
King Henry V (1/6)
Hamlet (2/6)

■ **1964, April 23. Shakespeare Festival**
Des: David Gentleman (3d to 1/6); Christopher and Robin Ironside (2/6). Printed in recess by Bradbury, Wilkinson (2/6). Perf: 11x12 (2/6). Wmk: Multiple St. Edward's Crown.
Non-phosphor issue
Set	2.25	2.50
First day cover	–	5.50

Phosphor issue (three bands on 3d, 6d, 1/3, 1/6)
Set	5.00	5.50
First day cover	–	10.00

Urban development: flats, Richmond Park (2½d)
Industrial activity: shipbuilding, Belfast (4d)
Forestry: Beddgelert Forest Park, Snowdonia (8d)
Technological development: nuclear reactor, Dounreay (1/6)

■ **1964, July 1. International Geographical Congress**
Des: Dennis Bailey. Wmk: Multiple St. Edward's Crown.
Non-phosphor issue
Set	2.00	2.25
First day cover	–	10.00

Phosphor issue (one band on 2½d, three bands on 4d, 8d, 1/6)
Set	13.00	14.00
First day cover	–	20.00

Spring gentian (3d)
Dog rose (6d)
Honeysuckle (9d)
Fringed water lily (1/3)

■ **1964, August 5. International Botanical Congress**
Des: Michael and Sylvia Goaman. Wmk: Multiple St. Edward's Crown.
Non-phosphor issue
Set	2.25	2.50
First day cover	–	11.00

Phosphor issue (three bands)
Set	16.00	18.00
First day cover	–	20.00

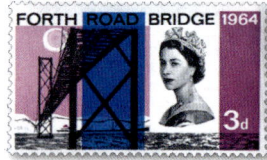

Forth Road Bridge (3d)
Forth Road Bridge and Foth Bridge (6d)

■ **1964, September 4. Opening of the Forth Road Bridge**
Des: Andrew Restall. Wmk: Multiple St. Edward's Crown.
Non-phosphor issue
Set	0.50	1.00
First day cover	–	3.50

Phosphor issue (three bands)
Set	2.75	2.75
First day cover	–	10.00

PRE-DECIMAL QUEEN ELIZABETH II

Sir Winston Churchill (4d, 1/3 with different designs)

1965, July 8. Churchill Commemoration
Des: David Gentleman and Rosalind Dease. Wmk: Multiple St. Edward's Crown.
Non-phosphor issue
Set	0.60	0.60
First day cover	–	5.00

Phosphor issue (three bands)
Set	1.25	1.75
First day cover	–	5.00

Printed on a Timson machine
4d	1.25	1.25

(*The Timson printing shows more detail on the Churchill portrait.)

Seal of Simon de Montfort (6d)
Parliament buildings (2/6)

1965, July 19. 700th Anniversary of Simon de Montfort's Parliament
Des: Stewart Black (6d), Richard Guyatt (2/6). Wmk: Multiple St. Edward's Crown.
Non-phosphor issue
Set	0.65	0.65
First day cover	–	7.00

Phosphor issue (three bands on 6d only)
6d	0.50	0.60
First day cover	–	20.00

Salvation Army band (3d)
Three Salvation Army members (1/6)

1965, August 9. Centenary of Salvation Army
Des: Michael Farrar-Bell (3d), Geoffrey Trenaman (1/6). Wmk: Multiple St. Edward's Crown.
Non-phosphor issue
Set	0.60	0.80
First day cover	–	10.00

Phosphor issue (one band on 3d, three bands on 1/6)
Set	1.35	1.50
First day cover	–	22.00

Carbolic spray (4d)
Joseph Lister (1/–)

1965, September 1. Centenary of Joseph Lister's Discovery of Antiseptic Surgery
Des: Peter Gauld (4d), Frank Ariss (1/–). Wmk: Multiple St. Edward's Crown.
Non-phosphor issue
Set	0.50	0.75
First day cover	–	5.00

Phosphor issue (three bands)
Set	1.50	1.75
First day cover	–	10.00

Trinidad carnival dancers (6d)
Canadian folk dancers (1/6)

1965, September 1. Commonwealth Arts Festival
Des: David Gentleman and Rosalind Dease. Wmk: Multiple St. Edward's Crown.
Non-phosphor issue
Set	0.60	0.80
First day cover	–	7.50

Phosphor issue (three bands)
Set	1.70	2.25
First day cover	–	15.00

QUEEN ELIZABETH II PRE-DECIMAL

Spitfires (4d)
Pilot in Hurricane (4d)
Overlapping wings (4d)
Spitfires attacking Heinkel bomber (4d)
Spitfire attacking Stuka bomber (4d)
Tail wing of Dornier bomber (4d)
Anti-aircraft artillery (9d)
St Paul's Cathedral (1/3)

■ **1965, September 13. 25th Anniversary of the Battle of Britain**
Des: David Gentleman and Rosalind Dease (4d, 1/3), Andrew Restall (9d). Wmk: Multiple St. Edward's Crown. Six 4d values se-tenant.
Non-phosphor issue

Set	6.00	8.00
First day cover	–	12.00

Phosphor issue (three bands)

Set	10.00	11.00
First day cover	–	16.00

Post Office Tower and Georgian buildings (3d)
Post Office Tower and Nash Terrace (1/3)

■ **1965, October 8. Opening of the Post Office Tower**
Des: Clive Abbott. Wmk: Multiple St. Edward's Crown.
Non-phosphor issue

Set	0.30	0.60
First day cover	–	3.00

Phosphor issue (one band on 3d, three bands on 1/3)

Set	0.40	0.50
First day cover	–	5.00

UN emblem (3d)
ICY emblem (1/6)

■ **1965, October 25. 20th Anniversary of United Nations and International Co-Operation Year**
Des: Jeffery Matthews. Wmk: Multiple St. Edward's Crown.
Non-phosphor issue

Set	0.50	0.60
First day cover	–	5.50

Phosphor issue (one band on 3d, three bands on 1/6)

Set	1.25	1.75
First day cover	–	10.00

Telecommunications (9d)
Radio waves (1/6)

■ **1965, November 15. International Telecommunication Union Centenary**
Des: Andrew Restall. Wmk: Multiple St. Edward's Crown.
Non-phosphor issue

Set	0.75	0.75
First day cover	–	8.50

Phosphor issue (three bands)

Set	2.50	3.75
First day cover	–	14.00

Robert Burns portrait by Skirving (4d)
Robert Burns portrait by Nasmyth (1/3)

■ **1966, January 25. Robert Burns**
Des: Gordon Huntly. Wmk: Multiple St. Edward's Crown.
Non-phosphor issue

Set	0.35	0.40
First day cover	–	1.50

Phosphor issue (three bands)

Set	1.25	1.50
First day cover	–	4.00

PRE-DECIMAL   QUEEN ELIZABETH II

Exterior of Westminster Abbey (3d)
Fan vaulting of Westminster Abbey (2/6)

■ 1966, February 28. 900th Anniversary of Westminster Abbey
Des: Sheila Robinson (3d), Bradbury Wilkinson (2/6). Printed in recess by Bradbury Wilkinson (2/6). Wmk: Multiple St. Edward's Crown. Perf: 11 x 12 (2/6)

Non-phosphor issue
Set	0.50	0.50
First day cover	–	2.75

Phosphor issue (one band on 3d only)
3d	0.20	0.20
First day cover	–	9.00

Sussex Downs (4d)
Antrim, Northern Ireland (6d)
Harlech Castle (1/3)
The Cairngorms (1/6)

■ 1966, May 2. Landscapes
Des: Leonard Rosoman. Wmk: Multiple St. Edward's Crown.

Non-phosphor issue
Set	0.60	0.75
First day cover	–	3.50

Phosphor issue (three bands)
Set	0.60	0.60
First day cover	–	5.00

Two footballers (4d)
Four footballers (6d)
Goalkeeper catching ball (1/3)

■ 1966, June 1. World Cup
Des: David Gentleman (4d), William Kempster (6d), David Caplan (1/3). Wmk: Multiple St. Edward's Crown.

Non-phosphor issue
Set	0.40	0.40
First day cover	–	10.00

Phosphor issue (two bands on 4d, three bands on 6d, 1/3)
Set	0.30	0.40
First day cover	–	12.00

Black-headed gull (4d)
Blue tit (4d)
Robin (4d)
Blackbird (4d)

■ 1966, August 8. British Birds
Des: John Norris Wood. Wmk: Multiple St. Edward's Crown. All four values in se-tenant blocks.

Non-phosphor issue
Set (in se-tenant block of four)	0.50	0.60
First day cover	–	4.00

Phosphor issue (three bands)
Set (in se-tenant block of four)	0.40	0.40
First day cover	–	4.50

Two footballers and 'England Winners' (4d)

■ 1966, August 18. England's World Cup Victory
As June 1 issue, with additional inscription 'ENGLAND WINNERS'.
Non-phosphor only.
4d	0.20	0.20
First day cover	–	7.50

BRITISH STAMP MARKET VALUES 2024   41

QUEEN ELIZABETH II PRE-DECIMAL

Jodrell Bank radiotelescope (4d)
Jaguar 'E' type and Mini cars (6d)
SR N6 hovercraft (1/3)
Windscale nuclear reactor (1/6)

■ **1966, September 19. British Technology**
Des: David and Ann Gillespie (4d, 6d), Andrew Restall (1/3, 1/6).
Wmk: Multiple St. Edward's Crown.
Non-phosphor issue
Set	0.40	0.60
First day cover	–	1.50

Phosphor issue (three bands)
Set	0.45	0.70
First day cover	–	3.00

Scenes from the Bayeux Tapestry (4d, 4d, 4d, 4d, 4d, 4d)
Norman ship (6d)
Norman cavalry attacking English infantry (1/3)

■ **1966, October 14. 900th Anniversary of the Battle of Hastings**
Des: David Gentleman. Wmk: Multiple St. Edward's Crown, sideways on 1/3 value. Six 4d values se-tenant.
Non-phosphor issue
Set	1.25	3.00
First day cover	–	2.50

Phosphor issue (three bands on 4d, 6d, four bands on 1/3)
Set	1.25	3.00
First day cover	–	3.75

King of the Orient (3d)
Snowman (1/6)

■ **1966, December 1. Christmas**
Des: Tasveer Shemza (3d), James Berry (1/6), both aged six.
Wmk: Multiple St. Edward's Crown, upright on both values.
Non-phosphor issue
Set	0.20	0.25
First day cover	–	1.00

Phosphor issue (one band on 3d, two bands on 1/6)
Set	0.20	0.30
First day cover	–	1.00

(*The phosphor 3d can be found with the band at left or right).

Loading freight on a ship (9d)
Loading freight on an aeroplane (1/6)

■ **1967, February 20. European Free Trade Association**
Des: Clive Abbott. Wmk: Multiple St. Edward's Crown.
Non-phosphor issue
Set	0.15	0.20
First day cover	–	6.00

Phosphor issue (three bands)
Set	0.20	0.25
First day cover	–	6.00

Hawthorn and bramble (4d)
Bindweed and viper's bugloss (4d)
Ox-eye daisy, coltsfoot and buttercup (4d)
Bluebell, red campion and wood anemone (4d)
Dog violet (9d)
Primrose (1/9)

■ **1967, April 24. British Wild Flowers**
Des: William Keble Martin (4d), Mary Grierson (9d, 1/9). Wmk: Multiple St. Edward's Crown. Four 4d values se-tenant.
Non-phosphor issue
Set	0.75	0.80
First day cover	–	1.50

Phosphor issue (three bands)
Set	0.40	0.80
First day cover	–	7.50

PRE-DECIMAL QUEEN ELIZABETH II

'Master Lambton' by Sir Thomas Lawrence (4d)
'Mares and Foals in a Landscape' by George Stubbs (9d)
'Children Coming Out of School' by L. S. Lowry (1/6)

■ **1967, July 10. British Paintings**
Des: Stuart Rose. No Wmk. Two phosphor bands.
Set	0.20	0.30
First day cover	–	1.50

Gipsy Moth IV (1/9)

■ **1967, July 24. Sir Francis Chichester's Single-Handed Voyage Around the World**
Des: Michael and Sylvia Goaman. No Wmk. Three phosphor bands.
1/9	0.10	0.15
First day cover	–	0.70

Radar screen (4d)
Penicillin mould (1/–)
Jet engine (1/6)
Television equipment (1/9)

■ **1967, September 19. British Discovery & Invention**
Des: Clive Abbott (4d, 1/–), Richard Negus and Philip Sharland (1/6, 1/9). Wmk: Multiple St. Edward's Crown. Three phosphor bands on the 4d.
Set	0.25	0.30
First day cover	–	1.00

'The Adoration of the Shepherds' by the School of Seville (3d)
'Madonna and Child' by Bartolomé Murillo (4d)
'The Adoration of the Shepherds' by Louis Le Nain (1/6)

■ **1967, October 18–November 27. Christmas**
Des: Stuart Rose. No Wmk. 3d has one central phosphor band. The 3d was released on November 27, the 4d on October 18, and the 1/6 on November 27.
Set	0.15	0.40
First day covers	–	3.00

Tarr Steps (4d)
Aberfeldy Bridge (9d)
Menai Bridge (1/6)
M4 Viaduct (1/9)

■ **1968, April 29. British Bridges**
Des: Jeffery Matthews (4d, 1/9), Andrew Restall (9d), Leonard Rosoman (1/6). No Wmk. Two phosphor bands.
Set	0.25	0.35
First day cover	–	1.00

Trades Union Congress (4d)
Votes for Women: Emmeline Pankhurst statue (9d)
Royal Air Force: Sopwith Camel and modern fighters (1/–)
James Cook's first voyage: signature and H.M.S. Endeavour (1/9)

■ **1968, May 29. Anniversaries**
Des: David Gentleman (4d), Clive Abbott (others). No Wmk.
Set	0.25	0.35
First day cover	–	2.25

BRITISH STAMP MARKET VALUES 2024

QUEEN ELIZABETH II PRE-DECIMAL

'Queen Elizabeth 1' by an unknown artist (4d)
'Pinkie' by Sir Thomas Lawrence (1/-)
'Ruins of St. Mary le Port' by John Piper (1/6)
'The Hay Wain' by John Constable (1/9)

■ **1968, August 12. British Paintings**
Des: Stuart Rose. No Wmk.
Set	0.25	0.30
First day cover	–	0.50

Boy and girl with rocking horse (4d)
Girl with doll's house (9d)
Boy with train set (1/6)

■ **1968, November 25. Christmas**
Des: Rosalind Dease. No Wmk.
Printed on a Rembrandt machine
Set	0.20	0.25
First day cover	–	1.25

Printed on a Thrissell machine (4d only)
4d	0.15	0.20

(*The Thrissell printing can be distinguished by the boy's pullover having a more mottled appearance.)

Queen Elizabeth 2 (5d)
Elizabethan galleon (9d)
East Indiaman (9d)
Cutty Sark (9d)
S.S. Great Britain (1/-)
R.M.S. Mauretania (1/-)

■ **1969, January 15. British Ships**
Des: David Gentleman. No Wmk. Three 9d values in se-tenant strip. Two 1/- values in se-tenant pair.
Set	0.75	1.20
First day cover	–	1.75

Concorde over Great Britain and France (4d)
Silhouettes of Concorde (9d)
Nose and tail of Concorde (1/6)

■ **1969, March 3. First Flight of Concorde**
Des: Michael and Sylvia Goaman (4d), David Gentleman (9d, 1/6). No Wmk.
Set	0.40	0.50
First day cover	–	4.00

First transatlantic flight: Vickers Vimy, Alcock & Brown (5d)
Europa/CEPT: emblems (9d)
International Labour Organisation: hand holding wrench (1/-)
NATO: flags of member countries (1/6)
First England–Australia Flight: Vickers Vimy, route on globe (1/9)

■ **1969, April 2. Anniversaries**
Des: Philip Sharland (5d, 1/-, 1/6), Michael and Sylvia Goaman (9d, 1/9). No Wmk.
Set	0.30	0.60
First day cover	–	1.25

PRE-DECIMAL **QUEEN ELIZABETH II**

Durham Cathedral (5d)
York Minster (5d)
St Giles' Cathedral, Edinburgh (5d)
Canterbury Cathedral (5d)
St Paul's Cathedral (9d)
Liverpool Metropolitan Cathedral (1/6)

■ **1969, May 28. British Cathedrals**
Des: Peter Gauld. No Wmk. Four 5d values se-tenant.
Set   0.65   0.85
First day cover   –   1.25

The King's Gate, Caernarfon Castle (5d)
The Eagle Tower, Caernarfon Castle (5d)
Queen Eleanor's Gate, Caernarfon Castle (5d)
Celtic cross, Margam Abbey (9d)
Charles, Prince of Wales (1/–)

■ **1969, July 1. Investiture of the Prince of Wales**
Des: David Gentleman. No Wmk. Three 5d values se-tenant.
Set   0.40   0.75
First day cover   –   1.00

Mahatma Gandhi and flag of India (1/6)

■ **1969, August 13. Gandhi Centenary Year**
Des: Biman Mullick.
1/6   0.30   0.40
First day cover   –   3.50

National Giro symbol (5d)
Telephone dials (9d)
Pulse code modulation (1/–)
Automatic sorting (1/6)

■ **1969, October 1. Post Office Technology**
Des: David Gentleman. Printed in litho by De La Rue. No Wmk. Perf: 13½x14.
Set   0.35   0.45
First day cover   –   0.75

Herald angel (4d)
Three shepherds (5d)
Three kings (1/6)

■ **1969, November 26. Christmas**
Des: Fritz Wegner. No Wmk.
Set   0.25   0.25
First day cover   –   0.50

Fife harling (5d)
Cotswold limestone (9d)
Welsh stucco (1/–)
Ulster thatch (1/6)

■ **1970, February 11. British Rural Architecture**
Des: David Gentleman (5d, 9d), Sheila Robinson (1/–, 1/6). No Wmk.
Set   0.40   0.50
First day cover   –   0.75

BRITISH STAMP MARKET VALUES 2024 **45**

QUEEN ELIZABETH II PRE-DECIMAL

Declaration of Arbroath: signing ceremony (5d)
Florence Nightingale: attending patients (9d)
International Co-operative Alliance: signing ceremony (1/–)
Sailing of the Mayflower: pilgrims and ship (1/6)
Royal Astronomical Society: Sir William Herschel, Francis Baily,
Sir John Herschel and telescope (1/9)

■ **1970, April 1. Anniversaries**
Des: Fritz Wegner (5d, 9d, 1/6), Marjorie Seynor (1/–, 1/9).
No Wmk.

Set	0.40	0.70
First day cover	–	1.00

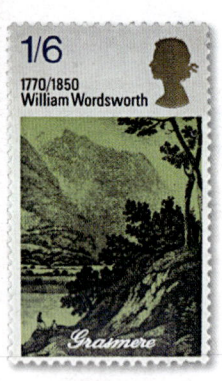

Mr Pickwick and Sam (5d)
Mr and Mrs Micawber (5d)
David Copperfield and Betsey Trotwood (5d)
Oliver Twist (5d)
Grasmere (1/6)

■ **1970, June 3. Literary Anniversaries**
Des: Rosalind Dease. No Wmk. Four 5d values se-tenant.

Set	0.60	0.75
First day cover	–	1.00

Runners (5d)
Swimmers (1/6)
Cyclists (1/9)

■ **1970, July 15. British Commonwealth Games**
Des: Andrew Restall. Printed in litho by De La Rue. No Wmk.
Perf: 13½x14.

Set	0.50	0.50
First day cover	–	0.75

1840 line-engraved Penny Black (5d)
1847 embossed 1/– green (9d)
1855 surface-printed 4d carmine (1/6)

■ **1970, September 18. Philympia 1970 International Stamp Exhibition**
Des: David Gentleman. No Wmk.

Set	0.50	0.40
First day cover	–	0.75

Angel appearing to shepherds (4d)
Mary, Joseph and Jesus (5d)
Wise men bringing gifts (1/6)

■ **1970, November 25. Christmas**
Des: Sally Stiff, based on the De Lisle Psalter. No Wmk.

Set	0.25	0.30
First day cover	–	0.75

46 BRITISH STAMP MARKET VALUES 2024

STAMP COLLECTIONS URGENTLY REQUIRED

best prices, fast friendly service

Whether it's for sale through one of our auctions, or a direct sale for immediate payment, we genuinely believe that we offer all the above and more - our reputation depends on it!

Visit our website for full details:

www.tonylester.co.uk

TONY LESTER Auctions

For a friendly and personal service just call **01926 634 809** and ask to speak to Tony

Tony Lester Auctions Limited, The Sidings, Birdingbury Road, Marton, Nr. Rugby CV23 9RX. Email: tonylester@btconnect.com
Web: www.tonylester.co.uk

We are long standing members of the Philatelic Traders' Society, complying with its strict code of ethics. We have been established for over 30 years, with a reputation for honesty and fair dealing.

MACHINS PRE-DECIMAL

PRE-DECIMAL MACHIN DEFINITIVES

In this section, prices are given for unmounted mint (left) and fine used (right). Exceptions are made where used prices are not applicable, for example booklet panes and gum varieties.

The Machin head of Queen Elizabeth II is so-called because it is based on a photograph of a sculpture by Arnold Machin. All designs in the series are similar, but small differences can be found in the head itself and in its setting in the design.

There are also varieties in the number and positioning of phosphor bands.

LOW VALUES

4d sepia

■ **1967–1969. Small format**
Des: Arnold Machin. Printed in photogravure by Harrisons. No wmk. Head A with two phosphor bands except where stated.

Gum Arabic

3d violet (August 8, 1967) (one band)	0.15	–
4d sepia (June 5, 1967)	0.15	–
head B	£2,000	–
4d red (one centre band)	1.00	–
9d green (August 8, 1967)	0.20	–
1/– pale violet (June 5, 1967)	0.20	–
1/– deep violet	1.00	–
1/6 green, deep blue (August 8, 1967)	0.30	–
1/9 orange, black (June 5, 1967)	0.35	–
First day cover (4d, 1/–, 1/9)	–	1.25
First day cover (3d, 9d, 1/6)	–	1.25

Coil stamps (August 27, 1969)

1d olive (head B, one band)	0.75	–
2d brown (head B, one band)	0.30	0.30
3d violet (head B, one band)	0.30	–
4d red (head B, one band)	0.20	–
Se-tenant coil of two **2d**, one **1d**, one **3d** and one **4d**	1.00	1.00

Booklet panes of six

Six **4d** sepia	8.00	–
Six **4d** red	£125	–

PVA gum

½d orange (February 5, 1968)	0.10	0.10
1d olive (February 5, 1968)	0.10	0.10
head B	0.10	0.10
head B (one centre band)	0.50	0.50
2d brown (February 5, 1968)	0.10	0.10
setting 2	0.10	0.30
3d violet (one centre band)	1.00	1.00
head B (one centre band)	2.00	2.00
3d violet	0.15	0.10
head B	0.50	0.10
4d sepia (shades)	0.15	0.10
head B	0.35	0.10
4d sepia (one centre band)	0.30	0.20
head B (one centre band)	0.10	0.10
4d red (January 6, 1969) (one centre band)	0.15	0.20
head B (one centre band)	0.10	0.10
head B (one band at left)	0.80	0.80
head B (one band at right)	1.50	1.50
5d blue (July 1, 1968)	0.20	0.30
head B	0.75	0.75
head B (two bands on 'all over' phosphor)	£275	–
6d purple (February 5, 1968)	0.20	0.20
head B	9.00	7.50
7d green (July 1, 1968) (head 2)	0.20	0.30
8d red (July 1, 1968)	0.20	0.25
8d light-blue (January 6, 1969) (head 2)	0.30	0.25
9d green	0.50	0.50
10d brown (July 1, 1968)	0.30	0.30
1/– deep violet	0.20	0.20
1/6 green, deep blue	0.30	0.20
phosphor-coated paper	0.50	0.45
1/9 orange, black	2.50	0.30
Set (one of each value)	6.00	6.00
First day cover (½d, 1d, 2d, 6d)	–	1.00
First day cover (5d, 7d, 8d red, 10d)	–	1.00
First day cover (4d red, 8d light blue)	–	2.50

Booklet panes of four

Four **4d** sepia (head B, two bands)	1.00	–
Four **4d** sepia (head B, one centre band)	1.00	–
Four **4d** red (head B, one centre band)	1.00	–
Two **1d** left of two **3d** (head B, two bands)	4.00	–
Two **1d** right of two **3d** (head B, two bands)	3.00	–
Two **4d** sepia (head B, one centre band), with two labels reading '£4,315 FOR YOU AT AGE 55' and 'SEE OTHER PAGES'	1.50	–
Two **4d** red (head B, one centre band), with two labels reading '£4,315 FOR YOU AT AGE 55' and 'SEE OTHER PAGES'	1.00	–

PRE-DECIMAL MACHINS

Booklet panes of six

Six **1d** olive (head B, two bands)	1.50	–
Six **3d** violet (head A, centre band)	5.00	–
Six **4d** sepia (head A, two bands)	5.00	–
Six **4d** sepia (head A, one centre band)	1.50	–
Six **4d** red (head A, one centre band)	1.25	–
Six **4d** red (head B, one centre band)	1.25	–
Six **5d** blue (head B, two bands)	1.50	–
Four **1d** olive (one centre band) with two **4d** sepia (head B, one centre band)	5.00	–
Four **1d** olive (two bands) with two **4d** red (head B, one left band)	6.00	–

Booklet panes of 15 (all head B)

Six **1d** olive (two bands) with three **4d** red (one band at left), three **4d** red (one band at right) and three **5d** blue, with recipe label	6.00	–
Fifteen **4d** red (one centre band), with 'Stuffed Cucumber' label	1.25	–
Fifteen **4d** red (one centre band), with 'Method' label	1.25	–
Fifteen **5d** blue (two bands), with recipe label	3.00	–

(*These panes come from the £1 Stamps For Cooks booklet and can be found with just four holes in the binding margin, where stapled together, or with a larger number of equally spaced holes, where stitched.)

HIGH VALUES

5/– brown-red

■ **1969, March 5. Large format**
Des: Arnold Machin. Printed in recess by Bradbury Wilkinson.
Perf: 12.

2/6 brown	0.25	0.20
5/– brown-red	1.00	0.50
10/– deep blue	3.00	4.00
£1 black	2.50	2.50
Set	5.50	5.00
First day cover	–	6.00

Griffin's
Auctioneers & Valuers

🌐 www.griffinsauctions.co.uk
✉ info@griffinsauctions.co.uk
📞 01926 505012

**Free auction valuations online or in person, for British, Commonwealth & World stamps, Postal History, Decimal Stamps, First Day Covers & Philatelic Literature.
Private treaty offers also available.**

Flexible rates of commission for higher value individual items & collections

Unit C2, Harris Road
Warwick, CV34 5JU

MACHINS DECIMAL

DECIMAL MACHIN DEFINITIVES

In this section, prices are given for unmounted mint (left) and fine used (right). Exceptions are made where used prices are not applicable, for example in the case of booklet panes and gum varieties.

All stamps have fluorescent-coated paper unless otherwise stated.

Gum
Gummed stamps can be found with three different gums. Gum Arabic is either colourless or yellow in appearance and is very shiny. Polyvinyl alcohol gum (PVA) is colourless but has a matt appearance. Polyvinyl alcohol with dextrin gum (PVAD) is also matt, but has a blueish or greenish tinge.

Self-adhesive definitives have become increasingly common since 1993.

Phosphor
Phosphor at first was applied in the form of vertical bands. When you hold a stamp up to the light and look along the surface, the paper itself appears shiny while the bands have a dull appearance.

Most stamps have two phosphor bands, on the two vertical edges; others have just one, which can be central or down the left or right vertical edge.

The width of the bands can vary, as can the size of the printing screen used to apply them, but these differences are beyond the scope of this publication.

Booklet panes, where stamps of the 2nd class rate (requiring a single phosphor band) have been printed se-tenant with other stamps (requiring two phosphor bands), have been found with the phosphor printed as bars rather than bands. Whereas bands extend across the perforations to the next stamp, these bars stop at the edge of the stamp design.

The term 'all over phosphor' is used where the phosphor was printed over the entire surface of the stamp, rather than in the form of bands. In some cases it was printed onto the paper before the stamp design was printed; in other cases it was printed afterwards.

The term 'no phosphor' is often applied to stamps with the phosphor omitted in error; such errors are outside the scope of this publication. However, the 50p and 75p values have been printed without phosphor in the normal course of events.

Paper
At first, from February 1971, these stamps were printed on what is now called 'original coated paper' (OCP), which gives a dull violet reaction when the front of the stamp is viewed under ultra-violet light.

This was gradually replaced from August 1971 by 'fluorescent coated paper' (FCP) which gives a bright reaction under ultra-violet light, and then from August 1979 by 'phosphor-coated paper' (PCP), which adds the after-glow of phosphor and makes the stamp appear uniformly shiny.

Note that stamps with phosphor omitted in error also have a uniformly shiny surface, so those with phosphor-coated paper can only be positively identified by their reaction under ultra-violet light.

The appearance of stamps with phosphor-coated paper can vary considerably due to variations in their drying time after printing. The abbreviation 'PCPI' is used to denote a dull appearance, and 'PCPII' a highly glazed appearance.

Some stamps with phosphor-coated paper have been found with the fluorescent brightener omitted. These still give a phosphor afterglow, but the paper gives a dull violet reaction similar to that found with original coated paper.

Attempts to standardise the paper produced what is known as 'advanced coated paper' (ACP), in use from March 1983. The visual difference between ACP and PCPI is minimal, but the former gives a brighter reaction under ultra-violet light.

Value and portrait
Minor changes can be noted in the position of the denomination of value in relation to the Queen's portrait, and the position of the portrait in relation to the base of the stamp.

Booklet panes
At first booklets were held together by stitching, so that a number of small holes can be found in the binding margin on the left hand side of panes. Later, the panes were stuck into booklet covers by the binding margins; in many such cases, panes can be found with the binding margin to the left or to the right.

In the case of stitched booklets, the booklet panes are recorded separately. Where the panes are stuck into the covers, most collectors prefer these as complete booklets, so the separate panes are not recorded.

Many of the early decimal booklet panes included non-postal labels se-tenant with the stamps in the pane, adjacent to the binding margin. At first these panes were perforated between the labels and the margin, but later they were not.

In 1987, as an experiment to counter complaints about the poor guillotining of panes, some booklet panes were produced with stamps with either the left or right-hand edge imperforate.

Coils
There are two different types of coils or rolls from which stamps may be found.

Where the source of a stamp is listed as 'coils', this refers to coils of the same value, usually 1st class or 2nd class, joined either horizontally or vertically. These were usually produced for use by businesses.

Where the source is listed as 'se-tenant coils', this refers to coils containing a mixture of values joined as a strip, These were usually produced for sale through vending machines.

Cartons
In an experiment staged in Scotland in 1976-78, 1st class and 2nd class definitives (including country definitives) were sold in cartons from vending machines. Sold at 30p or 60p, they contained either 6½p and 8½p, or 7p and 9p stamps.

DECIMAL MACHINS

LOW VALUES WITHOUT ELLIPTICAL PERFORATIONS, 1971–96

Des. Arnold Machin. Printed in photogravure by Harrisons except where stated. No Wmk. Perf: 15x14, except where stated.

■ ½p turquoise, February 15, 1971

gum Arabic, two phosphor bands, OCP	se-tenant coils	0.30	–
gum Arabic, two phosphor bands, OCP with silicone	se-tenant coils	30.00	–
gum Arabic, two phosphor bands, FCP	sheets	0.10	–
gum Arabic, two phosphor bands, FCP with silicone	se-tenant coils	0.40	–
PVA gum, two phosphor bands, OCP	sheets, se-tenant coils, booklets	0.20	–
PVA gum, two phosphor bands, FCP	sheets, booklets	0.50	–
PVA gum, one phosphor band (left)	prestige booklets	35.00	30.00
PVAD gum, two phosphor bands	sheets, se-tenant coils, booklets	0.10	0.15
PVAD gum, one phosphor band (centre)	se-tenant coils, booklets	0.20	0.15
PVAD gum, PCPI	sheets, se-tenant coils	0.10	0.10
PVAD gum, PCPII	sheets	0.15	0.15
PVAD gum, PCP, fluorescent brightener omitted (poor gum)	se-tenant coils	£125	30.00
PVAD gum, PCP, fluorescent brightener omitted (good gum)	se-tenant coils	£950	–

■ 1p crimson, February 15, 1971

gum Arabic, two phosphor bands, OCP	se-tenant coils	0.40	–
gum Arabic, two phosphor bands, OCP with silicone	se-tenant coils	30.00	–
gum Arabic, two phosphor bands, FCP	coils	0.60	–
gum Arabic, two phosphor bands, FCP with silicone	se-tenant coils	0.60	–
PVA gum, two phosphor bands, OCP	sheets	0.10	–
PVA gum, two phosphor bands, FCP	sheets, booklets	1.25	–
PVAD gum, two phosphor bands (value lower)	booklets	0.40	0.30
PVAD gum, two phosphor bands (value intermediate)	se-tenant coils, booklets	0.40	0.35
PVAD gum, two phosphor bands (value higher)	sheets, se-tenant coils	0.20	0.30
PVAD gum, one centre phosphor band (portrait higher)	se-tenant coils	0.10	0.15
PVAD gum, one centre phosphor band (portrait lower)	se-tenant coils, booklets	0.40	0.30
PVAD gum, all-over phosphor	sheets	0.20	0.20
PVAD gum, PCPI (portrait higher)	sheets	0.10	0.10
PVAD gum, PCPI (portrait lower)	sheets, se-tenant coils	0.20	0.15
PVAD gum, PCPII	sheets	0.30	0.25
PVAD gum, ACP	sheets	0.30	0.25
PVAD gum, one phosphor band (left)	booklets	0.60	0.60
PVAD gum, one phosphor band (right)	prestige booklets	4.00	4.00

■ 1½p black, February 15, 1971

PVA gum, two phosphor bands, OCP	sheets, booklets	0.20	0.10
PVA gum, two phosphor bands, FCP	sheets, booklets	0.90	0.50
PVAD gum, two phosphor bands	sheets, booklets	0.40	0.30

BRITISH STAMP MARKET VALUES 2024 51

MACHINS DECIMAL

■ 2p green, February 15, 1971
gum Arabic, two phosphor bands, OCP	se-tenant coils	2.00	–
gum Arabic, two phosphor bands, OCP with silicone	se-tenant coils	£120	–
gum Arabic, two phosphor bands, FCP with silicone	se-tenant coils	2.00	–
PVA gum, two phosphor bands, OCP	sheets, booklets	0.20	–
PVA gum, two phosphor bands, FCP	sheets, booklets	1.50	–
PVAD gum, two phosphor bands (portrait higher)	sheets, se-tenant coils, booklets	0.20	0.20
PVAD gum, two phosphor bands (portrait lower)	booklets	0.40	0.40
PVAD gum, all over phosphor	sheets	0.20	0.15
PVAD gum, PCPI	sheets	0.20	0.20
PVAD gum, PCPII	sheets	0.20	0.15
PVAD gum, PCP (litho by Questa, perf 13½x14)	sheets	0.20	0.20
PVAD gum, PCP (litho by Questa, perf 15x14)	sheets	0.20	0.20
PVAD gum, ACP (litho by Questa, perf 15x14)	sheets	0.30	0.40

■ 2p deep green, February 23, 1988
PVAD gum, PCP	sheets, booklets	0.20	0.20
PVA gum, PCP, litho by Walsall	booklets	1.00	1.00

■ 2½p pink, February 15, 1971
gum arabic, one centre phosphor band	sheets, coils	0.50	–
PVA gum, one centre phosphor band, OCP	sheets, coils, booklets	0.20	0.20
PVA gum, one centre phosphor band, FCP	sheets, booklets	0.50	0.50
PVA gum, one phosphor band (left), OCP	booklets	5.00	1.50
PVA gum, one phosphor band (left), FCP	booklets, prestige booklets	0.70	0.70
PVA gum, one phosphor band (right)	prestige booklets	1.00	1.00
PVAD gum, two phosphor bands	sheets	0.20	0.20
PVAD gum, one phosphor band (centre)	sheets	0.20	0.20

■ 2½p rose-red, January 14, 1981
PVAD gum, PCPI	sheets, se-tenant coils	0.40	0.40
PVAD gum, PCPII	sheets	0.20	0.20
PVAD gum, PCP, fluorescent brightener omitted	se-tenant coils	35.00	35.00
PVAD gum, two phosphor bands	booklets	0.30	0.30

■ 3p ultramarine, February 15, 1971
gum Arabic, two phosphor bands, OCP	coils	50.00	–
gum Arabic, two phosphor bands, FCP	sheets, coils	0.75	–
gum arabic, one phosphor band (centre)	sheets	0.40	–
PVA gum, two phosphor bands, OCP	sheets, coils, booklets	0.15	0.15
PVA gum, two phosphor bands, FCP	sheets, booklets	0.30	0.30
PVA gum, two phosphor bands, PCP	(only two examples known)	£1,200	–
PVA gum, one phosphor band (centre)	sheets, booklets	0.50	–
PVAD gum, one phosphor band (centre)	sheets, coils, booklets	0.20	0.20

■ 3p magenta, October 22, 1980
PVAD gum, PCPI	sheets, se-tenant coils	0.20	0.20
PVAD gum, PCPII	sheets, se-tenant coils	1.00	1.00
PVAD gum, PCP, fluorescent brightener omitted	se-tenant coils	5.00	4.00
PVAD gum, ACP	sheets, prestige booklets	0.25	0.25
PVAD gum, two phosphor bands	booklets, prestige booklets	0.20	0.20

■ 3½p olive-grey, February 15, 1971
PVA gum, two phosphor bands, OCP	sheets	0.25	0.25
PVA gum, two phosphor bands, FCP	sheets, booklets	1.50	–
PVAD gum, two phosphor bands, OCP	sheets	£120	50.00
PVAD gum, two phosphor bands, FCP	sheets, coils, booklets	0.50	0.25
PVAD gum, one phosphor band (centre)	sheets, coils, booklets	0.25	0.25

■ 3½p purple-brown, March 30, 1983
PVAD gum, PCPI	sheets	0.30	0.30

DECIMAL MACHINS

PVAD gum, ACP	prestige booklets	1.25	1.25
PVAD gum, one phosphor band (centre)	booklets	1.50	1.50

■ 4p bistre, February 15, 1971

gum arabic, two phosphor bands	sheets	0.50	–
PVA gum, two phosphor bands, OCP	sheets	0.30	0.20
PVA gum, two phosphor bands, FCP	sheets	3.50	–
PVAD gum, two phosphor bands	sheets	0.20	0.20

■ 4p greenish-blue, January 30, 1980

PVA gum, two phosphor bands (litho by Waddingtons)	sheets	0.20	0.15
PVAD gum, PCP (litho by Waddingtons)	sheets	0.30	0.20
PVA gum, PCP (litho by Questa, perf 15x14)	sheets	0.40	0.40
PVAD gum, two phosphor bands	booklets	2.00	2.00
PVAD gum, PCP	se-tenant coils	0.20	0.20
PVAD gum, PCP, fluorescent brightener omitted (perfect gum)	se-tenant coils	£370	35.00
PVAD gum, PCPI (value higher)	se-tenant coils	0.35	0.20
PVAD gum, one phosphor band (centre)	booklets	1.00	1.00
PVAD gum, one phosphor band (left)	prestige booklets	3.75	3.75
PVAD gum, one phosphor band (right)	prestige booklets	4.00	4.00

■ 4p bright blue, July 26, 1988

PVAD gum, ACP	sheets	0.30	0.30
PVAD gum, PCP	sheets, coils	0.25	0.25

■ 4½p grey-blue, October 24, 1973

PVAD gum, two phosphor bands	sheets, coils, booklets	0.20	0.20
PVAD gum, all-over phosphor, two phosphor bands	sheets	0.65	–

■ 5p pale violet, February 15, 1971

PVA gum, two phosphor bands, OCP	sheets	0.20	0.20
PVA gum, two phosphor bands, FCP	sheets	2.50	–
PVAD gum, two phosphor bands	sheets	0.20	0.20
PVAD gum, PCPI	sheets	0.20	0.20
PVAD gum, PCPII	sheets	0.50	0.35
PVAD gum, PCP (litho by Questa)	sheets	0.30	0.20
PVA gum, PCP (litho by Questa)	sheets	0.50	0.50

(*This stamp also appears in the 2017 Machin Definitive Golden Anniversary miniature sheet, printed by ISP. Price 0.50 mint or used.)

■ 5p red-brown, January 27, 1982

PVAD gum, PCP (litho by Questa, perf 13½x14)	sheets	0.40	0.40
PVAD gum, PCP (litho by Questa, perf 15x14)	sheets	0.50	0.40
PVAD gum, ACP (litho by Questa, perf 15x14)	sheets	0.45	0.40
PVAD gum, one phosphor band (centre)	booklets	1.00	1.00

■ 5½p violet, October 24, 1973

PVAD gum, two phosphor bands	sheets	0.30	0.30
PVAD gum, one phosphor band (centre)	sheets	0.20	0.20

■ 6p light green, February 15, 1971

gum arabic, two phosphor bands	sheets	1.75	–
PVA gum, two phosphor bands, OCP	sheets, se-tenant coils	0.30	–
PVA gum, two phosphor bands, FCP	sheets	25.00	–
PVAD gum, two phosphor bands	sheets, se-tenant coils, booklets	0.20	0.20

■ 6p yellow-olive, September 10, 1991

PVAD gum, ACP	sheets	0.20	0.20

■ 6½p greenish-blue, September 7, 1974

PVA gum, two phosphor bands	sheets	30.00	–
PVAD gum, two phosphor bands	sheets	0.30	0.30

BRITISH STAMP MARKET VALUES 2024

MACHINS DECIMAL

PVAD gum, one phosphor band (centre) (portrait higher)	sheets	0.30	0.30
PVAD gum, one phosphor band (centre) (portrait lower)	sheets, coils, booklets	0.50	0.50
PVAD gum, one phosphor band (left)	booklets	0.75	0.75
PVAD gum, one phosphor band (right)	booklets	0.75	0.75

■ 7p purple-brown, January 15, 1975

PVAD gum, two phosphor bands	sheets	0.30	0.30
PVAD gum, one phosphor band (centre) (portrait higher)	sheets, coils	0.30	0.30
PVAD gum, one phosphor band (centre) (portrait lower)	sheets, coils, se-tenant coils, booklets	0.50	0.50
PVAD gum, one phosphor band (left)	booklets	0.30	0.30
PVAD gum, one phosphor band (right)	booklets	0.40	0.50

■ 7p brownish-red, October 29, 1985

PVAD gum, PCP	sheets	1.00	0.90

■ 7½p pale chestnut, February 15, 1971

PVA gum, two phosphor bands, OCP	sheets	0.50	0.40
PVA gum, two phosphor bands, FCP	sheets	3.00	–
PVAD gum, two phosphor bands	sheets	0.25	0.25

■ 8p red, October 24, 1973

PVAD gum, two phosphor bands	sheets	0.20	0.20
PVAD gum, one phosphor band (centre) (portrait higher, value lower)	sheets	0.35	0.25
PVAD gum, one phosphor band (centre) (portrait lower, value higher)	sheets, coils, booklets	0.50	0.30
PVAD gum, one phosphor band (centre) (printed by Enschedé)	sheets	0.35	0.25
PVAD gum, one phosphor band (left)	booklets	0.50	0.50
PVAD gum, one phosphor band (right)	booklets	0.50	0.50

■ 8½p yellowish green, September 24, 1975

PVAD gum, two phosphor bands (value higher)	sheets, coils, booklets	0.30	0.30
PVAD gum, two phosphor bands (value lower)	booklets	0.50	0.50
PVAD gum, PCP	sheets	0.60	0.60

■ 9p orange and black, February 15, 1971

PVA gum, two phosphor bands, OCP	sheets	0.75	0.75
PVA gum, two phosphor bands, FCP	sheets	2.50	–
PVAD gum, two phosphor bands	sheets	0.40	0.40

■ 9p violet, February 25, 1976

PVAD gum, two phosphor bands	sheets, coils, booklets	0.30	0.30

■ 9½p purple, February 25, 1976

PVAD gum, two phosphor bands	sheets	0.30	0.30

■ 10p orange-brown and chestnut, August 11, 1971

PVA gum, two phosphor bands	sheets	0.30	–
PVAD gum, two phosphor bands	sheets	0.30	0.30

■ 10p orange-brown, February 25, 1976

PVAD gum, two phosphor bands (base of value above edge of bust)	sheets, booklets	0.30	0.20
PVAD gum, two phosphor bands (base of value at edge of bust)	booklets	0.30	0.25
PVAD gum, two phosphor bands (value narrower)	prestige booklets	12.00	12.00
PVAD gum, all-over phosphor	sheets, booklets	0.30	0.30
PVAD gum, PCPI	sheets	0.30	0.30
PVAD gum, ACP	sheets	0.30	0.25
PVAD gum, one phosphor band (centre)	sheets, booklets, prestige booklets	0.30	0.30
PVAD gum, one phosphor band (left)	booklets, prestige booklets	0.40	0.40
PVAD gum, one phosphor band (right)	booklets	1.00	1.20
PVAD gum, two phosphor bands, PCPI	sheets	0.50	–
PVAD gum, two phosphor bands, PCPI (gutter pair)	sheets	1.25	–

DECIMAL MACHINS

PVAD gum, two phosphor bands, FCP	sheets	0.45	0.35
PVAD gum, two phosphor bands, FCP (gutter pair)	sheets	1.00	1.50
PVAD gum, one phosphor band (centre), PCPI	sheets	1.00	–

■ 10$^{1}/_{2}$p yellow, February 25, 1976
PVAD gum, two phosphor bands	sheets	0.30	0.30

■ 10$^{1}/_{2}$p dull blue, April 26, 1978
PVAD gum, two phosphor bands	sheets	0.35	0.40

■ 11p brown-red, February 25, 1976
PVAD gum, two phosphor bands	sheets	0.30	0.30
PVAD gum, PCPI	sheets	0.50	0.50

■ 11$^{1}/_{2}$p ochre-brown, August 15, 1979
PVAD gum, PCP1	sheets	0.40	0.40

■ 11$^{1}/_{2}$p drab, January 14, 1981
PVAD gum, one phosphor band (centre)	sheets, coils, booklets	0.30	0.20
PVAD gum, one phosphor band (left)	booklets	0.40	0.40
PVAD gum, one phosphor band (right)	booklets	0.40	0.40

■ 12p yellowish green, January 30, 1980
PVAD gum, PCPI	sheets, coils, booklets	0.30	0.30
PVAD gum, PCPII	sheets	0.80	0.50
PVAD gum, two phosphor bands	booklets, prestige booklets	0.40	0.40

■ 12p bright emerald, October 29, 1985
PVAD gum, one phosphor band (centre)	sheets, booklets, prestige booklets	0.35	0.35
PVAD gum, one phosphor band (centre) (star on gummed side)	sheets	0.40	0.40
PVAD gum, one phosphor band (centre)	sheets	0.40	0.40
PVAD gum, one phosphor band (left)	booklets, prestige booklets	0.70	0.70
PVAD gum, one phosphor band (right)	booklets, prestige booklets	0.70	0.70

■ 12$^{1}/_{2}$p light emerald, January 27, 1982
PVAD gum, one phosphor band (centre)	sheets, coils, booklets, prestige booklets	0.40	0.40
PVAD gum, one phosphor band (centre), PCPI	sheets	7.50	–
PVAD gum, one phosphor band (left)	booklets, prestige booklets	0.50	0.50
PVAD gum, one phosphor band (right)	booklets, prestige booklets	0.50	0.50
PVAD gum, one phosphor band (centre) (star on gummed side)	booklets	0.70	0.70
PVAD gum, one phosphor band (centre) (simple star on gummed side)	booklets	0.70	0.70

■ 13p olive-grey, August 15, 1979
PVAD gum, PCPI	sheets	0.50	0.40

■ 13p chestnut, August 28, 1984
PVAD gum, one phosphor band (centre)	sheets, booklets, prestige booklets	0.40	0.40
PVAD gum, one phosphor band (centre) (star on gummed side)	booklets	0.70	–
PVAD gum, one phosphor band (centre)	sheets	0.30	0.30
PVAD gum, one phosphor band (left)	booklets, prestige booklets	0.50	0.50
PVAD gum, one phosphor band (right)	booklets, prestige booklets	0.50	0.50
PVA gum, one phosphor band (centre) (litho by Questa)	prestige booklets	0.50	0.50
PVA gum, one phosphor band (left) (litho by Questa)	prestige booklets	0.50	0.50
PVA gum, one phosphor band (right) (litho by Questa)	prestige booklets	0.50	0.50

■ 13$^{1}/_{2}$p red-brown, January 30, 1980
PVAD gum, PCPI	sheets	0.60	0.60

■ 14p grey-blue, January 14, 1981
PVAD gum, PCPI	sheets, coils, booklets	0.40	0.40

MACHINS DECIMAL

PVAD gum, PCPII	sheets, coils, booklets	0.50	0.50
PVAD gum, PCP, fluorescent brightener omitted	booklets	2.00	–
PVAD gum, two phosphor bands	booklets	1.00	1.00

■ 14p deep blue, August 23, 1988
PVAD gum, one phosphor band (centre)	sheets, booklets	0.40	0.40
PVAD gum, one phosphor band (right)	booklets	3.00	3.00
PVA gum, one phosphor band (centre) (litho by Questa)	booklets	2.25	2.25
PVA gum, one phosphor band (right) (litho by Walsall)	booklets	3.00	3.00

■ 15p ultramarine, August 15, 1979
PVAD gum, PCPI	sheets	0.50	0505
PVAD gum, PCPII	sheets	0.40	0.40

■ 15p bright blue, September 26, 1989
PVAD gum, one phosphor band (centre)	sheets, coils	0.50	0.50
PVAD gum, one phosphor band (left)	booklets	2.00	2.00
PVAD gum, one phosphor band (right)	prestige booklets	1.50	1.50

■ 15½p pale violet, January 14, 1981
PVAD gum, PCPI	sheets, coils, booklets	0.40	0.45
PVAD gum, PCPII	sheets	0.40	0.45
PVAD gum, PCP, fluorescent brightener omitted	sheets	15.00	–
PVAD gum, ACP	sheets	8.00	8.00
PVAD gum, two phosphor bands	booklets, prestige booklets	0.40	0.45
PVAD gum, two phosphor bands (star on gummed side)	booklets	0.50	0.45

■ 16p mushroom, March 30, 1983
PVAD gum, PCPI	sheets, coils, booklets, prestige booklets	0.50	0.50
PVAD gum, PCPI ('D' on gummed side)	booklets	0.65	0.65
PVAD gum, ACP	sheets, prestige booklets	0.60	0.45
PVAD gum, two phosphor bands	booklets	1.00	1.00

■ 16½p pale chestnut, January 27 1982
PVAD gum, PCPI	sheets	0.60	0.60
PVAD gum, PCPII	sheets	3.50	3.50

■ 17p light green, January 30, 1980
PVAD gum, PCPI	sheets	0.50	0.45
PVAD gum, PCPII	sheets	3.00	2.50
PVAD gum, PCP, fluorescent brightener omitted	sheets	1.50	–

■ 17p grey-blue, March 30, 1983
PVAD gum, PCPI	sheets, coils, booklets, prestige booklets	0.50	0.45
PVAD gum, PCPI ('D' on gummed side)	booklets	0.65	–
PVAD gum, ACP	sheets, booklets, prestige booklets	0.50	0.45
PVAD gum, two phosphor bands	booklets, prestige booklets	0.45	0.45
PVAD gum, two phosphor bands (stars on gummed side)	booklets	0.60	0.60

■ 17p deep blue, September 4, 1990
PVAD gum, one phosphor band (centre)	sheets, coils	0.60	0.60
PVAD gum, one phosphor band (left)	booklets	1.25	1.25
PVAD gum, one phosphor band (right)	booklets	10.00	10.00
PVA gum, one phosphor band (centre) (litho by Questa)	booklets	0.70	0.70

■ 17½p pale chestnut, January 30, 1979
PVAD gum, PCPI	sheets	0.50	0.50
PVAD gum, PCPII	sheets	2.00	1.75

■ 18p violet, January 14, 1981

BRITISH STAMP MARKET VALUES 2024

DECIMAL MACHINS

PVAD gum, PCPI	sheets	0.50	0.50
PVAD gum, PCPII	sheets	0.70	0.60

■ 18p grey-green, August 28, 1984
PVAD gum, ACP	sheets, coils, booklets, prestige booklets	0.50	0.50
PVAD gum, two phosphor bands	booklets, prestige booklets	0.50	0.50
PVAD gum, PCP	booklets, coils	0.75	0.75
PVAD gum, PCP (litho by Questa)	prestige booklets	0.50	0.50
PVAD gum, two phosphor bands (litho by Questa)	prestige booklets	5.50	5.50

■ 18p bright green, September 10, 1991
PVAD gum, one phosphor band (centre)	sheets	0.50	0.50
PVAD gum, one phosphor band (centre) (gravure by Enschedé)	sheets	0.50	0.50
PVA gum, one phosphor band (centre) (litho by Questa)	prestige booklets	0.75	0.75
PVA gum, one phosphor band (left) (litho by Questa)	prestige booklets	1.25	1.25
PVA gum, one phosphor band (right) (litho by Questa)	prestige booklets	1.00	1.00

■ 19p orange-red, August 23, 1988
PVAD gum, ACP	sheets, booklets	0.50	0.50
PVA gum, PCP (litho by Questa)	booklets	1.00	1.00
PVA gum, two phosphor bands (litho by Walsall)	booklets	1.00	1.00

■ 19½p olive grey, January 27, 1982
PVAD gum, PCPI	sheets	2.00	2.00

■ 20p dull purple, February 25, 1976
PVA gum, two phosphor bands (litho by Waddington)	sheets	1.25	1.25
PVAD gum, PCP (litho by Waddington)	sheets	1.25	1.25
PVAD gum, PCP (litho by Waddington) (dull purple and sepia)	sheets	1.75	1.75
PVAD gum, PCP (litho by Questa, perf 15x14)	sheets	1.00	1.00
PVAD gum, two phosphor bands	sheets	0.60	0.60
PVAD gum, PCPI	sheets	1.00	1.00
PVAD gum, PCPII	sheets	1.00	1.00

■ 20p turquoise, August 23, 1988
PVAD gum, ACP	sheets	0.60	0.60

■ 20p brownish-black, September 26, 1989
PVAD gum, ACP	sheets, coils, booklets	0.50	0.50
PVAD gum, two phosphor bands	booklets, prestige booklets	2.00	2.00

■ 20½p ultramarine, March 30, 1983
PVAD gum, PCPI	sheets	0.90	0.90

■ 22p deep blue, October 22, 1980
PVAD gum, PCPI	sheets	0.55	0.50
PVAD gum, PCPII	sheets	0.55	0.50
PVAD gum, experimental coated paper	sheets	2.50	2.00

■ 22p yellow-green, August 28, 1984
PVAD gum, ACP	sheets	0.55	0.50
PVA gum, two phosphor bands (litho by Questa)	prestige booklets	5.50	5.50

■ 22p orange-red, September 4, 1990
PVAD gum, ACP	sheets	0.55	0.55
PVAD gum, two phosphor bands	booklets	0.80	0.80
PVA gum, PCP (litho by Questa)	prestige booklets	0.60	0.50

■ 23p rose, March 30, 1983
PVAD gum, PCPI	sheets	1.25	1.25

MACHINS DECIMAL

■ 23p bright green, August 23, 1988
PVAD gum, ACP	sheets	1.00	1.00

■ 24p violet, August 28, 1984
PVAD gum, ACP	sheets	1.50	1.50

■ 24p red-brown, September 26, 1989
PVAD gum, ACP	sheets	2.00	2.00

■ 24p brown, September 10, 1991
PVAD gum, ACP	sheets, coils, booklets	0.60	0.60
PVA gum, ACP (litho by Questa)	prestige booklets	1.75	1.75
PVA gum, two phosphor bands (litho by Questa)	prestige booklets	1.50	1.50
PVA gum, ACP (litho by Walsall)	booklets	0.75	0.70

■ 25p purple, January 14, 1981
PVAD gum, PCPI	sheets	1.50	1.50
PVAD gum, PCPII	sheets	0.70	0.70

■ 25p rose red, February 6, 1996
PVAD gum, two phosphor bands	coils	7.50	7.50

■ 26p red, January 27, 1982
PVAD gum, PCPI	sheets	0.65	0.60
PVAD gum, ACP	sheets	0.65	0.50
PVAD gum, two phosphor bands	prestige booklets	6.50	6.50
PVAD gum, ACP, narrow value	booklets	5.50	5.50

■ 26p drab, September 4, 1990
PVAD gum, ACP	sheets	1.70	1.70

■ 27p chestnut, August 23, 1988
PVAD gum, ACP	sheets, booklets	0.70	0.70

■ 27p mauve, September 4, 1990
PVAD gum, ACP	sheets	0.70	0.70

■ 28p violet, March 30, 1983
PVAD gum, PCPI	sheets	0.80	0.90
PVAD gum, ACP	sheets	0.90	0.90

■ 28p yellow-ochre, August 23, 1988
PVAD gum, ACP	sheets	0.75	0.75

■ 28p blue-grey, September 10, 1991
PVAD gum , ACP	sheets	0.80	0.80

■ 29p ochre, January 27, 1982
PVAD gum, PCPI	sheets	2.50	2.50
PVAD gum, PCPII	sheets	4.00	4.00

■ 29p purple, September 26, 1989
PVAD gum, ACP	sheets	2.50	2.50
PVA gum, two phosphor bands (litho by Walsall)	booklets	3.00	3.00
PVA gum, ACP (litho by Walsall)	booklets	3.50	3.50

■ 30p olive-grey, September 26, 1989
PVAD gum, ACP	sheets	1.00	1.00

■ 31p mauve, March 30, 1983
PVAD gum, PCPI	sheets	1.25	1.25

DECIMAL MACHINS

PVAD gum, ACP	sheets	1.00	1.00
PVAD gum, two phosphor bands	prestige booklets	8.00	8.00

■ 31p ultramarine, September 4, 1990
PVAD gum, ACP	sheets	1.50	2.00
PVA gum, ACP (litho by Walsall)	booklets	1.75	1.75

■ 32p dark turquoise, August 23, 1988
PVAD gum, ACP	sheets	1.50	1.50

■ 33p emerald, September 4, 1990
PVAD gum, ACP	sheets, coils	1.00	1.00
PVA gum, ACP (litho by Questa)	prestige booklets	1.50	1.50
PVAD gum, two phosphor bands (litho by Questa)	prestige booklets	1.25	1.25
PVA gum, ACP (litho by Walsall)	booklets	1.75	1.75

■ 34p ochre, August 28, 1984
PVAD gum, PCP	sheets	1.00	1.50
PVAD gum, two phosphor bands	prestige booklets	5.50	6.00
PVAD gum, ACP	sheets	1.40	1.25
PVA gum, two phosphor bands (litho by Questa)	booklets	5.50	5.50

■ 34p blue-grey, September 26, 1989
PVAD gum, ACP	sheets	1.10	1.10

■ 34p purple, September 10, 1991
PVAD gum, ACP	sheets	2.00	2.50

■ 35p sepia, August 23, 1988
PVAD gum, ACP	sheets	1.80	1.80

■ 35p deep yellow, September 10, 1991
PVAD gum, ACP	sheets	2.00	2.50

■ 37p rosine, September 26, 1989
PVAD gum, ACP	sheets	2.00	2.50

■ 39p mauve, September 10, 1991
PVAD gum, ACP	sheets	1.40	1.40
PVAD gum, two phosphor bands (litho by Questa)	prestige booklets	2.25	2.25
PVA gum, phosphor paper (litho by Walsall)	booklets	1.50	1.50

■ 50p ochre-brown, February 2, 1977
PVAD gum, two phosphor bands	sheets	1.30	0.50
PVAD gum, no phosphor	sheets	2.25	1.50

■ 50p ochre, March 13, 1990
PVAD gum, ACP	sheets	13.00	13.00
PVAD gum, two phosphor bands	prestige booklets	2.75	2.75

■ 75p black, January 30, 1980
PVAD gum, no phosphor (litho by Questa, perf 13½x14)	sheets	2.25	2.00
PVA gum, no phosphor (litho by Questa, perf 15x14)	sheets	3.00	1.50
PVAD gum, no phosphor (litho by Questa, perf 15x14)	sheets	5.00	5.00
PVA gum, no phosphor (litho by Questa, perf 15x14, coated paper)	sheets	3.75	–

■ 75p brownish-grey and black, February 23, 1988
PVA gum (litho by Questa)	sheets	7.50	7.50

■ 75p grey-black, July 26, 1988
PVAD gum, no phosphor	sheets	3.50	3.50

MACHINS DECIMAL

FIRST DAY COVERS

First day cover (February 15, 1971)	
½p, 1p, 1½p, 2p, 2½p, 3p, 3½p, 4p, 5p, 6p, 7½p, 9p	2.50
First day cover (August 11, 1971)	
10p	1.00
First day cover (October 24, 1973)	
4½p, 5½p, 8p	1.25
First day cover (September 4, 1974)	
6½p	1.00
First day cover (January 15, 1975)	
7p	1.00
First day cover (September 24, 1975)	
8½p	1.00
First day cover (February 25, 1976)	
9p, 9½p, 10p, 10½p, 11p, 20p	1.50
First day cover (February 2, 1977)	
50p	1.50
First day cover (April 26, 1978)	
10½p	1.00
First day cover (August 15, 1979)	
11½p, 13p, 15p	1.00
First day cover (January 30, 1980)	
4p, 12p, 13½p, 17p, 17½p, 75p	1.50
First day cover (October 22, 1980)	
3p, 22p	1.00
First day cover (January 14, 1981)	
2½p, 11½p, 14p, 15½p, 18p, 25p	1.50
First day cover (January 27, 1982)	
5p, 12½p, 16½p, 19½p, 26p, 29p	1.75
First day cover (March 30, 1983)	
3½p, 16p, 17p, 20½p, 23p, 28p, 31p	2.00
First day cover (August 28, 1984)	
13p, 18p, 22p, 24p, 34p	2.00
First day cover (October 29, 1985)	
7p, 12p	1.00
First day cover (August 23, 1988)	
14p, 19p, 20p, 23p, 27p, 28p, 32p, 35p	2.50
First day cover (September 26, 1989)	
15p, 20p, 24p, 29p, 30p, 34p, 37p	3.00
First day cover (September 4, 1990)	
10p, 17p, 22p, 26p, 27p, 31p, 33p	3.00
First day cover (September 10, 1991)	
6p, 18p 24p, 28p, 34p, 35p, 39p	3.00
First day cover (February 6, 1996)	
25p	10.00

BOOKLET PANES WITHOUT ELLIPTICAL PERFORATIONS, 1971–93

■ **Panes of four with PVA gum**

Two **2p** with two ½p	
vertically se-tenant	3.00
horizontally se-tenant, OCP	3.00
horizontally se-tenant, FCP	0.75
Two **1p** with two **1½p**	
vertically se-tenant	3.00
horizontally se-tenant, OCP	3.00
horizontally se-tenant, FCP	1.25

■ **Panes of six with PVA gum**

Five ½p with label 'B ALAN LTD for GB STAMPS'	
perforated label	4.00
imperforate label	6.00
Five ½p with label 'LICK battery failure'	
perforated label	4.00
imperforate label	6.00
Five ½p with label 'MAKE YOUR LUCKY FIND PAY'	
imperforate label only	4.00
Four **2½p** (one centre band) with labels 'UNIFLO STAMPS' and 'STICK FIRMLY'	
perforated labels	3.50
imperforate labels	6.00
Five **2½p** (one centre band) with label 'STICK FIRMLY'	
perforated label	3.00
imperforate label	6.00
Five **2½p** (one centre band) with label 'TEAR OFF to ESSO'	
perforated label	3.00
imperforate label	8.00
Five **2½p** (one centre band) with label 'STAMP COLLECTIONS'	
imperforate label only	2.75
Four **2½p** (one centre band) with labels 'DO YOU COLLECT GB STAMPS' and 'BUYING OR SELLING'	
imperforate label only	4.00
Five **2½p** (one centre band) with label 'B ALAN'	
imperforate label only	3.00
Five **3p** (two bands) with label '£4,315 FOR YOU'	
perforated label	2.00
imperforate label, OCP	2.50
imperforate label, FCP	2.00
Four **3p** (two bands) with two **2½p** (one band at left)	
OCP	9.50
FCP	3.00
Six **3p** (two bands)	
OCP	4.00
FCP	2.00
Five **3p** (one centre band) with blank label	
imperforate label only	3.00
Five **3½p** (two bands) with blank label	
imperforate label only	3.00

■ **Panes of four with PVAD gum**

Two **2p** horizontally se-tenant with two ½p	1.25
Two **1p** horizontally se-tenant with two **1½p**	1.50

■ **Panes of six with PVAD gum**

Five **3p** (one centre band) with blank imperforate label	4.00
Five **3½p** (two bands) with blank imperforate label	3.00
Five **3½p** (one centre band) with blank imperforate label	4.00
Five **4½p** (two bands) with blank imperforate label	3.00

SE-TENANT COIL STRIPS WITHOUT ELLIPTICAL PERFORATIONS, 1971–95

DECIMAL MACHINS

■ **Strips with gum Arabic**
One **2p**, two **½p**, two **1p**

OCP	1.50
OCP with silicone	£200
FCP with silicone	3.50

■ **Strips with PVA gum**

One **6p**, one **2p**, one **1p**, two **½p** (two bands), OCP	2.75

■ **Strips with PVAD gum**

One **2p**, two **½p**, two **1p** (two bands), FCP	1.00
One **6p**, one **2p**, one **1p**, two **½p** (two bands), FCP	0.90
Two **½p**, one **7p**, two **1p** (one centre band), FCP	0.95
One **8p**, two **1p**, two labels (one centre band), FCP	0.90
One **2½p** rose, three **3p** pink, PCP	1.40
fluorescent brightener omitted	40.00
One **½p**, three **4p** blue, PCP	0.90
fluorescent brightener omitted	£150
perfect gum	£1,500
One **1p** and three **4p** blue, PCP	1.00
One **2p**, three **4p**, PCP	9.00
Three **4p**, one **3p**, PCP	2.00
Three **4p**, one **5p**, PCP	1.45
Two **5p**, two **4p**, PCP	1.45
Three **5p**, one **4p**, PCP	1.95

NON-VALUE INDICATORS WITHOUT ELLIPTICAL PERFORATIONS, 1989–93

From retail stamp books (at least one edge may be imperforate) or prestige stamp books (marked *).

■ **2nd bright blue (August 22, 1989)**
Printed in gravure by Harrison

with one centre phosphor band	2.00	2.00
with one phosphor band at right*	2.50	2.50

Printed in litho by Walsall

with one centre phosphor band	2.00	2.00

Printed in litho by Questa

with one centre phosphor band	2.00	2.00
with one phosphor band at left*	2.00	2.00
with one phosphor band at right*	2.25	2.25

■ **2nd deep blue (August 7, 1990)**
Printed in gravure by Harrison

with one centre phosphor band	1.50	1.50

Printed in litho by Walsall

with one centre phosphor band	1.50	1.50

Printed in litho by Questa

with one centre phosphor band	2.00	2.00

■ **1st brownish black (August 22, 1989)**
Printed in gravure by Harrison

on phosphor paper	1.75	1.75
with two phosphor bands*	2.25	2.25

Printed in litho by Walsall

with two phosphor bands	2.00	2.00

Printed in litho by Questa

on phosphor paper	2.00	2.00

■ **1st orange red (August 7, 1990)**
Printed in gravure by Harrison

on phosphor paper	1.75	1.75

Printed in litho by Walsall

on phosphor paper. Perf: 14	1.75	1.75
on phosphor paper. Perf: 13	3.50	3.50

Printed in litho by Questa

on phosphor paper	1.75	1.75
with two phosphor bands*	1.75	1.75

First day cover (August 22, 1989)
2nd bright blue, 1st brownish black — 1.50
First day cover (August 7, 1990)
2nd deep blue, 1st orange red — 1.50

HIGH VALUES WITHOUT ELLIPTICAL PERFORATIONS, 1970–77

■ **1970, June 17. Large format**
Des: Arnold Machin. Printed in recess by Bradbury, Wilkinson. No wmk. Perf: 12.

10p cerise, phosphor paper	0.40	0.35
20p olive-green	0.50	0.50
50p ultramarine	1.00	0.40
phosphor paper (Feb 1, 1973)	1.00	0.45
£1 black (Dec 6, 1972)	2.00	0.45
First day cover (10p, 20p, 50p)	–	2.50
First day cover (£1)	–	3.25

(*The £1 differs from the 1969 issue only in that the denomination is in a different typeface.)

MACHINS DECIMAL

■ 1977, February 2. Large format
Des: Arnold Machin. Printed in photogravure by Harrison. Perf: 14x15.

£1 olive, deep green	2.00	0.30
£1.30 steel blue, buff (Aug 3, 1983)	3.00	2.50
£1.33 lilac, deep blue (Aug 28, 1984)	3.50	3.00
£1.41 deep blue, pale blue, green (Sep 17, 1985)	4.00	3.50
£1.50 rose-lilac, blue-black (Sep 2, 1986)	3.25	2.50
£1.60 buff, blue-green (Sep 15, 1987)	3.25	2.75
£2 emerald, deep purple	3.00	0.50
£5 pink, blue	7.50	2.50
Set	24.00	24.00
Gutter pairs	£100	–
Traffic light gutter pairs	£110	–
First day cover (£1, £2, £5)	–	5.00
First day cover (£1.30)	–	3.00
First day cover (£1.33)	–	3.00
First day cover (£1.41)	–	3.00
First day cover (£1.50)	–	3.00
First day cover (£1.60)	–	3.00

SPECIAL ISSUES WITHOUT ELLIPTICAL PERFORATIONS, 1990–2017

■ 1990, January 10. 150th Anniversary of the Penny Black
Des: Jeffery Matthews. Issued in sheets and booklets; the stamps from booklets can have one or more edges imperforate.

Printed in photogravure by Harrison. Issued in sheets, booklets and, where marked *, in the London Life prestige stamp book

15p bright blue (one centre phosphor band)	0.60	0.60
(one phosphor band at left)*	4.00	4.00
(one phosphor band at right)*	1.75	1.75
20p brownish-black and cream (PCP)	1.00	1.00
(two phosphor bands)*	1.50	1.50
29p mauve (PCP)	1.50	1.50
(two phosphor bands)*	4.25	4.25
34p blue-grey	1.25	1.25
37p rosine	1.25	1.25
First day cover	–	3.00

Printed in litho by Walsall. Issued in booklets

15p bright blue (one centre phosphor band)	0.90	0.90
20p brownish-black and cream (PCP)	1.00	1.00

Printed in litho by Questa. Issued in booklets

15p bright blue (one centre phosphor band)	1.50	1.30
20p brownish-black and cream (PCP)	1.50	1.50

Printed in gravure by Walsall. Issued in the 2000 Special by Design prestige stamp book

1st brownish black and cream	1.75	1.75

(*The 1st class and 20p also appear in the 2009 Treasures of the Archive prestige stamp book, printed in litho by Cartor. The 20p also appears in the 2017 Machin Definitive Golden Anniversary miniature sheet, printed in gravure by ISP.)

■ 1999, February 6. Large format
Issued only in the Profile On Print prestige stamp book. Recess stamp engraved by C. Slania.

Printed in litho and embossed by Walsall. Self-adhesive

1st pale grey	2.00	2.00

Printed in recess by Enschedé. Two phosphor bands

1st grey-black	2.00	2.00

Printed in typography by Harrison. Two phosphor bands

1st black	2.00	2.00

■ 2017, June 5. Large format
Issued only in the Machin Definitive Golden Anniversary miniature sheet and the Machin Definitive 50th Anniversary prestige stamp book. Printed in gravure and embossed by International Security Printers.

£1 gold	4.00	4.00

DECIMAL MACHINS

LOW VALUES WITH ELLIPTICAL PERFORATIONS, 1993–2010

With an elliptical perforation towards the lower end of each vertical side.

■ 1993–2005. Printed in gravure by Enschedé
Issued in sheets except where stated. Two phosphor bands, except where stated.

1p crimson (June 8, 1993)	0.20	0.20
2p deep green (April 11, 1995)	0.25	0.25
4p new blue (December 14, 1993)	0.30	0.30
5p claret (June 8, 1993)	0.30	0.30
6p lime green (April 27, 1993)	1.00	1.00
10p orange (June 8, 1993)	0.40	0.40
20p sea green (December 14, 1993)	0.60	0.60
25p salmon pink (October 10, 1995)	0.65	0.70
29p light grey (October 26, 1993)	0.75	0.70
30p grey-green (July 27, 1993)	0.75	0.70
31p deep purple (June 25, 1996)	0.80	0.60
35p deep yellow (August 17, 1993)	0.80	0.80
35p lime-green (April 5, 2005) (one band)	0.80	0.80
35p lime-green (February 23, 2006)		
from Brunel prestige stamp book	1.00	1.00
36p ultramarine (October 26, 1993)	1.00	1.00
37p amethyst (June 25, 1996)	1.00	1.00
38p rosine (October 26, 1993)	1.10	1.10
39p magenta (June 25, 1996)	1.00	1.00
40p turquoise (February 23, 2006)		
from Brunel prestige stamp book	5.25	5.25
41p stone (October 26, 1993)	1.00	1.00
42p olive-grey (May 25, 2004)		
from Glory of the Garden prestige book	5.25	5.25
43p chocolate-brown (June 25, 1996)	1.50	1.50
47p turquoise green (May 25, 2004)		
from Glory of the Garden prestige book	5.25	5.25
50p ochre (December 14, 1993)	1.50	1.50
50p ochre (September 21, 2006)		
from Victoria Cross prestige stamp book	5.25	5.25
63p emerald (June 25, 1996)	1.60	1.60
£1 bluish-violet (August 22, 1995)	2.50	2.50
Stamp card (£1 stamp)	7.50	15.00

■ 1994–1996. Printed in litho by Questa
Issued in booklets and prestige stamp books. Two phosphor bands, except where stated.

1p crimson (July 8, 1995)		
from £1 booklets	0.25	0.25
6p lime-green (July 26, 1994)		
from Northern Ireland prestige stamp book	6.50	5.00
10p deep orange (April 25, 1995)		
from National Trust prestige stamp book	3.50	3.50
19p olive green (July 26, 1994) (one band at left)		
from Northern Ireland prestige stamp book and National Trust prestige stamp book (April 25, 1995) (one band at right)	0.80	0.80
from National Trust prestige stamp book	0.80	0.80
20p bright green (July 8, 1996) (one centre band)		
from £1 and £2 booklets	4.00	4.00
25p salmon-pink (July 26, 1994)		
from £1 and £2 booklets, and Northern Ireland and National Trust prestige stamp books	0.70	0.70
26p red-brown (July 8, 1996)		
from £1 and £2 booklets	0.65	0.65
30p grey-green (April 25, 1995)		
from National Trust prestige stamp book	2.25	2.25
35p deep yellow (April 25, 1995)		
from National Trust prestige stamp book	1.25	1.25
41p drab (April 25, 1995)		
from National Trust prestige stamp book	1.35	1.35

■ 1998–1999. Printed in gravure by Questa
Issued in booklets and prestige stamp books. Two phosphor bands, except where stated.

1p crimson (December 1, 1998)		
from £1 booklets and World Changers prestige stamp book	0.75	1.00
2p myrtle-green (April 26, 1999)		
from £1 booklets	5.00	5.00
19p olive green (Apr 26, 1999) (centre phosphor band)		
from £1 and £2 booklets and World Changers PSB	0.80	0.80
20p bright green (Dec 1, 1998) (one centre band)		
from £1 and £2 stamp booklets	17.50	17.50
26p red-brown (December 1, 1998)		
from £1 and £2 booklets and World Changers prestige stamp book	0.80	0.80

■ 1993–1996. Printed in litho by Walsall
Issued in booklets. Two phosphor bands.

25p salmon-pink (November 1, 1993)		
from £1 booklets	0.80	0.80
35p deep yellow (November 1, 1993)		
from £1.40 booklets	0.90	0.90
37p amethyst (July 8, 1996)		
from £1.48 booklets	2.50	1.50
41p stone (November 1, 1993)		
from £1.64 booklets	1.00	1.00
60p slate-blue (March 19, 1996)		
from £2.40 booklets	1.25	1.25
63p emerald (July 8, 1996)		
from £2.52 booklets	3.50	3.00

BRITISH STAMP MARKET VALUES 2024

MACHINS DECIMAL

■ 1997–2005. Printed in gravure by Walsall
Issued in booklets and prestige stamp books. Two phosphor bands, except where stated.

10p deep orange (October 13, 1998)		
from Breaking Barriers prestige stamp book	1.25	1.25
19p olive-green (Feb 15, 2000) (one band at right)		
from Special By Design prestige stamp book	0.75	0.75
30p grey-green (May 5, 1998)		
from £1.20 booklet	0.85	0.85
37p amethyst (August 26, 1997)		
from £1.48 booklets	1.00	1.00
38p ultramarine (April 26, 1999)		
from £1.52 booklet	1.25	1.25
38p ultramarine (February 15, 2000) (perf: 14)		
from Special By Design prestige stamp book	4.00	4.00
39p grey (February 24, 2005)		
from Bronte prestige stamp book	5.25	5.25
40p grey-blue (April 27, 2000)		
from £1.60 booklets	1.20	1.20
42p olive grey (February 24, 2005)		
from Bronte prestige stamp book	5.25	5.25
43p chocolate brown (October 13, 1998)		
from Breaking Barriers prestige stamp book	1.75	1.75
50p ochre (October 18, 2005)		
from Battle of Trafalgar prestige stamp book	5.25	5.25
63p emerald (August 26, 1997)		
from £2.52 booklets	1.60	1.60
64p sea-green (April 26, 1999)		
from £2.56 booklets	1.60	1.60
65p greenish blue (April 27, 2000)		
from £2.60 booklets	1.70	1.70
68p grey-brown (October 18, 2005)		
from Battle of Trafalgar prestige stamp book	5.25	5.25

■ 1993–2010. Printed in gravure initially by Harrisons, and later by De La Rue
Issued in sheets or coils. Two phosphor bands, except where stated.

1p crimson (April 1, 1997)	0.20	0.20
2p deep green (May 27, 1997)	0.25	0.25
4p new blue (May 27, 1997)	0.30	0.30
5p claret (May 27, 1997)	0.30	0.30
6p lime green (April 1, 1997)	0.40	0.40
7p light grey (April 20, 1999)	2.50	2.50
7p bright magenta (April 1, 2004)	0.35	0.35
8p deep yellow (April 25, 2000)	0.35	0.30
9p deep orange (April 5, 2005)	0.35	0.25
10p orange (May 8, 1997)	0.40	0.35
12p turquoise (August 1, 2006)	0.50	0.50
14p salmon pink (August 1, 2006)	0.50	0.50
15p shocking pink (April 1, 2008)	0.45	0.45
16p bright pink (March 27, 2007)	0.45	0.45
17p olive green (March 31, 2009)	0.50	0.30
19p olive (Oct 26, 1993) (one band)	0.50	0.50
20p bright green		
(June 25, 1996) (one centre band)	0.55	0.55
(September 23, 1997) (one band at right)	1.00	1.10
(April 20, 1999) (two bands)	0.50	0.50
22p stone (March 31, 2009)	0.65	0.35
25p salmon-pink		
(October 26, 1993) (PCP)	0.60	0.60
(December 20, 1994)	0.60	0.60
26p reddish brown (June 25, 1996)	0.60	0.60
26p gold (April 29, 1997)	0.70	0.70
30p grey-green (May 12, 1997)	0.75	0.75
31p deep mauve (August 26, 1997)	0.80	0.80
33p slate-blue (April 25, 2000)	0.80	0.80
34p lime green (May 6, 2003)	4.25	4.25
35p yellow (Nov 1, 1993) (PCP)	6.50	6.50
35p sepia (April 1, 2004)	0.90	0.90
35p lime-green		
(April 26, 2005) (one centre band)	1.00	1.00
37p amethyst (July 8, 1996)	2.50	2.50
37p bright mauve (August 7, 1997)	1.00	1.00
37p deep grey (July 4, 2002)	1.10	1.10
37p olive green (March 28, 2006)	1.10	1.10
38p ultramarine (April 20, 1999)	1.50	0.70
39p magenta (May 12, 1997)	1.00	1.00
39p grey (April 1, 2004)	1.20	1.20
40p greyish blue (April 20, 1999)	1.20	1.20
40p turquoise (April 1, 2004)	1.20	1.20
41p drab (Nov 1, 1993) (PCP)	6.50	6.50
41p rosine (April 20, 1999)	1.20	1.20
42p olive-grey (July 4, 2002)	1.00	1.00
43p chocolate-brown (July 8, 1996)	5.75	5.75
43p brown (March 21, 1997)	4.00	4.00
43p emerald (April 1, 2004)	1.60	1.60
44p stone (April 20, 1999)	3.50	3.50
44p ultramarine (March 28, 2006)	1.20	1.20
45p mauve (April 20, 1999)	1.20	1.20
46p yellow (April 5, 2005)	3.00	3.00
47p turquoise green (July 4, 2002)	1.25	1.25
48p purple (March 27, 2007)	1.50	1.50
49p rust (March 28, 2006)	3.00	3.00
50p ochre (April 1, 1997)	1.50	1.50
50p grey (March 27, 2007)	1.50	1.50
54p rust (March 27, 2007)	1.50	1.50
56p lime green (April 1, 2008)	1.60	1.60
60p emerald green (March 30, 2010)	3.00	3.00
62p red (March 31, 2009)	3.00	3.00
63p emerald (December 12, 1996)	1.60	1.60
64p sea green (April 20, 1999)	1.60	1.60
65p greenish blue (April 25, 2000)	1.85	1.85
67p rhododendron (March 30, 2010)	1.65	1.65
68p grey-brown (July 4, 2002)	1.75	1.75
72p red (March 28, 2006)	3.50	3.50
78p emerald green (March 27, 2007)	2.00	2.00
81p sea green (April 1, 2008)	1.85	1.85
88p shocking pink (March 30, 2010)	1.85	1.85
90p ultramarine (March 31, 2009)	1.90	1.90
97p mauve (March 30, 2010)	2.00	1.60
£1 bluish-violet (April 1, 1997)	2.50	2.50
£1 ruby (June 5, 2007)	2.25	2.25
£1.46 dark turquoise (March 30, 2010)	3.00	3.00
Stamp cards (24 values current in September 2008, including non-value-indicators)	30.00	50.00

(*The 2p, 5p, 37p deep grey, 46p, 48p and £1 ruby also appear in prestige stamp books, and the £1 ruby and £1 bluish-violet also appear in the 40th Anniversary of the Machin miniature sheet of 2007.)

DECIMAL MACHINS

2009. Printed in litho by De La Rue
Issued in prestige stamp books.

5p deep claret (February 12, 2009)		
from Darwin prestige stamp book	2.50	2.50
10p orange (February 12, 2009)		
from Darwin prestige stamp book	2.50	2.50
48p purple (February 12, 2009)		
from Darwin prestige stamp book	4.00	4.00

2009–2011. Printed in litho by Cartor
Issued in prestige stamp books.

1p crimson (September 17, 2009)		
from Royal Navy Uniforms prestige book	2.25	2.25
5p deep claret (February 25, 2010) with wrong font		
from Classic Album Covers prestige book	4.00	4.00
5p deep claret (May 13, 2010)		
from Britain Alone prestige book	2.50	2.50
5p lake brown (March 22, 2011)		
from WWF prestige book	2.40	2.40
10p orange-brown (February 25, 2010)		
from Classic Album Covers and Britain Alone prestige books	2.50	2.50
16p bright pink (January 13, 2009)		
from Design Classics prestige book	2.25	2.25
17p olive green (August 18, 2009)		
from Treasures of the Archive and Royal Navy Uniforms prestige books	2.25	2.25
20p bright green (February 25, 2010)		
from Classic Album Covers prestige book	2.25	2.25
22p stone (August 18, 2009)		
from Treasures of the Archive, Classic Album Covers and Royal Society prestige books	3.25	3.25
50p grey (January 13, 2009)		
from Design Classics prestige book	3.25	3.25
54p rust (February 25, 2010) with wrong font		
from Classic Album Covers and Royal Society prestige books	3.25	3.25
60p emerald-green (May 13, 2010)		
from Britain Alone prestige book	5.50	5.50
62p red (August 18, 2009)		
from Treasures of the Archive and Classic Album Covers prestige books	3.50	3.50
67p bright mauve (March 22, 2011)		
from WWF prestige book	8.25	8.25
90p ultramarine (September 17, 2009)		
from Royal Navy Uniforms prestige book	4.00	4.00
97p bluish violet (March 22, 2011)		
from WWF prestige book	8.50	8.50

(*Two prestige stamp books issued in 2010 included definitives using the wrong font for the '5' of 5p and '54' of 54p.)

First day cover (October 26, 1993)		
19p, 25p, 29p, 36p, 38p, 41p	–	3.00
First day cover (August 9, 1994)		
60p	–	2.00
First day cover (August 22, 1995)		
£1	–	2.00
First day cover (June 25, 1996)		
20p, 26p, 31p, 37p, 39p, 43p, 63p	–	4.25
First day cover (April 21, 1997)		
26p, together with 1st gold	–	2.00
First day cover (April 20, 1999)		
7p, 38p, 44p, 64p	–	3.50
First day cover (April 25, 2000)		
8p, 33p, 40p, 41p, 45p, 65p	–	3.50
First day cover (July 4, 2002)		
37p, 42p, 47p, 68p	–	4.00
First day cover (May 6, 2003)		
34p	–	2.00
First day cover (April 1, 2004)		
7p, 35p, 39p, 40p, 43p	–	4.00
First day cover (April 5, 2005)		
9p, 35p, 46p	–	3.50
First day cover (March 28, 2006)		
37p, 44p, 49p, 72p	–	4.00
First day cover (August 1, 2006)		
12p, 14p, with Pricing in Proportion stamps	–	4.50
First day cover (March 27, 2007)		
16p, 48p, 50p, 54p, 78p	–	4.00
First day cover (June 5, 2007)		
£1	–	4.00
First day cover (April 1, 2008)		
15p, 56p, 81p	–	3.50
First day cover (March 31, 2009)		
17p, 22p, 62p, 90p	–	3.50
First day cover (March 30, 2010)		
60p, 67p, 88p, 97p, £1.46, with Europe, Worldwide NVIs	–	7.00

NON-VALUE INDICATORS WITH ELLIPTICAL PERFORATIONS, 1993–2000

Issued in sheets, booklets or coils. 2nd class values have one centre phosphor band; the others have two phosphor bands, except where stated.

1993–1999. Printed in gravure by Harrison or (from 1999) De La Rue

2nd bright blue (September 7, 1993)	1.50	1.50
1st orange-red		
(April 6, 1993) (PCP)	1.75	1.25
(April 4, 1995) (two phosphor bands)	1.80	1.80
1st gold (April 21, 1997)	1.75	1.75
E deep blue (October 5, 1999)	3.00	3.00
Stamp card (1st gold)	2.50	7.00

MACHINS DECIMAL

■ 1993. Printed in litho by Walsall
2nd bright blue (April 6, 1993)	1.50	1.50
1st orange-red (April 6, 1993)	1.75	1.75

■ 1997–1999. Printed in gravure by Walsall
2nd bright blue (April 29, 1997)	1.50	1.50
1st gold (April 21, 1997)	1.75	1.75
1st orange-red (August 26, 1997)	1.75	1.75
E deep blue (January 19, 1999)	3.00	3.00

■ 1993. Printed in litho by Questa
2nd bright blue (April 6, 1993)	1.50	1.50
1st orange-red (April 6, 1993)	1.75	1.75

■ 1998–2000. Printed in gravure by Questa
2nd bright blue (Dec 1, 1998) (perf: 14)	1.60	1.60
2nd bright blue (Apr 27, 2000) (perf: 15x14)	1.75	1.75
1st orange-red (Dec 1, 1998) (perf: 14)	1.85	1.85
1st orange-red (Apr 27, 2000) (perf: 15x14)	2.00	2.00

First day cover (April 6, 1993)		
2nd bright blue, 1st orange-red	–	6.00
First day cover (April 21, 1997)		
1st gold, together with 26p	–	2.00
First day cover (January 19, 1999)		
E deep blue	–	2.00

(*The 2nd class bright blue printed in gravure by Enschedé and Walsall, the 1st class orange-red printed in gravure by Questa, the 1st class gold printed in gravure by De La Rue, Enschedé, Questa and Walsall, and the E deep blue printed in gravure by Enschedé and Questa also appear in prestige stamp books.)

NON-VALUE INDICATORS WITH ELLIPTICAL PERFORATIONS IN GREETINGS CARD SHEETLETS, 1994–97

Small sheets including one 1st class orange-red stamp sold in conjunction with greetings cards, through Boots and other retail outlets.

■ 1994–1995. Printed in litho by Questa
1st sheetlet with Boots logo (Aug 17, 1994)	1.95	1.95
1st sheetlet with no logo (Sep 11, 1995)	1.95	1.95

■ 1997. Printed in litho by Enschedé
1st sheetlet with no logo (Apr 29, 1997)	3.95	3.95

PRICING IN PROPORTION ISSUES WITH ELLIPTICAL PERFORATIONS, 2006–07

■ 2006–07. Printed in gravure by De La Rue or Enschedé
Issued in sheets, business sheets and coils.
2nd blue (August 1, 2006)	1.75	1.75
2nd Large blue (August 1, 2006)	2.25	2.25
1st gold (August 1, 2006)	1.95	1.95
1st Large gold (August 1, 2006)	3.00	3.00
First day cover (together with 12p, 14p)	–	5.00

(*All four values printed in gravure by De La Rue, and the 1st class printed in gravure by Enschedé, also appear in prestige stamp books.)

HIGH VALUES WITH ELLIPTICAL PERFORATIONS, 1999–2003

■ 1999. Printed in intaglio by Enschedé
£1.50 red (March 9, 1999)	3.25	3.25
£2 blue (March 9, 1999)	3.75	3.75
£3 violet (March 9, 1999)	5.00	4.00
£5 brown (March 9, 1999)	8.00	6.00
First day cover	–	12.50

■ 2000. Printed in intaglio by De La Rue
£1.50 red (April 11, 2000)	3.25	3.25
£2 blue (April 11, 2000)	3.75	3.75
£3 violet (April 11, 2000)	5.00	4.00
£5 brown (April 11, 2000)	8.00	7.00
First day cover	–	30.00

■ 2003. Printed in gravure by De La Rue
£1.50 brown-red (July 1, 2003)	2.50	2.50
£2 blue-green (July 1, 2003)	3.25	3.25
£3 mauve (July 1, 2003)	4.75	4.75
£5 grey-blue (July 1, 2003)	7.50	7.50
First day cover	–	15.00

DECIMAL MACHINS

SPECIAL ISSUES, 2000–17

■ **2000, January 6. Millennium definitive**
Des: R. Scholey.
Printed in gravure by De La Rue. Perf: 15x14. Issued in sheets
1st olive-brown 1.75 1.75
Printed in gravure by Walsall. Perf: 15x14. Issued in booklets
1st olive-brown 1.75 1.75
Printed in gravure by Walsall. Perf: 14. Issued in the Special By Design and Treasury Of Trees prestige stamp books
1st olive-brown 1.75 1.75
Printed in gravure by Questa. Perf: 14. Issued in booklets
1st olive-brown 1.75 1.75
Printed in gravure by Questa. Perf: 15x14. Issued in the Queen Elizabeth The Queen Mother prestige stamp book
1st olive-brown 1.75 1.75
First day cover – 2.00
Stamp card 9.00 30.00
(*This design also appears in the 2017 Machin Definitive Golden Anniversary miniature sheet and the 2017 Machin Definitive 50th Anniversary prestige stamp book, printed in gravure by ISP.)

■ **2000, May 22. Stamp Show 2000 Exhibition Souvenir**
Des: Jeffery Matthews. Printed by De La Rue. Phosphor paper. Miniature sheet comprising 4p blue, 5p claret, 6p lime green, 10p orange, 31p purple, 39p magenta, 64p sea-green, £1 bluish violet, plus labels featuring the Royal Mail crest and the Jeffery Matthews colour palette.
Miniature sheet 15.00 15.00
First day cover – 10.00

■ **2010, May 8. London 2010 Festival of Stamps Exhibition Souvenir**
Printed by De La Rue. Two phosphor bands. Miniature sheet comprising 1p, 2p, 5p, 9p, 10p, 20p, 60p, 67p, 88p, 97p, £1.46, plus a label featuring the London 2010: Festival of Stamps logo.
Miniature sheet 50.00 55.00
First day cover – 50.00

■ **2011, September 14. Centenary of the Birth of Arnold Machin**
Printed by Cartor. Miniature sheet comprising ten 1st class gold, with security overlay.
Miniature sheet 13.00 13.00
First day cover – 12.00

■ **2017, June 5. The Machin Definitive Golden Anniversary Celebration**
Des: Atelier Works. Printed in gravure by ISP. Miniature sheet comprising 5p violet (1971), 20p brownish-black and cream Penny Black Anniversary (1990), 1st orange-red (1993), 1st olive-brown (2000), 1st gold Pricing in Proportion (2006), 1st red (2013; source code MMIL, date code 17), £1 gold (2017).
Miniature sheet 15.00 15.00
First day cover – 12.00
Press sheet 50.00 –

BRITISH STAMP MARKET VALUES 2024 **67**

MACHINS SELF-ADHESIVE & SECURITY

SELF-ADHESIVES, 1993–2010

All stamps with die-cut elliptical 'perforations' except where otherwise stated.

■ 1993, October 19
Des: Jeffery Matthews. Printed in litho by Walsall. Horizontal format. Issued only in booklets of 20.

1st orange-red	1.50	1.50
Stamp card	6.00	7.00
First day cover	–	1.50

(*This design also appears, with standard gum, in the 2017 Machin Definitive Golden Anniversary miniature sheet, printed in gravure.)

■ 1997, March 18
Des: Jeffery Matthews. Printed in gravure by Enschedé. Horizontal format with 'st' or 'nd' in large size. Issued only in rolls of 100.

2nd bright blue	1.40	1.40
1st orange-red	1.40	1.40
First day cover	–	3.00

■ 1998, April 6
Printed in gravure by Enschedé in rolls of 200 and business sheets of 100, by Questa in business sheets of 100 (1st class only), and by Walsall in business sheets of 100 and booklets (from January 2001). Perf: 15x14 except where stated.

2nd bright blue	1.60	1.60
2nd bright blue (Perf: 14½x14)	£240	£240
1st orange-red	2.00	2.00
1st orange-red (Perf: 14½x14)	£195	£195

(*Perf: 14½x14 stamps were printed only by Walsall, and sold only individually through Royal Mail's philatelic service.)

■ 2002, June 5
Printed in gravure by De La Rue, Questa and Walsall in retail booklets, and by Enschedé and Walsall in business sheets of 100.

1st gold	2.00	2.00

■ 2002, July 4. Overseas rates
Printed in gravure by Walsall. Issued only in retail booklets.

E deep blue	3.00	3.00
42p olive-grey	4.50	4.00
68p grey-brown	5.00	5.00

■ 2003–2010. Overseas rates with airmail chevrons
Des: Sedley Place. Printed in gravure by Walsall. Issued only in booklets, although individual stamps were sold through Royal Mail's philatelic service.

Europe up to 40g (March 27, 2003)	4.00	3.50
Europe up to 20g (March 30, 2010)	3.50	3.50
Worldwide up to 40g (March 27, 2003)	5.00	5.00
Worldwide up to 20g (March 30, 2010)	4.00	4.00
Worldwide Postcard (April 1, 2004)	3.00	3.00
First day cover (March 27, 2003)	–	3.00
First day cover (April 1, 2004)	–	3.25
First day cover (March 30 2010, with other values)	–	7.00
Stamp cards (E40g, W40g)	2.50	10.00

■ 2006. Pricing in Proportion
Des: Mike Dempsey. Printed in gravure by Walsall and Enschedé. Issued in booklets, coils and business sheets.

2nd blue (September 12, 2006)	1.50	1.50
2nd Large blue (August 15, 2006)	2.00	2.00
1st gold (September 12, 2006)	2.00	2.00
1st Large gold (August 15, 2006)	2.20	2.20
First day cover (2nd Large, 1st Large)	–	3.00
First day cover (2nd, 1st)	–	3.00

SELF-ADHESIVE & SECURITY MACHINS

DEFINITIVES WITH ADDITIONAL SECURITY FEATURES, 2009–22

Stamps feature U-shaped security slits, and/or an iridescent wavy-line overlay text inscribed 'Royal Mail', with variant letters which indicate the source of the stamp (if not from counter sheets), and the year of production (from 2010).

Source codes are 'FOYAL' or 'MFIL' (booklets of four), 'MSIL' (booklets of six), 'MTIL' (booklets of 12), 'MCIL' (booklets which include special issues), 'ROYBL' or 'MBIL' (business sheets), 'MRIL' (rolls), 'MPIL' (prestige stamp books) and 'MMIL' (miniature sheets).

Year codes are 'MA10' (2010), 'MA11' or 'M11L' (2011), 'MA12' or 'M12L' (2012), 'MA13' or 'M13L' (2013), 'MA14' or 'M14L' (2014), 'M15L' (2015), 'M16L' (2016), 'M17L' (2017), 'M18L' (2018), 'M19L' (2019), 'M20L' (2020) and 'M21L' (2021).

From 2016, mint stamps came on security backing paper (SBP) with underlay text. This text can be found all upright, or upright and inverted in alternating double lines.

■ 2009 to date. Non-value indicators
Printed in gravure by De La Rue (sheets up to 2017) or Walsall (sheets from 2018, booklets and business sheets), or litho by Cartor (prestige stamp books). Self-adhesive, with slits and overlay text, except where stated.

2nd blue (February 17, 2009)

no source code, no date code	2.25	2.25
no source code, date code 10	6.00	6.00
no source code, date code 11	4.00	4.00
no source code, date code 12	1.75	1.75
no source code, date code 13	1.50	1.50
no source code, date code 14	1.50	1.50
no source code, date code 15	1.50	1.50
no source code, date code 16	1.50	1.50
no source code, date code 17	2.75	2.75
no source code, date code 17, SBP	1.60	–
no source code, date code 18, SBP	1.50	1.50
no source code, date code 19, SBP	1.60	1.60
no source code, date code 20, SBP	2.00	2.00
no source code, date code 21, SBP	7.50	7.50
source code MTIL, no date code	1.75	1.75
source code MTIL, date code 10	5.50	5.50
source code MTIL, date code 11	2.25	2.25
source code MTIL, date code 12	2.00	2.00
source code MTIL, date code 13	2.00	2.00
source code MTIL, date code 14	1.50	1.50
source code MTIL, date code 15	1.75	1.75
source code MTIL, date code 16, SBP	1.50	1.50
source code MTIL, date code 17, SBP	1.75	1.75
source code MTIL, date code 18, SBP	1.75	1.75
source code MTIL, date code 19, SBP	1.75	1.75
source code MTIL, date code 20, SBP	1.75	1.75
source code MTIL, date code 21, SBP	1.75	1.75
source code MBIL, no date code	2.25	2.25
source code MBIL, date code 10	5.00	5.00
source code MBIL, date code 11	3.25	3.25
source code MBIL, date code 12	2.00	2.00
source code MBIL, date code 13	2.25	2.25
source code MBIL, date code 14	5.00	4.50
source code MBIL, date code 15	3.50	3.50
source code MBIL, date code 15, SBP	3.25	–
source code MBIL, date code 16, SBP	2.00	2.00
source code MBIL, date code 17, SBP	2.25	2.25
source code MBIL, date code 18, SBP	2.00	2.00
source code MBIL, date code 19, SBP	2.00	2.00
source code MBIL, date code 20, SBP	2.00	2.00
source code MBIL, date code 21, SBP	25.00	25.00
source code MRIL, no date code	3.00	3.00
source code MRIL, date code 10	–	75.00
source code MRIL, date code 10, gum, no slits	5.75	5.75
source code MRIL, date code MA12	5.00	5.00
source code MRIL, date code M12L	4.00	4.00
source code MRIL, date code 15	3.75	3.75
source code MPIL, date code 10	5.00	5.00
source code MPIL, date code 15, gum, no slits	4.25	4.25
source code MPIL, date code 17, gum, no slits	2.25	2.25
source code MPIL, date code 19, gum, no slits	2.25	2.25
source code MPIL, date code 20, gum, no slits	2.25	2.25
source code MPIL, date code 21, gum, no slits	2.25	2.25

2nd Large blue (February 17, 2009)

no source code, no date code	2.25	2.25
no source code, date code 10	8.75	8.75
no source code, date code 11	2.60	2.60
no source code, date code 12	2.00	2.00
no source code, date code 13	2.00	2.00
no source code, date code 14	2.00	2.00
no source code, date code 15	2.00	2.00
no source code, date code 16	1.75	1.75
no source code, date code 17, SBP	2.00	2.00
no source code, date code 18, SBP	2.00	2.00
no source code, date code 19, SBP	2.00	2.00
no source code, date code 20, SBP	2.00	2.00
no source code, date code 21, SBP	2.25	2.25

BRITISH STAMP MARKET VALUES 2024

MACHINS SELF-ADHESIVE & SECURITY

source code FOYAL, no date code	2.50	2.50
source code MFIL, date code 10	35.00	35.00
source code MFIL, date code 11	1.75	1.75
source code MFIL, date code 12	3.00	3.00
source code MFIL, date code 13	4.00	4.00
source code MFIL, date code 14	1.75	1.75
source code MFIL, date code 15	4.50	4.50
source code MFIL, date code 16, SBP	2.25	2.25
source code MFIL, date code 17, SBP	9.00	9.00
source code MFIL, date code 18, SBP	8.00	8.00
source code MFIL, date code 19 SBP	3.00	3.00
source code MFIL, date code 20, SBP	3.00	3.00
source code MFIL, date code 21, SBP	3.00	3.00
source code ROYBL, no date code	2.50	2.50
source code MBIL, date code 10	16.00	16.00
source code MBIL, date code 11	12.00	12.00
source code MBIL, date code 12	2.75	2.75
source code MBIL, date code 13	3.50	3.50
source code MBIL, date code 14	2.25	2.25
source code MBIL, date code 15	4.50	4.50
source code MBIL, date code 16, SBP	2.00	2.00
source code MBIL, date code 17, SBP	3.00	3.00
source code MBIL, date code 18, SBP	2.50	2.50
source code MBIL, date code 19, SBP	2.75	2.75
source code MBIL, date code 20, SBP	2.75	2.75
source code MBIL, date code 21, SBP	2.75	2.75

source code MBIL, date code 11	3.00	3.00
source code MRIL, no date code	5.00	5.00
source code MRIL, date code 10	4.50	4.50
source code MRIL, date code 10, gum, no slits	6.00	6.00
source code MRIL, date code 12	3.00	3.00

(*The 1st gold also exists with slits but no overlay text, from rolls.)

1st Large gold (February 17, 2009)

no source code, no date code	2.50	2.50
no source code, date code 10	5.50	5.50
no source code, date code 11	6.00	6.00
source code FOYAL, no date code	3.00	3.00
source code MFIL, date code 10	5.25	5.25
source code MFIL, date code 11	2.00	2.00
source code ROYBL, no date code	2.75	2.75
source code MBIL, date code 10	9.75	9.75
source code MBIL, date code 11	2.75	2.75

1st gold (February 17, 2009)

no source code, no date code	2.50	2.50
no source code, date code 10	3.50	3.50
no source code, date code 11	2.75	2.75
source code MSIL, no date code	3.00	3.00
source code MSIL, date code 10	1.75	1.75
source code MSIL, date code 11	2.25	2.25
source code MTIL, no date code	1.75	1.75
source code MTIL, date code 10	3.00	3.00
source code MTIL, date code 11	2.25	2.25
source code MTIL, date code 12	5.50	5.50
source code MCIL, no date code	1.75	1.75
source code MCIL, date code 10	1.75	1.75
source code MCIL, date code 11	1.75	1.75
source code MPIL, date code 10	3.00	3.00
source code MPIL, date code 11, gum, no slits	5.00	5.00
source code MBIL, no date code	2.50	2.50
source code MBIL, date code 10	7.25	7.25

1st red (January 3, 2013)

no source code, date code 12	1.75	1.75
no source code, date code 13	2.25	2.25
no source code, date code 14	2.00	2.00
no source code, date code 15	3.25	3.25
no source code, date code 16	2.00	2.00
source code MBIL, date code 12	2.25	2.25
source code MBIL, date code 13	4.00	4.00
source code MBIL, date code 14	3.50	3.50
source code MBIL, date code 15	2.75	2.75
source code MBIL, date code 15, SBP	3.00	–
source code MBIL, date code 16, SBP	3.75	3.75
source code MSIL, date code 12	1.75	1.75
source code MSIL, date code 13	2.25	2.25
source code MSIL, date code 14	1.75	1.75
source code MSIL, date code 15	2.75	2.75
source code MTIL, date code 12	1.75	1.75

70 BRITISH STAMP MARKET VALUES 2024

SELF-ADHESIVE & SECURITY MACHINS

source code MTIL, date code 13	2.00	2.00
source code MTIL, date code 14	2.00	2.00
source code MTIL, date code 15	3.75	3.75
source code MTIL, date code 15, SBP	8.50	–
source code MTIL, date code 16, SBP	2.50	2.50
source code MCIL, date code 12	1.75	1.75
source code MCIL, date code 13	1.75	1.75
source code MCIL, date code 14	1.75	1.75
source code MCIL, date code 15	1.75	1.75
source code MRIL, date code 12	4.00	4.00
source code MRIL, date code 13	2.75	2.75
source code MPIL, date code 13, gum, no slits	1.75	1.00
source code MPIL, date code 15, gum, no slits	5.50	5.50
source code MPIL, date code 16, gum, no slits	2.25	2.25
source code MPIL, date code 17, gum, no slits	2.25	2.25
source code MPIL, date code 18, gum, no slits	2.00	2.00
source code MMIL, date code 17, gum, no slits	11.00	11.00

1st Large red (January 3, 2013)

no source code, date code 12	2.25	2.25
no source code, date code 13	3.00	3.00
no source code, date code 14	5.00	5.00
no source code, date code 15	2.00	2.00
no source code, date code 16	2.25	2.25
source code MBIL, date code 12	2.25	2.25
source code MBIL, date code 13	3.50	3.50
source code MBIL, date code 14	3.25	3.25
source code MBIL, date code 15	4.50	4.50
source code MBIL, date code 15, SBP	9.50	–
source code MBIL, date code 16, SBP	3.50	3.50
source code MFIL, date code 12	2.50	2.50
source code MFIL, date code 13	7.25	7.25
source code MFIL, date code 14	2.00	2.00
source code MFIL, date code 15	3.25	3.25
source code MFIL, date code 15, SBP	7.50	–
source code MFIL, date code 16, SBP	5.25	5.25

1st deep red (October 20, 2016)

no source code, date code 16, SBP	6.00	6.00
no source code, date code 17, SBP	1.75	1.75
no source code, date code 18, SBP	2.00	2.00
no source code, date code 19, SBP	2.00	2.00
no source code, date code 20, SBP	2.00	2.00
no source code, date code 21, SBP	2.00	2.00
source code MBIL, date code 16, SBP	3.25	3.25
source code MBIL, date code 17, SBP	2.00	2.00
source code MBIL, date code 18, SBP	2.00	2.00
source code MBIL, date code 19, SBP	2.25	2.25
source code MBIL, date code 20, SBP	2.25	2.25
source code MBIL, date code 21, SBP	2.25	2.25
source code MCIL, date code 16, SBP	1.75	1.75
source code MCIL, date code 17, SBP	1.75	1.75
source code MCIL, date code 18, SBP	1.75	1.75
source code MCIL, date code 19, SBP	1.75	1.75
source code MCIL, date code 20, SBP	2.00	2.00
source code MCIL, date code 21, SBP	2.00	2.00
source code MSIL, date code 16, SBP	2.00	2.00
source code MSIL, date code 17, SBP	1.75	1.75
source code MSIL, date code 18, SBP	2.00	2.00
source code MSIL, date code 19, SBP	2.00	2.00
source code MSIL, date code 20, SBP	2.25	2.25
source code MSIL, date code 21, SBP	3.75	3.75
source code MPIL, date code 16, gum, no slits	2.25	2.25
source code MPIL, date code 20, gum, no slits	2.25	2.25
source code MPIL, date code 21, gum, no slits	2.25	2.25
source code MTIL, date code 16, SBP	2.00	2.00
source code MTIL, date code 17, SBP	2.00	2.00
source code MTIL, date code 18, SBP	2.00	2.00
source code MTIL, date code 20, SBP	2.00	2.00
source code MTIL, date code 21, SBP	2.00	2.00

(*A pane comprising four of the 1st deep red, with no source code and date code 21, along with country definitives and a label inscribed '95', was issued on April 21, 2021 to mark the Queen's 95th birthday, but available only on a souvenir cover.)

1st Large deep red (October 20, 2016)

no source code, date code 17, SBP	2.25	2.25
no source code, date code 18, SBP	2.50	2.50
no source code, date code 19, SBP	2.50	2.50
no source code, date code 20, SBP	2.75	2.75
no source code, date code 21, SBP	2.75	2.75
source code MBIL, date code 16, SBP	2.40	2.40
source code MBIL, date code 17, SBP	9.00	9.00
source code MBIL, date code 18, SBP	2.75	2.75

BRITISH STAMP MARKET VALUES 2024

MACHINS SELF-ADHESIVE & SECURITY

source code MBIL, date code 19, SBP	2.75	2.75
source code MBIL, date code 20, SBP	3.00	3.00
source code MBIL, date code 21, SBP	3.00	3.00
source code MFIL, date code 16, SBP	7.50	7.50
source code MFIL, date code 17, SBP	4.75	4.75
source code MFIL, date code 18, SBP	2.75	2.75
source code MFIL, date code 19, SBP	3.00	3.00
source code MFIL, date code 20, SBP	4.00	4.00
source code MFIL, date code 21, SBP	4.00	4.00

■ **2009 to date. Denominated definitives**
Printed in gravure by De La Rue or Walsall/ISP (sheets), or litho by Cartor (prestige stamp books). Self-adhesive, with security slits and iridescent overlay text, except where stated.

1p dark maroon (March 8, 2011)

no overlay text	0.50	0.50
no source code, date code 12	0.30	0.30
no source code, date code 15	1.50	1.50
no source code, date code 16	0.30	0.30
no source code, date code 17, SBP	1.50	1.50
no source code, date code 18, SBP	0.40	0.40
no source code, date code 19, SBP	0.40	0.40
no source code, date code 20, SBP	0.40	0.40
no source code, date code 21, SBP	0.40	0.40
source code MPIL, date code 13, gum, no slits	1.00	1.00
source code MPIL, date code 14, gum, no slits	1.00	1.00
source code MPIL, date code 15, gum, no slits	1.00	1.00
source code MPIL, date code 18, gum, no slits	1.00	1.00
source code M IL, date code 18, gum, no slits	1.00	1.00
source code MPIL, date code 19, gum, no slits	1.00	1.00
source code MPIL, date code 20, gum, no slits	1.00	1.00

2p dark green (March 8, 2011)

no overlay text	0.40	0.40
no source code, date code 12	0.40	0.40
no source code, date code 14	1.50	1.50
no source code, date code 15	0.40	0.40
no source code, date code 16	1.50	1.50
no source code, date code 17	1.50	1.50
no source code, date code 17, SBP	0.50	0.50
no source code, date code 18, SBP	0.45	0.45
no source code, date code 19, SBP	0.40	0.40
no source code, date code 20, SBP	0.40	0.40
no source code, date code 21, SBP	0.40	0.40
source code MPIL, date code 13, gum, no slits	1.00	1.00
source code MPIL, date code 14, gum, no slits	1.00	1.00
source code MPIL, date code 16, gum, no slits	1.00	1.00
source code M IL, date code 18, gum, no slits	1.00	1.00
source code MPIL, date code 19, gum, no slits	1.00	1.00
source code MPIL, date code 20, gum, no slits	1.00	1.00
source code MPIL, date code 21, gum, no slits	1.00	1.00

(*The 2p also exists in gummed form, without overlay text, from a prestige stamp book.)

5p ash pink (March 8, 2011)

no overlay text	0.50	0.50
no source code, date code 12	0.40	0.40
no source code, date code 14	2.50	2.50
no source code, date code 15	2.50	2.50
no source code, date code 16	0.50	0.50
no source code, date code 17, SBP	0.40	0.40
no source code, date code 18, SBP	0.40	0.40
no source code, date code 19, SBP	0.40	0.40
no source code, date code 20, SBP	0.50	0.50
no source code, date code 21, SBP	0.50	0.50
source code MPIL, date code 12, gum, no slits	2.00	2.00
source code MPIL, date code 13, gum, no slits	1.00	1.00
source code MPIL, date code 15, gum, no slits	1.00	1.00
source code MPIL, date code 16, gum, no slits	1.00	1.00
source code MPIL, date code 17, gum, no slits	1.00	1.00
source code MPIL, date code 18, gum, no slits	1.25	1.25
source code MPIL, date code 19, gum, no slits	1.00	1.00
source code MPIL, date code 20, gum, no slits	1.00	1.00
source code MPIL, date code 21, gum, no slits	1.00	1.00
source code M IL, date code 18, gum, no slits	1.00	1.00

(*The 5p also exists in gummed form, without overlay text, from a prestige stamp book, and in gummed form, with source code MPIL and date code 13, with the elliptical perforation towards the top, from the Merchant Navy prestige stamp book.)

10p light tan (March 8, 2011)

no overlay text	0.60	0.60
no source code, date code 12	0.45	0.45
no source code, date code 13	1.00	1.00
no source code, date code 14	1.00	1.00
no source code, date code 15	1.25	1.25
no source code, date code 16	1.00	1.00
no source code, date code 17	4.00	4.00
no source code, date code 17, SBP	0.60	0.60
no source code, date code 18, SBP	0.60	0.60
no source code, date code 19, SBP	0.60	0.60
no source code, date code 20, SBP	0.60	0.60
no source code, date code 21, SBP	0.60	0.60
source code MPIL, date code 12, gum, no slits	2.00	2.00
source code MPIL, date code 13, gum, no slits	1.20	1.20
source code MPIL, date code 14, gum, no slits	1.00	1.00
source code MPIL, date code 15, gum, no slits	1.25	1.25
source code MPIL, date code 16, gum, no slits	1.00	1.00
source code MPIL, date code 18, gum, no slits	1.25	1.25
source code MPIL, date code 19, gum, no slits	1.20	1.20
source code MPIL, date code 21, gum, no slits	1.00	1.00

(*The 10p also exists in gummed form, without overlay text, from a prestige stamp book.)

20p light green (March 8, 2011)

no overlay text	0.75	0.75
no source code, date code 12	3.00	3.00
no source code, date code 13	1.20	1.20
no source code, date code 14	1.25	1.25
no source code, date code 15	1.00	1.00

SELF-ADHESIVE & SECURITY MACHINS

no source code, date code 16	0.70	0.70
no source code, date code 17, SBP	0.70	0.70
no source code, date code 18, SBP	0.70	0.70
no source code, date code 19, SBP	0.70	0.70
no source code, date code 20, SBP	0.70	0.70
no source code, date code 21, SBP	0.70	0.70
source code MPIL, date code 12, gum, no slits	3.00	3.00
source code MPIL, date code 14, gum, no slits	1.25	1.25
source code MPIL, date code 17, gum, no slits	2.00	2.00
source code MPIL, date code 18, gum, no slits	1.50	1.50
source code MPIL, date code 20, gum, no slits	1.25	1.25
source code MPIL, date code 21, gum, no slits	1.25	1.25
source code M IL, date code 18, gum, no slits	1.25	1.25

50p light grey (February 17, 2009)

no source code, no date code	1.25	1.25
source code MPIL, date code 10	6.00	6.00
source code MPIL, date code 11	5.00	5.00

50p slate-grey (January 3, 2013)

no source code, date code 12	1.35	1.35
no source code, date code 17, SBP	6.25	6.25
no source code, date code 19, SBP	1.50	1.50
source code MPIL, date code 13, gum, no slits	1.75	1.75
source code MPIL, date code 15, gum, no slits	2.00	2.00
source code MPIL, date code 18, gum, no slits	1.75	1.75
source code MPIL, date code 19, gum, no slits	1.75	1.75
source code MPIL, date code 20, gum, no slits	1.75	1.75
source code MPIL, date code 21, gum, no slits	1.75	1.75

(*The 50p with source code MPIL and date code 13 has the elliptical perforation towards the top; it comes from the Merchant Navy prestige stamp book.)

68p sea green (March 29, 2011)

no source code, date code 11	2.00	2.00
no source code, date code 12	7.00	7.00
source code MPIL, date code 11, gum, no slits	3.25	3.25

76p bright pink (March 29, 2011)

no source code, date code 11	1.85	1.85
no source code, date code 12	5.75	5.75
source code MPIL, date code 11, gum, no slits	9.00	9.00

78p orchard mauve (March 27, 2013)

no source code, date code 13 (Walsall)	1.50	1.50
no source code, date code 13 (De La Rue)	2.75	2.75

81p holly green (March 26, 2014)

no source code, date code 14	2.25	2.25

81p sea green (February 19, 2015)

source code MPIL, date code 14, gum, no slits	7.50	7.50

87p orange (April 25, 2012)

no source code, date code 12	4.25	4.25
source code MPIL, date code 12, gum, no slits	5.00	5.00

88p amber yellow (March 27, 2013)

no source code, date code 13 (Walsall)	1.75	1.75
no source code, date code 13 (De La Rue)	3.00	3.00

97p purple (March 26, 2014)

no source code, date code 14	2.40	2.40
source code MPIL, date code 14, gum, no slits	2.25	2.25

£1 ruby (February 17, 2009)

no source code, no date code	2.25	2.25
no source code, date code 11	29.50	29.50
no source code, date code 12	15.00	15.00
source code MPIL, date code 17, gum, no slits	23.00	23.00

£1 wood brown (January 3, 2013)

no source code, date code 12	6.00	6.00
no source code, date code 14	3.75	3.75
no source code, date code 15	3.25	3.25
no source code, date code 16	3.00	3.00
no source code, date code 18, SBP	2.75	2.75
no source code, date code 19, SBP	3.00	3.00
no source code, date code 21, SBP	3.00	3.00
source code MPIL, date code 14, gum, no slits	2.50	2.50
source code MPIL, date code 15, gum, no slits	2.50	2.50
source code MPIL, date code 21	2.50	2.50

£1.05 gooseberry green (March 22, 2016)

no source code, date code 16	2.25	2.25
source code MPIL, date code 16, gum, no slits	2.50	2.50

£1.10 lime green (March 29, 2011)

no source code, date code 11	2.50	2.50
no source code, date code 12	£450	–

£1.17 sunrise red (March 21, 2017)

no source code, date code 17	2.50	2.50
no source code, date code 17, SBP	2.75	2.75
source code MPIL, date code 17, gum, no slits	14.50	14.50
source code MPIL, date code 19, gum, no slits	3.60	3.60
source code M IL, date code 18, gum, no slits	3.60	3.60

£1.25 holly green (March 20, 2018)

no source code, date code 18, SBP	2.50	2.50
source code MPIL, date code 18, gum, no slits	2.85	2.85
source code M IL, date code 18, gum, no slits	2.50	2.50

£1.28 emerald green (April 25, 2012)

no source code, date code 12	3.75	3.75
no source code, date code 13	5.00	5.00
no source code, date code 14	12.00	12.00

£1.33 amber yellow (March 24, 2015)

no source code, date code 15	2.50	2.50
no source code, date code 16	4.50	4.50
source code MPIL, date code 15, gum, no slits	3.00	3.00

£1.35 orchid mauve (March 19, 2019)

no source code, date code 19, SBP	2.50	2.50
source code MPIL, date code 19, gum, no slits	5.00	5.00

£1.40 dark pine green (March 21, 2017)

no source code, date code 17	2.60	2.60
no source code, date code 17, SBP	3.00	3.00
source code MPIL, date code 17, gum, no slits	4.00	4.00

£1.42 garnet red (March 17, 2020)

no source code, date code 20, SBP	2.65	2.65

£1.45 dove grey (March 20, 2018)

no source code, date code 18, SBP	2.75	2.75

MACHINS SELF-ADHESIVE & SECURITY

source code M IL, date code 18, gum, no slits	7.00	7.00
£1.47 dove grey (March 26, 2014)		
no source code, date code 14	2.75	2.75
£1.50 brown-red (February 17, 2009)		
no source code, no date code	2.75	2.75
source code MPIL, date code 21, gum, no slits	12.50	12.50
£1.52 orchid mauve (March 24, 2015)		
no source code, date code 15	2.60	2.60
£1.55 marine turquoise (March 20, 2018)		
no source code, date code 18, SBP	2.85	2.85
no source code, date code 19, SBP	3.25	3.25
source code MPIL, date code 18, gum, no slits	14.50	14.50
£1.57 tarragon green (March 21, 2017)		
no source code, date code 17	2.65	2.65
no source code, date code 17, SBP	3.00	3.00
£1.60 amber yellow (March 19, 2019)		
no source code, date code 19, SBP	2.75	2.75
£1.63 sunset red (March 17, 2020)		
no source code, date code 20, SBP	3.00	3.00
source code MPIL, date code 20, gum, no slits	4.50	4.50
£1.65 sage green (March 29, 2011)		
no source code, date code 11	3.50	3.50
no source code, date code 12	£450	–
£1.68 tarragon green (March 17, 2020)		
no source code, date code 20, SBP	3.50	3.50
£1.70 marine turquoise (December 23, 2020)		
no source code, date code 21, SBP	3.50	3.50
source code MPIL, date code 21, gum, no slits	14.50	14.50
£1.88 sapphire blue (March 27, 2013)		
no source code, date code 13 (Walsall)	3.25	3.25
no source code, date code 13 (De La Rue)	4.25	4.25
£1.90 rhododendron (April 25, 2012)		
no source code, date code 12	3.75	3.75
£2 slate blue (February 17, 2009)		
no source code, no date code	3.50	3.50
no source code, date code 13	6.50	6.50
no source code, date code 19, SBP	3.50	3.50
£2.15 turquoise (March 26, 2014)		
no source code, date code 14	3.60	3.60
£2.25 plum purple (March 24, 2015)		
no source code, date code 15	3.25	3.25
no source code, date code 16	12.50	12.50
no source code, date code 18, SBP	3.50	3.50
£2.27 harvest gold (March 21, 2017)		
no source code, date code 17	3.50	3.50
no source code, date code 17, SBP	3.75	3.75
£2.30 gooseberry green (March 19, 2019)		
no source code, date code 19, SBP	3.50	3.50
£2.42 purple heather (March 17, 2020)		
no source code, date code 20, SBP	3.75	3.75
£2.45 spruce green (March 24, 2015)		
no source code, date code 15	3.65	3.65
£2.55 garnet red (March 21, 2017)		
no source code, date code 17	4.50	4.50
no source code, date code 17, SBP	5.25	5.25
no source code, date code 20, SBP	5.00	5.00
no source code, date code 21, SBP	5.00	5.00
£2.65 purple heather (March 20, 2018)		
no source code, date code 18, SBP	4.00	4.00
£2.80 spruce green (March 19, 2019)		

no source code, date code 19, SBP	4.20	4.20
£2.97 rose pink (March 17, 2020)		
no source code, date code 20, SBP	4.50	4.50
£3 mauve (February 17, 2009)		
no source code, no date code	4.75	4.75
no source code, date code 19, SBP	4.50	4.50
£3.15 aqua green (March 24, 2015)		
no source code, date code 15	4.50	4.50
£3.25 aqua green (December 23, 2020)		
no source code, date code 21, SBP	4.75	4.75
£3.30 rose pink (March 24, 2015)		
no source code, date code 15	4.75	4.75
£3.45 dark pine green (March 19, 2019)		
no source code, date code 19, SBP	4.85	4.85
£3.60 bright orange (March 19, 2019)		
no source code, date code 19, SBP	5.00	5.00
£3.66 harvest gold (March 17, 2020)		
no source code, date code 20, SBP	5.25	5.25
£3.82 holly green (March 17, 2020)		
no source code, date code 20, SBP	5.50	5.50
£4.20 plum purple (December 23, 2020)		
no source code, date code 21, SBP	6.25	6.25
£5 azure (February 17, 2009)		
no source code, no date code	8.00	8.00
no source code, date code 19, SBP	7.50	7.50

(*The 1p, 20p, £1.25 and £1.45 appear in the Marvel limited-edition prestige stamp book, source code MPIL, date code 19, with a printed cancellation.)

First day cover (February 17, 2009)		
2nd, 2nd Large, 1st, 1st Large, 50p, £1	–	5.00
First day cover (February 17, 2009)		
£1.50, £2, £3, £5	–	17.00
First day cover (March 29, 2011)		
1p, 2p, 5p, 10p, 20p	–	2.00
First day cover (March 29, 2011)		
68p, 76p, £1.10, £1.65	–	6.00
First day cover (April 25, 2012)		
87p, £1.28, £1.90, with 1st Large Diamond Jubilee	–	8.00
First day cover (January 3, 2013)		
1p, 2p, 5p, 10p, 20p, 50p, £1, 1st red, 1st Large red	–	6.00
First day cover (March 27, 2013)		
78p, 88p, £1.88, with 1st Signed For, 1st Large Signed For		7.00
First day cover (March 26, 2014)		
81p, 97p, £1.47, £2.15	–	9.00
First day cover (March 24, 2015)		
£1.33, £1.52, £2.25, £2.45, £3.15, £3.30	–	24.00
First day cover (March 22, 2016)		
£1.05	–	2.50
First day cover (March 21, 2017)		
£1.17, £1.40, £1.57, £2.27, £2.55	–	15.00
First day cover (March 20, 2018)		
£1.25, £1.45, £1.55, £2.65	–	16.00
First day cover (March 19, 2019)		
£1.35, £1.60, £2.30, £2.80, £3.45, £3.60	–	20.00
First day cover (March 17, 2020)		
£1.42, £1.63, £1.68, £2.42, £2.97, £3.66, £3.82	–	32.00
First day cover (December 23, 2020)		
£1.70, £3.25, £4.20	–	20.00

SELF-ADHESIVE & SECURITY **MACHINS**

PRIORITY SERVICE ISSUES WITH ADDITIONAL SECURITY FEATURES 2009–21

■ **2009, November 7. Recorded/Signed For**
Printed in gravure by De La Rue. Self-adhesive, with slits and iridescent overlay text.
1st orange-red and yellow
no source code, no date code	4.50	4.50
no source code, date code 10	12.50	12.50

1st Large orange-red and yellow
no source code, no date code	5.00	5.00
no source code, date code 10	29.50	29.50
First day cover	–	5.00

■ **2010, October 26. Special Delivery**
Printed in gravure by De La Rue (up to 2017) or ISP (from 2018). Self-adhesive, with slits and iridescent overlay text.
1st up to 100g silver and blue
no source code, date code 10	10.50	10.50
no source code, date code 14	20.00	20.00
no source code, date code 15	18.00	18.00
no source code, date code 16	20.00	20.00
no source code, date code 17	16.00	16.00
no source code, date code 17, SBP	18.00	–
no source code, date code 18, SBP	14.75	14.75
no source code, date code 19, SBP	14.75	14.75
no source code, date code 20, SBP	11.00	11.00

1st up to 500g blue and silver
no source code, date code 10	12.00	12.00
no source code, date code 14	17.00	17.00
no source code, date code 16	14.00	14.00
no source code, date code 18, SBP	14.00	14.00
no source code, date code 20, SBP	11.50	11.50
First day cover	–	15.00

■ **2013, March 27. Royal Mail/Signed For**
Printed in gravure by De La Rue (up to 2017) or ISP (from 2018). Self-adhesive, with slits and iridescent overlay text.
1st orange-red and yellow
no source code, date code 13	4.25	4.25
no source code, date code 15	6.00	6.00
no source code, date code 16	5.50	5.50
no source code, date code 17, SBP	4.75	4.75
no source code, date code 19, SBP	6.50	6.50
no source code, date code 20, SBP	5.75	5.75

1st Large orange-red and yellow
no source code, date code 13	4.75	4.75
no source code, date code 15	12.50	12.50
no source code, date code 16	8.75	8.75
no source code, date code 17	8.00	8.00
no source code, date code 18, SBP	7.50	7.50
no source code, date code 20, SBP	6.25	6.25
First day cover (with 78p, 88p, £1.88)	–	7.00

SPECIAL ISSUES WITH ADDITIONAL SECURITY FEATURES 2012–17

■ **2012, February 6. Diamond Jubilee**
Printed in gravure by De La Rue (counter sheets, business sheets) or Walsall (booklets, business sheets). Self-adhesive, with slits and overlay text reading 'DIAMOND JUBILEE'.
1st diamond blue
no source code (counter sheets)	1.75	1.75
source code MSND (booklets of 6)	1.75	1.75
source code MTND (booklets of 12)	1.75	1.75
source code MCND (special issue booklets)	1.60	1.60
source code MBND (business sheets)	2.25	2.25

BRITISH STAMP MARKET VALUES 2024 **75**

MACHINS SELF-ADHESIVE & SECURITY

source code MPND (PSBs), gum, no slits	3.00	3.00
source code MMND (mini sheet), gum, no slits	–	4.50
1st Large diamond blue (April 25, 2012)		
no source code (counter sheets)	2.50	2.50
source code JUBILFE (booklets of 4)	2.60	2.60
source code JUBILBE (business sheets)	4.00	4.00
First day cover (1st)	–	2.00
First day cover (1st Large, with 87p, £1.28, £1.90)	–	11.00

(*The 1st Large was released early by a number of post offices.)

■ 2015, September 9. Long To Reign Over Us
Printed in gravure by De La Rue (counter sheets) or ISP (booklets). Self-adhesive, with slits and overlay text reading 'LONG TO REIGN OVER US'.

1st amethyst purple

no source code, date code 15	1.60	1.60
no source code, date code 16	7.25	7.25
source code REIGS, date code 15	1.60	1.60
source code REIGS, date code 15, SBP	35.00	–
source code REIGS, date code 16, SBP	2.75	2.75
source code REIGC, date code 15	1.60	1.60
source code REIGC, date code 16	1.60	1.60
source code REIGP, date code 16, gum, no slits	2.50	2.50
First day cover	–	2.00

■ 2017, February 6. 65th Anniversary of the Accession
Printed in gravure by ISP. Gummed, with overlay text reading '65TH ANNIVERSARY OF ACCESSION'.

£5 sapphire blue	10.00	10.00
First day cover	–	10.00

SELF-ADHESIVE & SECURITY MACHINS

DEFINITIVES WITH DATA MATRIX CODES, 2021–22

In addition to U-shaped security slits, an iridescent wavy-line overlay text with source and year codes, and security backing paper (SBP), these stamps have a digital data matrix code adjacent to the Machin design, separated from it by a simulated perforation.

Source codes are 'MFIL' (booklets of four), 'MEIL' (booklets of eight) and 'MBIL' (business sheets). Stamps from counter sheets and prestige stamp books have no source code.

Year codes are 'M21L' (2021) and 'M22L' (2022).

■ 2021, March 23
Des: Royal Mail (using portrait by Arnold Machin and typography by Jeffery Matthews). Printed in gravure by ISP. Available only in business sheets of 50.

2nd blue
source code MBIL, date code 21, SBP	2.25	2.25
First day cover	–	3.00

■ 2022, February 1
Printed in gravure by ISP.

2nd holly green
no source code, date code 22, SBP (sideways)	1.60	1.60
source code MEIL, date code 22, SBP	1.65	1.65
source code MBIL, date code 22, SBP	2.25	2.25

1st plum purple
no source code, date code 22, SBP (sideways)	1.80	1.80
source code MEIL, date code 22, SBP	1.85	1.85
source code MFIL, date code 22, SBP	1.85	1.85
source code MBIL, date code 22, SBP	2.10	2.10

2nd Large dark pine green
no source code, date code 22, SBP (sideways)	1.95	1.95
source code MFIL, date code 22, SBP	2.25	2.25
source code MBIL, date code 22, SBP	2.40	2.40

1st Large marine turquoise
no source code, date code 22, SBP (sideways)	2.50	2.50
source code MFIL, date code 22, SBP	2.75	2.75
source code MBIL, date code 22, SBP	3.00	3.00
First day cover	–	7.50

■ 2022, April 4
Printed in gravure by ISP.

£1.85 wood brown
no source code, date code 22, SBP (sideways)	3.00	3.00

£2.55 sapphire blue
no source code, date code 22, SBP (sideways)	4.00	4.00

£3.25 purple
no source code, date code 22, SBP (sideways)	5.00	5.00

£4.20 light green
no source code, date code 22, SBP (sideways)	6.00	6.00
First day cover	–	17.50

■ 2022, April 4
Printed in gravure by ISP.

1p sapphire blue
no source code, date code 22, SBP (sideways)	0.25	0.25

2p dark green
no source code, date code 22, SBP (sideways)	0.30	0.30

5p purple heather
no source code, date code 22, SBP (sideways)	0.35	0.35

10p aqua green
no source code, date code 22, SBP (sideways)	0.40	0.40

20p light green
no source code, date code 22, SBP (sideways)	0.50	0.50

50p stone green
no source code, date code 22, SBP (sideways)	1.25	1.25

£1 wood brown
no source code, date code 22, SBP (sideways)	2.00	2.00

£2 bright blue
no source code, date code 22, SBP (sideways)	3.50	3.50

£3 purple
no source code, date code 22, SBP (sideways)	4.50	4.50

£5 spruce green
no source code, date code 22, SBP (sideways)	7.50	7.50
First day cover (1p to £1)	–	5.00
First day cover (£2, £3, £5)	–	15.00

BRITISH STAMP MARKET VALUES 2024

ATTENTION OWNERS OF LARGE/ VALUABLE COLLECTIONS –

from / respond to: **Andrew McGavin**

Are You THINKING of SELLING?

This is How The Stamp Trade Works

Philatelic Expert Lets You into his *Selling Secrets* so you can benefit from a *totally different* (and New) Selling Experience

1 If You want to learn how the stamp trade works, please read on… When I was 15, I did. I wondered if there was some secret source of supply? So, I bought my 1st stamp mixture, (wholesale I thought), broke it into 50 smaller units, advertised it in Stamp Magazine 'Classifieds', and waited for the orders to roll in… I'm still waiting, 51 years later !...
Wrong Offer ✗   Wrong Price ✗   Wrong Place ✗
(naïve seller) ✓ = 😊 me but I was only 15 at the time!

ANDREW PROMOTING PHILATELY ON THE ALAN TITCHMARSH SHOW ITV

About The Author ▶ Andrew found his Father's stamps at the age of 10. A year later at Senior School he immediately joined the School Stamp Club. He 'specialised'(!) in British, but soon was interested in Queen Victoria which he could not afford. The 2nd to last boy wearing short trousers in his school year, he religiously bought Post Office New Issues on Tuesdays with his pocket money. He soon found that he enjoyed swapping / trading stamps as much as collecting them. Aged 19, eschewing University he quickly found a philatelic career in London, leading to creating his own companies in stamps. Andrew has authored many internationally published Stamp 'Tips' articles, appearing on Local Radio and National TV promoting Philately with Alan Titchmarsh. Andrew's area of expertise is unusual – in so far as his grounding in collecting and wide philatelic knowledge has given him a deep understanding of Philately. He has studied Philately for the past 51 years, in combination with Commerce and Marketing Expertise, enabling him to create synergies in 'lifetime' interlinked Stamp Selling Systems, selling unit-priced stamps through to handling collections & Rarities up to £700,000 each. Today Andrew is fortunate to be co-owner with his Wife, of Universal Philatelic Auctions (aka UPA) – the Largest No Buyer's Premium Reducing-Estimate Stamp Auction in the World, creating records selling stamps to 2,261 different bidders from 54 different countries 'in his international auctions. Andrew stopped collecting stamps aged 18 reasoning that his enjoyment of stamps would be in handling them and selling them… He loves working in stamps and looks forward to each philatelic day

TIPS OF THE TRADE
REQUEST MY -TIPS OF THE TRADE FREE BOOKLET

2 Three years later, attending my first public stamp auctions I wondered how some bidders seemed to buy everything, paying the highest price? It didn't occur to me that they were probably Auction Bidding Agents, paid by absent (dealer) bidders to represent them. I wondered why two collectors sitting side by side muttered to each other **"he's a dealer"** as if that justified him paying the highest price…

…but did it really? What was the real reason? How could a Dealer pay a higher price than a Collector? It doesn't make sense, does it? Collectors are customers. Customers usually pay the highest price, unless… for a Collector, this was…
Wrong Presentation ✗   Wrong Place ✗
therefore Wrong Price ✗

3 Fast-forward 48 years later to a British Empire collection, lot #1 in an International Stamp Auction – Estimated at £3,000, but we were the highest bidder at £21,000 – **YES** – some 7×higher. Including Buyer's Premium in the extraordinary sum of £4,788 we actually paid GBP£25,788= upon a £3,000 estimate… **however,** we broke it down into sets, singles, mini-collections etc. We made a profit. Some might say it found its price. Others may say:
Wrong Estimate ✗ Wrong Presentation ✗
Wrong Structure ✗ Wrong Protection of Price ✗

– Lucky for the seller that 2 well-heeled bidders saw the potential value that day or it could have been given away… the seller could easily have lost out couldn't he? or she?

So, by un-peeling the layers of obfuscation, hopefully we can all agree:
The Secret is Simple – it's ALL ABOUT : TIMING
Plus the 3 Philatelic 'P's –
Presentation ✓ Place ✓ and Price ✓

4 Understanding the problem… I always remember the car trade had their own little 'bible' – Glass's Guide. I've no idea, I've not even looked - in this internet-dominated world, it may even have disappeared. Well, there's an insider Stamp Trade publication for Stamp Dealers called "The Philatelic Exporter". There's nothing that special about it – and you won't learn much or find massively reduced prices by subscribing – **BUT** – it is a forum, a paper focal point, a last 'bastion' in this on-line transparent world that we inhabit… whereby dealers (and auctioneers) can try and communicate with each other. I publish my own articles there…

Recently I discussed the outcome of my 10 years' simple research, asking dealers and auctioneers **'what is your biggest problem?'**

To a man, (why are we almost all men), they replied – **"my biggest problem is stock, if I can get more of the right stock I can sell it easily"**

Strange that, nobody ever asked me the same question back – because my answer would have been entirely different (and I don't treat it as a problem) – **I seek to satisfy more collector clients than any other stamp auction**

This is the reason why my company has such massive advertising. This is the reason why we spend up to 8% of turnover – up to £200,000 per annum in marketing costs. (Most dealers don't even sell £200K per annum).

5 Why is that? Because, as the world revolved **the Stamp Market, imperceptibly Changed, and incrementally – Massively**

So, although few will tell you this, it's clearly evident that the problem for most Sellers of Stamps today is no longer absent stock - but absent collectors in the place they choose to sell their stamps in. Simply put, other Dealers, Auctions, Stamp Fairs have not invested in marketing to have a strong Customer-core. To be fair, this is not true of all – but it is true of most – so that our former competitor 'Apex' had 800 bidders in a recent auction. In my most recent 20,000+ lot UPA 77th Auction we had 1,793 different bidders from 49 different countries, 95% of whom were Collectors. Some other well-advertised auctions only have 200 bidders (a high percentage of whom are dealers – so that, essentially they are Dealer-dominated auctions) – so that when you sell through them – you're paying up to 18% (including VAT) seller's commission and the buyer is paying up to 25% **and** more in Buyer's Premium, credit card fees, on-line bidding fee, delivery and insurance etc… **AND all of that so that your stamps may be sold, wait for it – TO DEALERS (and some collectors),** but Dealers, that naturally must make a profit to survive…

6 **Now, let's examine the cost implications – Example:** Your stamp collection sells in public auction for £800. Upon a 25% buyer's premium, the dealer pays £1,000 and it could be more. He breaks it into £2,000+ selling price (much lower and he'll go out of business). The auction charges you a seller's commission of up to 18% (VAT included) upon the £800 sale price. This is GBP£144. Therefore you receive approaching £656 – which is approximately 33% of the dealer's £2,000+/- retail selling price - **BUT… now that we have identified the problem…**

Isn't the Solution Staring us Right in The Face ?

7 **Why Pay an Auction to Sell to Dealers: Sell to Collectors instead?** In our example with buyer's premium, sellers commission, lotting fees, extra credit card charges, VAT and even insurance - you're already being charged in different ways up to 40% of the selling price to sell, possibly or probably, **to the wrong person.**

Why not direct that 40% cost you're paying to sell to Collectors instead? Sounds good, so why hasn't this been done before ?

8 **Truth is, it Has been done before…** Sometimes the 'old' ways are the best ways aren't they? But in today's enthusiasm to obscure the obvious so that money may be taken,

WE CAN SAFELY COLLECT YOUR STAMPS NOW

Contact UPA: 01451 861 111

UNSOLICITED TESTIMONIAL:

Dear Folk at UPA,

I've dealt with the public for 37 + years, and as both a consumer, and a businessman, I have created huge numbers of orders from all over the world from a complete range of suppliers from all aspects of our daily lives.

But I don't believe I have ever encountered such sensitivity, such kind thought, such understanding as I have with you in our initial meeting, our subsequent successful transaction, and now this.

I recall well the item you highlight, and realise that this one item has such colossal personal value, I could never part with it.

It has been an absolute pleasure dealing with yourself, and I am more than willing for you to use this e-mail as commendation to others who may be thinking of disposing of their collection.

Many, many thanks for a memorable experience, and I will try to emulate your thought and care in my own business sphere.

Yours sincerely
D. E. B. Bath, UK

almost surreptitiously, in numerous different ways, (without us apparently noticing until we see the cheque in our pocket) – the transparent 'seller pays' has been deliberately 'obscured' – so much so that, **amazingly,** the latest 2017 European Auction Selling Legislation just introduced – now requires auctions that charge 'buyer's premiums' **to warn the buyer in advance.** Just imagine going into the petrol station, and being warned that the price you're paying to put fuel in you tank is not the real price, you have to pay a premium! Obviously, there would be an uproar…

9 **How can you cut out the middleman and sell to Collectors instead?** Well, I can think of two ways. 1). **DIY** - Do It Yourself selling on eBay. That may be fine for lower grade material – but, would you risk auctioning relatively unprotected rare material on eBay ? We don't and we're professionals, so we should know what we're doing. Or 2). Cut out the extra middle-man. **Use my company UPA, which reaches collectors instead.** Here's how it works: Continuing from our previous **Example**:

The auction sold your stamps to a dealer for £1,000 – but You received circa £656

UPA sells them to collectors for you for up to £2,000 – even after 40% commission you receive up to £1,200. Up to £544 more. Now that's amazing, isn't it?

10 **Sounds Good Andrew, but Can You 'Deliver'?** Obviously, nothing is as simple as that, and as we auction stamps to collectors some collections may 'break' to the example £2,000+/- but the stamps may be sold for more or less – especially as we reserve all lots at 20% below, (Estimate £2,000 = £1,600 reserve) and not everything sells first or even 2nd time so prices may come down… Naturally, it's not that straightforward for a dealer either – he may sell at a discount to 'move' stock **OR**, like many dealers he may be sitting on the same unsold stamps, that you see time and time again, in dealer's stocks years later and still at the same unattractive prices… So, I think it is more reasonable for you to expect up to 36% to 50% more, indirectly or directly via my **Collector's Secret Weapon:** Universal Philatelic Auctions, which moves material more quickly, by incrementally reducing estimate (and reserve) price in a structured selling system…

Request Your Next FREE Catalogue NOW

86th Edition POSTAL AUCTION
Closing Date: 5pm Tuesday 5th July 2022
22,483 lots worth £2,053,980 estimates

Unique Reducing Estimate System

UNIVERSAL PHILATELIC AUCTIONS BSMV24
4 The Old Coalyard, West End, Northleach, Glos. GL54 3HE UK
Tel: 01451 861111 • Fax: 01451 861297
www.upastampauctions.co.uk • info@upastampauctions.co.uk

Continued on the outside back cover

QUEEN ELIZABETH II DECIMAL

QUEEN ELIZABETH II DECIMAL SPECIAL ISSUES

In this section, prices are quoted in two columns: unmounted mint (left) and fine used (right). Most issues, as well as gutter pairs and stamp cards, are priced for complete sets only except where stated.

Except where otherwise stated, all stamps were printed in photogravure by Harrison. Gutter pairs and traffic-light gutter pairs appear from November 1972, blue-tinted polyvinyl alcohol dextrin (PVAD) gum from November 1973 and phosphor-coated paper from September 1979.

'A Mountain Road' by T. P. Flanagan (3p)
'Deer's Meadow' by Tom Carr (7½p)
'Slieve na Brock' by Colin Middleton (9p)

■ 1971, June 16. Ulster Paintings
Des: S. Rose.
Set	0.50	0.60
First day cover	–	1.00

John Keats (3p)
Thomas Gray (5p)
Sir Walter Scott (7½p)

■ 1971, July 28. Literary Anniversaries
Des: Rosalind Dease.
Set	0.50	0.60
First day cover	–	1.00

British Legion: servicemen and nurse (3p)
City of York: Roman centurion (7½p)
Rugby Football Union: rugby players (9p)

■ 1971, August 25. Anniversaries
Des: F. Wegner.
Set	0.55	0.80
First day cover	–	1.75

University College, Aberystwyth (3p)
University of Southampton (5p)
University of Leicester (7½p)
University of Essex (9p)

■ 1971, September 22. Modern University Buildings
Des: N. Jenkins.
Set	0.85	1.00
First day cover	–	1.00

'Dream of the Wise Men' (2½p)
'Adoration of the Magi' (3p)
'Ride of the Magi' (7½p)

■ 1971, October 13. Christmas
Des: Clarke/Clements/Hughes, based on stained glass windows at Canterbury Cathedral.
Set	0.40	0.60
First day cover	–	1.00

Sir James Clarke Ross (3p)
Sir Martin Frobisher (5p)
Sir Henry Hudson (7½p)
Robert Scott (9p)

■ 1972, February 16. Polar Explorers
Des: Marjorie Seynor.
Set	0.50	1.00
First day cover	–	1.00

BRITISH STAMP MARKET VALUES 2024

DECIMAL QUEEN ELIZABETH II

Tutankhamun discovery: statuette (3p)
H.M. Coastguard: 19th-century coastguard (7½p)
Ralph Vaughan Williams: portrait and score (9p)

■ **1972, April 26. Anniversaries**
Des: Rosalind Dease (3p), F. Wegner (7½p), C. Abbott (9p)
Set	0.50	0.80
First day cover	–	1.00

St. Andrew's, Greensted-juxta-Ongar, Essex (3p)
All Saints, Earls Barton, Northamptonshire (4p)
St. Andrew's, Lethringsett, Norfolk (5p)
St. Andrew's, Helpringham, Lincolnshire (7½p)
St. Mary the Virgin, Huish Episcopi, Somerset (9p)

■ **1972, June 21. Village Churches**
Des: R. Maddox.
Set	0.60	1.40
First day cover	–	1.50

BBC: microphones (3p)
BBC: horn loudspeaker (5p)
BBC: colour television (7½p)
Marconi: oscillator and spark transmitter (9p)

■ **1972, September 13. Broadcasting Anniversaries**
Des: D. Gentleman.
Set	0.50	0.95
First day cover	–	1.25

Angel with trumpet (2½p)
Angel with lute (3p)
Angel with harp (7½p)

■ **1972, October 18. Christmas**
Des: Sally Stiff.
Set	0.50	0.60
First day cover	–	2.00

Queen Elizabeth II and Prince Phillip (3p, 20p)

■ **1972, November 20. Royal Silver Wedding**
Des: J. Matthews from photograph by Norman Parkinson.
All-over phosphor (3p), no phosphor (20p).
Printed on a Rembrandt machine
Set	0.90	1.25
First day cover	–	1.00

Printed on a Jumelle machine
3p	0.50	0.75
Gutter pair	1.00	–
Traffic light gutter pair	20.00	–

(*The portraits tend to be lighter on the Jumelle printing.)

Jigsaw pieces representing Europe (3p, 5p, 5p)

■ **1973, January 3. Britain's Entry into European Communities**
Des: P. Murdoch.
Set	0.50	1.00
First day cover	–	1.00

BRITISH STAMP MARKET VALUES 2024 **81**

QUEEN ELIZABETH II DECIMAL

Oak tree (9p)

■ **1973, February 28. British Trees (issue 1)**
Des: D. Gentleman.

9p	0.20	0.25
First day cover	–	0.50

David Livingstone (3p)
Henry Stanley (3p)
Sir Francis Drake (5p)
Sir Walter Raleigh (7½p)
Charles Sturt (9p)

■ **1973, April 18. British Explorers**
Des: Marjorie Seynor. All-over phosphor.

Set	0.80	1.10
First day cover	–	1.25

W. G. Grace batting (3p)
W. G. Grace watching the ball (7½p)
W. G. Grace leaving the wicket (9p)

■ **1973, May 16. Centenary of County Cricket**
Des: E Ripley, based on drawings by Harry Furniss.

Set	1.00	1.25
First day cover	–	1.50
Stamp card (of 3p design)	40.00	–

Self-portrait by Joshua Reynolds (3p)
Self-portrait by Henry Raeburn (5p)
'Nelly O'Brien' by Reynolds (7½p)
'The Skating Minister' by Raeburn (9p)

■ **1973, July 4. British Painters**
Des: S. Rose.

Set	0.70	0.80
First day cover	–	1.00

Court masque costumes (3p)
St Paul's Church, Covent Garden (3p)
Prince's Lodging, Newmarket (5p)
Court masque stage scene (5p)

■ **1973, August 15. 400th Anniversary of Birth of Inigo Jones**
Des: Rosalind Dease. Printed in litho and typo by Bradbury, Wilkinson.

Set	0.50	0.75
First day cover	–	1.00
Stamp card (of 3p St Paul's)	£100	£300

Palace of Westminster from Whitehall (8p)
Palace of Westminster from Millbank (10p)

■ **1973, September 12. Commonwealth Parliamentary Conference**
Des: R. Downer. Printed in recess and litho by Bradbury, Wilkinson.

Set	0.40	0.50
First day cover	–	0.75
Stamp card (of 8p design)	20.00	£175

DECIMAL QUEEN ELIZABETH II

Princess Anne and Captain Mark Phillips (3½p), (20p)

■ 1973, November 14. Royal Wedding
Des: C. Clements and E. Hughes, based on photograph by Lord Lichfield.

Set	0.50	0.55
Gutter pair	1.75	–
Traffic light gutter pair	70.00	–
First day cover	–	0.75
Stamp card (of 3½p design)	5.00	25.00

(*The 3½p exists from sheets guillotined in the wrong place, giving incorrect inscriptions within the gutter; price £30.)

Good King Wenceslas, the carol story (3p, 3p, 3p, 3p, 3p)
Good King Wenceslas, the page and the peasant (3½p)

■ 1973, November 28. Christmas
Des: D. Gentleman. 3p values have one phosphor band. These stamps exist with either gum Arabic (3p), PVA gum (3½p) or dextrin gum (both values); prices are the same.

Set	1.00	1.75
First day cover	–	1.25

Horse chestnut (10p)

■ 1974, February 27. British Trees (issue 2)
Des: D. Gentleman.

10p	0.25	0.25
Gutter pair	1.00	–
Traffic light gutter pair	50.00	–
First day cover	–	0.75
Stamp card	80.00	75.00

First motor fire engine, 1904 (3½p)
Prizewinning fire engine, 1863 (5½p)
First steam fire engine, 1830 (8p)
Fire engine, 1766 (10p)

■ 1974, April 24. Fire Service
Des: D. Gentleman. Dextrin gum except where stated.

Set	0.75	0.80
3½p with PVA gum	0.90	–
Gutter pairs	2.75	–
Traffic light gutter pairs	37.00	–
First day cover	–	1.50
Stamp card (of 3½p design)	67.00	70.00

P&O Packet Steamer 'Peninsular', 1888 (3½p)
First official airmail, 1911 (5½p)
Airmail van and postbox, 1930 (8p)
Imperial Airways flying boat, 1937 (10p)

■ 1974, June 12. Centenary of the UPU
Des: Rosalind Dease.

Set	0.55	0.75
Gutter pairs	1.75	–
Traffic light gutter pairs	30.00	–
First day cover	–	1.00

Robert the Bruce (4½p)
Owain Glyndwr (5½p)
King Henry V (8p)
The Black Prince (10p)

■ 1974, July 10. Great Britons
Des: F. Wegner.

Set	0.70	0.90
Gutter pairs	3.00	–
Traffic light gutter pairs	42.00	–
First day cover	–	1.50
Stamp cards	14.00	40.00

QUEEN ELIZABETH II DECIMAL

Lord Warden of the Cinque Ports (4½p)
Prime Minister (5½p)
Secretary for War and Air (8p)
War correspondent in South Africa (10p)

■ 1974, October 9. Birth Centenary of Sir Winston Churchill
Des: C. Clements and E. Hughes.

Set	1.00	1.25
8p with PVA gum	0.50	–
Gutter pairs	1.75	–
Traffic light gutter pairs	24.00	–
First day cover	–	1.00
Stamp card (of 5½p design)	3.00	20.00

'Peace: Burial at Sea' (4½p)
'Snowstorm' (5½p)
'The Arsenal, Venice' (8p)
'St. Laurent' (10p)

■ 1975, February 19. Bicentenary of the Birth of J. M. W. Turner
Des: S. Rose.

Set	0.50	0.60
Gutter pairs	1.25	–
Traffic light gutter pairs	10.00	–
First day cover	–	0.75
Stamp card (of 5½p design)	20.00	12.00

'Adoration of the Magi', York Minster (3½p)
'The Nativity', St. Helen's Church, Norwich (4½p)
'Virgin and Child', Ottery St. Mary Church (8p)
'Virgin and Child', Worcester Cathedral (10p)

■ 1974, November 27. Christmas
Des: Peter Hatch Partnership, based on church roof bosses.

3½p with phos band to right	0.20	0.25
Set	0.50	0.60
Gutter pairs	2.25	–
Traffic light gutter pairs	27.00	–
First day cover	–	1.00

Charlotte Square, Edinburgh (7p)
The Rows, Chester (7p)
Royal Observatory, Greenwich (8p)
St. George's Chapel, Windsor (10p)
National Theatre, London (12p)

■ 1975, April 23. European Architectural Heritage Year
Des: P. Gauld.

Set	0.80	1.00
Gutter pairs	3.50	–
Traffic light gutter pairs	15.00	–
First day cover	–	1.00
Stamp cards (of 7p and 8p designs)	6.00	25.00

Disabled person in wheelchair (4½p + 1½p)

■ 1975, January 22. Health and Handicap Charities
Des: P. Sharland. Surcharge donated to charity.

4½p + 1½p	0.15	0.30
Gutter pair	0.30	–
Traffic light gutter pair	2.50	–
First day cover	–	0.50

Sailing dinghies (7p)
Racing keel boats (8p)
Cruising yachts (10p)
Multihulls (12p)

84 BRITISH STAMP MARKET VALUES 2024

DECIMAL — QUEEN ELIZABETH II

■ 1975, June 11. Sailing
Des: A. Restall. Printed in photogravure and recess by Harrison.

Set	0.60	0.75
Gutter pairs	1.50	–
Traffic light gutter pairs	18.00	–
First day cover	–	1.00
Stamp card (of 8p design)	3.50	15.00

(*The 7p exists from sheets guillotined in the wrong place, giving gutter pairs with the wrong inscriptions, priced at £45.)

Stephenson's Locomotion, 1825 (7p)
Waverley class, 1876 (8p)
Caerphilly Castle, 1923 (10p)
Inter-City High Speed Train, 1975 (12p)

■ 1975, August 13. 150th Anniversary of Public Railways
Des: B. Cracker.

Set	0.80	1.00
Gutter Pairs	2.25	–
Traffic light gutter pairs	8.00	–
First day cover	–	1.00
Stamp cards (set)	32.00	35.00

Palace of Westminster (12p)

■ 1975, September 3. Inter-Parliamentary Union Conference
Des: R. Downer

12p	0.25	0.25
Gutter pair	0.60	–
Traffic light gutter pair	2.50	–
First day cover	–	0.50

Emma and Mr. Woodhouse, from Emma (8½p)
Catherine Morland, from Northanger Abbey (10p)
Mr. Darcy, from Pride and Prejudice (11p)
Mary and Henry Crawford, from Mansfield Park (13p)

■ 1975, October 22. Birth Bicentenary of Jane Austen
Des: Barbara Brown.

Set	0.80	1.00
Gutter pairs	1.40	–
Traffic light gutter pairs	7.50	–
First day cover	–	1.00
Stamp cards (set)	10.00	30.00

Angel with harp and lute (6½p)
Angel with mandolin (8½p)
Angel with horn (11p)
Angel with trumpet (13p)

■ 1975, November 25. Christmas
Des: R. Downer. Dextrin gum except where stated. The 8½p has the phosphor in the green printing ink

6½p with PVA gum	0.50	–
Set	0.75	1.00
Gutter pairs	1.40	–
Traffic light gutter pairs	5.50	–
First day cover	–	1.00

Housewife with telephone (8½p)
Policeman with telephone (10p)
District nurse with telephone (11p)
Industrialist with telephone (13p)

■ 1976, March 10. Centenary of First Telephone Call by Alexander Graham Bell
Des: P. Sharland.

Set	0.75	1.00
Gutter pairs	1.50	–
Traffic light gutter pairs	12.00	–
First day cover	–	0.75

QUEEN ELIZABETH II DECIMAL

Mining coal: Thomas Hepburn (8½p)
Machinery: Robert Owen (10p)
Sweeping a chimney: Lord Shaftesbury (11p)
Prison bars: Elizabeth Fry (13p)

■ **1976, April 28. Social Reformers**
Des: D. Gentleman.

Set	0.70	1.00
Gutter pairs	1.50	–
Traffic light gutter pairs	5.50	–
First day cover	–	0.75
Stamp card (of 8½p design)	3.00	7.50

Benjamin Franklin (11p)

■ **1976, June 2. Bicentennial of American Independence**
Des: P. Sharland.

11p	0.25	0.25
Gutter pair	0.50	–
Traffic light gutter pair	2.50	–
First day cover	–	0.75
Stamp card	2.50	10.00

Elizabeth of Glamis (8½p)
Grandpa Dickson (10p)
Rosa mundi (11p)
Sweet briar (13p)

■ **1976, June 30. Centenary of the Royal National Rose Society**
Des: Kristin Rosenberg.

Set	0.70	1.00
Gutter pairs	1.50	–
Traffic light gutter pairs	6.50	–
First day cover	–	1.00
Stamp cards	15.00	25.00

Royal National Eisteddfod of Wales: archdruid (8½p)
Morris dancing (10p)
Highland Gathering: piper (11p)
Royal National Eisteddfod of Wales: harpist (13p)

■ **1976, August 4. British Cultural Traditions**
Des: Marjorie Seynor.

Set	0.80	1.00
Gutter pairs	1.50	–
Traffic light gutter pairs	6.50	–
First day cover	–	0.75
Stamp cards	8.00	15.00

Woodcut from 'The Canterbury Tales' (8½p)
Extract from 'The Tretyse of Love' (10p)
Woodcut from 'The Game and Playe of Chesse' (11p)
Early printing press (13p)

■ **1976, September 29. 500th Anniversary of British Printing. William Caxton**
Des: R. Gay.

Set	0.80	1.00
Gutter pairs	1.50	–
Traffic light gutter pairs	5.50	–
First day cover	–	1.00
Stamp cards	6.00	15.00

DECIMAL   QUEEN ELIZABETH II

Virgin and child, embroidery c.1272 (6½p)
Angel with crown, embroidery c.1340 (8½p)
Angel appearing to shepherds, embroidery c.1320 (11p)
The three kings, embroidery c.1330 (13p)

■ **1976, November 24. Christmas.**
Des: Enid Marx, based on medieval English embroideries.
Set	0.80	1.00
6½p with one phos band	0.15	0.10
Gutter pairs	1.50	–
Traffic light gutter pairs	5.00	–
First day cover	–	0.75
Stamp cards	2.00	17.00

Lawn tennis (8½p)
Table tennis (10p)
Squash (11p)
Badminton (13p)

■ **1977, January 12. Racket Sports**
Des: A. Restall.
Set	0.75	1.00
Gutter pairs	1.75	–
Traffic light gutter pairs	6.00	–
First day cover	–	1.00
Stamp cards	4.00	12.00

Steroids: conformational analysis (8½p)
Vitamin C: synthesis (10p)
Starch: chromatography (11p)
Salt: crystallography (13p)

■ **1977, March 2. Centenary of the Royal Institute of Chemistry**
Des: J. Karo.
Set	0.75	1.00
Gutter pairs	1.75	–
Traffic light gutter pairs	6.00	–
First day cover	–	0.75
Stamp cards	4.00	10.00

'ER' and Queen Elizabeth II (8½p, 9p, 10p, 11p, 13p)

■ **1977, May 11. Silver Jubilee**
Des: Professor R. Guyatt. 9p issued on June 15.
Set	1.00	1.25
Gutter pairs	2.50	–
Traffic light gutter pairs	8.00	–
First day cover (8½p, 10p, 11p, 13p)	–	0.75
First day cover (9p)	–	0.50
Stamp cards	6.00	11.00

Symbol of meeting (13p)

■ **1977, June 8. Commonwealth Heads of Government Meeting, London**
Des: P. Murdoch. Printed in photogravure and recess by Harrison.
13p	0.25	0.35
Gutter pair	0.50	–
Traffic light gutter pair	2.50	–
First day cover	–	0.75
Stamp card	1.50	2.50

QUEEN ELIZABETH II DECIMAL

Hedgehog (9p)
Hare (9p)
Red squirrel (9p)
Otter (9p)
Badger (9p)

■ **1977, October 5. British Wildlife**
Des: P Oxenham.

Set (se-tenant strip of five)	0.90	1.40
Gutter strip	1.25	–
Traffic light gutter strip	5.50	–
First day cover	–	1.25
Stamp cards	2.00	5.50

(*Gutter strips normally comprise a horozontal strip of four designs separated from the fifth design by a gutter.)

Three hens, two turtle doves, a partridge in a pear tree (7p)
Six geese, five gold rings, four colly birds (7p)
Eight maids, seven swans (7p)
Ten pipers, nine drummers (7p)
Twelve lords, eleven ladies (7p)
Partridge in a pear tree (9p)

■ **1977, November 23. Christmas**
Des: D. Gentleman, based on the song 'The Twelve Days of Christmas'. The 7p values, issued se-tenant, have one phosphor band.

Set	0.75	1.25
Gutter strip	1.50	–
Traffic light gutter strip	4.00	–
First day cover	–	1.00
Stamp cards	2.00	5.00

(*Gutter strips of the 7p values comprise two horizontal se-tenant strips of five separated by a gutter.)

North Sea oil (9p)
Coal pithead (10½p)
Natural gas flame (11p)
Electricity (13p)

■ **1978, January 25. Energy**
Des: P. Murdoch.

Set	0.65	1.00
Gutter pairs	1.50	–
Traffic light gutter pairs	5.00	–
First day cover	–	0.75
Stamp cards	1.50	3.50

Tower of London (9p)
Palace of Holyroodhouse (10½p)
Caernarvon Castle (11p)
Hampton Court Palace (13p)

■ **1978, March 1. Historic Buildings**
Des: R. Maddox; miniature sheet by J. Matthews.

Set	0.75	1.00
Gutter pairs	1.60	–
Traffic light gutter pairs	4.50	–
First day cover	–	0.75
Stamp cards	1.50	3.50
Miniature sheet (one of each value)	1.25	1.50
Miniature sheet first day cover	–	1.25

(*The miniature sheet was sold at 53½p, the extra 10p being donated towards the cost of staging the International Stamp Exhibition. London 1980, which the sheet itself publicised.)

DECIMAL QUEEN ELIZABETH II

State Coach (9p)
St. Edward's Crown (10½p)
Sovereign's Orb (11p)
Imperial State Crown (13p)

■ **1978, May 31. 25th Anniversary of the Coronation**
Des: J. Matthews.
Set	0.75	1.00
Gutter pairs	1.50	–
Traffic light gutter pairs	4.50	–
First day cover	–	1.00
Stamp cards	1.50	3.50

Shire horse (9p)
Shetland pony (10½p)
Welsh pony (11p)
Thoroughbred (13p)

■ **1978, July 5. Horses**
Des: P. Oxenham.
Set	0.70	1.00
Gutter pairs	1.50	–
Traffic light gutter pairs	4.75	–
First day cover	–	0.75
Stamp cards	1.50	3.50

Penny Farthing and Safety Bicycle, 1884 (9p)
Touring bicycles, 1920 (10½p)
Modern small-wheel bicycles (11p)
Road racers, 1978 (13p)

■ **1978, August 2. Cycling**
Des: F. Wegner.
Set	0.70	1.00
Gutter pairs	1.50	–
Traffic light gutter pairs	4.50	–
First day cover	–	0.75
Stamp cards	1.50	3.50

Singing carols around a Christmas tree (7p)
The waits (9p)
18th-century carol singers (11p)
The boar's head carol (13p)

■ **1978, November 22. Christmas**
Des: Faith Jaques. 7p has one phosphor band.
Set	0.70	1.00
Gutter pairs	1.25	–
Traffic light gutter pairs	4.25	–
First day cover	–	0.75
Stamp cards	1.50	3.00

Old English sheepdog (9p)
Welsh springer spaniel (10½p)
West Highland terrier (11p)
Irish setter (13p)

■ **1979, February 7. British Dogs**
Des: P. Barrett.
Set	0.70	1.00
Gutter pairs	1.25	–
Traffic light gutter pairs	4.00	–
First day cover	–	0.75
Stamp cards	1.50	3.50

BRITISH STAMP MARKET VALUES 2024 **89**

QUEEN ELIZABETH II DECIMAL

Primrose (9p)
Daffodil (10½p)
Bluebell (11p)
Snowdrop (13p)

■ **1979, March 21. British Flowers**
Des: P. Newcombe.
Set	0.70	1.00
Gutter pairs	1.50	–
Traffic light gutter pairs	4.25	–
First day cover	–	0.75
Stamp cards	1.50	3.50

Hands placing flags into ballot boxes (9p, 10½p, 11p, 13p)

■ **1979, May 9. First Direct Elections to the European Assembly**
Des: S. Cliff.
Set	0.70	1.00
Gutter pairs	1.50	–
Traffic light gutter pairs	4.25	–
First day cover	–	0.75
Stamp cards	1.50	3.00

Saddling Mahmoud for the Derby, 1936 (9p)
Liverpool Great National Steeplechase, 1839 (10½p)
First Spring Meeting at Newmarket, 1793 (11p)
Racing at Dorsett Ferry, Windsor, 1684 (13p)

■ **1979, June 6. 200th Anniversary of the Derby. Horse Racing Paintings**
Des: S. Rose.
Set	0.70	1.00
Gutter pairs	1.50	–
Traffic light gutter pairs	4.75	–
First day cover	–	0.75
Stamp cards	1.50	3.00

'The Tale of Peter Rabbit' by Beatrix Potter (9p)
'The Wind in the Willows' by Kenneth Grahame (10½p)
'Winnie the Pooh' by A. A. Milne (11p)
'Alice's Adventures in Wonderland' by Lewis Carroll (13p)

■ **1979, July 11. International Year of the Child**
Des: E. Hughes.
Set	0.85	1.25
Gutter pairs	1.75	–
Traffic light gutter pairs	4.00	–
First day cover	–	0.75
Stamp cards	1.50	4.00

Sir Rowland Hill (10p)
General Post, 1839 (11½p)
London Post, 1839 (13p)
Uniform Penny Post, 1840 (15p)

DECIMAL   QUEEN ELIZABETH II

■ 1979, August 22. Centenary of the Death of Sir Rowland Hill
Des: E. Stemp (set) and J. Matthews (miniature sheet).

Set	0.75	1.00
Gutter pairs	1.60	–
Traffic light gutter pairs	4.00	–
First day cover	–	0.75
Stamp cards	1.50	3.50
Miniature sheet (one of each value)	1.00	1.50
Miniature sheet first day cover	–	1.00

(*The miniature sheet, issued on October 24, 1979, was sold at 59½p, the extra 10p being donated towards the cost of staging the International Stamp Exhibition, London 1980, which the sheet itself publicised.)

Policeman talking to two children (10p)
Street patrol (11½p)
Policewoman on horseback (13p)
River police (15p)

■ 1979, September 26. 150th Anniversary of the Metropolitan Police
Des: B. Sanders.

Set	0.80	1.00
Gutter pairs	1.60	–
Traffic light gutter pairs	4.25	–
First day cover	–	0.75
Stamp cards	1.50	3.00

Three kings following the star (8p)
Angel appearing to shepherds (10p)
Nativity (11½p)
Joseph and Mary travelling to Bethlehem (13p)
Annunciation (15p)

■ 1979, November 21. Christmas
Des: F. Wegner. 8p has one phosphor band.

Set	0.90	1.00
Gutter pairs	1.80	–
Traffic light gutter pairs	4.75	–
First day cover	–	0.75
Stamp cards	150	3.00

Kingfisher (10p)
Dipper (11½p)
Moorhen (13p)
Yellow wagtail (15p)

■ 1980, January 16. Water Birds
Des: Michael Warren.

Set	0.80	1.00
Gutter pairs	2.00	–
First day cover	–	1.00
Stamp cards	1.50	3.50

George Stephenson's Rocket (12p)
First and second class carriages (12p)
Third class carriage and cattle truck (12p)
Open coach on truck and horsebox (12p)
Goods wagon and mail coach (12p)

■ 1980, March 12. 150th Anniversary of the Liverpool & Manchester Railway
Des: D. Gentleman.

Se-tenant strip of five	1.00	1.25
Gutter strip	2.25	–
First day cover	–	1.00
Stamp cards	3.00	3.50

(*Gutter strips comprise two horizontal se-tenant strips separated by a gutter.)

BRITISH STAMP MARKET VALUES 2024   **91**

QUEEN ELIZABETH II DECIMAL

Montage of London buildings and monuments (50p)

■ **1980, April 9. London 1980 International Stamp Exhibition**
Des: J. Matthews. Printed in recess by Harrisons. No phosphor.

50p	0.80	1.00
Gutter pair	2.00	–
First day cover	–	0.75
Stamp card	0.75	1.75
Miniature sheet	1.00	1.50
Miniature sheet first day cover	–	1.25

(*The miniature sheet, issued on May 7, 1980, was sold at 75p, the extra 25p being donated towards the cost of staging the International Stamp Exhibition, London 1980. The stamp is known to exist in shades of green, caused by the speed of the ink-drying operation, and fakes of these shades exist.)

Buckingham Palace (10½p)
Albert Memorial (12p)
Royal Opera House (13½p)
Hampton Court (15p)
Kensington Palace (17½p)

■ **1980, May 7. London Landmarks**
Des: Sir Hugh Casson.

Set	1.00	1.25
Gutter pairs	2.50	–
First day cover	–	1.25
Stamp cards	1.50	3.00

Charlotte Brontë and 'Jane Eyre' (12p)
George Eliot and 'The Mill on the Floss' (13½p)
Emily Brontë and 'Wuthering Heights' (15p)
Elizabeth Gaskell and 'North and South' (17½p)

■ **1980, July 9. Famous Authoresses (Europa)**
Des: Barbara Brown.

Set	0.90	1.00
Gutter pairs	2.50	–
First day cover	–	1.00
Stamp cards	1.75	3.00

Queen Elizabeth, the Queen Mother (12p)

■ **1980, August 4. Queen Mother's 80th Birthday**
Des: Jeffery Matthews.

12p	0.40	0.40
Gutter pair	1.00	–
First day cover	–	0.75
Stamp card	0.75	1.75

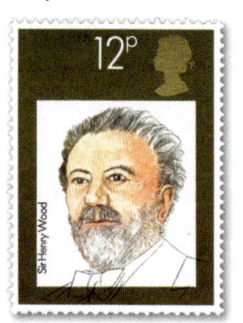

DECIMAL QUEEN ELIZABETH II

Sir Henry Wood (12p)
Sir Thomas Beecham (13½p)
Sir Malcolm Sargent (15p)
Sir John Barbirolli (17½p)

■ 1980, September 10. British Conductors
Des: Peter Gauld.

Set	0.90	1.00
Gutter pairs	2.25	–
First day cover	–	1.25
Stamp cards	1.50	2.75

(*These stamps exist on paper with differences in the degree of 'shine' on the surface.)

Athletics: Amateur Athletics Association (12p)
Rugby: Welsh Rugby Union (13½p)
Boxing: Amateur Boxing Association (15p)
Cricket: first England–Australia test match (17½p)

■ 1980, October 10. Sport Centenaries
Des: Robert Goldsmith. Printed in litho by Questa.

Set	0.90	1.00
Gutter pairs	2.25	–
First day cover	–	1.25
Stamp cards	1.50	2.75

Christmas tree (10p)
Candles, ivy and ribbon (12p)
Mistletoe and apples (13½p)
Paper chains with crown and bell (15p)
Holly wreath and ornaments (17½p)

■ 1980, November 10. Christmas
Des: Jeffery Matthews. 10p has one phosphor band.

Set	1.00	1.00
Gutter pairs	2.50	–
First day cover	–	1.25
Stamp cards	1.50	3.00

(*These stamps exist on paper with differences in the degree of 'shine' on the surface.)

St. Valentine's Day (14p)
Morris dancers (18p)
Lammastide (22p)
Medieval mummers (25p)

■ 1981, February 6. Folklore (Europa)
Des: Fritz Wegner.

Set	1.25	1.50
Gutter pairs	3.00	–
First day cover	–	1.25
Stamp cards	1.50	2.75

Blind man walking with guide dog (14p)
'Deaf' spelt in sign language (18p)
Man in wheelchair (22p)
Disabled artist foot painting (25p)

■ 1981, March 25. International Year of Disabled People
Des: John Gibbs.

Set	1.20	1.50
Gutter pairs	3.00	–
First day cover	–	1.00
Stamp cards	1.50	2.75

QUEEN ELIZABETH II DECIMAL

Small tortoiseshell (14p)
Large blue (18p)
Peacock (22p)
Chequered skipper (25p)

■ **1981, May 13. British Butterflies**
Des: Gordon Beningfield.
Set	1.25	1.50
Gutter pairs	3.50	–
First day cover	–	1.25
Stamp cards	1.50	2.75

Glenfinnan, Scotland (14p)
Derwentwater, England (18p)
Stackpole Head, Wales (20p)
Giant's Causeway, Northern Ireland (22p)
St. Kilda, Scotland (25p)

■ **1981, June 24. 50th Anniversary of the National Trust for Scotland. British Landscapes**
Des: Michael Fairclough.
Set	1.45	2.00
Gutter pairs	3.50	–
First day cover	–	1.50
Stamp cards	1.50	2.75

Prince Charles and Lady Diana Spencer (14p, 25p)

■ **1981, July 22. Wedding of Prince Charles and Lady Diana Spencer**
Des: Jeffery Matthews, from a portrait by Lord Snowdon.
Set	0.80	1.00
Gutter pair	2.00	–
First day cover	–	2.00
Stamp cards	1.50	2.75

Expeditions (14p)
Skills (18p)
Service (22p)
Recreation (25p)

■ **1981, August 12. 25th Anniversary of the Duke of Edinburgh's Award Scheme**
Des: Philip Sharland. Printed in litho by Waddingtons.
Set	1.25	1.50
Gutter pairs	3.50	–
First day cover	–	1.25
Stamp cards	1.50	2.75

Cockle dredging (14p)
Hauling side trawl net (18p)
Lobster potting (22p)
Hauling Seine net (25p)

■ **1981, September 23. Fishing Industry**
Des: Brian Sanders.
Set	1.25	1.50
Gutter pairs	3.50	–
First day cover	–	1.00
Stamp cards	1.50	2.75

DECIMAL QUEEN ELIZABETH II

Father Christmas with sacks of toys (11½p)
Jesus Christ (14p)
Angel in flight (18p)
Joseph and Mary with donkey (22p)
Three wise men on camels following the star (25p)

■ **1981, November 18. Christmas**
Des: Samantha Brown (11½p), Tracy Jenkins (14p), Lucinda Blackmore (18p), Stephen Moore (22p), Sophie Sharp (25p). The 11½p has one phosphor band.

Set	1.20	1.60
Gutter pairs	3.00	–
First day cover	–	1.00
Stamp cards	1.50	3.00

Darwin and giant tortoises (15½p)
Darwin and marine iguanas (19½p)
Darwin and finches (26p)
Darwin and prehistoric skulls (29p)

■ **1982, February 10. Centenary of the Death of Charles Darwin.**
Des: David Gentleman.

Set	1.40	1.60
Gutter pairs	3.50	–
First day cover	–	1.00
Stamp cards	1.50	3.50

Boys' Brigade (15½p)
Girls' Brigade (19½p)
Boy Scouts (26p)
Girl Guides and Brownies (29p)

■ **1982, March 24. Youth Organisations**
Des: Brian Sanders.

Set	1.40	1.60
Gutter pairs	3.50	–
First day cover	–	1.25
Stamp cards	1.50	3.50

Ballet (15½p)
Pantomime (19½p)
Shakespearean drama (26p)
Opera (29p)

■ **1982, April 28. British Theatre (Europa)**
Des: Adrian George.

Set	1.35	1.60
Gutter pairs	3.50	–
First day cover	–	1.25
Stamp cards	2.50	3.50

King Henry VIII and Mary Rose (15½p)
Admiral Blake and Triumph (19½p)
Lord Nelson and H.M.S. Victory (24p)
Lord Fisher and H.M.S. Dreadnought (26p)
Viscount Cunningham and H.M.S. Warspite (29p)

■ **1982, June 16. Maritime Heritage**
Des: Marjorie Seynor. Printed in recess and photogravure by Harrison.

Set	2.00	2.00
Gutter pairs	4.00	–
First day cover	–	1.25
Stamp cards	1.50	3.50

BRITISH STAMP MARKET VALUES 2024

QUEEN ELIZABETH II DECIMAL

'Strawberry Thief', 1883, by William Morris (15½p)
Untitled work 1906, by F. Steiner and Co (19½p)
'Cherry Orchard', 1930, by Paul Nash (26p)
'Chevrons', 1973, by Andrew Foster (29p)

■ **1982, July 23. British Textiles**
Des: Peter Hatch Patnership.
Set	1.40	1.60
Gutter pairs	3.00	–
First day cover	–	1.25
Stamp cards	3.25	3.50

History of communications (15½p)
Modern technology (26p)

■ **1982, September 8. Information Technology Year**
Des: Brian Delaney and Darrell Ireland.
Set	0.75	1.00
Gutter pair	2.00	–
First day cover	–	1.00
Stamp cards	1.00	3.50

Austin Seven and Metro (15½p)
Ford Model T and Escort (19½p)
Jaguar SS1 and XJ6 (26p)
Rolls Royce Silver Ghost and Silver Spirit (29p)

■ **1982, October 13. British Motor Cars**
Des: Stanley Paine. Printed in litho by Questa.
Set	1.50	1.70
Gutter pairs	3.50	–
First day cover	–	1.25
Stamp cards	1.50	3.50

'While Shepherds Watched' (12½p)
'The Holly and the Ivy' (15½p)
'I Saw Three Ships' (19½p)
'We Three Kings' (26p)
'Good King Wenceslas' (29p)

■ **1982, November 17. Christmas**
Des: Barbara Brown. 12½p has one phosphor band.
Set	1.50	1.80
Gutter pairs	3.50	–
First day cover	–	1.25
Stamp cards	1.50	3.50

Salmon (15½p)
Pike (19½p)
Trout (26p)
Perch (29p)

■ **1983, January 26. British River Fish**
Des: Alex Jardine.
Set	1.50	1.80
Gutter pairs	3.50	–
First day cover	–	1.25
Stamp cards	2.50	3.50

DECIMAL **QUEEN ELIZABETH II**

Tropical island (15½p)
Arid desert (19½p)
Lush arable land (26p)
Cold mountainous region (29p)

■ **1983, March 9. Commonwealth Day**
Des: Donald Hamilton Fraser.
Set	1.50	1.80
Gutter pairs	3.50	–
First day cover	–	1.25
Stamp cards	1.50	3.50

Humber Bridge (16p)
Thames Flood Barrier (20½p)
Iolair oilfield emergency support vessel (28p)

■ **1983, May 25. Engineering Achievements (Europa)**
Des: Michael Taylor.
Set	1.25	1.80
Gutter pairs	4.00	–
First day cover	–	1.25
Stamp cards	1.50	3.50

Musketeer and pikeman, Royal Scots, 1633 (16p)
Fusilier and ensign, Royal Welch Fusiliers, 18th century (20½p)
Riflemen, 95th Rifles (Royal Green Jackets), 1805 (26p)
Sergeant and guardsman, Irish Guards, 1900 (28p)
Paratroopers, Parachute Regiment, 1983 (31p)

■ **1983, July 6. British Army Uniforms**
Des: Eric Stemp.
Set	1.75	2.25
Gutter pairs	4.50	–
First day cover	–	1.75
Stamp cards	1.50	3.50

Sissinghurst, 20th century (16p)
Biddulph Grange, 19th century (20½p)
Blenheim Palace, 18th century (28p)
Pitmedden, 17th century (31p)

■ **1983, August 24. British Gardens**
Des: Liz Butler. Printed in litho by Waddingtons.
Set	1.50	1.80
Gutter pairs	4.00	–
First day cover	–	1.25
Stamp cards	1.50	3.50

Merry-go-round (16p)
Menagerie and fairground rides (20½p)
Side shows (28p)
Produce fair (31p)

■ **1983, October 5. British Fairs**
Des: Andrew Restall.
Set	1.40	1.80
Gutter pairs	3.25	–
First day cover	–	1.25
Stamp cards	1.50	3.50

BRITISH STAMP MARKET VALUES 2024

QUEEN ELIZABETH II DECIMAL

Birds posting Christmas cards (12½p)
Chimney pots with a dove and cat (16p)
Dove and blackbird under an umbrella (20½p)
Dove and blackbird under a street lamp (28p)
Hedge sculpture of dove (31p)

■ **1983, November 16. Christmas**
Des: Tony Meeuwissen. 12½p has one phosphor band.
Set	1.50	2.00
Gutter pairs	3.50	–
First day cover	–	1.25
Stamp cards	1.50	3.50

Arms of The College of Arms (16p)
Arms of King Richard III (20½p)
Arms of the Earl Marshal of England (28p)
Arms of the City of London (31p)

■ **1984, January 17. Quincentenary of the College of Arms**
Des: Jeffery Matthews.
Set	1.50	2.00
Gutter pairs	3.50	–
First day cover	–	1.50
Stamp cards	1.50	3.50

Highland cow (16p)
Chillingham wild bull (20½p)
Hereford bull (26p)
Welsh black bull (28p)
Irish moiled cow (31p)

■ **1984, March 6. British Cattle**
Des: Barry Driscoll.
Set	1.75	2.50
Gutter pairs	4.00	–
First day cover	–	1.50
Stamp cards	2.50	3.50

Liverpool: International Garden Festival (16p)
Durham: Milburngate Shopping Centre (20½p)
Bristol: Bush House, City Docks (28p)
Perth: Commercial Street Housing Scheme (31p)

■ **1984, April 19. Urban Renewal**
Des: Trickett and Webb, and Ronald Maddox.
Set	1.60	2.00
Gutter pairs	3.50	–
First day cover	–	1.25
Stamp cards	1.50	3.50

Europa 'bridge' and CEPT emblem (16p, 20½p)
Abduction of Europa and European Parliament emblem (16p, 20½p)

■ **1984, May 15. 25th Anniversary of CEPT and Second Elections to the European Parliament (Europa)**
Des: J. Larriviere (16p), Fritz Wegner (20½p). The two designs of each value were printed in se-tenant pairs.
Set	1.40	2.00
Gutter pairs	3.25	–
First day cover	–	1.50
Stamp cards	1.50	3.50

98 BRITISH STAMP MARKET VALUES 2024

DECIMAL   QUEEN ELIZABETH II

Lancaster House with flags of participating nations (31p)

■ **1984, June 5. London Economic Summit**
Des: Paul Hogarth.
31p	0.70	0.90
Gutter pair	1.75	–
First day cover	–	1.00
Stamp card	0.75	3.50

Earth from space (16p)
Navigational chart of the English Channel (20½p)
Aerial photograph of the Greenwich Observatory (28p)
Sir George Airy's transit circle telescope (31p)

■ **1984, June 21. Centenary of the Greenwich Meridian**
Des: J. Barney and H. Waller. Printed in litho by Questa.
Set	1.60	2.25
Gutter pairs	4.00	–
First day cover	–	1.25
Stamp cards	1.50	3.50

Bath mail coach, 1784 (16p)
Attack on the Exeter mail, 1816 (16p)
Norwich mail coach in a thunderstorm, 1827 (16p)
Holyhead and Liverpool mails leaving London, 1828 (16p)
Edinburgh mail coach snowbound, 1831 (16p)

■ **1984, July 31. 200th Anniversary of the First Mail Coach Run from Bristol and Bath to London**
Des: Keith Bassford and Stanley Paine. Printed in recess and photogravure by Harrison.
Set	1.50	2.00
Gutter strip	3.50	–
First day cover	–	1.50
Stamp cards	1.75	3.50

(*Gutter strips comprise two horizontal se-tenant strips of five separated by a gutter.)

Education for development, Nigeria (17p)
Promoting the arts, Greece (22p)
Technical training, Sri Lanka (31p)
Language and libraries, Middle East (34p)

■ **1984, September 25. 50th Anniversary of the British Council**
Des: Francis Newell, John Sorrell and Brian Sanders.
Set	1.50	2.00
Gutter pairs	3.75	–
First day cover	–	1.50
Stamp cards	2.00	3.50

(*Sheets of these stamps sold at the international stamp exhibition held in Melbourne, Australia, had the gutter margins overprinted with the exhibition logo.)

Holy family (13p)
Arrival in Bethlehem (17p)
Shepherd and lamb (22p)
Virgin and Child (31p)
Offering of frankincense (34p)

■ **1984, November 20. Christmas**
Des: Yvonne Gilbert. 13p has one centre phosphor band.
Set	1.75	2.50
13p (stars printed on gummed side)	0.60	–
Gutter pairs	4.00	–
First day cover	–	1.50
Stamp cards	1.75	3.50

(*The 13p exists with a five-pointed-star pattern printed on the gummed side, from a booklet sold at a discount.)

BRITISH STAMP MARKET VALUES 2024   **99**

QUEEN ELIZABETH II DECIMAL

Flying Scotsman, c.1947 (17p)
Golden Arrow, c.1960 (22p)
Cheltenham Flyer, c.1938 (29p)
Royal Scot, c.1959 (31p)
Cornish Riviera, c.1935 (34p)

■ **1985, January 22. Famous Trains**
Des: Terence Cuneo.
Set	2.50	3.50
Gutter pairs	6.50	–
First day cover	–	1.50
Stamp cards	4.00	6.00

Buff-tailed bumble bee (17p)
Seven-spotted ladybird (22p)
Wart-biter bush-cricket (29p)
Stag beetle (31p)
Emperor butterfly (34p)

■ **1985, March 12. Insects**
Des: Gordon Beningfield.
Set	2.00	2.50
Gutter pairs	5.00	–
First day cover	–	1.50
Stamp cards	2.00	3.00

'Water Music' by George Handel (17p)
'The Planets Suite' by Gustav Holst (22p)
'The First Cuckoo' by Frederick Delius (31p)
'Sea Pictures' by Edward Elgar (34p)

■ **1985, May 14. European Music Year. British Composers (Europa)**
Des: Wilson McLean.
Set	2.00	2.50
Gutter pairs	5.00	–
First day cover	–	1.50
Stamp cards	3.50	3.00

RNLI lifeboat and signal flags (17p)
Beachy Head Lighthouse and chart (22p)
MARECS A communications satellite and aerials (31p)
Trinity House buoyage (34p)

■ **1985, June 18. Safety at Sea**
Des: Newell and Sorell. Printed in litho by Waddingtons.
Set	1.60	2.25
Gutter pairs	4.00	–
First day cover	–	1.50
Stamp cards	1.50	3.00

Datapost motorcyclist and plane in London (17p)
Postbus in countryside (22p)
Parcel delivery by van in winter (31p)
Postman delivering letters on foot (34p)

■ **1985, July 30. 350th Anniversary of Royal Mail Service to the Public**
Des: Paul Hogarth.
Set	1.75	2.25
17p ('D' pattern on gummed side)	0.60	–
Gutter pairs	4.25	–
First day cover	–	1.50
Stamp cards	1.50	3.00

(*The 17p exists with a 'D' pattern printed on the gummed side, from a booklet sold at a discount.)

DECIMAL   QUEEN ELIZABETH II

King Arthur and Merlin (17p)
The Lady of the Lake (22p)
Queen Guinevere and Sir Lancelot (31p)
Sir Galahad (34p)

■ **1985, September 3. Arthurian Legend**
Des: Yvonne Gilbert.

Set	1.75	2.25
Gutter pairs	4.50	–
First day cover	–	1.50
Stamp cards	2.50	3.00

Peter Sellers, photographed by Bill Brandt (17p)
David Niven, photographed by Cornel Lucas (22p)
Charles Chaplin, photographed by Lord Snowdon (29p)
Vivien Leigh, photographed by Angus McBean (31p)
Alfred Hitchcock, photographed by Howard Coster (34p)

■ **1985, October 8. British Film Year**
Des: Keith Bassford.

Set	2.25	3.00
Gutter pairs	6.00	–
First day cover	–	2.25
Stamp cards	2.00	3.00

Principal boy (12p)
Genie (17p)
Pantomime dame (22p)
Good fairy (31p)
Pantomime cat (34p)

■ **1985, November 19. Christmas. Pantomime Characters**
Des: Adrian George. 12p has one phosphor band.

Set	1.75	2.25
12p (stars on gummed side)	0.55	–
Gutter pairs	5.00	–
First day cover	–	1.50
Stamp cards	1.50	3.00

(*The 12p exists with a star pattern printed on the gummed side, from a booklet sold at a discount.)

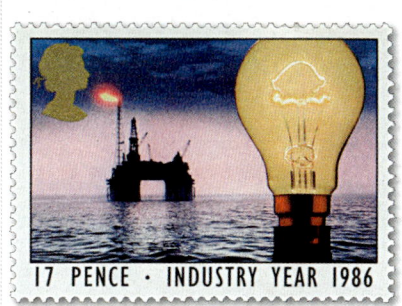

Energy: light bulb and North Sea oil rig (17p)
Health: thermometer and laboratory (22p)
Manufacture: garden hoe and steelworks (31p)
Agriculture: loaf of bread and cornfield (34p)

■ **1986, January 14. Industry Year**
Des: Keith Bassford. Printed in litho by Questa.

Set	1.75	2.25
Gutter pairs	5.00	–
First day cover	–	1.50
Stamp cards	1.50	3.00

Sir Edmond Halley as the comet (17p)
Giotto space probe approaching the comet (22p)
'Maybe twice in a lifetime' (31p)
The comet's orbit (34p)

■ **1986, February 18. Halley's Comet**
Des: Ralph Steadman.

Set	1.75	2.25
Gutter pairs	4.75	–
First day cover	–	1.50
Stamp cards	1.50	3.00

QUEEN ELIZABETH II DECIMAL

The Queen at the age of 2, 16 and 26 (17p, 34p)
The Queen at the age of 32, 47 and 56 (17p, 34p)

■ **1986, April 21. The Queen's 60th Birthday**
Des: Jeffery Matthews.
Set	2.25	3.50
Gutter pairs	5.00	–
First day cover	–	2.25
Stamp cards	1.50	3.00

Barn owl (17p)
Pine marten (22p)
Wild cat (31p)
Natterjack toad (34p)

■ **1986, May 20. Nature Conservation (Europa)**
Des: Ken Lilly.
Set	1.75	2.25
Gutter pairs	4.00	–
First day cover	–	1.75
Stamp cards	1.50	3.00

Peasants working the land (17p)
Freemen and their crafts (22p)
A knight and his retinue (31p)
A lord at a banquet (34p)

■ **1986, June 17. 900th Anniversary of the Domesday Book**
Des: Tayburn.
Set	1.75	2.25
Gutter pairs	5.00	–
First day cover	–	1.75
Stamp cards	1.50	3.00

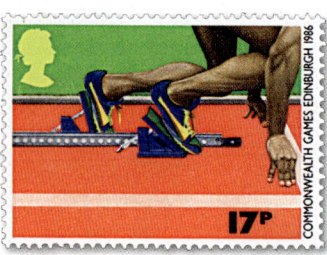

Athletics (17p)
Rowing (22p)
Weightlifting (29p)
Shooting (31p)
Hockey (34p)

■ **1986, July 15. Commonwealth Games, Edinburgh, and World Hockey Cup, London**
Des: Nick Cudworth.
Set	2.00	3.00
Gutter pairs	5.00	–
First day cover	–	2.00
Stamp cards	1.75	3.00

Prince Andrew and Sarah Ferguson (12p, 17p)

■ **1986, July 22. Royal Wedding**
Des: Jeffery Matthews.
Set	0.85	1.00
Gutter pairs	2.00	–
First day cover	–	1.00
Stamp cards	1.00	2.00

102 BRITISH STAMP MARKET VALUES 2024

DECIMAL QUEEN ELIZABETH II

Cross on ballot paper (34p)

■ **1986, August 19. Commonwealth Parliamentary Association Conference**
Des: John Gibbs. Printed in litho by Questa.

34p	0.75	0.80
Gutter pairs	2.00	–
First day cover	–	1.00
Stamp card	0.75	2.00

Lord Dowding and Hawker Hurricane (17p)
Lord Tedder and Hawker Typhoon (22p)
Lord Trenchard and De Havilland DH9A (29p)
Sir Arthur Harris and Avro Lancaster (31p)
Lord Portal and De Havilland Mosquito (34p)

■ **1986, September 16. Royal Air Force**
Des: Brian Sanders.

Set	2.25	3.00
Gutter pairs	5.00	–
First day cover	–	2.25
Stamp cards	1.75	3.00

The Glastonbury Thorn (12p, 13p)
The Tanad Valley Plygain (18p)
The Hebrides Tribute (22p)
The Dewsbury Church Knell (31p)
The Hereford Boy Bishop (34p)

■ **1986, November 18. Christmas. Folk Customs**
Des: Lynda Gray. 12p has one phosphor band and was issued on December 2, 1986; 13p has one phosphor band

Set	2.25	3.25
13p (stars on gummed side)	0.60	–
Gutter Pairs	4.50	–
First day covers	–	2.25
Stamp cards	1.75	3.00

(*The 13p exists with a star pattern printed on the gummed side, from a booklet and a pack sold at a discount.)

Gaillardia (18p)
Echinops (22p)
Echeveria (31p)
Colchicum (34p)

■ **1987, January 6. Flowers**
Des: Jeffery Matthews from photographs by Alfred Lammer.

Set	1.75	2.25
Gutter pairs	4.50	–
First day cover	–	1.75
Stamp cards	1.50	3.00

'Principia Mathematica': apple (18p)
Motion of bodies in ellipses: planets orbiting around sun (22p)
'Optick Treatise': flask of water refracting light (31p)
'The System of the World': Earth and artificial satellite (34p)

■ **1987, March 24. Sir Isaac Newton**
Des: Sarah Goodwin.

Set	1.75	2.25
Gutter pairs	4.50	–
First day cover	–	1.75
Stamp cards	1.75	3.00

BRITISH STAMP MARKET VALUES 2024 **103**

QUEEN ELIZABETH II DECIMAL

Willis Faber Dumas Building, Ipswich (18p)
Pompidou Centre, Paris (22p)
Staatgalerie, Stuttgart (31p)
European Investment Bank, Luxembourg (34p)

■ **1987, May 12. British Architects in Europe (Europa)**
Des: Minale Tattersfield Studio.

Set	1.75	2.25
Gutter pairs	4.50	–
First day cover	–	1.75
Stamp cards	1.50	3.00

Arms of the Lord Lyon, King of Arms (18p)
Arms of the Duke of Rothesay (22p)
Arms of the Royal Scottish Academy of Painting, Sculpture and Architecture (31p)
Arms of the Royal Society of Edinburgh (34p)

■ **1987, July 21. 300th Anniversary of the Revival of the Order of the Thistle**
Des: Jeffery Matthews.

Set	1.75	2.25
Gutter pairs	4.50	–
First day cover	–	1.75
Stamp cards	1.50	3.00

First aid duties, 1887 (18p)
First aid in wartime, 1940 (22p)
First aid at events, 1965 (31p)
Transporting transplant organs by air, 1987 (34p)

■ **1987, June 16. St John Ambulance Centenary**
Des: Debbie Cook. Printed in litho by Questa.

Set	1.75	2.25
Gutter pairs	4.50	–
First day cover	–	1.75
Stamp cards	1.50	3.00

Landseer's painting 'Monarch of the Glen', the Great Exhibition, Grace Darling (18p)
Brunel's S.S. Great Eastern, Mrs Beeton's 'Book of Household Management', Prince Albert (22p)
Albert Memorial, Benjamin Disraeli, the first ballot box (31p)
Marconi's broadcast to Paris, the Diamond Jubilee, the Relief of Mafeking (34p)

■ **1987, September 8. 150th Anniversary of the Accession of Queen Victoria**
Des: Carroll and Dempsey Studio. Printed in recess and photogravure by Harrison.

Set	1.75	2.25
Gutter pairs	4.50	–
First day cover	–	1.75
Stamp cards	1.75	3.00

DECIMAL   QUEEN ELIZABETH II

Pot by Bernard Leach (18p)
Pot by Elizabeth Fritsch (26p)
Pot by Lucie Rie (31p)
Pot by Hans Coper (34p)

■ **1987, October 13. Studio Pottery**
Des: Tony Evans.

Set	1.75	2.25
Gutter pairs	4.50	–
First day cover	–	1.75
Stamp cards	3.50	3.00

Child decorating a Christmas tree (13p)
Child looking out of a window (18p)
Child sleeping, and Father Christmas in his sleigh (26p)
Child reading a book surrounded by toys (31p)
Child playing a recorder, watched by snowman (34p)

■ **1987, November 17. Christmas**
Des: M. Foreman. 13p has one phosphor band.

Set	1.75	2.25
13p (stars on gummed side)	0.70	–
Gutter pairs	4.50	–
First day cover	–	1.75
Stamp cards	1.75	3.00

(*The 13p exists with a star pattern printed on the gummed side, from a pack sold at a discount.)

Short-spined sea scorpion (18p)
Yellow waterlily (26p)
Bewick's swan (31p)
Morel mushroom (34p)

■ **1988, January 19. Bicentenary of the Linnean Society**
Des: E. Hughes.

Set	1.75	2.25
Gutter pairs	4.50	–
First day cover	–	1.75
Stamp cards	1.50	3.00

Reverend William Morgan, Bible translator 1588 (18p)
William Salesbury, New Testament translator 1567 (26p)
Bishop Richard Davies, New Testament translator 1567 (31p)
Bishop Richard Parry, Welsh Bible editor 1620 (34p)

■ **1988, March 1. 400th Anniversary of the Welsh Bible**
Des: K. Bowen.

Set	1.75	2.25
Gutter pairs	4.50	–
First day cover	–	1.75
Stamp cards	1.50	3.00

Gymnastics: British Amateur Gymnastics Association (18p)
Skiing: Ski Club of Great Britain (26p)
Tennis: Lawn Tennis Association (31p)
Football: Football League (34p)

■ **1988, March 22. Sports Organisations**
Des: J. Sutton.

Set	1.75	2.25
Gutter pairs	4.50	–
First day cover	–	1.75
Stamp cards	1.50	3.00

BRITISH STAMP MARKET VALUES 2024

QUEEN ELIZABETH II DECIMAL

Mallard train and mailbags (18p)
Queen Elizabeth liner and transatlantic mail (26p)
Glasgow tram and pillar box (31p)
Imperial Airways Handley Page HP45 and airmail (34p)

■ **1988, May 10. Transport and Mail Services (Europa)**
Des: M. Dempsey.

Set	1.75	2.25
Gutter pairs	4.50	–
First day cover	–	1.75
Stamp cards	1.50	3.00

(*The Handley Page design also exists as an imprinted 33p value on a set of airmail postal cards issued on March 2, 1993; price £5.)

Early settler and sailing clipper (18p)
British and Australian parliaments and Queen Elizabeth II (18p)
W. G. Grace and tennis racquet (34p)
Shakespeare, John Lennon and Sydney Opera House (34p)

■ **1988, June 21. Bicentenary of Australian Settlement**
Des: G. Emery. Printed in litho by Questa.

Set (two se-tenant pairs)	1.80	2.25
Gutter pairs	4.00	–
First day cover	–	1.75
Stamp cards	1.50	3.00

Spanish ship off The Lizard (18p)
English fleet leaving Plymouth (18p)
Engagement off the Isle of Wight (18p)
English fire-ships attack off Calais (18p)
Spanish ships in North Sea storm (18p)

■ **1988, July 19. 400th anniversary of the Spanish Armada**
Des: G. Evernden.

Set (se-tenant strip of five)	1.75	2.25
Gutter pairs	4.00	–
First day cover	–	1.75
Stamp cards	1.75	3.00

'The owl and the pussy cat went to sea' (19p)
Self-portrait of Edward Lear as a bird (27p)
'Cat' (32p)
'There was a young lady whose bonnet...' (35p)

■ **1988, September 6. Centenary of the Death of Edward Lear**
Des: M. Swatridge and S. Dew.

Set	1.75	2.25
Gutter pairs	4.50	–
First day cover	–	1.75
Stamp cards	1.50	3.00
Miniature sheet (one of each value)	3.75	4.75
Miniature sheet first day cover	–	4.00

(*The miniature sheet, issued on September 27, 1988, was sold with a surcharge towards the cost of staging the international stamp exhibition, Stamp World London 90.)

Carrickfergus Castle (£1)
Caernarfon Castle (£1.50)
Edinburgh Castle (£2)
Windsor Castle (£5)

■ **1988, October 18. Castle high value definitives**
Engraved by C. Matthews from photographs by Prince Andrew. Recess-printed by Harrison.

Set	16.00	4.50
Gutter pairs	35.00	–
Gutter blocks of four (centre cross)	75.00	–
First day cover	–	20.00

106 BRITISH STAMP MARKET VALUES 2024

DECIMAL   QUEEN ELIZABETH II

Journeying to Bethlehem (14p)
Shepherds following the star (19p)
Three wise men (27p)
Nativity (32p)
Annunciation (35p)

■ **1988, November 15. Christmas. Christmas Cards**
Des: L. Trickett. 14p has one phosphor band.
Set	1.90	2.25
Gutter pairs	4.00	–
First day cover	–	1.75
Stamp cards	1.75	3.00

(*Examples of the 14p are known with the denomination of 13p in error.)

Atlantic puffin (19p)
Avocet (27p)
Oystercatcher (32p)
Northern gannet (35p)

■ **1989, January 17. Centenary of the Royal Society for the Protection of Birds**
Des: D. Cordery.
Set	1.75	2.25
Gutter pairs	5.00	–
First day cover	–	1.75
Stamp cards	2.75	3.00

Teddy bear (19p)
Rose (19p)
Cupid (19p)
Yachts (19p)
Fruit (19p)

■ **1989, January 31. Greetings (issue 1)**
Des: P. Sutton. Se-tenant strip of five. Issued in booklets in panes of ten containing two of each design.
Set (se-tenant strip of five)	10.00	15.00
Booklet pane (of 10)	23.00	–
Booklet	25.00	–
First day cover	–	9.00
Stamp cards	5.00	10.00

Fruit and vegetables (19p)
Meat products (27p)
Dairy products (32p)
Cereal products (35p)

■ **1989, March 7. Food and Farming Year**
Des: Sedley Place.
Set	1.75	2.25
Gutter pairs	4.50	–
First day cover	–	1.75
Stamp cards	1.50	3.00

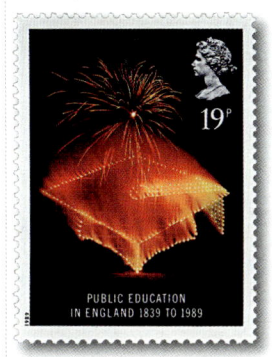

150th anniversary of public education: mortar board (19p)
Third elections to European Parliament: cross on ballot (19p)
26th Postal, Telegraph and Telephone Congress: posthorn (35p)
Inter-Parliamentary Union Conference: globe (35p)

■ **1989, April 11. Anniversaries and Events**
Des: Lewis Moberly. 19p and 35p issued in se-tenant pairs.
Set (two se-tenant pairs)	1.75	2.25
Gutter pairs	4.50	–
First day cover	–	1.75
Stamp cards	1.50	3.00

BRITISH STAMP MARKET VALUES 2024

QUEEN ELIZABETH II DECIMAL

Toy aeroplane and locomotive (19p)
Building bricks (27p)
Board games and dice (32p)
Toy robot, boat and doll's house (35p)

■ **1989, May 16. Games and Toys (Europa)**
Des: D. Fern.
Set	1.75	2.25
Gutter pairs	4.50	–
First day cover	–	1.75
Stamp cards	1.50	3.00

Snowflake (19p)
Fly (27p)
Blood cells (32p)
Microchip (35p)

■ **1989, September 5. 150th Anniversary of the Royal Microscopical Society**
Des: K. Bassford. Printed in litho by Questa.
Set	1.75	2.25
Gutter pairs	4.50	–
First day cover	–	1.75
Stamp cards	1.50	3.00

Ironbridge, Shropshire (19p)
Tin mine, St Agnes Head, Cornwall (27p)
Cotton Mills, New Lanark, Strathclyde (32p)
Pontcysyllte Aqueduct, Clwyd (35p)

■ **1989, July 4. Industrial Archaeology**
Des: R. Maddox.
Set	1.75	2.25
Gutter pairs	4.00	–
First day cover	–	1.75
Stamp cards	1.50	3.00
Miniature sheet	3.50	4.00
Miniature sheet first day cover	–	3.50

(*The miniature sheet, issued on July 25, 1989, contained one of each value but with the designs in a horizontal format, with a surcharge towards the cost of staging the international stamp exhibition, Stamp World London 90.)

Royal Mail coach (20p)
Escort of the Blues and Royals (20p)
Lord Mayor's coach (20p)
St Paul's Cathedral (20p)
Blues and Royals drum horse (20p)

■ **1989, October 17. 800th Anniversary of the Mayoralty of London. The Lord Mayor's Show**
Des: P. Cox.
Set (se-tenant strip of five)	1.75	2.25
Gutter pairs	4.00	–
First day cover	–	1.70
Stamp cards	1.75	3.00

(*The Royal Mail Coach design also appears in the Treasures of the Archive prestige stamp book issued on August 18, 2009, printed in litho.)

DECIMAL QUEEN ELIZABETH II

14th-century peasants, from stained glass window (15p)
Arches and roundels from West Front (15p+1p)
Octagon Tower (20p+1p)
Arcade from West Transept (34p+1p)
Triple arch from West Front (37p+1p)

■ **1989, November 14. Christmas. 800th Anniversary of Ely Cathedral**
Des: D. Gentleman. 15p and 15p+1p have one phosphor band.

Set	2.25	2.50
Gutter pairs	5.00	–
First day cover	–	1.75
Stamp cards	2.25	3.00

(*Four of these stamps carried a surcharge for charity.)

■ **1990, January 10. 150th Anniversary of the Penny Black**
See under Decimal Machin definitives.

Kitten (20p)
Rabbit (29p)
Duckling (34p)
Puppy (37p)

■ **1990, January 23. 150th Anniversary of the Royal Society for the Prevention of Cruelty to Animals**
Des: T. Evans. Printed in litho by Questa.

Set	2.00	2.50
Gutter pairs	5.00	–
First day cover	–	1.75
Stamp cards	1.75	3.00

Teddy Bear (20p)
Dennis the Menace (20p)
Punch (20p)
Cheshire Cat (20p)
The Man in the Moon (20p)
The Laughing Policeman (20p)
Clown (20p)
Mona Lisa (20p)
Queen of Hearts (20p)
Stan Laurel (20p)

■ **1990, February 6. Greetings (issue 2): Smiles**
Des: Michael Peters and Partners. Issued se-tenant in booklet panes of ten comprising one of each design.

Booklet pane (of 10)	12.00	14.50
Booklet	14.00	–
First day cover	–	11.00

Alexandra Palace, London (20p)
School of Art, Glasgow (20p)
British Philatelic Bureau, Edinburgh (29p)
Templeton Carpet Factory, Glasgow (37p)

■ **1990, March 6. Glasgow 1990 European City of Culture and Stamp World Exhibition (Europa)**
Des: P. Hogarth.

Set	1.75	2.25
Gutter pairs	4.25	–
First day cover	–	1.75
Stamp cards	1.50	3.00

(*The 20p Alexandra Palace design also appears in the £5 London Life prestige stamp book issued on March 20, 1990.)

BRITISH STAMP MARKET VALUES 2024   **109**

QUEEN ELIZABETH II DECIMAL

Export Achievement Award (20p and 37p)
Technological Achievement Award (20p and 37p)

■ **1990, April 10. 25th Anniversary of The Queen's Awards for Export and Technology**
Des: S. Broom. Printed in litho by Questa.

Set (two se-tenant pairs)	1.75	2.25
Gutter pairs	4.00	–
First day cover	–	1.80
Stamp cards	1.50	3.00

Portraits of Queen Victoria and Queen Elizabeth II (20p)

■ **1990, May 3. Stamp World London 90 International Exhibition**
Des: Sedley Place Design; engraved by C. Matthews. Printed in recess and photogravure by Harrison.

Miniature sheet	2.50	3.25
First day cover	–	2.75

(*The border illustrates the 1840 Penny Black but this was not valid for postage. The sheets were sold at £1 each, the surcharge going towards the cost of staging the exhibition.)

Cycad and Sir Joseph Banks Building (20p)
Stone pine and Princess of Wales Conservatory (29p)
Willow tree and Palm House (34p)
Cedar tree and Pagoda (37p)

■ **1990, June 5. 150th Anniversary of Kew Gardens**
Des: P. Leith.

Set	1.75	2.25
Gutter pairs	4.00	–
First day cover	–	1.75
Stamp cards	1.50	3.00

Thomas Hardy and Clyffe Clump, Dorset (20p)

■ **1990, July 10. 150th Anniversary of the Birth of Thomas Hardy**
Des: J. Gibbs.

20p	0.40	0.60
Gutter pair	1.00	–
First day cover	–	1.00
Stamp card	1.00	1.50

Queen Elizabeth as The Queen Mother (20p)
Queen Elizabeth as Queen (29p)
Queen Elizabeth as Duchess of York (34p)
Queen Elizabeth as Lady Elizabeth Bowes-Lyon (37p)

DECIMAL QUEEN ELIZABETH II

■ 1990, August 2. 90th Birthday of Queen Elizabeth, The Queen Mother
Des: J. Gorham from photographs by Norman Parkinson, Dorothy Wilding, B. Park and Rita Martin.

Set	2.75	4.00
Gutter pairs	7.00	–
First day cover	–	2.50
Stamp cards	1.50	3.00

(*The same designs were used in the Queen Mother Memorial issue of April 2002, but with the borders changed to black.)

Victoria Cross (20p)
George Cross (20p)
Distinguished Service Cross, Distinguished Service Medal (20p)
Military Cross and Military Medal (20p)
Distinguished Flying Cross, Distinguished Flying Medal (20p)

■ 1990, September 11. Gallantry Awards
Des: J. Gibbs and J. Harwood.

Set	1.75	2.25
Gutter pairs	4.50	–
First day cover	–	2.00
Stamp cards	2.25	3.00

(*The 20p also appears in the miniature sheet and the prestige stamp book with the Victoria Cross issue on September 21, 2006.)

Armagh Observatory, Jodrell Bank & La Palma telescopes (22p)
Early telescope and moon and tides diagram by Newton (26p)
Greenwich Old Observatory and astronomical equipment (31p)
Stonehenge, armillary sphere and navigation by the stars (37p)

■ 1990, October 16. Astronomy
Des: J. Fisher. Printed in litho by Questa.

Set	1.75	2.25
Gutter pairs	4.50	–
First day cover	–	2.00
Stamp cards	1.50	3.00

Building a snowman (17p)
Fetching a Christmas tree (22p)
Carol singers (26p)
Tobogganing (31p)
Ice-skating (37p)

■ 1990, November 13. Christmas
Des: J. Gorham and A. Davidson. The 17p has one phosphor band.

Set	2.00	2.60
Gutter pairs	5.00	–
First day cover	–	1.75
Stamp cards	1.75	3.00

(*The 17p was also sold in booklets.)

'King Charles Spaniel' (22p)
'A Pointer' (26p)
'Two Hounds in a Landscape' (31p)
'A Rough Dog' (33p)
'Fino and Tiny' (37p)

■ 1991, January 8. Dogs. Paintings by George Stubbs
Des: Carroll, Dempsey and Thirkell.

Set	1.85	2.75
Gutter pairs	4.00	–
First day cover	–	2.25
Stamp cards	1.75	3.00

QUEEN ELIZABETH II DECIMAL

Thrush's nest (1st)
Shooting star and rainbow (1st)
Magpies and charm bracelet (1st)
Black cat (1st)
Kingfisher and key (1st)
Mallard and frog (1st)
Four-leaf clover, boot and matchbox (1st)
Pot of gold at the end of the rainbow (1st)
Butterflies (1st)
Wishing well and sixpence (1st)

■ **1991, February 5. Greetings (issue 3): Good Luck**
Des: T. Meeuwissen. Issued se-tenant in booklet panes of 10 containing one of each design.

Booklet pane (of 10)	13.00	13.00
Booklet	13.00	–
First day cover	–	10.00

Michael Faraday, electricity (22p)
Charles Babbage, computer (22p)
Robert Watson Watt, radar (31p)
Frank Whittle, jet engine: Gloster Whittle E28/39 aircraft (37p)

■ **1991, March 5. Scientific Achievements**
Des: P. Till (22p, 22p), J. Harwood (31p, 37p).

Set	2.00	2.60
Gutter pairs	5.00	–
First day cover	–	1.75
Stamp cards	1.50	3.00

■ **1991, March 26. Greetings: Smiles**
Designs as for the Greetings stamps of February 6, 1990, but with all values changed to 1st class. Issued se-tenant in booklet panes of ten containing one of each design.

Booklet pane (of 10)	13.00	13.00
Booklet	13.00	–
First day cover	–	10.00

(*These designs were also used for Smilers sheets in 2000 and 2001.)

Man looking at space (22p, 22p)
Space looking at man (37p, 37p)

■ **1991, April 23. Europe in Space (Europa)**
Des: J-M. Folon.

Set (two se-tenant pairs)	2.25	2.75
Gutter pairs	6.00	–
First day cover	–	2.50
Stamp cards	1.50	3.00

Fencing (22p)
Hurdling (26p)
Diving (31p)
Rugby (37p)

■ **1991, June 11. World Student Games, Sheffield, and Rugby World Cup**
Des: Huntley Muir Partners.

Set	2.00	2.75
Gutter pairs	5.00	–
First day cover	–	2.25
Stamp cards	1.50	3.00

112 BRITISH STAMP MARKET VALUES 2024

DECIMAL QUEEN ELIZABETH II

Silver Jubilee rose (22p)
Madame Alfred Carrière rose (26p)
Rosa Moyesii rose (31p)
Harvest Fayre rose (33p)
Mutabilis rose (37p)

■ 1991, July 16. World Congress of Roses, Belfast
Des: Yvonne Skargon. Printed in litho by Questa.

Set	2.25	3.00
Gutter pairs	5.00	–
First day cover	–	2.25
Stamp cards	2.00	3.00

Iguanodon (22p)
Stegosaurus (26p)
Tyrannosaurus (31p)
Protoceratops (33p)
Triceratops (37p)

■ 1991, August 20. 150th Anniversary of the Identification of Dinosaurs by Richard Owen
Des: B. Kneale.

Set	2.50	3.00
Gutter pairs	6.00	–
First day cover	–	3.00
Stamp cards	2.00	3.00

Map of Hamstreet, Kent, in 1816 (24p)
Map of Hamstreet, Kent, in 1906 (28p)
Map of Hamstreet, Kent, in 1959 (33p)
Map of Hamstreet, Kent, in 1991 (39p)

■ 1991, September 17. Bicentenary of Ordnance Survey
Des: H. Brown. Printed in recess and litho by Harrison (24p), in litho by Harrison (28p), and in litho by Questa (33p, 39p).

Set	2.25	2.75
Gutter pairs	6.00	–
First day cover	–	2.50
Stamp cards	1.50	3.00

(*Examples of the 28p are known with the denomination of 26p, from supplies printed before an increase in postage rates and issued in error.)

Adoration of the Magi (18p)
Mary with Jesus in stable (24p)
Holy family and angel (28p)
Annunciation (33p)
Flight into Egypt (39p)

■ 1991, November 12. Christmas
Des: D. Driver, from the Acts Of Mary & Jesus illuminated manuscript. The 18p has one phosphor band.

Set	2.25	2.75
Gutter pairs	6.00	–
First day cover	–	2.50
Stamp cards	1.75	3.00

(*The 18p was also sold in booklets.)

Fallow deer in Scottish forest (18p)
Hare on North Yorkshire moors (24p)
Fox in the Fens (28p)
Redwing in the Home Counties (33p)
Welsh mountain sheep in Snowdonia (39p)

■ 1992, January 14. The Four Seasons: Wintertime
Des: J. Gorham and K. Bowen. 18p has one phosphor band.

Set	2.25	3.25
Gutter pairs	5.00	–
First day cover	–	2.25
Stamp cards	1.75	3.75

(*The 39p also appears in the Cymru Wales prestige stamp booklet issued on February 25, 1992.)

QUEEN ELIZABETH II DECIMAL

Spray of flowers (1st)
Double locket (1st)
Key (1st)
Toy car and cigarette cards (1st)
Compass and map (1st)
Pocket watch (1st)
Penny Red stamp and pen (1st)
Pearl necklace (1st)
Marbles (1st)
Starfish and a bucket and spade (1st)

■ **1992, January 28. Greetings (issue 4): Memories**
Des: Trickett and Webb Ltd. Issued se-tenant in booklet panes of ten, containing one of each design.

Booklet pane (of 10)	13.00	13.00
Booklet	13.00	–
First day cover	–	10.00

Queen Elizabeth II, in Coronation robes (24p)
Queen Elizabeth II, in Garter robes (24p)
Queen Elizabeth II, with Prince Andrew as a baby (24p)
Queen Elizabeth II, at Trooping of the Colour (24p)
Queen Elizabeth II, with emblem of the Commonwealth (24p)

■ **1992, February 6. 40th Anniversary of the Accession**
Des: Why Not Associates. Printed in litho by Questa.

Set (se-tenant strip of five)	3.00	4.00
Gutter pairs	7.50	–
First day cover	–	3.50
Stamp cards	1.75	3.75

Tennyson in 1888 and 'The Beguiling of Merlin' by Burne-Jones (24p)
Tennyson in 1856 and 'April Love' by Hughes (28p)
Tennyson in 1864 and 'I Am Sick Of The Shadows' by Waterhouse (33p)
Tennyson as a young man and 'Mariana' by Rossetti (39p)

■ **1992, March 10. Centenary of the Death of Alfred, Lord Tennyson**
Des: Irene von Treskow.

Set	2.25	3.00
Gutter pairs	5.00	–
First day cover	–	2.25
Stamp cards	1.50	3.75

Barcelona Olympics: British Olympic Association logo (24p)
Barcelona Paralympics: British Paralympic Association logo (24p)
Discovery of America by Columbus: 'Santa Maria' (24p)
Operation Raleigh Grand Regatta: 'Kaisei' (39p)
Expo '92 in Seville: British Pavilion (39p)

■ **1992, April 7. International Events (Europa)**
Des: K. Bassford (Olympics, Paralympics and Expo), K. Bassford and S. Paine (Columbus and Raleigh). Printed in litho by Questa (Olympics, Paralympics and Expo) or in recess and litho by Harrison (Columbus and Raleigh). The Olympics and Paralympics designs were issued as a se-tenant pair.

Set	2.50	3.25
Gutter pairs	6.00	–
First day cover	–	2.50
Stamp cards	1.75	3.75

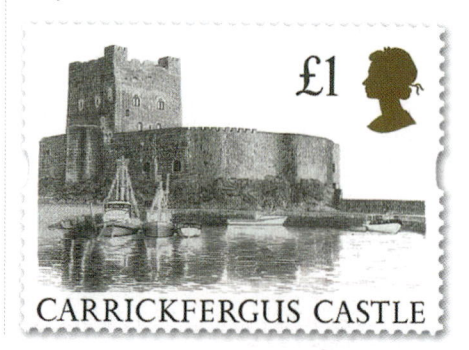

114 BRITISH STAMP MARKET VALUES 2024

DECIMAL **QUEEN ELIZABETH II**

Carrickfergus Castle (£1)
Caernarfon Castle (£1.50)
Edinburgh Castle (£2)
Windsor Castle (£5)

■ **1992, March 24. Castle high value definitives**
As issue of October 18, 1988, but with the Queen's head in silhouette, printed in optically variable ink which changes colour from gold to green depending on the angle at which it is viewed, and with an elliptical perforation along each side.

Set	23.00	6.00
Gutter pairs	50.00	–
Gutter blocks of four (centre cross)	£120	
First day cover	–	15.00
Stamp cards	8.00	55.00

(*The £1.50, £2 and £5 exist with either blue-tinted PVAD gum or white PVA gum.)

Pikeman (24p)
Drummer (28p)
Musketeer (33p)
Standard bearer (39p)

■ **1992, June 16. 350th Anniversary of the Civil War**
Des: J. Sancha.

Set	2.25	3.00
Gutter pairs	6.00	–
First day cover	–	2.25
Stamp cards	2.50	3.75

'The Yeoman of the Guard' (18p)
'The Gondoliers' (24p)
'The Mikado' (28p)
'The Pirates of Penzance' (33p)
'Iolanthe' (39p)

■ **1992, July 21. Gilbert and Sullivan Operas**
Des: Lynda Gray. 18p has one phosphor band.

Set	2.25	3.25
Gutter pairs	5.50	–
First day cover	–	2.50
Stamp cards	1.75	3.75

Acid rain kills (24p)
Ozone layer (28p)
Greenhouse effect (33p)
Bird of hope (39p)

■ **1992, September 15. Protection of the Environment**
Des: C. Hall (24p), L. Fowler (28p), S. Warren (33p) and A. Newton-Mold (39p). All paintings by children, in conjunction with the BBC Television programme 'Blue Peter'.

Set	2.00	3.00
Gutter pairs	4.50	–
First day cover	–	2.25
Stamp cards	1.50	3.75

European star (24p)

■ **1992, October 13. Single European Market**
Des: D. Hockney.

24p	0.50	0.60
Gutter pair	1.50	–
First day cover	–	1.00
Stamp card	1.00	2.50

BRITISH STAMP MARKET VALUES 2024

QUEEN ELIZABETH II DECIMAL

Angel Gabriel, from St. James's, Pangbourne (18p)
Madonna and Child, from St. Mary's, Bibury (24p)
King with gold, from Our Lady and St. Peter, Leatherhead (28p)
Shepherds, from All Saints, Porthcawl (33p)
Kings with gifts, from Our Lady and St. Peter, Leatherhead (39p)

■ **1992, November 10. Christmas. Stained-Glass Windows**
Des: Carroll, Dempsey and Thirkell. The 18p has one phosphor band.

Set	2.25	3.25
Gutter pairs	5.00	–
First day cover	–	2.50
Stamp cards	1.75	3.75

(*The 18p was also sold in booklets.)

Mute swan cob and St. Catherine's Chapel (18p)
Cygnet and decoy (24p)
Swans and cygnet (28p)
Eggs in nest and Tithe Barn (33p)
Young swan (39p)

■ **1993, January 19. 600th Anniversary of Abbotsbury Swannery**
Des: David Gentleman. The 18p has one phosphor band.

Set	4.00	5.00
Gutter pairs	10.00	–
First day cover	–	4.00
Stamp cards	1.75	5.00

William (1st)
Long John Silver (1st)
Tweedledum and Tweedledee (1st)
Mole and Toad (1st)
Teacher and Wilfred (1st)
Peter Rabbit and Mrs Rabbit (1st)
Snowman and Father Christmas (1st)
The Big Friendly Giant and Sophie (1st)
Bill Badger and Rupert Bear (1st)
Aladdin and the Genie (1st)

■ **1993, February 2. Greetings (issue 5): Gift Giving**
Des: Newell and Sorrell. Issued se-tenant in booklet panes of ten containing one of each design.

Booklet pane (of 10)	13.00	13.00
Booklet	13.00	–
First day cover	–	10.00
Stamp cards	8.00	15.50

(*The Peter Rabbit and Mrs Rabbit design also appears in the Story of Beatrix Potter prestige stamp book issued on August 10, 1993.)

H4 chronometer: decorated enamel dial (24p)
H4 chronometer: escapement, remontoire and fusée (28p)
H4 chronometer: balance and spring (33p)
H4 chronometer: movement seen from back (39p)

■ **1993, February 16. 300th Anniversary of the Birth of John Harrison**
Des: H. Brown and D. Penny. Printed in litho by Questa.

Set	2.00	3.00
Gutter pairs	4.50	–
First day cover	–	2.25
Stamp cards	1.75	5.00

Britannia (£10)

DECIMAL — QUEEN ELIZABETH II

■ 1993, March 2. £10 definitive
Des: M. Denney and B. Craddock. Printed in litho by Questa, with die-stamping and braille embossing.

£10	20.00	8.50
First day cover	–	15.00
Stamp card	4.50	50.00

Dendrobium hellwigianum (18p)
Paphiopedilum Maudiae 'Magnificum' (24p)
Cymbidium lowianum (28p)
Vanda Rothschildiana (33p)
Dendrobium vexillarius var. albiviride (39p)

■ 1993, March 16. World Orchid Conference, Glasgow
Des: Pandora Sellars. The 18p has one phosphor band.

Set	2.25	3.25
Gutter pairs	5.50	–
First day cover	–	2.25
Stamp cards	1.75	5.00

'Family Group' by Henry Moore (24p)
'Kew Gardens' by Edward Bawden (28p)
'St Francis and the Birds' by Stanley Spencer (33p)
'Still Life: Odyssey 1' by Ben Nicholson (39p)

■ 1993, May 11. Contemporary Art (Europa)
Des: A. Dastor.

Set	2.25	3.00
Gutter pairs	6.00	–
First day cover	–	2.25
Stamp cards	1.50	5.00

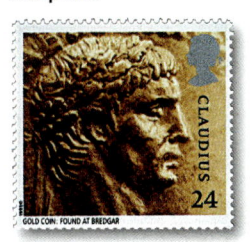

Emperor Claudius, from gold coin (24p)
Emperor Hadrian, from bronze head (28p)
Goddess Roma, from gemstone (33p)
Christ, from mosaic at Hinton St. Mary (39p)

■ 1993, June 15. Roman Britain
Des: J. Gibbs.

Set	2.25	3.00
Gutter pairs	6.00	–
First day cover	–	2.25
Stamp cards	1.50	5.00

Narrowboats on Grand Junction Canal (24p)
Humber keels on Stainforth and Keadby Canal (28p)
Horse-drawn barges on Brecknock and Abergavenny Canal (33p)
Steam barges and fishing boats on Crinan Canal (39p)

■ 1993, July 20. Inland Waterways
Des: T. Lewery. Printed in litho by Questa.

Set	2.00	3.00
Gutter pairs	4.50	–
First day cover	–	2.25
Stamp cards	2.00	5.00

Horse chestnut (18p)
Blackberry (24p)
Hazel (28p)
Rowan (33p)
Pear (39p)

■ 1993, September 14. The Four Seasons: Autumn
Des: Charlotte Knox. The 18p has one phosphor band.

Set	2.25	3.25
Gutter pairs	6.00	–
First day cover	–	2.25
Stamp cards	2.00	5.00

BRITISH STAMP MARKET VALUES 2024

QUEEN ELIZABETH II DECIMAL

'The Reigate Squire' (24p)
'The Hound of the Baskervilles' (24p)
'The Six Napoleons' (24p)
'The Greek Interpreter' (24p)
'The Final Problem' (24p)

■ **1993, October 12. Sherlock Holmes**
Des: A. Davidson. Printed in litho by Questa.

Set (se-tenant strip of five)	2.50	3.50
Gutter pairs	5.50	–
First day cover	–	3.00
Stamp cards	5.00	4.50

Bob Cratchit and Tiny Tim (19p)
Mr. and Mrs. Fezziwig (25p)
Mr. Scrooge (30p)
The prize turkey (35p)
Mr. Scrooge's nephew (41p)

■ **1993, November 9. Christmas. 150th Anniversary of 'A Christmas Carol' by Charles Dickens**
Des: Q. Blake. The 19p has one phosphor band.

Set	2.40	3.25
Gutter pairs	6.00	–
First day cover	–	2.75
Stamp cards	2.50	5.00

(*The 19p and 25p were also sold in booklets.)

Class 5 and Class B1 on the West Highland Line (19p)
Class A1 at Kings Cross (25p)
Class 4 at Blyth North (30p)
Class 4 near Wigan Central (35p)
Castle class crossing Worcester & Birmingham Canal (41p)

■ **1994, January 18. The Age of Steam**
Des: B. Delaney, from photographs by Colin Gifford. The 19p has one phosphor band.

Set	2.40	3.50
Gutter pairs	6.00	–
First day cover	–	2.50
Stamp cards	3.00	5.50

Dan Dare (1st)
The Three Bears (1st)
Rupert Bear (1st)
Alice in Wonderland (1st)
Noggin and the Ice Dragon (1st)
Peter Rabbit (1st)
Little Red Riding Hood (1st)
Orlando the Marmalade Cat (1st)
Biggles (1st)
Paddington Bear (1st)

■ **1994, February 1. Greetings (issue 6): Messages**
Des: Newell and Sorrell. Issued se-tenant in booklet panes of ten containing one of each design.

Booklet pane (of 10)	13.00	13.00
Booklet	13.00	
First day cover	–	10.00
Stamp cards	8.00	15.50

Chirk Castle, Clwyd, Wales (19p)
Ben Arkle, Sutherland, Scotland (25p)
Mourne Mountains, County Down, Northern Ireland (30p)
Dersingham, Norfolk, England (35p)
Dolwyddelan, Gwynedd, Wales (41p)

DECIMAL QUEEN ELIZABETH II

■ **1994, March 1. 25th Anniversary of the Investiture of The Prince of Wales**
Des: paintings by the Prince of Wales. The 19p has one phosphor band.

Set	2.40	3.25
Gutter pairs	6.00	–
First day cover	–	2.75
Stamp cards	2.50	5.50

(*The 30p also appears in the Northern Ireland prestige stamp book issued on July 26, 1994.)

Bathing at Blackpool (19p)
'Where's my little lad?' (25p)
'Wish you were here' (30p)
Punch and Judy show (35p)
Tower Crane machine (41p)

■ **1994, April 12. Centenary of Picture Postcards**
Des: M. Dempsey and B. Dare. Printed in litho by Questa. The 19p has one phosphor band, and the other values have two.

Set	2.40	3.25
Gutter pairs	6.50	–
First day cover	–	2.75
Stamp cards	2.00	5.50

British lion and French cockerel (25p, 41p)
Hands over a train (25p, 41p)

■ **1994, May 3. Opening of the Channel Tunnel**
Des: G. Hardie (lion and cockerel), J.-P. Cousin (hands and train).

Set (two se-tenant pairs)	2.50	3.25
Gutter pairs	6.50	–
First day cover	–	2.75
Stamp cards	2.00	5.50

Ground crew servicing Douglas Boston aircraft (25p)
HMS Warspite (25p)
Commandos on Gold Beach (25p)
Infantry on Sword Beach (25p)
Tank and infantry at Ouistreham (25p)

■ **1994, June 6. 50th Anniversary of D-Day**
Des: K. Bassford. Printed in litho by Questa.

Set (se-tenant strip of five)	3.00	4.00
Gutter pairs	6.50	–
First day cover	–	3.00
Stamp cards	2.50	5.50

St. Andrew's, old course (19p)
Muirfield, 18th hole (25p)
Carnoustie, 15th hole (30p)
Royal Troon, 8th hole (35p)
Turnberry, 9th hole (41p)

■ **1994, July 5. Scottish Golf Courses**
Des: P. Hogarth. The 19p has one phosphor band.

Set	2.25	3.25
Gutter pairs	5.00	–
First day cover	–	2.50
Stamp cards	2.50	5.50

Royal Welsh Show, Llanelwedd (19p)
All England Tennis Championships, Wimbledon (25p)
Cowes Week (30p)
Test Match, Lord's (35p)
Braemar Gathering (41p)

■ **1994, August 2. The Four Seasons: Summertime**
Des: M. Cook. The 19p has one phosphor band.

Set	2.25	3.25
Gutter pairs	6.00	–
First day cover	–	2.50
Stamp cards	3.25	5.50

QUEEN ELIZABETH II DECIMAL

Ultrasonic imaging (25p)
Scanning electron microscopy (30p)
Magnetic resonance imaging (35p)
Computed tomography (41p)

■ **1994, September 27. Medical Discoveries (Europa)**
Des: P. Vermier and J.-P. Tibbles. Printed in photogravure by Enschedé.

Set	2.25	3.25
Gutter pairs	6.00	–
First day cover	–	2.50
Stamp cards	2.00	5.50

Mary and Joseph (19p)
Three wise men (25p)
Mary with doll (30p)
Shepherds (35p)
Angels (41p)

■ **1994, November 1. Christmas. Children's Nativity Plays**
Des: Yvonne Gilbert. The 19p has one phosphor band.

Set	2.40	3.25
Gutter pairs	6.00	–
First day cover	–	2.50
Stamp cards	2.50	5.50

(*The 19p and 25p were also sold in booklets.)

Black cat (19p)
Siamese and tabby cat (25p)
Ginger cat (30p)
Tortoiseshell and Abyssinian cat (35p)
Black and white cat (41p)

■ **1995, January 17. Cats**
Des: Elizabeth Blackadder. Printed in litho by Questa. The 19p has one phosphor band, other values two phosphor bands.

Set	2.50	3.25
Gutter pairs	6.00	–
First day cover	–	2.50
Stamp cards	3.00	6.50

Dandelions (19p)
Chestnut leaves (25p)
Garlic leaves (30p)
Hazel leaves (35p)
Spring grass (41p)

■ **1995, March 14. The Four Seasons: Springtime**
Des: plant sculptures by Andy Goldsworthy. The 19p has one phosphor band, other values two phosphor bands.

Set	2.25	3.25
Gutter pairs	6.00	–
First day cover	–	2.50
Stamp cards	2.50	6.50

'La Danse à la Campagne' by Pierre-Auguste Renoir (1st)
'Troilus and Criseyde' by Peter Brookes (1st)
'The Kiss' by Auguste Rodin (1st)
'Girls on the Town' by Beryl Cook (1st)
'Jazz' by Andrew Mockett (1st)
'Girls Performing a Kathak Dance' (1st)
'Alice Keppel With Her Daughter' by Alice Hughes (1st)
'Children Playing' by L. S. Lowry (1st)
'Circus Clowns' by Emily Firmin and Justin Mitchell (1st)
'All the Love Poems of Shakespeare' by Eric Gill (1st)

120 BRITISH STAMP MARKET VALUES 2024

DECIMAL QUEEN ELIZABETH II

■ 1995, March 21. Greetings (issue 7): Art
Des: Newell and Sorrell. Printed in litho by Walsall. Issued se-tenant in booklet panes of ten containing one of each design.

Booklet pane (of 10)	13.00	13.00
Booklet	13.00	–
First day cover	–	10.00
Stamp cards	9.00	15.50

Fireplace decoration (19p)
Oak seedling (25p)
Carved table leg (30p)
St David's Head, Dyfed, Wales (35p)
Elizabethan window (41p)

■ 1995, April 11. Centenary of The National Trust
Des: T. Evans. The 19p has one phosphor band, the 25p and 35p two phosphor bands, the 30p and 41p phosphor paper.

Set	2.25	3.25
Gutter pairs	6.00	–
First day cover	–	2.50
Stamp cards	2.50	6.50

(*The 25p also appears in the National Trust prestige stamp book issued on April 25, 1995.)

End of World War II: British troops and French civilians (19p)
British Red Cross: symbolic hands and Red Cross emblem (19p)
Victory: searchlights in a 'V' over St. Paul's Cathedral (25p)
United Nations: hand releasing dove of peace (25p)
United Nations: symbolic hands uplifted (30p)

■ 1995, May 2. Peace & Freedom (Europa)
Des: J–M. Folon (Red Cross 19p, Dove 25p, 30p), J. Gorham (Troops 19p, Seachlights 25p). The 19p has one phosphor band, other values two phosphor bands.

Set	2.25	3.25
Gutter pairs	6.00	–
First day cover	–	2.50
Stamp cards	3.00	6.50

(*The St Paul's Cathedral design was also used as a 1st class stamp in the End of the War miniature sheet in 2005.)

'The Time Machine' (25p)
'The First Men in the Moon' (30p)
'The War of the Worlds' (35p)
'The Shape of Things to Come' (41p)

■ 1995, June 6. Novels of H. G. Wells
Des: Siobhan Keaney. Printed in litho by Questa.

Set	2.25	3.25
Gutter pairs	5.00	–
First day cover	–	2.50
Stamp cards	3.00	6.50

The Swan Theatre, 1595 (25p)
The Rose Theatre, 1592 (25p)
The Globe Theatre, 1599 (25p)
The Hope Theatre, 1613 (25p)
The Globe Theatre, 1614 (25p)

■ 1995, August 8. Reconstruction of Shakespeare's Globe Theatre
Des: C. Hodges. Printed in litho by Walsall.

Set (se-tenant strip of five)	2.25	3.25
Gutter pairs	5.00	–
First day cover	–	2.50
Stamp cards	3.00	6.50

BRITISH STAMP MARKET VALUES 2024 **121**

QUEEN ELIZABETH II DECIMAL

■ 1995, August 22. Castle high-value definitive
Des: as issue of March 24, 1992, but new value, replacing the £1.

£3	8.50	1.75
Gutter pair	20.00	–
Gutter block of four (centre cross)	40.00	–
First day cover	–	5.00
Stamp card	8.00	21.00

(*This stamp exists with either blue tinted PVAD gum or white PVA gum.)

Sir Rowland Hill and Uniform Penny Postage petition (19p)
Sir Rowland Hill and Penny Black (25p)
Guglielmo Marconi and early wireless (41p)
Guglielmo Marconi and the sinking of the 'Titanic' (60p)

■ 1995, September 5. Pioneers of Communications
Des: The Four Hundred; engraved by C. Slania. Printed in recess and litho by Harrison. The 19p has one phosphor band.

Set	2.25	3.25
Gutter pairs	5.00	–
First day cover	–	2.50
Stamp cards	2.50	6.50

Harold Wagstaff (19p)
Gus Risman (25p)
Jim Sullivan (30p)
Billy Batten (35p)
Brian Bevan (41p)

■ 1995, October 3. Centenary of Rugby League
Des: C. Birmingham. The 19p has one phosphor band, other values two phosphor bands.

Set	2.25	3.25
Gutter pairs	6.00	–
First day cover	–	2.50
Stamp cards	2.50	6.50

Robin in letter box (19p)
Robin on railings (25p)
Robin on milk bottles (30p)
Robin on road sign (41p)
Robin on door handle (60p)

■ 1995, October 30. Christmas. Robins
Des: K. Lilly. The 19p has one phosphor band, other values two phosphor bands.

Set	2.50	3.50
Gutter pairs	6.00	–
First day cover	–	2.80
Stamp cards	3.25	6.50

(*The 19p, 25p and 60p were also sold in booklets, and the 19p was used in Smilers sheets in 2000 and 2001.)

'Wee, fleeket, cowran, tim'rous beastie' (19p)
'O, my love's like a red, red rose' (25p)
'Scots, wha hae wi Wallace bled' (41p)
'Should auld acquaintance be forgot' (60p)

■ 1996, January 25. Bicentenary of the Death of Robert Burns
Des: Tayburn Consultancy. Printed in litho by Questa. The 19p has one phosphor band, other values two phosphor bands.

Set	2.25	3.25
Gutter pairs	5.50	–
First day cover	–	2.50
Stamp cards	2.50	6.50

DECIMAL   QUEEN ELIZABETH II

'I'm writing to you because you don't listen to a word I say' (1st)
'More! Love' (1st)
'Sincerely' (1st)
'Do you have something for the human condition?' (1st)
'Mental floss' (1st)
'4:55pm. Don't ring' (1st)
'Dear lottery prize winner' (1st)
'Fetch this, fetch that. Let the cat do it' (1st)
'My day starts before I'm ready for it' (1st)
'The cheque in the post' (1st)

Odeon, Harrogate (19p)
Laurence Olivier and Vivien Leigh in 'Lady Hamilton' (25p)
Cinema ticket (30p)
Pathé News (35p)
Cinema sign, Odeon, Manchester (41p)

■ **1996, February 26. Greetings (issue 8): Cartoons**
Des: M. Wolff. Printed in litho by Walsall. All-over phosphor. Issued se-tenant in booklet panes of ten containing one of each design.

Booklet pane (of 10)	13.00	13.00
Booklet	13.00	–
First day cover	–	9.00
Stamp cards	9.00	16.00

■ **1996, April 16. Centenary of Cinema**
Des: The Chase. The 19p has one phosphor band, other values two phosphor bands.

Set	2.25	3.25
Gutter pairs	5.00	–
First day cover	–	2.75
Stamp cards	4.00	6.50

Muscovy duck (19p)
Lapwing (25p)
White-front goose (30p)
Bittern (35p)
Whooper swan (41p)

Dixie Dean (19p)
Bobby Moore (25p)
Duncan Edwards (30p)
Billy Wright (35p)
Danny Blanchflower (41p)

■ **1996, March 12. 50th Anniversary of the Wildfowl and Wetlands Trust**
Des: Moseley Webb, from paintings by C. F. Tunnicliffe. The 19p has one phosphor band.

Set	2.25	3.25
Gutter pairs	6.00	–
First day cover	–	2.75
Stamp cards	3.00	6.50

■ **1996, May 14. European Football Championship**
Des: H. Brown. Printed in litho by Questa. The 19p has one phosphor band, other values two phosphor bands.

Set	2.75	3.75
Gutter pairs	6.50	–
First day cover	–	3.00
Stamp cards	4.00	6.50

(*All five values also appear in the European Football Championship prestige stamp book issued on May 14, 1996.)

QUEEN ELIZABETH II DECIMAL

Athlete on starting blocks (26p)
Throwing the javelin (26p)
Basketball (26p)
Swimming (26p)
Athlete and Olympic rings (26p)

■ **1996, July 9. Olympic and Paralympic Games, Atlanta, USA**
Des: N. Knight. Printed in litho by Questa.

Set (se-tenant strip of five)	2.25	3.25
Gutter pairs	5.00	–
First day cover	–	2.75
Stamp cards	3.00	6.50

Dorothy Hodgkin, chemist (20p)
Margot Fonteyn, ballerina (26p)
Elisabeth Frink, sculptor (31p)
Daphne du Maurier, author (37p)
Marea Hartman, sports administrator (43p)

■ **1996, August 6. Famous Women (Europa)**
Des: Stephanie Nash. The 20p has one phosphor band, other values two phosphor bands.

Set	2.50	3.50
Gutter pairs	6.50	–
First day cover	–	3.00
Stamp cards	2.50	6.50

Muffin the Mule (20p)
Sooty (26p)
Stingray (31p)
The Clangers (37p)
Dangermouse (43p)

■ **1996, September 3. 50th Anniversary of Children's Television**
Des: Tutssels. Printed in photogravure by Enschedé. The 20p has one phosphor band, other values two phosphor bands.

Set	2.50	3.50
Gutter pairs	6.50	–
First day cover	–	3.00
Stamp cards	3.00	6.50

(*The 20p also appears in the 75th Anniversary of the BBC prestige stamp booklet issued on September 23, 1997, printed in photogravure by Harrison; price £1.00 mint or used.)

Triumph TR3 (20p)
MG TD (26p)
Austin Healey 100 (37p)
Jaguar XK120 (43p)
Morgan Plus 4 (63p)

■ **1996, October 1. Classic Sports Cars**
Des: S. Clay. The 20p has one phosphor band, other values two phosphor bands.

Set	3.00	5.00
Gutter pairs	8.50	–
First day cover	–	3.50
Stamp cards	5.00	6.50

124 BRITISH STAMP MARKET VALUES 2024

DECIMAL QUEEN ELIZABETH II

Three kings (2nd)
Annunciation (1st)
Journey to Bethlehem (31p)
Nativity (43p)
Shepherds (63p)

■ 1996, October 28. Christmas
Des: Laura Stoddart. The 2nd class has one phosphor band, other values two phosphor bands.

Set	4.00	5.00
Gutter pairs	8.50	–
First day cover	–	3.50
Stamp cards	3.50	6.50

(*The 2nd class and 1st class were also sold in booklets.)

■ 1996, November 11. Greetings: Cartoons
As issue of February 26, but with two phosphor bands. Issued se-tenant in booklet panes of ten containing one of each design.

Booklet pane (of 10)	25.00	27.00
Booklet	25.00	–

(*These designs were also used for Smilers sheets in 2001 and 2002.)

Iris latifolia (1st)
Gentiana acaulis (1st)
Magnolia grandiflora (1st)
Camellia japonica (1st)
Tulipa (1st)
Fuchsia 'Princess of Wales' (1st)
Tulipa gesneriana (1st)
Gazania splendens (1st)
Hippeastrum rutilum (1st)
Passiflora coerulea (1st)

■ 1997, January 6. Greetings (issue 9): 19th-Century Flower Paintings
Des: Tutssels. Printed in litho by Walsall. Two phosphor bands. Issued se-tenant in booklet panes of ten containing one of each design.

Booklet pane (of 10)	13.00	13.00
Booklet	13.00	–
First day cover	–	11.00
Stamp cards	12.00	20.00

(*The *Gentiana acaulis*, *Tulipa* and *Iris latifolia* designs also appear in the Glory of the Garden prestige stamp book of 2004, and the *Tulipa* and *Iris latifolia* designs in the 50th Anniversary of NAFAS booklet of May 21, 2009, in self adhesive form. All the designs were also used in a Smilers sheet issued in 2003.)

King Henry VIII (26p)
Catherine of Aragon (26p)
Anne Boleyn (26p)
Jane Seymour (26p)
Anne of Cleves (26p)
Catherine Howard (26p)
Catherine Parr (26p)

■ 1997, February 21. 450th Anniversary of the Death of King Henry VIII
Des: Kate Stephens. Two phosphor bands. The wives designs were issued in a se-tenant strip of six.

Set	3.50	4.75
Gutter pairs	9.00	–
First day cover	–	4.00
Stamp cards	7.50	6.50

St Columba in boat (26p)
St Columba on Iona (37p)
St Augustine with King Ethelbert (43p)
St Augustine with a model of cathedral (63p)

■ 1997, March 11. Religious Anniversaries
Des: Claire Melinsky. Printed in photogravure by Enschedé. Two phosphor bands.

Set	2.75	3.75
Gutter pairs	7.00	–
First day cover	–	3.50
Stamp cards	2.50	6.50

BRITISH STAMP MARKET VALUES 2024

QUEEN ELIZABETH II DECIMAL

Dracula (26p)
Frankenstein (31p)
Dr Jekyll and Mr Hyde (37p)
The Hound of the Baskervilles (43p)

■ **1997, May 13. Horror Stories (Europa)**
Des: J. Pollock. Printed in photogravure by Walsall. Two phosphor bands and features printed in fluorescent ink which are visible only under ultra-violet light.

Set	2.50	3.50
Gutter pairs	6.50	–
First day cover	–	3.00
Stamp cards	2.50	6.50

Supermarine Spitfire MkIIA and Reginald Mitchell (20p)
Avro Lancaster MkI and Roy Chadwick (26p)
De Havilland Mosquito B MkXVI and Ronald Bishop (37p)
Gloster Meteor T Mk7 and George Carter (43p)
Hawker Hunter FGA Mk9 and Sir Sydney Camm (63p)

■ **1997, June 10. British Aircraft Designers**
Des: Turner Duckworth. The 20p has one phosphor band, other values two phosphor bands.

Set	3.25	4.00
Gutter pairs	8.00	–
First day cover	–	3.25
Stamp cards	3.00	6.50

(*The 20p value also appears in the Pilot To Plane: RAF Uniforms prestige stamp book issued on September 18, 2008.)

Carriage horse (20p)
Lifeguards horse (26p)
Blues and Royals drum horse (43p)
Duke of Edinburgh's horse (63p)

■ **1997, July 8. All The Queen's Horses. 50th Anniversary of the British Horse Society**
Des: J.-L. Benard. Printed in litho by Walsall. The 20p has one phosphor band, other values two phosphor bands.

Set	2.50	3.50
Gutter pairs	7.00	–
First day cover	–	3.00
Stamp cards	2.50	6.50

Caernarfon Castle (£1.50)
Edinburgh Castle (£2)
Carrickfergus Castle (£3)
Windsor Castle (£5)

■ **1997, July 29. Castle high-value definitives**
Des: as the issues of March 24, 1992, and August 22, 1995, but re-engraved by Inge Madlé. Printed in recess and silk screen (for Queen's portrait) by Enschedé.

Set	45.00	13.00
Gutter pairs	£100	–
Gutter blocks of four (centre cross)	£250	–
First day cover	–	25.00

Haroldswick, Shetland (20p)
Painswick, Gloucestershire (26p)
Beddgelert, Gwynedd (43p)
Ballyroney, County Down (63p)

BRITISH STAMP MARKET VALUES 2024

DECIMAL QUEEN ELIZABETH II

■ 1997, August 12. Sub Post Offices
Des: T. Millington. Printed in photogravure by Enschedé. The 20p has one phosphor band, other values two phosphor bands.

Set	2.50	3.50
Gutter pairs	7.00	–
First day cover	–	3.00
Stamp cards	2.00	6.50

'Noddy' (20p)
'Famous Five' (26p)
'Secret Seven' (37p)
'Faraway Tree' (43p)
'Malory Towers' (63p)

■ 1997, September 9. Centenary of the Birth of Enid Blyton
Des: C. Birmingham. Printed in photogravure by Enschedé. The 20p has one phosphor band, other values two phosphor bands.

Set	2.75	3.75
Gutter pairs	7.00	–
First day cover	–	3.00
Stamp cards	3.00	6.50

Father Christmas and children pulling a cracker (2nd)
Father Christmas holding a cracker (1st)
Father Christmas riding on a cracker (31p)
Father Christmas riding on a snowball (43p)
Father Christmas on a chimney (63p)

■ 1997, October 27. Christmas. 150th Anniversary of the Christmas Cracker
Des: M. Thomas (1st) and J. Gorham (others). The 2nd class has one phosphor band, other values two phosphor bands.

Set	3.00	3.75
Gutter pairs	7.50	–
First day cover	–	3.25
Stamp cards	3.25	6.50

(*The 2nd class and 1st class also appear in booklets, and the 1st class was used in Smilers sheets in 2000 and 2001.)

Queen Elizabeth II and Prince Philip, wedding photograph of 1947 (20p, 43p)
Queen Elizabeth II and Prince Philip, photographed in 1997 (26p, 63p)

■ 1997, November 13. Royal Golden Wedding
Des: D. Driver (20p, 43p), Lord Snowdon (26p, 63p). The 20p has one phosphor band, other values two phosphor bands.

Set	4.50	5.50
Gutter pairs	10.00	–
First day cover	–	3.25
Stamp cards	2.50	6.50

Common dormouse (20p)
Lady's slipper orchid (26p)
Song thrush (31p)
Shining ram's-horn snail (37p)
Mole cricket (43p)
Devil's bolette (63p)

■ 1998, January 20. Endangered Species
Des: R. Maude. Printed in litho by Questa. The 20p has one phosphor band, other values two phosphor bands.

Set	4.00	4.00
Gutter pairs	10.00	–
First day cover	–	3.75
Stamp cards	3.50	6.50

BRITISH STAMP MARKET VALUES 2024   127

QUEEN ELIZABETH II DECIMAL

Princess Diana wearing necklace, 1997 (26p)
Princess Diana dressed in blue, 1997 (26p)
Princess Diana wearing tiara, 1991 (26p)
Princess Diana dressed in black and white checks, 1995 (26p)
Princess Diana wearing black evening dress, 1986 (26p)

■ **1998, February 3. Diana, Princess of Wales Memorial**
Des: B. Robinson. Two phosphor bands.
Set (se-tenant strip of five)	2.25	3.00
Gutter pairs	6.00	–
First day cover	–	3.50

Lion of England and Griffin of Edward III (26p)
Falcon of Plantagenet and Bull of Clarence (26p)
Lion of Mortimer and Yale of Beaufort (26p)
Greyhound of Richmond and Dragon of Wales (26p)
Unicorn of Scotland and Horse of Hanover (26p)

■ **1998, February 24. The Queen's Beasts. 650th Anniversary of the Order of the Garter**
Des: Jeffery Matthews. Printed in recess and litho by Harrison. Two phosphor bands.
Set (se-tenant strip of five)	2.25	3.25
Gutter pairs	5.00	–
First day cover	–	3.00
Stamp cards	3.00	6.50

Wilding design of 1952–67 (20p, 26p, 37p)

■ **1998, March 10. Wilding definitives**
Des: Dew Gibbons Design Group, from original design by G. Knipe. Printed in gravure by Walsall. Issued only in the Wilding Definitives prestige stamp book.
20p light green (phos band at left)	0.70	0.75
20p light green (phos band at right)	0.70	0.75
26p red-brown	0.75	0.80
37p light purple	1.75	1.85

St John's Point lighthouse, Co. Down (20p)
Smalls lighthouse, Pembrokeshire (26p)
Needles Rock lighthouse, Isle of Wight (37p)
Bell Rock lighthouse, Angus (43p)
Eddystone lighthouse, Cornwall (63p)

■ **1998, March 24. Lighthouses**
Des: D. Davis and J. Boon. Printed in litho by Questa. The 20p has one phosphor band, other values two phosphor bands.
Set	3.25	4.00
Gutter pairs	8.50	–
First day cover	–	3.25
Stamp cards	2.50	6.50

Tommy Cooper (20p)
Eric Morecambe (26p)
Joyce Grenfell (37p)
Les Dawson (43p)
Peter Cook (63p)

■ **1998, April 23. Comedians**
Des: Gerald Scarfe. Printed in litho by Questa. The 20p has one phosphor band, other values two phosphor bands.
Set	3.25	4.00
Gutter pairs	8.00	–
First day cover	–	3.25
Stamp cards	3.00	6.50

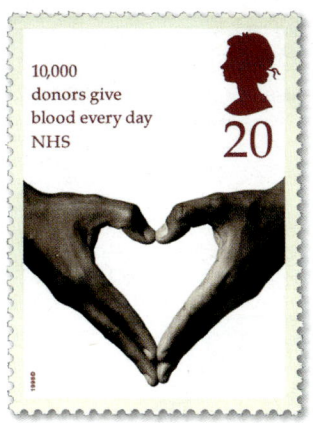

DECIMAL QUEEN ELIZABETH II

Hands forming the shape of a heart (20p)
Adult holding the hand of a child (26p)
Hands forming a cradle (43p)
Hand taking a pulse (63p)

■ 1998, June 23. 50th Anniversary of the National Health Service
Des: V. Frost, using photographs by A. Wilson. Printed in litho by Questa. The 20p has one phosphor band, other values two phosphor bands.

Set	2.25	3.25
Gutter pairs	5.00	–
First day cover	–	3.25
Stamp cards	3.50	6.50

'The Hobbit' by J. R. R. Tolkien (20p)
'The Lion, The Witch and The Wardrobe' by C. S. Lewis (26p)
'The Phoenix and the Carpet' by E. Nesbit (37p)
'The Borrowers' by Mary Norton (43p)
'Through The Looking Glass' by Lewis Carroll (63p)

■ 1998, July 21. Children's Fantasy Novels
Des: P. Malone. Printed in photogravure by De La Rue. The 20p has one phosphor band, other values two phosphor bands.

Set	3.25	4.00
Gutter pairs	7.50	–
First day cover	–	3.25
Stamp cards	5.00	6.50

Woman in costume of yellow feathers (20p)
Woman in blue costume (26p)
Children in white and gold robes (43p)
Child dressed as a tree (63p)

■ 1998, August 25. Notting Hill Carnival (Europa)
Des: T. Hazael. Printed in photogravure by Walsall. The 20p has one phosphor band, other values two phosphor bands.

Set	2.75	3.50
Gutter pairs	7.00	–
First day cover	–	3.25
Stamp cards	2.00	6.50

Bluebird of Sir Malcolm Campbell, 1925 (20p)
Sunbeam of Sir Henry Segrave, 1926 (26p)
Babs of John Parry Thomas, 1926 (30p)
Railton Mobil Special of John Cobb, 1947 (43p)
Bluebird CN7 of Donald Campbell, 1964 (63p)

■ 1998, September 29. British Land Speed Records
Des: Roundel Design Group. Printed in photogravure by De La Rue. The 20p has one phosphor band, other values two phosphor bands.

Set	3.00	3.75
Gutter pairs	7.50	–
First day cover	–	3.25
Stamp cards	2.50	6.50

(*The 20p also appears in the Breaking Barriers prestige stamp book issued on October 13, 1988, but printed in photogravure by Walsall, and with one phosphor band printed on the left or right of the stamp; price £1.00 each mint or used)

BRITISH STAMP MARKET VALUES 2024

QUEEN ELIZABETH II DECIMAL

Angel with hands in blessing (20p)
Angel praying (26p)
Angel playing lute (30p)
Angel playing flute (43p)
Angel praying (63p)

■ **1998, November 2. Christmas. Angels**
Des: Irene von Treskow. Printed in photogravure by De La Rue. The 20p has one phosphor band, other values two phosphor bands.

Set	3.25	4.00
Gutter pairs	9.00	–
First day cover	–	3.25
Stamp cards	2.50	6.50

(*The 20p and 26p values were also sold in booklets.)

During 1999 and 2000 Royal Mail produced a series of special stamp issues to mark the new millennium. Each design includes the inscription 'Millennium', the year of issue and a serial number. The designs for 1999 looked back over the previous millennium under 12 different themes. The designs for 2000 highlighted projects undertaken to celebrate the millennium.

Timekeeping: Greenwich Meridian and clock face (20p)
Steam Power: worker and blast furnace (26p)
Photography: photograph of leaves (43p)
Computers: computer inside head (63p)

■ **1999, January 12. The Inventors' Tale**
Des: David Gentleman (20p), P. Howson (26p), Z. and B. Baran (43p), E. Paolozzi (63p). Printed in photogravure by Enschedé (26p), or De La Rue (20p, 43p, 63p). The 20p has one phosphor band, other values two phosphor bands.

Set	2.50	3.75
Gutter pairs	6.00	–
First day cover	–	4.50
Stamp cards	2.00	6.50

(*The 63p value also appears in the World Changers prestige stamp book issued on September 21, 1999, but printed in photogravure by Questa; price £2.25 mint or used.)

Jet Travel: globe surrounded by aircraft (20p)
Liberation By Bike: woman on bicycle (26p)
Linking The Nation: railway station (43p)
Cook's Endeavour: Captain Cook and Maori (63p)

■ **1999, February 2. The Travellers' Tale**
Des: G. Hardie (20p), S. Fanelli (26p), J. Lawrence (43p), A. Klimowski (63p). Printed in photogravure by Enschedé (20p, 63p) or De La Rue (26p), or litho by Enschedé (43p). The 20p has one phosphor band, other values two phosphor bands.

Set	2.50	3.75
Gutter pairs	6.00	–
First day cover	–	3.75
Stamp cards	2.00	6.50

Jenner's Vaccination: cow with markings of vaccinated child (20p)
Nursing Care: patient on trolley (26p)
Fleming's Penicillin: penicillin mould (43p)
Test Tube Baby: sculpture of baby (63p)

130 BRITISH STAMP MARKET VALUES 2024

DECIMAL **QUEEN ELIZABETH II**

■ **1999, March 2. The Patients' Tale**
Des: P. Brookes (20p), S. Macfarlane (26p), M. Dempsey (43p), A. Gormley (63p. Printed in photogravure by Questa. The 20p has one phosphor band, other values two phosphor bands.

Set	2.50	3.75
Gutter pairs	6.00	–
First day cover	–	3.75
Stamp cards	3.00	6.50

(*The 20p also appears in the World Changers prestige stamp book issued on September 21, 1999.)

Migration To Scotland: Norman settler and dove (20p)
Pilgrim Fathers: settlers and Red Indian (26p)
Destination Australia: sailing ship and aspects of settlement (43p)
Migration To UK: face superimposed on hummingbird (63p)

■ **1999, April 6. The Settlers' Tale**
Des: J. Byrne (20p), W. McLean (26p), J. Fisher (43p), G. Powell (63p). Printed in litho (20p) or photogravure (26p, 43p, 63p) by Walsall. The 20p has one phosphor band, other values two phosphor bands.

Set	2.50	3.75
Gutter pairs	6.00	–
First day cover	–	3.75
Stamp cards	2.00	6.50

(*The 26p also appears in a booklet issued on May 12, 1999.)

Weaver's Craft: woven threads (19p)
Mill Towns: Salts Mill, Saltaire (26p)
Shipbuilding: hull on slipway (44p)
City Finance: Lloyd's Building, London (64p)

■ **1999, May 4. The Workers' Tale**
Des: P. Collingwood (19p), D. Hockney (26p), R. Sanderson (44p), B. Neiland (64p). Printed in litho (19p) or photogravure (26p, 44p, 64p) by De La Rue. The 19p has one phosphor band, other values two phosphor bands.

Set	2.50	3.75
Gutter pairs	6.00	–
First day cover	–	3.75
Stamp cards	3.00	6.50

(*The 26p also appears in a booklet issued on May 12, 1999, printed in photogravure by Walsall; price £1.75 mint or used.)

Mercury's Magic: Freddie Mercury of Queen on stage (19p)
World Cup: Bobby Moore holding the trophy (26p)
Doctor Who: dalek (44p)
Chaplin's Genius: Charlie Chaplin (64p)

■ **1999, June 1. The Entertainers' Tale**
Des: P. Blake (19p), M. White (26p), Lord Snowdon (44p), R. Steadman (64p). Printed in photogravure by Enschedé. The 19p has one phosphor band, other values two phosphor bands.

Set	2.50	3.75
Gutter pairs	6.00	–
First day cover	–	3.75
Stamp cards	4.50	6.50

Prince Edward and Miss Sophie Rhys–Jones facing front (26p)
Prince Edward and Miss Sophie Rhys–Jones facing sideways (64p)

■ **1999, June 15. Royal Wedding**
Des: J. Gibbs, from photographs by John Swannell. Printed in photogravure by De La Rue.

Set	1.50	2.75
Gutter pairs	4.00	–
First day cover	–	2.50
Stamp cards	2.50	3.50

BRITISH STAMP MARKET VALUES 2024   **131**

QUEEN ELIZABETH II DECIMAL

Equal Rights: suffragette behind bars (19p)
Right To Health: tap (26p)
Right To Learn: children at school (44p)
First Rights: Magna Carta (64p)

■ **1999, July 6. The Citizens' Tale**
Des: N. Kerr (19p), M. Craig-Martin (26p), A. Drummond (44p), A. Kitching (64p). Printed in photogravure by De La Rue. The 19p has one phosphor band, other values two phosphor bands.

Set	2.50	3.75
Gutter pairs	6.00	–
First day cover	–	3.75
Stamp cards	2.00	6.50

Decoding DNA: molecular structures (19p)
Darwin's Theory: Galapagos finch and skeleton (26p)
Faraday's Electricity: light polarised by magnetism (44p)
Newton: Saturn, from Hubble Space Telescope (64p)

■ **1999, August 3. The Scientists' Tale**
Des: M. Curtis (19p), R. Harris Ching (26p), C. Gray (44p), photograph (64p). Printed in photogravure (19p, 64p) or litho (26p, 44p) by Questa. The 19p has one phosphor band, other values two phosphor bands.

Set	2.50	3.75
Gutter pairs	6.00	–
First day cover	–	3.75
Stamp cards	2.00	6.50

(*The 26p and 44p also appear in the World Changers prestige stamp book of September 21, 1999; price £3.50 for the pair. The 64p also appears in the miniature sheet of August 11, 1999.)

Saturn, from Hubble Space Telescope (64p)

■ **1999, August 11. Solar Eclipse**
Des: four 64p values from the issue of August 3. Printed in photogravure by De La Rue.

Miniature sheet	12.00	18.00
First day cover	–	12.50

Strip Farming: upland landscape (19p)
Mechanical Farming: horse-drawn seed drill (26p)
Food From Afar: peeling potato (44p)
Satellite Agriculture: combine harvester in field (64p)

■ **1999, September 7. The Farmers' Tale**
Des: D. Tress (19p), C. Wormell (26p), T. Traeger (44p), R. Cooke (64p). Printed in photogravure by De La Rue. The 19p has one phosphor band, other values two phosphor bands.

Set	2.50	3.75
Gutter pairs	6.00	–
First day cover	–	3.75
Stamp cards	2.00	6.50

(*The 26p also appears in a booklet issued on September 21, 1999, printed in gravure by Walsall; price £2.00 mint or used.)

Bannockburn: Robert the Bruce (19p)
Civil War: cavalier and horse (26p)
World Wars: war graves (44p)
Peace-Keeping: soldiers with boy (64p)

■ **1999, October 5. The Soldiers' Tale**
Des: A. Davidson (19p), R. Kelly (26p), D. McCullin (44p), C. Corr (64p). Printed in litho (19p) or photogravure (26p, 44p, 64p) by Walsall. The 19p has one phosphor band, other values two phosphor bands.

Set	2.50	3.75
Gutter pairs	6.00	–
First day cover	–	3.75
Stamp cards	2.00	6.50

DECIMAL QUEEN ELIZABETH II

Wesley: 'Hark the Herald Angels Sing' (19p)
King James Bible: King James I and Authorised Version (26p)
St. Andrews Pilgrimage: St. Andrews Cathedral, Fife (44p)
First Christmas: nativity (64p)

■ 1999, November 2. The Christians' Tale
Des: B. Neuenschwander (19p), C. Melinsky (26p), C. Yass (44p), C. Aitchison (64p). Printed in photogravure by De La Rue. The 19p has one phosphor band, other values two phosphor bands.

Set	2.50	3.75
Gutter pairs	6.00	–
First day cover	–	3.75
Stamp cards	2.00	6.50

(*The 19p and 26p were also sold in booklets.)

World Of The Stage: dancers behind curtain (19p)
World Of Music: coloured stripes (26p)
World Of Literature: untitled book (44p)
New Worlds: rainbow abstract (64p)

■ 1999, December 7. The Artists' Tale
Des: A. Jones (19p), B. Riley (26p), L. Milroy (44p), Sir H. Hodgkin (64p). Printed in photogravure by Walsall. The 19p has one phosphor band, other values two phosphor bands.

Set	2.50	3.75
Gutter pairs	6.00	–
First day cover	–	3.75
Stamp cards	2.00	6.50

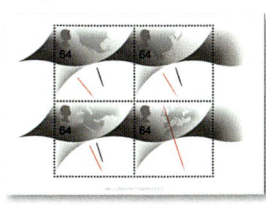

Clock face and globe showing North America (64p)
Clock face and globe showing Asia (64p)
Clock face and globe showing Middle East (64p)
Clock face and globe showing Europe (64p)

■ 1999, December 14. Millennium Timekeeper
Des: David Gentleman. Printed in gravure by De La Rue.

Miniature sheet	12.00	18.00
First day cover		11.00
Stamp cards	11.00	19.00

(*The miniature sheet also exists with the margin overprinted 'Earls Court, London 22–28 May 2000 The Stamp Show 2000', sold at £10 with tickets to the exhibition from March 1, 2000; price £18.00 mint.)

Third Millennium, Muncaster: barn owl (19p)
National Space Centre, Leicester: night sky (26p)
Torrs Walkway, New Mills: River Goyt and textile mills (44p)
Seabird Centre, North Berwick: cape gannets (64p)

■ 2000, January 18. Above and Beyond
Printed in litho (44p) and gravure (19p, 26p, 64p) by Questa. The 19p has one phosphor band, other values two phosphor bands.

Set	3.50	4.50
Gutter pairs	8.50	–
First day cover	–	4.50
Stamp cards	2.00	6.50

(*The 26p design also appears, as a 1st class value, in a booklet issued on May 26, 2000, printed in gravure by Walsall; price £3.00 mint.)

Beacons Across The Land: millennium beacon (19p)
Rheilffordd Eryri, Snowdonia: Garratt locomotive and train (26p)
Dynamic Earth Centre, Edinburgh: lightning (44p)
Lighting Croydon's Skyline: floodlighting (64p)

■ 2000, February 1. Fire and Light
Printed in gravure by De La Rue. The 19p has one phosphor band, other values two phosphor bands.

Set	3.50	4.50
Gutter pairs	8.50	–
First day cover	–	4.50
Stamp cards	2.50	6.50

QUEEN ELIZABETH II DECIMAL

Turning The Tide, Durham: beach pebbles (19p)
National Pondlife Centre, Merseyside: frog's legs and lilies (26p)
Parc Arfordirol, Llanelli: cliff boardwalk (44p)
Portsmouth Harbour: reflections in water (64p)

■ **2000, March 7. Water and Coast**
Printed in litho (44p) or gravure (19p, 26p, 64p) by Walsall. The 19p has one phosphor band, other values two phosphor bands.

Set	3.50	4.50
Gutter pairs	8.50	–
First day cover	–	4.50
Stamp cards	2.50	6.50

ECOS, Ballymena: River Braid reed beds (2nd)
Web Of Life, London Zoo: leaf-cutter ants (1st)
Earth Centre, Doncaster: solar sensors (44p)
Project Suzy, Teesside: hydroponic leaves (64p)

■ **2000, April 4. Life and Earth**
Printed in gravure by De La Rue. The 2nd class has one phosphor band, other values two phosphor bands.

Set	3.50	4.50
Gutter pairs	9.50	–
First day cover	–	4.50
Stamp cards	2.50	6.50

(*The 1st class also appears in a booklet issued on May 26, 2000.)

Ceramica Museum, Stoke-on-Trent: pottery glaze (2nd)
Tate Modern, London: bankside galleries (1st)
Cycle Network: road markings for bicycles (45p)
Lowry Centre, Salford: people in Salford (65p)

■ **2000, May 2. Art and Craft**
Printed in gravure by Enschedé. The 2nd class has one phosphor band, other values two phosphor bands.

Set	3.50	4.50
Gutter pairs	9.50	–
First day cover	–	4.50
Stamp cards	2.50	6.50

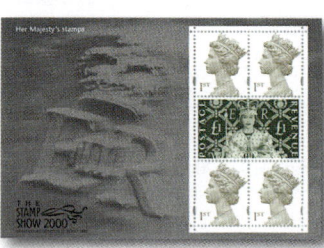

Coronation design of 1953 (£1)
Definitives (1st, 1st. 1st, 1st)

■ **2000, May 23. Her Majesty's Stamps. Stamp Show 2000**
Des: Delaney Design Consultants, the £1 based on the 1953 Coronation 1/3 design by Edmund Dulac. Printed in gravure by De La Rue.

Miniature sheet	10.00	12.50
First day cover	–	10.00
Stamp cards	11.00	35.00

Millennium Greens Project: children playing (2nd)
Millennium Bridge, Gateshead: bridge (1st)
Mile End Park, London: daisies (45p)
On The Meridian Line: African hut and thatched cottage (65p)

■ **2000, June 6. People and Places**
Printed in gravure (2nd, 45p) or litho (1st, 65p) by Walsall. The 2nd class has one phosphor band, other values two bands.

Set	3.50	4.50
Gutter pairs	9.50	–
First day cover	–	4.50
Stamp cards	2.50	6.50

DECIMAL QUEEN ELIZABETH II

Strangford Stone, Killyleagh: raising the stone (2nd)
Trans–Pennine Trail, Derbyshire: horse's hooves (1st)
Kingdom Of Fife Cycle Ways: cyclist and reflection (45p)
Groundwork's Changing Places: bluebell wood (65p)

■ 2000, July 4. Stone and Soil
Printed in gravure in Enschedé. The 2nd class has one phosphor band, other values two phosphor bands.

Set	3.50	4.50
Gutter pairs	9.50	–
First day cover	–	4.50
Stamp cards	2.50	6.50

(*The 1st class also appears in a booklet issued on September 5, 2000, printed in gravure by Walsall; price 75p mint. The 65p design also appears in the Treasury of Trees prestige stamp book issued on September 18, 2000, printed in gravure by Walsall; price £1.50 mint.)

Yews For The Millennium: tree roots (2nd)
Eden Project, St. Austell: sunflower (1st)
Millennium Seed Bank, Ardingly: sycamore seeds (45p)
Forest For Scotland: highland forest (65p)

■ 2000, August 1. Tree and Leaf
Printed in gravure in De La Rue. The 2nd class has one phosphor band, other values two phosphor bands.

Set	3.50	4.50
Gutter pairs	9.50	–
First day cover	–	4.50
Stamp cards	2.50	6.50

(*The 1st class also appears in a booklet issued on September 5, 2000, printed in gravure by Walsall; price 75p mint. The 2nd, 45p and 65p also appear in the Treasury of Trees prestige stamp book issued on September 18, 2000, printed in gravure by Walsall; price £3 each mint.)

Queen Elizabeth II (27p)
Prince William (27p)
The Queen Mother (27p)
Prince Charles (27p)

■ 2000, August 4. 100th Birthday of The Queen Mother
Des: J. Gibbs. Photograph by J. Swannell. Printed in gravure by De La Rue.

Miniature sheet	6.00	8.00
First day cover	–	6.00
Stamp cards	10.00	11.50

(*The Queen Mother design, and the entire miniature sheet but in a slightly larger size, also appear in the Life Of The Century prestige stamp book issued on August 4, 2000, printed in gravure; price £1.50 mint or used.)

Wildscreen At Bristol: head of ant (2nd)
Norfolk & Norwich Project: gathering water lilies on Broads (1st)
Millennium Point, Birmingham: X-ray of hand on mouse (45p)
Scottish Cultural Resources Network: tartan wool holder (65p)

■ 2000, September 5. Mind and Matter
Printed in litho by Walsall. The 2nd class has one phosphor band, other values two phosphor bands.

Set	3.50	4.50
Gutter pairs	9.50	–
First day cover	–	4.50
Stamp cards	2.50	6.50

Body Zone, Millennium Dome: acrobats (2nd)
Hampden Park, Glasgow: footballers (1st)
Bath Spa Project: bather (45p)
Centre For Life, Newcastle: hen's egg under magnification (65p)

■ 2000, October 3. Body and Bone
Printed in litho (2nd) or gravure (1st, 45p, 65p) by Questa. The 2nd class has one phosphor band, other values two phosphor bands.

Set	3.50	4.50
Gutter pairs	9.50	–
First day cover	–	4.50
Stamp cards	2.50	6.50

BRITISH STAMP MARKET VALUES 2024 **135**

QUEEN ELIZABETH II DECIMAL

St. Edmundsbury Cathedral, Suffolk: stained glass window (2nd)
Church Floodlighting: St. Peter and St. Paul, Overstowey (1st)
St. Patrick Centre, Downpatrick: Latin gradual (45p)
Mystery Plays, York Minster: Chapter House ceiling (65p)

■ **2000, November 7. Spirit and Faith**
Printed in gravure by De La Rue. The 2nd class has one phosphor band, other values two phosphor bands.

Set	3.50	4.50
Gutter pairs	9.50	–
First day cover	–	4.50
Stamp cards	2.50	6.50

(*The 2nd class and 1st class also appear in booklets.)

Ringing In The Millennium: church bells (2nd)
Year Of The Artist: eye (1st)
Canolfan Mileniwm, Cardiff: top of a harp (45p)
Talent & Skills 2000: figure in latticework (65p)

■ **2000, December 5. Sound and Vision**
Printed in gravure by De La Rue. The 2nd class has one phosphor band, other values two phosphor bands.

Set	3.50	4.50
Gutter pairs	9.00	–
First day cover	–	4.50
Stamp cards	2.50	6.50

Nurture children: face painting of flower (2nd)
Listen to children: face painting of tiger (1st)
Teach children: face painting of owl (45p)
Ensure children's freedom: face painting of butterfly (65p)

■ **2001, January 16. Hopes for the Future. Rights of the Child**
Des: Why Not Associates. Printed in gravure by De La Rue. The 2nd class has one phosphor band, other values two phosphor bands.

Set	3.50	4.50
Gutter pairs	8.50	–
First day cover	–	3.75
Stamp cards	3.25	6.50

Hallmark: 'Love' (1st)
Hallmark: 'Thanks' (1st)
Hallmark: 'ABC' (1st)
Hallmark: 'Welcome' (1st)
Hallmark: 'Cheers' (1st)

■ **2001, February 6. Occasions (issue 1)**
Des: Springpoint Design. Printed in gravure by Enschedé.

Set	7.00	9.00
Gutter pairs	17.00	–
First day cover	–	5.00
Stamp cards	4.50	7.50

(*These designs were also used for Smilers sheets in 2001.)

Dog in bath (1st)
Dog and man on a bench (1st)
Dog at dog show (1st)
Cat in handbag (1st)
Cat on gate (1st)
Dog in car (1st)
Cat at window (1st)
Dog looking over fence (1st)
Cat watching bird (1st)
Cat in wash basin (1st)

■ **2001, February 13. Cats and Dogs**
Des: Johnson Banks. Printed in gravure by Walsall. Self-adhesive. Issued as a sheetlet which could be folded to form a booklet, containing one of each of the ten designs.

Sheetlet	13.00	15.00
First day cover	–	8.00
Stamp cards	5.00	16.00

(*All these designs, along with two 1st class definitives, also appear in a booklet issued on February 13, 2001.)

DECIMAL QUEEN ELIZABETH II

Quadrant of a barometer: rain (19p)
Quadrant of a barometer: fair (27p)
Quadrant of a barometer: stormy (45p)
Quadrant of a barometer: very dry (65p)

■ **2001, March 13. The Weather**
Des: H. Brown and T. Meeuwissen. Printed in gravure by De La Rue. The 19p has one phosphor band, other values two phosphor bands.

Set	3.50	4.50
Gutter pairs	8.50	–
First day cover	–	3.50
Miniature sheet (one of each value)	11.00	12.00
Miniature sheet first day cover	–	11.00
Stamp cards	4.00	9.00

Vanguard class submarine (2nd)
Swiftsure class submarine (1st)
Unity class submarine (45p)
Holland class submarine (65p)

■ **2001, April 10. Centenary of Royal Navy Submarine Service (issue 1)**
Des: D. Davis. Printed in gravure by Questa. Perf: 15x14. PVA gum. The 2nd class has one phosphor band, other values two phosphor bands.

Set	3.25	4.00
Gutter pairs	7.50	–
First day cover	–	3.50
Stamp cards	4.00	6.50

(*All four stamps also appear in the Unseen And Unheard prestige stamp book issued on October 22, 2001, perf: 15x15; price £10.00 mint or used. The 1st class also appears in self-adhesive form in a booklet issued on April 17, 2001; price £35 mint or used. See also the issue of October 22, 2001.)

Leyland X2, B Type, Leyland Titan TD1, AEC Regent I (1st)
AEC Regent I, Daimler COG5, Guy Arab II, AEC Regent III (1st)
AEC Regent III, Bristol K, AEC Routemaster, Bristol Lodekka FSF (1st)
Bristol Lodekka FSF, Leyland PD3, Leyland Atlantean, Daimler Fleetline (1st)
Daimler Fleetline, MCW Metrobus, Leyland Olympian, Dennis Trident (1st)

■ **2001, May 15. 150th Anniversary of the Double-Decker Bus**
Des: M. English. Printed in gravure by Questa. The illustrations extend into the sheet margins, and across the sheet, so that some of the illustrations span two stamps.

Set (se-tenant strip of five)	4.75	5.50
Gutter pairs	11.50	–
First day cover	–	5.00
Miniature sheet (one of each value)	7.00	7.50
Miniature sheet first day cover	–	8.00
Stamp cards	6.50	16.00

Toque hat by Pip Hackett (1st)
Butterfly hat by Dai Rees (E)
Top hat by Stephen Jones (45p)
Spiral hat by Philip Treacy (65p)

■ **2001, June 19. Fabulous Hats**
Des: Rose Design, from photographs by N. Knight. Printed in litho by Enschedé.

Set	3.50	4.50
Gutter pairs	9.00	–
First day cover	–	3.50
Stamp cards	3.00	6.50

BRITISH STAMP MARKET VALUES 2024 **137**

QUEEN ELIZABETH II DECIMAL

Common frog (1st)
Great diving beetle (E)
Three-spined stickleback (45p)
Southern hawker dragonfly (65p)

■ **2001, July 10. Pond Life (Europa)**
Des: J. Gibbs. Printed in gravure by De La Rue.

Set	3.75	4.50
Gutter pairs	9.00	–
First day cover	–	5.25
Stamp cards	3.00	6.50

Policeman (1st)
Mr Punch (1st)
Clown (1st)
Judy (1st)
Beadle (1st)
Crocodile (1st)

■ **2001, September 4. Punch and Judy**
Des: Keith Bernstein, from puppets made by Bryan Clarke. Printed in gravure by Walsall. PVA gum. Perf: 14x15.

Set (se-tenant strip of six)	8.00	11.00
Gutter pairs	17.50	–
First day cover	–	7.00
Stamp cards	4.75	8.50

(*The Mr Punch and Judy designs also appear in self-adhesive form in a booklet issued on September 4, 2001, printed in gravure by Questa, perf: 14x15½; price £15 mint per pair.)

Prize for Chemistry: carbon molecule (2nd)
Prize for Economic Sciences: globe (1st)
Prize for Peace: dove (E)
Prize for Physiology or Medicine: green cross (40p)
Prize for Literature: 'The Addressing of Cats' by T. S. Eliot (45p)
Prize for Physics: boron atom (65p)

■ **2001, October 2. Centenary of Nobel Prizes**
Des: Pierre Vermeir, with engraving by Inge Madle (1st). Printed in litho by Enschedé with additional silk screen and thermochromic ink (2nd), recess (1st), embossing (E), scented beads (40p), micro-printing (45p) and hologram (65p). The 2nd class has one phosphor band, other values a phosphor frame.

Set	8.50	10.00
Gutter pairs	22.00	–
First day cover	–	6.50
Stamp cards	10.00	8.50

White Ensign (1st)
Union Flag (1st)
Jolly Roger from HMS Proteus (1st)
Flag of Chief of Defence Staff (1st)

■ **2001, October 22. Centenary of Royal Navy Submarine Service (issue 2). Flags and Ensigns**
Des: D. Davis. Printed in gravure by Questa. PVA gum.

Miniature sheet	6.00	8.50
First day cover	–	5.50
Stamp cards	7.00	14.00

(*The White Ensign and Jolly Roger designs also appear in self-adhesive form in a booklet issued on October 22, 2001; price £16 mint or used per pair. The Union Jack and White Ensign designs were used in Smilers sheets from 2005, and also appear in the Ian Fleming's James Bond prestige stamp book issued on January 8, 2008. See also the issue of April 10, 2001.)

DECIMAL — QUEEN ELIZABETH II

Robins with snowman (2nd)
Robins on bird table (1st)
Robins skating on bird bath (E)
Robins with Christmas pudding hanging from tree (45p)
Robins in nest made of paper chains (65p)

■ 2001, November 6. Christmas. Robins
Des: A. Robins and H. Brown. Printed in gravure by De La Rue. Self-adhesive.

Set	4.50	5.50
First day cover	–	4.50
Stamp cards	3.50	7.50

(*The 2nd class and 1st class values also appear in booklets, and were used for Smilers sheets in 2003 and 2005.)

'The Elephant's Child' (1st)
'How the Whale got his Throat' (1st)
'How the Camel got his Hump' (1st)
'How the Rhinoceros got his Skin' (1st)
'How the Leopard got his Spots' (1st)
'The Sing Song of Old Man Kangaroo' (1st)
'The Beginning of the Armadillos' (1st)
'The Crab that Played with the Sea' (1st)
'The Cat that Walked by Himself' (1st)
'The Butterfly that Stamped' (1st)

■ 2002, January 15. Centenary of the Just So Stories by Rudyard Kipling
Des: I. Cohen. Printed in gravure by Walsall. Self-adhesive. Issued as a sheetlet which could be folded to form a booklet, containing one of each of the ten designs.

Sheetlet	14.00	16.00
First day cover	–	10.00
Stamp cards	5.00	20.00

Queen Elizabeth II in 1952, by Dorothy Wilding (2nd)
Queen Elizabeth II in 1968, by Cecil Beaton (1st)
Queen Elizabeth II in 1978, by Lord Snowdon (E)
Queen Elizabeth II in 1984, by Yousef Karsh (45p)
Queen Elizabeth II in 1996, by Tim Graham (65p)

■ 2002, February 6. Golden Jubilee
Des: Kate Stephens. Printed in gravure by De La Rue. Wmk: 50 (sideways). The 2nd class has one phosphor band, other values two phosphor bands.

Set	7.00	9.00
Gutter pairs	17.00	–
First day cover	–	5.00
Stamp cards	2.50	7.00

(*All the stamps also appear in the Gracious Accession prestige book, but with the Wmk upright; price £11 mint, £11 used.)

Wilding design of 1952–67 (2nd)
Wilding design of 1952–67 (1st)

■ 2002, February 6. Wilding definitives
Des: M. Farrar-Bell (2nd), Enid Marx (1st). Printed in gravure by Enschedé. Wmk: 50. The 2nd class has one phosphor band, the 1st class two phosphor bands. Issued only in the £7.29 Gracious Accession prestige stamp book. One pane had a tilted stamp, resulting in a diagonal watermark.

2nd carmine-red	1.50	1.50
2nd carmine-red (Wmk diagonal)	2.50	2.50
1st green	1.25	1.25

Love (1st)
Rabbits, inscribed 'a new baby' (1st)
'Hello' written in sky (1st)
Bear pulling topiary tree in shape of house (1st)
Flowers inscribed 'best wishes' (1st)

■ 2002, March 5. Occasions (issue 2)
Des: I. Bilbey (Rabbits and Flowers), A. Kitching (Love), Hoop Associates (Hello), G. Percy (Bear). Printed in litho by Questa.

Set	7.00	9.00
Gutter pairs	12.00	–
First day cover	–	5.75
Stamp cards	3.25	7.00

(*The Hello design also appears, in self-adhesive form, in a booklet issued on March 4, 2003; price £3.50 mint or used. All designs were also used in Smilers sheets.)

BRITISH STAMP MARKET VALUES 2024   139

QUEEN ELIZABETH II DECIMAL

Studland Bay, Dorset (27p)
Luskentyre, South Harris (27p)
Cliffs of Dover, Kent (27p)
Padstow Harbour, Cornwall (27p)
Broadstairs, Kent (27p)
St Abb's Head, Berwickshire (27p)
Dunster Beach, Somerset (27p)
Newquay Beach, Cornwall (27p)
Portrush, County Antrim (27p)
Sand spit, Conwy, (27p)

■ **2002, March 19. British Coastlines**
Des: R. Cooke. Printed in litho by Walsall.
Set (se-tenant block of ten)	4.50	5.50
Gutter pairs	13.00	–
First day cover	–	5.00
Stamp cards	4.50	13.50

Slack wire act (2nd)
Lion tamer (1st)
Trick tricyclists (E)
Krazy kar (45p)
Equestrienne (65p)

■ **2002, April 10. Circus (Europa)**
Des: R. Fuller. Printed in gravure by Questa. The 2nd class has one phosphor band, other values two phosphor bands.
Set	4.50	5.50
Gutter pairs	11.00	–
First day cover	–	4.75
Stamp cards	3.25	7.50

Queen Mother: 20p design from the 1990 issue (1st)
Queen Mother: 29p design from the 1990 issue (E)
Queen Mother: 34p design from the 1990 issue (45p)
Queen Mother: 37p design from the 1990 issue (65p)

■ **2002, April 25. Queen Mother Memorial**
Des: J. Gorham, as the issue of August 2, 1990, but with frames and Queen's head in black. Printed in gravure by De La Rue.
Set	6.00	8.00
Gutter pairs	15.00	–
First day cover	–	4.25

Airbus A340-600, 2002 (2nd)
Concorde, 1976 (1st)
Trident, 1964 (E)
VC10, 1964 (45p)
Comet, 1952 (65p)

■ **2002, May 2. Airliners**
Des: Roundel. Printed in gravure by De La Rue. The 2nd class has one phosphor band, other values two phosphor bands.
Set	6.00	7.00
Gutter pairs	15.00	–
First day cover	–	4.25
Miniature sheet (one of each value)	8.00	8.50
Miniature sheet first day cover	–	8.00
Stamp cards	3.50	14.00

(*The 1st class design also appears in self-adhesive form in a booklet issued on May 2, 2002, printed in gravure; price £3.50 mint or used. It also appears in the British Design Classics prestige stamp book issued on January 13, 2009.)

Lion with shield of St. George (1st)
Top left quarter of English flag with football (1st)
Top right quarter of English flag with football (1st)
Bottom left quarter of English flag with football (1st)
Bottom right quarter of English flag with football (1st)

140 BRITISH STAMP MARKET VALUES 2024

DECIMAL QUEEN ELIZABETH II

■ 2002, May 21. Football World Cup, Japan and Korea

Des: Sedley Place (lion), H. Brown (flag). Printed in gravure by Walsall. The St. George design was issued in counter sheets, and all five designs in a miniature sheet.

1st (St. George design)	1.50	1.50
Gutter pair (St. George design)	4.00	–
First day cover	–	2.75
Miniature sheet	5.50	6.50
Miniature sheet first day cover	–	6.00
Stamp cards (set of six)	3.50	11.00

(*The 1st class designs showing the top left and top right of the flag also appear in self-adhesive form in a booklet issued on May 21, 2002; price £5.50 per pair. The 1st class design showing the bottom right of the flag was used in Smilers sheets.)

Swimming (2nd)
Running (1st)
Cycling (E)
Long jump (47p)
Wheelchair racing (68p)

■ 2002, July 16. 17th Commonwealth Games, Manchester

Des: Madeleine Bennett. Printed in gravure by Enschedé. The 2nd class has one phosphor band, other values two phosphor bands.

Set	7.00	9.00
Gutter pairs	17.00	–
First day cover	–	4.50
Stamp cards	3.00	10.00

Tinkerbell (2nd)
Wendy, John and Michael Darling flying past Big Ben (1st)
Crocodile and the alarm clock (E)
Captain Hook (47p)
Peter Pan (68p)

■ 2002, August 20. Peter Pan

Des: Tutsells. Printed in gravure by De La Rue. The 2nd class has one phosphor band, other values two phosphor bands.

Set	5.00	6.50
Gutter pairs	12.00	–
First day cover	–	6.00
Stamp cards	4.00	8.00

Millennium Bridge, 2001 (2nd)
Tower Bridge, 1894 (1st)
Westminster Bridge, 1864 (E)
Blackfriars Bridge, 1800 (47p)
London Bridge, 1670 (68p)

■ 2002, September 10. Bridges of London

Des: Sarah Davies and Robert Maude. Printed in litho by Questa. The 2nd class has one phosphor band, other values two phosphor bands.

Set	6.50	7.50
Gutter pairs	15.00	–
First day cover	–	5.50
Stamp cards	3.50	10.00

(*The 1st class design also appears in self-adhesive form in a booklet issued on September 10, 2002, printed in gravure by Questa; price £3.50 mint or used.)

Planetary nebula in Aquila (1st)
Seyfert 2 galaxy in Pegasus (1st)
Planetary nebula in Norma (1st)
Seyfert 2 galaxy in Circinus (1st)

■ 2002, September 24. Astronomy

Des: Rose. Printed in gravure by Questa.

Miniature sheet	5.50	7.00
First day cover	–	5.50
Stamp cards	3.50	10.00

(*The miniature sheet also appears, in a larger format, in the Across The Universe prestige stamp book issued on September 21, 2002.)

QUEEN ELIZABETH II DECIMAL

Green pillar box, 1857 (2nd)
Horizontal-aperture pillar box, 1874 (1st)
Blue air mail box, 1934 (E)
Double-aperture pillar box, 1939 (47p)
Modern pillar box, 1980 (68p)

■ **2002, October 8. 150th Anniversary of the First Pillar Box**
Des: Silk Pearce; engraved by C. Slania. Printed in recess and litho by Enschedé. The 2nd class has one phosphor band, other values two phosphor bands.

Set	7.00	9.00
Gutter pairs	17.00	–
First day cover	–	5.50
Stamp cards	3.50	7.50

Blue spruce (2nd)
Holly (1st)
Ivy (E)
Mistletoe (47p)
Pine cone (68p)

■ **2002, November 5. Christmas**
Des: Rose. Printed in gravure by De La Rue. Self-adhesive. The 2nd class has one phosphor band, other values two phosphor bands.

Set	5.50	6.00
First day cover	–	5.00
Stamp cards	3.50	7.50

(*The 2nd class and 1st class stamps also appear in booklets.)

Wilding designs of 1952–67 (1p, 2p, 5p, 2nd, 1st, 33p, 37p, 47p, 50p)

■ **2002, December 5. 50th Anniversary of the Wilding Definitives (1st issue)**
Des: Rose (based on the original designs of 1952). Printed in gravure by De La Rue. Wmk: 50. The 2nd class has one phosphor band, other values two phosphor bands.

Miniature sheet	5.50	5.50
First day cover	–	5.00
Stamp cards	5.00	15.50

(*The 47p value also appears in the Perfect Coronation prestige stamp book issued on June 2, 2003.)

Barn owl in flight, five different views (1st, 1st, 1st, 1st, 1st)
Kestrel in flight, five different views (1st, 1st, 1st, 1st, 1st)

■ **2003, January 14. Birds of Prey**
Des: J. Gibbs, from photographs by S. Dalton. Printed in litho by Walsall.

Set (se-tenant block of ten)	13.00	15.00
Gutter pairs	30.00	–
First day cover	–	9.50
Stamp cards	5.50	15.00

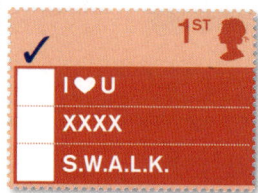

Gold star, See me, Playtime (1st)
I 'love' U, XXXX, S.W.A.L.K. (1st)
Angel, Poppet, Little terror (1st)
Yes, No, Maybe (1st)
Oops! Sorry, Will try harder (1st)
I did it! You did it! We did it! (1st)

142 BRITISH STAMP MARKET VALUES 2024

DECIMAL   QUEEN ELIZABETH II

■ **2003, February 4. Occasions (issue 3)**
Des: UNA, S. Wiegand and M. Exon. Printed in litho by Questa.

Set (se-tenant block of six)	8.00	10.00
Gutter pairs	21.00	–
First day cover	–	6.00
Stamp cards	3.50	9.00

(*All these designs were used in Smilers sheets.)

End of the beginning: the genetic jigsaw (2nd)
Comparative genetics: ape with scientist (1st)
Cracking the code: DNA snakes and ladders (E)
Genetic engineering: animals cross-bred with scientists (47p)
Medical futures: looking into a DNA crystal ball (68p)

■ **2003, February 25. 50th Anniversary of the Discovery of the Structure of DNA. The Secret of Life**
Des: William Murray Hamm and P. Brookes. Printed in litho by Enschedé. The 2nd class has one phosphor band, other values two phosphor bands.

Set	5.25	6.50
Gutter pairs	14.00	–
First day cover	–	5.00
Stamp cards	3.00	8.50

(*The 2nd class and E designs also appear in the Microcosmos prestige stamp book issued on February 25, 2003.)

Red pepper (1st)
Strawberry (1st)
Potato (1st)
Apple (1st)
Pear (1st)
Orange (1st)
Tomato (1st)
Lemon (1st)
Brussels sprout (1st)
Aubergine (1st)

■ **2003, March 25. Fun Fruit and Veg**
Des: Johnson Banks. Printed in gravure by Walsall. Issued as a self-adhesive sheetlet containing one each of the ten designs.

Sheetlet	13.00	15.00
First day cover	–	9.50
Stamp cards	7.50	22.00

(*This sheetlet came with a pane of self-adhesive stickers, such as of eyes, ears and mouths, so that the fruit and vegetables could be customised to resemble faces. These designs were also used in Smilers sheets.)

Amy Johnson with biplane (2nd)
The 1953 Everest team in the Himalayas (1st)
Freya Stark in the Arabian desert (E)
Ernest Shackleton in the Antarctic (42p)
Francis Chichester with 'Gipsy Moth IV' (47p)
Robert Falcon Scott at the South Pole (68p)

■ **2003, April 29. Extreme Endeavours**
Des: H. Brown. Printed in gravure by Questa. The 2nd class has one phosphor band, other values two phosphor bands. Perf: 15x14½.

Set	6.00	7.00
Gutter pairs	15.00	–
First day cover	–	6.00
Stamp cards	3.00	10.00

(*The 1st class design also appears, in self adhesive form, in a booklet issued on April 29, 2003, printed in gravure by De La Rue, Perf: 14½; price £3.50 mint, £3.50 used.)

Wilding designs of 1952–67 (4p, 8p, 10p, 20p, 28p, 34p, E, 42p, 68p)

■ **2003, May 20. 50th Anniversary of the Wilding Definitives (2nd issue)**
Des: Rose (based on the original designs of 1952). Printed in gravure by De La Rue. Wmk: 50. The 20p has one phosphor band, other values two phosphor bands.

Miniature sheet	5.00	5.50
First day cover	–	6.50

(*The 68p value also appears in the Perfect Coronation prestige stamp book issued on June 2, 2003.)

BRITISH STAMP MARKET VALUES 2024   143

QUEEN ELIZABETH II DECIMAL

Coronation procession (1st)
Children reading poster (1st)
Queen seated in the Coronation Chair (1st)
Children producing royal montage (1st)
Queen in Coronation robes, by Cecil Beaton (1st)
Children racing during street party (1st)
Gold State Coach passing through Admiralty Arch (1st)
Children in fancy dress (1st)
Gold State Coach outside Buckingham Palace (1st)
Children at street party (1st)

■ **2003, June 2. 50th Anniversary of the Coronation**
Des: Kate Stephens. Printed in gravure by De La Rue.
Set (se-tenant block of ten)	13.00	15.00
Gutter pairs	28.00	–
First day cover	–	9.00
Stamp cards	6.00	19.00

(*Eight of these designs also appear in the Perfect Coronation prestige stamp book issued on June 2, 2003.)

Photograph of Prince William by Brendan Beirne (28p)
Photograph of Prince William by Tim Graham (E)
Photograph of Prince William by Camera Press (47p)
Photograph of Prince William by Tim Graham (68p)

■ **2003, June 17. 21st Birthday of Prince William**
Des: Madeleine Bennett. Printed in gravure by Walsall.
Set	6.50	7.50
Gutter pairs	15.00	–
First day cover	–	5.00
Stamp cards	4.00	19.00

Loch Assynt, Sutherland (2nd)
Ben More, Isle of Mull (1st)
Rothiemurchus, Cairngorms (E)
Dalveen Pass, Lowther Hills (42p)
Glenfinnan Viaduct, Lochaber (47p)
Papa Little, Shetland Islands (68p)

■ **2003, July 15. A British Journey: Scotland**
Des: Phelan Barker. Printed in gravure by De La Rue. The 2nd class has one phosphor band, other values two phosphor bands.
Set	5.50	7.00
Gutter pairs	14.00	–
First day cover	–	6.00
Stamp cards	3.00	9.50

(*The 1st class design also appears, in self adhesive form, in a booklet issued on July 15, 2003; price £3.50 mint or used.)

The Station (1st)
Black Swan (E)
The Cross Keys (42p)
The Mayflower (47p)
The Barley Sheaf (68p)

■ **2003, August 12. Pub Signs (Europa)**
Des: Elmwood. Printed in gravure by De La Rue.
Set	5.25	7.50
Gutter pairs	12.50	–
First day cover	–	5.25
Stamp cards	3.00	7.50

(*The 1st class design also appears in the Letters By Night prestige stamp book issued on March 16, 2004.)

DECIMAL QUEEN ELIZABETH II

Meccano constructor biplane, 1931 (1st)
Wells-Brimtoy clockwork double-decker bus, 1938 (E)
Hornby M1 clockwork locomotive, 1948 (42p)
Dinky Toys Ford Zephyr, 1956 (47p)
Mettoy friction-drive Eagle space ship, 1960 (68p)

■ 2003, September 18. Classic Transport Toys
Des: Trickett and Webb. Printed in gravure by Enschedé.

Set	5.25	6.00
Gutter pairs	12.00	–
First day cover	–	5.25
Miniature sheet (one of each value)	4.50	6.00
Miniature sheet first day cover	–	7.50
Stamp cards	3.50	13.50

(*The 1st class design also appears, in self-adhesive form, in a booklet issued on September 18, 2003, printed in gravure by De La Rue; price £3.25 mint or used.)

Coffin of Denytenamun, Egypt, c.900 BC (2nd)
Sculpture of Alexander the Great, Greece, c.200 BC (1st)
Anglo-Saxon helmet, Sutton Hoo, c.600 AD (E)
Sculpture of Parvati, India, c.1550 AD (42p)
Aztec mask of Xiuhtecuhtli, Mexico, c.1500 AD (47p)
Statue of Hoa Hakananai'a, Easter Island, c.1000 AD (68p)

■ 2003, October 7. 250th Anniversary of the British Museum
Des: Rose. Printed in gravure by Walsall. The 2nd class has one centre phosphor band, the 42p and 68p one phosphor band at right, other values two phosphor bands.

Set	5.50	7.50
Gutter pairs	14.00	–
First day cover	–	5.75
Stamp cards	3.25	9.50

Ice spiral (2nd)
Icicle star (1st)
Wall of ice blocks (E)
Ice ball (53p)
Ice hole (68p)
Snow pyramids (£1.12)

■ 2003, November 4. Christmas. Ice Sculptures
Des: D. Davis, from ice sculptures by Andy Goldsworthy. Printed in gravure by De La Rue. Self-adhesive. The 2nd class has one phosphor band, other values two phosphor bands.

Set	6.50	8.00
First day cover	–	8.00
Stamp cards	8.00	12.00

(*The 1st class and 2nd class designs also appear in booklets, and were used in Smilers sheets.)

England fans and England flag (1st)
England team huddled in a circle before the final (1st)
Rugby World Cup held aloft (68p)
England team members from the back after the final (68p)

■ 2003, December 19. England's Victory in the Rugby World Cup
Des: Why Not Associates. Printed in litho by Walsall.

Miniature sheet	10.00	11.00
First day cover	–	10.00

BRITISH STAMP MARKET VALUES 2024

QUEEN ELIZABETH II DECIMAL

'Dolgoch' on the Talyllyn Railway (20p)
CR 439 on the Bo'ness and Kinneil Railway (28p)
GCR 8K on the Great Central Railway (E)
GWR Manor on the Severn Valley Railway (42p)
SR West Country on the Bluebell Railway (47p)
BR Standard on the Keighley and Worth Valley Railway (68p)

■ **2004, January 13. Classic Locomotives**
Des: Roundel. Printed in litho by De La Rue. The 2nd class has one phosphor band, other values two phosphor bands.

Set	5.50	7.50
Gutter pairs	14.00	–
First day cover	–	6.00
Miniature sheet (one of each value)	15.00	17.50
Miniature sheet first day cover		15.00
Stamp cards	6.50	25.00

(*The 28p, E and 42p designs also appear in the Letters by Night prestige stamp book issued on March 16, 2004.)

Postman (1st)
Face (1st)
Duck (1st)
Baby (1st)
Aircraft (1st)

■ **2004, February 3. Occasions (issue 4)**
Des: S. Kambayashi. Printed in litho by De La Rue.

Set (se-tenant strip of five)	7.00	9.00
Gutter pairs	17.50	–
First day cover	–	7.00
Stamp cards	3.00	7.50

(*These designs were used in Smilers sheets.)

Middle Earth (1st)
Forest of Lothlórien (1st)
The Fellowship of the Ring (1st)
Rivendell (1st)
The Hall at Bag End (1st)
Orthanc (1st)
Doors of Durin (1st)
Barad-dûr (1st)
Minas Tirith (1st)
Fangorn Forest (1st)

■ **2004, February 26. The Lord of The Rings by J. R. R. Tolkien**
Des: HGV Design. Printed in litho by Walsall.

Set (se-tenant block of ten)	14.00	16.00
Gutter pairs	30.00	–
First day cover	–	10.00
Stamp cards	6.50	15.00

Ely Island, Lower Lough Erne (2nd)
Giant's Causeway, Antrim (1st)
Slemish, Antrim (E)
Banns Road, Mourne Mountains (42p)
Glenelly Valley, Sperrins (47p)
Islandmore, Strangford Lough (68p)

■ **2004, March 16. A British Journey: Northern Ireland**
Des: Phelan Barker. Printed in gravure by Enschedé. The 2nd class has one phosphor band, other values two phosphor bands.

Set	6.00	8.00
Gutter pairs	15.00	–
First day cover	–	5.00
Stamp cards	3.50	9.50

(*The 28p design also appears, in self-adhesive form, in a booklet issued on March 16, 2004; price £3.50 mint or used.)

'Lace 1 (trial proof) 1968' by Sir Terry Frost (28p)
'Coccinelle' by Sonia Delaunay (57p)

146 BRITISH STAMP MARKET VALUES 2024

DECIMAL — QUEEN ELIZABETH II

■ 2004, April 6. Centenary of the Entente Cordiale
Des: Rose. Printed in gravure by Walsall.

Set	2.00	3.00
Gutter pairs	4.50	–
Traffic light gutter pairs	11.00	–
First day cover	–	2.50
Stamp cards	6.00	10.00

(*This was a joint issue with La Poste of France.)

RMS 'Queen Mary 2', 2004 (1st)
SS 'Canberra', 1961 (E)
RMS 'Queen Mary', 1936 (42p)
RMS 'Mauretania', 1907 (47p)
SS 'City of New York', 1888 (57p)
PS 'Great Western', 1838 (68p)

■ 2004, April 13. Ocean Liners
Des: J. Gibbs. Printed in gravure by De La Rue.

Set	6.00	8.00
Gutter pairs	15.00	–
First day cover	–	6.00
Miniature sheet (one of each value)	8.00	9.50
Miniature sheet first day cover	–	7.50
Stamp cards	4.00	16.50

(*The 1st class also appears, in self-adhesive form, in a booklet issued on April 13, 2004; price £3.50 mint or used.)

Dianthus Allwoodii group (2nd)
Dahlia 'Garden Princess' (1st)
Clematis 'Arabella' (E)
Miltonia 'French Lake' (42p)
Lilium 'Lemon Pride' (47p)
Delphinium 'Clifford Sky' (68p)

■ 2004, May 25. Bicentenary of the Royal Horticultural Society
Des: Rose. Printed in gravure by Enschedé. The 2nd class has one phosphor band, other values two phosphor bands.

Set	5.50	7.00
Gutter pairs	14.00	–
First day cover	–	6.00
Miniature sheet (one of each value)	7.00	8.50
Miniature sheet first day cover	–	7.50
Stamp cards	4.00	16.50

(*All values also appear in the Glory of the Garden prestige book issued on May 25, 2004, and the 1st class in Smilers sheets.)

Barmouth Bridge (2nd)
Hyddgen, Plynlimon (1st)
Brecon Beacons (40p)
Pen-pych, Rhondda Valley (43p)
Rhewl, Dee Valley (47p)
Marloes Sands, Pembrokeshire (68p)

■ 2004, June 15. A British Journey: Wales (Europa)
Des: Phelan Barker. Printed in gravure by De La Rue. The 2nd class has one phosphor band, other values two phosphor bands.

Set	4.50	5.50
Gutter pairs	12.00	–
First day cover	–	5.00
Stamp cards	3.50	9.50

(*The 1st class design also appears, in self-adhesive form, in a booklet of June 15, 2004; price £4.50 mint or used.)

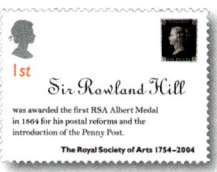

Penny Black and citation to Sir Rowland Hill (1st)
William Shipley, founder of the RSA (40p)
R, S and A as typewriter keys and shorthand notation (43p)
George Smart's brush for sweeping chimneys (47p)
Eric Gill's typeface (57p)
'Zero Waste' manifesto (68p)

■ 2004, August 10. 250th Anniversary of the Royal Society of Arts
Des: D. Birdsall. Printed in litho by Walsall.

Set	5.50	7.50
Gutter pairs	14.00	–
First day cover	–	6.00
Stamp cards	3.00	9.50

QUEEN ELIZABETH II DECIMAL

Pine marten (1st)
Roe deer (1st)
Badger (1st)
Yellow-necked mouse (1st)
Wild cat (1st)
Red squirrel (1st)
Stoat (1st)
Natterer's bat (1st)
Mole (1st)
Fox (1st)

■ **2004, September 16. Woodland Animals**
Des: Kate Stephens. Printed in gravure by Enschedé.

Set (se-tenant block of ten)	14.00	16.00
Gutter pairs	30.00	–
Traffic light gutter blocks	70.00	–
First day cover	–	9.00
Stamp cards	5.50	15.00

Scotland definitives (40p, 1st, 2nd, 1st, 40p)

■ **2004, October 5. Opening of the Scottish Parliament Building, Edinburgh**
Des: H. Brown. Printed in gravure by De La Rue.

Miniature sheet	4.50	4.50
First day cover	–	4.50

Private McNamara, 5th Dragoon Guards (2nd)
Piper Muir, 42nd Regiment of Foot (1st)
Sergeant Major Edwards, Scots Fusilier Guards (40p)
Sergeant Powell, 1st Regiment of Foot Guards (57p)
Sergeant Major Poole, Royal Sappers and Miners (68p)
Sergeant Glasgow, Royal Artillery (£1.12)

■ **2004, October 12. The Crimean War**
Des: Atelier Works, from period photographs. Printed in litho by Walsall. The 2nd class has one phosphor band, other values two phosphor bands.

Set	6.50	7.50
Gutter pairs	16.00	–
Traffic light gutter pairs	40.00	–
First day cover	–	5.50
Stamp cards	3.50	9.50

Father Christmas on roof (2nd)
Father Christmas welcoming the sunrise (1st)
Father Christmas battling against the wind (40p)
Father Christmas holding an umbrella (57p)
Father Christmas holding a torch (68p)
Father Christmas sheltering behind a chimney (£1.12)

■ **2004, November 2. Christmas**
Des: R. Briggs. Printed in gravure by De La Rue. Counter stamps self-adhesive, miniature sheet gummed. The 2nd class has one phosphor band, other values two phosphor bands.

Set	5.50	7.00
First day cover	–	6.00
Miniature sheet (one of each value)	7.00	8.00
Miniature sheet first day cover	–	7.00
Stamp cards	5.50	15.00

(*The 1st class and 2nd class designs also appear in booklets, and were used in Smilers sheets.)

DECIMAL QUEEN ELIZABETH II

Emden geese (1st)
British saddleback pigs (1st)
Khaki Campbell ducks (1st)
Clydeside mare and foal (1st)
Dairy shorthorn cattle (1st)
Border collie dog (1st)
Light Sussex chickens (1st)
Suffolk sheep (1st)
Bagot goat (1st)
Norfolk black turkeys (1st)

■ 2005, January 11. Farm Animals
Des: Rose, from illustrations by C. Wormell. Printed in gravure by Enschedé.

Set (se-tenant block of ten)	14.00	16.00
Gutter pairs	30.00	–
Traffic light gutter blocks	70.00	–
First day cover	–	8.00
Stamp cards	5.00	15.50

Old Harry Rocks, Studland Bay, Dorset (2nd)
Wheal Coates, St Agnes, Cornwall (1st)
Start Point, Start Bay, Devon (40p)
Horton Down, Wiltshire (43p)
Chiselcombe, Exmoor, Devon (57p)
St James's Stone, Lundy Island (68p)

■ 2005, February 8. A British Journey: South-West England
Des: J. Phelan and L. Barker. Printed in gravure by De La Rue. The 2nd class has one phosphor band, other values two phosphor bands.

Set	5.25	6.50
Gutter pairs	12.50	–
First day cover	–	5.50
Stamp cards	3.75	9.50

Scene from 'Jane Eyre': Mr. Rochester (2nd)
Scene from 'Jane Eyre': come to me (1st)
Scene from 'Jane Eyre': in the comfort of her bonnet (40p)
Scene from 'Jane Eyre': La Ligne des Rats (57p)
Scene from 'Jane Eyre': refectory (68p)
Scene from 'Jane Eyre': inspection (£1.12)

■ 2005, February 24. 150th Anniversary of the Death of Charlotte Brontë
Des: P. Willberg, from illustrations by Paula Rego. Printed in litho by Walsall. The 2nd class has one phosphor band, other values two phosphor bands.

Set	6.50	8.00
Gutter pairs	16.00	–
Traffic light gutter blocks	50.00	–
First day cover	–	6.25
Miniature sheet (one of each value)	6.50	8.00
Miniature sheet first day cover	–	6.00
Stamp cards	4.00	15.00

(*All designs also appear in the Brontë Sisters prestige stamp book issued on February 24, 2005.)

Spinning coin trick (1st)
Rabbit and top hat trick (40p)
Knotted scarf trick (47p)
Card trick (68p)
Pyramids under fezzes trick (£1.12)

■ 2005, March 15. Centenary of the Magic Circle
Des: Tathem Design, from illustrations by G. Hardie. Printed in gravure by Walsall. Rubbing the 1st class stamp with a coin reveals either the head or tail of a coin; parts of the 47p and £1.12 designs fade temporarily when exposed to heat.

Set	5.75	7.00
Gutter pairs	15.00	–
First day cover	–	5.50
Stamp cards	3.00	7.50

(*The 1st class design was used in Smilers sheets.)

Carrickfergus Castle (50p)
Caernarvon Castle (£1)
Edinburgh Castle (£1)
Windsor Castle (50p)

■ 2005, March 22. 50th Anniversary of the Castles Definitives
Des: Sedley Place, based on designs of 1955-58 by Lynton Lamb but with new values. Printed by intaglio and litho by Enschedé.

Miniature sheet	4.75	6.50
First day cover	–	6.00
Stamp cards	7.00	15.00

(*The 50p design also appears in the First UK Aerial Post prestige stamp book issued on September 9, 2011.)

QUEEN ELIZABETH II DECIMAL

Prince Charles and Camilla at the Highland Games (30p, 30p)
Prince Charles and Camilla at Birkhall (68p, 68p)

■ 2005, April 8. The Wedding of Prince Charles and Camilla Parker Bowles
Des: Rose, from photographs by Christopher Furlong (30p) and Carolyn Robb (68p). Printed in litho by Enschedé.

Miniature sheet	4.75	6.50
First day cover	–	5.50

(*Whilst the miniature sheet and first day handstamps are dated April 8, the wedding took place on April 9.)

Hadrian's Wall, England (2nd)
Uluru Kata Tjuta National Park, Australia (2nd)
Stonehenge, England (1st)
Wet Tropics of Queensland, Australia (1st)
Blenheim Palace, England (47p)
Greater Blue Mountains, Australia (47p)
Heart of Neolithic Orkney, Scotland (68p)
Pumululu National Park, Australia (68p)

■ 2005, April 21. World Heritage Sites
Des: Jason Godfrey from photographs by Peter Marlow. Litho printed by Enschedé. The 2nd class has one phosphor band, other values two phosphor bands.

Set (four se-tenant pairs)	6.50	9.00
Gutter pairs	16.00	–
Traffic light gutter blocks	35.00	–
First day cover	–	8.00
Stamp cards	4.00	12.50

(*This was a joint issue with Australia Post.)

Ensign of the Scots Guards (2nd)
The Queen taking the salute, 1983 (1st)
Trumpeter of the Household Cavalry (42p)
Welsh Guardsmann (60p)
The Queen on horseback, 1972 (68p)
The Queen and Duke of Edinburgh in carriage, 2004 (£1.12)

■ 2005, June 7. Trooping the Colour
Des: Why Not Associates. Printed in litho by Walsall. The 2nd class has one phosphor band, other values two phosphor bands.

Set	5.50	7.00
Gutter pairs	14.00	–
First day cover	–	6.50
Miniature sheet (one of each value)	5.50	7.50
Miniature sheet first day cover	–	6.00
Stamp cards	3.50	17.50

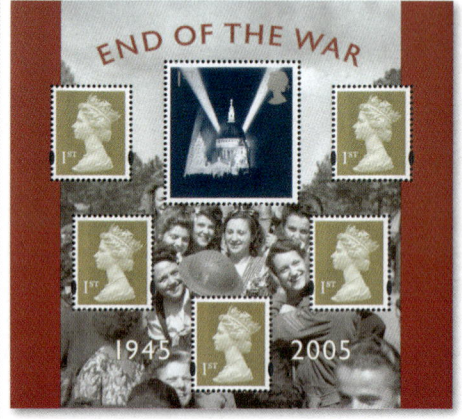

Searchlights in a 'V' over St. Paul's Cathedral (1st)
Definitives (1st, 1st, 1st, 1st, 1st)

DECIMAL QUEEN ELIZABETH II

■ **2005, July 5. 60th Anniversary of the End of World War II**
Des: Jeffery Matthews, using the St. Paul's stamp designed by J. Gorham and originally issued on May 2, 1995. Printed in gravure by Enschedé.

Miniature sheet	8.50	10.00
First day cover	–	6.00

Norton F1, 1991 (1st)
BSA Rocket 3, 1969 (40p)
Vincent Black Shadow, 1949 (42p)
Triumph Speed Twin, 1938 (47p)
Brough Superior, 1930 (60p)
Royal Enfield, 1914 (68p)

■ **2005, July 19. Motorcycles**
Des: Atelier Works, with illustrations by Michael English. Printed in litho by Walsall.

Set	5.00	6.50
Gutter pairs	12.50	–
First day cover	–	6.00
Stamp cards	3.50	9.50

Woman eating rice (2nd)
Woman drinking tea (1st)
Boy eating sushi (42p)
Woman eating pasta (47p)
Woman eating chips (60p)
Boy eating apple (68p)

■ **2005, August 23. Changing Tastes in Britain (Europa)**
Des: Rose, with illustrations by Catell Ronca. Printed in gravure by Enschedé. The 2nd class has one phosphor band, other values two phosphor bands.

Set	5.00	6.50
Gutter pairs	12.50	–
First day cover	–	5.50
Stamp cards	3.00	9.50

'Inspector Morse' (2nd)
'Emmerdale' (1st)
'Rising Damp' (42p)
'The Avengers' (47p)
'The South Bank Show' (60p)
'Who Wants To Be A Millionaire?' (68p)

■ **2005, September 15. Classic ITV Programmes**
Des: Kate Stephens. Printed in litho by De La Rue. The 2nd class has one phosphor band, other values two phosphor bands.

Set	4.50	6.50
Gutter pairs	11.00	–
First day cover	–	5.50
Stamp cards	3.75	9.00

(*The 1st class design was used in Smilers sheets.)

Athletes (1st, 1st, 1st, 1st, 1st, 1st)

■ **2005, August 12. London 2012**
Des: one of each of the five designs issued on July 9, 1996, plus a second of one design, but with Olympic rings omitted and new values. Printed in litho by Walsall.

Miniature sheet	7.50	10.00
First day cover	–	6.00

QUEEN ELIZABETH II DECIMAL

Gazania splendens (1st)
Hello (1st)
Love (1st)
Union flag (1st)
Teddy bear (1st)
Robin looking through pillar box slit (1st)

■ **2005, October 4. Smilers (issue 1)**
Printed by litho by Walsall. Self-adhesive. Issued in booklets containing one of each of the six designs.
Set	10.00	11.00
Booklet (without PiP information)	10.00	–
Booklet (with PiP information)	9.00	–
First day cover	–	9.50

(*These designs were also used in Smilers sheets. For the same designs with elliptical perforations, see the issues of January 16, 2007, and February 28, 2008.)

England team celebrating with Ashes trophy (1st)
Kevin Pietersen, Michael Vaughan and Andrew Flintoff (1st)
Michael Vaughan batting (68p)
Action from Second Test at Edgbaston (68p)

■ **2005, October 6. The Ashes**
Des: Why Not Associates. Printed in litho by Cartor.
Miniature sheet	4.50	5.50
First day cover	–	5.50

HMS 'Entreprenante' and HMS 'Belle Isle' (1st)
Nelson wounded on HMS 'Victory' (1st)
HMS 'Entreprenante' and burning French ship 'Achille' (42p)
HMS 'Pickle' and cutter (42p)
British fleet attacking in two columns (68p)
Franco-Spanish fleet putting to sea from Cadiz (68p)

■ **2005, October 18. Bicentenary of the Battle of Trafalgar**
Des: Dick Davis from a painting by William Heath. Printed in litho by Walsall. Issued in se-tenant pairs.

Set (three se-tenant pairs)	5.25	7.50
Gutter pairs	14.00	–
First day cover	–	6.00
Stamp cards	3.50	25.00
Miniature sheet (one of each value)	5.50	7.00
Miniature sheet first day cover	–	6.50

(*All values also appear in the Battle of Trafalgar prestige stamp book issued on October 18, 2005.)

Madonna and Child painting, Haitian (2nd)
Madonna and Child painting, European (1st)
Madonna and Child painting, European (42p)
Madonna and Child painting, North American Indian (60p)
Madonna and Child painting, Indian (68p)
Madonna and Child painting, Australian Aboriginal (£1.12)

■ **2005, November 1. Christmas**
Des: Irene von Treskow. Printed in gravure by De La Rue. Counter stamps self-adhesive, miniature sheet gummed. The 2nd class has one phosphor band, other values two phosphor bands.
Set	6.00	7.50
First day cover	–	6.50
Miniature sheet (one of each value)	6.00	7.50
Miniature sheet first day cover	–	6.50
Stamp cards	5.00	18.50

(*The 2nd class and 1st class stamps also appear in booklets.)

'The Tale of Mr Jeremy Fisher' by Beatrix Potter (2nd)
'Kipper' by Mick Inkpen (2nd)
'The Enormous Crocodile' by Roald Dahl (1st)
'More About Paddington' by Michael Bond (1st)
'Comic Adventures of Boots' by Satoshi Kitamura (42p)
'Alice's Adventures in Wonderland' by Lewis Carroll (42p)
'The Very Hungry Caterpillar' by Eric Carle (68p)
'Maisy's ABC' by Lucy Cousins (68p)

■ **2006. January 10. Animal Tales**
Des: Rose. Printed in litho by De La Rue. Issued in se-tenant pairs.
Set (four se-tenant pairs)	6.50	9.50
Gutter pairs	15.00	–
Traffic light gutter blocks	55.00	–
First day cover	–	8.00
Stamp cards	5.00	12.50

(*This was a joint issue with the United States Postal Service.)

QUEEN ELIZABETH II DECIMAL

Carding Mill Valley, Shropshire (1st)
Beachy Head, Sussex (1st)
St. Paul's Cathedral, London (1st)
Brancaster, Norfolk (1st)
Derwent Edge, Peak District (1st)
Robin Hood's Bay, Yorkshire (1st)
Buttermere, Lake District (1st)
Chipping Campden, Cotswolds (1st)
St Boniface Down, Isle of Wight (1st)
Chamberlain Square, Birmingham (1st)

■ 2006, February 7. A British Journey: England
Des: Phelan Parker Design Consultants. Printed in gravure by De La Rue.

Set (se-tenant block of 10)	14.00	15.00
Gutter pairs	30.00	–
First day cover	–	10.00
Stamp cards	5.50	15.00

Royal Albert Bridge (1st)
Box Tunnel (40p)
Paddington Station (42p)
PSS 'Great Britain' (47p)
Clifton Suspension Bridge (60p)
Maidenhead Bridge (68p)

■ 2006, February 23. Bicentenary of the Birth of Isambard Kingdom Brunel
Des: Hat-Trick Design. Printed in litho by Enschedé.

Set	5.00	6.50
Gutter pairs	12.50	–
First day cover	–	6.00
Miniature sheet (one of each value)	5.50	7.00
Miniature sheet first day cover	–	6.00
Stamp cards	5.00	25.00

(*All values also appear in a prestige stamp book.)

Wales definitives (68p, 1st, 2nd, 1st, 68p)

■ 2006, March 1. Opening of the Welsh Assembly Building, Cardiff
Des: Silk Pearce. Printed in gravure by De La Rue.

Miniature sheet	5.00	5.00
First day cover	–	5.50

Sabre-tooth cat (1st)
Giant deer (42p)
Woolly rhino (47p)
Woolly mammoth (68p)
Cave bear (£1.12)

■ 2006, March 21. Ice Age Animals
Des: Howard Brown from illustrations by Andrew Davidson. Printed in litho by Enschedé.

Set	5.25	7.00
Gutter pairs	14.00	–
First day cover	–	6.00
Stamp cards	4.00	8.50

The Queen in 1972 (2nd)
The Queen in 1985 (2nd)
The Queen in 1931 with Duchess of York (1st)
The Queen in 2001 (1st)
The Queen in 1951 (44p)
The Queen in 1960 (44p)
The Queen in 1940 (72p)
The Queen in 1951 with Duke of Edinburgh (72p)

■ 2006, April 18. The Queen's 80th Birthday
Des: Sedley Place. Printed in gravure by Enschedé.

Set	6.50	8.00
Gutter pairs	17.00	–
First day cover	–	6.50
Stamp cards	5.00	16.00

QUEEN ELIZABETH II DECIMAL

T. S. Eliot by Patrick Heron (1st)
Sir Winston Churchill by Walter Sickert (1st)
Sir Joshua Reynolds, self-portrait (1st)
Emmeline Pankhurst by Georgina Brackenbury (1st)
Virginia Woolf by George Beresford (1st)
Sir Walter Scott by Sir Francis Chantry (1st)
Mary Seacole by Albert Challen (1st)
William Shakespeare by John Taylor (1st)
Dame Cicely Saunders by Catherine Goodman (1st)
Charles Darwin by John Collier (1st)

■ 2006, July 18. 150th Anniversary of the National Portrait Gallery
Des: Peter Willberg. Printed in gravure by De La Rue.

Set (se-tenant block of 10)	14.00	15.00
Gutter pairs	30.00	–
Traffic light gutter blocks	55.00	–
First day cover	–	9.50
Stamp cards	8.00	18.00

England (1st)
Italy (42p)
Argentina (44p)
Germany (50p)
France (64p)
Brazil (72p)

■ 2006, June 6. World Cup Winners
Des: Getty Images. Printed in litho by Walsall.

Set	6.00	7.50
Gutter pairs	14.00	–
First day cover	–	6.00
Stamp cards	4.00	11.00

Definitive (£3)

■ 2006, August 31. The Year of the Three Kings
Des: Together Design. Printed in gravure by De La Rue.

Miniature sheet	5.75	7.50
First day cover	–	6.00

(*The border illustrates 1d stamps of George V, Edward VIII and George VI, but these are not valid for postage.)

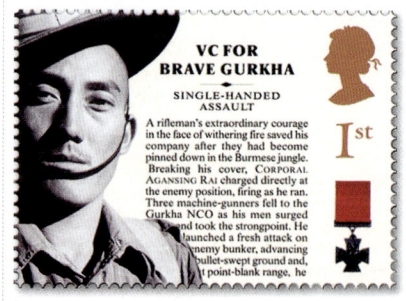

30 St Mary Axe, London (1st)
Maggie's Centre, Dundee (42p)
Selfridges, Birmingham (44p)
Downland Gridshell, Chichester (50p)
An Turas, Isle of Tiree (64p)
The Deep, Hull (72p)

■ 2006, June 20. Modern Architecture
Des: Roundel. Printed in gravure by Walsall.

Set	5.25	7.00
Gutter pairs	13.00	–
First day cover	–	6.25
Stamp cards	3.50	10.00

Corporal Agansing Rai (1st)
Boy Seaman First Class Jack Cornwell (1st)
Midshipman Charles Lucas (64p)
Captain Noel Chavasse (64p)
Captain Albert Ball (72p)
Captain Charles Upham (72p)

DECIMAL QUEEN ELIZABETH II

■ **2006, September 21. Victoria Cross**
Des: Atelier Works. Printed in litho by Enschedé.
Set	6.50	8.00
Gutter pairs	15.00	–
First day cover	–	7.00
Miniature sheet (one of each value, plus the Victoria Cross 20p of September 1990)	7.00	8.50
Miniature sheet first day cover	–	7.00
Press sheet	75.00	–
Stamp cards	4.00	20.00

Asian sitar and dancer (1st)
Caribbean base guitar and drum (42p)
Irish fiddle and harp (50p)
Black American saxophone and blues guitar (72p)
Latin American maracas and salsa dancers (£1.19)

■ **2006, October 3. Sounds of Britain (Europa)**
Des: CDT. Printed in litho by Cartor
Set	5.75	7.50
Gutter pairs	14.00	–
Traffic light gutter blocks	40.00	–
First day cover	–	6.50
Stamp cards	4.00	8.00

New baby (1st)
Best wishes (1st)
Thank you (1st)
Balloons (1st)
Firework (1st)
Champagne, flowers and butterflies (1st)

■ **2006, October 17. Smilers (issue 2)**
Des: NB Studio. Printed by litho by Walsall. Self-adhesive. Issued in booklets containing one of each of the six designs.
Set	7.50	10.00
Booklet	8.00	–
First day cover	–	7.00
Stamp cards	7.00	21.00

(*These designs were used in Smilers sheets. For the same designs with elliptical perforations, see the issue of February 28, 2008.)

Snowman (2nd, 2nd Large)
Father Christmas sitting on chimney (1st, 1st Large)
Reindeer (72p)
Christmas tree (£1.19)

■ **2006, November 7. Christmas**
Des: CDT. Printed in litho by De La Rue. Counter sheets self-adhesive, miniature sheet gummed. The 2nd class has one phosphor band, other values two phosphor bands.
Set	10.00	12.00
First day cover	–	7.50
Miniature sheet (one of each value)	7.00	8.50
Miniature sheet first day cover	–	7.50
Stamp cards	6.00	18.00

(*The 2nd class and 1st class designs also appear in booklets.)

Poppies on barbed wire (1st)
Country definitives (72p, 72p, 72p, 72p)

■ **2006, November 9. Lest We Forget (issue 1)**
Des: Hat-Trick Design. Printed in gravure by De La Rue.
Miniature sheet	6.00	7.50
First day cover	–	6.50

(*The 1st class design was used in Smilers sheets.)

Scotland definitive (1st)
Scottish flag (1st)
St Andrew (72p)
Edinburgh Castle (72p)

■ **2006, November 30. Celebrating Scotland**
Des: P. Crowther and C. Melinsky, Silk Pearce. Printed in gravure by De La Rue.
Miniature sheet	4.50	4.50
First day cover	–	5.00
Stamp cards	4.00	15.00

(*The 1st class Scottish Flag design also appears in the Football Heroes prestige stamp book of 2013 and the Classic Locomotives of the UK prestige stamp book of 2014.)

QUEEN ELIZABETH II DECIMAL

Album cover: 'With The Beatles' (1st)
Album cover: 'Sgt Pepper's Lonely Hearts Club Band' (1st)
Album cover: 'Help!' (64p)
Album cover: 'Abbey Road' (64p)
Album cover: 'Revolver' (72p)
Album cover: 'Let It Be' (72p)

■ 2007, January 9. The Beatles
Des: Johnson Banks, from album sleeve covers. Printed in gravure by Walsall. Self-adhesive, in freeform shape. Available in horizontal pairs.

Set	6.50	6.50
First day cover	–	7.00
Stamp cards (set & miniature sheet)	6.00	22.00

Guitar and badge (1st)
'Yellow Submarine' lunch box and key rings (1st)
'Love Me Do' vinyl record (1st)
Tea tray and badges (1st)

■ 2007, January 9. The Beatles
Des: Johnson Banks. Printed in litho by Walsall.

Miniature sheet	4.50	4.50
First day cover	–	7.00

■ 2007, January 16. Smilers (issue 3)
Printed in litho by Walsall. Self-adhesive. Design as the 'Love' 1st class stamp of October 4, 2005, but with elliptical perforations along vertical sides. Issued in booklets of six, along with five 1st class definitives.

1st	6.00	6.00
Booklet	35.00	–

(*This design also appears in a booklet issued on January 15, 2008, and in Smilers sheets.)

Moon jellyfish (1st)
Common starfish (1st)
Beadlet anemone (1st)
Bass (1st)
Thornback ray (1st)
Lesser octopus (1st)
Common mussels (1st)
Grey seal (1st)
Shore crab (1st)
Common sun star (1st)

■ 2007, February 1. Sea Life
Des: A. Ross. Printed in litho by Cartor.

Set (se-tenant block of ten)	14.00	14.00
Gutter pairs	30.00	–
First day cover	–	10.00
Stamp cards	5.00	16.00

Saturn nebula C55 (1st)
Eskimo nebula C39 (1st)
Cat's Eye nebula C6 (50p)
Helix nebula C63 (50p)
Flaming Star nebula C31 (72p)
The Spindle galaxy C53 (72p)

■ 2007, February 13. The Sky at Night
Des: D. Davis. Printed in gravure by Walsall. Self-adhesive. Available in horizontal pairs. Stamps have description of designs on the backing paper.

Set	6.50	6.50
First day cover	–	6.50
Stamp cards	4.50	13.00

DECIMAL   QUEEN ELIZABETH II

Bridge building: iron bridge in Thomas Telford's imagination (1st)
Railways: locomotive billowing track as steam (1st)
Communications: Britain and Australia close on map (64p)
Television: reporter on camera and viewer with screen (64p)
E-mail and internet: world wide web as globe (72p)
Space tourism: couple carrying suitcases on the Moon (72p)

■ 2007, March 1. World of Invention
Des: P. Willberg. Printed in gravure by De La Rue. Counter stamps self-adhesive, with description of designs on the backing paper. Miniature sheet gummed.

Set	6.50	6.50
Gutter pairs	16.00	–
First day cover	–	6.50
Miniature sheet (one of each value)	12.50	12.50
Miniature sheet first day cover	–	6.50
Stamp cards	4.25	22.00

(*All designs also appear, in gummed form, in the World of Invention prestige stamp book issued on March 1, 2007.)

William Wilberforce and abolitionist poster (1st)
Olaudah Equiano and map of slave trade routes (1st)
Granville Sharp and slave ship (50p)
Thomas Clarkson and diagram of slave ship (50p)
Hannah More and title page of 'The Sorrows of Yamba' (72p)
Ignatius Sancho and business card (72p)

■ 2007, March 22. Bicentenary of the Abolition of the Slave Trade
Des: Howard Brown. Printed in litho by Cartor. Issued in se-tenant pairs.

Set	5.50	5.50
Gutter pairs	14.00	–
Traffic light gutter blocks	45.00	–
First day cover	–	6.00
Stamp cards	4.00	13.00

England definitive (1st)
English flag (1st)
St. George (78p)
Houses of Parliament (78p)

■ 2007, April 23. Celebrating England
Des: P. Crowther and C. Melinsky, Silk Pearce. Printed in gravure by De La Rue.

Miniature sheet	4.50	4.50
First day cover	–	5.00
Stamp cards	3.25	14.00

(*The 1st class English Flag design also appears in the Football Heroes prestige stamp book of 2013 and the Classic Locomotives of the UK prestige stamp book of 2014.)

Ice cream cone (1st)
Sand castle (46p)
Merry-go-round (48p)
Beach huts (54p)
Deckchairs (69p)
Donkeys (78p)

■ 2007, May 15. Beside the Seaside
Des: Phelan Barker Design Consultants. Printed in gravure by De La Rue.

Set	5.50	5.50
Gutter pairs	14.00	–
First day cover	–	6.00
Stamp cards	4.00	11.00

(* The 1st class design also appears, in self-adhesive form, in a booklet issued on May 13, 2008: price £2.50 mint.)

Lion with shield of St. George (1st)
England definitives (2nd, 2nd, 78p, 78p)

■ 2007, May 17. Opening of the New Wembley Stadium, London
Des: Roundel. Printed in gravure by De La Rue.

Miniature sheet	6.50	8.50
First day cover	–	5.50

(*The 1st class design was previously issued on May 21, 2002, with an inscription, and was used in Smilers sheets.)

QUEEN ELIZABETH II DECIMAL

Arnold Machin (1st)
4d Machin olive sepia-brown (1st)
Definitive (£1 bluish-violet)
Definitive (£1 ruby)

■ **2007, June 5. 40th Anniversary of the Machin Definitives**
Des: J. Matthews and Together Design. Printed in gravure by De La Rue.

Miniature sheet	5.00	5.50
Press sheet	75.00	–
First day cover	–	5.50
Stamp cards	3.50	16.00

(* The two 1st class designs also appear in The Making of a Masterpiece prestige stamp book. The Arnold Machin design was also used in a generic Smilers sheet.)

Stirling Moss and Vanwall 2.5L, 1957 (1st)
Graham Hill and BRM P57, 1962 (1st)
Jim Clark and Lotus-Climax 25, 1963 (54p)
Jackie Stewart and Tyrrell-Cosworth 006, 1973 (54p)
James Hunt and McLaren-Cosworth M23, 1976 (78p)
Nigel Mansell and Williams-Honda FW11, 1986 (78p)

■ **2007, July 3. Grand Prix**
Des: True North, from photographs by James Callaghan. Printed in litho by Cartor.

Set	5.75	5.75
Gutter pairs	15.00	–
First day cover	–	6.50
Stamp cards	4.50	11.00

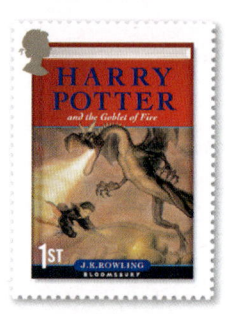

'Harry Potter and the Philosopher's Stone' (1st)
'Harry Potter and the Chamber of Secrets' (1st)
'Harry Potter and the Prisoner of Azkaban' (1st)
'Harry Potter and the Goblet of Fire' (1st)
'Harry Potter and the Order of the Phoenix' (1st)
'Harry Potter and the Half-Blood Prince' (1st)
'Harry Potter and the Deathly Hallows' (1st)

■ **2007, July 17. Harry Potter**
Des: True North, from book covers. Printed in litho by Walsall.

Set	10.00	10.00
Gutter pairs	22.00	–
Traffic light gutter pairs	35.00	–
First day cover	–	6.50
Stamp cards	15.00	42.00

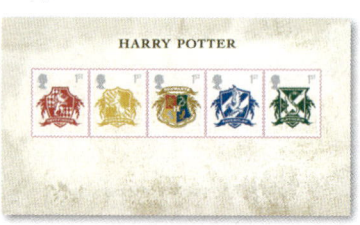

Symbol of Gryffindor house (1st)
Symbol of Hufflepuff house (1st)
Crest of Hogwarts School (1st)
Symbol of Ravenclaw house (1st)
Symbol of Slytherin house (1st)

■ **2007, July 17. Harry Potter**
Des: True North. Printed in litho by Walsall.

Miniature sheet	6.50	6.50
First day cover	–	6.00

(*These designs were also used in a generic Smilers sheet.)

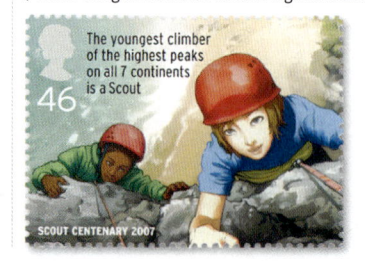

158 BRITISH STAMP MARKET VALUES 2024

DECIMAL QUEEN ELIZABETH II

Scout looking at the Moon (1st)
Scouts conquering a mountain (46p)
Scout planting a tree (48p)
Scout learning archery (54p)
Scout piloting a glider (69p)
Scouts from many nations (78p)

■ 2007, July 26. Centenary of Scouting (Europa)
Des: The Workroom. Printed in litho by Enschedé.

Set	5.75	6.00
Gutter pairs	14.00	–
First day cover	–	6.50
Stamp cards	4.00	11.00

White-tailed eagle (1st)
Bearded tit (1st)
Red kite (1st)
Cirl bunting (1st)
Marsh harrier (1st)
Avocet (1st)
Bittern (1st)
Dartford warbler (1st)
Corncrake (1st)
Peregrine (1st)

■ 2007, September 4. Endangered Species. Birds
Des: Kate Stephens. Printed in litho by De La Rue. Issued in a se-tenant block.

Set (se-tenant block of ten)	14.00	14.00
Gutter pairs	23.00	–
First day cover	–	9.50
Stamp cards	5.00	16.00

NCO, British Military Police, 1999 (1st)
Tank Commander, 5th Royal Tank Regiment, 1944 (1st)
Observer, Royal Field Artillery, 1917 (1st)
Rifleman, 95th Rifles, 1813 (78p)

Grenadier, Royal Regiment of Foot of Ireland, 1704 (78p)
Trooper, Earl of Oxford's Horse, 1661 (78p)

■ 2007, September 20. British Army Uniforms
Des: Atelier Works, from paintings by Graham Turner. Printed in litho by Enschedé. Issued in se-tenant strips of three.

Set (two se-tenant strips of three)	6.50	6.50
Gutter pairs	14.00	–
Traffic light gutter pairs	32.00	–
First day cover	–	7.50
Stamp cards	3.75	11.00

(*All six stamps also appear in the British Army Uniforms prestige stamp book. The 1st class Observer stamp also appears in the Great War 1915 prestige stamp book issued on May 14, 2015.)

The Queen and Prince Philip, 2006 (1st)
The Queen and Prince Philip, 1997 (1st)
The Queen and Prince Philip, 1980 (54p)
The Queen and Prince Philip, 1969 (54p)
The Queen and Prince Philip, 1961 (78p)
The Queen and Prince Philip, 1947 (78p)

■ 2007, October 16. Royal Diamond Wedding Anniversary
Des: Pentagram. Printed in gravure by Walsall. Issued in se-tenant pairs.

Set (three se-tenant pairs)	8.00	10.00
Gutter pairs	20.00	–
First day cover	–	8.00
Stamp cards	6.00	28.00

The royal family at Balmoral, 1972 (1st)
Queen Elizabeth and Prince Philip at Buckingham Palace, 2007 (1st)
The royal family at Windsor Castle, 1965 (69p)
The royal family at Clarence House, 1951 (78p)

■ 2007, October 16. Royal Diamond Wedding Anniversary
Des: Pentagram. Printed in gravure by Walsall. Self-adhesive. The reverse of the sheet shows photographs of the royal couple leading up to their marriage.

Miniature sheet	5.00	5.00
Press sheet	60.00	–
First day cover	–	6.00

QUEEN ELIZABETH II DECIMAL

Peace: angel playing trumpet (2nd, 2nd Large)
Goodwill: angel playing lute (1st, 1st Large)
Joy: angel playing flute (78p)
Glory: angel playing tambourine (£1.24)

■ **2007, November 6. Christmas. Angels**
Des: Rose, with illustrations by Marco Ventura. Printed in gravure by De La Rue. Counter stamps self-adhesive, miniature sheet gummed.

Set	7.50	7.50
First day cover	–	9.50
Miniature sheet (one of each value)	7.00	7.00
Miniature sheet first day cover	–	7.50
Stamp cards	5.00	17.50

(*The 2nd class and 1st class designs also appear in booklets, and the 2nd, 1st and 78p were used in Smilers sheets.)

'Madonna & Child' by William Dyce (2nd)
'The Madonna of Humility' by Lippo di Dalmasio (1st)

■ **2007, November 6. Christmas. Madonna and Child**
Des: Peter Willberg, from paintings. Printed in gravure by De La Rue. Self-adhesive.

Set	2.25	2.25
Gutter pairs	6.00	–
First day cover	–	3.50

(*These stamps were re-issued at Christmas in 2008–2012.)

Soldiers in poppy (1st)
Country definitives (78p, 78p, 78p, 78p)

■ **2007, November 8. Lest We Forget (issue 2)**
Des: Hat-Trick Design. Printed in gravure by De La Rue.

Miniature sheet	6.50	6.50
First day cover	–	7.00

(*The 1st class design was also used in a Smilers generic sheet.)

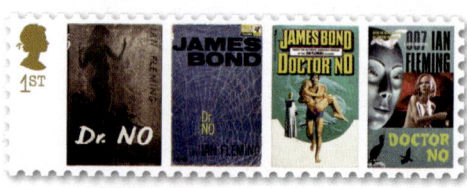

Book covers of 'Casino Royale' (1st)
Book covers of 'Dr No' (1st)
Book covers of 'Goldfinger' (54p)
Book covers of 'Diamonds Are Forever' (54p)
Book covers of 'For Your Eyes Only' (78p)
Book covers of 'From Russia With Love' (78p)

■ **2008, January 8. Centenary of the Birth of Ian Fleming. James Bond Books**
Des: A2. Printed in litho by De La Rue.

Set	6.00	7.50
Gutter pairs	15.00	–
First day cover	–	7.00
Miniature sheet	10.00	12.00
Miniature sheet first day cover	–	8.00
Press sheet	75.00	
Stamp cards (set and miniature sheet)	6.00	25.00

(*All values also appear in the Ian Fleming's James Bond prestige stamp book, issued on January 8, 2008.)

Assistance dog with letter (1st)
Mountain rescue dog (46p)
Police dog (48p)
Customs dog (54p)
Sheepdog (69p)
Guide dog (78p)

■ **2008, February 5. Working Dogs**
Des: Redpath Design. Printed in litho by Cartor.

Set	5.75	7.50
Gutter pairs	14.00	–
First day cover	–	6.50
Stamp cards	5.00	14.00

DECIMAL QUEEN ELIZABETH II

King Henry IV, 1399–1413 (1st)
King Henry V, 1413–22 (1st)
King Henry VI, 1422–61 and 1470–71 (54p)
King Edward IV, 1461–70 and 1471–83 (54p)
King Edward V, 1483 (69p)
King Richard III, 1483–85 (69p)

■ **2008, February 28. Kings and Queens. Houses of Lancaster and York**
Des: Ian Chilvers, Atelier Works. Printed in litho by Walsall.
Set	5.25	7.50
Gutter pairs	14.00	–
Traffic light gutter blocks	35.00	–
First day cover	–	7.50
Stamp cards	7.00	26.00

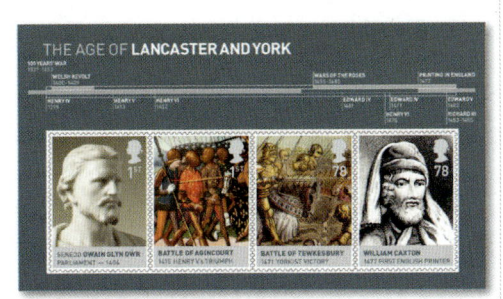

Owain Glyndwr's parliament, 1404 (1st)
Battle of Agincourt, 1415 (1st)
Battle of Tewkesbury, 1471 (78p)
William Caxton, first English printer, 1477 (78p)

■ **2008, February 28. The Age of Lancaster and York**
Des: Ian Chilvers. Printed in litho by Walsall.
Miniature sheet	4.25	6.50
First day cover	–	5.25
Press sheet	90.00	–

■ **2008, February 28. Smilers (issue 4)**
Printed in litho by Walsall. Self-adhesive. As designs of Hello, Gazania Splendens and Union Flag 1st class of October 4, 2005, and Champagne, Flowers and Butterfly, Firework and New baby 1st class of October 17, 2006, but with elliptical perforations on vertical sides. Issued in booklets of six.
Set	32.00	35.00
Booklet	32.00	–
First day cover	–	32.00

(*These designs also appear in Smilers sheets.)

Carrickfergus Castle (1st)
Giant's Causeway (1st)
St Patrick (78p)
Queen's Bridge, Belfast (78p)

■ **2008, March 11. Celebrating Northern Ireland**
Des: Silk Pearce (sheet) and David Lyons, Clare Melinsky, Tony Pleavin and Ric Ergenbright (stamps). Printed in litho by De La Rue.
Miniature sheet	4.50	4.50
First day cover	–	5.00
Stamp cards	3.25	15.00

Lifeboat at Barra (1st)
Lifeboat and dinghy at Appledore (46p)
Helicopter rescue at Portland (48p)
Lifeboat at St Ives (54p)
Rescue helicopter at Lee-on-Solent (69p)
Lifeboat at Dinbych-y-Pysgod, Tenby (78p)

■ **2008, March 13. Rescue at Sea**
Des: Hat Trick Design. Printed in litho by Walsall. 'Dot' and 'dash' shaped perforations at top and bottom.
Set	5.50	7.50
Gutter pairs	14.00	–
First day cover	–	7.00
Stamp cards	4.25	13.00

BRITISH STAMP MARKET VALUES 2024

QUEEN ELIZABETH II DECIMAL

Adonis blue butterfly (1st)
Southern damselfly (1st)
Red-barded ant (1st)
Barberry carpet moth (1st)
Stag beetle (1st)
Hazel pot beetle (1st)
Field cricket (1st)
Silver-spotted skipper (1st)
Purbeck mason wasp (1st)
Noble chafer beetle (1st)

Composite view inside St Paul's Cathedral (1st, 1st, 81p, 81p)

■ 2008, May 13. 300th Anniversary of St. Paul's Cathedral
Des: Howard Brown. Printed in litho by Enschedé.
Miniature sheet	4.50	6.00
First day cover	–	5.50
Press sheet	70.00	–

■ 2008, April 15. Endangered Species. Insects
Des: Andrew Ross. Printed in litho by De La Rue. Issued in se-tenant blocks of ten.
Set	14.00	15.00
Gutter pairs	30.00	–
First day cover	–	9.00
Stamp cards	7.00	22.00

Poster promoting 'Carry On Sergeant' (1st)
Poster promoting 'Dracula' (48p)
Poster promoting 'Carry on Cleo' (50p)
Poster promoting 'The Curse of Frankenstein' (56p)
Poster promoting 'Carry On Screaming' (72p)
Poster promoting 'The Mummy' (81p)

Lichfield Cathedral (1st)
Belfast Cathedral (48p)
Gloucester Cathedral (50p)
St. Davids Cathedral (56p)
Westminster Cathedral (72p)
St. Magnus Cathedral, Kirkwall, Orkney (81p)

■ 2008, June 10. Classic Carry On and Hammer Films
Des: Elmwood Design Group, from film posters. Printed in litho by Walsall.
Set	5.75	7.50
Gutter pairs	14.00	–
First day cover	–	6.50
Stamp cards	4.00	14.00
Postcards and stamps set	30.00	–

(*The postcards and stamps set comprised six cards showing the stamp designs against a brick background, together with a folder containing three 1st class and three 56p values.)

■ 2008, May 13. Cathedrals
Des: Howard Brown. Printed in litho by Enschedé.
Set	6.50	8.00
Gutter pairs	17.00	–
Traffic light gutter pairs	35.00	–
First day cover	–	7.25
Stamp cards	6.50	27.50

DECIMAL QUEEN ELIZABETH II

Red Arrows aerobatic display, 2006 (1st)
RAF Falcons parachute display, 2006 (48p)
Spectators watching the Red Arrows, 2006 (50p)
Avro Vulcan prototypes and Avro 707S, 1953 (56p)
Parachutist Robert Wyndham and Avro 504, 1933 (72p)
Hendon air race, 1912 (81p)

■ 2008, July 17. Air Displays
Des: Roundel. Printed in litho by Cartor.

Set	6.00	7.50
Gutter pairs	15.00	–
First day cover	–	7.00
Stamp cards	4.00	14.00

(*The 1st class design also appears in the Pilot To Plane: RAF Uniforms prestige stamp book of September 18, 2008, and was used in Smilers sheets.)

National Stadium, Beijing (1st)
London Eye (1st)
Tower of London (1st)
Corner Tower the Forbidden City, Beijing (1st)

■ 2008, August 22. Handover of the Olympic Flag from Beijing to London
Des: Why Not Associates. Printed in litho by Walsall, with the Olympic rings in a silk screen varnish.

Miniature sheet	5.50	7.00
First day cover	–	5.50
Stamp cards	3.00	15.00

Drum Major, RAF Central Band, 2007 (1st)
Helicopter rescue winchman, 1984 (1st)
Hawker Hunter pilot, 1951 (1st)
Lancaster air gunner, 1944 (81p)
WAAF plotter, 1940 (81p)
Pilot, 1918 (81p)

■ 2008, September 18. RAF Uniforms
Des: Atelier Works, from paintings by Graham Turner. Printed in litho by Walsall. Issued in se-tenant strips of three.

Set	6.50	8.00
Gutter pairs	15.00	–
Traffic light gutter pairs	30.00	–
First day cover	–	7.50
Stamp cards	4.00	14.00

(*All values also appear in the Pilot To Plane: RAF Uniforms prestige stamp book issued on September 18, 2008.)

Northern Ireland 3d design, 1958 (1st)
Northern Ireland 6d design, 1958 (1st)
Northern Ireland 1s 3d design, 1958 (1st)
Scotland 3d design, 1958 (1st)
Scotland 6d design, 1958 (1st)
Scotland 1s 3d design, 1958 (1st)
Wales 3d design, 1958 (1st)
Wales 6d design, 1958 (1st)
Wales 1s 3d design, 1958 (1st)

■ 2008, September 29. 50th Anniversary of the Country Definitives
As the 1958 regional stamps of Northern Ireland, Scotland and Wales, with new values. Printed in gravure by De La Rue.

Miniature sheet	12.50	12.50
Press sheet	80.00	–
First day cover	–	10.00
Stamp cards	11.00	35.00

(*All designs also appear in the Heraldry and Symbol prestige stamp book issued on September 29, 2008.)

BRITISH STAMP MARKET VALUES 2024

QUEEN ELIZABETH II DECIMAL

Millicent Garrett Fawcett: votes for women (1st)
Elizabeth Garrett Anderson: women's health (48p)
Marie Stopes: family planning (50p)
Eleanor Rathbone: family allowance (56p)
Claudia Jones: civil rights (72p)
Barbara Castle: equal pay for women (81p)

■ **2008, October 14. Women of Distinction**
Des: Together Design. Printed in gravure by Walsall.
Set	5.75	7.50
Gutter pairs	15.00	–
First day cover	–	7.00
Stamp cards	4.00	14.00

The Ugly Sisters from 'Cinderella' (2nd, 2nd Large)
The Genie from 'Aladdin' (1st, 1st Large)
Captain Hook from 'Peter Pan' (50p)
The Wicked Queen from 'Snow White' (81p)

■ **2008, November 4. Christmas. Pantomime**
Des: Steve Haskins, from photographs by Peter Thorpe. Printed in gravure by De La Rue. Counter stamps self-adhesive, miniature sheet gummed.
Set	6.75	8.50
First day cover	–	7.00
Miniature sheet (one of each value)	6.00	7.50
Miniature sheet first day cover	–	6.00
Stamp cards	4.25	19.00

(*The 1st class and 2nd class designs also appear in booklets, and the 2nd, 1st and 81p designs were used in Smilers sheets.)

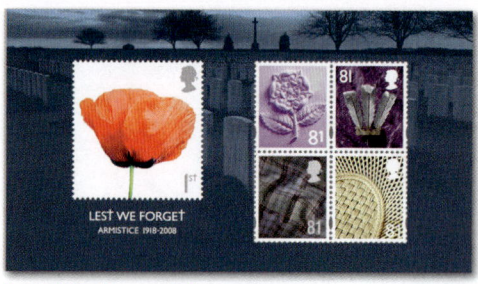

Soldier's face in poppy (1st)
Country definitives (81p, 81p, 81p, 81p)

■ **2008, November 6. Lest We Forget (issue 3)**
Des: Hat-Trick Design. Printed in litho by De La Rue.
Miniature sheet	6.50	8.00
First day cover	–	7.50

(*The 1st class design was used in a Smilers generic sheet.)

■ **2008, November 6. Lest We Forget**
The Poppy designs of November 6, 2006, November 8, 2007, and November 6, 2008, but in se-tenant strips in counter sheets. Printed in litho by De La Rue.
Set (se-tenant strip of three)	3.50	5.00
Gutter pairs	9.00	–
Traffic light gutter pairs	26.00	–
First day cover	–	4.00
Stamp cards (3 stamps, 3 miniature sheets)	10.00	27.00

Supermarine Spitfire by R. J. Mitchell (1st)
Mini skirt by Mary Quant (1st)
Mini by Sir Alec Issigonis (1st)
Anglepoise lamp by George Carwardine (1st)
Concorde by BAC and Aerospatiale (1st)
K2 telephone kiosk by Sir Giles Gilbert Scott (1st)
Polypropylene chair by Robin Day (1st)
Penguin book cover by Edward Young (1st)
London Underground map by Harry Beck (1st)
Routemaster bus by A.A.M. Durrant (1st)

164 BRITISH STAMP MARKET VALUES 2024

DECIMAL   QUEEN ELIZABETH II

■ **2009, January 13. British Design Classics**
Des: HGV Design. Printed in litho by Cartor. Issued in se-tenant blocks of 10.

Set	13.00	15.00
Gutter pairs	30.00	–
First day cover	–	10.00
Stamp cards	5.50	22.00
Postcards and stamps set	22.00	–

(*The postcards and stamps set comprises 10 cards reproducing the stamp designs against a Union Flag background, and a set of the stamps. All designs also appear in the British Design Classics prestige stamp book. The Routemaster Bus, Telephone Kiosk, Mini, Concorde, Spitfire and Mini Skirt designs also appear, in self-adhesive form, in booklets; price £3 mint and £5 used for the Routemaster and Kiosk stamps, £1.50 mint of used for the others. The Mini and Concorde designs also appear in Smilers sheets.)

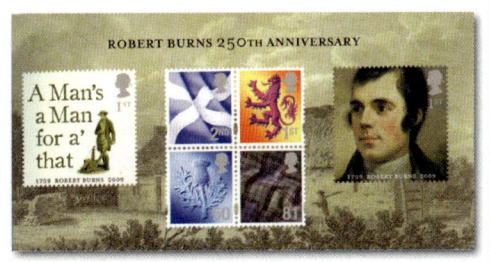

'A Man's a Man for a' That' (1st)
Portrait of Burns by Alexander Nasmyth (1st)
Scotland definitives (2nd, 1st, 50p, 81p)

■ **2009, January 22. 250th Anniversary of the Birth of Robert Burns**
Des: Tayburn. Printed in gravure by Enschedé.

Miniature sheet	5.50	5.50
First day cover	–	6.00
Press sheet	90.00	–
Stamp cards	2.50	12.50

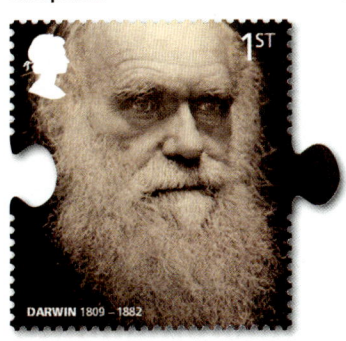

Charles Darwin (1st)
Marine iguana (48p)
Finches (50p)
Atoll (56p)
Bee orchid (72p)
Orang-utan (81p)

■ **2009, February 12. Bicentenary of the Birth of Charles Darwin**
Des: Hat-Trick Design. Printed in gravure by De La Rue. Self-adhesive, in freeform shape to resemble jigsaw pieces.

Set	7.50	7.75
Gutter pairs	18.00	–
First day cover	–	8.50
Stamp cards	7.00	28.00

(*All values also appear, in gummed form, in the Charles Darwin prestige stamp book issued on February 12, 2009.)

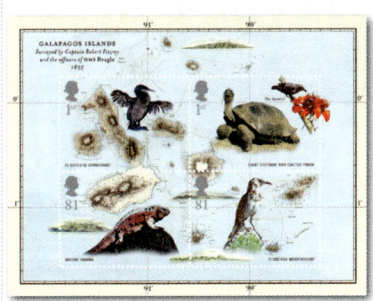

Flightless cormorant and Galapagos Islands (1st)
Giant tortoise, cactus finch and Galapagos Islands (1st)
Marine iguana and Galapagos Islands (81p)
Floreana mockingbird and Galapagos Islands (81p)

■ **2009, February 12. Bicentenary of the Birth of Charles Darwin. The Galapagos Islands**
Des: Howard Brown. Printed in litho by De La Rue.

Miniature sheet	5.00	5.00
First day cover	–	5.50
Press sheet	55.00	–

(*The miniature sheet also appears in the Charles Darwin prestige stamp book issued on February 12, 2009.)

Welsh flag (1st)
Wales definitive (1st)
St. David (81p)
National Assembly for Wales, Cardiff (81p)

■ **2009, February 26. Celebrating Wales**
Des: Silk Pearce. Printed in litho by De La Rue.

Miniature sheet	4.50	4.75
First day cover	–	6.00
Stamp cards	3.75	15.00

(*The 1st class Welsh Flag design also appears in the Football Heroes prestige stamp book of 2013 and the Classic Locomotives of the UK prestige stamp book of 2014.)

QUEEN ELIZABETH II DECIMAL

Matthew Boulton, manufacturing (1st)
James Watt, engineering (1st)
Richard Arkwright, textiles (50p)
Josiah Wedgwood, ceramics (50p)
George Stephenson, railways (56p)
Henry Maudslay, machine-making (56p)
James Brindley, canal engineering (72p)
John McAdam, road building (72p)

■ **2009, March 17. Pioneers of the Industrial Revolution**
Des: Webb & Webb. Printed in litho by Enschedé. Issued in se-tenant pairs.

Set	7.00	7.00
Gutter pairs	17.00	–
First day cover	–	8.00
Stamp cards	5.00	20.00

King Henry VII, 1485–1509 (1st)
King Henry VIII, 1509–47 (1st)
King Edward VI, 1547–53 (62p)
Lady Jane Grey, 1553 (62p)
Queen Mary 1, 1553–58 (81p)
Queen Elizabeth I, 1558–1603 (81p)

■ **2009, April 21. Kings and Queens. The House of Tudor**
Des: Ian Chilvers, Atelier Works. Printed in litho by Walsall.

Set	5.50	5.50
Gutter pairs	15.00	–
Traffic light gutter pairs	32.50	–
First day cover	–	7.00
Stamp cards	6.50	30.00

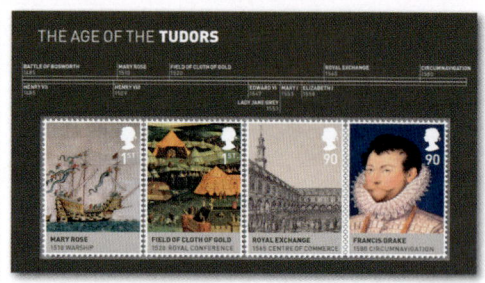

'Mary Rose' warship, 1510 (1st)
Field of Cloth of Gold conference, 1520 (1st)
Royal Exchange commercial centre, 1565 (90p)
Francis Drake's circumnavigation, 1580 (90p)

■ **2009, April 21. The Age of the Tudors**
Des: Ian Chilvers, Atelier Works. Printed in litho by Walsall.

Miniature sheet	4.50	4.50
First day cover	–	6.00
Press sheet	90.00	–

Round-headed leek (1st)
Floating water-plantain (1st)
Lady's slipper orchid (1st)
Dwarf milkwort (1st)
Marsh saxifrage (1st)
Downy woundwort (1st)
Upright spurge (1st)
Plymouth pear (1st)
Sea knotgrass (1st)
Deptford pink (1st)

■ **2009, May 19. Endangered Species: Plants**
Des: Studio Dempsey. Printed in litho by Cartor. Issued in se-tenant blocks of ten.

Set	13.00	14.00
Gutter pairs	30.00	–
First day cover	–	11.00
Stamp cards	8.00	35.00

166 BRITISH STAMP MARKET VALUES 2024

DECIMAL   QUEEN ELIZABETH II

Palm House, Kew Gardens (1st)
Millennium Seed Bank, Wakehurst Place (1st)
Pagoda, Kew Gardens (90p)
Sackler Crossing, Kew Gardens (90p)

■ **2009, May 19. 250th Anniversary of the Royal Botanic Gardens, Kew**
Des: Studio Dempsey. Printed in litho by Cartor.

Miniature sheet	4.75	5.00
First day cover	–	6.00
Maximum cards set	12.00	–
Press sheet	70.00	–

(*The maximum cards set comprises four postcards, each with one stamp from the miniature sheet affixed and cancelled on the picture side, sold in a pack with a mint miniature sheet.)

Dragons (1st)
Unicorns (1st)
Giants (62p)
Pixies (62p)
Mermaids (90p)
Fairies (90p)

■ **2009, June 16. Mythical Creatures**
Des: Morgan Radcliffe, from illustrations by Dave McKean. Printed in gravure by De La Rue.

Set	6.50	6.50
Gutter pairs	16.00	–
First day cover	–	8.50
Stamp cards	4.00	17.00

George V type B wall box, 1933, at Cookham Rise (1st)
Edward VII Ludlow box, 1901, at Bodiam post office (56p)
Victorian lamp box, 1896, at Hythe (81p)
Elizabeth II type A wall box, 1962, at Slaithwaite sorting office (90p)

■ **2009, August 18. Post Boxes**
Des: Elmwood Design Group, from photographs by Peter Marlow. Printed in litho by Cartor.

Miniature sheet	5.00	5.00
First day cover	–	5.50
Press sheet	70.00	–
Stamp cards	3.50	17.00

(*All designs also appear in the Treasures of the Archive prestige stamp book issued on August 18, 2009, and the 1st class design was used in a Smilers generic sheet.)

Firefighting (1st)
Chemical fire (54p)
Emergency rescue (56p)
Flood rescue (62p)
Search and rescue (81p)
Fire safety (90p)

■ **2009, September 1. Fire and Rescue Services**
Des: Rose. Printed in gravure by De La Rue.

Set	6.00	6.00
Gutter pairs	15.00	–
First day cover	–	8.00
Stamp cards	3.75	17.00

QUEEN ELIZABETH II DECIMAL

Flight Deck Officer, 2009 (1st)
Captain, 1941 (1st)
Second Officer WRNS, 1918 (1st)
Able Seaman, 1880 (90p)
Royal Marine, 1805 (90p)
Admiral, 1795 (90p)

■ **2009, September 17. Royal Navy Uniforms**
Des: Atelier Works, from paintings by Graham Turner. Printed in litho by Cartor. Issued in se-tenant strips of three.

Set	7.00	7.00
Gutter pairs	17.00	–
Traffic light gutter pairs	32.50	–
First day cover	–	9.00
Stamp cards	3.75	17.00

(*All values also appear in the Royal Navy Uniforms prestige stamp book issued on September 17, 2009.)

Fred Perry, tennis player (1st)
Henry Purcell, composer (1st)
Sir Matt Busby, football manager (1st)
William Gladstone, statesman (1st)
Mary Wollstonecraft, pioneering feminist (1st)
Sir Arthur Conan Doyle, author (1st)
Donald Campbell, water speed record breaker (1st)
Judy Fryd, founder of Mencap (1st)
Samuel Johnson, lexicographer (1st)
Sir Martin Ryle, radio astronomer (1st)

■ **2009, October 8. Eminent Britons**
Des: Together Design. Printed in litho by Cartor. Issued in strips of five se-tenant designs, in two different sheets.

Set	13.00	15.00
Gutter pairs	28.00	–
First day cover	–	10.00
Stamp cards	6.00	26.00

Canoe slalom (1st)
Paralympic archery (1st)
Track athletics (1st)
Aquatics (1st)
Paralympic boccia (1st)
Judo (1st)
Paralympic equestrianism (1st)
Badminton (1st)
Weightlifting (1st)
Basketball (1st)

■ **2009, October 22. London 2012 Olympic and Paralympic Games (issue 1)**
Des: John Royle (Canoe), George Hardie (Archery), Nathalie Guinamard (Athletics), Julian Opie (Aquatics), David Doyle (Boccia), Paul Slater (Judo), Andrew Davidson (Equestrian), David Holmes (Badminton), Guy Billout (Weightlifting), Huntley Muir (Basketball), Studio David Hillman (set). Printed in litho by Cartor. Issued in strips of five se-tenant designs in two different sheets.

Set	13.00	15.00
Gutter pairs	28.00	–
First day cover	–	10.00
Postcard and stamp set (Athletics)	9.00	–
Postcard and stamp set (Badminton)	9.00	–
Postcard and stamp set (Equestrian)	9.00	–
Postcard and stamp set (Judo)	9.00	–
Stamp cards	7.00	26.00

(All values also appear in a commemorative sheet. The Judo, Archery, Track Athletics and Basketball designs also appear, in self-adhesive from, in booklets; price £7 each mint or £8 used.)

DECIMAL **QUEEN ELIZABETH II**

Angel by William Morris (2nd, 2nd large)
Madonna & Child by Henry Holiday (1st, 1st Large)
Joseph by Henry Holiday (56p)
Wise Man by Sir Edward Burne-Jones (90p)
Shepherd by Henry Holiday (£1.35)

■ 2009, November 3. Christmas
Des: Andrew Ross, from stained glass windows. Printed in gravure by De La Rue. Counter sheets self-adhesive, miniature sheet gummed.

Set	8.75	8.75
First day cover	–	9.50
Miniature sheet (one of each value)	7.50	7.50
Miniature sheet first day cover	–	8.50
Stamp cards	5.00	27.50

(*The 1st class and 2nd class designs also appear in booklets, and the 2nd, 1st, 56p and 90p designs were used in Smilers sheets.)

'The Division Bell' by Pink Floyd, 1994 (1st)
'A Rush of Blood to the Head' by Coldplay, 2002 (1st)
'Parklife' by Blur, 1994 (1st)
'Power, Corruption and Lies' by New Order, 1983 (1st)
'Let It Bleed' by The Rolling Stones, 1969 (1st)
'London Calling' by The Clash, 1979 (1st)
'Tubular Bells' by Mike Oldfield 1973 (1st)
'IV' by Led Zepplin, 1971 (1st)
'Screamadelica' by Primal Scream, 1991 (1st)
'The Rise & Fall of Ziggy Stardust' by David Bowie, 1972 (1st)

■ 2010, January 7. Classic Album Covers
Des: Studio Dempsey. Counter sheets printed in gravure by De La Rue, self-adhesive in freeform shape, in strips of five in two different sheets. Miniature sheet printed in litho by Cartor, gummed.

Set	14.00	16.00
First day cover	–	10.00
Miniature sheet (one of each value)	25.00	26.00
Miniature sheet first day cover	–	30.00
Stamp cards	10.00	26.00

(*The stamps also appear in the Classic Album Covers prestige stamp book, litho-printed. A souvenir sheet of 10 of the Division Bell design was issued on March 6, 2010, but was not available from post offices; price £6.50.)

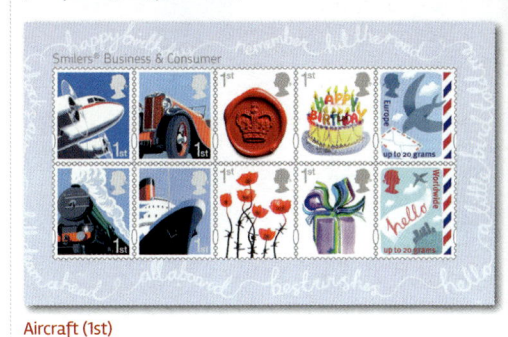

Aircraft (1st)
Sports car (1st)
Wax seal with crown (1st)
Birthday cake with 'Happy birthday' message (1st)
Bird with envelope (Europe up to 20g)
Steam locomotive (1st)
Ocean liner (1st)
Poppies on barbed wire (1st)
Wrapped present (1st)
Aircraft with 'Hello' message (Worldwide up to 20g)

■ 2010, January 26. Smilers (issue 5): stamps for business and consumer customised sheets
Des: Andrew Davidson (Aircraft, Sports car, Steam locomotive, Ocean liner), Hat-Trick (Seal, Poppies), Annabel Wright (Cake, Present) and Lucy Davey (Europe, Worldwide). Printed in litho by Cartor.

Miniature sheet	16.00	17.50
First day cover	–	9.00
Stamp cards	10.00	35.00

(*These designs were issued primarily for use in Smilers sheets, where they are self-adhesive. The Poppies design was also issued in self-adhesive counter sheets in 2012.)

Rainbows and activities (1st)
Brownies and activities (56p)
Guides and activities (81p)
Senior Section and activities (90p)

■ 2010, February 2. Centenary of Girlguiding
Des: Together Design. Printed in litho by Cartor.

Miniature sheet	5.00	5.00
First day cover	–	6.00
Stamp cards	3.00	22.00

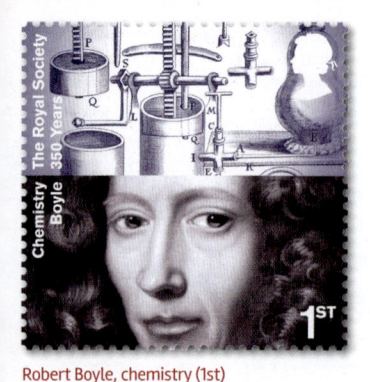

QUEEN ELIZABETH II DECIMAL

Robert Boyle, chemistry (1st)
Isaac Newton, optics (1st)
Benjamin Franklin, electricity (1st)
Edward Jenner, vaccination (1st)
Charles Babbage, computing (1st)
Alfred Russel Wallace, evolution (1st)
Joseph Lister, antiseptic surgery (1st)
Ernest Rutherford, atomic structure (1st)
Dorothy Hodgkin, crystallography (1st)
Nicholas Shackleton, earth science (1st)

■ **2010, February 25. 350th Anniversary of The Royal Society**
Des: Hat-Trick. Printed in litho by Cartor. Issued in se-tenant blocks of ten.

Set (se-tenant block of 10)	13.00	15.00
Gutter pairs	28.00	–
First day cover	–	11.00
Stamp cards	6.25	25.00

(* All designs also appear in The Royal Society prestige stamp book.)

Pixie, mastiff cross (1st)
Button, cat (1st)
Herbie, mongrel (1st)
Mr Tumnus, cat (1st)
Tafka, border collie (1st)
Boris, bulldog cross (1st)
Casey, lurcher (1st)
Tigger, cat (1st)
Leonard, Jack Russell cross (1st)
Tia, terrier cross (1st)

■ **2010, March 11. 150th Anniversary of Battersea Dogs & Cats Home**
Des: CDT Design Ltd. Printed in litho by Cartor. Issued in se-tenant blocks of ten.

Set (se-tenant block of 10)	13.00	15.00
Gutter pairs	28.00	–
First day cover	–	11.00
Stamp cards	6.25	25.00

King James I of Scotland, 1406–37 (1st)
King James II of Scotland, 1437–60 (1st)
King James III of Scotland, 1460–88 (1st)
King James IV of Scotland, 1488–1513 (62p)
King James V of Scotland, 1513–42 (62p)
Mary Queen of Scots, 1542–67 (81p)
King James VI of Scotland, 1567–1625 (81p)

■ **2010, March 23. Kings and Queens. The House of Stewart**
Des: Atelier Works. Printed in litho by Cartor.

Set	8.50	10.50
Gutter pairs	20.00	–
Traffic light gutter pairs	42.00	–
First day cover	–	8.50
Stamp cards	7.00	35.00

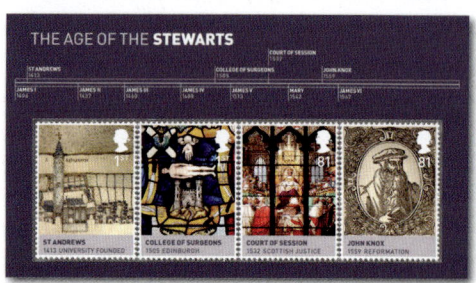

St. Andrews University, 1413 (1st)
College of Surgeons, 1505 (1st)
Court of Session, 1532 (81p)
John Knox and the Reformation, 1559 (81p)

■ **2010, March 23. The Age of the Stewarts**
Des: Atelier Works. Printed in litho by Cartor.

Miniature sheet	5.00	5.00
First day cover	–	6.00
Press sheet	75.00	–

DECIMAL   QUEEN ELIZABETH II

CENTRE, LONDON, 8–15 May 2010'; price £11.00 mint, £13.00 on first day cover. Stamp cards showing the stamps and miniature sheets of this issue were included in the issue of May 8.)

Humpback whale (1st)
Wildcat (1st)
Brown long-eared bat (1st)
Polecat (1st)
Sperm whale (1st)
Water vole (1st)
Greater horseshoe bat (1st)
Otter (1st)
Dormouse (1st)
Hedgehog (1st)

1924 British Empire Exhibition 1d stamp (1st)
1924 British Empire Exhibition 1½d stamp (1st)
1913–34 'Seahorses' £1 definitive (£1)
1913–34 'Seahorses' 10/– definitive (£1)

■ **2010, April 13. Endangered Species. Mammals**
Des: Jason Godfrey. Printed in litho by Cartor. Issued in se-tenant blocks of ten.

Set	14.00	14.00
Gutter pairs	25.00	–
First day cover	–	11.00
Stamp cards	6.25	25.00

(* The Otter and Hedgehog designs also appear, in self-adhesive form, in booklets; price £5 each mint or £6 used.)

■ **2010, May 8. London 2010 Festival of Stamps. The King's Stamps**
Des: Sedley Place. Printed in intaglio and litho by Enschedé.

Miniature sheet	6.00	7.00
First day cover	–	12.50
Press sheet	40.00	–
Stamp cards (issues of May 6 and May 8)	5.00	28.00

(*All designs also appear in the King George V prestige stamp book.)

Machin portrait of Queen Elizabeth II and Mackennal portrait of King George V (1st)
Mackennal and Downey portraits of King George V (£1)

■ **2010, May 6. London 2010 Festival of Stamps. Centenary of the Accession of King George V**
Des: Sedley Place. Printed in litho by Cartor. 1st class design printed in sheets; 1st and £1 designs issued in miniature sheets.

1st class	2.00	2.00
Gutter pair (1st class)	5.00	–
First day cover	–	4.00
Miniature sheet	4.50	4.50
Miniature sheet first day cover	–	12.50
Press sheet	45.00	–

(*These stamps also appear in the King George V prestige stamp book. The miniature sheet was issued on May 8, 2010, with an additional overprint in the border reading 'BUSINESS DESIGN

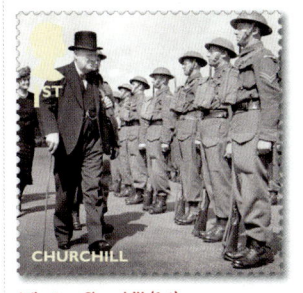

Winston Churchill (1st)
Land girls (1st)
Home Guard (60p)
Evacuees (60p)
Air raid wardens (67p)
Women in factories (67p)
Royal broadcast, 1940 (97p)
Fire service (97p)

■ **2010, May 13. Britain Alone**
Des: Why Not Associates. Printed in litho by Cartor.

Set	8.00	8.00
Gutter pairs	20.00	–
First day cover	–	12.00
Stamp cards	7.50	37.50

(*All values also appear in the Britain Alone prestige stamp book.)

QUEEN ELIZABETH II   DECIMAL

Evacuation of British soldiers from Dunkirk (1st)
Vessels involved in 'Operation Dynamo' (60p)
British soldiers on board a Royal Navy destroyer (88p)
Two boats from the Dunkirk evacuation (97p)

■ **2010, May 13. 70th Anniversary of the Evacuation of Dunkirk**
Des: Why Not Associates. Printed in litho by Cartor.
Miniature sheet	5.50	5.50
First day cover	–	6.00

(*All values also appear in the Britain Alone prestige stamp book.)

King James I, 1603–25 (1st)
King Charles I, 1625–49 (1st)
King Charles II, 1660–85 (60p)
King James II, 1685–88 (60p)
King William III, 1689–1702 (67p)
Queen Mary II, 1689–94 (67p)
Queen Anne, 1702–14 (88p)

■ **2010, June 15. Kings and Queens. The House of Stuart**
Des: Atelier Works. Printed in litho by Cartor.
Set	6.75	6.75
Gutter pairs	20.00	–
Traffic light gutter pairs	50.00	–
First day cover	–	9.00
Stamp cards	7.00	35.00

William Harvey and discovery of blood circulation, 1628 (1st)
Battle of Naseby, 1645 (60p)
John Milton and 'Paradise Lost', 1667 (88p)
John Vanbrugh and Castle Howard, 1712 (97p)

■ **2010, June 15. The Age of the Stuarts**
Des: Atelier Works. Printed in litho by Cartor.
Miniature sheet	5.50	5.50
First day cover	–	5.75
Press sheet	85.00	–

Paralympic rowing (1st)
Shooting (1st)
Modern pentathlon (1st)
Taekwondo (1st)
Cycling (1st)
Paralympic table tennis (1st)
Hockey (1st)
Football (1st)
Paralympic goalball (1st)
Boxing (1st)

■ **2010, July 27. London 2012 Olympic and Paralympic Games (issue 2)**
Des: Marian Hill (Rowing), David Hillman (Shooting), Katherine Baxter (Modern pentathlon), James Fryer (Taekwondo), Matthew Dennis (Cycling), Michael Craig-Martin (Table tennis), Darren Hopes (Hockey), Alex Williamson (Football), Tobatron (Goalball), Stephen Ledwidge (Boxing), Studio David Hillman (set). Printed in litho by Cartor. Issued in se-tenant strips of five in two different sheets.
Set	13.00	15.00
Gutter pairs	28.00	–
First day cover	–	10.00
Postcard and stamp set (Boxing)	9.00	–
Postcard and stamp set (Rowing)	9.00	–
Stamp cards	6.00	25.00

(*The Rowing, Table Tennis, Football and Cycling designs also appear, in self-adhesive form, in booklets; price £7 each mint or £8 used. All values also appear in a commemorative sheet.)

DECIMAL   QUEEN ELIZABETH II

LMS: Coronation Class locomotive (1st)
BR: Class 9F locomotive (1st)
GWR: King Class locomotive (67p)
LNER: Class A1 locomotive (67p)
SR: King Arthur Class locomotive (97p)
LMS: NCC Class WT locomotive (97p)

■ **2010, August 19. Great British Railways**
Des: Delaney Design Consultants. Printed in gravure by De La Rue.

Set	6.50	6.50
Gutter pairs	20.00	–
First day cover	–	7.00
Stamp cards	7.50	17.50

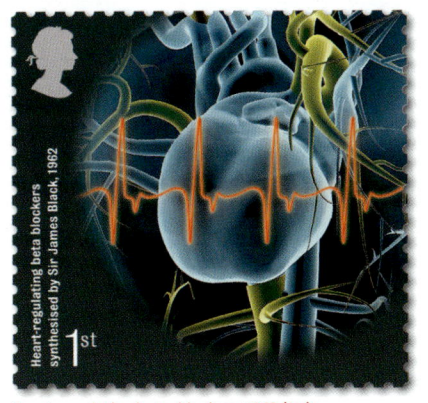

Heart-regulating beta-blockers, 1962 (1st)
Discovery of antibiotic properties of penicillin, 1928 (58p)
Total hip replacement, 1962 (60p)
Artificial lens implant surgery, 1949 (67p)
Proof of malaria transmission by mosquitoes, 1897 (88p)
Computed tomography scanning, 1971 (97p)

■ **2010, September 16. Medical Breakthroughs**
Des: Howard Brown. Printed in litho by Cartor.

Set	6.50	6.50
Gutter pairs	20.00	–
First day cover	–	9.00
Stamp cards	4.00	17.50

(*The Beta-Blockers design also appears, in self-adhesive form, in booklets; price £2.00 mint or used.)

Winnie-the-Pooh, Piglet and Christopher Robin (1st)
Winnie-the-Pooh and Piglet (58p)
Winnie-the-Pooh and Rabbit (60p)
Winnie-the-Pooh and Eeyore (67p)
Winnie-the-Pooh and Friends (88p)
Winnie-the-Pooh and Tigger (97p)

■ **2010, October 12. Winnie-the-Pooh (Europa)**
Des: Magpie Studio, from the illustrations of E. H. Shepard. Printed in litho by Cartor.

Set	6.50	6.50
Gutter pairs	20.00	–
First day cover	–	9.00
Stamp cards	9.00	36.00

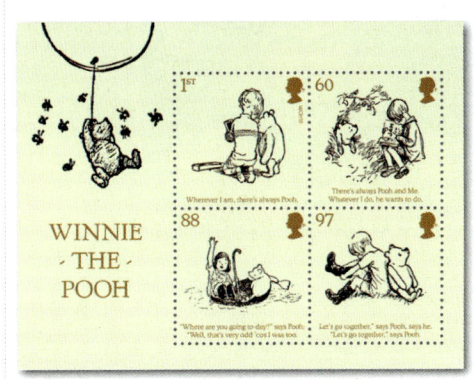

Winnie-the-Pooh and Christopher Robin (1st)
Christopher Robin reads to Winnie-the-Pooh (60p)
Winnie-the-Pooh and Christopher Robin set sail (88p)
Christopher Robin pulls on his wellingtons (97p)

■ **2010, October 12. Winnie-the-Pooh**
Des: Magpie Studio, from the illustrations of E. H. Shepard. Printed in litho by Cartor.

Miniature sheet	5.00	5.00
First day cover	–	7.00

QUEEN ELIZABETH II DECIMAL

Wallace and Gromit singing carols (2nd, 2nd Large)
Gromit posting Christmas cards (1st, 1st Large)
Wallace and Gromit decorating a Christmas tree (60p)
Gromit carrying a Christmas pudding (97p)
Gromit wearing a sweater (£1.46)

■ **2010, November 2. Christmas. Wallace and Gromit**
Des: Aardman Animations and Nick Park. Printed in gravure by De La Rue. Counter stamps self-adhesive; miniature sheet gummed.

Set	10.00	12.00
Gutter pairs	22.00	
First day cover	–	10.00
Miniature sheet (one of each design)	10.00	12.00
Miniature sheet first day cover	–	10.00
Stamp cards	13.00	30.00

(*The 2nd and 1st class designs also appear in booklets. The 2nd, 1st, 60p and 97p designs were used in Smilers sheets.)

'Joe 90' (1st)
'Captain Scarlet' (1st)
'Thunderbirds' (1st)
'Stingray' (97p)
'Fireball XL5' (97p)
'Supercar' (97p)

■ **2011, January 11. FAB. The Genius of Gerry Anderson**
Des: GBH. Printed in litho by Cartor. Issued in se-tenant strips for each denomination.

Set (se-tenant strips of three)	7.00	7.00
Gutter pairs	17.00	–
First day cover	–	9.00
Stamp cards	11.00	35.00

(*The Thunderbirds design also appears, in self-adhesive form, in a booklet: price £1.75 mint or used.)

Thunderbird 4 (41p)
Thunderbird 3 (60p)
Thunderbird 2 (88p)
Thunderbird 1 (97p)

■ **2011, January 11. Thunderbirds**
Des: GBH. Printed with microlenticular technology by Cartor and Outer Aspect, New Zealand.

Miniature sheet	5.50	6.00
First day cover	–	6.50

BR Dean Goods (1st)
Peckett R2 Thor (60p)
Lancashire and Yorkshire Railway 1093 (88p)
BR WD (97p)

■ **2011, February 1. Classic Locomotives of England**
Des: Delaney Design Consultants. Printed in litho by Cartor.

Miniature sheet	7.00	7.00
First day cover	–	7.50
Stamp cards	4.00	22.00

(*The 1st class design also appears, in self-adhesive form, in booklets; price £2 mint.)

174 BRITISH STAMP MARKET VALUES 2024

DECIMAL QUEEN ELIZABETH II

'Oliver' (1st)
'Blood Brothers' (1st)
'We Will Rock You' (1st)
'Spamalot' (1st)
'Rocky Horror Show' (97p)
'Me and My Girl' (97p)
'Return to the Forbidden Planet' (97p)
'Billy Elliot' (97p)

■ 2011, February 24. Musicals
Des: Webb and Webb. Printed in litho by Cartor.

Set	11.00	11.00
Gutter pairs	24.00	–
Traffic light gutter pairs	27.50	–
First day cover	–	10.00
Stamp cards	6.00	22.00

Rincewind from Terry Pratchett's Discworld series (1st)
Nanny Ogg from Terry Pratchett's Discworld series (1st)
Dumbledore from J. K. Rowling's Harry Potter series (1st)
Lord Voldemort from J. K. Rowling's Harry Potter series (1st)
Merlin from Arthurian legend (60p)
Morgan Le Fay from Arthurian legend (60p)
Aslan from C. S. Lewis's Narnia series (97p)
White Witch from C. S. Lewis's Narnia series (97p)

■ 2011, March 8. Magical Realms
Des: So Design Consultants. Printed in gravure by De La Rue. Issued in vertical se-tenant pairs.

Set	10.00	12.00
Gutter pairs	18.00	–
First day cover	–	10.00
Stamp cards	6.00	20.00

African elephant (1st)
Mountain gorilla (1st)
Siberian tiger (1st)
Polar bear (1st)
Amur leopard (1st)
Iberian lynx (1st)
Red panda (1st)
Black rhinoceros (1st)
African wild dog (1st)
Golden lion tamarin (1st)

■ 2011, March 22. 50th Anniversary of WWF
Des: Rose Design Consultants. Printed in litho by Cartor. Issued in se-tenant strips of five, in two different sheets.

Set	14.00	14.00
Gutter pairs	30.00	–
First day cover	–	10.00
Stamp cards	9.00	35.00

(*All designs also appear in the WWF prestige stamp book.)

Spider monkey in Amazon rainforest (1st)
Hyacinth macaw in Amazon rainforest (60p)
Poison dart frog in Amazon rainforest (88p)
Jaguar in Amazon rainforest (97p)

■ 2011, March 22. Amazon Alive (Europa)
Des: Janice Nicholson and Rose Design Consultants. Printed in litho by Cartor.

Miniature sheet	5.00	5.00
First day cover	–	6.00

(*The whole sheet also appears in the WWF prestige stamp book.)

'Hamlet' (1st)
'The Tempest' (66p)
'Henry VI' (68p)
'King Lear' (76p)
'A Midsummer's Night Dream' (£1)
'Romeo and Juliet' (£1.10)

■ 2011, April 12. 50th Anniversary of the Royal Shakespeare Company
Des: Hat-Trick Design. Printed in gravure by Walsall.

Set	7.00	7.00
Gutter pairs	17.00	–
First day cover	–	8.50
Stamp cards	7.50	33.00

BRITISH STAMP MARKET VALUES 2024

QUEEN ELIZABETH II DECIMAL

Royal Shakespeare Theatre, Stratford-upon-Avon (1st)
Swan Theatre, Stratford-upon-Avon (68p)
The Courtyard Theatre, Stratford-upon-Avon (76p)
The Other Place, Stratford-upon-Avon (£1)

■ **2011, April 12. 50th Anniversary of the Royal Shakespeare Company**
Des: Hat-Trick. Printed in litho by Cartor.
Miniature sheet	5.00	5.00
First day cover	–	6.00

Prince William and Catherine Middleton, informal (1st, 1st)
Prince William and Catherine Middleton, formal (£1.10, £1.10)

■ **2011, April 21. Royal Wedding of Prince William and Catherine Middleton**
Des: Atelier Works, from portraits by Mario Testino. Printed in gravure by Walsall.
Miniature sheet	6.00	6.00
First day cover	–	7.50

'Cray' by William Morris, 1884 (1st)
'Cherries' by Philip Webb, 1867 (1st)
'Seaweed' by John Henry Dearle, 1901 (76p)
'Peony' by Kate Faulkner, 1877 (76p)
'Acanthus' by William Morris and William de Morgan, 1876 (£1.10)
'The Merchant's Daughter' by Edward Burne-Jones, c1864 (£1.10)

■ **2011, May 5. Morris and Co**
Des: Kate Stevens. Printed in litho by Cartor.
Set	7.00	7.00
Gutter pairs	17.00	–
First day cover	–	8.50
Stamp cards	5.00	17.50

(*All values also appear in the Morris & Co prestige stamp book.)

Thomas (1st)
James (66p)
Percy (68p)
Daisy (76p)
Toby (£1)
Gordon (£1.10)

■ **2011, June 14. Thomas the Tank Engine**
Des: Elmwood, from television stills. Printed in litho by Cartor.
Set	7.50	7.50
Gutter pairs	18.00	–
First day cover	–	8.50
Stamp cards	7.50	35.00

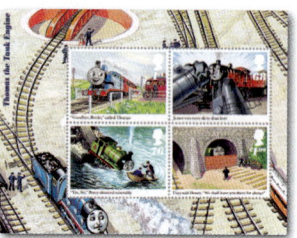

Thomas racing Bertie the Bus (1st)
James has a crash (68p)
Percy ends up in the sea (76p)
Henry walled up in a tunnel (£1)

■ **2011, June 14. Thomas the Tank Engine**
Des: Elmwood, from book illustrations by Reginald Dalby and John Kenney. Printed in litho by Cartor.
Miniature sheet	4.50	5.00
First day cover	–	6.00

(*The 1st class design also appears, in self-adhesive form, in booklets; price £1.75 mint or used.)

DECIMAL QUEEN ELIZABETH II

Paralympic sailing (1st)
Field athletics (1st)
Volleyball (1st)
Wheelchair rugby (1st)
Wrestling (1st)
Wheelchair tennis (1st)
Fencing (1st)
Gymnastics (1st)
Triathlon (1st)
Handball (1st)

■ **2011, July 27. London 2012 Olympic and Paralympic Games (issue 3)**
Des: Lara Harwood (Sailing), Anthony Pike (Field), Ben Dalling (Volleyball), Matthew Hollings (Wheelchair rugby), Daniel Stolle (Wrestling), David McConochie (Wheelchair tennis), Lyndon Hayes (Fencing), Kathy Wyatt (Gymnastics), Adam Simpson (Triathlon), David Cutter (Handball), Studio David Hillman (set). Printed in litho by Cartor. Issued in se-tenant strips of five in two different sheets.

Set (se-tenant strips of five)	14.00	14.00
Gutter pairs	30.00	–
First day cover	–	11.00
Postcard and stamp set (Sailing)	9.00	–
Postcard and stamp set (Gymnastics)	9.00	–
Composite sheet (entire series of 30)	40.00	50.00
Stamp cards	7.00	23.00

(*The composite sheet comprises one of each design in the Olympic and Paralympic Games series. The Wheelchair rugby, Paralympic sailing, Gymnastics and Fencing designs also appear, in self-adhesive form, in booklets; price £7 each mint or £8 used. All values also appear in a commemorative sheet.)

Sovereign's Sceptre with Cross (1st)
St. Edward's Crown (1st)
Rod and Sceptre with Doves (68p)
Queen Mary's Crown (68p)
The Sovereign's Orb (76p)
Jewelled Sword of Offering (76p)
Imperial State Crown (£1.10)
Coronation Spoon (£1.10)

■ **2011, August 23. The Crown Jewels**
Des: Purpose. Printed in litho by Cartor.

Set	9.00	9.50
Gutter pairs	23.00	–
First day cover	–	11.00
Stamp cards	6.00	25.00

Gustav Hamel receives first mailbag (1st)
Hamel ready to leave Hendon (68p)
Greswell's Blériot at Windsor (£1)
Airmail delivered at Windsor (£1.10)

■ **2011, September 9. Centenary of the First UK Aerial Post**
Des: Robert Maude and Sarah Davies, from photography by Geoff Dann. Printed in litho by Cartor.

Miniature sheet	5.50	6.00
Miniature sheet first day cover	–	6.50
Press sheet	£100	–
Stamp cards	4.75	20.00

(*The £1 and £1.10 designs also appear in the First UK Aerial Post prestige stamp book.)

King George I, 1714–27 (1st)
King George II, 1727–60 (1st)
King George III, 1760–1820 (76p)
King George IV, 1820–30 (76p)
King William IV, 1830–37 (£1.10)
Queen Victoria, 1837–1901 (£1.10)

■ **2011, September 15. Kings and Queens. The House of Hanover**
Des: Ian Chilvers, Atelier Works. Printed in litho by Cartor.

Set	7.00	8.50
Gutter pairs	17.00	–
Traffic light gutter pairs	55.00	–
First day cover	–	9.00
Stamp cards	7.50	35.00

QUEEN ELIZABETH II DECIMAL

Robert Walpole, first Prime Minister, 1721 (1st)
Ceiling of Kedleston Hall by Robert Adam, 1763 (68p)
Penny Black and Uniform Penny Postage, 1840 (76p)
Queen Victoria's Diamond Jubilee, 1897 (£1)

■ **2011, September 15. The Age of the Hanoverians**
Des: Ian Chilvers, Atelier Works. Printed in litho by Cartor.

Miniature sheet	5.00	5.00
First day cover	–	6.00
Press sheet	90.00	–

Angel of the North (1st)
Blackpool Tower (1st)
Carrick-a-Rede (1st)
Downing Street, London (1st)
Edinburgh Castle (1st)
Forth Railway Bridge (1st)
Glastonbury Tor (1st)
Harlech Castle (1st)
Ironbridge (1st)
Jodrell Bank (1st)
Kursaal, Southend (1st)
Lindisfarne Priory (1st)

■ **2011, October 13. UK A–Z (issue 1)**
Des: Robert Maude and Sarah Davies. Printed in litho by Cartor.
Issued in se-tenant strips of six in two different sheets.

Set (se-tenant strips of six)	13.00	13.00
Gutter pairs	28.00	–
Traffic light gutter pairs	70.00	–
First day cover	–	1200
Stamp cards	9.00	27.00

The angel visits Joseph, from Matthew 1:21 (2nd, 2nd Large)
Madonna and child, from Matthew 1:23 (1st, 1st Large)
Jesus in the manger, from Luke 2:7 (68p)
The angel visits the shepherds, from Luke 2:10 (£1.10)
The wise men and the star, from Matthew 2:10 (£1.65)

■ **2011, November 8. Christmas. 400th Anniversary of the King James Bible**
Des: Peter Malone, The Artworks and Together Design. Printed in gravure by De La Rue. Counter stamps self-adhesive; miniature sheet gummed.

Set	9.00	9.00
First day cover	–	11.00
Miniature sheet (one of each design)	12.00	13.00
Miniature sheet first day cover	–	12.00
Stamp cards	6.25	32.00

(*The 2nd and 1st class also appear in booklets, the 2nd, 1st, 68p, £1.10 and £1.50 in generic Smilers sheets, and the 2nd, 1st, 68p and £1.10 in customised Smilers sheets.)

Olympic Games logo (1st, Worldwide up to 20g)
Paralympic Games logo (1st, Worldwide up to 20g)

■ **2012, January 5. Olympic and Paralympic Games definitives**
Des: Studio Dempsey. Printed in gravure by De La Rue. Self-adhesive. The two designs for each value are arranged in a checkerboard fashion in sheets, with the order alternating.

Set	15.00	15.00
Gutter pairs (1st class)	40.00	–
First day cover	–	15.00
Stamp cards	10.00	22.00

(*The 1st class values also appear in booklets, printed by Walsall.)

DECIMAL — QUEEN ELIZABETH II

'Charlie and The Chocolate Factory' (1st)
'Fantastic Mr Fox' (66p)
'James and The Giant Peach' (68p)
'Matilda' (76p)
'The Twits' (£1)
'The Witches' (£1.10)

■ 2012, January 10. Roald Dahl
Des: Magpie Studios. Printed in litho by Cartor.

Set	7.00	7.25
Gutter pairs	17.00	–
Traffic light gutter pairs	42.00	–
First day cover	–	9.50
Stamp cards	8.00	33.00

(*All values also appear in the Roald Dahl prestige stamp book.)

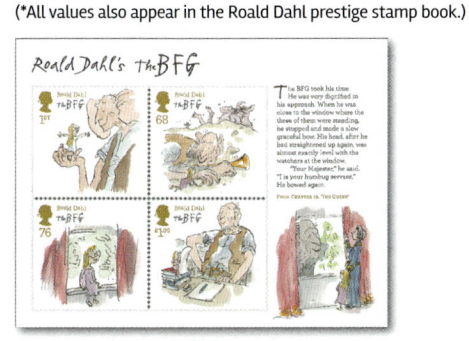

The BFG carrying Sophie (1st)
The BFG and the giants (68p)
Sophie sitting on the Queen's window-sill (76p)
The BFG and Sophie at the writing desk (£1)

■ 2012, January 10. Roald Dahl's The BFG
Des: Magpie Studios. Printed in litho by Cartor.

Miniature sheet	14.00	16.00
Miniature sheet first day cover	–	8.00

(*All values also appear in the Roald Dahl prestige stamp book.)

King Edward VII, 1901–10 (1st)
King George V, 1910–36 (68p)
King Edward VIII, 1936 (76p)
King George VI, 1936–52 (£1)
Queen Elizabeth II, 1952– (£1.10)

■ 2012, February 2. Kings and Queens. The House of Windsor
Des: Ian Chilvers, Atelier Works. Printed in litho by Cartor.

Set	7.00	7.00
Gutter pairs	20.00	–
Traffic light gutter pairs	37.00	–
First day cover	–	7.50
Stamp cards	8.00	32.00

Scott Expedition to the South Pole, 1912 (1st)
Bomb damage in World War I, 1939–45 (68p)
England World Cup winning team, 1966 (76p)
Channel Tunnel opened, 1994 (£1)

■ 2012, February 2. The Age of the Windsors and Saxe-Coburg-Gotha
Des: Ian Chilvers, Atelier Works. Printed in litho by Cartor.

Miniature sheet	5.00	5.00
First day cover	–	6.00
Press sheet	90.00	–

Dorothy Wilding stamp portrait, 1953 (1st)
Robert Austin banknote portrait., 1960 (1st)
Harry Eccleston banknote portrait, 1971 (1st)
Mary Gillick coinage portrait, 1953 (1st)
Arnold Machin coinage portrait, 1968 (1st)
Arnold Machin stamp portrait, 1967 (1st)

■ 2012, February 6. Diamond Jubilee
Printed in gravure by Walsall. The Arnold Machin stamp portrait design has overlay text reading 'Diamond Jubilee' and source code 'MMND'.

Miniature sheet	8.00	9.50
First day cover	–	6.50
Press sheet	60.00	–
Stamp cards	5.00	20.00

(*The Arnold Machin Stamp Portrait design also appears, in self-adhesive form, in counter sheets, business sheets and booklets. The Dorothy Wilding and Arnold Machin Stamp Portrait designs also appear in the Diamond Jubilee prestige stamp book.)

BRITISH STAMP MARKET VALUES 2024   179

QUEEN ELIZABETH II DECIMAL

Coventry Cathedral by Sir Basil Spence (1st)
Frederick Delius, composer (1st)
'Orange Tree' embroidery by Mary 'May' Morris (1st)
Odette Hallowes, wartime secret agent (1st)
Atmospheric steam engine by Thomas Newcomen (1st)
Kathleen Ferrier, opera singer (1st)
Interior of Palace of Westminster by Augustus Pugin (1st)
Montague Rhodes James, author (1st)
Bombe code-breaking machine by Alan Turing (1st)
Joan Mary Fry, social reformer (1st)

■ 2012, February 23. Britons of Distinction
Des: Purpose. Printed in litho by Cartor. Issued in se-tenant strips of five in two separate sheets.

Set	14.00	15.00
Gutter pairs	30.00	–
First day cover	–	9.50
Stamp cards	8.00	22.00

(*The 1st class Bombe design also appears in the Inventive Britain prestige stamp book of February 19, 2015.)

BR Class D34 locomotive (1st)
BR Class D40 locomotive (68p)
Andrew Barclay No807 locomotive (£1)
BR Class 4P locomotive (£1.10)

■ 2012, March 8. Classic Locomotives of Scotland
Des: Delaney Design Consultants. Printed in litho by Cartor.

Miniature sheet	7.50	7.50
Miniature sheet first day cover	–	8.50
Stamp cards	4.50	23.00

'The Dandy' and Desperate Dan (1st)
'The Beano' and Dennis the Menace (1st)
'Eagle' and Dan Dare(1st)
'The Topper' and Beryl the Peril (1st)
'Tiger' and Roy of the Rovers (1st)
'Bunty' and The Four Marys (1st)
'Buster' and Buster(1st)
'Valiant' and The Steel Claw (1st)
'Twinkle' and Nurse Nancy (1st)
'2000AD' and Judge Dredd (1st)

■ 2012, March 20. Comics
Des: The Chase. Printed in litho by Cartor. Issued in se-tenant strips of five in two separate sheets.

Set	14.00	16.00
Gutter pairs	30.00	–
First day cover	–	16.00
Stamp cards	7.00	23.00

Manchester Town Hall (1st)
Narrow Water Castle (1st)
Old Bailey (1st)
Portmeirion (1st)
Queen's College, Oxford (1st)
Roman Baths (1st)
Stirling Castle (1st)
Tyne Bridge (1st)
Urquhart Castle (1st)
Victoria and Albert Museum (1st)
White Cliffs of Dover (1st)
Station X, Bletchley Park (1st)
York Minster (1st)
ZSL London Zoo (1st)

■ 2012, April 10. UK A–Z (issue 2) (Europa)
Des: Robert Maude and Sarah Davies. Printed in litho by Cartor. Issued in se-tenant strips of six (M-R and S-X), and in se-tenant pairs (Y-Z), in three different sheets.

Set (se-tenant strips and pairs)	15.00	15.00
Gutter pairs	35.00	–
Traffic light gutter pairs	80.00	–
First day cover	–	16.00
Stamp cards	10.00	37.00
Composite sheet (entire series of 26)	£120	–

(*The 1st class Station X design also appears in the Inventive Britain prestige stamp book of February 19, 2015.)

DECIMAL **QUEEN ELIZABETH II**

Ladies' suit by Hardy Amies (1st)
Ladies' outfit by Norman Hartnell (1st)
Men's jacket by Granny Takes A Trip (1st)
Ladies' outfit by Ossie Clark (1st)
Men's suit by Tommy Nutter (1st)
Ladies' outfit by Jean Muir (1st)
Ladies' dress by Zandra Rhodes (1st)
Ladies' dress by Vivienne Westwood (1st)
Men's suit by Paul Smith (1st)
Ladies' dress by Alexander McQueen (1st)

■ **2012, May 15. Great British Fashion**
Des: Johnson Banks. Printed in litho by Cartor. Printed in se-tenant strips of five in two separate sheets.

Set (se-tenant strips of five)	13.00	13.00
Gutter pairs	28.00	–
Traffic light gutter pairs	60.00	–
First day cover	–	12.50
Stamp cards	9.00	24.00

The Queen during her Golden Jubilee, 2002 (1st)
The Queen at the Trooping of the Colour, 1967 (1st)
The Queen inspecting troops of the Royal Welsh, 2007 (77p)
The Queen making her first Christmas TV broadcast, 1957 (77p)
The Queen on a Silver Jubilee Walkabout, 1977 (87p)
The Queen at the Order of the Garter Ceremony, 1997 (87p)
The Queen addressing the United Nations, 1957 (£1.28)
The Queen at the Commonwealth Games, 1982 (£1.28)

■ **2012, May 31. Diamond Jubilee**
Des: Kate Stephens. Printed in litho by Cartor. Issued in se-tenant pairs of each denomination.

Set	11.00	11.00
Gutter pairs	27.00	–
First day cover	–	15.00
Stamp cards	5.00	23.00

(*All values also appear in the Diamond Jubilee prestige stamp book. The Golden Jubilee design also appears, in self-adhesive form, in a booklet; price £2.25 mint or used. The Golden Jubilee and Trooping the Colour designs also appear in the Platinum Jubilee prestige stamp book issued in 2022.)

Mr Bumble from 'Oliver Twist' (2nd)
Mr Pickwick from 'The Pickwick Papers' (1st)
The Marchioness from 'The Old Curiosity Shop' (77p)
Mrs Gamp from 'Martin Chuzzlewit' (87p)
Captain Cuttle from 'Dombey & Son' (£1.28)
Mr Micawber from 'David Copperfield' (£1.90)

■ **2012, June 19. Bicentenary of the Birth of Charles Dickens**
Des: Howard Brown, from illustrations by 'Kyd' (Joseph Clayton Clarke). Printed in litho by Cartor.

Set	9.00	9.00
Gutter pairs	23.00	–
Traffic light gutter pairs	40.00	–
First day cover	–	12.00
Stamp cards	8.00	40.00

Scene from 'Nicholas Nickleby' (1st)
Scene from 'Bleak House' (1st)
Scene from 'Little Dorrit' (1st)
Scene from 'A Tale of Two Cities' (1st)

■ **2012, June 19. Bicentenary of the Birth of Charles Dickens**
Des: Howard Brown, from illustrations by 'Phiz' (Hablot Knight Brown). Printed in litho by Cartor.

Miniature sheet	4.50	4.50
Miniature sheet first day cover	–	5.00

BRITISH STAMP MARKET VALUES 2024   **181**

QUEEN ELIZABETH II DECIMAL

Miniature sheet (1st, 1st, 1st, 1st, 1st, 1st): 29 different sheet designs

■ **2012, July 27–August 12. London 2012 Olympic Games Gold Medal Winners**
Des: True North. Base design printed in litho by Walsall (at Cartor), with photographic image and event-specific inscriptions added in litho by regional printers Acorn Press (Swindon), Allander Print (Edinburgh), Aquatint BSC (London), B&D (Preston), Breckland (Attleborough) and Crescent (Solihull). Self-adhesive miniature sheets comprising six 1st class stamps, issued the day after each gold medal win and initially available from 518 selected post offices.

	Mint	Used	FDC
Miniature sheet Rowing, women's pairs: Heather Stanning, Helen Glover (Aug 2)	7.00	7.00	10.00
Miniature sheet Cycling, men's time trial: Bradley Wiggins (Aug 2)	7.00	7.00	10.00
Miniature sheet Canoeing, men's double slalom: Etienne Stott, Tim Baillie (Aug 3)	7.00	7.00	10.00
Miniature sheet Shooting, men's double trap: Peter Wilson (Aug 3)	7.00	7.00	10.00
Miniature sheet Cycling, men's team sprint: Philip Hindes, Chris Hoy, Jason Kenny (Aug 3)	7.00	7.00	10.00
Miniature sheet Rowing, women's double sculls: Anna Watkins, Katherine Grainger (Aug 4)	7.00	7.00	10.00
Miniature sheet Cycling, men's pursuit: Ed Clancy, Geraint Thomas, Steven Burke, Peter Kennaugh (Aug 4)	7.00	7.00	10.00
Miniature sheet Cycling, women's keirin: Victoria Pendleton (Aug 4)	7.00	7.00	10.00
Miniature sheet Rowing, men's four: Alex Gregory, Tom James, Pete Reed, Andrew Triggs-Hodge (Aug 5)	7.00	7.00	10.00
Miniature sheet Rowing, women's lightweight double sculls: Kat Copeland, Sophie Hosking (Aug 5)	7.00	7.00	10.00
Miniature sheet Cycling, women's team pursuit: Danielle King, Joanna Rowsell, Laura Trott (Aug 5)	7.00	7.00	10.00
Miniature sheet Athletics, women's heptathlon: Jessica Ennis (Aug 5)	7.00	7.00	10.00
Miniature sheet Athletics, men's long jump: Greg Rutherford (Aug 5)	7.00	7.00	10.00
Miniature sheet Athletics, men's 10,000 metres: Mo Farah (Aug 5)	7.00	7.00	10.00
Miniature sheet Sailing, finn class: Ben Ainslie (Aug 6)	7.00	7.00	10.00
Miniature sheet Tennis, men's singles: Andy Murray (Aug 6)	7.00	7.00	10.00
Miniature sheet Equestrian, team show-jumping: Scott Brash, Peter Charles, Ben Maher, Nick Skelton (Aug 7)	7.00	7.00	10.00
Miniature sheet Cycling, men's sprint: Jason Kenny (Aug 7)	7.00	7.00	10.00
Miniature sheet Athletics, men's triathlon: Alistair Brownlee (Aug 8)	7.00	7.00	10.00
Miniature sheet Equestrian, team dressage: Laura Bechtolsheimer, Charlotte Dujardin, Carl Hester (Aug 8)	7.00	7.00	10.00
Miniature sheet Cycling, women's omnium: Laura Trott (Aug 8)	7.00	7.00	10.00
Miniature sheet Cycling, men's keirin: Chris Hoy (Aug 8)	7.00	7.00	10.00
Miniature sheet Equestrian, individual dressage: Charlotte Dujardin (Aug 10)	7.00	7.00	10.00
Miniature sheet Boxing, women's flyweight: Nicola Adams (Aug 10)	7.00	7.00	10.00
Miniature sheet Taekwando, women's under 57kg: Jade Jones (Aug 10)	7.00	7.00	10.00
Miniature sheet Kayaking, men's K1 sprint: Ed McKeever (Aug 12)	7.00	7.00	10.00
Miniature sheet Athletics, men's 5,000 metres: Mo Farah (Aug 12)	7.00	7.00	10.00
Miniature sheet Boxing, men's bantamweight: Luke Campbell (Aug 12)	7.00	7.00	10.00
Miniature sheet Boxing, men's super heavyweight: Anthony Joshua (Aug 13)	7.00	7.00	10.00

DECIMAL QUEEN ELIZABETH II

Miniature sheet (1st, 1st): 34 different sheet designs

2012, August 31–September 10. London 2012 Paralympic Games Gold Medal Winners

Des: True North. Base design printed in litho by Walsall (at Cartor), with photographic image and event-specific inscriptions added in litho by regional printers Acorn Press (Swindon), Allander Print (Edinburgh), Aquatint BSC (London), B&D (Preston), Breckland (Attleborough) and Crescent (Solihull). Self-adhesive miniature sheets comprising two 1st class stamps, issued within four days of each gold medal win and initially available from 518 selected post offices.

	Mint	Used	FDC
Miniature sheet Cycling, women's C5 pursuit: Sarah Storey (Aug 31)	2.75	3.00	4.50
Miniature sheet Swimming, men's S7 100m backstroke: Jonathan Fox (Sep 1)	2.75	3.00	4.50
Miniature sheet Cycling, men's C1 pursuit: Mark Colbourne (Sep 3)	2.75	3.00	4.50
Miniature sheet Athletics, women's T34 100m: Hannah Cockcroft (Sep 3)	2.75	3.00	4.50
Miniature sheet Cycling, men's 1km time trial B: Neil Fachie, Barney Storey (Sep 3)	2.75	3.00	4.50
Miniature sheet Athletics, men's T42 200m: Richard Whitehead (Sep 3)	2.75	3.00	4.50
Miniature sheet Equestrian, individual championship test, grade II: Natasha Baker (Sep 3)	2.75	3.00	4.50
Miniature sheet Cycling, women's 500m time trial C4–5: Sarah Storey (Sep 3)	2.75	3.00	4.50
Miniature sheet Swimming, women's 400m freestyle S6: Ellie Simmonds (Sep 3)	2.75	3.00	4.50
Miniature sheet Rowing, coxed four: Pam Relph, Naomi Riches, David Smith, James Roe, Lily Broecke (Sep 4)	2.75	3.00	4.50
Miniature sheet Athletics, men's F42 discus: Aled Davies (Sep 4)	2.75	3.00	4.50
Miniature sheet Cycling, men's individual sprint B: Anthony Kappes, Craig MacLean (Sep 4)	2.75	3.00	4.50
Miniature sheet Swimming, women's S14 200m freestyle: Jessica-Jane Applegate (Sep 4)	2.75	3.00	4.50
Miniature sheet Equestrian, individual championship test grade Ia: Sophie Christiansen (Sep 4)	2.75	3.00	4.50
Miniature sheet Athletics, men's 5000m T54: David Weir (Sep 4)	2.75	3.00	4.50
Miniature sheet Equestrian, individual freestyle test grade II: Natasha Baker (Sep 4)	2.75	3.00	4.50
Miniature sheet Swimming, women's 200m individual medley SM6: Ellie Simmonds (Sep 4)	2.75	3.00	4.50
Miniature sheet Athletics, men's 100m T53: Mickey Bushell (Sep 5)	2.75	3.00	4.50
Miniature sheet Archery, women's individual compound open: Danielle Brown (Sep 5)	2.75	3.00	4.50
Miniature sheet Swimming, women's 100m backstroke S8: Heather Frederiksen (Sep 5)	2.75	3.00	4.50
Miniature sheet Equestrian, individual freestyle test grade Ia: Sophie Christiansen (Sep 5)	2.75	3.00	4.50
Miniature sheet Athletics, men's T54 1500m: David Weir (Sep 7)	2.75	3.00	4.50
Miniature sheet Cycling, women's time trial C5: Sarah Storey (Sep 7)	2.75	3.00	4.50
Miniature sheet Swimming, men's 200m individual medley SM8: Oliver Hynd (Sep 7)	2.75	3.00	4.50
Miniature sheet Equestrian, team: Sophie Christiansen, Deborah Criddle, Lee Pearson, Sophie Wells (Sep 7)	2.75	3.00	4.50
Miniature sheet Sailing, 2.4mR single-person keelboat: Helena Lucas (Sep 8)	2.75	3.00	4.50
Miniature sheet Cycling, women's C4–5 road race: Sarah Storey (Sep 8)	2.75	3.00	4.50
Miniature sheet Swimming, men's S7 400m freestyle: Josef Craig (Sep 8)	2.75	3.00	4.50
Miniature sheet Athletics, women's T34 200m: Hannah Cockcroft (Sep 8)	2.75	3.00	4.50
Miniature sheet Athletics, men's 800m T54: David Weir (Sep 10)	2.75	3.00	4.50
Miniature sheet Athletics, men's 100m T44: Jonnie Peacock (Sep 10)	2.75	3.00	4.50
Miniature sheet Athletics, women's discus F51/52/53: Josie Pearson (Sep 10)	2.75	3.00	4.50
Miniature sheet Cycling, mixed road race T1–2: David Stone (Sep 10)	2.75	3.00	4.50
Miniature sheet Athletics, men's marathon T54: David Weir (Sep 10)	2.75	3.00	4.50

QUEEN ELIZABETH II DECIMAL

Fencer and Tower Bridge (1st)
Track athletes and Olympic Stadium (1st)
Diver and Tate Modern (£1.28)
Track cyclist and London Eye (£1.28)

■ **2012, July 27. Welcome to the London 2012 Olympic Games**
Des: Hat-Trick. Printed in litho by Cartor.

Miniature sheet	6.00	6.00
Miniature sheet first day cover	–	11.00
Stamp cards	8.50	25.00

Amputee athlete and Olympic Stadium (1st)
Wheelchair basketball player and Houses of Parliament (1st)
Weightlifter and St. Paul's Cathedral (£1.28)
Cyclist and London Eye (£1.28)

■ **2012, August 29. Welcome to the London 2012 Paralympic Games**
Des: Hat-Trick. Printed in litho by Cartor.

Miniature sheet	6.00	6.00
Miniature sheet first day cover	–	11.00
Stamp cards	8.50	25.00

Paralympic Games: ParalympicsGB team (1st)
Olympic Games: games makers (1st)
Paralympic Games: opening ceremony (£1.28)
Olympic Games: closing ceremony (£1.28)

■ **2012, September 27. Memories of London 2012**
Des: The Chase. Printed in litho by Walsall (at Cartor).

Miniature sheet	10.00	10.00
Miniature sheet first day cover	–	14.00
Stamp cards	12.00	25.00

Sun (1st)
Venus (1st)
Mars (77p)
Lutetia (77p)
Saturn (£1.28)
Titan (£1.28)

■ **2012, October 16. Space Science.**
Des: Osborne Ross Design. Printed in litho by Cartor.

Set	8.00	8.00
Gutter pairs	20.00	–
First day cover	–	11.00
Stamp cards	4.50	25.00

Poppies (1st)

■ **2012, October 23. Lest We Forget**
Des: Hat-Trick Design. Printed in gravure by Walsall. Design as the Poppies 1st class of January 26, 2010, but self-adhesive.

1st	1.75	1.75
Gutter pair	4.50	–

Reindeer (2nd, 2nd Large)
Father Christmas with robin (1st, 1st Large)
Snowman with penguin (87p)
Robin holding star (£1.28)
Christmas tree with cat and mouse (£1.90)

DECIMAL QUEEN ELIZABETH II

■ 2012, November 6. Christmas
Des: Brian Webb from illustrations by Axel Scheffler. Printed in gravure by De La Rue. Counter sheets self-adhesive; miniature sheet gummed.

Set	10.00	10.50
First day cover	–	13.00
Miniature sheet	10.00	10.50
Miniature sheet first day cover	–	13.00
Stamp cards	5.50	35.00

(*The 2nd class and 1st class values also appear in booklets, printed by Walsall. The 2nd class, 1st class, 87p and £1.28 were used in generic and customised Smilers sheets.)

Metropolitan Railway opens, 1863 (2nd)
Tunnelling beneath London, 1898 (2nd)
Commute from the suburbs, 1911 (1st)
Boston Manor station, 1934 (1st)
Classic rolling stock, 1938 (£1.28)
Canary Wharf station, 1999 (£1.28)

■ 2013, January 9. 150th Anniversary of the London Underground
Des: Hat-Trick. Printed in litho by Cartor.

Set	7.50	8.00
Gutter pairs	18.00	–
First day cover	–	10.00
Stamp cards	8.00	45.00

(*The 1st class Boston Manor design also appears, in self-adhesive form, in a booklet; price £2.00, mint or used.)

Posters: Golders Green; To Fresh Air; Summer Sales (1st)
Posters: For The Zoo; Power; The Seen (77p)
Posters: Every 90 Seconds; Thanks; Cut Travelling Time (87p)
Posters: Transport Collection; London Zoo; Tate Gallery (£1.28)

■ 2013, January 9. Art on the London Underground
Des: NB Studios. Printed in litho by Cartor.

Miniature sheet	5.75	6.00
Miniature sheet first day cover	–	7.00

'Pride & Prejudice' (1st)
'Sense & Sensibility' (1st)
'Mansfield Park' (77p)
'Emma' (77p)
'Northanger Abbey' (£1.28)
'Persuasion' (£1.28)

■ 2013, February 21. Jane Austen
Des: Angela Barrett. Printed in litho by Cartor.

Set	9.00	10.50
Gutter pairs	20.00	–
Traffic light gutter pairs	35.00	–
First day cover	–	11.00
Stamp cards	4.50	18.00

The 11th Doctor, played by Matt Smith (1st)
The 10th Doctor, played by David Tennant (1st)
The 9th Doctor, played by Christopher Eccleston (1st)
The 8th Doctor, played by Paul McGann (1st)
The 7th Doctor, played by Sylvester McCoy (1st)
The 6th Doctor, played by Colin Baker (1st)
The 5th Doctor, played by Peter Davison (1st)
The 4th Doctor, played by Tom Baker (1st)
The 3rd Doctor, played by Jon Pertwee (1st)
The 2nd Doctor, played by Patrick Troughton (1st)
The 1st Doctor, played by William Hartnell (1st)

■ 2013, March 26. 50 Years of Doctor Who
Des: GBH. Printed in litho by Cartor. Issued in se-tenant strips of three, four and four in three separate sheets.

Set	15.00	15.00
Gutter pairs	35.00	–
First day covers (set of two)	–	13.00
Stamp cards	20.00	50.00

(*All designs also appear in the 50 Years of Doctor Who prestige stamp book. The Matt Smith and William Hartnell designs also appear, in self-adhesive form, in a retail booklet; price £7 each mint, £8 each used.)

BRITISH STAMP MARKET VALUES 2024 185

QUEEN ELIZABETH II DECIMAL

The Ood (2nd)
Cyberman (2nd)
Weeping Angel (2nd)
Dalek (2nd)
Tardis (1st)

■ **2013, March 26. 50 Years of Doctor Who**
Des: GBH. Printed in litho by Cartor. Self-adhesive.
Miniature sheet	9.00	9.00
Miniature sheet first day cover	–	6.00

(*The 1st class design also appears in a booklet and in Smilers sheets. It also appears, in gummed form, in the 50 Years of Doctor Who prestige stamp book; price £2.50 mint or used.)

Norman Parkinson (1st)
Vivien Leigh (1st)
Peter Cushing (1st)
David Lloyd George (1st)
Elizabeth David (1st)
John Archer (1st)
Benjamin Britten (1st)
Mary Leakey (1st)
Bill Shankly (1st)
Richard Dimbleby (1st)

■ **2013, April 16. Great Britons**
Des: Together Design. Printed in litho by Cartor. Issued in se-tenant strips of five in two separate sheets.
Set (se-tenant strips of five)	14.00	14.00
Gutter pairs	23.00	–
First day cover	–	12.00
Stamp cards	8.00	25.00

Jimmy Greaves (1st)
John Charles (1st)
Gordon Banks (1st)
George Best (1st)
John Barnes (1st)
Kevin Keegan (1st)
Denis Law (1st)
Bobby Moore (1st)
Bryan Robson (1st)
Dave Mackay (1st)
Bobby Charlton (1st)

■ **2013, May 9. Football Heroes**
Des: Andrew Kinsman. Printed in litho by Cartor. Issued in se-tenant strips of five and six, in two separate sheets.
Set	15.00	17.00
Gutter pairs	35.00	–
First day cover	–	13.00
Miniature sheet (all 11 designs)	15.00	17.00
Miniature sheet first day cover	–	13.00
Stamp cards	8.50	50.00

(*All designs also appear in the Football Heroes prestige stamp book. The George Best, Bobby Moore, John Charles and Dave Mackay designs also appear, in self-adhesive form, in booklets; price £7 each mint, £8 each used.)

Portrait of Queen Elizabeth II by Terence Cuneo, 1953 (2nd)
Portrait of Queen Elizabeth II by Nicola Philipps, 2013 (1st)
Portrait of Queen Elizabeth II by Andrew Festing, 1999 (78p)
Portrait of Queen Elizabeth II by Pietro Annigoni, 1955 (88p)
Portrait of Queen Elizabeth II by Sergei Pavlenko, 2000 (£1.28)
Portrait of Queen Elizabeth II by Richard Stone, 1992 (£1.88)

DECIMAL — QUEEN ELIZABETH II

■ **2013, May 30. 60th Anniversary of the Coronation. Royal Portraits**
Des: Atelier Works. Printed in gravure by Walsall.
Set	10.00	12.00
Gutter pairs	23.00	–
Traffic light gutter pairs	37.50	–
First day cover	–	12.00
Stamp cards	5.00	20.00

UTA W No.103 (1st)
UTA SG3 No.35 (78p)
Peckett No.2 (88p)
CDRJC Class 5 No.4 (£1.28)

■ **2013, June 18. Classic Locomotives of Northern Ireland**
Des: Delaney Design Consultants. Printed in litho by Cartor.
Miniature sheet	7.00	8.00
Miniature sheet first day cover	–	9.50
Stamp cards	4.00	25.00

(*The 1st class design also appears, in self-adhesive form, in a booklet; price £1.50, mint or used.)

Comma (1st)
Orange-tip (1st)
Small copper (1st)
Chalkhill blue (1st)
Swallowtail (1st)
Purple emperor (1st)
Marsh fritillary (1st)
Brimstone (1st)
Red admiral (1st)
Marbled white (1st)

■ **2013, July 11. Butterflies**
Des: Marc & Anna. Printed in litho by Cartor. Issued in se-tenant strips of five in two separate sheets.
Set (in se-tenant strips of 5)	14.00	14.00
Gutter pairs	23.00	–
First day cover	–	13.00
Stamp cards	7.75	25.00

(*The Chalkhill Blue and Comma designs also appear, in self-adhesive form, in a booklet; price £2.50 each, mint or used.)

Andy Murray kissing the championship trophy (1st)
Andy Murray serving (1st)
Andy Murray returning with a backhand (£1.28)
Andy Murray holding the championship trophy (£1.28)

■ **2013. August 8. Andy Murray, Gentlemen's Singles Champion, Wimbledon 2013**
Des: Hat-Trick. Printed in litho by International Security Printers.
Miniature sheet	6.00	6.00
Miniature sheet first day cover	–	7.50

Jaguar E-Type, 1961 (1st)
Rolls-Royce Silver Shadow, 1965 (1st)
Aston Martin DB5, 1963 (1st)
MG MGB, 1962 (£1.28)
Morgan Plus 8, 1968 (£1.28)
Lotus Esprit, 1976 (£1.28)

■ **2013, August 13. British Auto Legends**
Des: Why Not Associates. Printed in litho by Cartor. Issued in se-tenant strips of three in two separate sheets.
Set	10.00	12.00
Gutter pairs	22.00	–
First day cover	–	11.00
Stamp cards	7.50	42.00

Morris Minor van operated by Royal Mail (1st)
Austin FX4 operated as a taxi (1st)
Ford Anglia 105E operated by the police (1st)
Land Rover Defender 110 operated by HM Coastguard (1st)

■ **2013, August 13. British Auto Legends: The Workhorses (Europa)**
Des: Robert Maude and Sarah Davies. Printed in litho by Cartor.
Miniature sheet	6.00	7.00
Miniature sheet first day cover	–	5.00
Press sheet	50.00	–

(*The Morris Minor design also appears, in self-adhesive form, in a booklet printed in gravure by Walsall; price £24 mint, £20 used.)

BRITISH STAMP MARKET VALUES 2024   187

QUEEN ELIZABETH II DECIMAL

East Indiaman 'Atlas', 1813 (1st)
Royal Mail ship 'Britannia', 1840 (1st)
Tea clipper 'Cutty Sark', 1870 (1st)
Cargo liner 'Clan Matheson', 1919 (£1.28)
Royal Mail ship 'Queen Elizabeth', 1940 (£1.28)
Bulk carrier 'Lord Hinton', 1986 (£1.28)

■ 2013, September 19. The Merchant Navy
Des: Silk Pearce. Printed in litho by International Security Printers.

Set	9.00	9.00
Gutter pairs	22.00	–
First day cover	–	11.00
Stamp cards	7.50	30.00

(*All designs also appear in the Merchant Navy prestige stamp book, printed by Enschedé. The 1st class Britannia design also appears, in self-adhesive form, in a booklet printed in gravure by Walsall; price £10 mint or used.)

Polacanthus (1st)
Ichthyosaurus (1st)
Iguanodon (1st)
Ornithocheirus (1st)
Baryonyx (1st)
Dimorphodon (1st)
Hypsilophodon (1st)
Cetiosaurus (1st)
Megalosaurus (1st)
Plesiosaurus (1st)

■ 2013, October 10. Dinosaurs
Des: John Sibbick and Why Not Associates. Printed in litho by International Security Printers. Self-adhesive. Issued in strips of five in two separate sheets.

Set	14.00	15.00
First day cover	–	12.00
Stamp cards	8.00	25.00

HMS 'Vanoc' escorting Atlantic convoy (1st)
Merchant ship in the Thames Estuary (1st)
Clearing ice on HMS 'King George V' in Arctic waters (1st)
Naval convoy in the North Sea (1st)

■ 2013, September 19. The Merchant Navy: The Atlantic and Arctic Convoys
Des: Silk Pearce. Printed in litho by Enschedé.

Miniature sheet	4.50	4.50
Miniature sheet first day cover	–	5.50

(*All designs also appear in the Merchant Navy prestige stamp book.)

'Virgin and Child with the Young St. John the Baptist', by Antoniazzo Romano (2nd, 2nd Large)
'Madonna and Child', by Francesco Granacci (1st, 1st Large)
'St. Roch Praying to the Virgin for an End to the Plague', by Jacques-Louis David (88p)
'The Virgin of the Lilies', by William-Adolphe Bouguereau (£1.28)
'Theotokos, Mother of God', by Fadi Mikhail (£1.88)

■ 2013, November 5. Christmas. Madonna and Child
Des: Robert Maude and Sarah Davies. Printed in gravure by De La Rue. Counter sheets self-adhesive; miniature sheet gummed.

DECIMAL QUEEN ELIZABETH II

Set	11.00	11.00
First day cover	–	13.00
Miniature sheet	16.00	17.00
Miniature sheet first day cover	–	12.50
Stamp cards	5.50	35.00

(*The 2nd class and 1st class designs also appear in booklets, printed by Walsall. The 2nd, 1st, 88p, £1.28 and £1.88 were used in Smilers sheets. The 2nd and 1st were reissued in 2014 and 2016.)

Three Singing Angels (2nd)
A Jolly Father Christmas (1st)

■ 2013, November 5. Children's Christmas

Des: Rosie Hargreaves, aged 10 (2nd), and Molly Robson, aged 7 (1st). Printed in gravure by International Security Printers. Self-adhesive.

Set	3.50	4.50
First day cover	–	5.50

Andy Pandy (1st)
Ivor the Engine (1st)
Dougal from The Magic Roundabout (1st)
Windy Miller from Camberwick Green (1st)
Mr Benn (1st)
Great Uncle Bulgaria from The Wombles (1st)
Bagpuss (1st)
Paddington Bear (1st)
Postman Pat (1st)
Bob the Builder (1st)
Peppa Pig (1st)
Shaun the Sheep (1st)

■ 2014, January 7. Classic Children's TV

Des: Interabang. Printed in gravure by International Security Printers. Self-adhesive. Issued in strips of six in two separate sheets.

Set	16.00	17.00
Gutter pairs	27.00	–
First day cover	–	14.00
Stamp cards	8.00	30.00

Riding for the Disabled Association (1st)
The King's Troop ceremonial horses (1st)
Dray horses (88p)
Royal Mews carriage horses (88p)
Police horses (£1.28)
Forestry horse (£1.28)

■ 2014, February 4. Working Horses

Des: Michael Denny and Harold Batten. Printed in litho by International Security Printers.

Set	8.50	8.50
Gutter pairs	21.00	–
First day cover	–	11.00
Stamp cards	5.50	18.00

LMS 2F No7720 (1st)
Ffestiniog Railway Hunslet No589 'Blanche' (78p)
W&LLR No822 'The Earl' (88p)
BR 5600 No5652 (£1.28)

■ 2014, February 20. Classic Locomotives of Wales

Des: Delaney Design Consultants. Printed in litho by International Security Printers.

Miniature sheet	8.00	8.00
Miniature sheet first day cover	–	9.00
Stamp cards	5.00	25.00

(*All values also appear in the Classic Locomotives of the UK prestige stamp book, printed by Enschedé. The 1st class design also appears, in self-adhesive form, in a booklet, printed in gravure by Walsall; price £2.50 mint or used.)

BRITISH STAMP MARKET VALUES 2024 189

QUEEN ELIZABETH II DECIMAL

Roy Plomley (1st)
Barbara Ward (1st)
Joe Mercer (1st)
Kenneth More (1st)
Dylan Thomas (1st)
Sir Alec Guinness (1st)
Noorunissa Inayat Khan (1st)
Max Perutz (1st)
Joan Littlewood (1st)
Abram Games (1st)

■ **2014, March 25. Remarkable Lives**
Des: Purpose. Printed in litho by International Security Printers. Issued in se-tenant strips of five.

Set	14.00	15.00
Gutter pairs	23.00	–
First day cover	–	12.00
Stamp cards	8.00	25.00

Buckingham House, c1700 (1st)
Buckingham House, 1714 (1st)
Buckingham House, 1819 (1st)
Buckingham Palace, 1846 (1st)
Buckingham Palace, c1862 (1st)
Buckingham Palace, 2014 (1st)

■ **2014, April 15. Buckingham Palace**
Des: Howard Brown. Printed in litho by International Security Printers. Issued in se-tenant strips of three.

Set	8.00	8.50
Gutter pairs	20.00	–
First day cover	–	11.00
Stamp cards	8.50	30.00

(*All designs also appear in the Buckingham Palace prestige stamp book.)

The Throne Room (1st)
The Grand Staircase (1st)
The Blue Drawing Room (1st)
The Green Drawing Room (1st)

■ **2014, April 15. Buckingham Palace**
Des: Robert Maude and Sarah Davies. Printed in litho by Enschedé.

Miniature sheet	4.00	4.00
Miniature sheet first day cover	–	5.00

(*This miniature sheet and subsequent miniature sheets come with a barcode in the selvedge when sold individually, but without this when sold in packs. All designs also appear in the Buckingham Palace prestige stamp book. The Grand Staircase and Throne Room designs also appear, in self-adhesive form, in a booklet printed in gravure by Walsall; price £2.50 each mint or used.)

'A Matter of Life and Death' (1st)
'Lawrence of Arabia' (1st)
'2001: A Space Odyssey' (1st)
'Chariots of Fire' (£1.28)
'Secrets & Lies' (£1.28)
'Bend It Like Beckham' (£1.28)

■ **2014, May 13. Great British Film**
Des: Johnson Banks. Printed in litho by International Security Printers. Issued in se-tenant strips of three.

Set	8.50	9.00
Gutter pairs	22.00	–
First day cover	–	11.50
Stamp cards	8.50	33.00

190 BRITISH STAMP MARKET VALUES 2024

DECIMAL QUEEN ELIZABETH II

'Night Mail', 1936 (1st)
'Love on the Wing', 1938 (1st)
'The Colour Box', 1935 (1st)
'Spare Time', 1939 (1st)

■ 2014, May 13. The GPO Film Unit
Des: Magpie Studio. Printed in litho by Enschedé.

Miniature sheet	5.00	5.00
Miniature sheet first day cover	–	5.50

Herring (1st)
Red gunard (1st)
Dab (1st)
Pouting (1st)
Cornish sardine (1st)
Common skate (1st)
Spiny dogfish (1st)
Wolffish (1st)
Sturgeon (1st)
Conger eel (1st)

■ 2014, June 5. Sustainable Fish
Des: Kate Stephens. Printed in litho by International Security Printers. Issued in se-tenant strips of five.

Set	14.00	14.00
Gutter pairs	23.00	–
First day cover	–	12.00
Stamp cards	8.00	25.00

(*The Common Skate and Cornish Sardine designs also appear, in self-adhesive form, in a booklet, printed in gravure by Walsall; price £7 each mint or £8 used.)

Judo (2nd)
Swimming (1st)
Marathon (97p)
Squash (£1.28)
Netball (£1.47)
Para-sport track cycling (£2.15)

■ 2014, July 17. Commonwealth Games, Glasgow
Des: Howard Brown and Nanette Hoogslag. Printed in litho by International Security Printers.

Set	10.50	10.50
Gutter pairs	24.00	–
First day cover	–	12.50
Stamp cards	7.00	22.00

(*The Swimming design also appears, in self-adhesive form, in a booklet, printed in gravure by Walsall; price £2.50 mint or used.)

Poppy, by Fiona Strickland (1st)
'For The Fallen', by Laurence Binyon (1st)
Private William Cecil Tickle (1st)
'A Star Shell', by C. R. W. Nevinson (£1.47)
'The Response', by William Goscombe John (£1.47)
Princess Mary's Gift Fund Box (£1.47)

■ 2014, July 28. First World War, 1914
Des: Hat-Trick. Printed in litho by International Security Printers.

Set	10.00	10.00
Gutter pairs	22.50	–
First day cover	–	12.50
Stamp cards	6.00	20.00

(*All designs also appear in the Great War 1914 prestige stamp book. The 1st class Poppy design also appears, in self-adhesive form, in a booklet issued in 2018.)

BRITISH STAMP MARKET VALUES 2024

QUEEN ELIZABETH II DECIMAL

Eastbourne bandstand (1st)
Tinside Lido, Plymouth (1st)
Bangor Pier (97p)
Southwold Lighthouse (97p)
Blackpool Pleasure Beach (£1.28)
Bexhill-on-Sea shelter (£1.28)

■ **2014, September 18. Seaside Architecture (Europa)**
Des: Why Not Associates, after photography by Lee Mawdsley.
Printed in litho by International Security Printers.

Set	9.00	9.00
Gutter pairs	23.00	–
First day cover	–	11.50
Stamp cards	8.50	38.00

Margaret Thatcher (1st)
Harold Wilson (1st)
Clement Attlee (1st)
Winston Churchill (1st)
William Gladstone (1st)
Robert Peel (1st)
Charles Grey (1st)
William Pitt the Younger (1st)

■ **2014, October 14. Prime Ministers**
Des: Together. Printed in litho by International Security Printers.
Issued in se-tenant strips of four.

Set	11.00	12.00
Gutter pairs	23.00	–
First day cover	–	12.50
Stamp cards	6.50	22.00

Llandudno Pier (1st)
Worthing Pier (1st)
Dunoon Pier (£1.28)
Brighton Pier (£1.28)

■ **2014, September 18. Seaside Architecture. British Piers**
Des: Why Not Associates, after photography by Lee Mawdsley.
Printed in litho by Enschedé.

Miniature sheet	8.00	8.50
Miniature sheet first day cover	–	8.00

Taking home the Christmas tree (2nd, 2nd Large)
Posting cards into a pillar box (1st, 1st Large)
Decorating a snowman (£1.28)
Singing carols (£1.47)
Skating (£2.15)

■ **2014, November 4. Christmas**
Des: True North, after illustrations by Andrew Bannecker. Printed
in gravure by De La Rue. Counter sheets self-adhesive; miniature
sheet gummed.

Set	11.50	11.50
First day cover	–	15.00
Miniature sheet	11.50	11.50
Miniature sheet first day cover	–	15.00
Stamp cards	7.00	38.00

(*The 2nd class and 1st class values also appear in booklets,
printed by International Security Printers. The 2nd, 1st, £1.28 and
£1.47 designs were used in Smilers sheets.)

192 BRITISH STAMP MARKET VALUES 2024

DECIMAL QUEEN ELIZABETH II

The White Rabbit (2nd)
Down the rabbit hole (2nd)
'Drink Me' (1st)
The White Rabbit's house (1st)
The Cheshire Cat (81p)
A mad tea party (81p)
The Queen of Hearts (£1.28)
The game of croquet (£1.28)
Alice's evidence (£1.47)
A pack of cards (£1.47)

■ **2015, January 6. Alice in Wonderland**
Des: Godfrey Design, after illustrations by Grahame Baker-Smith. Printed in litho by International Security Printers. Issued in vertical se-tenant pairs.

Set	18.00	21.00
Gutter pairs	45.00	–
First day cover	–	19.00
Stamp cards	7.50	30.00

(*The 1st class designs also appear, in self-adhesive form, in booklets printed in gravure by Walsall; price £15 each, mint or used.)

Well done: '1st' (1st)
Mum: 'Mum Mummy Mother' (1st)
New baby: baby with envelope as nappy (1st)
Wedding: three-tiered cake (1st)
Happy birthday: three smiling candles (1st)
Dad: 'DAD' (1st)
Grandparent: child's hand in adult's hand (1st)
Love: birds in a heart shape (1st)

■ **2015, January 20. Smilers (issue 6)**
Des: Webb & Webb (Well Done and DAD), The Chase (Mum), NB Studio (New Baby, Happy Birthday and Grandparent), Caroline Gardner (Wedding), Rebecca Sutherland (Love). Printed in litho by International Security Printers.

Miniature sheet	10.00	11.00
Miniature sheet first day cover	–	10.00
Stamp cards	7.50	30.00

(*All designs also appear, in self-adhesive form, in a booklet. All values were used in Smilers sheets.)

Colossus (1st)
World Wide Web (1st)
Catseyes (81p)
Fibre optics (81p)
Stainless steel (£1.28)
Carbon fibre (£1.28)
DNA sequencing (£1.47)
i-Limb (£1.47)

■ **2015, February 19. Inventive Britain**
Des: GBH. Printed in litho by International Security Printers. Issued in horizontal se-tenant pairs.

Set	13.00	14.00
Gutter pairs	30.00	–
First day cover	–	17.00
Stamp cards	7.00	26.00

(*All designs also appear in the Inventive Britain prestige stamp book.)

Tarr Steps, River Barle (1st)
Row Bridge, Mosedale Beck (1st)
Pulteney Bridge, River Avon (1st)
Craigellachie Bridge, River Spey (1st)
Menai Suspension Bridge, Menai Strait (1st)
High Level Bridge, River Tyne (1st)
Royal Border Bridge, River Tweed (1st)
Tees Transporter Bridge, River Tees (1st)
Humber Bridge, River Humber (1st)
Peace Bridge, River Foyle (1st)

■ **2015, March 6. Bridges**
Des: GBH. Printed in litho by International Security Printers. Issued in se-tenant strips of five.

Set	13.00	14.00
Gutter pairs	28.00	–
Traffic light gutter pairs	35.00	–
First day cover	–	12.00
Stamp cards	8.00	25.00

BRITISH STAMP MARKET VALUES 2024

QUEEN ELIZABETH II DECIMAL

Spike Milligan (1st)
The Two Ronnies (1st)
Billy Connolly (1st)
Morecambe & Wise (1st)
Norman Wisdom (1st)
Lenny Henry (1st)
Peter Cook & Dudley Moore (1st)
Monty Python (1st)
French & Saunders (1st)
Victoria Wood (1st)

■ **2015, April 1. Comedy Greats**
Des: The Chase. Printed in litho by International Security Printers. Issued in se-tenant strips of five.

Set	10.00	11.00
Gutter pairs	25.00	–
First day cover	–	12.00
Stamp cards	7.50	25.00

(*The Norman Wisdom and Morecambe & Wise designs also appear, in self-adhesive form, in a booklet printed in gravure by International Security Printers; price £15 each, mint or used.)

Penny Black (1st, 1st)
Twopenny Blue (1st, 1st)

■ **2015, May 6. 175th Anniversary of the Penny Black**
Printed in litho by International Security Printers.

Miniature sheet	6.00	8.00
Miniature sheet first day cover	–	5.50
Press sheet	55.00	–
Stamp cards	4.00	17.50

(* The miniature sheet also exists with the frame around the stamps inscribed for the London 2015 Europhilex international stamp exhibition, and a serial number, sold only at the exhibition in a special pack in a limited edition of 7,500. The Penny Black design also exists, in self-adhesive form, in retail booklets printed in gravure; price £5.00 mint or used. It was reissued in a sheetlet of 25 in 2020. Both designs were used in Smilers sheets, and in the Queen Victoria prestige stamp book of 2019.)

Poppy, by Howard Hodgkin (1st)
'All the Hills & Vales Along', by C. H. Sorley (1st)
Rifleman Kulbir Thapa (1st)
'The Kensingtons at Laventie', by Eric Kennington (£1.52)
Cape Helles, Gallipoli, Turkey (£1.52)
London Irish Rifles' football from Loos (£1.52)

■ **2015, May 14. First World War, 1915**
Des: Hat-Trick. Printed in litho by International Security Printers.

Set	10.00	10.00
Gutter pairs	23.00	–
First day cover	–	13.00
Stamp cards	6.50	22.00

(*All designs also appear in the Great War 1915 prestige stamp book.)

Magna Carta, 1215 (1st)
Simon de Montfort's Parliament, 1265 (1st)
Bill of Rights, 1689 (£1.33)
American Bill of Rights, 1791 (£1.33)
Universal Declaration of Human Rights, 1948 (£1.52)
Charter of the Commonwealth, 2013 (£1.52)

■ **2015, June 2. 800th Anniversary of Magna Carta**
Des: Howard Brown. Printed in litho by International Security Printers.

Set	10.50	10.50
Gutter pairs	24.00	–
First day cover	–	13.50
Stamp cards	5.00	21.00

DECIMAL QUEEN ELIZABETH II

Pilots scramble to their Hawker Hurricanes (1st)
Supermarine Spitfires on patrol (1st)
Armourer replaces ammunition boxes (1st)
Spotters of the Auxiliary Territorial Service (£1.33)
Operations Room at Bentley Priory (£1.33)
Pilots of 32 Squadron await orders (£1.33)

■ **2015, July 16. 75th Anniversary of the Battle of Britain**
Des: Supple Studio. Printed in litho by International Security Printers.

Miniature sheet	11.00	13.00
Miniature sheet first day cover	–	12.00
Stamp cards	8.00	25.00

(*The 1st class designs also appear in the RAF Centenary prestige stamp book issued on March 20., 2018.)

The defence of Hougoumont (1st)
The Scots Greys during the charge of the Union Brigade (1st)
The French cavalry's assault on Allied defensive squares (£1.00)
The defence of La Haye Sainte by the King's German Legion (£1.00)
The capture of Plancenoit by the Prussians (£1.52)
The French Imperial Guard's final assault (£1.52)

■ **2015, June 18. 200th Anniversary of the Battle of Waterloo**
Des: Silk Pearce. Printed in litho by International Security Printers.

Set	9.00	9.00
Gutter pairs	22.50	–
First day cover	–	12.50
Stamp cards	10.00	40.00

(*All designs also appear in the Battle of Waterloo prestige stamp book.)

Scabious bee (2nd)
Great yellow bumblebee (1st)
Northern colletes bee (£1.00)
Bilberry bumblebee (£1.33)
Large mason bee (£1.52)
Potter flower bee (£1.28)

■ **2015, August 18. Bees**
Des: Anna Ekelund, after illustrations by Richard Lewington. Printed in litho by International Security Printers.

Set	11.50	12.00
Gutter pairs	25.00	–
First day cover	–	13.50
Stamp cards	7.50	50.00

(*The 1st class design also appears, in self-adhesive form, in booklets; price £2.00, mint or used.)

15th Infantry Regiment, IV Corps, Prussian Army (1st)
Light Infantry, King's German Legion, Anglo-Allied Army (1st)
92nd Gordon Highlanders, Anglo-Allied Army (£1.33)
Grenadiers, Imperial Guard, French Army (£1.33)

■ **2015, June 18. 200th Anniversary of the Battle of Waterloo**
Des: Webb and Webb, after illustrations by Chris Collingwood. Printed in litho by International Security Printers.

Miniature sheet	6.00	6.00
Miniature sheet first day cover	–	8.00

(*All designs also appear in the Battle of Waterloo prestige stamp book.)

Waggle dance (1st)
Pollination (1st)
Making honey (£1.33)
Tending young (£1.33)

■ **2015, August 18. The Honeybee**
Des: Interabang, after illustrations by Andy English. Printed in litho by International Security Printers.

Miniature sheet	7.50	8.00
Miniature sheet first day cover	–	7.50

BRITISH STAMP MARKET VALUES 2024

QUEEN ELIZABETH II DECIMAL

William Wyon's City Medal and Machin portrait (1st)
Wilding portrait and Machin portrait (1st)
Machin definitive, amethyst purple (1st)
Badge of the House of Windsor and Machin portrait (£1.33)
The Queen's personal flag and Machin portrait (£1.33)

■ **2015, September 9. Long To Reign Over Us**
Des: Sedley Place. Printed in intaglio and gravure by International Security Printers.

Miniature sheet	8.50	8.50
Miniature sheet first day cover	–	11.00
Press sheet	50.00	–
Stamp cards	6.00	30.00

(*The Machin definitive in amethyst purple was also issued in counter sheets and booklets.)

Tackle (2nd)
Scrum (2nd)
Try (1st)
Conversion (1st)
Pass (£1.00)
Drop goal (£1.00)
Ruck (£1.52)
Line-out (£1.52)

■ **2015, September 18. Rugby World Cup**
Des: Hat-trick; illustrations by Geoff Appleton. Printed in litho by International Security Printers. Issued in se-tenant pairs.

Set	11.00	11.50
Gutter pairs	28.00	–
First day cover	–	14.50
Stamp cards	6.50	24.00

(*The two 1st class designs also appear, in self-adhesive form, in a booklet; price £10 each, mint or used.)

Darth Vader (1st)   Yoda (1st)
Obi-Wan Kenobi (1st)   Stormtrooper (1st)
Han Solo (1st)   Rey (1st)
Princess Leia (1st)   The Emperor (1st)
Luke Skywalker (1st)   Boba Fett (1st)
Finn (1st)   Kylo Renn (1st)

■ **2015, October 20. Star Wars (issue 1): The Force Awakens**
Des: Interabang, from illustrations by Malcolm Tween. Printed in litho by International Security Printers. Issued in se-tenant strips of six in two separate sheets.

Set	13.00	15.00
Gutter pairs	30.00	–
First day cover	–	15.00
Stamp cards	18.00	67.50

(*All designs also appear in the Making of Star Wars prestige stamp book issued on December 17, 2015. The Han Solo, Yoda, Darth Vader and Stormtrooper designs were used in Smilers sheets.)

X-Wing T-65 Starfighter (1st)
X-Wing T-70 Starfighter (1st)
Millennium Falcon (1st)
Single-seater TIE Fighter (1st)
Two-seater TIE Fighter (1st)
AT-AT Walker (1st)

■ **2015, October 20. Star Wars: The Vehicles**
Des: GBH. Printed in litho by International Security Printers. Self-adhesive.

Miniature sheet	9.00	9.00
Miniature sheet first day cover	–	7.50

(*All design also appear in the Making of Star Wars prestige stamp book issued on December 17, 2015.)

DECIMAL QUEEN ELIZABETH II

The journey to Bethlehem (2nd, 2nd Large)
The Nativity (1st, 1st Large)
The animals of the Nativity (£1.00)
The Shepherds (£1.33)
The Three Wise Men (£1.52)
The Annunciation (£2.25)

■ 2015, November 3. Christmas
Des: Studio David Hillman, from illustrations by David Holmes. Printed in gravure by De La Rue. Counter stamps self-adhesive; miniature sheet gummed.

Set	13.00	13.50
First day cover	–	17.50
Miniature sheet	16.00	18.00
Miniature sheet first day cover	–	17.50
Stamp cards	7.50	50.00

(*The 2nd and 1st class designs also appear in booklets, printed by International Security Printers. The 2nd, 1st, £1.00, £1.33, £1.52 and £2.25 designs were used in Smilers sheets.)

Entering the Antarctic ice, December 1914 (1st)
'Endurance' frozen in pack ice, January 1915 (1st)
Striving to free 'Endurance', February 1915 (£1.00)
Trapped in a pressure crack, October 1915 (£1.00)
Patience Camp, December 1915, April 1916 (£1.33)
Safe arrival at Elephant Island, April 1916 (£1.33)
Setting out for South Georgia, April 1916 (£1.52)
Rescue of 'Endurance' crew, August 1916 (£1.52)

■ 2016, January 7. Shackleton and the Endurance Expedition
Des: Robert Maude and Sarah Davies. Printed in litho by International Security Printers. Issued in se-tenant pairs.

Set	15.00	17.00
Gutter pairs	35.00	–
First day cover	–	17.50
Stamp cards	7.50	27.00

Sir Brian Tuke: Master of the Posts in 1516 (1st)
Packet ship: 'Mail Packet off Eastbourne' by Victor Howes (1st)
Penfold pillar box: hexagonal postbox of 1866 (1st)
River post: river postwoman in World War I (£1.52)
Mail coach: London–Glasgow horse-drawn coach (£1.52)
Medway Mail Centre: sorting machines (£1.52)

■ 2016, February 17. Royal Mail 500
Des: Atelier Works. Printed in litho by International Security Printers.

Set	12.00	14.00
Gutter pairs	27.00	–
Traffic light gutter pairs	22.50	–
First day cover	–	13.00
Stamp cards	9.00	37.00

(*All values also appear in the 500 Years of Royal Mail prestige stamp book.)

'Quickest Way by Airmail' (1st)
'Address Your Letters Plainly' (1st)
'Pack your Parcels Carefully' (£1.33)
'Stamps in Books Save Time' (£1.33)

■ 2016, February 17. Classic GPO Posters
Des: Purpose. Printed in litho by International Security Printers.

Miniature sheet	10.00	12.00
Miniature sheet first day cover	–	8.00

(*All values also appear in the 500 Years of Royal Mail prestige stamp book. The miniature sheet also exists with the border inscribed 'Spring Stampex, 17–20 February 2016', sold only in a special pack at the exhibition.)

BRITISH STAMP MARKET VALUES 2024 197

QUEEN ELIZABETH II DECIMAL

Penny Red (1st)

■ **2016, February 18. 175th Anniversary of the Penny Red**
Printed in litho by International Security Printers. Self-adhesive. Issued in booklets of six.

1st	2.50	2.50
First day cover	–	4.00

(*This design also appears, in gummed form, in the 500 Years of Royal Mail prestige stamp book of 2016, and the Queen Victoria prestige stamp book issued on May 24, 2019. It was reissued in a retail booklet in 2020, and also used in Smilers sheets.)

Nicholas Winton (1st)
Sue Ryder (1st)
John Boyd Orr (1st)
Eglantyne Jebb (£1.33)
Joseph Rowntree (£1.33)
Josephine Butler (£1.33)

■ **2016, March 15. British Humanitarians**
Des: Hat-Trick Design. Printed in litho by International Security Printers. Issued in se-tenant strips of three.

Set	11.00	13.00
Gutter pairs	25.00	–
First day cover	–	12.00
Stamp cards	5.50	20.00

'To thine own self be true' from Hamlet (1st)
'Cowards die many times...' from Julius Caesar (1st)
'Love is a smoke...' from Romeo and Juliet (1st)
'The fool doth think he is wise...' from As You Like It (1st)
'There was a star danced...' from Much Ado About Nothing (1st)
'But if the while I think on thee...' from Sonnet 30 (1st)
'Love comforteth like sunshine after rain' from Venus and Adonis (1st)
'We are such stuff...' from The Tempest (1st)
'Life's but a walking shadow...' from Macbeth (1st)
'I wasted time...' from Richard II (1st)

■ **2016, April 5. 400th Anniversary of the Death of William Shakespeare**
Des: The Chase. Printed in litho by International Security Printers. Issued in se-tenant strips of five in two separate sheets.

Set	17.00	20.00
Gutter pairs	40.00	–
First day cover	–	15.00
Stamp cards	9.00	25.00

Princess Elizabeth II with King George VI, c.1930 (1st)
Queen Elizabeth at the State Opening of Parliament, 2012 (1st)
Queen Elizabeth with Princess Anne and Prince Charles, 1952 (1st)
Queen Elizabeth visiting New Zealand, 1977 (£1.52)
Queen Elizabeth with the Duke of Edinburgh, 1957 (£1.52)
Queen Elizabeth with Nelson Mandela, 1996 (£1.52)

■ **2016, April 21. The Queen's 90th Birthday**
Des: Kate Stephens. Printed in litho by International Security Printers. Issued in se-tenant strips of three.

Set	12.00	14.00
Gutter pairs	25.00	–
First day cover	–	13.00
Stamp cards	8.00	45.00

(*All values also appear in the Queen's 90th Birthday prestige stamp book. The State Opening of Parliament and Princess Anne and Prince Charles designs also appear in the Platinum Jubilee prestige stamp book issued in 2022.)

DECIMAL QUEEN ELIZABETH II

Prince Charles (1st)
Queen Elizabeth II (1st)
Prince George (1st)
Prince William (1st)

■ 2016, April 21. The Queen's 90th Birthday
Des: photograph by Ranald Mackechnie. Printed in litho by International Security Printers.

Miniature sheet	9.00	10.00
Miniature sheet first day cover	–	9.00
Press sheet	55.00	–

(*This miniature sheet also appears in the Queen's 90th Birthday prestige stamp book. All four designs also appear, in self-adhesive form, in retail booklets; price £16 mint, £20 used for the Prince Charles and Queen Elizabeth II stamps, and £3 mint, £4 used for the Prince George and Prince William stamps.)

Woodpecker (1st)
Snake holding a stamp (1st)
Chimpanzee (£1.05)
Bat (£1.05)
Orangutan (£1.33)
Koala with baby (£1.33)

■ 2016, May 17. Animail
Des: Magpie Studio. Printed in litho by International Security Printers. Self-adhesive.

Miniature sheet	10.00	12.00
Miniature sheet first day cover	–	12.00
Stamp cards	6.00	37.00

'Battlefield Poppy', by Giles Revell (1st)
'To My Brother', by Vera Brittain (1st)
Munitions worker Lottie Meade (1st)
'Travoys Arriving With wounded', by Stanley Spencer (£1.52)
Thiepval Memorial, Somme, France (£1.52)
Captain A. C. Green's Battle of Jutland commemorative medal (£1.52)

■ 2016, June 21. First World War, 1916
Des: Hat-Trick. Printed in litho by International Security Printers.

Set	12.00	14.00
Gutter pairs	27.00	
First day cover	–	13.00
Stamp cards	10.00	37.50

(*All designs also appear in the Great War 1916 prestige stamp book.)

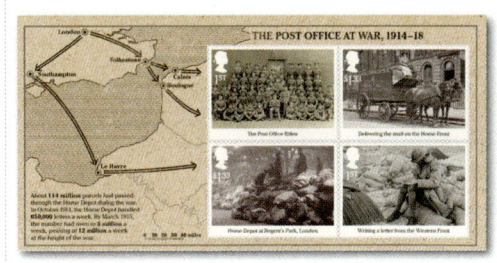

The Post Office Rifles (1st)
Writing a letter from the Western Front (1st)
Home Depot at Regent's Park, London (£1.33)
Delivering the mail on the Home Front (£1.33)

■ 2016, June 21. The Post Office at War, 1914–1918
Des: Hat-Trick. Printed in litho by International Security Printers.

Miniature sheet	8.00	10.00
Miniature sheet first day cover	–	8.00

(*All designs also appear in the Great War 1916 prestige stamp book.)

'The Piper at the Gates of Dawn' album cover (1st)
'Atom Heart Mother' album cover (1st)
'The Dark Side of the Moon' album cover (1st)
'Wish You Were Here' album cover (£1.52)
'Animals' album cover (£1.52)
'The Endless River' album cover (£1.52)

■ 2016, July 7. Music Giants (issue 1). Pink Floyd
Based on design by Studio Dempsey. Printed in gravure by International Security Printers. Self-adhesive in free-form shape.

Set	19.00	20.00
First day cover	–	13.00
Stamp cards	11.00	50.00

(*The Dark Side of the Moon design also appears in a souvenir sheet of 10, not available from post offices; price £12.95.)

QUEEN ELIZABETH II DECIMAL

On stage at the UFO Club, 1966 (1st)
The Dark Side of the Moon tour, 1973 (1st)
The Wall tour, 1981 (£1.52)
The Division Bell tour, 1994 (£1.52)

■ **2016, July 7. Pink Floyd Live**
Printed in litho by International Security Printers.
Miniature sheet	8.00	10.00
Miniature sheet first day cover	–	8.50

'The Tale of Peter Rabbit' (1st)
'The Tale of Mrs Tiggy-Winkle' (1st)
'The Tale of Squirrel Nutkin' (£1.33)
'The Tale of Jemima Puddle-Duck' (£1.33)
'The Tale of Tom Kitten' (£1.52)
'The Tale of Benjamin Bunny' (£1.52)

■ **2016, July 28. 150th Anniversary of the Birth of Beatrix Potter**
Des: Charlie Smith Design. Printed in litho by International Security Printers. Issued in se-tenant pairs.
Set	12.00	14.00
Gutter pairs (each of two designs)	14.00	–
Traffic light gutter pairs	21.00	–
First day cover	–	14.00
Stamp cards	8.50	35.00

(*All designs also appear in the Beatrix Potter prestige stamp book. The two 1st class designs also appear, in self-adhesive form, in a booklet printed in gravure; price £14 each mint, £16 used.)

Peter Rabbit with his mother (1st)
Peter Rabbit entering Mr. McGregor's garden (1st)
Peter Rabbit feeling sick after eating too much (£1.33)
Peter Rabbit escaping from Mr. McGregor (£1.33)

■ **2016, July 28. The Tale of Peter Rabbit**
Printed in litho by International Security Printers.
Miniature sheet	18.00	21.00
Miniature sheet first day cover	–	11.00

(*All designs also appear in the Beatrix Potter prestige stamp book.)

Blenheim Palace (2nd)
Longleat (2nd)
Compton Verney (1st)
Highclere Castle (1st)
Alnwick Castle (£1.05)
Berrington Hall (£1.05)
Stowe (£1.33)
Croome Park (£1.33)

■ **2016, August 16. 300th Anniversary of the Birth of Capability Brown: Landscape Gardens**
Des: Robert Maude and Sarah Davies. Printed in litho by International Security Printers. Issued in se-tenant pairs.
Set	13.00	15.00
Gutter pairs	30.00	–
First day cover	–	14.00
Stamp cards	7.00	23.00

(*The two 1st class designs also appear, in self-adhesive form, in a retail booklet printed in gravure; price £10.00 for the Compton Verney stamp, £5.00 for the Highclere Castle stamp, mint or used.)

DECIMAL QUEEN ELIZABETH II

Mr. Happy (1st)
Little Miss Naughty (1st)
Mr. Bump (1st)
Little Miss Sunshine (1st)
Mr. Tickle (1st)
Mr. Grumpy (1st)
Little Miss Princess (1st)
Mr. Strong (1st)
Little Miss Christmas (1st)
Mr. Messy (1st)

Sunday, 2nd September 1666. Fire breaks out (1st)
Sunday, 2nd September 1666. Fire spreads rapidly (1st)
Monday, 3rd September 1666. Houses are pulled down (£1.05)
Tuesday, 4th September 1666. Fire reaches St. Paul's (£1.05)
Wednesday, 5th September 1666. Fire dies out (£1.52)
Tuesday, 11th September 1666. Wren develops plans (£1.52)

■ 2016, October 20. Mr. Men and Little Miss
Des: Supple Studio. Printed in litho by International Security Printers. Issued in se-tenant strips of five in two separate sheets.

Set	14.00	16.00
Gutter pairs	23.00	–
First day cover	–	12.50
Stamp cards	8.00	25.00

(*The Mr. Happy and Mr. Tickle designs also appear, in self-adhesive form, in a booklet printed in gravure: price £6 each, mint or used. All designs were used, in self-adhesive form, in Smilers sheets.)

■ 2016, September 2. 350th Anniversary of the Great Fire of London
Des: The Chase; illustrations by John Higgins. Printed in litho by International Security Printers. Issued in se-tenant pairs.

Set	12.00	14.00
Gutter pairs	28.00	–
First day cover	–	13.00
Stamp cards	6.00	22.00

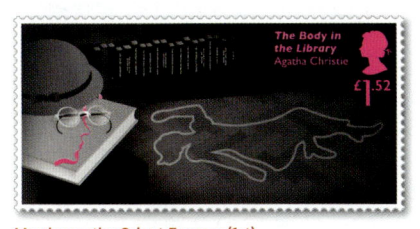

Murder on the Orient Express (1st)
And Then There Were None (1st)
The Mysterious Affair at Styles (£1.33)
The Murder of Roger Ackroyd (£1.33)
The Body in the Library (£1.52)
A Murder is Announced (£1.52)

■ 2016, September 15. Agatha Christie
Des: Studio Sutherland; illustrations by Neil Webb. Printed in litho by International Security Printers. Issued in vertically se-tenant pairs.

Set	13.00	15.00
Gutter pairs (each of two designs)	14.00	–
First day cover	–	14.00
Stamp cards	5.50	23.00

Snowman (2nd, 2nd Large)
Robin (1st, 1st Large)
Christmas tree (£1.05)
Lantern (£1.33)
Stocking full of toys (£1.52)
Christmas pudding (£2.25)

■ 2016, November 8. Christmas
Des: The Chase; paper cuts by Helen Musselwhite, photography by Jonathan Beer. Printed in gravure by De La Rue. Counter stamps self-adhesive; miniature sheet gummed.

Set	15.00	19.00
First day cover	–	17.50
Miniature sheet	16.00	17.00
Miniature sheet first day cover	–	17.50
Stamp cards	7.50	52.00

(*The 2nd class and 1st class also appear in booklets, printed by International Security Printers. The 2nd, 1st, £1.05, £1.33, £1.52 and £2.25 designs were used in Smilers sheets.)

QUEEN ELIZABETH II DECIMAL

Battersea shield, London (1st)
Skara Brae village, Orkney Islands (1st)
Star Carr headdress, Yorkshire (£1.05)
Maiden Castle hill fort, Dorset (£1.05)
Avebury stone circles, Wiltshire (£1.33)
Drumbest horns, County Antrim (£1.33)
Grime's Graves flint mines, Norfolk (£1.52)
Mold cape, Flintshire (£1.52)

■ **2017, January 17. Ancient Britain**
Des: True North; illustrations by Rebecca Strickson. Printed in litho by International Security Printers. Issued in se-tenant pairs.

Set	14.50	14.50
Gutter pairs	33.00	–
First day cover	–	17.50
Stamp cards	7.25	28.00

Nave: Sir Reginald Bray roof boss (1st)
Nave: fan-vaulted roof (1st)
Quire: Garter banners (£1.33)
Quire: St George's Cross roof boss (£1.33)

■ **2017, February 15. Windsor Castle: St George's Chapel**
Des: Up. Printed in litho by International Security Printers.

Miniature sheet	6.50	7.00
Miniature sheet first day cover	–	8.00
Press sheet	95.00	–

(*All designs also appear in the Windsor Castle prestige stamp book. The two 1st class designs also appear, in self-adhesive form, in a booklet printed in gravure: price £5 each mint or used. The miniature sheet also exists with the border inscribed 'Spring Stampex 15–18 February 2017', sold only in a special pack at the exhibition.)

The Long Walk (1st)
The Round Tower (1st)
The Norman Gate (1st)
St George's Hall (£1.52)
The Queen's Ballroom (£1.52)
The Waterloo Chamber (£1.52)

■ **2017, February 15. Windsor Castle (Europa)**
Des: Up. Printed in litho by International Security Printers. Issued in se-tenant strips of three.

Set	11.00	11.00
Gutter pairs	24.00	–
First day cover	–	12.50
Stamp cards	8.50	42.00

(*All values also appear in the Windsor Castle prestige stamp book.)

'Hunky Dory' album cover (1st)
'Aladdin Sane' album cover (1st)
'Heroes' album cover (1st)
'Let's Dance' album cover (£1.52)
'Earthling' album cover (£1.52)
'Blackstar' album cover (£1.52)

■ **2017, March 14. Music Giants (issue 2). David Bowie**
Studio Dempsey. Printed in gravure by International Security Printers. Self-adhesive.

Set	10.50	11.00
First day cover	–	12.00
Stamp cards	11.00	43.00

202 BRITISH STAMP MARKET VALUES 2024

DECIMAL QUEEN ELIZABETH II

(*The Aladdin Sane and Heroes designs also appear in a booklet, printed by International Security Printers: price £4 each mint or used. All six designs also appear, in gummed form, in four different 'fan sheets' which were sold at a premium and were available only from the philatelic service.)

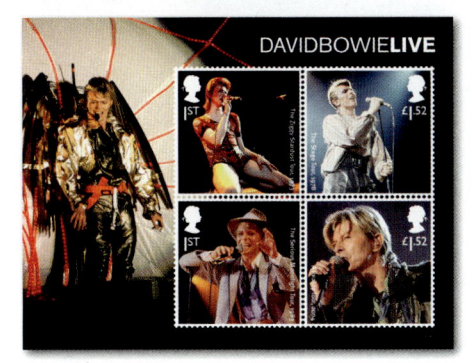

Ziggy Stardust Tour, 1973 (1st)
Serious Moonlight Tour, 1983 (1st)
Stage Tour, 1978 (£1.52)
A Reality Tour, 2006 (£1.52)

■ **2017, March 14. David Bowie Live**
Printed in litho by International Security Printers.
Miniature sheet	9.00	10.00
Miniature sheet first day cover	–	8.50

Frankel (1st)
Red Rum (1st)
Shergar (£1.17)
Kauto Star (£1.17)
Desert Orchid (£1.40)
Brigadier Gerard (£1.40)
Arkle (£1.57)
Estimate (£1.57)

■ **2017, April 6. Racehorse Legends**
Des: Together Design; illustrations by Mike Heslop. Printed in litho by International Security Printers.
Set	15.00	16.00
Gutter pairs	33.00	–
First day cover	–	19.00
Stamp cards	7.25	29.00

Great tit (1st)
Wren (1st)
Willow warbler (1st)
Goldcrest (1st)
Skylark (1st)
Blackcap (1st)
Song thrush (1st)
Nightingale (1st)
Cuckoo (1st)
Yellowhammer (1st)

■ **2017, May 4. Songbirds**
Des: Osborne Ross; illustrations by Federico Gemma. Printed in litho by International Security Printers. Issued in se-tenant strips of five in two separate sheets.
Set	13.00	16.00
Gutter pairs	28.00	–
First day cover	–	12.50
Stamp cards	10.00	25.00

Preliminary sketch by Arnold Machin, January 1966 (1st)
Photograph of coin mould, February 1966 (1st)
Essay with coinage head and symbols, April/May 1966 (1st)
Essay with coinage head simplified, October 1966 (1st)
Photograph by John Hedgecoe, August 1966 (1st)
Essay of first plaster cast of the 'Diadem' head, October 1966 (1st)

■ **2017, June 5. The Machin Definitive. 50 Years of a Design Icon**
Des: Atelier Works. Printed in gravure and embossing by International Security Printers.
Miniature sheet	11.50	13.00
Miniature sheet first day cover	–	15.00
Press sheet	50.00	–
Stamp cards	7.50	50.00

(*All designs also appear in the Machin Definitive 50th Anniversary prestige stamp book. The set of stamp cards includes that of the Machin Definitive Golden Anniversary miniature sheet, which is listed in the Machins section of this guide).

BRITISH STAMP MARKET VALUES 2024 203

QUEEN ELIZABETH II DECIMAL

Nutley Windmill, East Sussex (1st)
New Abbey Corn Mill, Dumfries and Galloway (1st)
Ballycopeland Windmill, County Down (£1.40)
Cheddleton Flint Mill, Staffordshire (£1.40)
Woodchurch Windmill, Kent (£1.57)
Felin Cochwillan Mill, Gwynedd (£1.57)

■ **2017, June 20. Windmills and Watermills**
Des: Atelier Works; photographs by Philip Sayer. Printed in litho by International Security Printers. Issued in vertical se-tenant pairs.

Set	11.00	11.00
Gutter pairs	24.00	–
First day cover	–	14.00
Stamp cards	5.25	23.00

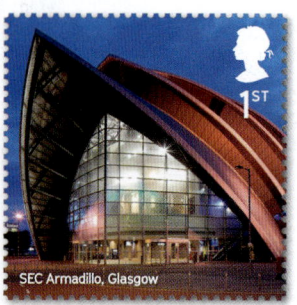

London Aquatics Centre (1st)
Library of Birmingham (1st)
SEC Armadillo, Glasgow (1st)
Scottish Parliament, Edinburgh (1st)
Giant's Causeway Visitor Centre, County Antrim (1st)
National Assembly for Wales, Cardiff (1st)
Eden Project, St Austell, Cornwall (1st)
Everyman Theatre, Liverpool (1st)
Imperial War Museum North, Manchester (1st)
Switch House, Tate Modern, London (1st)

■ **2017, July 13. Landmark Buildings**
Des: GBH. Printed in litho by International Security Printers. Issued in se-tenant strips of five.

Set	14.00	14.00
Gutter pairs	24.00	–
First day cover	–	12.50
Stamp cards	10.00	25.00

'Shattered Poppy', by John Ross (1st)
'Dead Man's Dump', by Isaac Rosenberg (1st)
Nurses Elsie Knocker and Mairi Chisholm (1st)
'Dry Docked for Scaling and Painting', by Edward Wadsworth (£1.57)
Tyne Cot Cemetery, Belgium (£1.57)
Private Lemuel Thomas Rees's life-saving Bible (£1.57)

■ **2017, July 31. First World War, 1917**
Des: Hat-Trick. Printed in litho by International Security Printers.

Set	10.00	10.00
Gutter pairs	23.00	–
First day cover	–	13.00
Stamp cards	4.50	35.00

(*All designs also appear in the Great War 1917 prestige stamp book.)

Merrythought bear (1st)
Sindy Weekender doll (1st)
Spirograph (1st)
Stickle Bricks (1st)
William Britain Herald Trojan warriors (1st)
Spacehopper (1st)
Fuzzy-Felt farm set (1st)
Meccano ferris wheel (1st)
Action Man Red Devil (1st)
Hornby Dublo TPO mail van (1st)

■ **2017, August 22. Classic Toys**
Des: Interabang. Printed in litho by International Security Printers. Issued in se-tenant strips of five.

Set	14.00	14.00
Gutter pairs	24.00	–
First day cover	–	12.50
Stamp cards	10.00	25.00

204 BRITISH STAMP MARKET VALUES 2024

DECIMAL **QUEEN ELIZABETH II**

Adventures From History series (2nd)
Well-Loved Tales series (2nd)
Key Words Reading Scheme series (1st)
Early Tales and Rhymes series (1st)
Hobbies and How It Works series (£1.40)
People At Work series (£1.40)
Nature and Conservation series (£1.57)
Achievements series (£1.57)

■ **2017, September 14. Ladybird Books**
Des: True North. Printed in litho by International Security Printers. Issued in se-tenant pairs.

Set	14.00	16.00
Gutter pairs	32.00	–
First day cover	–	16.00
Stamp cards	7.00	29.00

Maz Kanata (1st)   **Chewbacca (1st)**
Supreme Leader Snoke (1st)   **Porg (1st)**
BB-8 (1st)   **R2-D2 (1st)**
C-3PO (1st)   **K-2SO (1st)**

■ **2017, October 12. Star Wars (issue 2). Droids and Aliens**
Des: Royal Mail Group Ltd. Printed in litho by International Security Printers. Issued in se-tenant strips of four.

Set	10.50	12.50
Gutter pairs	20.00	–
First day cover	–	10.00
Stamp cards	9.00	25.00
Composite sheet (entire series of 20)	32.00	47.50

(*All designs also appear in the Star Wars: The Making of the Droids, Aliens and Creatures prestige stamp book issued on December 14, 2017. The BB-8, R2-D2, Maz Kanata and Chewbacca designs appear, in self-adhesive form, in booklets, printed in gravure; price £15 mint or used for the BB-8 and R2-D2 stamps, £10 mint or used for the Maz Kanata and Chewbacca stamps. All designs were also used in Smilers sheets.)

'Virgin and Child', attributed to Gerard David (2nd, 2nd Large)
'Madonna and Child', by William Dyce (1st, 1st Large)
'Virgin Mary with Child', attributed to Quinten Matsijs (£1.17)
'The Small Cowper Madonna', by Raphael (£1.40)
'The Sleep of the Infant Jesus', by Giovanni Battista Salvi (£1.57)
'St Luke Painting the Virgin', by Eduard Jakob von Steinle (£2.27)

■ **2017, November 7. Christmas. Madonna and Child Paintings**
Des: Royal Mail Group Ltd, from a concept by Kate Stevens. Printed in gravure by De La Rue. Counter stamps self-adhesive; miniature sheet gummed. 2nd, 2nd Large, 1st and 1st Large values printed in mixed sheets with Children's Competition designs, resulting in vertical se-tenant pairs.

Set	14.00	14.00
Se-tenant pairs (2nd, 2nd L, 1st, 1st L)	12.00	–
First day cover	–	23.00
Miniature sheet	14.00	14.00
Miniature sheet first day cover	–	18.00
Stamp cards	10.00	55.00

(*The 2nd class and 1st class designs also appear in booklets, printed by International Security Printers. The 2nd, 1st, £1.17, £1.40, £1.57 and £2.27 designs were used in Smilers sheets. The 2nd and 1st class were reissued on November 1, 2018, printed by ISP.)

Arwen Wilson, age 9

'Snow Family' (2nd, 2nd Large)
'Santa Claus on his Sleigh on a Starry Night' (1st, 1st Large)

■ **2017, November 7. Christmas. Children's Competition**
Des: Arwen Wilson, aged 9 (2nd), and Ted Lewis Clark, aged 10 (1st). Printed in gravure by De La Rue. Self-adhesive. Printed in mixed sheets with Madonna and Child designs, resulting in vertical se-tenant pairs.

Set	6.00	6.00
Se-tenant pairs	12.00	–
First day cover	–	10.00

(*The 2nd class and 1st class designs also appear in booklets, printed by International Security Printers, and in Smilers sheets.)

BRITISH STAMP MARKET VALUES 2024   **205**

QUEEN ELIZABETH II DECIMAL

Engagement of Princess Elizabeth and Philip Mountbatten (1st)
Wedding (1st)
Honeymoon (1st)
Engagement (£1.57)
Wedding (£1.57)
Honeymoon (£1.57)

■ **2017, November 20. The Royal Wedding: Platinum Anniversary**
Design: Mytton Williams. Printed in gravure by International Security Printers.

Miniature sheet	13.00	13.00
Miniature sheet first day cover	–	13.00
Press sheet	£150	–
Stamp cards	6.00	35.00

Sansa Stark (1st)
Jon Snow (1st)
Eddard Stark (1st)
Olenna Tyrell (1st)
Tywin Lannister (1st)
Tyrion Lannister (1st)
Cersei Lannister (1st)
Arya Stark (1st)
Jaime Lannister (1st)
Daenerys Targaryen (1st)

■ **2018, January 23. Game of Thrones**
Des: GBH. Printed in litho by International Security Printers. Issued in se-tenant strips of five.

Set	14.00	18.00
Gutter pairs	23.00	–
First day cover	–	12.50
Stamp cards	11.00	40.00

(*All designs also appear in the Game of Thrones prestige stamp book. All designs were used, in self-adhesive form, in a generic Smilers sheet.)

The Iron Throne (1st)
The Night King and white walkers (1st)
Giants (1st)
Direwolves (1st)
Dragons (1st)

■ **2018, January 23. Game of Thrones**
Des: GBH. Printed in litho by International Security Printers. Self-adhesive.

Miniature sheet	5.50	7.50
Miniature sheet first day cover	–	8.00

(*The Iron Throne design also appears in a booklet. All the designs also appear, in gummed form, in the Game of Thrones prestige stamp book.)

Lone suffragette in Whitehall, c.1908 (2nd)
The Great Pilgrimage of Suffragists, 1913 (2nd)
Suffragette leaders at Earl's Court, 1908 (1st)
Women's Freedom League poster parade, c.1907 (1st)
Welsh suffragettes at coronation procession (£1.40)
Mary Leigh and Edith New released from prison, 1908 (£1.40)
Sophia Duleep Singh sells 'The Suffragette', 1913 (£1.57)
Suffragette prisoners' pageant, 1911 (£1.57)

■ **2018, February 15. 100th Anniversary of Votes for Women**
Des: Supple Studio. Printed in litho by International Security Printers. Issued in se-tenant pairs.

Set	12.50	14.00
Gutter pairs	28.00	–
First day cover	–	16.00
Stamp cards	6.00	29.00

206 BRITISH STAMP MARKET VALUES 2024

DECIMAL **QUEEN ELIZABETH II**

Lightning F6 (1st)
Hurricane Mk1 (1st)
Vulcan B2 (£1.40)
Typhoon FGR4 (£1.40)
Sopwith Camel F1 (£1.57)
Nimrod MR2 (£1.57)

■ 2018, March 20. Centenary of the Royal Air Force
Des: Royal Mail Group Ltd, from paintings by Michael Turner. Printed in litho by International Security Printers. Issued in se-tenant pairs.

Set	11.50	15.50
Gutter pairs	26.00	–
First day cover	–	14.00
Stamp cards	8.00	35.00

(*All the designs also appear in the RAF Centenary prestige stamp book. The two 1st class designs also appear, in self-adhesive form, in a retail booklet; price £4 each, mint or used.)

'Flypast' formation (1st)
'Swan' formation (1st)
'Synchro' formation (£1.40)
'Python' formation (£1.40)

■ 2018, March 20. Red Arrows
Des: Turner Duckworth. Printed in litho by International Security Printers.

Miniature sheet	7.00	9.00
Miniature sheet first day cover	–	8.00
Press sheet	75.00	–

(*All the designs also appear in the RAF Centenary prestige stamp book. The two 1st class designs also appear, in self-adhesive form, in a retail booklet; price £12 mint, £14 used.)

Osprey (1st)
Large blue butterfly (1st)
Eurasian beaver (£1.45)
Pool frog (£1.45)
Stinking hawk's-beard (£1.55)
Sand lizard (£1.55)

■ 2018, April 17. Reintroduced Species
Des: Godfrey Design, from illustrations by Tanya Lock. Printed in litho by International Security Printers. Issued in se-tenant pairs.

Set	11.50	15.50
Gutter pairs	26.00	–
First day cover	–	14.50
Stamp cards	4.50	22.00

Barn owl, adult (1st)
Little owl, adult (1st)
Tawny owl, adult (1st)
Short-eared owl, adult (1st)
Long-eared owl, adult (1st)
Barn owl, juveniles (1st)
Little owl, juveniles (1st)
Tawny owl, juvenile (1st)
Short-eared owl, juvenile (1st)
Long-eared owl, juvenile (1st)

■ 2018, May 11. Owls
Des: Atelier Works. Printed in litho by International Security Printers. Issued in se-tenant strips of five.

Set	14.00	18.00
Gutter pairs	24.00	–
Traffic light gutter pairs	40.00	–
First day cover	–	13.00
Stamp cards	7.50	25.00

Prince Harry and Meghan Markle, formal portrait (1st, 1st)
Meghan Markle and Prince Harry, informal (£1.55, £1.55)

■ 2018, May 19. Royal Wedding of Prince Henry of Wales and Meghan Markle
Des: The Chase, from photographs by Alexi Lubomirski. Printed in litho by International Security Printers.

Miniature sheet	8.00	10.00
Miniature sheet first day cover	–	9.00
Press sheet	75.00	–

BRITISH STAMP MARKET VALUES 2024   207

QUEEN ELIZABETH II DECIMAL

'Summer Exhibition', by Grayson Perry (1st)
'Queen of the Sky', by Fiona Rae (1st)
'St Kilda: The Great Sea Stacs', by Norman Ackroyd (£1.25)
'Inverleith Allotments and Edinburgh Castle', by Barbara Rae (£1.25)
'Queuing at the RA', by Yinka Shonibare (£1.55)
'Saying Goodbye', by Tracey Emin (£1.55)

■ 2018, June 5. 250th Anniversary of the Royal Academy of Arts
Des: Royal Mail Group Ltd, from artwork by members of the Royal Academy. Printed in litho by International Security Printers. Issued in vertical se-tenant pairs.

Set	11.00	14.50
Gutter pairs (each of two designs)	12.00	–
First day cover	–	13.50
Stamp cards	4.50	25.00

Sergeant Wilson (2nd)
Private Pike (2nd)
Captain Mainwaring (1st)
Lance Corporal Jones (1st)
Private Walker (£1.45)
Private Frazer (£1.45)
Private Godfrey (£1.55)
Chief Warden Hodges (£1.55)

■ 2018, June 26. 50th Anniversary of Dad's Army
Des: Up. Printed in litho by International Security Printers. Issued in se-tenant pairs.

Set	12.50	17.00
Gutter pairs	28.00	–
First day cover	–	16.60
Stamp cards	6.00	29.00

(*The two 1st class designs also appear, in self-adhesive form, in a booklet; price £12 mint, £14 used, the pair. All designs were used in a generic Smilers sheet.)

South Front (1st)
West Front (1st)
East Front (1st)
Pond Gardens (£1.55)
Maze (£1.55)
Great Fountain Garden (£1.55)

■ 2018, July 31. Hampton Court Palace
Des: Osborne Ross. Printed in litho by International Security Printers. Issued in se-tenant strips of three.

Set	9.00	12.50
Gutter pairs	25.00	–
First day cover	–	12.00
Stamp cards	8.00	25.00

Great Hall (1st)
King's Great Bedchamber (1st)
Chapel Royal (£1.45)
King's Staircase (£1.45)

■ 2018, July 31. Hampton Court Palace
Des: Osborne Ross. Printed in litho by International Security Printers.

Miniature sheet	7.00	9.50
Miniature sheet first day cover	–	9.00
Press sheet	70.00	–

(*The two 1st class designs also appear, in self-adhesive form, in a booklet; price £16 mint, £20 used.)

208 BRITISH STAMP MARKET VALUES 2024

DECIMAL   QUEEN ELIZABETH II

Joseph Banks, red passion flower and red-tailed tropicbird (2nd)
The Chief Mourner of Tahiti, palm trees and canoe (2nd)
Captain James Cook and HMB Endeavour (1st)
The transit of Venus, 1769, and sextant (1st)
Scarlet clianthus and Maori chief with facial moko (£1.45)
Sydney Parkinson and blue-black grassquit plant (£1.45)

■ **2018, August 16. Captain Cook and the Endeavour Voyage**
Des: Howard Brown. Printed in litho by International Security Printers. Issued in se-tenant pairs.

Set	8.00	12.00
Gutter pairs	20.00	–
First day cover	–	11.00
Stamp cards	8.00	25.00

Route of HMB Endeavour to New Zealand and Australia (1st)
Boathouse and canoes on Raiatea, Society Islands (1st)
Maori clifftop fortress in New Zealand (£1.45)
Repairing Endeavour on Australia's Great Barrier Reef (£1.45)

■ **2018, August 16. Captain Cook and the Endeavour Voyage**
Des: Webb & Webb Design. Printed in litho by International Security Printers.

Miniature sheet	6.50	9.00
Miniature sheet first day cover	–	8.00

'The Dance of Death', 1967, with Laurence Olivier (1st)
'King Lear', 2016, with Glenda Jackson (1st)
'Hamlet', 1975, with Albert Finney (£1.25)
'Hedda Gabler', 1970, with Maggie Smith (£1.25)
'No Man's Land', 1975, with John Gielgud and Ralph Richardson (£1.45)
'Carmen Jones', 1991, with Sharon Benson (£1.45)
'Romeo & Juliet', 1960, with Judi Dench and John Stride (£1.55)
'Henry V', 1955, with Richard Burton (£1.55)

■ **2018, August 30. The Old Vic**
Des: Hat-Trick Design. Printed in litho by International Security Printers. Issued in se-tenant pairs.

Set	15.00	20.00
Gutter pairs (each of two designs)	16.00	–
Traffic-light gutter pairs	30.00	–
First day cover	–	19.00
Stamp cards	5.00	30.00

'100 Poppies', by Zafer and Barbara Baran (1st)
'Anthem for Doomed Youth', by Wilfred Owen (1st)
Second Lieutenant Walter Tull (1st)
'We Are Making A New World', by Paul Nash (£1.55)
The Grave of the Unknown Warrior, Westminster Abbey (£1.55)
Lieutenant Francis Hopgood's goggles (£1.55)

■ **2018, September 13. First World War, 1918**
Des: Hat-Trick. Printed in litho by International Security Printers.

Set	10.00	15.00
Gutter pairs	23.00	–
First day cover	–	13.00
Stamp cards	4.50	25.00
Composite sheet (entire series 2014–18)	50.00	–

(*All the designs also appear in the Great War 1918 prestige stamp book. The 100 Poppies 1st class design also appears, in self-adhesive form, in a booklet.)

BRITISH STAMP MARKET VALUES 2024   209

QUEEN ELIZABETH II DECIMAL

Hermione Granger (1st)
Hogwarts Express (1st)
Harry Potter (1st)
Flying Ford Anglia (1st)
Ron Weasley (1st)
Hagrid's motorbike (1st)
Ginny Weasley (1st)
Triwizard Cup (1st)
Neville Longbottom (1st)
Knight bus (1st)

■ **2018, October 16. Harry Potter**
Des: True North. Printed in litho by International Security Printers. Issued in se-tenant strips of five.

Set	14.00	21.00
Gutter pairs	32.00	–
First day cover	–	13.00
Stamp cards	10.00	30.00

(*All designs also appear in the Harry Potter prestige stamp book issued on December 4, 2018. The Hermione Granger and Harry Potter designs also appear, in self-adhesive form, in a booklet; price £2 mint, £3 used, each. All designs appear in a collector's sheet.)

Pomona Sprout (1st)
Horace Slughorn (1st)
Sybill Trelawney (1st)
Remus Lupin (1st)
Severus Snape (1st)

■ **2018, October 16. Harry Potter**
Des: The Chase. Printed in litho by International Security Printers. Self-adhesive.

Miniature sheet	7.50	11.00
Miniature sheet first day cover	–	7.00
Press sheet	90.00	–

(*All the designs also appear in the Harry Potter prestige stamp book issued on December 4, 2018.)

King Edward VII wall box (2nd, 2nd Large)
Queen Elizabeth II double-aperture box (1st, 1st Large)
King George VI lamp box (£1.25)
Queen Victoria Penfold box (£1.45)
King Edward VIII pillar box (£1.55)
King George V lamp box (£2.25)

■ **2018, November 1. Christmas: Postboxes**
Des: Andrew Davidson. Printed in gravure by International Security Printers. Counter sheets self-adhesive; miniature sheet gummed.

Set	15.00	21.00
Se-tenant pairs (2018 with 2017 designs)	20.00	–
First day cover	–	18.00
Miniature sheet	18.50	21.00
Miniature sheet first day cover	–	18.00
Stamp cards	7.00	35.00

(* As well as in sheets of 50, the 2nd and 1st designs were additionally printed as the lower 25 stamps in sheets of 50 with the reissued Madonna & Child 2nd and 1st designs of 2017, resulting in vertically se-tenant pairs; price £12. The 2nd and 1st class designs also appear in booklets. All designs were used in a generic Smilers sheet.)

Prince of Wales in civilian dress (1st)
Prince of Wales and Duchess of Cornwall (1st)
Prince of Wales, Duke of Cambridge and Duke of Sussex (1st)
Prince of Wales, Duke of Cambridge and Duke of Sussex at Cirencester Park Polo Club (£1.55)
Prince of Wales at the Castle of Mey (£1.55)
Prince of Wales and schoolchildren in Wales (£1.55)

■ **2018, November 14. 70th Birthday of the Prince of Wales**
Design: Davies Maude. Printed in gravure by International Security Printers.

Miniature sheet	10.00	14.50
Miniature sheet first day cover	–	13.00
Press sheet	£125	–
Stamp cards	5.00	25.00

DECIMAL   QUEEN ELIZABETH II

Queen Victoria 1891 £1 green (1st)
King Edward VII 1910 2d Tyrian plum (1st)
King George V 1913 2s 6d brown (1st)
King Edward VIII 1936 1½d red-brown (£1.55)
King George VI 1940 Penny Black Centenary ½d green (£1.55)
Queen Elizabeth II 1953 Coronation 2½d red (£1.55)

■ **2019, January 15. Stamp Classics**
Des: Hat-Trick Design. Printed in litho by International Security Printers.

Miniature sheet	10.00	14.50
Miniature sheet first day cover	–	13.00
Press sheet	£125	–
Stamp cards	5.00	25.00

(*The miniature sheet exists with the additional text 'Stampex International 13–16 February 2019' in the border, and a serial number, sold only at the exhibition in a limited edition of 5,000.)

The skull sectioned (1st)
A sprig of guelder rose (1st)
Studies of cats (1st)
The anatomy of the shoulder and foot (1st)
A star-of-Bethlehem and other plants (1st)
The head of Leda (1st)
The head of a bearded man (1st)
The skeleton (1st)
The head of St Philip (1st)
A woman in a landscape (1st)
A design for an equestrian monument (1st)
The fall of light on a face (1st)

■ **2019, February 13. Leonardo da Vinci**
Des: Kate Stephens, from drawings by Leonardo da Vinci held by the Royal Collection. Printed in litho by International Security Printers. Issued in se-tenant strips of six.

Set	16.00	21.00
Gutter pairs	25.00	–
First day cover	–	16.00
Stamp cards	8.00	26.00

(*These stamps also appear in the Leonardo da Vinci prestige stamp book.)

Spider-Man (1st)
Captain Marvel (1st)
Hulk (1st)
Doctor Strange (1st)
Captain Britain (1st)
Peggy Carter (1st)
Iron Man (1st)
Union Jack (1st)
Black Panther (1st)
Thor (1st)

■ **2019, March 14. Marvel**
Des: Interabang, from illustrations by Alan Davis. Printed in litho by International Security Printers. Issued in se-tenant strips of five.

Set	11.50	15.50
Gutter pairs	23.00	–
First day cover	–	13.50
Stamp cards	10.00	35.00

(* All designs also appear in the Make Mine Marvel prestige stamp book. The Spider-Man and Hulk designs appear, in self-adhesive form, in a retail booklet, printed in gravure; price £10 mint or used.)

Captain Britain spies a portal opening (£1.45)
Thanos emerges from the portal (1st)
Thor, Doctor Strange and Iron Man deflect a cosmic ray (1st)
Hulk, Spider-Man, Black Panther and Iron Man retaliate (1st)
Captain Britain and the superheroes proclaim their unity (£1.45)

■ **2019, March 14. Marvel Heroes UK**
Des: Interabang, from illustrations by Alan Davis. Printed in litho by International Security Printers.

Miniature sheet	7.50	11.00
Miniature sheet first day cover	–	10.00
Press sheet	£130	–

(*The miniature sheet also appears in the Make Mine Marvel prestige stamp book.)

BRITISH STAMP MARKET VALUES 2024   211

QUEEN ELIZABETH II DECIMAL

White-tailed eagle (1st)
Merlin (1st)
Hobby (1st)
Buzzard (1st)
Golden eagle (1st)
Kestrel (1st)
Goshawk (1st)
Sparrowhawk (1st)
Red kite (1st)
Peregrine falcon (1st)

■ **2019, April 4. Birds of Prey**
Des: Royal Mail and GBH, from photography by Tim Flach. Printed in litho by International Security Printers. Issued in se-tenant strips of five.

Set	14.00	16.00
Gutter pairs	32.00	–
First day cover	–	13.50
Stamp cards	7.00	20.00

(*The Buzzard and Hobby designs also appear, in self-adhesive form, in a retail booklet; price £50 mint, £60 used the pair.)

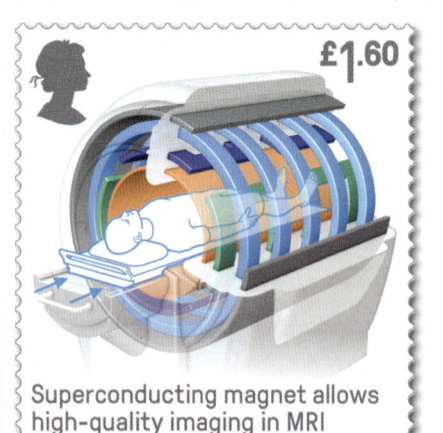

Raspberry Pi microcomputer (1st)
Falkirk Wheel (1st)
Three-way catalytic converter (£1.55)
Crossrail (£1.55)
Superconducting magnets in MRI scanner (£1.60)
Synthetic bone graft material (£1.60)

■ **2019, May 2. British Engineering**
Des: Common Curiosity. Printed in litho by International Security Printers. Issued in se-tenant pairs.

Set	11.50	16.50
Gutter pairs (each of two designs)	12.00	–
Traffic-light gutter pairs	24.00	–
First day cover	–	15.00
Stamp cards	8.00	25.00

Harrier GR3: short take-off (1st)
Harrier GR3: conventional flight (1st)
Harrier GR3: transition to landing (£1.55)
Harrier GR3: vertical landing (£1.55)

■ **2019, May 2. 50th Anniversary of the Harrier Jump Jet**
Des: Turner Duckworth, from photography by Richard Cooke. Printed in litho by International Security Printers.

Miniature sheet	7.00	10.00
Miniature sheet first day cover	–	9.00
Press sheet	90.00	–

Queen Victoria portrait by Heinrich Von Angeli, 1890 (1st)
Queen Victoria and Benjamin Disraeli at Osborne House, 1878 (1st)
Queen Victoria on horseback with servant John Brown, 1876 (£1.35)
Queen Victoria wearing her Robes of State, 1859 (£1.35)
Marriage of Queen Victoria and Prince Albert, 1840 (£1.60)
Princess Victoria aged 11, 1830 (£1.60)

DECIMAL   QUEEN ELIZABETH II

■ **2019, May 24. Bicentenary of the Birth of Queen Victoria**
Des: Webb & Webb Design. Printed in litho by International Security Printers. Issued in se-tenant pairs.

Set	14.00	20.00
Gutter pairs	30.00	–
First day cover	–	14.00
Stamp cards	8.00	25.00

(*All values also appear in the Victoria: A Long & Glorious Reign prestige stamp book.)

Model Lodge, Kennington (1st)
Balmoral Castle, Scotland (1st)
The New Crystal Palace, Sydenham (£1.55)
Royal Albert Hall, London (£1.55)

■ **2019, May 24. The Legacy of Prince Albert**
Des: Common Curiosity. Printed in litho by International Security Printers.

Miniature sheet	20.00	26.00
Miniature sheet first day cover	–	9.00
Press sheet	£100	–

(*All designs also appear in the Victoria: A Long & Glorious Reign prestige stamp book.)

British soldiers are briefed before embarkation (1st)
HMS Warspite shelling in support of beach landings (1st)
Paratroopers synchronising watches (£1.35)
Soldiers wade ashore on Juno (£1.35)
An American light bomber provides air support (£1.60)
British troops take cover as they advance inland (£1.60)

■ **2019, June 6. 75th Anniversary of D-Day**
Des: Baxter & Bailey. Printed in litho by International Security Printers. Issued in se-tenant pairs.

Set	11.00	16.00
Gutter pairs (each of two designs)	12.00	–
First day cover	–	14.00
Stamp cards	8.00	25.00

Utah beach (1st)
Omaha beach (1st)
Gold beach (1st)
Juno beach (1st)
Sword beach (1st)

■ **2019, June 6. 75th Anniversary of D-Day: The Normandy Landings**
Des: Baxter & Bailey. Printed in litho by International Security Printers.

Miniature sheet	7.00	9.00
Miniature sheet first day cover	–	7.00

(*The Gold and Sword designs also appear, in self-adhesive form, in a retail booklet; price £7 mint, £9 used.)

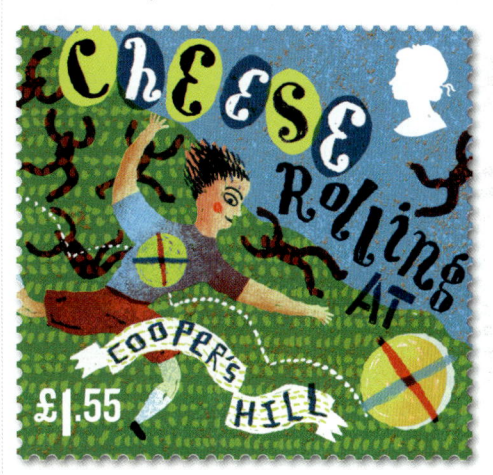

Burning the Clocks, Brighton (2nd)
'Obby 'Oss, Padstow (2nd)
World Gurning Championships, Egremont (1st)
Up Helly Aa, Lerwick (1st)
Cheese Rolling, Cooper's Hill, Brockworth (£1.55)
Halloween, Derry/Londonderry (£1.55)
Horn Dance, Abbots Bromley (£1.60)
Bog Snorkelling, Llanwrtyd Wells (£1.60)

■ **2019, July 9. Curious Customs**
Des: NB Studio. from illustrations by Jonny Hannah. Printed in litho by International Security Printers. Issued in se-tenant pairs.

Set	13.00	18.50
Gutter pairs	28.00	–
First day cover	–	17.00
Stamp cards	6.00	20.00

BRITISH STAMP MARKET VALUES 2024   213

QUEEN ELIZABETH II DECIMAL

Glen Affric (1st)
Westonbirt, The National Arboretum (1st)
Sherwood Forest (£1.55)
Coed y Brenin (£1.55)
Glenariff Forest (£1.60)
Kielder Forest (£1.60)

■ **2019, August 13. Forests**
Des: Up. Printed in litho by International Security Printers. Issued in se-tenant pairs.

Set	11.50	16.00
Gutter pairs (each of two designs)	13.00	–
First day cover	–	15.00
Stamp cards	4.50	25.00

'Honky Château' album cover (1st)
'Goodbye Yellow Brick Road' album cover (1st)
'Caribou' album cover (1st)
'Captain Fantastic & The Brown Dirt Cowboy' album cover (1st)
'Sleeping With The Past' album cover (£1.55)
'The One' album cover (£1.55)
'Made in England' album cover (£1.55)
'Songs From The West Coast' album cover (£1.55)

■ **2019, September 3. Music Giants (issue 3). Elton John**
Des: Royal Mail Group, based on a concept by Studio Dempsey. Printed in litho by International Security Printers. Issued in se-tenant strips of four.

Set	13.00	20.00
Gutter pairs	28.00	–
First day cover	–	17.50
Stamp cards	9.00	35.00

(*The Goodbye Yellow Brick Road and Captain Fantastic & The Brown Dirt Cowboy designs also appear, in self-adhesive form, in a retail booklet; price £12 mint, £14 used the pair. The designs also appear on three 'fan sheets', sold at a premium by the philatelic service only.)

Madison Square Garden, 2018 (1st)
Dodger Stadium, 1975 (1st)
Hammersmith Odeon, 1975 (£1.55)
Buckingham Palace, 2012 (£1.55)

■ **2019, September 3. Elton John Live**
Des: Royal Mail Group. Printed in litho by International Security Printers.

Miniature sheet	7.00	10.00
Miniature sheet first day cover	–	9.00
Press sheet	£110	–

Mary Rose, 1511 (1st)
HMS Queen Elizabeth, 2014 (1st)
HMS Victory, 1765 (£1.35)
HMS Dreadnought, 1906 (£1.35)
HMS Warrior, 1860 (£1.55)
Sovereign of the Seas, 1637 (£1.55)
HMS King George V, 1939 (£1.60)
HMS Beagle, 1820 (£1.60)

■ **2019, September 19. Royal Navy Ships**
Des: Hat-Trick Design. Printed in litho by International Security Printers. Issued in se-tenant pairs.

Set	15.00	22.00
Gutter pairs	32.00	–
First day cover	–	20.00
Stamp cards	5.00	30.00

(*The Mary Rose and HMS Queen Elizabeth designs also appear, in self-adhesive form, in a retail booklet; price £50 mint, £60 used the pair.)

DECIMAL QUEEN ELIZABETH II

England team with the trophy on the pitch (1st)
England players congratulating Anya Shrubsole (1st)
England captain Heather Knight and team-mates (£1.60)
England team with the trophy on the balcony (£1.60)

■ **2019, September 26. England ICC Women's World Cup 2017 Winners**
Des: Royal Mail Group. Printed in litho by International Security Printers.

Miniature sheet	7.00	10.00
Miniature sheet first day cover	–	9.00

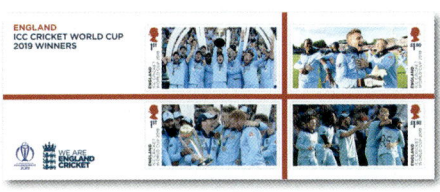

England team lifting the trophy (1st)
England captain Eoin Morgan and team-mates (1st)
England players celebrating at the end of the game (£1.60)
England players congratulating Ben Stokes (£1.60)

■ **2019, September 26. England ICC Cricket World Cup 2019 Winners**
Des: Royal Mail Group. Printed in litho by International Security Printers.

Miniature sheet	7.00	10.00
Miniature sheet first day cover	–	9.00

Scrambled snake! (1st)
Gruffalo crumble! (1st)
All was quiet in the deep dark wood (1st)
A mouse took a stroll (£1.60)
Roasted fox! (£1.60)
Owl ice cream? (£1.60)

■ **2019, October 10. 20th Anniversary of the Publication of The Gruffalo by Julia Donaldson**
Des: Rose, from illustrations by Axel Scheffler. Printed in litho by International Security Printers. Issued in se-tenant strips of three.

Set	10.00	15.00
Gutter pairs	22.00	–
First day cover	–	13.00
Stamp cards	8.00	30.00

Owl (1st)
Mouse (1st)
Snake (£1.55)
Fox (£1.55)

■ **2019, October 10. The Gruffalo**
Des: Rose, from illustrations by Axel Scheffler. Printed in litho by International Security Printers.

Miniature sheet	7.00	10.00
Miniature sheet first day cover	–	10.00
Press sheet	£120	–

(*The designs also appear in a collector's sheet.)

The angel Gabriel (2nd, 2nd Large)
Mary and Jesus (1st, 1st Large)
Joseph (£1.35)
Jesus in the manger (£1.55)
The shepherds (£1.60)
The three wise men (£2.30)

■ **2019, November 5. Christmas**
Des: Charlie Smith Design, from illustrations by Harikrishman Panicker and Deepti Nair. Printed in gravure by International Security Printers. Counter stamps self-adhesive; miniature sheet gummed.

Set	17.00	22.00
First day cover	–	19.00
Stamp cards	7.00	35.00
Miniature sheet	17.00	22.00
Miniature sheet first day cover	–	19.00

(*The 2nd class and 1st class designs also appear in retail booklets. All designs also appear in a collector's sheet.)

QUEEN ELIZABETH II DECIMAL

Count Dooku (1st)
Lando Calrissian (1st)
Sith Trooper (1st)
Jannah (1st)
Captain Moff Tarkin (1st)
Darth Maul (1st)
Zorii (1st)
Wicket W Warrick (1st)
Poe Dameron (1st)
Queen Amidala (1st)

■ **2019, November 26. Star Wars (issue 3). The Rise of Skywalker**
Des: Interabang. Printed in litho by International Security Printers. Issued in se-tenant strips of five.

Set	14.00	18.00
Gutter pairs	30.00	–
First day cover	–	15.00
Stamp cards	11.00	30.00
Composite sheet (entire series of 30)	36.00	52.00

(*All designs also appear in the Star Wars: The Making Of The Vehicles prestige stamp book. The Poe Dameron and Sith Trooper designs also appear, in self-adhesive form, in a retail stamp book; price £9 mint, £11 used the pair. All designs also appear in a collector's sheet.)

Poe's X-Wing Fighter (1st)
Jedi Starfighter (1st)
Slave 1 (1st)
TIE Silencer (1st)
Podracers (1st)
Speeder Bikes (1st)

■ **2019, November 26. Star Wars: The Vehicles**
Des: Interabang. Printed in litho by International Security Printers.

Miniature sheet	8.00	11.00
Miniature sheet first day cover	–	9.00
Press sheet	£120	–

(*All designs also appear in the Star Wars: The Making Of The Vehicles prestige stamp book.)

Elite, 1984 (2nd)
Worms, 1995 (2nd)
Sensible Soccer, 1992 (1st)
Lemmings, 1991 (1st)
Wipeout, 1995 (£1.55)
Micro Machines, 1991 (£1.55)
Dizzy, 1987 (£1.60)
Populous, 1989 (£1.60)

■ **2020, January 21. Video Games**
Des: Supple Studio and Bitmap Books. Printed in litho by International Security Printers. Issued in se-tenant pairs.

Set	13.00	20.00
Gutter pairs	28.00	–
First day cover	–	17.00
Stamp cards	9.00	30.00

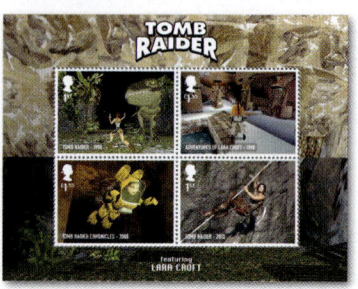

Tomb Raider, 1996 (1st)
Tomb Raider, 2013 (1st)
Adventures of Lara Croft, 1998 (£1.55)
Tomb Raider Chronicles, 2000 (£1.55)

■ **2020, January 21. Tomb Raider**
Des: Supple Studio and Bitmap Books. Printed in litho by International Security Printers.

Miniature sheet	7.00	10.50
Miniature sheet first day cover	–	9.50

(*The Tomb Raider 1996 and Tomb Raider 2013 designs also appear, in self-adhesive form, in a retail booklet; price £14 mint, £16 used the pair. All four designs also appear in a collector's sheet.)

DECIMAL QUEEN ELIZABETH II

Cat's Eye nebula (2nd)
Enceladus (2nd)
Pulsars (1st)
Black holes (1st)
Jupiter's auroras (£1.55)
Gravitational lensing (£1.55)
Comet 67P (£1.60)
Cygnus A galaxy (£1.60)

■ 2020, February 11. Visions of the Universe
Des: True North. Printed in litho by International Security Printers. Issued in se-tenant pairs.

Set	13.00	20.00
Gutter pairs	28.00	–
First day cover	–	17.50
Stamp cards	6.00	25.00

(*All designs also appear in the Visions Of The Universe prestige stamp book.)

Daniel Craig in 'Casino Royale', 2006 (1st)
Pierce Brosnan in 'GoldenEye', 1995 (1st)
Timothy Dalton in 'The Living Daylights' 1987 (1st)
Roger Moore in 'Live And Let Die', 1973 (£1.60)
George Lazenby in 'On Her Majesty's Secret Service', 1969 (£1.60)
Sean Connery in 'Goldfinger', 1964 (£1.60)

■ 2020, March 17. James Bond Films
Des: Interabang. Printed in litho by International Security Printers. Issued in se-tenant strips of three.

Set	11.00	16.00
Gutter pairs	24.00	–
First day cover	–	14.00
Stamp cards	8.00	35.00

(*All designs also appear in the Behind The Scenes Of James Bond prestige stamp book, and in a collector's sheet.)

Bell-Textron jet pack (1st)
Aston Martin DB5 car (1st)
Lotus Esprit submarine (£1.55)
Little Nellie autogyro (£1.55)

■ 2020, March 17. James Bond: Q Branch
Des: Interabang. Printed in litho by International Security Printers.

Miniature sheet	7.00	10.50
Miniature sheet first day cover	–	9.50
Press sheet	80.00	–

(*All designs also appear in the Behind The Scenes Of James Bond prestige stamp book. The Bell-Textron Jet Pack and Aston Martin DB5 designs also appear, in self-adhesive form, in a retail booklet; price £15 mint, £16 used the pair. The Aston Martin DB5 design also appears in a collector's sheet issued on November 3, 2020.)

Scotland definitives (2nd, 1st, £1.42, £1.63)

■ 2020, April 6. 700th Anniversary of the Declaration of Arbroath
Printed in litho by International Security Printers.

Miniature sheet	7.00	10.00
Miniature sheet first day cover	–	10.00

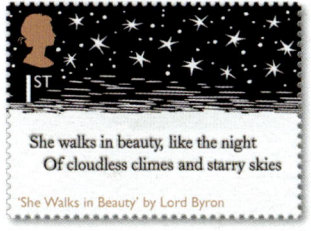

'The Progress of Rhyme' by John Clare (1st)
'Frost at Midnight' by Samuel Taylor Coleridge (1st)
'Auguries of Innocence' by William Blake (1st)
'The Lady of the Lake' by Walter Scott (1st)
'To a Skylark' by Percy Bysshe Shelley (1st)
'The Rainbow' by William Wordsworth (1st)
'Ode to the Snowdrop' by Mary Robinson (1st)
'The Fate of Adelaide' by Letitia Elizabeth Landon (1st)
'Ode to a Grecian Urn' by John Keats (1st)
'She Walks in Beauty' by Lord Byron (1st)

■ 2020, April 7. The Romantic Poets
Des: The Chase, with illustrations by Linda Farquharson. Printed in litho by International Security Printers. Issued in se-tenant strips of five.

Set	13.00	20.00
Gutter pairs	28.00	–
First day cover	–	15.00
Stamp cards	7.00	30.00

QUEEN ELIZABETH II DECIMAL

Servicemen welcomed home, 1945 (2nd)
Nurses celebrate, 1945 (2nd)
Jubilant public, 1945 (1st)
Evacuees return home, 1945 (1st)
Troops parade, 1945 (£1.42)
Demobilised servicemen, 1945 (£1.42)
Allied prisoners-of-war liberated, 1945 (£1.63)
Navy personnel celebrate, 1945 (£1.63)

Ena Sharples and Elsie Tanner (2nd)
Stan and Hilda Ogden (2nd)
Vera and Jack Duckworth (1st)
Deirdre and Ken Barlow (1st)
Rita Sullivan and Norris Cole (£1.42)
Hayley and Roy Cropper (£1.42)
Sunita and Dev Alahan (£1.63)
Tracy Barlow and Steve McDonald (£1.63)

■ 2020, May 8. 75th Anniversary of the End of the Second World War
Des: Hat-Trick Design, from photographs colourised by Royston Leonard. Printed in litho by International Security Printers. Issued in se-tenant pairs.

Set	13.00	20.00
Gutter pairs	28.00	–
First day cover	–	17.50
Stamp cards	8.00	30.00

(*All designs also appear in the End of the Second World War prestige stamp book.)

■ 2020, May 28. 60th Anniversary of Coronation Street
Des: The Chase. Printed in litho by International Security Printers. Issued in se-tenant pairs.

Set	13.00	20.00
Gutter pairs	28.00	–
First day cover	–	17.50
Stamp cards	9.00	35.00

(*The Vera and Jack Duckworth and Deirdre and Ken Barlow designs also appear in a collector's sheet. They also appear, in self-adhesive form, in a retail stamp book; price £5 mint, £6.50 used the pair.)

Hall of Names, Holocaust History Museum, Israel (1st)
Runnymede Memorial (1st)
Plymouth Naval Memorial (£1.55)
Rangoon Memorial, Myanmar (£1.55)

■ 2020, May 8. In Remembrance. End of the Second World War
Des: Hat-Trick Design. Printed in litho by International Security Printers.

Miniature sheet	7.50	10.50
Miniature sheet first day cover	–	9.50
Press sheet	£125	–

(*All designs also appear in the End of the Second World War prestige stamp book.)

Bet Lynch (1st)
Raquel Watts (1st)
Liz McDonald (£1.55)
Gemma Winter (£1.55)

■ 2020, May 28. Rovers Return Inn
Des: The Chase. Printed in litho by International Security Printers.

Miniature sheet	7.00	10.00
Miniature sheet first day cover	–	9.50
Press sheet	70.00	–

DECIMAL **QUEEN ELIZABETH II**

Dover Lighthouse (2nd)
Bignor mosaic (2nd)
Amphitheatre at Caerleon (1st)
Ribchester helmet (1st)
Bridgeness distance slab (£1.63)
Warrior god figurine, Cambridgeshire (£1.63)
Gorgon's head sculpture, Bath (£1.68)
Hadrian's Wall (£1.68)

■ 2020, June 18. Roman Britain
Des: Up. Printed in litho by International Security Printers. Issued in se-tenant pairs.

Set	14.00	21.00
Gutter pairs (each of two designs)	16.00	–
Traffic lights gutter pairs	32.00	–
First day cover	–	18.50
Stamp cards	6.00	305.00

'Queen II' album cover (1st)
'Sheer Heart Attack' album cover (1st)
'A Night At The Opera' album cover (1st)
'News Of The World' album cover (1st)
'The Game' album cover (£1.63)
'Greatest Hits' album cover (£1.63)
'The Works' album cover (£1.63)
'Innuendo' album cover (£1.63)

■ 2020, July 9. Music Giants (issue 4). Queen
Des: Royal Mail Group, based on a concept by Studio Dempsey. Printed in litho by International Security Printers. Issued in se-tenant strips of four.

Set	14.50	21.00
Gutter pairs	31.00	–
First day cover	–	19.00
Stamp cards	10.00	35.00

(* All designs appear in the Queen prestige stamp book. The Queen II and A Night At The Opera designs also appear, in self-adhesive form, in a retail stamp book; price £14 mint, £16 used the pair. The designs also appear in a collector's sheet, and in two 'fan sheets' sold at a premium by the philatelic service only.)

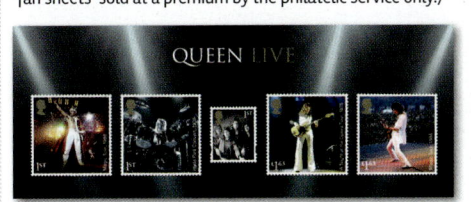

Freddie Mercury during the Magic Tour, 1986 (1st)
Roger Taylor at Hyde Park Concert, 1976 (1st)
Studio photograph, 1974 (1st)
John Deacon during the A Night At The Opera Tour, 1975 (£1.55)
Brian May during the Magic Tour, 1986 (£1.55)

■ 2020, July 9. Queen Live
Des: Royal Mail Group and Baxter & Bailey. Printed in litho by International Security Printers.

Miniature sheet	8.50	12.50
Miniature sheet first day cover	–	11.00
Press sheet	£140	

(* All designs appear in the Queen prestige stamp book. The studio photograph design also appears, in self-adhesive form, in a retail stamp book issued on March 29, 2021; price £2 mint or used. It also appears in a collector's sheet.)

View from Old Palace Yard (1st)
River Thames view (1st)
Elizabeth Tower (1st)
Commons Chamber (£1.68)
Central Lobby (£1.68)
Lords Chamber (£1.68)

■ 2020, July 30. Palace of Westminster
Des: Steers McGillan Eves. Printed in litho by International Security Printers. Issued in se-tenant strips of three.

Set	11.00	16.00
Gutter pairs	24.00	–
First day cover	–	14.50
Stamp cards	8.00	30.00

QUEEN ELIZABETH II DECIMAL

Norman Porch (1st)
Chapel of St. Mary Undercroft (1st)
St. Stephen's Hall (£1.63)
Royal Gallery (£1.63)

■ **2020, July 30. Palace of Westminster**
Des: Steers McGillan Eves. Printed in litho by International Security Printers.
Miniature sheet	7.50	11.00
Miniature sheet first day cover	–	10.00
Press sheet	£100	–

The Reichenbach Fall (1st)
A Study in Pink (1st)
The Great Game (£1.42)
The Empty Hearse (£1.42)
A Scandal in Belgravia (£1.68)
The Final Problem (£1.68)

■ **2020, August 18. Sherlock**
Des: So Design Consultants, from stills from the BBC television series. Printed in litho by International Security Printers. Issued in se-tenant pairs.
Set	12.00	17.00
Gutter pairs (each of two designs)	13.00	–
First day cover	–	15.00
Stamp cards	9.00	25.00

(*All designs also appear in a collector's sheet.)

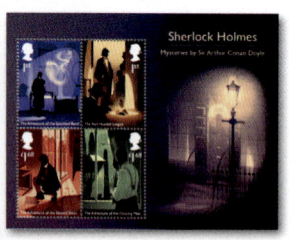

The Adventure of the Speckled Band (1st)
The Red-Headed League (1st)
The Adventure of the Second Stain (£1.68)
The Adventure of the Dancing Men (£1.68)

■ **2020, August 18. Sherlock Holmes**
Des: NB Studio, from illustrations by Karolis Strautniekas. Printed in litho by International Security Printers.
Miniature sheet	7.50	11.00
Miniature sheet first day cover	–	10.00

(*The Adventure of the Speckled Band and The Red-Headed League designs also appear, in self-adhesive form, in a retail booklet; price £5 mint or £6.50 used the pair.)

'The water bursts in' from Rupert's Rainy Adventure, 1944 (2nd)
'The bath is rocked' from Rupert's Rainy Adventure, 1944 (2nd)
'Algy looks a trifle glum' from Rupert & The Mare's Nest, 1952 (1st)
'The large bird' from Rupert & The Mare's Nest, 1952 (1st)
'Please tell me too' from Rupert & The Lost Cuckoo, 1963 (£1.45)
'My cuckoo's back' from Rupert & The Lost Cuckoo, 1963 (£1.45)
'Rupert searches' from Rupert's Christmas Tree, 1947 (£1.70)
'A lovely sight' from Rupert's Christmas Tree, 1947 (£1.70)

■ **2020, September 3. 100th Anniversary of Rupert Bear**
Des: Rose, from original comic strip artwork by Alfred Bestall. Printed in litho by International Security Printers. Issued in se-tenant pairs.
Set	13.50	20.50
Gutter pairs (each of two designs)	15.00	–
Traffic light gutter pairs	35.00	–
First day cover	–	17.50
Stamp cards	6.00	25.00

Common carder bee (1st)
Painted lady butterfly (1st)
Longhorn beetle (£1.45)
Elephant hawk-moth (£1.45)
Marmalade hoverfly (£1.70)
Ruby-tailed wasp (£1.70)

DECIMAL QUEEN ELIZABETH II

■ **2020, October 1. Brilliant Bugs**
Des: Royal Mail Group, from illustrations by Richard Lewington. Printed in litho by International Security Printers. Issued in se-tenant pairs.

Set	12.00	17.50
Gutter pairs	26.00	–
First day cover	–	15.50
Stamp cards	5.00	25.00

Adoration of the Magi, St Andrew's Church, East Lexham (2nd, 2nd L)
Virgin and Child, St Andrew's Church, Coln Rogers (1st, 1st L)
Virgin and Child, Church of St James, Hollowell (£1.45)
Virgin and Child, All Saints' Church, Otley (£1.70)
The Holy Family, St Columba's Church, Topcliffe (£2.50)
Virgin and Child, Christ Church, Coalville (£2.55)

■ **2020, November 3. Christmas: Stained Glass Windows**
Des: Royal Mail Group and Up. Printed in gravure by International Security Printers. Counter stamps self-adhesive; miniature sheet gummed.

Set	19.00	26.00
First day cover	–	22.50
Stamp cards	6.00	35.00
Miniature sheet	19.00	26.00
Miniature sheet first day cover	–	22.50

(*The 2nd class and 1st class designs also appear in retail booklets. All designs also appear in a collector's sheet.)

■ **2020, November 13. Star Trek**
Des: Interabang, from illustrations by Freya Betts. Printed in litho by International Security Printers. Issued in se-tenant strips of six.

Set	15.50	23.00
Gutter pairs	33.00	–
First day cover	–	17.50
Stamp cards	14.00	35.00

James T Kirk (1st)
Jean-Luc Picard (1st)
Benjamin Sisko (1st)
Kathryn Janeway (1st)
Jonathan Archer (1st)
Gabriel Lorca (1st)
Spock (1st)
Deanna Troi (1st)
Julian Bashir (1st)
Malcolm Reed (1st)
Michael Burnham (1st)
Ash Tyler (1st)

(*All designs also appear in the Star Trek prestige stamp book. The Kirk and Picard designs appear, in self-adhesive form, in a retail booklet; price £5 mint, £6.50 used the pair. The Kirk, Picard, Sisko, Janeway, Archer and Lorca designs also appear in a collector's sheet.)

Montgomery Scott (1st)
Shinzon (1st)
Tolian Soran (1st)
Chancellor Gorkon (1st)
Carol Marcus (1st)
Krall (1st)

■ **2020, November 13. Star Trek: The Movies**
Des: Interabang. Printed in litho by International Security Printers.

Miniature sheet	8.00	12.00
Miniature sheet first day cover	–	10.00
Press sheet	£175	–

(*All designs also appear in the Star Trek prestige stamp book.)

Dartmoor National Park (1st)
New Forest National Park (1st)
Lake District National Park (1st)
Loch Lomond & The Trossachs National Park (1st)
Snowdonia National Park (1st)
North York Moors National Park (1st)
South Downs National Park (1st)
Peak District National Park (1st)
Pembrokeshire Coast National Park (1st)
Broads National Park (1st)

■ **2021, January 14. National Parks**
Des: Studio Mean. Printed in litho by International Security Printers. Issued in se-tenant strips of five.

Set	17.50	26.00
Gutter pairs	40.00	–
First day cover	–	16.50
Stamp cards	7.00	30.00

(*The Peak District and Snowdonia designs also appear, in self-adhesive form, in a retail booklet; price £8 mint, £12 used the pair.)

BRITISH STAMP MARKET VALUES 2024 **221**

QUEEN ELIZABETH II DECIMAL

Great sport (1st)
Great creativity (1st)
Great community (£1.70)
Great industry and innovation (£1.70)

■ **2021, January 26. United Kingdom: A Celebration**
Des: Hat-Trick Design. Printed in litho by International Security Printers.

Miniature sheet	8.00	12.00
Miniature sheet first day cover	–	10.50
Stamp cards	4.00	20.00

Scenes from 'A Losing Streak', 1982 (1st)
Scenes from 'Sleeping Dogs Lie', 1985 (1st)
Scenes from 'Yuppy Love', 1989 (1st)
Scenes from 'A Touch of Glass', 1982 (1st)
Scenes from 'The Jolly Boys' Outing', 1989 (£1.70)
Scenes from 'The Unlucky Winner Is…', 1989 (£1.70)
Scenes from 'Three Men, a Woman and a Baby', 1991 (£1.70)
Scenes from 'Time on Our Hands', 1996 (£1.70)

■ **2021, February 16. Only Fools & Horses**
Des: Interabang, from stills from episodes of the BBC television series. Printed in litho by International Security Printers. Issued in se-tenant pairs.

Set	15.00	22.00
Gutter pairs (each of two designs)	16.00	–
First day cover	–	20.00
Stamp cards	9.00	35.00

(*All designs also appear in the Only Fools & Horses prestige stamp book.)

Del Boy (1st)
Rodney (1st)
Uncle Albert (£1.70)
Grandad (£1.70)

■ **2021, February 16. Only Fools & Horses**
Des: Interabang. Printed in litho by International Security Printers.

Miniature sheet	8.00	12.00
Miniature sheet first day cover	–	10.50
Press sheet	£120	–

(*The Del Boy and Rodney designs also appear, in self-adhesive form, in a retail booklet; price £12 mint or used the pair. They also appear in a collector's sheet.)

Merlin and the baby Arthur (1st)
Arthur draws the sword from the stone (1st)
Arthur takes Excalibur (1st)
Arthur marries Guinevere (1st)
Sir Gawain and the Green Knight (1st)
Knights of the Round Table (£1.70)
Sir Lancelot defeats the dragon (£1.70)
Sir Galahad and the Holy Grail (£1.70)
Arthur battles Mordred (£1.70)
The death of King Arthur (£1.70)

■ **2021, March 16. The Legend of King Arthur**
Des: Godfrey Design, from illustrations by Jaime Jones. Printed in litho by International Security Printers. Issued in se-tenant strips of five.

Set	19.00	28.00
Gutter pairs	40.00	–
First day cover	–	26.00
Stamp cards	7.00	30.00

'Frankenstein' by Mary Shelley (1st)
'The Time Machine' by H. G. Wells (1st)
'Brave New World' by Aldous Huxley (£1.70)
'The Day of the Triffids' by John Wyndham (£1.70)
'Childhood's End' by Arthur C. Clarke (£2.55)
'Shikasta' by Doris Lessing (£2.55)

DECIMAL — QUEEN ELIZABETH II

■ **2021, April 15. Classic Science Fiction**
Des: Webb & Webb Design, from illustrations by Sabina Sinko (Frankenstein), Francisco Rodriguez (Time Machine), Thomas Danthony (Brave New World), Mick Brownfield (Day of the Triffids), Matt Murphy (Childhood's End) and Sarah Jones (Shikasta). Printed in litho by International Security Printers. Issued in se-tenant pairs.

Set	16.00	23.00
Gutter pairs	34.00	–
First day cover	–	20.00
Stamp cards	4.00	25.00

Battle of Bosworth, 1485 (2nd)
Battle of Tewkesbury, 1471 (2nd)
Battle of Barnet, 1471 (1st)
Battle of Edgecote Moor, 1469 (1st)
Battle of Towton, 1461 (£1.70)
Battle of Wakefield, 1460 (£1.70)
Battle of Northampton, 1460 (£2.55)
First Battle of St. Albans, 1455 (£2.55)

■ **2021, May 4. The Wars of the Roses**
Des: Royal Mail Group, from illustrations by Graham Turner. Printed in litho by International Security Printers. Issued in se-tenant pairs.

Set	17.00	24.50
Gutter pairs	24.00	–
First day cover	–	23.00
Stamp cards	6.00	30.00

'McCartney' album cover (1st)
'RAM' album cover (1st)
'Venus & Mars' album cover (1st)
'McCartney II' album cover (1st)
'Tug of War' album cover (£1.70)
'Flaming Pie' album cover (£1.70)
'Egypt Station' album cover (£1.70)
'McCartney III' album cover (£1.70)

■ **2021, May 28. Music Giants (issue 5). Paul McCartney**
Des: Royal Mail Group and Baxter & Bailey. Printed in litho by International Security Printers. Issued in se-tenant strips of four.

Set	16.00	23.00
Gutter pairs	34.00	–
First day cover	–	21.00
Stamp cards	9.00	35.00

(*All designs also appear in the Paul McCartney prestige stamp book, and in a collector's sheet. The McCartney and Tug of War designs appear, in self-adhesive form, in a retail stamp book; price £5 mint, £6.50 used the pair. All designs also appear in three 'fan sheets', sold at a premium from the philatelic service only.)

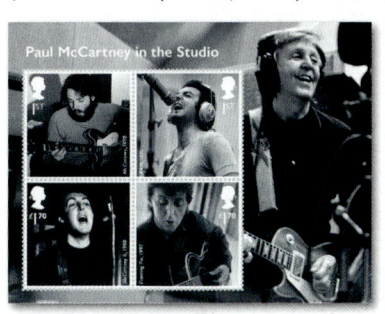

Recording 'McCartney', 1970 (1st)
Recording 'RAM', 1971 (1st)
Recording 'McCartney II', 1980 (£1.70)
Recording 'Flaming Pie', 1997 (£1.70)

■ **2021, May 28. Paul McCartney In The Studio**
Des: Royal Mail Group and Baxter & Bailey. Printed in litho by International Security Printers.

Miniature sheet	8.00	11.50
Miniature sheet first day cover	–	10.00
Press sheet	£130	–

(*All designs also appear in the Paul McCartney prestige stamp book.)

Portrait of Prince Philip by Baron, 1940s (2nd)
Prince Philip at Dartmouth Naval College, 1980 (1st)
Prince Philip at the Royal Windsor Horse Show, 1980s (£1.70)
Portrait of Prince Philip by Terry O'Neill (£2.55)

■ **2021, June 24. In Memoriam: Prince Philip, Duke of Edinburgh**
Des: Kate Stephens and Royal Mail Group. Printed in litho by International Security Printers.

Miniature sheet	10.00	13.00
Miniature sheet first day cover	–	11.50
Press sheet	75.00	–
Stamp cards	4.00	22.00

QUEEN ELIZABETH II DECIMAL

Dennis's first comic strip, 1951 (1st)
Dennis adopts Gnasher, 1968 (1st)
Dennis's front cover debut, 1974 (1st)
Dennis adopts Rasher the Pig, 1979 (£1.70)
Dennis meets his sister Bea, 1998 (£1.70)
Dennis reveals Dad was Dennis, 2015 (£1.70)

■ **2021, July 1. Dennis & Gnasher**
Des: The Chase. Printed in litho by International Security Printers. Issued in se-tenant strips of three.

Set	11.00	16.50
Gutter pairs	24.00	–
First day cover	–	15.50
Stamp cards	8.00	30.00

Dennis (1st)
Gnasher (1st)
Minnie the Minx (£1.70)
Family portrait (£1.70)

■ **2021, July 1. Happy Birthday Dennis**
Des: Rose, illustrated by Nigel Parkinson. Printed in litho by International Security Printers.

Miniature sheet	8.00	12.00
Miniature sheet first day cover	–	11.00
Press sheet	£140	

(*The Dennis and Gnasher designs appear, in self-adhesive form, in a retail booklet; price £5 mint, £6 used the pair. Both designs also appear in a collector's sheet.)

Northern gannet (1st)
Common cuttlefish (1st)
Grey seal (1st)
Bottlenose dolphin (1st)
Spiny spider crab (1st)
Long-snouted seahorse (1st)
Orca (1st)
Fried-egg anemone (1st)
Cuckoo wrasse (1st)
Cold-water coral reef (1st)

■ **2021, July 22. Wild Coasts**
Des: Steers McGillan Eves. Printed in litho by International Security Printers. Issued in se-tenant strips of five.

Set	13.50	19.00
Gutter pairs	30.00	–
First day cover	–	17.00
Stamp cards	7.00	30.00

(*The Orca and Grey Seal designs also appear, in self-adhesive form, in a retail stamp book; price £5 mint, £6.50 used the pair. All designs also appear in a collector's sheet.)

Phytoplankton (1st)
Zooplankton (1st)
Atlantic herring (£1.70)
Harbour porpoise (£1.70)

■ **2021, July 22. Marine Food Chain**
Des: Maité Franchi. Printed in litho by International Security Printers.

Miniature sheet	8.00	12.00
Miniature sheet first day cover	–	10.50
Press sheet	£110	–
Stamp cards	4.00	20.00

Bessemer process, 1856 (2nd)
Watt's rotative steam engine, 1780s (2nd)
Penydarren locomotive, 1804 (1st)
Spinning jenny, c1764 (1st)
Lombe's silk mill, c1721 (£1.70)
Portland cement, 1824 (£1.70)

DECIMAL — QUEEN ELIZABETH II

■ 2021, August 12. Industrial Revolutions
Des: Common Curiosity. Printed in litho by International Security Printers. Issued in se-tenant pairs.

Set	10.00	15.00
Gutter pairs	22.00	–
First day cover	–	13.00
Stamp cards	7.50	35.00

(*All designs also appear in the Industrial Revolutions prestige stamp book.)

Faraday generates electricity, 1831 (2nd)
Transatlantic cable, 1858 (1st)
Deptford power station, 1889 (£1.70)
Incandescent light bulb, 1880 (£2.55)

■ 2021, August 12. The Electric Revolution
Des: Common Curiosity. Printed in litho by International Security Printers.

Miniature sheet	8.50	13.00
Miniature sheet first day cover	–	12.00

(*All designs also appear in the Industrial Revolutions prestige stamp book.)

MkIV (1st)
Matilda MkII (1st)
Churchill AVRE (1st)
Centurion Mk9 (1st)
Scorpion (£1.70)
Chieftain Mk5 (£1.70)
Challenger 2 (£1.70)
Ajax (£1.70)

■ 2021, September 2. British Army Vehicles
Des: Royal Mail Group, from illustrations by Mick Graham. Printed in litho by International Security Printers. Issued in se-tenant strips of four.

Set	15.00	22.00
Gutter pairs	32.00	–
First day cover	–	21.00
Stamp cards	9.00	30.00

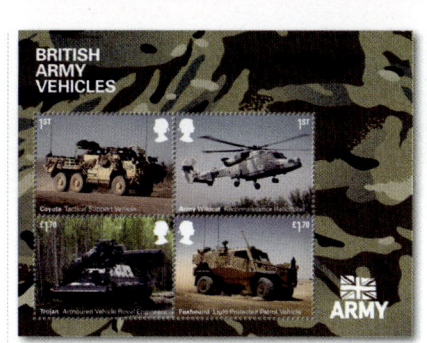

Coyote tactical support vehicle (1st)
Army Wildcat reconnaissance helicopter (1st)
Trojan AVRE (£1.70)
Foxhound light protected patrol vehicle (£1.70)

■ 2021, September 2. British Army Vehicles
Des: Studio Up. Printed in litho by International Security Printers.

Miniature sheet	7.50	11.00
Miniature sheet first day cover	–	10.50

Batman (1st)
Batwoman (1st)
Robin (1st)
Batgirl (1st)
Alfred (1st)
Nightwing (1st)
The Joker (1st)
Harley Quinn (1st)
The Penguin (1st)
Poison Ivy (1st)
Catwoman (1st)
The Riddler (1st)

■ 2021, September 17. DC Collection
Des: Interabang, from illustrations by Jim Cheung. Printed in litho by International Security Printers. Issued in se-tenant strips of six.

Set	16.00	22.00
Gutter pairs	34.00	–
First day cover	–	21.00
Stamp cards	12.00	40.00

(*All designs also appear in the DC Collection prestige stamp book and in a collectors sheet. The Batman and Robin designs appear, in self-adhesive form, in a retail stamp book; price £5 mint or £6 used the pair.)

QUEEN ELIZABETH II DECIMAL

Batman (1st)
Green Lantern and The Flash (1st)
Wonder Woman (1st)
Superman (1st)
Cyborg and Aquaman (1st)
Supergirl and Shazam! (1st)

■ **2021, September 17. Justice League**
Des: Interabang, from illustrations by Jim Cheung. Printed in litho by International Security Printers.

Miniature sheet	9.00	12.00
Miniature sheet first day cover	–	10.50
Press sheet	£100	–

(*All designs also appear in the DC Collection prestige stamp book. The Wonder Woman design appears, in self-adhesive form, in a retail stamp book; price £3 mint or used.)

Women's Rugby World Cup Final, 2014 (2nd)
Five Nations Championship, 1970 (2nd)
Women's Six Nations Championship, 2015 (1st)
Five Nations Championship, 1984 (1st)
Women's Home Nations Championship, 1998 (£1.70)
Five Nations Championship, 1994 (£1.70)
Women's Six Nations Championship, 2009 (£2.55)
Rugby World Cup Final, 2003 (£2.55)

■ **2021, October 19. 150th Anniversary of Rugby Union**
Des: True North. Printed in litho by International Security Printers. Issued in se-tenant pairs.

Set	17.00	25.00
Gutter pairs	38.00	–
First day cover	–	23.00
Stamp cards	6.00	25.00

Herald angels (2nd, small format)
Herald angels (2nd, large format with data matrix code)
Road to Bethlehem (2nd Large, with data matrix code)
Mary and Jesus (1st, small format)
Mary and Jesus (1st, large format with data matrix code)
Shepherds with flocks (1st Large, with data matrix code)
The Magi following the star (£1.70)
Adoration of the shepherds (£2.55)

■ **2021, November 2. Christmas**
Des: Supple Studio, from illustrations by Jorge Cocco Santangelo. Printed in gravure by International Security Printers. Self-adhesive.

Set	20.00	21.00
First day cover	–	19.50
Stamp cards	6.00	25.00
Miniature sheet	20.00	21.00
Miniature sheet first day cover	–	19.50

(*The small-format 2nd class and 1st class stamps were available only in the miniature sheet, in retail booklets or in complete sets from the philatelic service, in the latter case with the backing paper unprinted. The four designs without data matrix codes also appear in a collector's sheet.)

Hyde Park, London, 1969 (1st)
East Rutherford, New Jersey, USA, 2019 (1st)
Rotterdam, Netherlands, 1995 (1st)
Tokyo, Japan, 1995 (1st)
New York City, USA, 1972 (£1.70)
Oslo, Norway, 2014 (£1.70)
Knebworth, Hertfordshire, 1976 (£1.70)
Düsseldorf, Germany, 2017 (£1.70)

■ **2022, January 20. The Rolling Stones**
Des: Baxter & Bailey. Printed in litho by International Security Printers. Issued in se-tenant strips of four.

Set	15.00	22.00
Gutter pairs	32.00	–
First day cover	–	18.00
Stamp cards	9.00	30.00

(*All designs appear in The Rolling Stones prestige stamp book, and in two collector's sheets. The London 1969 and Tokyo 1995 designs also appear in two 'fan sheets', sold at a premium by the philatelic service.)

DECIMAL QUEEN ELIZABETH II

Group portrait in the USA, 2005 (1st)
Group portrait in Paris, 2017 (1st)
Posters for the 1990 Europe Tour and 1975 Americas Tour (£1.70)
Posters for the 1971 UK Tour and 1981 American Tour (£1.70)

■ **2022, January 20. The Rolling Stones**
Des: Brown & Bailey. Printed in litho by International Security Printers.

Miniature sheet	9.00	13.00
Miniature sheet first day cover	–	10.00
Press sheet	£110	–

(*All designs appear in The Rolling Stones prestige stamp book.)

The Queen visiting MI5 in London, 2020 (1st)
The Queen and Duke of Edinburgh in Washington, USA, 1957 (1st)
The Queen visiting Worcester, 1980 (1st)
The Queen at Trooping the Colour, 1978 (1st)
The Queen at the Provincial Museum of Alberta, Canada, 2005 (£1.70)
The Queen in London during Silver Jubilee celebrations, 1977 (£1.70)
The Queen visiting St Vincent, 1966 (£1.70)
The Queen during the Order of the Garter ceremony, 1999 (£1.70)

■ **2022, February 4. Platinum Jubilee**
Des: Kate Stephens. Printed in litho by Cartor Security Printers. Issued in se-tenant strips of four.

Set	15.00	22.00
Gutter pairs	32.00	–
First day cover	–	21.00
Stamp cards	6.00	25.00

(*All designs appear in the Platinum Jubilee prestige stamp book.)

1962 National Productivity Year 3d stamp (2nd)
1969 British Ships 9d stamp (2nd)
1973 British Trees 9p stamp (1st)
1976 Social Reformers 8½p stamp (1st)
1966 Battle of Hastings 6d stamp (£1.70)
1965 Battle of Britain 4d stamp (£1.70)

■ **2022, February 14. The Stamp Designs of David Gentleman**
Des: Hat-Trick Design. Printed in litho by Cartor Security Printers.

Miniature sheet	10.00	14.00
Miniature sheet first day cover	–	13.00
Press sheet	£125	–
Stamp cards	5.00	25.00

(*This miniature sheet exists with an additional 'London 2022' logo in the border, and a serial number, sold only at the exhibition in a limited edition of 10,000.)

Lifting the Cup: Arsenal in 1971 (1st)
Wembley stadium: crowds in 1923 (1st)
A big day out: supporters in 1968 (£1.70)
Classic finals: Coventry City in 1987 (£1.70)
Cup upsets: Lincoln City in 2017 (£2.55)
Royal patronage: presenting the Cup in 1937 (£2.55)

■ **2022, March 8. 150th Anniversary of the FA Cup**
Des: The Chase. Printed in litho by Cartor Security Printers. Issued in vertical se-tenant pairs.

Set	16.00	22.00
Gutter pairs	34.00	–
First day cover	–	21.00
Stamp cards	8.00	30.00

Supporters' memorabilia (1st)
Winner's medal and trophy (1st)
Official match-day items (£1.70)
Cup Final souvenirs (£1.70)

■ **2022, March 8. The FA Cup: Artefacts from the National Football Museum**
Des: The Chase. Printed in litho by International Security Printers.

Miniature sheet	8.00	12.00
Miniature sheet first day cover	–	10.00
Press sheet	£100	–

BRITISH STAMP MARKET VALUES 2024   227

QUEEN ELIZABETH II DECIMAL

NHS workers, by Jessica Roberts, aged 14 (1st)
Captain Sir Tom Moore, by Shachow Ali, aged 11 (1st)
NHS hospital cleaners, by Raphael Valle Martin, aged 14 (1st)
NHS/my mum, by Alfie Craddock, aged 12 (1st)
Lab technician, by Logan Pearson, aged 11 (1st)
Delivery driver, by Isabella Grover, aged 7 (1st)
The NHS, by Connie Stuart, aged 14 (1st)
Doctors, nurses, by Ishan Bains, aged 7 (1st)

■ **2022, March 23. Heroes of the Covid Pandemic**
Des: Royal Mail Group, from paintings by children. Printed in litho by Cartor Security Printers. Issued in se-tenant strips of four.

Set	11.00	15.00
Gutter pairs	24.00	–
First day cover	–	14.00
Stamp cards	6.00	25.00

Nightjar (1st)
Pied flycatcher (1st)
Swift (1st)
Yellow wagtail (1st)
Arctic skua (1st)
Stone-curlew (1st)
Arctic tern (1st)
Swallow (1st)
Turtle dove (1st)
Montagu's harrier (1st)

■ **2022, April 7. Migratory Birds**
Des: Hat-Trick Design, from illustrations by Killian Mullarney. Printed in litho by Cartor Security Printers. Issued in se-tenant strips of five.

Set	14.00	21.00
Gutter pairs	24.00	–
First day cover	–	19.50
Stamp cards	7.00	25.00

Protecting civilians: ARP (1st)
Nursing on the front line: QAIMNS (1st)
Repairing army vehicles: ATS (1st)
Arming the fleet: WRNS (1st)
Powering the war effort: factory worker (1st)
Deciphering enemy messages: codebreakers (1st)
Supplying military production: WVS (1st)
Lighting the way to victory: ATS (1st)
Maintaining RAF aircraft: WAAF (1st)
Meeting Britain's demand: WLA (1st)

■ **2022, May 5. Unsung Heroes: Women of World War II**
Des: Supple Studio. Printed in litho by Cartor Security Printers. Issued in se-tenant strips of five.

Set	14.00	21.00
Gutter pairs	24.00	–
First day cover	–	19.00
Stamp cards	10.00	35.00

(*All designs appear in the Unsung Heroes prestige stamp book.)

Pilots meeting in ferry pool briefing room (1st)
Pilot climbing into cockpit of Supermarine Spitfire (1st)
Pilot completing post-flight paperwork (£1.85)
Pilots disembarking from Avro Anson (£1.85)

■ **2022, May 5. 'Spitfire Women': Ferry Pilots of the Air Transport Auxiliary**
Des: Supple Studio. Printed in litho by International Security Printers.

Miniature sheet	9.00	13.00
Miniature sheet first day cover	–	11.50
Press sheet	£120	–

(*All designs appear in the Unsung Heroes prestige stamp book.)

Siamese cat grooming (2nd)
Tabby cat stalking (2nd)
Ginger cat playing (1st)
British shorthair cat sleeping (1st)
Maine coon cat staring (£1.85)
Back-and-white cat on alert (£1.85)
Bengal cat being curious (£2.55)
Tabby-and-white cat stretching (£2.55)

DECIMAL **QUEEN ELIZABETH II**

■ **2022, June 9. Cats**
Des: Studio Up. Printed in litho by Cartor Security Printers. Issued in se-tenant pairs.

Set	17.50	26.00
Gutter pairs	38.00	–
First day cover	–	25.00
Stamp cards	6.00	25.00

(*All designs also appear in a collector's sheet.)

Pride marchers and couple kissing (1st)
Pride marchers and 'Love' banner (1st)
Pride marchers and Transgender pride banner (1st)
Pride marchers and Progress Pride flag (1st)
Pride marchers and 'Gay pride' banner (£1.85)
Pride marchers and 'Glad to be gay' banner (£1.85)
Pride marchers and 'Gay liberation' banner (£1.85)
Pride marchers and 'Love always wins' banner (£1.85)

■ **2022, July 1. Pride**
Des: NB Studio, from illustrations by Sofie Birkin. Printed in litho by Cartor Security Printers. Issued in se-tenant pairs.

Set	16.50	24.00
Gutter pairs	36.00	–
First day cover	–	22.50
Stamp cards	6.00	25.00

(*All designs also appear in a collector's sheet.)

Synchronised diving (1st)
Boxing (1st)
Para table tennis (1st)
Para powerlifting (1st)
Artistic gymnastics (£1.85)
Mountain biking (£1.85)
Athletics (£1.85)
Wheelchair basketball (£1.85)

■ **2022, July 28. Birmingham 2022 Commonwealth Games**
Des: Interabang, from illustrations by Charis Tsevis. Printed in litho by Cartor Security Printers. Issued in se-tenant pairs.

Set	16.00	24.00
Gutter pairs	34.00	–
First day cover	–	24.00
Stamp cards	6.00	30.00

Optimus Prime (1st)   Grimlock (£1.85)
Megatron (1st)   Shockwave (£1.85)
Bumblebee (1st)   Arcee (£1.85)
Starscream (1st)   Soundwave (£1.85)

■ **2022, September 1. Transformers**
Des: The Chase, from illustrations by Andrew Wildman, Stephen Baskerville and John-Paul Bove. Printed in litho by Cartor Security Printers. Issued in se-tenant pairs.

Set	16.00	24.00
Gutter pairs	34.00	–
First day cover	–	22.00
Stamp cards	9.00	45.00

(*All designs appear in the Transformers prestige stamp book, and in a collector's sheet. The Optimus Prime, Megatron and Bumblebee designs also appear in 'fan sheets', sold at a premium by the philatelic service.)

Swoop (2nd)
Slug (1st)
Sludge (1st)
Grimlock (1st)
Snarl (£1.85)

■ **2022, September 1. Transformers: The Dinobots**
Des: The Chase, from illustrations by Andrew Wildman, Stephen Baskerville and John-Paul Bove. Printed in litho by Cartor Security Printers. Self-adhesive.

Miniature sheet	8.50	12.00
Miniature sheet first day cover	–	11.00
Press sheet	£100	–

(*All designs appear in the Transformers prestige stamp book.)

QUEEN ELIZABETH II DECIMAL

Aviation operations (1st)
Cold-weather operations (1st)
Mountain operations (1st)
Arid-climate operations (1st)
Commando training (£1.85)
Band security (£1.85)
Amphibious operations (£1.85)
Maritime security operations (£1.85)

■ **2022, September 29. Royal Marines**
Des: Osborne Ross. Printed in litho by Cartor Security Printers. Issued in se-tenant strips of four.

Set	16.00	24.00
Gutter pairs	34.00	–
First day cover	–	22.00
Stamp cards	9.00	45.00

Sea Soldier, Duke of York & Albany's Maritime Regiment, 1644 (1st)
Grenadier, Chatham Division, HM Marine Forces, 1775 (1st)
Sergeant, 4th Battalion, Royal Marines, 1918 (£1.85)
Officer, 48th Royal Marine Commando, 1944 (£1.85)

■ **2022, September 29. Royal Marines: Uniforms**
Des: Webb & Webb Design, from illustrations by Graham Turner. Printed in litho by Cartor Security Printers.

Miniature sheet	8.00	12.00
Miniature sheet first day cover	–	11.00
Press sheet	£120	–

Rocky and Ginger, from Chicken Run (2nd)
Feathers McGraw, from The Wrong Trousers (2nd)
Wallace and Gromit (1st)
Frank, from Creature Comforts (1st)
Timmy, from Shaun The Sheep and Timmy Time (£1.85)
Morph and Chas, from The Amazing Adventures of Morph (£1.85)
Robin, from Robin Robin (£2.55)
Shaun and Bitzer, from Shaun The Sheep (£2.55)

■ **2022, October 19. Aardman Classics**
Des: Studio Up and Royal Mail Group. Printed in litho by Cartor Security Printers. Self-adhesive. Issued in se-tenant pairs.

Set	18.00	26.00
Gutter pairs	38.00	–
First day cover	–	24.00
Stamp cards	9.00	45.00

(*All designs also appear in a collector's sheet.)

A Close Shave (1st)
A Matter of Loaf and Death (1st)
The Wrong Trousers (£1.85)
A Grand Day Out (£1.85)

■ **2022, October 19. Wallace and Gromit: Cracking Moments**
Des: Aardman Animations, Studio Up and Royal Mail Group. Printed in litho by Cartor Security Printers.

Miniature sheet	8.00	12.00
Miniature sheet first day cover	–	11.00
Press sheet	£110	–

Annunciation (2nd)
Journey to Bethlehem (2nd Large)
Holy family (1st)
Angel (1st Large)
Angel and shepherds (£1.85)
Magi (£2.55)

■ **2022, November 3. Christmas**
Des: Baxter & Bailey, from illustrations by Katie Ponder. Printed in gravure by Cartor Security Printers. Self-adhesive.

DECIMAL QUEEN ELIZABETH II

Set	13.00	19.00
First day cover	-	17.00
Stamp cards	5.00	35.00
Miniature sheet	13.00	19.00
Miniature sheet first day cover	-	17.00

(*The 2nd class and 1st class stamps also appear in retail stamp books. All values appear in a collector's sheet.)

Photograph by Dorothy Wilding, 1952 (2nd)
Photograph by Cecil Beaton, 1968 (1st)
Photograph by Yousuf Karsh, 1984 (£1.85)
Photograph by Tim Graham, 1996 (£2.55)

■ **2022, November 10. In Memoriam: Queen Elizabeth II**
Des: Kate Stephens. Printed in litho by Cartor Security Printers.

Set	9.00	13.00
Gutter pairs	20.00	-
First day cover	-	12.00
Stamp cards	3.00	17.50

(*All four photographs were previously used in the Golden Jubilee set issued on February 6, 2002.)

Head of the king (2nd)
Inlaid fan (2nd)
Gold mask (1st)
Falcon pendant (1st)
Lion couch (£1.85)
Throne (£1.85)
Boat model (£2.55)
Guardian statue (£2.55)

■ **2022, November 24. 100th Anniversary of the Discovery of the Tomb of Tutankhamun**
Des: Andy Altmann. Printed in litho by Cartor Security Printers. Issued in se-tenant pairs.

Set	18.00	26.00
Gutter pairs	38.00	-
First day cover	-	24.00
Stamp cards	9.00	45.00

(*All designs appear in the Tutankhamun: Finding a Pharaoh prestige stamp book.)

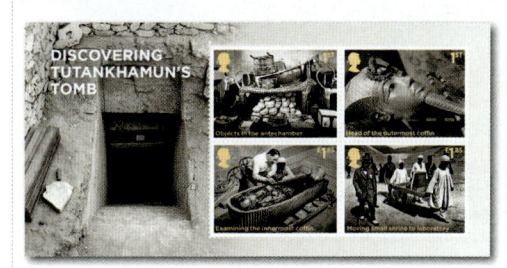

Objects in the antechamber (1st)
Head of the outermost coffin (1st)
Examining the innermost coffin (£1.85)
Moving small shrine to laboratory (£1.85)

■ **2022, November 24. Discovering Tutankhamun's Tomb**
Des: Andy Altmann. Printed in litho by Cartor Security Printers.

Miniature sheet	8.00	12.00
Miniature sheet first day cover	-	11.00
Press sheet	£150	-

(*All designs appear in the Tutankhamun: Finding a Pharaoh prestige stamp book.)

Steve Harris, Vancouver, 2010 (1st)
Bruce Dickinson, Hammersmith, 1983 (1st)
Dave Murray, Adrian Smith and Steve Harris, Pamplona, 1988 (1st)
Nicko McBrain, Quito, 2009 (1st)
Dave Murray, Bruce Dickinson and Janick Gers, Rio, 2001 (£1.85)
Adrian Smith and Steve Harris, Helsinki, 2018 (£1.85)
Iron Maiden, Twickenham, 2008 (£1.85)
Bruce Dickinson and Eddie, Birmingham, 2018 (£1.85)

■ **2023, January 12. Iron Maiden**
Des: Royal Mail Group. Printed in litho by Cartor Security Printers. Issued in se-tenant strips of four.

Set	16.00	24.00
Gutter pairs	34.00	-
First day cover	-	22.00
Stamp cards	9.00	45.00

(*All designs appear, in self-adhesive form, in two collector's sheets. The Rio de Janeiro, Quito and Helsinki designs also appear in a 'fan sheet' sold at a premium by the philatelic service.)

QUEEN ELIZABETH II DECIMAL

'The Trooper' Eddie (1st)
'Aces High' Eddie (1st)
'Iron Maiden' Eddie (£1.85)
'Senjutsu' Eddie (£1.85)

■ **2023, January 12. Iron Maiden: Eddie**
Des: Royal Mail Group. Printed in litho by Cartor Security Printers.
Miniature sheet	8.00	12.00
Miniature sheet first day cover	–	11.00
Press sheet	£130	–

(*The Trooper, Aces High and Senjutsu designs also appear on a 'fan sheet', sold at a premium by the philatelic service.)

Professor X (2nd)   Wolverine (1st)
Kitty Pryde (2nd)   Jean Grey (1st)
Angel (2nd)   Iceman (1st)
Colossus (2nd)   Storm (1st)
Jubilee (2nd)   Beast (1st)
Cyclops (2nd)   Rogue (1st)

■ **2023, February 16. X-Men**
Des: Interabang. Printed in litho by Cartor Security Printers. Issued in se-tenant strips of six.
Set	15.00	20.00
Gutter pairs	32.00	–
First day cover	–	20.00
Stamp cards	12.00	45.00

(*All designs appear in the X-Men prestige stamp book and collector's sheet. The Wolverine and Jean Grey designs also appear in 'fan sheets', sold at a premium by the philatelic service.)

Juggernaut (1st)   Sabretooth (1st)
Mystique (1st)   Magneto (£1.85)
Emma Frost (1st)

■ **2023, February 16. X-Men**
Des: Interabang. Printed in litho by Cartor Security Printers. Self-adhesive.
Miniature sheet	8.50	12.00
Miniature sheet first day cover	–	12.00
Press sheet	£100	–

(*All designs appear in the X-Men prestige stamp book.)

The Flying Scotsman headboard (1st)
The Flying Scotsman in the Yorkshire Dales (1st)
The Flying Scotsman crossing the Ribblehead Viaduct (1st)
The Flying Scotsman in Blyth (1st)
The Flying Scotsman at Heap Bridge (£1.85)
The Flying Scotsman crossing the Royal Border Bridge (£1.85)
The Flying Scotsman at Victoria Station (£1.85)
The Flying Scotsman at Shildon (£1.85)

■ **2023, March 9. Centenary of The Flying Scotsman'**
Des: Steers McGillan Eves. Printed in litho by Cartor Security Printers. Issued in se-tenant pairs.
Set	16.00	24.00
Gutter pairs	34.00	–
First day cover	–	22.00
Stamp cards	9.00	45.00

(*All designs appear in the Flying Scotsman prestige stamp book.)

Scotland by the Night Scotsman, 1932 (1st)
LNER service to and from England, 1923 (1st)
Edinburgh by LNER, 1935 (£1.85)
Refuelling the Flying Scotsman, 1932 (£1.85)

■ **2023, March 9. Flying Scotsman: Posters and Advertisements**
Des: Steers McGillan Eves. Printed in litho by Cartor Security Printers.
Miniature sheet	8.50	12.00
Miniature sheet first day cover	–	11.00
Press sheet	£130	–

(*All designs appear in the Flying Scotsman prestige stamp book.)

232 BRITISH STAMP MARKET VALUES 2024

Top-rated Internet Stamp Dealers – Galashiels

Buying GB Decimal Collections

Selling Discount GB Postage
for latest prices visit: **www.philatelink.co.uk**

Buying GB & Commonwealth Collections

We urgently want to buy good GB collections from 1840 to present day, especially Wildings, Machin's and modern postage material. Top prices paid.

We buy and sell almost ANYTHING Philatelic

HOME VALUATION SERVICE
PREPARED TO TRAVEL UK WIDE TO BUY LARGE OR VALUABLE PROPERTIES
WE OFFER BETTER PRICES THAN YOU WOULD GET AT AUCTION

PHILATELINK eBay Shop & Auctions

WE HOLD HUNDREDS OF AUCTIONS EVERY MONTH
often via our CLIENT SELLING SERVICE (ask for Details)
http://stores.ebay.co.uk/PHILATELINK
Auctions start at just £0.99 and P&P is FREE to UK bidders

philatelink
The GB discount postage specialists

Web: www.philatelink.co.uk • Email philatelink@btinternet.com
☎ Landline: 01896 759703 or Mobile 07510 312271
DAVID WALDIE (PHILATELINK) 13 REDPATH CRESCENT,
GALASHIELS, BORDERS, TD1 2OG, UK

ORIGINAL ARTWORK REPRODUCED BY PERMISSION OF PHIL STAMP COVERS

KING CHARLES III

In this section, prices are quoted in two columns: unmounted mint (left) and fine used (right). Issues are priced for complete sets only, except where stated.

Definitives have U-shaped security slits, an iridescent wavy-line overlay text with source and year codes, a digital data matrix code separated from the design by a simulated perforation, and security backing paper (SBP) with the wavy-line underlay text sideways.

Source codes are 'MFIL' (booklets of four), 'MEIL' (booklets of eight) and 'MBIL' (business sheets). Stamps from counter sheets and prestige stamp books have no source code.

Year codes are 'M23L' (2023).

■ 2023. Definitives
Des: Royal Mail, from a portrait by Martin Jennings. Self-adhesive, with a data matrix code, on security backing paper (sideways). Printed in gravure by Cartor.

2nd holly green (April 4, 2023)
no source code, date code 23	1.25	1.25
source code MEIL, date code 23	1.25	1.25
source code MBIL, date code 23	1.25	1.25

2nd Large dark pine green (April 4, 2023)
no source code, date code 23	2.00	2.00
source code MFIL, date code 23	2.00	2.00
source code MBIL, date code 23	2.00	2.00

1st plum purple (April 4, 2023)
no source code, date code 23	2.00	2.00
source code MEIL, date code 23	2.00	2.00
source code MFIL, date code 23	2.00	2.00
source code MBIL, date code 23	2.00	2.00

1st Large marine turquoise (April 4, 2023)
no source code, date code 23	2.40	2.40
source code MFIL, date code 23	2.40	2.40

£2.20 dark green (April 4, 2023)
no source code, date code 23, SBP2 (sideways)	3.25	3.25

First day cover (April 4, 2023)
2nd, 2nd Large, 1st, 1st Large	–	10.00

First day cover (April 4, 2023)
£2.20	–	5.00

KING CHARLES III

Sweet pea (1st)
Iris (1st)
Lily (1st)
Sunflower (1st)
Fuchsia (1st)
Tulip (1st)
Peony (1st)
Nasturtium (1st)
Rose (1st)
Dahlia (1st)

■ **2023, March 23. Flowers**
Des: Charlie Smith Design. Printed in litho by Cartor Security Printers. Issued in se-tenant strips of five.

Set	15.00	21.00
Gutter pairs	32.00	–
First day cover	–	20.00
Stamp cards	7.00	30.00

Robin Hood is declared an outlaw (1st)
Robin Hood meets Little John (1st)
Friar Tuck carries Robin Hood (1st)
Robin Hood robs the rich (1st)
Robin Hood wins the archery contest (1st)
Robin Hood captures the Sheriff (1st)
Robin Hood helps Maid Marian escape (1st)
Robin Hood and Maid Marian marry (1st)
King Richard removes his disguise (1st)
Robin Hood shoots his last arrow (1st)

■ **2023, April 13. The Legend of Robin Hood**
Des: Godfrey Design Illustrations. Printed in litho by Cartor Security Printers. Issued in se-tenant strips of five.

Set	16.00	22.00
Gutter pairs	32.00	–
First day cover	–	21.00
Stamp cards	7.00	30.00

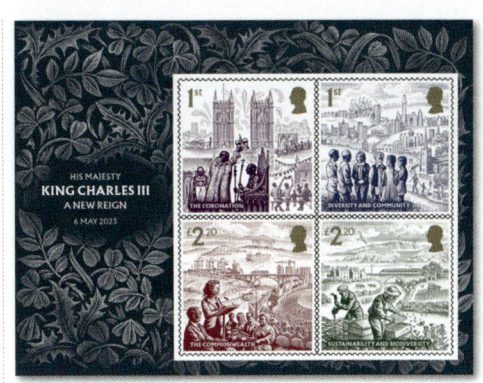

The Coronation (1st)
Diversity and community (1st)
The Commonwealth (£2.20)
Sustainability and biodiversity (£2.20)

■ **2023, May 6. King Charles III: A New Reign**
Des: Andrew Davidson. Printed in litho by Cartor Security Printers.

Miniature sheet	10.00	15.00
Miniature sheet first day cover	–	15.00
Press sheet	£140	–
Stamp cards	4.00	20.00

(*All designs also appear in a collector's sheet.)

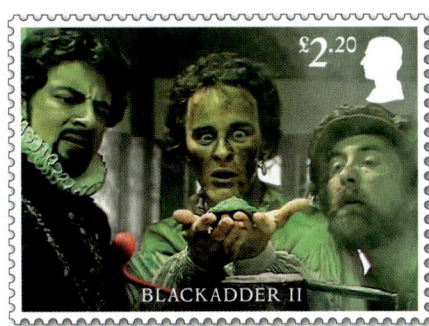

Blackadder the Third: Nob and Nobility (2nd)
Blackadder the Third: Duel and Duality (2nd)
Blackadder Goes Forth: Goodbyeee (1st)
Blackadder Goes Forth: Goodbyeee (1st)
The Black Adder: Born to be King (£2)
The Black Adder: The Archbishop (£2)
Blackadder II: Bells (£2.20)
Blackadder II: Money (£2.20)

■ **2023, May 17. Blackadder**
Des: True North. Printed in litho by Cartor Security Printers. Issued in se-tenant pairs.

Set	18.00	26.00
Gutter pairs	38.00	–
First day cover	–	24.00
Stamp cards	9.00	45.00

(*All designs also appear in a collector's sheet.)

KING CHARLES III

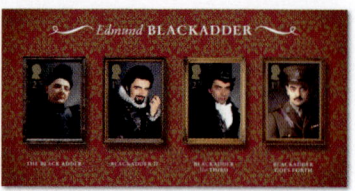

Prince Edmund, The Black Adder (£2.20)
Lord Edmund Blackadder (1st)
Mr E. Blackadder (£2.20)
Captain Blackadder (1st)

■ **2023, May 17. Edmund Blackadder**
Des: True North. Printed in litho by Cartor Security Printers.

Miniature sheet	10.00	15.00
Miniature sheet first day cover	–	15.00
Press sheet	£150	–

Warhammer 40,000: Space Marines (1st)
Warhammer 40,000: Orks (1st)
Warhammer Age of Sigmar: Stormcast Eternals (£2)
Warhammer Age of Sigmar: Slaves to Darkness (£2)
Warhammer The Old World: High Elves (£2.20)
Warhammer The Old World: Dwarfs (£2.20)

■ **2023, June 8. Warhammer**
Des: Common Curiosity. Printed in litho by Cartor Security Printers. Issued in vertical se-tenant pairs.

Set	15.00	23.00
Gutter pairs	32.00	–
First day cover	–	24.00
Stamp cards	7.50	35.00

(*All designs also appear, in self-adhesive form, in a collector's sheet. The Space Marines and Stormcast Eternals designs also appear on two fan sheets.)

Warhammer 40,000: Rogue Trader (1st)
Warhammer The Old World: Battle for Skull Pass (1st)
Warhammer The Horus Heresy: The Emperor of Mankind (£2.20)
Warhammer Age of Sigmar: Yndrasta, the celestial spear (£2.20)

■ **2023, June 8. Warhammer**
Des: Common Curiosity. Printed in litho by Cartor Security Printers.

Miniature sheet	10.00	15.00
Miniature sheet first day cover	–	15.00
Press sheet	£120	–

(*All designs also appear, in self-adhesive form, in a collector's sheet.)

'From Small Island Life to Big Island Dreams' by Kareen Cox (1st)
'Ode to Saturday Schools' by Tomekah George (1st)
'Carnival Come Thru!' By Bokiba (£1)
'Basking in the Sun After a Hard Day's Work', by Emma Prempeh (£1)
'The March', by Emma Prempeh (£2)
'Here We Come', by Bokiba (£2)
'Taste the Caribbean', by Kareen Cox (£2.20)
'Dancehall Rhythms', by Alvin Kofi (£2.20)

■ **2023, June 22. Windrush: 75 Years**
Des: The Chase and Supple Studio. Printed in litho by Cartor Security Printers. Issued in se-tenant pairs.

Set	18.00	26.00
Gutter pairs	38.00	–
First day cover	–	24.00
Stamp cards	6.00	30.00

Beaver (2nd)
Atlantic salmon (2nd)
Kingfisher (2nd)
Beautiful demoiselle (2nd)
Water vole (2nd)
Grey wagtail (1st)
Common mayfly (1st)
Otter (1st)
Brown trout (1st)
Dipper (1st)

■ **2023, July 13. River Wildlife**
Des: Stand Up. Printed in litho by Cartor Security Printers. Issued in se-tenant strips of five.

Set	15.00	21.00
Gutter pairs	32.00	–
First day cover	–	20.00
Stamp cards	7.00	30.00

(*All designs also appear in a collector's sheet.)

KGV

At Rowland Hill Stamps we have a large stock of King George V stamps from the vast majority of Commonwealth countries.

ASK NOW TO START RECEIVING OUR FREE COMMONWEALTH LISTS

ROWLAND HILL STAMPS
Hill House, Cookley,
Kidderminster, DY10 3UW
01562 851101
sales@rowlandhillstamps.co.uk
www.rowlandhillstamps.co.uk

A FAMILY RUN BUSINESS ESTABLISHED OVER 50 YEARS

---

cddstamps.com
Commemorative Definitive Decimal Stamps

- Offering GB, British Commonwealth and selected other countries,
- over 10,000 GB including 2500 Machins,
- from over 30,000 + listings,
- mostly listed by SG and Scott,
- with reverse scans wherever possible.
- We are a member of the Internet Philatelic Dealers Association, the APS and the GBPS
- With over 65,000 positive feedbacks.
- Buy with confidence – please visit

www.hipstamp.com/store/cddstamps

GREAT BRITAIN 1840-2010

Our latest catalogue covers all periods of G.B. from Penny Blacks to modern Machins

Included are Booklets, Booklet Panes, First Day Covers, and a wide range of Definitives and Commemorative stamps in unmounted and fine condition. For a friendly, personal service, why not request a **FREE** copy today or send us a list of your requirements. Whether buying or selling we look forward to receiving your enquiries.

We have comprehensive stocks of Wildings and Machins and we attend most of the major fairs in the UK. Visit our website for full details.

ARUN STAMPS
P.O. Box 15, Fakenham, Norfolk, NR21 0EU
Telephone: (01328) 829318
Email:arunstampspobox15@gmail.com
www.arunstamps.co.uk

REGIONAL ISSUES GUERNSEY, ISLE OF MAN, JERSEY

REGIONAL ISSUES

Prices in this section are quoted in two columns: mint (left) and fine used (right).
The definitive issues for Guernsey, the Isle of Man and Jersey pre-date their postal independence in 1969, 1973 and 1969 respectively.

CHANNEL ISLANDS

Gathering seaweed (1d)

Islanders gathering seaweed (2½d)

■ **1948, May 10. Third Anniversary of Liberation**
Des: J.R.R. Stobie (1d), E. Blampied (2½d). Printed in gravure by Harrison. Wmk: Multiple Crowns and GVIR. Perf: 15x14.

Set	0.15	0.20
First day cover	–	17.50

GUERNSEY

2½d

3d, 4d, 5d

■ **1958–1969**
Des: E.A. Piprell. Printed in gravure by Harrison. Perf: 15x14.

Wmk: Multiple St. Edward's Crown. Non phosphor, except where stated

2½d red (June 8, 1964)	0.30	0.35
3d lilac (August 18, 1958)	0.30	0.30
one centre phos band (May 24, 1967)	0.10	0.15
4d ultramarine (February 7, 1966)	0.20	0.25
two phos bands (October 24, 1967)	0.10	0.15
First day cover (2½d)	–	25.00
First day cover (3d)	–	20.00
First day cover (4d)	–	10.00

No watermark. Chalky paper. Two phosphor bands, except where stated

4d ultramarine (April 16, 1968)	0.10	0.15
4d sepia (September 4, 1968)		
one centre phosphor band	0.10	0.15
4d red (February 26, 1969)		
one centre phosphor band	0.10	0.20
5d deep blue (September 4, 1968)	0.10	0.20
First day cover (4d sepia, 5d)	–	2.00
First day cover (4d red)	–	1.50

ISLE OF MAN

2½d

GUERNSEY, ISLE OF MAN, JERSEY REGIONAL ISSUES

JERSEY

3d, 4d, 5d

■ 1958–1969
Des: J. Nicholson. Printed in gravure by Harrison. Perf: 15x14.

Wmk: Multiple St. Edward's Crown. Non phosphor, except where stated

2½d carmine-red (June 8, 1964)	0.20	0.35
3d lilac (August 18, 1958)	0.15	0.20
chalky paper (May 17, 1964)	4.50	4.00
one centre phos band (June 27, 1968)	0.10	0.15
4d ultramarine (February 7, 1966)	0.75	0.75
a) two phosphor bands (July 5, 1967)	0.10	0.15
First day cover (2½d)	–	25.00
First day cover (3d)	–	30.00
First day cover (4d)	–	10.00

No watermark. Chalky paper. Two phosphor bands, except where stated

4d ultramarine (June 24, 1968)	0.10	0.15
4d sepia (September 4, 1968)		
one centre phosphor band	0.10	0.15
4d red (February 26, 1969)		
one centre phosphor band	0.20	0.30
5d deep blue (September 4, 1968)	0.20	0.30
First day cover (4d sepia, 5d)	–	2.00
First day cover (4d red)	–	1.50

■ 1971–1973
Des: J. Matthews. Printed in gravure by Harrison. Perf: 15x14.

2½p magenta (July 7, 1971)	0.15	0.15
3p ultramarine (July 7, 1971)	0.20	0.20
5p violet (July 7, 1971)	0.50	0.50
7½p pale brown (July 7, 1971)	0.60	0.60
First day cover	–	2.50

(*The 2½p and 3p exist on either ordinary coated paper or fluorescent-coated paper.)

2½d

3d, 4d, 5d

■ 1958–1969
Des: E. Blampied (2½d), W.M. Gardner (others). Printed in gravure by Harrison. Perf: 15x14.

Wmk: Multiple St. Edward's Crown. Non phosphor, except where stated

2½d carmine-red (June 8, 1964)	0.20	0.25
3d lilac (August 18, 1958)	0.25	0.25
one centre phos band (June 9, 1967)	0.10	0.15
4d ultramarine (February 7, 1966)	0.20	0.25
two phos bands (September 5, 1967)	0.10	0.15
First day cover (2½d)	–	25.00
First day cover (3d)	–	20.00
First day cover (4d)	–	10.00

No watermark. Chalky paper, PVA gum. One centre phosphor band (4d), or two phosphor bands (5d).

4d sepia (September 4, 1968)	0.10	0.15
4d red (February 26, 1969)	0.10	0.20
5d deep blue (September 4, 1968)	0.10	0.20
First day cover (4d sepia, 5d)	–	2.00
First day cover (4d red)	–	1.50

BRITISH STAMP MARKET VALUES 2024 239

NORTHERN IRELAND DEFINITIVES

Prices in this section are quoted in two columns: mint (left) and fine used (right).

PRE-DECIMAL WILDING ISSUES

3d lilac, 4d blue, 5d blue

6d purple, 9d green

1/3 green, 1/6 grey–blue

■ 1958–1969
Des: W. Hollywood (3d, 4d, 5d), L.Philton (6d, 9d), T. Collins (1/3, 1/6). Printed in gravure by Harrisons. Perf 15x14.

Wmk: Multiple St. Edward's Crown. Non-phosphor except where stated

3d lilac (August 18, 1958)	0.15	0.15
3d lilac, one phos band	0.15	0.20
4d blue (February 7, 1966)	0.15	0.15
4d blue, two phos bands	0.15	0.15
6d purple (September 29, 1958)	0.25	0.25
9d green (March 1, 1967). two phos bands	0.35	0.40
1/3 green (September 29, 1958)	0.35	0.40
1/6 grey–blue (March 1, 1967), two phos bands	0.40	0.40
First day cover (3d)	–	25.00
First day cover (6d, 1/3)	–	30.00
First day cover (4d)	–	7.50
First day cover (9d, 1/6)	–	4.00

No wmk. Two phosphor bands and PVA gum except where stated

4d blue, gum Arabic (June 27, 1968)	0.15	0.15
4d sepia (September 4, 1968), one phos band	0.15	0.25
4d red (February 26, 1969), one phos band	0.20	0.30
5d blue (September 4, 1968)	0.20	0.20
1/6 grey–blue (May 20, 1969)	1.50	1.40
First day cover (4d sepia, 5d)	–	2.50
First day cover (4d red)	–	1.00

(*The 4d blue also exists with PVA gum, but this was not placed on sale in Northern Ireland; price £8.50 mint.)

DECIMAL MACHIN ISSUES WITHOUT ELLIPTICAL PERFORATIONS

3p blue

Des: J. Matthews. Type I has the symbol close to the top of the design; type II (1983) has the symbol redrawn and edged down.

■ 1971–1980. Printed in gravure by Harrisons
Perf 15x14. Two phosphor bands except where stated.

Original coated paper. PVA gum

2½p pink (July 7, 1971), one phos band	0.40	0.40
3p blue (July 7, 1971)	0.20	0.20
5p violet (July 7, 1971)	0.75	0.75
7½p brown (July 7, 1971)	1.50	1.50

Fluorescent coated paper. PVA gum

2½p pink (June 1973), one phos band	5.25	4.00
3p blue (April 1973)	7.50	7.00
3p blue, one centre band	0.35	0.30

Fluorescent coated paper. PVAD gum

3p blue (January 23, 1974), one phos band	1.00	1.00
3½p green (January 23, 1974)	0.20	0.20
3½p green, one centre band	0.20	0.20
4½p grey–blue (November 6, 1974)	0.20	0.20
5½p deep violet (January 23, 1974)	0.20	0.20
5½p deep violet, one centre band	0.20	0.20
6½p green–blue (January 14, 1976), one band	0.20	0.20
7p red-brown (January 18, 1978), one band	0.20	0.20
8p red (January 23, 1974)	0.25	0.25
8½p green (January 14, 1976)	0.25	0.25
9p violet-blue (January 18, 1978)	0.25	0.25

NORTHERN IRELAND COUNTRY DEFINITIVES

10p orange (October 20, 1976)	0.25	0.25
10p orange, one phos band	0.25	0.25
10½p grey-blue (January 18, 1978)	0.30	0.30
11p red (October 20, 1976)	0.30	0.30

Phosphor coated paper. PVAD gum

12p yellow-green (July 23, 1980)	0.35	0.35
13½p red-brown (July 23, 1980)	0.40	0.40
15p blue (July 23, 1980)	0.40	0.40
First day cover (2½p, 3p, 5p, 7½p)	–	1.70
First day cover (3½p, 5½p, 8p)	–	1.40
First day cover (4½p)	–	1.25
First day cover (6½p, 8½p)	–	1.00
First day cover (10p, 11p)	–	1.00
First day cover (7p, 9p, 10½p)	–	1.00
First day cover (12p, 13½p, 15p)	–	1.00

■ 1981–1993. Printed in litho by Questa
Perf: 13½x14. Phosphor coated paper, except 11½p and 12½p (left side band). PVA gum (11½p, 14p, 18p, 22p), PVAD gum (others)

11½p mushroom (April 8, 1981)	0.50	0.50
12½p light green (February 24, 1982)	0.35	0.30
14p steel-blue (April 8, 1981)	0.50	0.50
15½p pale violet (February 24, 1982)	0.50	0.50
16p light mushroom (April 27, 1983)	0.70	0.70
18p mauve (April 8, 1981)	0.60	0.60
19½p grey-green (February 24, 1982)	1.25	1.25
20½p bright blue (April 27, 1983)	2.50	2.50
22p deep blue (April 8, 1981)	0.60	0.60
26p red (February 24, 1982), type I	0.70	0.70
28p blue (April 27, 1983), type I	0.70	0.70

Perf: 15x14. One phosphor band (12p, 12½p, 13p, 14p, 15p), phosphor coated paper (16p, 17p, 18p, 19p, 20p, 22p, 23p, 24p, 31p, 32p, 34p, 37p, 39p), advanced coated paper (22p, 26p, 28p), or as stated. PVAD gum except where stated.

12p emerald green (January 7, 1986)	0.60	0.60
12½p light green (February 28, 1984)	3.00	3.00
12½p light green, PVA gum	3.00	–
13p red-brown (October 23, 1984), type I	0.60	0.60
13p deep brown, type II	1.00	1.00
14p deep blue (November 8, 1988)	0.40	0.40
15p bright blue (November 28, 1989)	0.40	0.40
16p light mushroom (February 28, 1984)	4.25	4.25
17p steel blue (October 23, 1984), type I	1.25	1.25
17p steel blue, type I, advanced coated paper	0.50	0.50
17p steel blue, type II, advanced coated paper	£140	£140
17p deep blue (December 4, 1990)	0.50	0.50
18p deep green (January 6, 1987)	0.60	0.60
18p bright green, centre phos band	0.60	0.60
18p bright green, perf 14	5.00	5.00
18p bright green, left phos band	1.75	1.75
19p orange-red (November 8, 1988)	0.60	0.60
20p brownish-black (November 28, 1989)	0.60	0.50
22p yellowish-green (October 23, 1984)	0.60	0.60
22p orange-red (December 4, 1990)	0.60	0.60
23p bright green (November 8, 1988)	0.60	0.60
24p deep red (November 28, 1989)	0.70	0.70
24p chestnut (August 10, 1993), two bands	1.50	1.50
26p red (January 27, 1987), type II	2.00	2.00
26p drab (December 4, 1990), phos paper	0.90	0.90
28p blue (January 27, 1987), type II	1.50	1.50
28p blue-grey (Dec 3, 1991), phos paper	0.80	0.80
31p purple (October 23, 1984), type I	1.00	1.00
31p purple (April 14, 1987), type II	1.60	1.60
32p greenish blue (November 8, 1988)	1.00	1.00
34p bluish grey (November 28, 1989)	1.00	1.00
37p rosine (December 4, 1990)	1.40	1.40
39p mauve (December 3, 1991)	1.50	1.50

(*The 18p with left phosphor band and 24p chestnut with two phosphor bands come from prestige stamp books. The 13p also exists printed on paper supplied by Coated Papers Ltd, with PVA gum, in 1987)

First day cover (11½p, 14p, 18p, 22p)	–	1.00
First day cover (12½p, 15½p, 19½p, 26p)	–	1.50
First day cover (16p, 20½p, 28p)	–	1.50
First day cover (13p, 17p, 22p, 31p)	–	1.50
First day cover (12p)	–	1.00
First day cover (18p)	–	1.00
First day cover (14p, 19p, 23p, 32p)	–	2.00
First day cover (15p, 20p, 24p, 34p)	–	2.00
First day cover (17p, 22p, 26p, 37p)	–	2.25
First day cover (18p, 24p, 28p, 39p)	–	2.25

DECIMAL MACHIN ISSUES WITH ELLIPTICAL PERFORATIONS

1st red

■ 1993–1996. Printed in litho by Questa
Perf 15x14. One phosphor band (19p and 20p), or two phosphor bands (others).

19p bistre (December 7, 1993), left phos band	1.00	1.00
19p bistre, right phos band	1.75	1.75
20p bright green (July 23, 1996)	1.00	1.40
25p red (December 7, 1993)	0.60	0.60
26p red-brown (July 23, 1996)	1.50	1.50
30p olive-grey (December 7, 1993)	0.90	0.90
37p mauve (July 23, 1996)	2.20	2.20
41p grey-brown (December 7, 1993)	1.00	1.00
63p emerald (July 23, 1996)	2.75	2.50

COUNTRY DEFINITIVES NORTHERN IRELAND

(*The 19p with phosphor band to right comes from the 1995 National Trust prestige stamp book.)

■ **1997–2000. Printed in gravure by Walsall**
Perf 15x14. One phosphor band (19p and 20p), two phosphor bands (others)

19p bistre (June 8, 1999)	2.00	2.00
20p bright green (July 1, 1997)	2.00	2.00
26p chestnut (July 1, 1997)	1.85	1.85
37p mauve (July 1, 1987)	2.00	2.00
38p ultramarine (June 8, 1999)	5.00	5.00
40p azure (April 25, 2000)	3.25	3.25
63p emerald (July 1, 1997)	3.00	3.00
64p turquoise (June 8, 1999)	5.50	5.50
65p greenish blue (April 25, 2000)	3.00	3.00

(*The 20p with right phosphor band, the 26p perf 15x14 and perf 14, and the 37p also exist printed by Harrisons, from prestige stamp books.)

Perf 15x14 except where stated. One phosphor band

1st orange-red (February 15, 2000), perf 14	2.25	2.20
1st orange-red (April 25, 2000)	6.50	6.50

(*The perf 14 stamp was issued only in the Special By Design prestige stamp book.)

First day cover (19p, 25p, 30p, 41p)	–	2.50
First day cover (20p, 26p, 37p, 63p)	–	2.50
First day cover (19p, 38p, 64p)	–	3.00
First day cover (1st, 40p, 65p)	–	3.00

PICTORIAL ISSUES WITHOUT WHITE BORDERS

Basalt columns (2nd)

Patchwork of fields (1st)

Linen slip case (E)

Pattern on vase (65p, 68p)

■ **2001–2002**
Des: Rodney Miller Associates. Printed in litho by Walsall (2nd, 1st, E, 65p), De La Rue (E, 68p), or Enschedé (2nd, 1st). Perf 15x14. One phosphor band (2nd), two phosphor bands (others).

2nd (March 6, 2001, Walsall)	1.20	1.20
2nd (February 25, 2003, Enschedé)	4.50	4.50
1st (March 6, 2001, Walsall)	1.80	1.80
1st (February 25, 2003, Enschedé)	4.50	4.50
E (March 6, 2001, Walsall)	2.50	2.50
E (October 15, 2002, De La Rue)	2.50	2.50
65p (March 6, 2001)	2.20	2.20
68p (July 4, 2002)	2.30	2.30

(*The 2nd and 1st printed by Enschedé come from the 2003 Microcosmos prestige stamp book.)

First day cover (2nd, 1st, E, 65p)	–	3.00
First day cover (68p)	–	2.00
Stamp cards	8.00	13.00

PICTORIAL ISSUES WITH WHITE BORDERS

Basalt columns (2nd)

Patchwork of fields (1st)

Linen slip case (E, 40p, 42p, 44p, 48p, 50p, 56p, 60p, 87p, 88p, 97p, £1.00, £1.05)

Pattern on vase (68p, 72p, 78p, 81p, 90p, 97p, £1.10, £1.28, £1.33)

■ **2003–2016**
Des: Rodney Miller Associates. Printed in litho by De La Rue (2nd, 1st, E, 40p, 42p, 44p, 68p, 72p, 78p, 81p), in litho by Walsall (42p), in gravure by De La Rue (2nd, 1st, 48p, 50p, 56p, 60p, 72p, 78p, 81p, 90p, 97p), in litho by Enschedé (1st, in prestige stamp books only) or in litho by Cartor (2nd, 1st, 68p, 87p, 88p, £1.00, £1.05, £1.10, £1.28, £1.33). Perf 15x14. One phosphor band (2nd) or two phosphor bands (others).

242 BRITISH STAMP MARKET VALUES 2024

NORTHERN IRELAND COUNTRY DEFINITIVES

2nd (October 14, 2003, De La Rue)	1.20	1.20
2nd (January 3, 2013, Cartor)	1.20	1.20
1st (October 14, 2003, De La Rue)	1.80	1.80
1st (January 3, 2013, Cartor)	1.80	1.80
E (October 14, 2003)	2.50	2.50
40p (May 11, 2004)	1.90	1.90
42p (Walsall, April 5, 2005)	1.90	1.90
42p (De La Rue, July 26, 2005)	2.25	2.25
44p (March 25, 2006)	1.50	1.50
48p (March 27, 2007)	1.00	1.00
50p (April 1, 2008)	1.40	1.40
56p (March 31, 2009)	1.20	1.20
60p (March 30, 2010)	1.75	1.75
68p (October 14, 2003, De La Rue)	2.20	2.20
68p (March 29, 2011, Cartor)	2.00	2.00
72p (March 28, 2006)	2.30	2.30
78p (March 27, 2007)	1.60	1.60
81p (April 1, 2008)	1.75	1.75
87p (April 25, 2012)	2.00	2.00
88p (March 27, 2013)	2.00	2.00
90p (March 31, 2009)	1.85	1.85
97p (March 30, 2010)	2.00	2.00
97p (March 26, 2014)	3.00	3.00
£1.00 (March 24, 2015)	2.25	2.25
£1.05 (March 22, 2016)	2.60	2.60
£1.10 (March 29, 2011)	2.20	2.20
£1.28 (April 25, 2012)	2.25	2.25
£1.33 (March 24, 2015)	2.40	2.40

(*Various values have also appeared in miniature sheets and prestige stamp books. The 1st class also exists, self-adhesive, in Smilers sheets. Although January 3, 2013, was the official date of issue of the 1st class and 2nd class printed by Cartor, both stamps were available earlier from post offices.)

First day cover (2nd, 1st, E, 68p)	–	3.00
First day cover (40p)	–	1.50
First day cover (42p)	–	1.50
First day cover (44p, 72p)	–	2.00
First day cover (48p, 78p)	–	2.50
First day cover (50p, 81p)	–	2.50
First day cover (56p, 90p)	–	3.00
First day cover (60p, 97p)	–	3.60
First day cover (68p, £1.10)	–	3.00
First day cover (87p, £1.28)	–	4.00
First day cover (88p)	–	2.00
First day cover (97p)	–	2.25
First day cover (£1.00, £1.33)	–	4.50
First day cover (£1.05)	–	2.25
Stamp cards	5.00	12.00

Basalt columns (2nd)

Patchwork of fields (1st)

Linen slip case (£1.17, £1.25, £1.35, £1.42, £1.70)

Pattern on vase (£1.40, £1.45, £1.55, £1.63)

■ **2017–2020**
Designs as previous issue but with revised typeface for denomination. Printed in litho by Cartor. Perf 15 x 14. One phosphor band (2nd) or two phosphor bands (others).

2nd (March 20, 2018)	1.75	1.75
1st (March 20, 2018)	1.85	1.85
£1.17 (March 21, 2017)	2.25	2.25
£1.25 (March 20, 2018)	2.40	2.40
£1.35 (March 19, 2019)	2.50	2.50
£1.40 (March 21, 2017)	2.50	2.50
£1.42 (March 17, 2020)	2.75	2.75
£1.45 (March 20, 2018)	2.75	2.75
£1.55 (March 19, 2019)	2.75	2.75
£1.63 (March 17, 2020)	3.00	3.00
£1.70 (December 23, 2020)	3.45	3.45
First day cover (£1.17, £1.40)	–	5.00
First day cover (2nd, 1st, £1.25, £1.45)	–	7.00
First day cover (£1.35, £1.55)	–	5.00
First day cover (£1.42, £1.63)	–	6.00
First day cover (£1.70)	–	4.00

COUNTRY DEFINITIVES NORTHERN IRELAND

PICTORIAL ISSUES WITH DATA MATRIX CODES

Basalt columns (2nd)

Patchwork of fields (1st)

Linen slip case (£1.85)

■ **2022**
Printed in litho by Cartor. One phosphor band (2nd) or two phosphor bands (others). Self-adhesive.

2nd (August 11, 2022)	2.25	3.50
1st (August 11, 2022)	2.50	3.75
£1.85 (August 11, 2022)	3.00	4.00
First day cover	–	10.00

(*The stamps found on Royal Mail first day covers were from a separate printing that differed in relation to the phosphor bands.)

244 BRITISH STAMP MARKET VALUES 2024

SCOTLAND COUNTRY DEFINITIVES

SCOTLAND DEFINITIVES

Prices in this section are quoted in two columns: mint (left) and fine used (right).

PRE-DECIMAL WILDING ISSUES

3d lilac, 4d blue, 5d blue

6d purple, 9d green

1/3 green, 1/6 grey-blue

■ 1958–1970
Des: G. F. Huntly (3d, 4d, 5d), J. B. Fleming (6d, 9d), A. B. Imrie (1/3, 1/6). Printed in gravure by Harrisons. Perf 15x14.

Wmk: Multiple St Edward's Crown. Non-phosphor except where stated

3d lilac (August 18, 1958)	0.15	0.15
3d lilac, two phos bands	6.00	4.00
3d lilac, one left band	0.20	0.35
3d lilac, one right band	0.20	0.35
3d lilac, one centre band	0.20	0.30
4d blue (February 7, 1966)	0.15	0.15
4d blue, two phos bands	0.15	0.15
6d purple (September 29, 1958)	0.15	0.15
6d purple, two phos bands	0.20	0.25
9d green (March 1, 1967), two phos bands	0.35	0.40
1/3 green (September 29, 1958)	0.35	0.25
1/3 green, two phos bands	0.35	0.40
1/6 grey-blue (March 1, 1967), two phos bands	0.40	0.50
First day cover (3d)	–	10.00
First day cover (6d, 1/3)	–	20.00
First day cover (3d, 6d, 1/3 phosphor)	–	£100
First day cover (4d)	–	10.00
First day cover (9d, 1/6)	–	2.75

No watermark. Two phosphor bands except where stated. PVA gum except where stated

3d lilac (May 16, 1968), one band, gum Arabic	0.15	—
3d lilac, one centre band (July 11, 1968)	0.15	0.20
4d blue (November 28, 1967), gum Arabic	0.15	—
4d blue (July 25, 1968)	0.15	0.20
4d sepia (September 4, 1968), one band	0.15	0.20
4d red (February 26, 1969), one band	0.20	0.20
5d blue (September 4, 1968)	0.20	0.25
9d green (September 28, 1970)	3.25	3.25
1/6 grey-blue (December 12, 1968)	1.00	1.00
First day cover (4d sepia, 5d)	–	2.50
First day cover (4d red)	–	1.00

DECIMAL MACHIN ISSUES WITHOUT ELLIPTICAL PERFORATIONS

3½p green

Des: J. Matthews. Type I has the eye on the lion symbol appearing as a circle, while the tongue and claws are thin; type II (1983) has a solid eye and thicker tongue and claws.

■ 1971–1980. Printed in gravure by Harrisons
Perf 15x14. Two phosphor bands except where stated.

Original coated paper. PVA gum

2½p pink (July 7, 1971), one phos band	0.20	0.20
3p blue (July 7, 1971)	0.20	0.20
5p violet (July 7, 1971)	0.75	0.75
7½p brown (July 7, 1971)	0.85	0.85

Fluorescent coated paper. Gum Arabic

2½p pink (Sep 22, 1972), one phos band	0.50	–
3p blue (December 14, 1972)	0.50	–

Fluorescent coated paper. PVA gum

2½p pink (January 1973), one phos band	5.00	5.00
3p blue (January 23, 1974)	11.00	10.50
3p blue, one phos band	0.35	0.30
3½p green (January 23, 1974)	7.50	–
5p violet (January 23, 1974)	15.00	15.00
7½p brown (January 23, 1974)	75.00	75.00

Fluorescent coated paper. PVAD gum

3p blue (November 6, 1974), one phos band	0.75	–
3½p green (November 6, 1974)	0.20	0.20
3½p green, one phos band	0.20	0.20
4½p grey-blue (November 6, 1974)	0.20	0.20

COUNTRY DEFINITIVES SCOTLAND

5½p deep violet (January 23, 1974)	0.20	0.20
5½p deep violet, one phos band	0.20	0.20
6½p green-blue (January 14, 1976), one band	0.20	0.20
7p red-brown (January 18, 1974), one band	0.20	0.20
8p red (January 23, 1974)	0.20	0.30
8½p green (January 14, 1976)	0.25	0.25
9p violet-blue (January 18, 1978)	0.25	0.25
10p orange (October 20, 1976)	0.25	0.25
10p orange, one phos band	0.30	0.30
10½p grey-blue (January 18, 1978)	0.30	0.35
11p red (October 20, 1976)	0.30	0.35

Phosphor coated paper. PVAD gum

12p yellow-green (July 23, 1980)	0.40	0.40
13½p red-brown (July 23, 1980)	0.70	0.70
15p blue (July 23, 1980)	0.50	0.50
First day cover (2½p, 3p, 5p, 7½p)	–	1.70
First day cover (3½p, 5½p, 8p)	–	1.00
First day cover (4½p)	–	1.25
First day cover (6½p, 8½p)	–	1.00
First day cover (10p, 11p)	–	1.00
First day cover (7p, 9p, 10½p)	–	1.00
First day cover (12p, 13½p, 15p)	–	1.00

■ 1981–1986. Printed in litho by Waddingtons

Perf 13½x14. Phosphor coated paper, except 11½p, 12p, 12½p, 13p (left side phosphor band), 22p (advanced coated paper). PVAD gum except 11½p, 12½p (PVA).

11½p mushroom (April 8, 1981)	0.70	0.70
12p emerald-green (January 7, 1986)	1.00	1.00
12½p light green (February 24, 1982)	0.50	0.50
13p light brown (Oct 23, 1984), type I	0.60	0.60
13p light brown, type II	6.00	6.00
14p grey-blue (April 8, 1981)	0.40	0.40
15½p pale-violet (February 24, 1982)	0.70	0.70
16p light mushroom (April 27, 1983)	0.70	0.70
17p steel blue (October 23, 1984), type I	0.90	0.90
17p steel blue, type II	0.70	0.70
17p steel blue, type II, PVA gum	1.00	1.00
18p violet (April 8, 1981)	0.50	0.50
19½p grey-green (February 24, 1982)	1.00	1.00
20½p bright blue (April 27, 1983)	2.00	2.00
22p deep blue (April 8, 1981)	0.60	0.60
22p yellowish green (Oct 23, 1984), type I	2.00	2.00
22p yellowish green, type II	16.00	16.00
26p red (February 24, 1982), type I	0.60	0.60
28p blue (April 27, 1983), type I	0.60	0.60
31p purple (October 23, 1984), type I	1.20	1.20
31p purple, type II	£135	£100

(*The 16p also exists printed by Harrisons on advanced coated paper in 1983; price £4 mint, £3.75 used.)

First day cover (11½p, 14p, 18p, 22p)	–	1.00
First day cover (12½p, 15½p, 19½p, 26p)	–	1.50
First day cover (16p, 20½p, 28p)	–	1.50
First day cover (13p, 17p, 22p, 31p)	–	1.50
First day cover (12p)	–	1.10

■ 1986–1993. Printed in litho by Questa

Perf 15x14. One centre phosphor band (12p, 13p, 14p, 18p), phosphor coated paper (19p, 20p, 23p, 24p, 26p, 28p, 32p, 34p, 37p, 39p), or as indicated. PVAD gum.

12p emerald-green (April 29, 1986)	1.00	1.00
13p light brown (November 4, 1986)	0.60	0.60
14p deep blue (November 8, 1988)	0.40	0.40
14p deep blue, left band	0.50	0.50
15p bright blue (Nov 28, 1989)	0.40	0.40
17p steel blue (April 29, 1986)	1.80	1.80
17p deep blue (December 4, 1990)	0.50	0.50
18p deep green (January 6, 1987)	0.60	0.60
18p bright green (December 3, 1991)	0.60	0.60
18p bright green, perf 14	0.75	0.75
18p bright green, left band	1.20	1.20
19p orange-red (November 8, 1988)	0.50	0.50
19p orange-red, two bands	1.25	1.25
20p brownish-black (November 28, 1989)	0.50	0.50
22p green (Jan 27, 1987), advanced coated paper	0.85	0.85
22p orange-red (Dec 4, 1990), phos paper	0.60	0.60
23p bright green (November 8, 1988)	0.60	0.60
23p bright green, two bands	6.00	6.00
24p deep red (November 28, 1989)	0.60	0.60
24p chestnut (December 3, 1991)	0.70	0.70
24p chestnut, perf 14	5.00	5.00
24p chestnut, two bands	1.25	1.25
26p red (Jan 27, 1987), advanced coated paper	2.00	2.00
26p drab (December 4, 1990)	0.75	0.75
28p blue (Jan 27, 1987), advanced coated paper	1.10	1.10
28p bluish grey (December 3, 1991)	0.80	0.80
28p bluish grey, perf 14	9.00	9.00
31p purple (April 29, 1986)	1.20	1.20
32p greenish blue (November 8, 1988)	0.80	0.80
34p bluish grey (November 28, 1989)	1.00	1.00
37p rosine (December 4, 1990)	1.00	1.00
39p mauve (December 3, 1991)	1.20	1.20
39p mauve, perf 14	10.00	10.00

(*The 19p and 23p with two bands come from the 1989 Scots Connection prestige stamp book. The 13p also exists printed on paper supplied by Coated Papers Ltd, with PVA gum, in 1987)

First day cover (12p, 17p, 31p)	–	10.00
First day cover (13p)	–	9.00
First day cover (18p)	–	1.00
First day cover (22p, 26p, 28p)	–	1.50
First day cover (14p, 19p, 23p, 32p)	–	2.00
First day cover (15p, 20p, 24p, 34p)	–	2.00
First day cover (17p, 22p, 26p, 37p)	–	2.50
First day cover (18p, 24p, 28p, 39p)	–	2.90

DECIMAL MACHIN ISSUES WITH ELLIPTICAL PERFORATIONS

37p mauve

SCOTLAND COUNTRY DEFINITIVES

■ 1993–1996. Printed in litho by Questa
Perf 15x14. One phosphor band (19p and 20p), or two phosphor bands (others).

19p bistre (December 7, 1993)	0.60	0.60
19p bistre, one right band	2.00	2.00
20p bright green (July 23, 1996)	1.00	1.00
25p red (December 7, 1993)	0.80	0.80
26p red-brown (July 23, 1996)	1.10	1.10
30p olive-grey (December 7, 1993)	1.00	1.00
37p mauve (July 23, 1996)	1.50	1.50
41p grey-brown (December 7, 1993)	1.10	1.10
63p emerald (July 23, 1996)	2.50	2.50

(* The 19p with phosphor band to right comes from the 1995 National Trust prestige stamp book.)

■ 1997–2000. Printed in gravure by Walsall
Perf 15x14. except where stated. One phosphor band (20p), or two phosphor bands (others)

20p bright green (July 1, 1997)	0.75	0.75
26p chestnut (July 1, 1997)	1.20	1.20
37p mauve (July 1, 1997)	1.40	1.40
63p emerald (July 1, 1997)	3.00	3.00

(*The 20p with right phosphor band, the 26p perf 15x14 and perf 14, and the 37p also exist printed by Harrisons, from prestige stamp books.)

Perf 15x14. One phosphor band

1st orange-red (February 15, 2000)	2.00	2.00

(*Issued only in the Special By Design prestige stamp book.)

First day cover (19p, 25p, 30p, 41p)	–	3.00
First day cover (20p, 26p, 37p, 63p)	–	3.00

■ 1999–2002
Des: A. Morris (2nd), F. Pottinger and T. Chalk (1st, E), Tayburn (64p), all adapted by Tayburn. Printed in gravure by Walsall (2nd, 1st, E, 64p, 65p), Questa (2nd, 1st, E, 65p), or De La Rue (2nd, 1st, 68p). Perf 15x14. One phosphor band (2nd), two phosphor bands (others).

2nd (June 8, 1999, Walsall)	1.20	1.20
2nd (August 4, 2000, Questa)	1.20	1.20
2nd (June 5, 2002, De La Rue)	1.50	1.50
1st (June 8, 1999, Walsall)	2.00	2.00
1st (October 22, 2001, Questa)	1.40	1.40
1st (June 5, 2002, De La Rue)	1.40	1.40
E (June 8, 1999, Walsall)	3.20	3.20
E (October 22, 2001, Questa)	3.20	3.20
64p (June 8, 1999)	5.00	5.00
65p (April 25, 2000, Walsall)	2.00	2.00
65p (August 4, 2000, Questa)	2.00	2.00
68p (July 4, 2002)	2.30	2.30

(*The 2nd, 1st, E and 65p printed by Questa come from the 2000 Queen Mother and 2001 Unseen and Unheard prestige stamp books.)

First day cover (2nd, 1st E, 64p)	–	4.00
First day cover (65p)	–	2.00
First day cover (68p)	–	2.00
Stamp cards	5.00	14.00

PICTORIAL ISSUES WITH WHITE BORDERS

Scottish flag (2nd)

Scottish lion (1st)

Thistle (E, 40p, 42p, 44p, 48p, 50p, 56p, 60p, 87p, 88p, 97p, £1.00, £1.05)

Tartan (68p, 72p, 78p, 81p, 90p, 97p, £1.10, £1.28, £1.33)

PICTORIAL ISSUES WITHOUT WHITE BORDERS

Scottish flag (2nd)

Scottish lion (1st)

Thistle (E)

Tartan (64p, 65p, 68p)

BRITISH STAMP MARKET VALUES 2024 247

COUNTRY DEFINITIVES SCOTLAND

■ 2003–2016

Des: A. Morris (2nd), F. Pottinger and T. Chalk (1st, E), Tayburn (68p), all adapted by Tayburn. Printed in gravure by De La Rue (2nd, 1st, E, 40p, 42p, 44p, 48p, 50p, 56p, 60p, 68p, 72p, 78p, 81p, 90p, 97p), in gravure by Walsall (42p), in gravure by Enschedé (2nd, 1st, 50p, 81p), in litho by De La Rue (1st, 78p, 81p), in litho by Enschedé (1st, in prestige stamp books only) or in litho by Cartor (2nd, 1st, 68p, 87p, 88p, £1.00, £1.05, £1.10, £1.28, £1.33). Perf 15x14. One phosphor band (2nd) or two phosphor bands (others).

2nd (October 14, 2003, De La Rue)	1.20	1.20
2nd (January 3, 2013, Cartor), silver head	1.40	1.40
2nd (2016, Cartor), grey head	1.75	1.75
1st (October 14, 2003, De La Rue)	1.80	1.80
1st (January 3, 2013, Cartor)	1.80	1.80
E (October 14, 2003)	2.30	2.30
40p (May 11, 2004)	1.10	1.10
42p (April 5, 2005, Walsall)	1.50	1.50
42p (May 10, 2005, De La Rue)	1.50	1.50
44p (March 28, 2006)	1.40	1.40
48p (March 27, 2007)	1.00	1.00
50p (April 1, 2008)	1.25	1.25
56p (March 31, 2009)	1.40	1.40
60p (March 30, 2010)	1.50	1.50
68p (October 14, 2003, De La Rue)	1.40	1.40
68p (March 29, 2011, Cartor)	1.60	1.60
72p (March 28, 2006)	1.70	1.70
78p (March 27, 2007)	1.50	1.50
81p (April 1, 2008)	1.80	1.80
87p (April 25, 2012)	2.00	2.00
88p (March 27, 2013)	1.90	1.90
90p (March 31, 2009)	2.20	2.20
97p (March 30, 2010)	2.00	2.00
97p (March 26, 2014)	2.50	2.50
£1.00 (March 24, 2015)	2.20	2.20
£1.05 (March 22, 2016)	2.25	2.25
£1.10 (March 29, 2011)	2.20	2.20
£1.28 (April 25, 2012)	2.25	2.25
£1.33 (March 24, 2015)	2.25	2.25

(*Various values have also appeared in miniature sheets and prestige stamp books. The 1st class also exists, self-adhesive, in Smilers sheets. Although January 3, 2013, was the official date of issue of the 1st class and 2nd class printed by Cartor, both stamps were available earlier from post offices.)

First day cover (2nd, 1st, E, 68p)	–	3.50
First day cover (40p)	–	2.00
First day cover (42p)	–	2.00
First day cover (44p, 72p)	–	2.50
First day cover (48p, 78p)	–	2.50
First day cover (50p, 81p)	–	3.50
First day cover (56p, 90p)	–	3.50
First day cover (60p, 97p)	–	3.50
First day cover (68p, £1.10)	–	3.50
First day cover (87p, £1.28)	–	4.50
First day cover (88p)	–	2.00
First day cover (97p)	–	2.25
First day cover (£1.00, £1.33)	–	4.00
First day cover (£1.05)	–	2.25
Stamp cards	5.00	11.00

Scottish flag (2nd)

Scottish lion (1st)

Thistle (£1.17, £1.25, £1.35, £1.42, £1.70)

Tartan (£1.40, £1.45, £1.55, £1.63)

■ 2017–2020

As previous issue but with revised typeface for denomination. Printed in litho by Cartor. Perf 15 x 14. One phosphor band (2nd) or two phosphor bands (others).

2nd (March 20, 2018)	1.75	1.75
1st (March 20, 2018)	1.85	1.85
£1.17 (March 21, 2017)	2.25	2.25
£1.25 (March 20, 2018)	2.40	2.40
£1.35 (March 19, 2019)	2.50	2.50
£1.40 (March 21, 2017)	2.50	2.50
£1.42 (March 17, 2020)	2.75	2.75
£1.45 (March 20, 2018)	2.75	2.75
£1.55 (March 19, 2019)	2.75	2.75
£1.63 (March 17, 2020)	3.00	3.00
£1.70 (December 23, 2020)	3.50	3.50
First day cover (£1.17, £1.40)	–	5.00
First day cover (2nd, 1st, £1.25, £1.45)	–	7.00
First day cover (£1.35, £1.55)	–	5.00
First day cover (£1.42, £1.63)	–	6.00
First day cover (£1.70)	–	4.00

SCOTLAND COUNTRY DEFINITIVES

PICTORIAL ISSUES WITH DATA MATRIX CODES

Scottish flag (2nd)

Scottish lion (1st)

Thistle (£1.85)

■ **2022**
Printed in litho by Cartor. One phosphor band (2nd) or two phosphor bands (others). Self-adhesive.

2nd (August 11, 2022)	2.25	3.50
1st (August 11, 2022)	2.50	3.75
£1.85 (August 11, 2022)	3.00	4.00
First day cover	–	10.00

(*The stamps found on Royal Mail first day covers were from a separate printing that differed in relation to the phosphor bands.)

BRITISH STAMP MARKET VALUES 2024   **249**

COUNTRY DEFINITIVES WALES

WALES DEFINITIVES

Prices in this section are quoted in two columns: mint (left) and fine used (right).

PRE-DECIMAL WILDING ISSUES

3d lilac, 4d blue, 5d blue

6d purple, 9d green

1/3 green, 1/6 grey-blue

■ **1958–1969**
Des: Reynolds Stone. Printed in gravure by Harrisons. Perf 15x14.

Wmk: Multiple St. Edward's Crown. Non-phosphor except where stated

3d lilac (August 18, 1958)	0.15	0.15
3d lilac, one phos band	0.15	0.20
4d blue (February 7, 1966)	0.20	0.15
4d blue, two phos bands	0.15	0.15
6d purple (September 29, 1958)	0.25	0.25
9d green (March 1, 1967), two phos bands	0.35	0.30
1/3 green (September 29, 1958)	0.45	0.40
1/6 grey-blue (March 1, 1967), two bands	0.40	0.30
First day cover (3d)	–	10.00
First day cover (6d, 1/3)	–	20.00
First day cover (4d)	–	7.50
First day cover (9d, 1/6)	–	2.75

No watermark. Two phosphor bands except where stated. PVA gum except where stated

3d lilac (June 6, 1967), one band, gum Arabic	0.20	0.20
4d blue (June 21, 1968)	0.20	0.30
4d sepia (September 4, 1968), one band	0.15	0.15
4d red (February 26, 1969), one band	0.25	0.25
5d blue (September 4, 1968)	0.30	0.25
1/6 grey-blue (December 12, 1968)	2.25	2.25
First day cover (4d sepia, 5d)	–	2.50
First day cover (4d red)	–	1.00

DECIMAL MACHIN ISSUES WITHOUT ELLIPTICAL PERFORATIONS

3p blue

Des: J. Matthews. Type I has the eye on the dragon symbol appearing as a circle, while the tongue, claws and tail are thin; type II (1983) has a solid eye, and thicker tongue, claws and tail.

■ **1971–1980. Printed in gravure by Harrisons**
Perf 15x14. Two phosphor bands except where stated.

Original coated paper. PVA gum

2½p pink (July 7, 1971), one phos band	0.25	0.25
3p blue (July 7, 1971)	0.20	0.20
5p violet (July 7, 1971)	0.60	0.60
7½p brown (July 7, 1971)	1.20	1.20

Fluorescent coated paper. Gum Arabic

2½p pink (September 22, 1972), one band	0.35	–
3p blue (June 6, 1973)	0.35	–

Fluorescent coated paper. PVA gum

2½p pink (1973), one phos band	2.50	2.50
3p blue (February 1973)	9.00	7.00
3p blue (January 1, 1974), one phos band	0.35	0.30
5p violet (June 1973)	20.00	20.00

Fluorescent coated paper. PVAD gum

3½p green (January 23, 1974)	0.20	0.20
3½p green, one phos band	0.20	0.20
4½p grey-blue (November 6, 1974)	0.20	0.20
5½p deep violet (January 23, 1974)	0.20	0.20
5½p deep violet, one phos band	0.20	0.20
6½p green-blue (January 14, 1976), one band	0.20	0.35
7p red-brown (January 18, 1978), one band	0.20	0.30
8p red (January 23, 1974)	0.25	0.25
8½p green (January 14, 1976)	0.25	0.25

250 BRITISH STAMP MARKET VALUES 2024

WALES COUNTRY DEFINITIVES

9p violet-blue (January 18, 1978)	0.25	0.25
10p orange (October 20, 1976)	0.25	0.25
10p orange, one phos band	0.30	0.30
10½p grey-blue (January 18, 1978)	0.30	0.30
11p red (October 20, 1976)	0.30	0.30

Phosphor coated paper. PVAD gum

12p yellow-green (July 23, 1980)	0.35	0.35
13½p red-brown (July 23, 1980)	0.40	0.40
15p blue (July 23, 1980)	0.45	0.45
First day cover (2½p, 3p, 5p, 7½p)	–	1.70
First day cover (3½p, 5½p, 8p)	–	1.00
First day cover (4½p)	–	1.25
First day cover (6½p, 8½p)	–	1.00
First day cover (10p, 11p)	–	1.00
First day cover (7p, 9p, 10½p)	–	1.00
First day cover (12p 13½p, 15p)	–	1.00

■ **1981-1991. Printed in litho by Questa**
Perf 13½x14. Phosphor coated paper, except 11½p and 12½p (left side band). PVA gum (11½p, 14p, 18p, 22p), PVAD gum (others)

11½p mushroom (April 8, 1981)	0.45	0.45
12½p light green (February 24, 1982)	0.45	0.45
14p steel-blue (April 8, 1981)	0.45	0.45
15½p pale-violet (February 24, 1982)	0.65	0.65
16p light mushroom (April 27, 1983)	1.00	1.00
18p mauve (April 8, 1981)	0.70	0.75
19½p grey-green (February 24, 1982)	1.20	1.20
20½p bright blue (April 27, 1983)	2.20	2.20
22p deep blue (April 8, 1981)	0.65	0.65
26p red (February 24, 1982), type I	0.65	0.65
28p blue (April 27, 1983), type I	0.65	0.65

Perf 15x14. One side phosphor band (12p, 12½p, 13p), phosphor coated paper (16p, 17p, 19p, 20p, 22p, 23p, 24p, 26p, 28p, 31p, 32p, 34p, 37p, 39p), or as indicated. PVAD gum

12p emerald-green (January 7, 1986)	0.80	0.80
12½p light green (January 10, 1984)	2.50	2.50
13p reddish-brown (Oct 23, 1984), type I	0.50	0.50
13p deep brown, type II	1.20	1.20
14p deep blue (November 8, 1988)	0.50	0.50
15p bright blue (November 28, 1989)	0.65	0.65
16p light mushroom (January 10, 1984)	1.00	1.00
17p steel-blue (October 23, 1984), type I	0.60	0.60
17p steel-blue, type I, advanced coated paper	1.00	1.00
17p steel-blue, type II	40.00	40.00
17p deep blue (December 4, 1990), one band	0.50	0.50
18p deep green (January 6, 1987)	0.60	0.60
18p bright green (December 3, 1991), cent band	0.50	0.50
18p bright green, left band	1.35	1.35
18p bright green, right band	1.50	1.50
18p bright green, perf 14	5.50	5.50
19p orange-red (November 8, 1988)	0.65	0.65
20p brownish-black (November 28, 1989)	0.65	0.65
22p green (Oct 23, 1984), advanced paper	0.65	0.65
22p orange-red (December 4, 1990)	0.65	0.65
23p bright green (November 8, 1988)	0.70	0.70
24p deep red (November 28, 1989)	0.75	0.75
24p chestnut (December 3, 1991)	0.60	0.60
24p chestnut, two bands	1.00	1.00
24p chestnut, perf 14	5.25	5.25
26p red (Jan 27, 1987), type II, advanced paper	2.50	2.50
26p drab (December 4, 1990)	1.00	1.00
28p blue (Jan 27, 1987), type II, advanced paper	1.00	1.00
28p bluish grey (December 3, 1991)	0.70	0.70
31p purple (October 23, 1984)	0.90	0.90
31p purple, advanced coated paper	1.50	1.50
32p greenish blue (November 8, 1988)	1.00	1.20
34p bluish grey (November 28, 1989)	1.20	1.20
37p rosine (December 4, 1990)	1.20	1.20
39p mauve (December 3, 1991)	1.20	1.20

(*The 18p with one band at left or right comes from prestige stamp books. The 13p also exists printed on paper supplied by Coated Papers Ltd, with PVA gum, in 1987)

First day cover (11½p, 14p, 18p, 22p)	–	1.00
First day cover (12½p, 15½p. 19½p, 26p)	–	1.00
First day cover (16p, 20½p, 28p)	–	1.50
First day cover (12p, 17p, 22p, 31p)	–	1.50
First day cover (12p)	–	1.00
First day cover (18p)	–	1.00
First day cover (14p, 19p, 23p, 32p)	–	2.00
First day cover (15p, 20p, 24p, 34p)	–	2.00
First day cover (17p, 22p, 26p, 37p)	–	2.00
First day cover (18p, 24p, 28p, 39p)	–	2.00

DECIMAL MACHIN ISSUES WITH ELLIPTICAL PERFORATIONS

30p olive-grey

■ **1993-1996. Printed in litho by Questa**
Perf 15x14. One phosphor band (19p and 20p), two phosphor bands (others).

19p bistre (December 7, 1993)	0.60	0.70
19p bistre, right band	2.00	2.00
20p bright green (July 23, 1996)	0.90	0.90
25p red (December 7, 1993)	0.85	0.80
26p red-brown (July 23, 1996)	1.00	1.00
30p olive-grey (December 7, 1993)	0.80	0.80
37p mauve (July 23, 1996)	1.50	1.50
41p grey-brown (December 7, 1993)	1.30	1.80
63p emerald (July 23, 1996)	3.20	3.20

(*The 19p with phosphor band to right comes from the 1995 National Trust prestige stamp book.)

COUNTRY DEFINITIVES WALES

26p chestnut

1997–2000. Printed in gravure by Walsall
Perf 15x14. One phosphor band (19p and 20p), two phosphor bands (others)

20p bright green (July 1, 1997)	0.65	0.65
26p chestnut (July 1, 1997)	1.25	1.25
37p mauve (July 1, 1997)	1.70	1.70
63p emerald (July 1, 1997)	3.20	3.20

(*The 20p with right phosphor band, the 26p perf 15x14 and perf 14, and the 37p also exist printed by Harrisons, from prestige stamp books.)

Perf 15x14. One phosphor band

1st orange-red (February 15, 2000)	2.00	2.00

(*This stamp was issued only in the Special By Design prestige stamp book.)

First day cover (19p, 25p, 30p, 41p)	–	2.50
First day cover (20p, 26p, 37p, 63p)	–	3.00

PICTORIAL ISSUES WITHOUT WHITE BORDERS

Leek (2nd)

Welsh dragon (1st)

Daffodil (E)

Prince of Wales' feathers (64p, 65p, 68p)

1999–2002
Des: D. Petersen (2nd), T. and G. Petersen (1st), I. Rees (E), R. Evans (64p), all adapted by Tutssels. Printed in gravure by Walsall (2nd, 1st, E, 64p, 65p) or De La Rue (2nd, 1st, 68p). Perf 15x14. One phosphor band (2nd), two phosphor bands (others).

2nd (June 8, 1999, Walsall)	1.60	1.60
2nd (September 18, 2000, Walsall), right band	2.25	2.25
2nd (May 28, 2003, De La Rue)	1.60	1.60
1st (June 8, 1999, Walsall)	1.80	1.80
1st (March 4, 2003, De La Rue)	1.80	1.80
E (June 8, 1999)	2.30	2.30
64p (June 8, 1999)	5.00	5.00
65p (April 25, 2000)	2.25	2.25
68p (July 4, 2002)	2.00	2.00

(*The 2nd class with band at right comes from the 2000 Treasury of Trees prestige stamp book.)

First day cover (2nd, 1st, E, 64p)	–	2.00
First day cover (65p)	–	2.00
First day cover (68p)	–	2.00
Stamp cards	5.00	15.00

PICTORIAL ISSUES WITH WHITE BORDERS

Leek (2nd)

Welsh dragon (1st)

Daffodil (E, 40p, 42p, 44p, 48p, 50p, 56p, 60p, 87p, 88p, 97p, £1.00, £1.05)

Prince of Wales' feathers (68p, 72p, 78p, 81p, 90p, 97p, £1.10, £1.28, £1.33)

2003–2016
Des: D. Petersen (2nd), T. and G. Petersen (1st), I. Rees (E), R. Evans (68p), all adapted by Tutssels. Printed in gravure by De La Rue (2nd, 1st, E, 40p, 42p, 44p, 48p, 50p, 56p, 60p, 68p, 72p, 78p,

252 BRITISH STAMP MARKET VALUES 2024

WALES COUNTRY DEFINITIVES

81p, 90p, 97p), in gravure by Walsall (42p), in litho by De La Rue (1st, 78p, 81p), in litho by Enschedé (1st, in prestige stamp books only) or in litho by Cartor (2nd, 1st, 68p, 87p, 88p, £1.00, £1.05, £1.10, £1.28, £1.33). Perf 15x14. One phosphor band (2nd) or two phosphor bands (others).

2nd (October 14, 2003, De La Rue)	1.50	1.50
2nd (January 3, 2013, Cartor)	1.50	1.50
1st (October 14, 2003, De La Rue)	1.70	1.70
1st (January 3, 2013, Cartor)	1.70	1.70
E (October 14, 2003)	2.30	2.30
40p (May 11, 2004)	1.20	1.20
42p (April 5, 2005, Walsall)	2.50	2.50
42p (May 10, 2005, De La Rue)	2.30	2.30
44p (March 28, 2006)	1.50	1.50
48p (March 27, 2007)	1.00	1.00
50p (April 1, 2008)	1.20	1.20
56p (March 31, 2009)	1.50	1.50
60p (March 30, 2010)	1.50	1.50
68p (October 14, 2003, De La Rue)	1.50	1.50
68p (March 29, 2011, Cartor)	1.90	1.90
72p (March 28, 2006)	1.50	1.50
78p (March 27, 2007)	2.20	2.20
81p (April 1, 2008)	2.40	2.40
87p (April 25, 2012)	2.30	2.30
88p (March 27, 2013)	2.30	2.30
90p (March 31, 2009)	1.80	1.80
97p (March 30, 2010)	2.25	2.25
97p (March 26, 2014)	2.50	2.50
£1.00 (March 24, 2015)	2.20	2.20
£1.05 (March 22, 2016)	2.50	2.50
£1.10 (March 29, 2011)	2.20	2.20
£1.28 (April 25, 2012)	2.50	2.50
£1.33 (March 24, 2015)	2.60	2.60

(*Various values have also appeared in miniature sheets and prestige stamp books. The 1st class also exists, self-adhesive, in Smilers sheets. Although January 3, 2013, was the official date of issue of the 1st class and 2nd class printed by Cartor, both stamps were available earlier from post offices.)

First day cover (2nd, 1st, E, 68p)	–	3.00
First day cover (40p)	–	2.00
First day cover (42p)	–	2.00
First day cover (44p, 72p)	–	2.50
First day cover (48p, 78p)	–	3.00
First day cover (50p, 81p)	–	3.00
First day cover (56p, 90p)	–	3.00
First day cover (60p, 97p)	–	3.00
First day cover (68p, £1.10)	–	3.00
First day cover (87p, £1.28)	–	4.00
First day cover (88p)	–	2.00
First day cover (97p)	–	2.25
First day cover (£1.00, £1.33)	–	4.00
First day cover (£1.05)	–	2.25
Stamp cards	5.00	11.00

Leek (2nd)

Welsh dragon (1st)

Daffodil (£1.17, £1.25, £1.35, £1.42, £1.70)

Prince of Wales' feathers (£1.40, £1.45, £1.55, £1.63)

■ **2017–2020**
As previous issue but with revised typeface for denomination. Printed in litho by Cartor. Perf 15 x 14. One phosphor band (2nd) or two phosphor bands (others).

2nd (March 20, 2018)	1.75	1.75
1st (March 20, 2018)	1.85	1.85
£1.17 (March 21, 2017)	2.25	2.25
£1.25 (March 20, 2018)	2.40	2.40
£1.35 (March 19, 2019)	2.50	2.50
£1.40 (March 21, 2017)	2.50	2.50
£1.42 (March 17, 2020)	2.75	2.75
£1.45 (March 20, 2018)	2.75	2.75
£1.55 (March 19, 2019)	2.75	2.75
£1.63 (March 17, 2020)	3.00	3.00
£1.70 (December 23, 2020)	3.50	3.50
First day cover (£1.17, £1.40)	–	5.00
First day cover (2nd, 1st, £1.25, £1.45)	–	7.00
First day cover (£1.35, £1.55)	–	5.00
First day cover (£1.42, £1.63)	–	6.00
First day cover (£1.70)	–	4.00

Ideal for GB collectors

BRITISH STAMP MARKET VALUES 2024 253

COUNTRY DEFINITIVES WALES

PICTORIAL ISSUES WITH DATA MATRIX CODES

Leek (2nd)

Welsh dragon (1st)

Daffodil (£1.85)

■ **2022**
Printed in litho by Cartor. One phosphor band (2nd) or two phosphor bands (others). Self-adhesive.

2nd (August 11, 2022)	2.25	3.50
1st (August 11, 2022)	2.50	3.75
£1.85 (August 11, 2022)	3.00	4.00
First day cover	–	15.00

(*The stamps found on Royal Mail first day covers were from a separate printing that differed in relation to the phosphor bands; the Welsh version of the denomination on the 1st class stamp also used a different typeface.)

Plumridge & Co.
PHILATELIC AUCTIONEERS

Established 1898
The oldest name in Stamp Auctioneering in the world

One Hundred and Twenty Years of Selling Stamps by Auction
is an assurance to prospective sellers that their stamps
will be entrusted to a firm that will obtain the maximum realisation

---

OBLIGATION FREE AUCTION APPRAISALS

We provide free auction estimates and advice to potential vendors

Our commission rates are very competitive and negotiable for larger consignments

We promise timely settlement and first class service throughout

---

View auction catalogues, register and bid online via our website
www.plumridge.co.uk

Plumridge & Co *Philatelic Auctioneers*
P.O.Box 7831, Northants, NN17 9HL, UK
email: plumridge@plumridge.co.uk
Telephone: +44(0)208 857 3161

COUNTRY DEFINITIVES ENGLAND

ENGLAND DEFINITIVES

Prices in this section are quoted in two columns: mint (left) and fine used (right).

PICTORIAL ISSUES WITHOUT WHITE BORDERS

Three lions (2nd)

Crowned lion and shield (1st)

Oak tree (E)

Tudor rose (65p, 68p)

■ **2001–2002**

Des: Sedley Place, after sculptures by D. Dathan. Printed in gravure by De La Rue. Perf 15x14. One phosphor band (2nd), two phosphor bands (others).

2nd (April 23, 2001)	1.65	1.65
1st (April 23, 2001)	1.85	1.85
E (April 23, 2001)	2.50	2.50
65p (April 23, 2001)	1.75	1.75
68p (July 4, 2002)	1.75	1.60

(*The 2nd and 1st class also exist printed in gravure by Questa, from the 2002 Across The Universe prestige stamp book.)

First day cover (2nd, 1st, E, 65p)	–	3.00
First day cover (68p)	–	2.50
Stamp cards	6.00	14.00

PICTORIAL ISSUES WITH WHITE BORDERS

Three lions (2nd)

Crowned lion and shield (1st)

Oak tree (E, 40p, 42p, 44p, 48p, 50p, 56p, 60p, 87p, 88p, 97p, £1.00, £1.05)

Tudor rose (68p, 72p, 78p, 81p, 90p, 97p, £1.10, £1.28, £1.33)

■ **2003–2016**

Des: Sedley Place, after sculptures by D. Dathan. Printed in gravure by De La Rue (2nd, 1st, E, 40p, 42p, 44p, 48p, 50p, 56p, 60p, 68p, 72p, 78p, 81p, 90p, 97p), in gravure by Walsall (2nd, 42p), in litho by De La Rue (1st, 78p, 81p), in litho by Enschedé (1st, in prestige stamp books only) or in litho by Cartor (2nd, 1st, 68p, 87p, 88p, £1.00, £1.05, £1.10, £1.28, £1.33). Perf 15x14. One phosphor band (2nd) or two phosphor bands (others).

2nd (October 14, 2003, De La Rue)	1.65	1.65
2nd (January 3, 2013, Cartor)	1.65	1.65
1st (October 14, 2003, De La Rue)	1.85	1.85
1st (January 3, 2013, Cartor)	1.85	1.85
E (October 14, 2003)	2.50	2.50
40p (May 11, 2004)	1.10	1.25
42p (April 5, 2005, Walsall)	2.50	2.50
42p (May 10, 2005, De La Rue)	2.30	2.30
44p (May 28, 2006)	1.50	1.50
48p (Mar 27, 2007)	1.00	1.00
50p (April 1, 2008)	1.00	1.00
56p (March 31, 2009)	1.20	1.20
60p (March 30, 2010)	1.30	1.30
68p (October 14, 2003, De La Rue)	1.75	1.75
68p (March 29, 2011, Cartor)	1.75	1.75
72p (March 28, 2006)	1.60	1.60
78p (March 27, 2007)	1.75	1.75
81p (April 1, 2008)	1.75	1.75
87p (April 25, 2012)	1.90	1.90
88p (March 27, 2013)	1.90	1.90
90p (March 31, 2009)	1.90	1.90
97p (March 30, 2010)	2.25	2.25
97p (March 26, 2014)	2.25	2.25
£1.00 (March 24, 2015)	2.20	2.20
£1.05 (March 22, 2016)	2.20	2.20
£1.10 (March 29, 2011)	2.20	2.20
£1.28 (April 25, 2012)	2.50	2.50
£1.33 (March 24, 2015)	2.60	2.60

(*Various values have also appeared in miniature sheets and prestige stamp books. The 1st class also exists, self-adhesive, from Smilers sheets. Although January 3, 2013, was the official date of issue of the 1st class and 2nd class printed by Cartor, both stamps were available earlier from post offices.)

First day cover (2nd, 1st, E, 68p)	–	3.50
First day cover (40p)	–	2.50
First day cover (42p)	–	2.00
First day cover (44p, 72p)	–	2.50

ENGLAND COUNTRY DEFINITIVES

First day cover (48p, 78p)	–	3.00
First day cover (50p, 81p)	–	3.00
First day cover (56p, 90p)	–	3.00
First day cover (60p, 97p)	–	3.00
First day cover (68p, £1.10)	–	3.50
First day cover (87p, £1.28)	–	4.50
First day cover (88p)	–	2.00
First day cover (97p)	–	2.25
First day cover (£1.00, £1.33)	–	4.00
First day cover (£1.05)	–	2.25
Stamp cards	5.00	11.00

Three lions (2nd)

Crowned lion and shield (1st)

Oak tree (£1.17, £1.25, £1.35, £1.42, £1.70)

Tudor rose (£1.40, £1.45, £1.55, £1.63)

■ 2017–2020
As previous issue but with revised typeface for denomination. Printed in litho by Cartor. Perf 15 x 14. One phosphor band (2nd) or two phosphor bands (others).

2nd (March 20, 2018)	1.75	1.75
1st (March 20, 2018)	1.85	1.85
£1.17 (March 21, 2017)	2.25	2.25
£1.25 (March 20, 2018)	2.40	2.40
£1.35 (March 19, 2019)	2.50	2.50
£1.40 (March 21, 2017)	2.75	2.75
£1.42 (March 17, 2020)	2.75	2.75
£1.45 (March 20, 2018)	2.75	2.75
£1.55 (March 19, 2019)	2.75	2.75
£1.63 (March 17, 2020)	3.00	3.00
£1.70 (December 23, 2020)	3.50	3.50
First day cover (£1.17, £1.40)	–	5.00
First day cover (2nd, 1st, £1.25, £1.45)	–	7.00
First day cover (£1.35, £1.55)	–	5.00
First day cover (£1.42, £1.63)	–	6.00
First day cover (£1.70)	–	4.00

PICTORIAL ISSUES WITH DATA MATRIX CODES

Three lions (2nd)

Crowned lion and shield (1st)

Oak tree (£1.85)

■ 2022
Printed in litho by Cartor. One phosphor band (2nd) or two phosphor bands (others). Self-adhesive.

2nd (August 11, 2022)	2.25	3.50
1st (August 11, 2022)	2.50	3.75
£1.85 (August 11, 2022)	3.00	4.00
First day cover	–	10.00

(*The stamps found on Royal Mail first day covers were from a separate printing that differed in relation to the phosphor bands.)

BOOKLETS STITCHED OR STAPLED

STITCHED OR STAPLED BOOKLETS

In this section, items are priced in very fine mint condition only.

Booklets were bound with staples until 1917 and thereafter by stitching, although there are examples of subsequent issues where failed stitching was repaired using staples.

From 1913–43, an edition number was inscribed on most booklet covers, usually towards the top left or right corner. This related to the Post Office's internal classification system, which divided the issues into eight different series, although the series numbers were not inscribed. From 1943, edition numbers were discontinued but most booklets had the month and year of issue inscribed on the back cover.

Trade advertisements were introduced on interleaves in 1909, on booklet covers in 1917, and on labels in stamp panes in 1924. Booklets designed for dispense from vending machines were introduced in 1937.

EDWARD VII, 1904–10

■ 2/– booklets
24 x 1d (sold at 2s ½d). Printed by De La Rue, 1904	£250
12 x 1d, 23 x ½d. Printed by De La Rue, 1906	£1,000
18 x 1d, 11 x ½d. Printed by De La Rue, 1907–09	£1,100
18 x 1d, 11 x ½d. Printed by Harrison, 1911	£1,250

GEORGE V, 1910–35

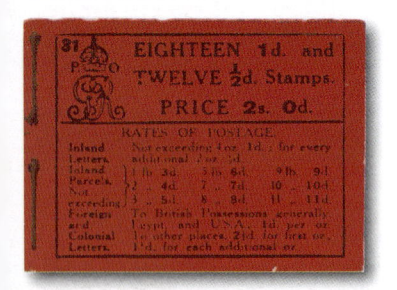

■ 2/– booklets (Downey head stamps)
18 x 1d, 12 x ½d. Wmk: Imperial Crown printed by Harrison, 1911. Red cover	£900
18 x 1d, 12 x ½d. Wmk: Simple Royal Cypher printed by Harrison, 1912. Red cover	£750

■ 2/– booklets (Mackennal head stamps, typography)
18 x 1d, 12 x ½d. Wmk: Simple Royal Cypher printed by Harrison, 1913–17. Red cover	£650
10 x 1½d, 6 x 1d, 6 x ½d. Wmk: Simple Royal Cypher printed by Harrison, 1924. Red-orange cover	£1,300
10 x 1½d, 6 x 1d, 6 x ½d. Wmk: Block GVR printed by Waterlow, 1924–33. Blue cover	£600
10 x 1½d, 6 x 1d, 6 x ½d. Wmk: Block GVR printed by Harrison, 1934. Blue cover	£650

■ 2/– booklets (Mackennal head stamps, photogravure)
10 x 1½d, 6 x 1d, 6 x ½d (intermediate). Wmk: Block GVR printed by Harrison, 1935. Blue cover	£2,250
10 x 1½d, 6 x 1d, 6 x ½d (small). Wmk: Block GVR printed by Harrison, 1935. Blue cover	£400

■ 2/– booklets (Postal Union Congress stamps)
10 x 1½d, 6 x 1d, 6 x ½d printed by Waterlow, 1929. Blue on buff cover	£400

■ 2/– booklets (Silver Jubilee stamps)
12 x 1½d, 4 x 1d, 4 x ½d printed by Harrison, 1935. Blue on buff cover	65.00

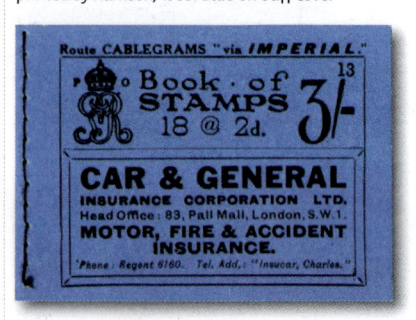

■ 3/– booklets (Mackennal head stamps, typography)
12 x 1½d, 12 x 1d, 12 x ½d. Wmk: Simple Royal Cypher printed by Harrison, 1918. Orange cover	£900
18 x 1½d, 6 x 1d, 6 x ½d. Wmk: Simple Royal Cypher printed by Harrison, 1919. Orange cover	£900
18 x 2d. Wmk: Simple Royal Cypher printed by Harrison, 1921. Blue cover	£1,200
24 x 1½d. Wmk: Simple Royal Cypher printed by Harrison, 1922. Blue cover	£1,200
18 x 1½d, 6 x 1d, 6 x ½d. Wmk: Block GVR printed by Waterlow, 1924–33. Red cover	£350
18 x 1½d, 6 x 1d, 6 x ½d. Wmk: Block GVR printed by Harrison, 1934. Red cover	£450

■ 3/– booklets (Mackennal head stamps, photogravure)
18 x 1½d, 6 x 1d, 6 x ½d (intermediate). Wmk: Block GVR printed by Harrison, 1935. Red cover	£1,750
18 x 1½d, 6 x 1d, 6 x ½d (small). Wmk: Block GVR printed by Harrison, 1935. Red cover	£350

■ 3/– booklets (Postal Union Congress stamps)
18 x 1½d, 6 x 1d, 6 x ½d printed by Waterlow, 1929. Red on buff cover	£325

258 BRITISH STAMP MARKET VALUES 2024

STITCHED OR STAPLED BOOKLETS

3/- booklets (Silver Jubilee stamps)
20 x 1½d, 4 x 1d, 4 x ½d
printed by Harrison, 1935. Red on buff cover — 55.00

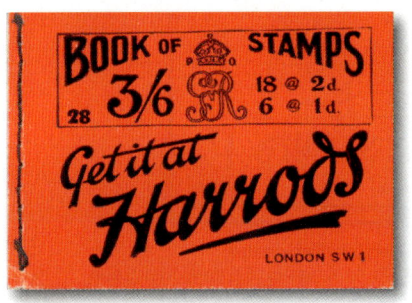

3/6 booklets (Mackennal head stamps, typography)
18 x 2d, 6 x 1d. Wmk: Simple Royal Cypher
printed by Harrison, 1920. Orange-red cover — £1,100
12 x 2d, 6 x 1½d, 6 x 1d, 6 x ½d. Wmk: Simple Royal Cypher
printed by Harrison, 1921. Orange-red cover — £1,100

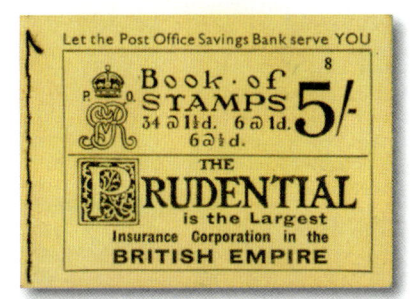

5/- booklets (Mackennal head stamps, typography)
34 x 1½d, 6 x 1d, 6 x ½d.
printed by Waterlow, 1931. Green cover — £3,750
34 x 1½d, 6 x 1d, 6 x ½d.
printed by Waterlow, 1932. Buff cover — £3,000
34 x 1½d, 6 x 1d, 6 x ½d
printed by Harrison, 1934. Buff cover — £1,200

5/- booklets (Mackennal head, stamps photogravure)
34 x 1½d, 6 x 1d, 6 x ½d (intermediate). Wmk: Block GVR
printed by Harrison, 1935. Buff cover — £4,000
34 x 1½d, 6 x 1d, 6 x ½d (small). Wmk: Block GVR
printed by Harrison, 1935. Buff cover — £400

EDWARD VIII, 1936

6d booklets (machine-vended)
4 x 1½d (panes of two)
printed by Harrison, 1937. Plain buff cover — 30.00

2/- booklets
10 x 1½d, 6 x 1d, 6 x ½d
printed by Harrison, 1936. Blue cover — 95.00

3/- booklets
18 x 1½d, 6 x 1d, 6 x ½d
printed by Harrison, 1936. Red cover — 85.00

5/- booklets
34 x 1½d, 6 x 1d, 6 x ½d
printed by Harrison, 1937. Buff cover — £175

GEORGE VI, 1937–52

6d booklets (machine-vended)
4 x 1½d (panes of two)
printed by Harrison, 1938. Plain buff cover — 55.00
2 x 1½d, 2 x 1d, 2 x ½d (panes of two)
printed by Harrison, 1938. Plain pink cover — £200
4 x 1d, 4 x ½d (panes of four)
printed by Harrison, 1940. Plain green cover — 90.00

1/- booklets (machine-vended)
4 x 1½d, 4 x 1d, 4 x ½d (panes of 2) (pale shades)
printed by Harrison, 1947. Plain cream cover — 15.00

BOOKLETS STITCHED OR STAPLED

4 x 1½d, 4 x 1d, 4 x ½d (panes of 4) (pale shades)
printed by Harrison, 1948. Plain cream cover £4,000
4 x 1½d, 4 x 1d, 4 x ½d (panes of 2) (changed colours)
printed by Harrison, 1951. Plain cream cover 16.00
4 x 1½d, 4 x 1d, 4 x ½d (panes of 4) (changed colours)
printed by Harrison, 1951. Plain cream cover 12.00
4 x 1½d, 4 x 1d, 4 x ½d (panes of 4) (changed colours)
printed by Harrison, 1952. Cream cover, circular emblem 10.00
4 x 1½d, 4 x 1d, 4 x ½d (panes of 4) (changed colours)
printed by Harrison, 1954. Cream cover, oval emblem 12.00

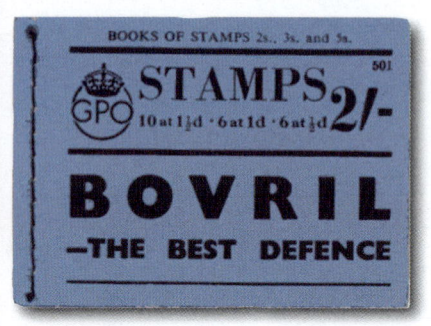

■ 2/- booklets

10 x 1½d, 6 x 1d, 6 x ½d
printed by Harrison, 1937. Blue cover, royal cypher £600
10 x 1½d, 6 x 1d, 6 x ½d
printed by Harrison, 1938. Blue cover, GPO emblem £600

■ 2/6 booklets

6 x 2½d, 6 x 2d, 6 x ½d (dark shades)
printed by Harrison, 1940. Red cover £950
6 x 2½d, 6 x 2d, 6 x ½d (dark shades)
printed by Harrison, 1940. Blue cover £950
6 x 2½d, 6 x 2d, 6 x ½d (dark shades)
printed by Harrison, 1940. Green cover £575
6 x 2½d, 6 x 2d, 6 x ½d (pale shades)
printed by Harrison, 1942. Green cover £550
6 x 2½d, 6 x 2d, 6 x ½d (pale shades)
printed by Harrison, 1943. Green cover, no advertisement 80.00
6 x 2½d, 6 x 2d, 6 x ½d (changed colours)
printed by Harrison, 1951. Green cover, no advertisement 45.00
6 x 2½d, 6 x 1½d, 3 x 1d, 6 x ½d
printed by Harrison, 1952. Green cover, no advertisement 25.00

■ 3/- booklets

18 x 1½d, 6 x 1d, 6 x ½d
printed by Harrison, 1937. Red cover, royal cypher £950
18 x 1½d, 6 x 1d, 6 x ½d
printed by Harrison, 1938 Red cover, GPO emblem £950

■ 5/- booklets

34 x 1½d, 6 x 1d, 6 x ½d (dark shades)
printed by Harrison, 1937. Buff cover, royal cypher £1,100
34 x 1½d, 6 x 1d, 6 x ½d (dark shades)
printed by Harrison, 1938. Buff cover, GPO emblem £1,100
18 x 2½d, 6 x 2d, 6 x ½d (dark shades)
printed by Harrison, 1940. Buff cover, GPO emblem £1,100

18 x 2½d, 6 x 2d, 6 x ½d (pale shades)
printed by Harrison, 1942. Buff cover, GPO emblem £1,100
18 x 2½d, 6 x 2d, 6 x ½d (pale shades)
printed by Harrison, 1943. Buff cover, no advertisement £120
18 x 2½d, 6 x 2d, 6 x ½d (changed colours)
printed by Harrison, 1951. Buff cover, no advertisement 40.00
18 x 2½d, 6 x 1½d, 3 x 1d, 6 x ½d
printed by Harrison, 1952. Buff cover, no advertisement 35.00
12 x 2½d, 6 x 2d, 6 x 1½d, 6 x 1d, 6 x ½d
printed by Harrison, 1953. Buff cover, no advertisement 40.00

ELIZABETH II (WILDINGS), 1953–68

■ 1/- booklets (machine-vended)

4 x 1½d, 4 x 1d, 4 x ½d (panes of 2). Wmk: Tudor Crown
printed by Harrison, 1953. Plain white cover 3.00
4 x 1½d, 4 x 1d, 4 x ½d (panes of 4). Wmk: Tudor Crown
printed by Harrison, 1954. White cover, GPO emblem 6.00
4 x 1½d, 4 x 1d, 4 x ½d (panes of 4). Wmk: St. Edward's Crown
printed by Harrison, 1956. White cover, GPO emblem 4.00
4 x 1½d, 4 x 1d, 4 x ½d (panes of 2). Wmk: St. Edward's Crown
printed by Harrison, 1957. Plain white cover 30.00
4 x 1½d, 4 x 1d, 4 x ½d (panes of 4). Wmk: Multiple Crowns
printed by Harrison, 1959. White cover, GPO emblem 3.00

■ 2/- booklets (machine-vended)

4 x 3d, 4 x 1½d, 4 x 1d, 4 x ½d. Wmk: St. Edward's Crown
printed by Harrison, 1959. Pink cover 4.00
4 x 3d, 4 x 1½d, 4 x 1d, 4 x ½d. Wmk: Multiple Crowns (upright)
printed by Harrison, 1960. Pink cover 4.00
4 x 3d, 4 x 1½d, 4 x 1d, 4 x ½d. Wmk: Multiple Crowns (upright)
printed by Harrison, 1961. Yellow cover 3.00
4 x 3d, 4 x 1½d, 4 x 1d, 4 x ½d. Wmk: Multiple Crowns (sideways)
printed by Harrison, 1961–65. Yellow cover 30.00
4 x 3d, 4 x 1½d, 4 x 1d, 4 x ½d, with phosphor bands
printed by Harrison, 1961–65. Yellow cover 55.00
4 x 4d, 2 x 1d se-tenant with 2 x 3d; 3d with no phosphor band
printed by Harrison, 1965–67. Orange-yellow cover 4.00
4 x 4d, 2 x 1d se-tenant with 2 x 3d; 3d with one phosphor band
printed by Harrison, 1965–67. Orange-yellow cover 8.00
4 x 4d, 2 x 1d se-tenant with 2 x 3d; 3d with two phosphor bands
printed by Harrison, 1968. Orange-yellow cover 3.00
8 x 2½d, 3 x ½d se-tenant with 1 x 2½d. Wmk: Multiple Crowns
printed by Harrison, 1963. Red on yellow cover 3.00
8 x ½d, 8 x 2½d, se-tenant in panes. Wmk: Multiple Crowns
printed by Harrison, 1964. Red on yellow cover 2.00
8 x 3d. Wmk: Multiple Crowns (sideways)
printed by Harrison, 1965. Red on yellow cover 1.00

STITCHED OR STAPLED BOOKLETS

■ 2/6 booklets
6 x 2½d, 6 x 1½d (QEII), 3 x 1d, 6 x ½d (KGVI)
printed by Harrison, 1953-54. Green cover 40.00
6 x 2½d, 6 x 1½d, 6 x ½d (QEII), 3 x 1d (KGVI)
printed by Harrison, 1954. Green cover £350
6 x 2½d, 6 x 1½d, 3x 1d, 6 x ½d. Wmk: Tudor Crown
printed by Harrison, 1954-55. Green cover 35.00
6 x 2½d, 6 x 1½d, 3x 1d, 6 x ½d. Wmk: St Edward's Crown
printed by Harrison, 1955-57. Green cover 25.00
6 x 2½d, 6 x 2d, 6 x ½d, Wmk: St Edward's Crown
printed by Harrison, 1957. Green cover 20.00

■ 3/- booklets
6 x 3d, 6 x 1½d, 6 x 1d, 6 x ½d. Wmk: St Edward's Crown
printed by Harrison, 1958. Red cover 15.00
6 x 3d, 6 x 1½d, 6 x 1d, 6 x ½d. Wmk: Multiple Crowns
printed by Harrison, 1959-65. Red cover 30.00
6 x 3d, 6 x 1½d, 6 x 1d, 6 x ½d, with graphite lines
printed by Harrison, 1959-60. Red cover £200
6 x 3d, 6 x 1½d, 6 x 1d, 6 x ½d, with phosphor bands
printed by Harrison, 1960-65. Red cover 60.00

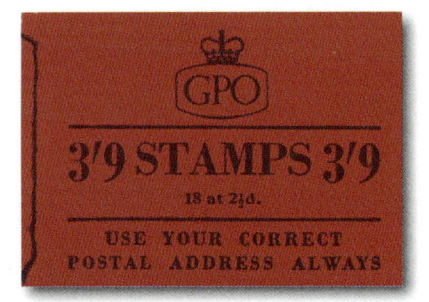

■ 3/9 booklets
18 x 2½d. Wmk: Tudor Crown
printed by Harrison, 1953-55. Red cover 25.00
18 x 2½d. Wmk: St Edward's Crown
printed by Harrison, 1956-57. Red cover 18.00

■ 4/6 booklets
18 x 3d. Wmk: St Edward's Crown
printed by Harrison, 1957-58. Violet cover 20.00
18 x 3d. Wmk: Multiple Crowns
printed by Harrison, 1959. Violet cover 25.00
18 x 3d, with graphite lines. Wmk: Multiple Crowns
printed by Harrison, 1959-60. Violet cover 20.00
18 x 3d, with phosphor bands. Wmk: Multiple Crowns
printed by Harrison, 1960-65. Violet cover 45.00
12 x 4d, 6 x 1d, no phosphor bands. Wmk: Multiple Crowns
printed by Harrison, 1965-67. Slate-blue cover 22.00
12 x 4d, 6 x 1d, with phosphor bands. Wmk: Multiple Crowns
printed by Harrison, 1965-68. Slate-blue cover 20.00

■ 5/- booklets
12 x 2½d, 6 x 1½d (QEII), 6 x 2d, 6 x 1d, 6 x ½d (KGVI)
printed by Harrison, 1953-54. Buff cover 35.00
12 x 2½d, 6 x 1½d, 6 x ½d (QEII), 6 x 2d, 6 x 1d (KGVI)
printed by Harrison, 1954. Buff cover £500

12 x 2½d, 6 x 1½d, 6 x ½d, 6 x 1d (QEII), 6 x 2d (KGVI)
printed by Harrison, 1954. Buff cover £250
12 x 2½d, 6 x 1½d, 6 x ½d, 6 x 1d, 6 x 2d. Wmk: Tudor Crown
printed by Harrison, 1954-55. Buff cover 80.00
12 x 2½d, 6 x 1½d, 6 x ½d, 6 x 1d, 6 x 2d. Wmk: St Edward's Crown
printed by Harrison, 1955-57. Buff cover 25.00
12 x 3d, 6 x 2½d, 6 x 1½d, 6 x ½d. Wmk: St Edward's Crown
printed by Harrison, 1958. Blue cover 20.00
12 x 3d, 6 x 2½d, 6 x 1½d, 6 x ½d. Wmk: Multiple Crowns
printed by Harrison, 1959-65. Blue cover 30.00
12 x 3d, 6 x 2½d, 6 x 1½d, 6 x ½d, with graphite lines
printed by Harrison, 1959-60. Blue cover 70.00
12 x 3d, 6 x 2½d, 6 x 1½d, 6 x ½d; 2½d with two phosphor bands
printed by Harrison, 1960-62. Blue cover £150
12 x 3d, 6 x 2½d, 6 x 1½d, 6 x ½d; 2½d with one phosphor band
printed by Harrison, 1962-65. Blue cover £160

■ 6/- booklets
18 x 4d, with no phosphor bands. Wmk: Multiple Crowns
printed by Harrison, 1965-67. Claret cover 30.00
18 x 4d, with phosphor bands. Wmk: Multiple Crowns
printed by Harrison, 1965-67. Claret cover 30.00

■ 10/- booklets
30 x 3d, 6 x 2d, 6 x 1½d, 6 x 1d, 6 x ½d
printed by Harrison, 1961. Green cover 80.00
30 x 3d, 6 x 2½d, 6 x 1½d, 6 x 1d
printed by Harrison, 1962-64. Green cover 90.00
24 x 4d, 6 x 3d, 6 x 1d
printed by Harrison, 1965-66. Ochre cover 40.00
24 x 4d, 6 x 3d, 6 x 1d; 3d with side phosphor band
printed by Harrison, 1967. Ochre cover 5.00
24 x 4d, 6 x 3d, 6 x 1d; 3d with centre phosphor band
printed by Harrison, 1967-68. Ochre cover 5.00

ELIZABETH II (PRE-DECIMAL MACHINS), 1968-70

■ 2/- booklets (machine-vended)
4 x 4d sepia (two phosphor bands), 2 x 1d se-tenant with 2 x 3d (two phosphor bands)
printed by Harrison, 1968. Yellow cover 0.80
4 x 4d sepia (two phosphor bands), 2 x 4d sepia (centre phosphor band) se-tenant with two labels
printed by Harrison, 1968-70. Grey cover 0.65
4 x 4d sepia (centre phosphor band), 2 x 4d sepia (centre phosphor band) se-tenant with two labels
printed by Harrison, 1968-69. Grey cover 1.00

BOOKLETS STITCHED OR STAPLED

4 x 4d red (centre phosphor band) 2 x 4d red (centre phosphor band) se-tenant with two labels
printed by Harrison, 1969-70. Grey cover ... 1.00

■ **4/6 booklet**
6 x 4d sepia, 6 x 4d sepia (two phosphor bands), 6 x 1d
printed by Harrison, 1968. Blue cover ... 3.00

■ **4/6 booklets. Ships series**
6 x 4d sepia, 6 x 4d sepia (two phosphor bands), 6 x 1d
printed by Harrison, 1968. Cutty Sark cover ... 1.00
6 x 4d sepia, 6 x 4d sepia (centre phosphor band), 6 x 1d
printed by Harrison, 1968. Golden Hind cover ... 1.00
6 x 4d sepia, 6 x 4d sepia (centre phosphor band), 6 x 1d
printed by Harrison, 1968. Discovery cover ... 1.00
6 x 4d red, 6 x 4d red (centre phosphor band), 6 x 1d
printed by Harrison, 1969. Queen Elizabeth 2 cover ... 1.25
6 x 4d red, 6 x 4d red (centre phosphor band), 6 x 1d
printed by Harrison, 1969. Sirius cover ... 2.00
6 x 4d red, 6 x 4d red (centre phosphor band), 6 x 1d
printed by Harrison, 1969. Dreadnought cover ... 1.50
6 x 4d red, 6 x 4d red (centre phosphor band), 6 x 1d
printed by Harrison, 1969-70. Mauretania cover ... 2.00
6 x 4d red, 6 x 4d red (centre phosphor band), 6 x 1d
printed by Harrison, 1970. Victory cover ... 2.00
6 x 4d red, 6 x 4d red (centre phosphor band), 6 x 1d
printed by Harrison, 1970. Sovereign of the Seas cover ... 4.50

■ **5/- booklets. English Homes series**
6 x 5d, 6 x 5d
printed by Harrison, 1968. Ightham Mote cover ... 2.00
6 x 5d, 6 x 5d
printed by Harrison, 1969. Little Moreton Hall cover ... 2.00
6 x 5d, 6 x 5d
printed by Harrison, 1969. Long Melford Hall cover ... 2.50

6 x 5d, 6 x 5d
printed by Harrison, 1969. Mompesson House cover ... 2.50
6 x 5d, 6 x 5d
printed by Harrison, 1970. Cumberland Terrace cover ... 2.00
6 x 5d, 6 x 5d
printed by Harrison, 1970. Vineyard, Saffron Walden cover ... 2.50
6 x 5d, 6 x 5d
printed by Harrison, 1970. Mereworth Castle cover ... 3.25

■ **5/- booklet. Philympia**
6 x 5d, 6 x 5d
printed by Harrison, 1970. Philympia 1970 cover ... 2.00

■ **6/- booklets**
6 x 4d sepia, 6 x 4d sepia, 6 x 4d sepia (phos bands), gum arabic
printed by Harrison, 1967-68. Purple cover ... 45.00
6 x 4d sepia, 6 x 4d sepia, 6 x 4d sepia (phos bands), PVA gum
printed by Harrison, 1970. Purple cover ... £475

■ **6/- booklets. Birds series**
6 x 4d sepia, 6 x 4d sepia, 6 x 4d sepia (two phos bands)
printed by Harrison, 1968. Kingfisher cover ... 2.00
6 x 4d sepia, 6 x 4d sepia, 6 x 4d sepia (two phos bands)
printed by Harrison, 1968. Peregrine Falcon cover ... 2.00
6 x 4d sepia, 6 x 4d sepia, 6 x 4d sepia (centre phos band)
printed by Harrison, 1968. Peregrine Falcon cover ... 2.00
6 x 4d sepia, 6 x 4d sepia, 6 x 4d sepia (centre phos band)
printed by Harrison, 1968. Pied Woodpecker cover ... 2.00
6 x 4d sepia, 6 x 4d sepia, 6 x 4d sepia (centre phos band)
printed by Harrison, 1968. Great Crested Grebe cover ... 2.00
6 x 4d sepia, 6 x 4d sepia, 6 x 4d sepia (centre phos band)
printed by Harrison, 1969. Barn Owl cover ... 3.00
6 x 4d red, 6 x 4d red, 6 x 4d red (centre phos band)
printed by Harrison, 1969. Barn Owl cover ... 3.50
6 x 4d red, 6 x 4d red, 6 x 4d red (centre phos band)
printed by Harrison, 1969. Jay cover ... 3.00

STITCHED OR STAPLED BOOKLETS

6 x 4d red, 6 x 4d red, 6 x 4d red (centre phos band)
printed by Harrison, 1969. Puffin cover — 3.00
6 x 4d red, 6 x 4d red, 6 x 4d red (centre phos band)
printed by Harrison, 1969–70. Cormorant cover — 3.50
6 x 4d red, 6 x 4d red, 6 x 4d red (centre phos band)
printed by Harrison, 1970. Wren cover — 3.00
6 x 4d red, 6 x 4d red, 6 x 4d red (centre phos band)
printed by Harrison, 1970. Golden Eagle cover — 3.00

■ **10/– booklets. Explorers series**
6 x 4d sepia, 6 x 4d sepia, 6 x 4d sepia, 6 x 4d sepia (two phos bands), 6 x 3d, 6 x 1d
printed by Harrison, 1968. Livingstone cover — 4.50
6 x 5d, 6 x 5d, 6 x 4d sepia, 6 x 4d sepia (centre phos band), 4 x 1d se-tenant with 2 x 4d sepia (one phos band)
printed by Harrison, 1968. Scott cover — 3.50
6 x 5d, 6 x 5d, 6 x 4d red, 6 x 4d red (centre phos band), 4 x 1d se-tenant with 2 x 4d red (one phos band)
printed by Harrison, 1969. Kingsley cover — 3.50
6 x 5d, 6 x 5d, 6 x 4d red, 6 x 4d red (centre phos band), 4 x 1d se-tenant with 2 x 4d red (one phos band)
printed by Harrison, 1969. Shackleton cover — 4.00
6 x 5d, 6 x 5d, 6 x 4d red, 6 x 4d red (centre phos band), 4 x 1d se-tenant with 2 x 4d red (one phos band)
printed by Harrison, 1970. Frobisher cover — 5.50
6 x 5d, 6 x 5d, 6 x 4d red, 6 x 4d red (centre phos band), 4 x 1d se-tenant with 2 x 4d red (one phos band)
printed by Harrison, 1970. Cook cover — 6.00

ELIZABETH II (DECIMAL MACHINS), 1971–76

■ **10p booklets (machine-vended). Pillar Boxes series**
2 x ½p, 2 x 1p, 2 x 1½p, 2 x 2p
printed by Harrison, 1971. London's first box 1855 cover — 1.00
2 x ½p, 2 x 1p, 2 x 1½p, 2 x 2p
printed by Harrison, 1971. Pillar box 1856 cover — 1.50
2 x ½p, 2 x 1p, 2 x 1½p, 2 x 2p
printed by Harrison, 1971. Urban pillar box 1857 cover — 2.00
2 x ½p, 2 x 1p, 2 x 1½p, 2 x 2p
printed by Harrison, 1971–72. Penfold box 1866 cover — 2.50
2 x ½p, 2 x 1p, 2 x 1½p, 2 x 2p
printed by Harrison, 1972. Double-aperture box 1899 cover — 2.00
2 x ½p, 2 x 1p, 2 x 1½p, 2 x 2p
printed by Harrison, 1972. Mellor box 1968 cover — 2.00
2 x ½p, 2 x 1p, 2 x 1½p, 2 x 2p
printed by Harrison, 1973. Edward VIII box 1936 cover — 2.50
2 x ½p, 2 x 1p, 2 x 1½p, 2 x 2p
printed by Harrison, 1973. Elizabeth II box 1952 cover — 2.50
2 x ½p, 2 x 1p, 2 x 1½p, 2 x 2p
printed by Harrison, 1973. Double-aperture box 1973 cover — 2.00
2 x ½p, 2 x 1p, 2 x 1½p, 2 x 2p
printed by Harrison, 1974. Philatelic box 1974 cover — 2.00

■ **10p booklets (machine-vended). Postal Uniforms series**
2 x ½p, 2 x 1p, 2 x 1½p, 2 x 2p
printed by Harrison, 1974. Letter carrier 1793 cover — 1.00
2 x ½p, 2 x 1p, 2 x 1½p, 2 x 2p
printed by Harrison, 1974. Letter carrier 1837 cover — 1.00
2 x ½p, 2 x 1p, 2 x 1½p, 2 x 2p
printed by Harrison, 1975–76. Letter carrier 1855 cover — 0.75

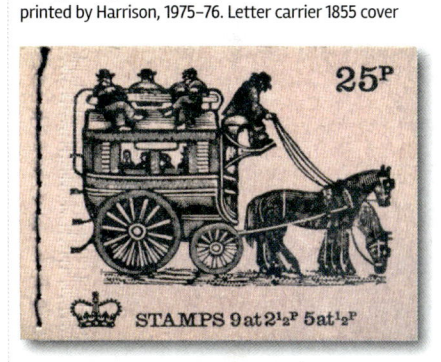

■ **25p booklets. Veteran Transport series**
5 x ½p, 9 x 2½p
printed by Harrison, 1971. Knifeboard Omnibus cover — 3.50
5 x ½p, 9 x 2½p
printed by Harrison, 1971. B-type Omnibus cover — 4.00
5 x ½p, 9 x 2½p
printed by Harrison, 1971. Showman's Engine cover — 8.00
5 x ½p, 9 x 2½p
printed by Harrison, 1972. Royal Mail Van 1913 cover — 5.00
5 x ½p, 9 x 2½p
printed by Harrison, 1972. Motor Wagonette 1901 cover — 4.50
5 x ½p, 9 x 2½p
printed by Harrison, 1972. London Taxi Cab 1931 cover — 6.00
5 x ½p, 9 x 2½p
printed by Harrison, 1973. Electric Tramcar cover — 6.00

■ **25p booklets. 80 Years of British Stamp Books Exhibition**
5 x ½p, 9 x 2½p
printed by Harrison, 1971. Stamp Books cover (purple) — 4.00

BOOKLETS STITCHED OR STAPLED

■ 25p booklets. Save The Children Fund
5 x ½p, 9 x 2½p
printed by Harrison, 1973. Save The Children cover (mauve)   6.00

■ 30p booklets. British Birds series
10 x 3p
printed by Harrison, 1971. Curlew cover   3.00
10 x 3p
printed by Harrison, 1971. Lapwing cover   4.00
10 x 3p
printed by Harrison, 1971. Robin cover   4.50
10 x 3p
printed by Harrison, 1971-72. Pied Wagtail cover   4.00
10 x 3p
printed by Harrison, 1972. Kestrel cover   4.50
10 x 3p
printed by Harrison, 1972. Black Grouse cover   4.50
10 x 3p
printed by Harrison, 1973. Skylark cover   4.50
10 x 3p
printed by Harrison, 1973. Oystercatcher cover (purple)   5.00
10 x 3p
printed by Harrison, 1973. Oystercatcher cover (bistre)   5.50

■ 30p booklets. 80 Years of British Stamp Books
10 x 3p
printed by Harrison, 1971. Stamp Books cover (purple)   4.00

■ 30p booklets. Save The Children Fund
10 x 3p
printed by Harrison, 1974. Save The Children cover (red)   3.50

■ 30p booklets. Canada Life Assurance
10 x 3p
printed by Harrison, 1974. Canada Life advert cover (red)   4.00

■ 35p booklets. British Coins series
10 x 3½p
printed by Harrison, 1973-74. Cuthred Penny cover   3.00
10 x 3½p
printed by Harrison, 1974. Edward I Silver Groat cover   3.00

■ 35p booklets. Canada Life Assurance
10 x 3½p
printed by Harrison, 1974. Canada Life advert cover (blue)   3.00

■ 45p booklets. British Coins series
10 x 4½p
printed by Harrison, 1974. Elizabeth Gold Crown cover   3.50

■ 50p booklets. British Flowers series
5 x ½p, 7 x 2½p, 10 x 3p
printed by Harrison, 1971. Large Bindweed cover   5.00
5 x ½p, 7 x 2½p, 10 x 3p
printed by Harrison, 1971. Primrose cover   6.00
5 x ½p, 7 x 2½p, 10 x 3p
printed by Harrison, 1971. Honeysuckle cover   6.00
5 x ½p, 7 x 2½p, 10 x 3p
printed by Harrison, 1971. Hop cover   6.50
5 x ½p, 7 x 2½p, 10 x 3p
printed by Harrison, 1971. Common Violet cover   6.50
5 x ½p, 7 x 2½p, 10 x 3p
printed by Harrison, 1972. Lords-and-Ladies cover   6.50
5 x ½p, 7 x 2½p, 10 x 3p
printed by Harrison, 1972. Wood Anemone cover   6.50
5 x ½p, 7 x 2½p, 10 x 3p
printed by Harrison, 1972. Deadly Nightshade cover   6.00

■ 50p booklets. Canada Life Assurance
5 x ½p, 7 x 2½p, 10 x 3p
printed by Harrison, 1973. Canada Life cover (blue-green)   5.50
5 x 3p, 10 x 3½p
printed by Harrison, 1973. Canada Life cover (deep green)   4.50

■ 85p booklets. Canada Life Assurance
5 x 3½p, 15 x 4½p
printed by Harrison, 1973. Canada Life advert cover (purple)   6.50

UPA VIP Series: 'Because' ...

Sometimes Collectors Get a Raw Deal, don't they?

The problem with most stamp auctions is not what they sell, but how they sell it...

1.▶ Imagine, you drive into a Petrol Station, with fuel at 150p per litre it is expensive, so you limit your fuel purchase by putting £50 worth fuel into your tank. Then you go in to pay, and the cashier asks you for £65 ... how can that be? Yes, **£15 (30%) more.** You are infuriated, £65 for £50 worth of fuel! No chance ... you would rather empty your tank first, than pay such an iniquitous premium.

2.▶ That's the reason why in 2017 European Auction Selling Legislation introduced – required auctions that charge 'buyer's premiums' **to warn the buyer in advance.** Of course, we are no longer in the EU, but that has not stopped Buyer's Premiums and other charges lifting the hammer cost of your stamps, by as much as a further 30% above the 'hammer' price that the stamps were actually sold to you at.

3.▶ You really don't need to imagine – because this is still what happens in most stamp auctions. Further, there is no distinction between when you are buying stamps that are actually owned by that auction, and when you are buying stamps that are being sold on behalf of a vendor. Is this fair?

4.▶ That is why Universal Philatelic Auctions (UPA) steadfastly refuses to charge any buyer's premium or other charges, because at UPA collectors are treated like the Very Important Philatelists (VIPs) that they are.

5.▶ If you feel the same as we do about extra levies upon our philatelic pastime, you may wish to learn a little more about UPA. Each quarter UPA offers a 20,000+/- lot auction catalogue with NO extra buyer's premiums or hidden charges, lightweight auction lots delivered insured and loyalty post-free. Furthermore, ALL lots won are Guaranteed, which may account for why more than 2,000 different collectors from 54 different countries regularly bid in their auctions.

6.▶ If you would like a complimentary catalogue of their next auction, plus your 1st £55 auction winnings free when you win £75+, please visit: upastampauctions.co.uk and ...

7.▶ Determine how You wish to be treated Here ...

PHILATELIC ROUTE-FINDER

VISIT
upastampauctions.co.uk

or if you prefer, telephone: 01451 861111

UPA VIP | **Putting Collectors Like You First**

UNIVERSAL PHILATELIC AUCTIONS
4 The Old Coalyard, West End, Northleach, Glos. GL54 3HE·UK

BOOKLETS FOLDED

FOLDED BOOKLETS

In this section, items are priced in mint condition only.

MACHINE-VENDED BOOKLETS OF MACHIN DEFINITIVES, 1976–2000

These booklets were sold from vending machines. They contain panes attached to covers by their top selvedge, so the Queen's portrait is face-down. In most cases, panes are folded along their perforations.

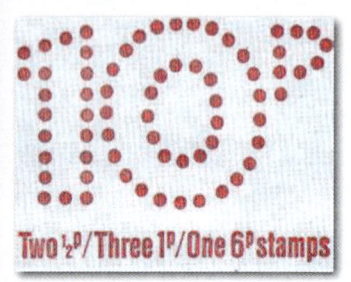

■ **10p booklet**
2 x ½p, 3 x 1p, 1 x 6p
printed by Harrison, 1976–77; dotted '10p' cover — 0.60

■ **10p booklets. Farm Buildings series**
2 x ½p, 2 x 1p, 1x 7p
printed by Harrison, 1978; Kent buildings cover — 0.40
2 x ½p, 2 x 1p, 1x 7p
printed by Harrison, 1978; N Ireland buildings cover — 0.40
2 x ½p, 2 x 1p, 1x 7p
printed by Harrison, 1978; Yorkshire buildings cover — 0.40
2 x ½p, 2 x 1p, 1x 7p
printed by Harrison, 1978; Wales buildings cover — 0.40
2 x ½p, 2 x 1p, 1x 7p
printed by Harrison, 1979; Scotland buildings cover — 0.40
2 x ½p, 2 x 1p, 1x 7p
printed by Harrison, 1979; Sussex buildings cover — 0.40

■ **10p booklet. London 1980 Exhibition**
2 x 1p, 1 x 8p
printed by Harrison, 1979–80; London 1980 cover — 0.45
(*This booklet exists with differing postal rates quoted on its inside covers.)

■ **50p booklets**
2 x ½p, 2 x 1p, 2 x 6½p (phos band at left), 4 x 8½p
printed by Harrison, 1977; bold '50p' cover — 1.40
2 x ½p, 2 x 1p, 2 x 6½p (phos band at right), 4 x 8½p
printed by Harrison, 1977; bold '50p' cover — 1.40
2 x 1p, 3 x 7p (phos band at left), 3 x 9p
printed by Harrison, 1977; bold '50p' cover — 2.00
2 x 1p, 3 x 7p (phos band at right), 3 x 9p
printed by Harrison, 1977; bold '50p' cover — 3.00

■ **50p booklets. Commercial Vehicles series**
2 x 1p, 3 x 7p (phos band at left), 3 x 9p
printed by Harrison, 1978; Clement Talbot Van cover — 2.00
2 x 1p, 3 x 7p (phos band at right), 3 x 9p
printed by Harrison, 1978; Clement Talbot Van cover — 3.00
2 x 1p, 3 x 7p (phos band at left), 3 x 9p
printed by Harrison, 1978; Austin Cape Taxi cover — 2.00
2 x 1p, 3 x 7p (phos band at right), 3 x 9p
printed by Harrison, 1978; Austin Cape Taxi cover — 3.00
2 x 1p, 3 x 7p (phos band at left), 3 x 9p
printed by Harrison, 1978; Morris Royal Mail Van cover — 2.00
2 x 1p, 3 x 7p (phos band at right), 3 x 9p
printed by Harrison, 1978; Morris Royal Mail Van cover — 3.00
2 x 1p, 3 x 7p (phos band at left), 3 x 9p
printed by Harrison, 1978; Guy Electric Dustcart cover — 2.00
2 x 1p, 3 x 7p (phos band at right), 3 x 9p
printed by Harrison, 1978; Guy Electric Dustcart cover — 4.00
2 x 1p, 3 x 7p (phos band at left), 3 x 9p
printed by Harrison, 1979; Albion Van cover — 4.00
2 x 1p, 3 x 7p (phos band at right), 3 x 9p
printed by Harrison, 1979; Albion Van cover — 4.00
2 x 1p, 3 x 7p (phos band at left), 3 x 9p
printed by Harrison, 1979; Leyland Fire Engine cover — 4.00
2 x 1p, 3 x 7p (phos band at right), 3 x 9p

FOLDED BOOKLETS

printed by Harrison, 1979; Leyland Fire Engine cover 4.00
2 x 2p, 2 x 8p (phos band at left or right), 3 x 10p
printed by Harrison, 1979; Leyland Fire Engine cover 2.00

■ 50p booklets. Veteran Cars series
2 x 2p, 2 x 8p (phos band left or right), 3 x 10p
printed by Harrison, 1979; Rolls Royce Silver Ghost cover 1.50
3 x 2p, 2 x 10p (phos band left or right), 2 x 12p
printed by Harrison, 1980; Grand Prix Austin cover 1.75
3 x 2p, 2 x 10p (phos band left or right), 2 x 12p
printed by Harrison, 1980; Vauxhall cover 1.50
3 x 2p, 2 x 10p (phos band left or right), 2 x 12p
printed by Harrison, 1980; Daimler cover 1.50
1 x ½p, 1 x 1p, 1 x 14p, 3 x 11½p (phos band left or right)
printed by Harrison, 1981; Lanchester cover 1.50
1 x ½p, 1 x 1p, 1 x 14p, 3 x 11½p (phos band left or right)
printed by Harrison, 1981; Bullnose Morris cover 1.75

■ 50p booklets. Follies series
1 x ½p, 1 x 1p, 1 x 14p, 3 x 11½p (phos band left or right)
printed by Harrison, 1981; Mugdock Castle cover 1.50
3 x 2½p, 2 x 4p, 3 x 11½p (phos band at left)
printed by Harrison, 1981; Mugdock Castle cover 7.00
3 x 2½p, 2 x 4p, 3 x 11½p (phos band at right)
printed by Harrison, 1981; Mugdock Castle cover 5.50
3 x 2½p, 2 x 4p, 3 x 11½p (phos band at left)
printed by Harrison, 1981; Mow Cop Castle cover 5.50
3 x 2½p, 2 x 4p, 3 x 11½p (phos band at right)
printed by Harrison, 1981; Mow Cop Castle cover 4.00
1 x ½p, 4 x 3p pink, 3 x 12½p (phos band left or right)
printed by Harrison, 1982; Paxton's Tower cover 2.00
1 x ½p, 4 x 3p pink, 3 x 12½p (phos band left or right)
printed by Harrison, 1982; Temple of the Winds cover 2.00
1 x ½p, 4 x 3p pink, 3 x 12½p (phos band left or right)
printed by Harrison, 1982; Temple of the Sun cover 2.00
1 x ½p, 4 x 3p pink, 3 x 12½p (phos band left or right)
printed by Harrison, 1982; Water Garden cover 2.00

■ 50p booklets. Rare Farm Animals series
1 x ½p, 4 x 3p pink, 3 x 12½p (phos band left or right)
printed by Harrison, 1983; Bagot Goat cover 2.00
2 x 1p, 3 x 3½p, 3 x 12½p (all with centre phos band)
printed by Harrison, 1983; Gloucester Old Spot Pig cover 3.50
2 x 1p, 3 x 3½p, 3 x 12½p (all with centre phos band)
printed by Harrison, 1983; Gloucester Old Spot Pig cover
with postal rate information corrected 12.00
2 x 1p, 3 x 3½p, 3 x 12½p (all with centre phos band)
printed by Harrison, 1983; Toulouse Goose cover 4.00
2 x 1p, 3 x 3½p, 3 x 12½p (all with centre phos band)
printed by Harrison, 1983; Orkney Sheep cover 4.00

■ 50p booklets. Orchids series
3 x 1p, 2 x 4p, 3 x 13p (all with centre phos band)
printed by Harrison, 1984; Dendrobium Nobile cover 2.50
3 x 1p, 2 x 4p, 3 x 13p (all with centre phos band)
printed by Harrison, 1985; Cypripedium and Ophrys cover 2.50
3 x 1p, 2 x 4p, 3 x 13p (all with centre phos band)
printed by Harrison, 1985; Bifienasia and Vandatricolour 2.50
3 x 1p, 2 x 4p, 3 x 13p (all with centre phos band)
printed by Harrison, 1985; Cymbidium and Arpophyllum 2.50

■ 50p booklet. Pillar Box
3 x 17p (two phos bands, stars printed on gummed side)
printed by Harrison, 1985; Pillar box cover 3.00

■ 50p booklets. Pond Life series
3 x 17p (two phos bands, stars printed on gummed side)
printed by Harrison, 1986; Emperor Dragonfly cover 2.00
3 x 17p (two phos bands, stars printed on gummed side)
printed by Harrison, 1986; Common Frog cover 2.50
3 x 17p (two phos bands, without stars on gummed side)
printed by Harrison, 1986; Common Frog cover 2.50
1 x 1p, 2 x 5p, 3 x 13p (all with centre phos band)
printed by Harrison, 1986; Moorhen and Dabchicks cover 3.50
1 x 1p, 2 x 5p, 3 x 13p (all with centre phos band)
printed by Harrison, 1987; Giant Pond Snail cover 3.50

■ 50p booklets. Roman Britain series
2 x 1p, 4 x 12p emerald-green (all with centre phos band)
printed by Harrison, 1986; Hadrian's Wall cover 6.50
1 x 1p (right band), 1 x 13p (left band), 2 x 18p (two bands)
printed by Harrison, 1986; Roman Theatre cover 2.50
1 x 1p (right band), 1 x 13p (left band), 2 x 18p (two bands)
printed by Harrison, 1987; Portchester Castle cover 2.50

■ 50p booklets. Marylebone Cricket Club series
1 x 1p (right band), 1 x 13p (left band), 2 x 18p (two bands)
printed by Harrison, 1987; Weather Vane at Lord's cover 1.75
1 x 1p (right band), 1 x 13p (left band), 2 x 18p (two bands)
printed by Harrison, 1987; Ashes Urn cover 1.75
1 x 1p (right band), 1 x 13p (left band), 2 x 18p (two bands)
printed by Harrison, 1987; Lord's pavilion cover 1.75
1 x 1p (right band), 1 x 13p (left band), 2 x 18p (two bands)
printed by Harrison, 1988; Lord's New Stand cover 1.75

■ 50p booklets. Botanical Gardens series
1 x 1p, 2 x 5p, 3 x 13p (all with centre phos band)
printed by Harrison, 1987; Bodnant Gardens cover 3.25
1 x 1p, 2 x 5p, 3 x 13p (all with centre phos band)
printed by Harrison, 1987; Edinburgh Gardens cover 3.25
1 x 1p, 2 x 5p, 3 x 13p (centre phos bands, side edges imperf)
printed by Harrison, 1987; Mount Stuart cover 2.00
1 x 1p, 2 x 5p, 3 x 13p (all with centre phos band)
printed by Harrison, 1987; Mount Stewart (corrected) 2.25
1 x 1p, 2 x 5p, 3 x 13p (all with centre phos band)
printed by Harrison, 1988; Kew Gardens cover 2.00

■ 50p booklets. London Zoo series
1 x 1p, 1 x 13p, 2 x 18p
printed by Harrison, 1988; Pigs cover 2.00
1 x 1p, 1 x 13p, 2 x 18p
printed by Harrison, 1988; Birds cover 2.00
1 x 1p, 1 x 13p, 2 x 18p
printed by Harrison, 1988; Elephants cover 2.00

■ 50p booklets. Marine Life series
1 x 1p, 2 x 5p, 3 x 13p (all with centre phos band)
printed by Harrison, 1988; Anenome, Whelk, Jellyfish cover 2.00
1 x 14p, 2 x 19p
printed by Harrison, 1989; Crab, Bladderwrack cover 5.00

BOOKLETS FOLDED

■ 50p booklets. Gilbert & Sullivan Operas series
1 x 14p, 2 x 19p
printed by Harrison, 1988; Yeomen of the Guard cover   4.50
1 x 14p, 2 x 19p
printed by Harrison, 1989; Pirates of Penzance cover   4.50
1 x 14p, 2 x 19p
printed by Harrison, 1989; Mikado cover   4.50

■ 50p booklets. Aircraft series
2 x 15p, 1 x 20p
printed by Harrison, 1989; AW Atalanta & DH Dragon   8.00
2 x 15p, 1 x 20p (Penny Black Anniversary stamps)
printed by Harrison, 1990; Vickers Viscount & DH Comet   10.00
2 x 15p, 1 x 20p
printed by Harrison, 1990; BAC 1-11 & VC10   10.00
2 x 15p, 1 x 20p
printed by Harrison, 1991; BAe ATP 146 & Concorde   10.00

■ 50p booklets. Archaeology series
2 x 1p, 2 x 24p
printed by Harrison, 1991; Sir Arthur Evans at Crete   2.00
2 x 1p, 2 x 24p
printed by Harrison, 1992; Howard Carter, Tutankhamun   2.00
2 x 1p, 2 x 24p
printed by Harrison, 1992; Sir Austen Layard in Assyria   2.00
2 x 1p, 2 x 24p
printed by Harrison, 1992; Sir Flinders Petrie at Giza   2.00

■ 50p booklet. Sheriff's Millennium
2 x 1p, 2 x 24p
printed by Harrison, 1992; Sheriff's millennium cover   2.00

■ 50p booklets. Postal History series
2 x 1p, 2 x 24p
printed by Harrison, 1993; Airmail markings cover   1.50
2 x 1p, 2 x 24p
printed by Harrison, 1993; Ship mail markings cover   1.50
2 x 1p, 2 x 24p
printed by Harrison, 1993; Registered mail cover   1.50
2 x 25p
printed by Harrison, 1993; 'Paid' marking cover   1.50

■ 50p booklets. Coaching Inns series
2 x 25p
printed by Harrison, 1994; Swan With Two Necks cover   1.50
2 x 25p
printed by Harrison, 1994; Bull & Mouth cover   1.50
2 x 25p
printed by Harrison, 1994; Golden Cross cover   1.50
2 x 25p
printed by Harrison, 1994; Pheasant Inn cover   1.50

■ 50p booklets. Sea Charts series
2 x 25p
printed by Harrison, 1995; John O'Groats cover   1.50
2 x 25p
printed by Harrison, 1995; Land's End cover   1.50
2 x 25p
printed by Harrison, 1995; St. David's Head cover   2.00
2 x 25p
printed by Harrison, 1995; Giant's Causeway cover   2.00

■ £1 booklets. Musical Instruments series
6 x 17p (advanced coated paper)
printed by Harrison, 1986; Violin cover   3.00
1 x 13p (phos band at right), 5 x 18p (two phos bands)
printed by Harrison, 1986; French Horn cover   3.00
1 x 13p (phos band at right), 5 x 18p (two phos bands)
printed by Harrison, 1987; Bass Clarinet cover   3.00

■ £1 booklets. Sherlock Holmes series
1 x 13p (phos band at right), 5 x 18p (two phos bands)
printed by Harrison, 1987; A Study in Scarlet cover   3.00
1 x 13p (phos band at right), 5 x 18p (two phos bands)
printed by Harrison, 1987; Hound of the Baskervilles cover   3.00
1 x 13p (band at right), 5 x 18p (two bands), edges imperf
printed by Harrison, 1987; Adventure of the Speckled Band   3.00
1 x 13p (band at right), 5 x 18p (two bands), edges imperf
printed by Harrison, 1988; The Final Problem cover   3.00

■ £1 booklet. London Zoo series
1 x 13p (phos band at right), 5 x 18p (two phos bands)
printed by Harrison, 1988; Bears   3.00

■ £1 booklets. Charles Dickens series
1 x 13p (phos band at right), 5 x 18p (two phos bands)
printed by Harrison, 1988; Oliver Twist cover   4.00
2 x 14p (phos band at right), 4 x 19p (two phos bands)
printed by Harrison, 1988; Nicholas Nickleby cover   4.00
2 x 14p (phos band at right), 4 x 19p (two phos bands)
printed by Harrison, 1989; David Copperfield cover   4.00
2 x 14p (phos band at right), 4 x 19p (two phos bands)
printed by Walsall, 1989; Great Expectations cover   8.50

■ £1 booklet. Marine Life series
2 x 14p (phos band at right), 4 x 19p (two phos bands)
printed by Harrison, 1989; Sea urchin, starfish, crab   4.00

■ £1 booklets. Mills series
5 x 20p
printed by Harrison, 1989; Wicken Fen cover (matt)   4.00
5 x 20p (Penny Black Anniversary stamps)
printed by Walsall, 1990; Wicken Fen cover (glossy)   10.00
5 x 20p (Penny Black Anniversary stamps)
printed by Harrison, 1990; Click Mill cover   6.00
2 x 17p, 3 x 22p
printed by Harrison, 1990; Jack & Jill Mills cover   3.00
2 x 17p, 3 x 22p
printed by Harrison, 1991 Howell Mill cover   3.00

FOLDED BOOKLETS

■ **£1 booklets. Punch Magazine series**
2 x 2p, 4 x 24p
printed by Harrison, 1991; illustrations by Doyle, Hoffnung   2.00
2 x 2p, 4 x 24p
printed by Harrison, 1992; illustrations by Tenniel, Burgin   2.00
2 x 2p, 4 x 24p
printed by Harrison, 1992; illustrations by Tenniel, Anton   2.00
2 x 2p, 4 x 24p
printed by Harrison, 1992; illustrations by Tenniel, Hewison   2.00

■ **£1 booklet. Sheriff's Millennium**
2 x 2p, 4 x 24p
printed by Harrison, 1992; Sheriff's Millennium cover   2.00

■ **£1 booklets. Educational Institutions series**
2 x 2p, 4 x 24p
printed by Walsall, 1993; University of Wales cover   4.00
2 x 2p, 4 x 24p
printed by Walsall, 1993; St. Hilda's College, Oxford   4.00
2 x 2p, 4 x 24p
printed by Walsall, 1993; Marlborough College cover   4.00
4 x 25p
printed by Walsall, 1993; Free Church of Scotland College   4.00

■ **£1 booklets. Prime Ministers series**
4 x 25p
printed by Walsall, 1994; Herbert Asquith cover   2.00
4 x 25p
printed by Harrison, 1994; David Lloyd-George cover   2.00
4 x 25p
printed by Harrison, 1994; Winston Churchill cover   2.00
4 x 25p
printed by Harrison, 1994; Clement Attlee cover   2.00

■ **£1 booklets. Second World War series**
4 x 25p
printed by Harrison, 1995; Violette Szabo cover   2.00
4 x 25p
printed by Harrison, 1995; Dame Vera Lynn cover   2.00
4 x 25p
printed by Harrison, 1995; R. J. Mitchell cover   2.00
4 x 25p
printed by Harrison, 1995; Archibald McIndoe cover   2.25

■ **£1 booklets. Red cover series**
4 x 25p (litho)
printed by Questa, 1996; Royal Mail cruciform cover   4.00
2 x 1p, 1 x 20p, 3 x 26p (litho)
printed by Questa, 1996–97; Royal Mail cruciform cover   3.50
2 x 1p, 1 x 20p, 3 x 26p (gravure)
printed by Questa, 1998; Royal Mail cruciform cover   19.00
1 x 1p, 1 x 2p, 1 x 19p, 3 x 26p (gravure)
printed by Questa, 1999; Royal Mail cruciform cover   6.00
1 x 2nd, 3 x 1st (gravure)
printed by Questa, 2000–01; Royal Mail cruciform cover   7.00

■ **£2 booklets. Postal Vehicles series**
8 x 25p
printed by Harrison, 1993; Motorised Cycle cover   3.50
8 x 25p
printed by Harrison, 1994; Motor Mail Van cover   4.00
8 x 25p
printed by Harrison, 1994; Electric Mail Van cover   4.00

■ **£2 booklets. Sir Rowland Hill series**
8 x 25p
printed by Harrison, 1995; London & Brighton Railway   3.50
8 x 25p
printed by Harrison, 1995; Hazlewood School   3.50
8 x 25p
printed by Harrison, 1995; Secretary to the Post Office   3.75
8 x 25p
printed by Harrison, 1995; Uniform Penny Postage   3.75

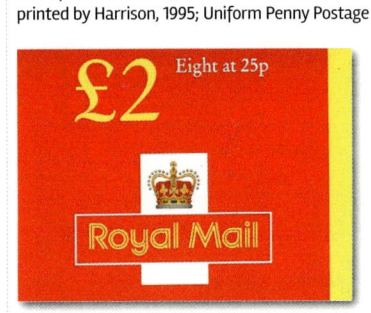

■ **£2 booklets. Red cover series**
8 x 25p
printed by Questa, 1996; Royal Mail cruciform cover   4.00
1 x 20p, 7 x 26p (litho)
printed by Questa, 1996; Royal Mail cruciform cover   5.00
1 x 20p, 7 x 26p (gravure)
printed by Questa, 1998; Royal Mail cruciform cover   19.50
1 x 19p, 7 x 26p
printed by Questa, 1999; Royal Mail cruciform cover   6.50
2 x 2nd, 6 x 1st
printed by Questa, 2000; Royal Mail cruciform cover   6.50

BOOKLETS FOLDED

COUNTER BOOKLETS OF MACHIN DEFINITIVES, 1976–89

These booklets were sold over post office counters. They contain panes attached to covers by their side selvedge, so the Queen's portrait appears upright. Panes can have a margin to the left or right; prices are the same for both, except where stated.

■ 65p booklets
10 x 6½p (right margin)
printed by Harrison, 1976; bold '65p' cover — 5.50
10 x 6½p (left margin)
printed by Harrison, 1976; bold '65p' cover — 10.00

■ 70p booklet
10 x 7p
printed by Harrison, 1977; bold '70p' cover — 4.00

■ 70p booklets. Country Crafts series
10 x 7p (right margin)
printed by Harrison, 1978; Horse–Shoeing cover — 3.00
10 x 7p (left margin)
printed by Harrison, 1978; Horse–Shoeing cover — 35.00
10 x 7p (right margin)
printed by Harrison, 1978; Thatching cover — 3.00
10 x 7p (left margin)
printed by Harrison, 1978; Thatching cover — £180
10 x 7p (right margin)
printed by Harrison, 1978; Dry-Stone Walling cover — 3.00
10 x 7p (left margin)
printed by Harrison, 1978; Dry-Stone Walling cover — £165
10 x 7p (right margin)
printed by Harrison, 1978; Wheel-Making cover — 4.50
10 x 7p (left margin)
printed by Harrison, 1978; Wheel-Making cover — 5.75
10 x 7p (right margin)
printed by Harrison, 1979; Wattle Fence-Making cover — 4.00
10 x 7p (left margin)
printed by Harrison, 1979; Wattle Fence-Making cover — 11.00
10 x 7p (right margin)
printed by Harrison, 1979; Basket-Making cover — 3.00
10 x 7p (left margin)
printed by Harrison, 1979; Basket-Making cover — 6.00

■ 70p booklet. Derby Letter Office series
10 x 7p
printed by Harrison, 1979; Kedleston Hall cover — 5.50

■ 80p booklet. Military Aircraft series
10 x 8p
printed by Harrison, 1979; Vickers Gun Bus cover — 2.50

■ 85p booklets
10 x 8½p (right margin)
printed by Harrison, 1976; bold '85p' cover — 7.50
10 x 8½p (left margin)
printed by Harrison, 1976; bold '85p' cover — 7.00

■ 90p booklets
10 x 9p (left margin)
printed by Harrison, 1977; bold '90p' cover — 4.00
10 x 9p (right margin)
printed by Harrison, 1977; bold '90p' cover — 6.00

FOLDED BOOKLETS

■ **90p booklets. British Canals series**
10 x 9p (right margin)
printed by Harrison, 1978; Grand Union Canal cover 4.00
10 x 9p (left margin)
printed by Harrison, 1978; Grand Union Canal cover 22.00
10 x 9p (right margin)
printed by Harrison, 1978; Llangollen Canal cover £330
10 x 9p (left margin)
printed by Harrison, 1978; Llangollen Canal cover 3.25
10 x 9p (right margin)
printed by Harrison, 1978; Kennet & Avon Canal cover 8.00
10 x 9p (left margin)
printed by Harrison, 1978; Kennet & Avon Canal cover 10.00
10 x 9p (right margin)
printed by Harrison, 1978; Caledonian Canal cover 5.00
10 x 9p (left margin)
printed by Harrison, 1978; Caledonian Canal cover 6.00
10 x 9p (right margin)
printed by Harrison, 1979; Regent's Canal cover 6.50
10 x 9p (left margin)
printed by Harrison, 1979; Regent's Canal cover 10.00
10 x 9p
printed by Harrison, 1979; Leeds & Liverpool Canal cover 4.00

■ **90p booklet. Derby Letter Office series**
10 x 9p
printed by Harrison, 1979; Tramway Museum, Crich, cover 7.00

■ **£1 booklets. Industrial Archaeology series**
10 x 10p (all-over phosphor)
printed by Harrison, 1979; Ironbridge, Telford, cover 3.00

■ **£1 booklets. Military Aircraft series**
10 x 10p (one centre phos band)
printed by Harrison, 1980; Sopwith Camel, Vickers Vimy cover 2.50
10 x 10p (one centre phos band)
printed by Harrison, 1980; Hawker Fury, HP Heyford cover 3.50
10 x 10p (one centre phos band)
printed by Harrison, 1980; Wellington, Hurricane cover 2.50

■ **£1.15 booklets. Military Aircraft series**
10 x 11½p (one centre phos band)
printed by Harrison, 1981; Spitfire, Lancaster cover 3.50
10 x 11½p (one centre phos band)
printed by Harrison, 1981; Lightning, Vulcan cover 3.50

■ **£1.15 booklets. Museums series**
10 x 11½p (one centre phos band)
printed by Harrison, 1981; Natural History Museum cover 3.50
10 x 11½p (one centre phos band)
printed by Harrison, 1981; Museum of Antiquities cover 3.50

■ **£1.20 booklets. Industrial Archaeology series**
10 x 12p yellow-green
printed by Harrison, 1980; Beetle Mill cover 3.50
10 x 12p yellow-green
printed by Harrison, 1980; Tin Mines cover 3.50
10 x 12p yellow-green
printed by Harrison, 1980; Bottle Kilns cover 3.50

■ **£1.20 booklets**
10 x 12p emerald-green (one centre phos band)
printed by Harrison, 1986; Pillar Box cover 4.50
10 x 12p emerald-green (one centre phos band)
printed by Harrison, 1986; National Gallery cover 4.25
10 x 12p emerald-green (one centre phos band)
printed by Harrison, 1986; 'Maybe' cover 4.25

■ **£1.25 booklets. Museums series**
10 x 12½p (one centre phos band)
printed by Harrison, 1982; Ashmolean Museum cover 4.50
10 x 12½p (one centre phos band)
printed by Harrison, 1982; National Museum of Wales cover 4.50
10 x 12½p (one centre phos band)
printed by Harrison, 1982; Ulster Museum, Belfast, cover 4.50
10 x 12½p (one centre phos band)
printed by Harrison, 1982; Castle Museum, York, cover 4.50

BOOKLETS FOLDED

■ **£1.25 booklets. Railway Engines series**
10 x 12½p (one centre phos band)
printed by Harrison, 1983; GWR IK Brunel cover 4.00
10 x 12½p (one centre phos band)
printed by Harrison, 1983; LMS Class 4P cover 4.75
10 x 12½p (one centre phos band)
printed by Harrison, 1983; LNER Mallard cover 4.00
10 x 12½p (one centre phos band)
printed by Harrison, 1983; SR/BR Clan Line cover 4.00

■ **£1.30 booklets. Postal History series**
6 x 14p (two phos bands), 2 x 11½p (left phos band),
2 x 11½p (right phos band) (right margin)
printed by Harrison, 1981; Penny Black cover 3.50
6 x 14p (two phos bands), 2 x 11½p (left phos band),
2 x 11½p (right phos band) (left margin)
printed by Harrison, 1981; Penny Black cover 4.00
6 x 14p (two phos bands), 2 x 11½p (left phos band),
2 x 11½p (right phos band) (left margin)
printed by Harrison, 1981; Downey Head cover 5.00
6 x 14p (two phos bands), 2 x 11½p (left phos band),
2 x 11½p (right phos band) (right margin)
printed by Harrison, 1981; Downey Head cover 15.50

■ **£1.30 booklets. Trams series**
10 x 13p (one centre band)
printed by Harrison, 1984; Swansea Car cover 3.25
10 x 13p (one centre band)
printed by Harrison, 1985; Glasgow Car cover 3.25
10 x 13p (one centre band)
printed by Harrison, 1985; Blackpool Car cover 3.25
10 x 13p (one centre band)
printed by Harrison, 1985; London Car cover 3.25

■ **£1.30 booklets. Special Offers series**
10 x 13p (one centre band)
printed by Harrison, 1986; Books For Children offer 3.00
10 x 13p (one centre band)
printed by Harrison, 1987; 'Keep In Touch' Pack offer 3.00
10 x 13p (one centre band)
printed by Harrison, 1987; 'Ideas For Your Garden' offer 3.00
10 x 13p (one centre band)
printed by Harrison, 1987; 'Brighter Writer' Pack offer 3.00
10 x 13p (one centre band)
printed by Harrison, 1987; 'Jolly Postman' Pack offer 3.00
10 x 13p (one centre band)
printed by Harrison, 1988; Natural History Postcards offer 3.50

10 x 13p (one centre band)
printed by Harrison, 1988; Recipe Cards offer 3.00
10 x 13p (one centre band)
printed by Harrison, 1988; Children's Party Pack offer 3.00

■ **£1.40 booklets. Industrial Archaeology series**
10 x 14p (phos-coated paper)
printed by Harrison, 1981; Preston Mill cover 3.00
10 x 14p (phos-coated paper)
printed by Harrison, 1981; Talyllyn Railway cover 3.00

■ **£1.40 booklets. Women's Costumes series**
10 x 14p (phos-coated paper)
printed by Harrison, 1981; Costumes of 1800–1815 cover 3.00
10 x 14p (phos-coated paper)
printed by Harrison, 1981; Costumes of 1815–1830 cover 4.00

■ **£1.40 booklet. Special Offers series**
10 x 14p (phos-coated paper)
printed by Harrison, 1988; Pocket Planner offer 3.00

■ **£1.40 booklet. Fox Talbot Photography**
10 x 14p (phos-coated paper)
printed by Harrison, 1989; photography equipment cover 3.50

■ **£1.43 booklets. Postal History series**
6 x 15½p (two bands), 2 x 12½p (left band), 2 x 12½p (right band)
printed by Harrison, 1982; James Chalmers cover 3.00
6 x 15½p (two bands), 2 x 12½p (left band), 2 x 12½p (right band)
printed by Harrison, 1982; Edmund Dulac cover 3.00
6 x 15½p (two bands), 2 x 12½p (left band), 2 x 12½p (right band)
printed by Harrison, 1982; Forces Postal Service cover 3.00
6 x 15½p (two bands), 2 x 12½p (left band), 2 x 12½p (right band)
printed by Harrison, 1982; £5 Orange cover 3.00
6 x 15½p (two bands), 2 x 12½p (left band), 2 x 12½p (right band)
printed by Harrison, 1983; Postmark History cover 3.00

FOLDED BOOKLETS

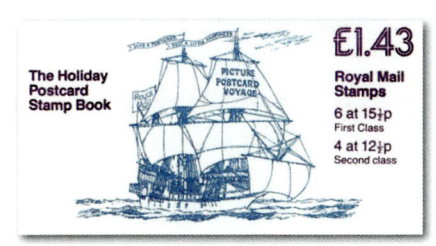

■ £1.43 booklets. Holiday Postcard Stamp Book
6 x 15½p (two bands), 2 x 12½p (left band),
2 x 12½p (right band)
printed by Harrison, 1982; Golden Hinde cover — 3.75

■ £1.45 booklet. Britain's Countryside
10 x 16p (phos-coated paper, 'D' printed on the gummed side) printed by Harrison, 1983; Lyme Regis cover — 4.75
(*This booklet was sold at a discount of 15p off face value.)

■ £1.46 booklets. Postal History series
6 x 16p (two bands), 2 x 12½p (left band), 2 x 12½p (right band)
printed by Harrison, 1983; Seahorses cover — 5.75
6 x 16p (two bands), 2 x 12½p (left band), 2 x 12½p (right band)
printed by Harrison, 1983; Parcel Post cover — 5.00
6 x 16p (two bands), 2 x 12½p (left band), 2 x 12½p (right band)
printed by Harrison, 1983; Regional Stamps cover — 5.00
(*Panes have either four 12½p followed by one 16p on the bottom row, or one 16p followed by four 12½p.)

■ £1.50 booklets. Special Offers series
6 x 17p (two bands), 2 x 12p (left band), 2 x 12p (right band)
printed by Harrison, 1986; 'Write Now' letter pack offer — 4.20
6 x 17p (two bands), 2 x 12p (left band), 2 x 12p (right band)
printed by Harrison, 1986; National Gallery offer — 4.20
6 x 17p (two bands), 2 x 12p (left band), 2 x 12p (right band)
printed by Harrison, 1986; 'No' Graphology offer — 4.20
(*Panes have either four 12p followed by one 17p on the bottom row, or one 17p followed by four 12p.)

■ £1.54 booklets. Postal History series
6 x 17p (two bands), 2 x 13p (left band), 2 x 13p (right band)
printed by Harrison, 1984; To Pay Labels cover — 3.00
6 x 17p (two bands), 2 x 13p (left band), 2 x 13p (right band)
printed by Harrison, 1985; Embossed Stamps cover — 3.00
6 x 17p (two bands), 2 x 13p (left band), 2 x 13p (right band)
printed by Harrison, 1985; Surface-Printed Stamps cover — 3.00
6 x 17p (two bands), 2 x 13p (left band), 2 x 13p (right band)
printed by Harrison, 1985; 350 Years of Service cover — 3.00
(*Panes have either four 13p followed by one 17p on the bottom row, or one 17p followed by four 13p.)

■ £1.55 booklets. Women's Costumes series
10 x 15½p (phos-coated paper)
printed by Harrison, 1982; Costumes of 1830–1850 cover — 3.00
10 x 15½p (phos-coated paper)
printed by Harrison, 1982; Costumes of 1850–1860 cover — 3.00
10 x 15½p (phos-coated paper)
printed by Harrison, 1982; Costumes of 1860–1880 cover — 3.00
10 x 15½p (phos-coated paper)
printed by Harrison, 1982; Costumes of 1880–1900 cover — 3.00

■ £1.55 booklet. Social Letter Writing series
10 x 17p (phos-coated paper, 'D' printed on gummed side)
printed by Harrison, 1985; Paper Boat and Plane cover — 6.00
(*This booklet was sold at a discount of 15p off face value.)

BRITISH STAMP MARKET VALUES 2024   273

BOOKLETS FOLDED

■ £1.60 booklets. Special Offers series
10 x 16p (phos-coated paper)
printed by Harrison, 1983; Birthday Box offer   4.00
10 x 16p (phos-coated paper)
printed by Harrison, 1984; 'Write It' wallet offer   4.00

■ £1.60 booklet. Britain's Countryside series
10 x 16p (phos-coated paper)
printed by Harrison, 1983; Weavers' Cottages cover   4.00

■ £1.70 booklets. Social Letter Writing series
10 x 17p (phos-coated paper)
printed by Harrison, 1984; Love Letters cover   4.00
10 x 17p (phos-coated paper)
printed by Harrison, 1984; Fan Letters cover   4.00

■ £1.70 booklets. Special Offers series
10 x 17p (phos-coated paper)
printed by Harrison, 1985; 'Write Now' pack offer   4.00
10 x 17p (phos-coated paper)
printed by Harrison, 1986; National Gallery offer   4.00
10 x 17p (phos-coated paper)
printed by Harrison, 1986; 'Yes' Graphology offer   4.00

■ £1.80 booklets. Special Offers series
10 x 18p (phos-coated paper)
printed by Harrison, 1986; Books For Children offer   4.25
10 x 18p (phos-coated paper)
printed by Harrison, 1987; 'Keep In Touch' Pack offer   4.25
10 x 18p (phos-coated paper)
printed by Harrison, 1987; 'Ideas For Your Garden' offer   4.25
10 x 18p (phos-coated paper)
printed by Harrison, 1987; 'Brighter Writer' Pack offer   4.25
10 x 18p (phos-coated paper)
printed by Harrison, 1987; 'Jolly Postman' Pack offer   4.25
10 x 18p (phos-coated paper)
printed by Harrison, 1988; Natural History Postcards offer   4.25
10 x 18p (phos-coated paper)
printed by Harrison, 1988; Recipe Cards offer   4.25
10 x 18p (phos-coated paper)
printed by Harrison, 1988; Children's Party Pack offer   4.25

■ £1.90 booklet. Special Offers series
10 x 19p
printed by Harrison, 1988; Pocket Planner offer   4.50

■ £1.90 booklet. Fox Talbot Photography
10 x 19p
printed by Harrison, 1989; Fox Talbot with camera cover   4.50

COUNTER BOOKLETS OF ROYAL MAIL COMMEMORATIVES, 1985

■ £1.53 booklet. 350th Anniversary of Royal Mail Service to the Public
10 x 17p 350th Anniversary stamp ('D' pattern on gummed side)
printed by Harrison, 1985; van, plane, Concorde cover   4.00
(*This booklet was sold at a discount of 17p off face value.)

274 BRITISH STAMP MARKET VALUES 2024

HWI

For your philatelic insurance requirements, contact H W Wood Limited, the preferred insurance broker for stamp collectors and dealers worldwide.

Whether you require insurance at home, for your business, at exhibitions and/or in transit*, we have a range of tailored insurance products to best cater to your needs.
Please contact us using the information below.

Telephone: +44 (0)20 7398 9000
Email: collectibles@hwint.com
Visit us online at www.hwinternational.com/uk/

European based clients are looked after by HWI Europe, a branch of HWI France, based in the UK.
Email: fineart@hwieurope.com

(*transit only cover not available, terms and conditions apply).

"Australia - 1953 Queen Elizabeth The Second Coronation Die Proofs dated in Note Printing Branch handstamps on the reverse - '28-8-53'. Recipient of proof: Director-General Chippendall of the Postmaster-General Department."

"Jamaica -2nd June 1953 'Coronation' - Design Bradbury Wilkinson: Printed by De La Rue, Watermark Multiple Script C4. Perforation 13 1/2 x 13

H W Wood Limited is authorised and regulated by the Financial Conduct Authority (FCA).
FCA register number 309408. For confirmation of our regulatory status please visit the FCA website www.fca.org.uk
HWI France is registered in the UK, with Companies House No. BR021326. Registered Office, 1 Lloyd's Avenue, London EC3N 3DQ
Authorised by the FCA with FRN; 972814

BOOKLETS RETAIL, GUMMED

RETAIL STAMP BOOKS

In this section, items are priced in mint condition only.

These booklets were intended to be sold not only over post office counters, but also through alternative retail outlets. All have a barcode on the outside back cover, and contain stamps with conventional gum.

BOOKLETS OF DEFINITIVES WITHOUT ELLIPTICAL PERFORATIONS, 1987–93

Booklets with a 'window' in the cover, through which one of the stamps can be seen, and with the panes surrounded by a white margin.

■ **4 x 13p**
August 4, 1987. Printed by Harrison — 2.75

■ **10 x 13p**
August 4, 1987. Printed by Harrison — 3.75

■ **4 x 14p**
August 23, 1988. Printed by Harrison — 4.00
October 11, 1988. Stamps by Harrison; cover by Walsall — 5.25

■ **10 x 14p**
August 23, 1988. Printed by Harrison — 9.50
October 11, 1988. Printed by Questa — 10.00

■ **4 x 18p**
August 4, 1987. Printed by Harrison — 3.00

■ **10 x 18p**
August 4, 1987. Printed by Harrison — 5.00

■ **4 x 19p**
August 23, 1988. Printed by Harrison — 4.25
October 11, 1988. Stamps by Harrison; cover by Walsall — 4.50

■ **10 x 19p**
August 23, 1988. Printed by Harrison — 7.00

October 11, 1988. Printed by Questa — 12.50

■ **4 x 26p**
August 4, 1987. Printed by Harrison — 10.00

■ **4 x 27p**
August 23, 1988. Printed by Harrison — 8.00

Booklets with an illustration of the contents in place of the 'window' on the cover, containing panes with no margin, and with either the top and bottom or all three edges imperforate.

■ **4 x 14p**
October 11, 1988. Printed by Harrison — 4.50
January 24, 1989. Stamps by printed Harrison, cover printed by Walsall — 19.50

■ **10 x 14p**
October 11, 1988. Printed by Harrison — 9.00
October 11, 1988. Printed by Questa — 11.00

■ **4 x 19p**
October 11, 1988. Printed by Harrison — 5.00
January 24, 1989. Stamps by printed Harrison, cover printed by Walsalll — 19.50

■ **10 x 19p**
October 11, 1988. Printed by Harrison — 7.00
October 11, 1988. Printed by Questa — 12.50

■ **4 x 27p**
October 11, 1988. Printed by Harrison — 18.00

■ **4 x 29p**
October 2, 1989. Printed by Walsall (two phos bands) — 9.00
April 17, 1990. Printed by Walsall (phos paper) — 10.50

■ **4 x 31p**
September 17, 1990. Printed by Walsall — 4.00

■ **4 x 33p**
September 16, 1991. Printed by Walsall — 4.00
September 8, 1992. Printed by Walsall (yellow strip at right is inscribed 'For Worldwide Postcards') — 7.00

RETAIL, GUMMED BOOKLETS

■ **2 x 39p**
July 28, 1992. Printed by Harrison — 2.50

■ **4 x 39p**
September 16, 1991. Printed by Walsall — 6.00

Booklets with an illustration of the contents on the cover, containing non-value indicator stamps in panes with no margin, and with either the top and bottom edges or all three edges imperforate.

■ **4 x 2nd bright blue**
August 22, 1989. Printed by Walsall	6.00
November 28, 1989. Stamps printed by Harrison; cover by Walsall	22.00
August 6, 1991. Printed by Walsall Cover features Royal Mail cruciform	5.00
January 21, 1992. Printed by Walsall Cover features logos of Olympic and Paralympic Games	5.00

■ **10 x 2nd bright blue**
August 22, 1989. Printed by Harrison	10.00
September 19, 1989. Printed by Questa	10.00
August 6, 1991. Printed by Walsall Cover features Royal Mail cruciform	10.00
August 6, 1991. Printed by Questa Cover features Royal Mail cruciform	10.00
January 21, 1992. Printed by Walsall Cover features logos of Olympic and Paralympic Games	10.00
March 31, 1992. Printed by Questa Cover features logos of Olympic and Paralympic Games	10.00
September 22, 1992. Printed by Harrison Cover features Royal Mail cruciform	10.00

■ **4 x 2nd deep blue**
August 7, 1990. Printed by Walsall — 5.00

■ **10 x 2nd deep blue**
August 7, 1990. Printed by Harrison	10.00
August 7, 1990. Printed by Questa	10.00
August 7, 1990. Printed by Walsall	10.00

■ **4 x 1st brownish-black**
August 22, 1989. Printed by Walsall	7.75
December 5, 1989. Stamps by Harrison; cover by Walsall	25.00

■ **10 x 1st brownish-black**
August 22, 1989. Printed by Harrison	13.00
September 19, 1989. Printed by Questa	13.00

■ **4 x 1st orange-red**
August 7, 1990. Printed by Walsall	6.00
August 7, 1990. Printed by Walsall. Perf: 13	10.00
January 21, 1992. Printed by Walsall Cover features logos of Olympic and Paralympic Games	6.00

■ **10 x 1st orange-red**
August 7, 1990. Printed by Harrison	13.00
August 7, 1990. Printed by Questa	13.00
August 7, 1990. Printed by Walsall	13.00
January 21, 1992. Printed by Harrison Cover features logos of Olympic and Paralympic Games	13.00
January 21, 1992. Printed by Walsall Cover features logos of Olympic and Paralympic Games	13.00
February 9, 1993. Printed by Walsall Cover features Royal Mail cruciform; back cover has advertisement for Greetings stamps	13.00

BOOKLETS OF PENNY BLACK ANNIVERSARY DEFINITIVES, 1990

Booklets with an illustration of the contents on the cover, containing denominated stamps in panes with all four edges perforated, or with either two or three edges imperforate.

■ **4 x 15p**
January 30, 1990. Printed by Walsall — 4.50

■ **10 x 15p**
January 30, 1990. Printed by Harrison	6.00
April 17, 1990. Printed by Questa	11.00
June 12, 1990. Printed by Walsall	6.50

■ **4 x 20p**
January 30, 1990. Printed by Walsall	5.00
April 17, 1990. Stamps by Harrison; cover by Walsall	12.00

■ **10 x 20p**
January 30, 1990. Printed by Harrison	6.25
April 17, 1990. Printed by Questa	12.00
June 12, 1990. Printed by Walsall	10.00

BOOKLETS RETAIL, GUMMED

BOOKLETS OF DEFINITIVES WITH ELLIPTICAL PERFORATIONS, 1993–2000

■ 4 x 2nd bright blue
April 6, 1993. Printed by Walsall
Cover shows a single stamp — 5.00
September 7, 1993. Printed by Harrison
Cover shows a single stamp — 5.00
January 10, 1995. Printed by Harrison
Cover has white lines through block of stamps — 5.00
December 12, 1995. Printed by Walsall
Cover shows block of stamps — 5.00
February 6, 1996. Printed by Walsall
Back cover features Olympic symbols — 5.00
February 4, 1997. Printed by Walsall (litho)
Cover has no line through block of stamps — 5.00
August 26, 1997. Printed by Walsall (gravure)
Cover has no line through block of stamps — 5.00

■ 10 x 2nd bright blue
April 6, 1993. Printed by Questa
Cover shows a single stamp — 10.00
November 1, 1993. Printed by Walsall
Cover shows a single stamp — 10.00
January 10, 1995. Printed by Questa
Cover has white lines through block of stamps — 10.00
December 12, 1995. Printed by Harrison
Cover shows block of stamps — 10.00
February 6, 1996. Printed by Harrison
Back cover features Olympic symbols — 10.00
February 6, 1996. Printed by Questa
Back cover features Olympic symbols — 10.00
August 6, 1996. Printed by Harrison
Cover has no white line through block of stamps
Back cover features Olympic symbols — 10.00
August 6, 1996. Printed by Questa
Cover has no white line through block of stamps
Back cover features Olympic symbols — 10.00
February 4, 1997. Printed by Harrison
Cover has no white line through block of stamps — 10.00
February 4, 1997. Printed by Questa
Cover has no white line through block of stamps — 10.00
May 5, 1998. Printed by De La Rue
Cover has no white line through block of stamps — 10.00
December 1, 1998. Printed by Questa (gravure)
Cover has no white line through block of stamps — 10.00

■ 4 x 1st orange-red
April 6, 1993. Printed by Harrison
Cover shows a single stamp — 6.00
August 17, 1993. Printed by Walsall
Cover shows a single stamp — 6.00
January 10, 1995. Printed by Walsall
Cover has white lines through block of stamps — 6.00
February 6, 1996. Printed by Walsall
Back cover features Olympic symbols — 6.00
February 4, 1997. Printed by Walsall (litho)
Cover has no white line through block of stamps — 6.00
August 26, 1997. Printed by Walsall (gravure)
Cover has no white line through block of stamps — 6.00

■ 4 x 1st orange-red
with commemorative label
July 27, 1994. Printed by Questa
Label marks 300th anniversary of Bank of England — 6.00
May 16, 1995. Printed by Walsall
Label marks centenary of birth of R. J. Mitchell — 6.00
April 16, 1996. Printed by Walsall
Label marks 70th birthday of Queen Elizabeth II — 6.00
February 12, 1997. Printed by Walsall
Label marks Hong Kong '97 stamp exhibition — 6.00
October 21, 1997. Printed by Walsall
Label marks Commonwealth Heads of Government Meeting — 6.25
November 14, 1998. Printed by Walsall
Label marks 50th birthday of the Prince of Wales — 6.00
May 12, 1999. Printed by Walsall
Label marks 50th anniversary of the Berlin Airlift — 6.00
October 1, 1999. Printed by Walsall
Label marks the Rugby World Cup — 6.00
(*Stamp cards were produced illustrating the Bank of England, R. J. Mitchell, Elizabeth II, Berlin Airlift and Rugby World Cup labels; price £10–£16 each mint, £35 postally used.)

■ 4 x 1st olive-brown
with commemorative label
March 21, 2000. Printed by Walsall
Label shows Postman Pat — 6.00
April 4, 2000. Printed by Walsall
Label shows National Botanic Garden of Wales — 6.00
(*Stamp cards were produced illustrating the Postman Pat and National Botanic Garden of Wales labels; price £13–£16 mint, £30–£35 postally used.)

RETAIL, GUMMED BOOKLETS

■ **10 x 1st orange-red**

April 6, 1993. Printed by Harrison
Cover shows a single stamp — 13.00
April 6, 1993. Printed by Walsall
Cover shows a single stamp — 13.00
November 1, 1993. Printed by Questa
Cover shows a single stamp — 13.00
November 1, 1993. Printed by Walsall
Back cover has advertisement for Greetings stamps — 13.00
February 22, 1994. Printed by Walsall
Yellow strip has 'Free postcards' — 13.00
July 1, 1994. Printed by Walsall
Yellow strip has 'Open now, chance to win a kite', and inside back cover has 'Better luck next time' — 13.00
July 1, 1994. Printed by Walsall
Yellow strip has 'Open now, chance to win a kite', and inside back cover has 'You've won' — 13.00
September 20, 1994. Printed by Walsall
Cover has 'Stampers' and 'Do not open until' — 13.00
September 20, 1994. Printed by Walsall
Cover has 'Stampers' and 'Keep in touch' — 13.00
September 20, 1994. Printed by Walsall
Cover has 'Stampers' and 'Happy birthday' — 13.00
September 20, 1994. Printed by Walsall
Cover has 'Stampers' and 'What's happenin'?' — 13.00
January 10, 1995. Printed by Harrison
Cover has white lines through block of stamps — 13.00
January 10, 1995. Printed by Questa
Cover has white lines through block of stamps — 13.00
January 10, 1995. Printed by Walsall
Cover has white lines through block of stamps — 13.00
February 14, 1995. Printed by Walsall
Cover has 'Brighten up someone's day' — 13.00
April 4, 1995. Printed by Harrison
Stamps have two phosphor bands — 13.00
April 24, 1995. Printed by Walsall
Yellow strip has 'W H Smith Special Offer' — 13.00
June 26, 1995. Printed by Questa
Yellow strip has 'Sainsbury's Promotion' — 13.00
September 4, 1995. Printed by Harrison
Cover shows Benjy Bear and Harry Hedgehog — 13.00
February 6, 1996. Printed by Walsall
Back cover features Olympic symbols — 13.00
February 19, 1996. Printed by Harrison
Cover shows Walt Disney World — 13.00
March 19, 1996. Printed by Harrison
Back cover features Olympic symbols — 13.00
May 13, 1996. Printed by Harrison
Cover has 'Will you be at the Olympics?'
Back cover shows shot put — 13.00
May 13, 1996. Printed by Harrison
Cover has 'Will you be at the Olympics?'
Back cover shows hurdling — 13.00
May 13, 1996. Printed by Harrison
Cover has 'Will you be at the Olympics?'
Back cover shows archery — 13.00
July 15, 1996. Printed by Walsall
Yellow strip has 'W H Smith Offer Inside' — 13.00
August 16, 1996. Printed by Harrison
Cover has no white line through block of stamps — 13.00

Back cover features Olympic symbols — 13.00
August 16, 1996. Printed by Walsall
Cover has no white line through block of stamps
Back cover features Olympic symbols — 13.00
September 9, 1996. Printed by Walsall
Cover shows iced cakes — 13.00
October 7, 1996. Printed by Walsall
Yellow strip has 'Offer Inside' — 13.00
February 4, 1997. Printed by Harrison
Cover has no white line through block of stamps — 13.00
February 4, 1997. Printed by Walsall (litho)
Cover has no white line through block of stamps — 13.00
November 8, 1997. Printed by Walsall (gravure)
Cover has no white line through block of stamps — 13.00
February 2, 1998. Printed by De La Rue
Cover has 'Win an adventure holiday' — 13.00
April 27, 1998. Printed by De La Rue
Cover has 'Stick one of these on your drive' — 13.00
May 5, 1998. Printed by De La Rue
Cover has no white line through block of stamps — 13.00
July 1, 1998. Printed by De La Rue
Cover has 'Zoom out with one of these' — 13.00
August 3, 1998. Printed by De La Rue
Cover inscribed 'Make their post memorable' — 13.00
September 7, 1998. Printed by Questa (litho)
Cover has no white line through block of stamps — 13.00
December 1, 1998. Printed by Questa (gravure)
Cover has no white line through block of stamps — 13.00

■ **10 x 1st gold**

April 21, 1997. Printed by Harrison
Cover shows a block of stamps — 13.00
April 21, 1997. Printed by Walsall
Cover shows a block of stamps — 13.00
September 15, 1997. Printed by Harrison
Cover shows a beach, and 'First class travel' — 13.00

■ **10 x 1st olive-brown**

January 6, 2000. Printed by Questa
Cover shows a block of stamps — 13.00
January 6, 2000. Printed by Walsall
Cover shows a block of stamps — 13.00

■ **4 x E dark blue**

January 19, 1999. Printed by Walsall
Cover shows a block of stamps and
'By Air Mail' label — 11.00

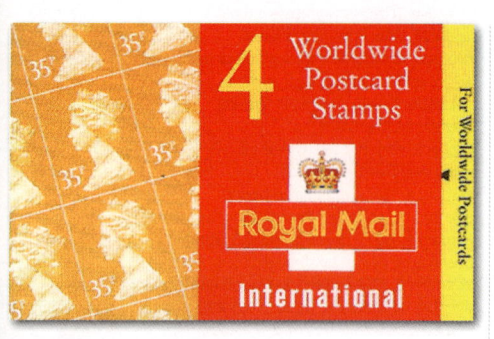

BOOKLETS RETAIL, GUMMED

■ **4 x 30p**
May 5, 1998. Printed by Walsall
Cover shows a block of stamps 3.00
August 3, 1998. Printed by Walsall
Cover inscribed 'Make their post memorable' 3.00

■ **4 x 35p**
November 1, 1993. Printed by Walsall
Cover shows a single stamp 4.25
May 16, 1995. Printed by Walsall
Cover shows a block of stamps 4.00
March 19, 1996. Printed by Walsall
Back cover features Olympic symbols 4.00

■ **4 x 37p**
July 8, 1996. Printed by Walsall
Back cover features Olympic symbols 5.25
February 4, 1997. Printed by Walsall
Back cover features no Olympic symbols 5.25
August 26, 1997. Printed by Walsall
Cover shows street names in London 4.00
August 3, 1998. Printed by Walsall
Cover inscribed 'Make their post memorable' 4.00

■ **4 x 38p**
April 26, 1999. Printed by Walsall
Cover shows a block of stamps 4.00

■ **4 x 40p**
April 27, 2000. Printed by Walsall
Cover shows a block of stamps 4.00

■ **4 x 41p**
November 1, 1993. Printed by Walsall
Cover shows a single stamp 4.00
May 16, 1995. Printed by Walsall
Cover shows a block of stamps 4.00
March 19, 1996. Printed by Walsall
Back cover features Olympic symbols 4.00

■ **4 x 60p**
August 9, 1994. Printed by Walsall
Cover shows a single stamp 5.50
October 4, 1994. Printed by Walsall
Cover inscribed 'Worldwide Airmail Stamps' 5.00

May 16, 1995. Printed by Walsall
Cover shows a block of stamps 5.00
March 19, 1996. Printed by Walsall
Back cover features Olympic symbols 5.00

■ **4 x 63p**
July 8, 1996. Printed by Walsall
Back cover features Olympic symbols 8.00
February 4, 1997. Printed by Walsall (litho)
Cover shows a block of stamps 8.00
August 26, 1997. Printed by Walsall (gravure)
Cover shows a block of stamps 5.00
May 5, 1998. Printed by Walsall
Cover shows airmail label below block of stamps 5.00

■ **4 x 64p**
April 26, 1999. Printed by Walsall
Cover shows a block of stamps 6.00

■ **4 x 65p**
April 27, 2000. Printed by Walsall
Cover shows a block of stamps 6.00

BOOKLETS OF DEFINITIVES & MILLENNIUM COMMEMORATIVES, 1999–2000

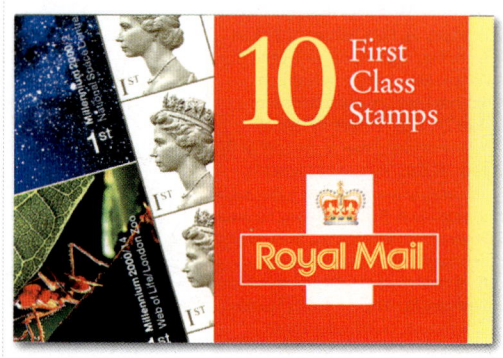

■ **8 x 1st orange–red, 1 x 26p Settlers' Tale, 1 x 26p Workers' Tale**
May 12, 1999. Printed by Walsall 14.00

■ **8 x 1st orange–red, 2 x 26p Farmers' Tale**
September 21, 1999. Printed by Walsall 14.00

■ **8 x 1st olive–brown, 1 x 1st Above & Beyond, 1 x 1st Life & Earth**
May 26, 2000. Printed by Walsall 14.00

■ **8 x 1st olive–brown, 1 x 1st Stone & Soil, 1 x 1st Tree & Leaf**
September 5, 2000. Printed by Walsall 14.00

JERWOOD PHILATELICS

(Established 2010)

Established dealer specialising in:

* Stitched Booklets
* Folded Booklets
* Window Booklets
* Prestige Booklets
* Greetings & Christmas Booklets
* Machins, including Cylinder, Date Blocks etc.
* Smilers™ Sheets, inc. Business Customised Sheets
* Post & Go™ stamps
* Modern commemoratives, inc. errors & varieties
* Royal Mail Year Books & Year Packs
* Accessories, including stockcards, mounts etc.
* Selected material from earlier reigns

Collections & quality single items bought

Detailed booklet listings using both the Stanley Gibbons and Modern British Philatelic Circle catalogues.

Website: www.jerwoodphilatelics.co.uk
Email: dave@jerwoodphilatelics.co.uk
Telephone: (0121) 249 5277

Insert bsmv24 at checkout to receive a 10% discount on any order over £25. Free P&P on all UK orders.

MBPC catalogue numbers are used with kind permission. For more information on the Circle's activities and benefits of membership, please visit www.mbp-circle.co.uk

Member of the Philatelic Traders Society
(Membership Number: 6026)

BOOKLETS RETAIL, SELF-ADHESIVE

SELF-ADHESIVE BOOKLETS

In this section, items are priced in mint condition only.
These booklets were sold over post office counters and other retail outlets. All have a barcode on the back cover.

BOOKLETS OF SELF-ADHESIVE DEFINITIVES, 1993–2010

Booklets with experimental format.

■ **20 x 1st orange–red**
October 19, 1993. Printed by Walsall — 24.00

Booklets with a mainly red cover, and an illustration of the contents.

■ **6 x 2nd bright blue**
January 29, 2001. Printed by Walsall — 6.50

■ **10 x 2nd bright blue**
January 29, 2001. Printed by Questa — 10.00

■ **12 x 2nd bright blue**
January 29, 2001. Printed by Questa — 13.00

■ **6 x 1st orange–red and commemorative label**
January 29, 2001. Printed by Walsall
Label marks centenary of the death of Queen Victoria — 12.00

■ **6 x 1st orange–red**
January 29, 2001. Printed by Walsall — 8.00
July 4, 2002. Printed by Questa — 8.00

■ **10 x 1st orange–red**
January 29, 2001. Printed by Questa — 13.00

■ **12 x 1st orange–red**
January 29, 2001. Printed by Questa — 16.00
January 29, 2001. Printed by Walsall — 16.00

Booklets with a cover the colour of the stamps, and with one notch (1st class), two notches (2nd class) or no notches (other values) along the right hand edge.

■ **12 x 2nd bright blue**
July 4, 2002. Printed by Questa — 13.00
March 27, 2003. Printed by Walsall
Inscription 'The Real Network' under Royal Mail cruciform — 13.00
June 15, 2004. Printed by Walsall
No 'The Real Network' inscription — 13.00
June 5, 2007. Printed by Walsall
Includes PiP information — 13.00

■ **6 x 1st gold**
June 5, 2002. Printed by Questa — 8.00
June 5, 2002. Printed by Walsall — 8.00
March 27, 2003. Printed by Walsall
Inscription 'The Real Network' under Royal Mail cruciform — 8.00
June 15, 2004. Printed by Walsall
Inscription 'Supporting London 2012' — 8.00
March 22, 2005. Printed by Walsall
Advertisement for Smilers on inside front cover — 8.00
June 5, 2007. Printed by Walsall
Includes PiP information — 8.00
June 5, 2007. Printed by Walsall
Includes facsimile of Arnold Machin's signature — 8.00
August 28, 2007. Printed by Walsall
Advertisement for Harry Potter stamps — 8.00
September 29, 2007. Printed by Walsall
Improved postcode information — 8.00
June 10, 2008. Printed by Walsall
Advertisement for Classic Carry On & Hammer stamps — 8.00

■ **12 x 1st gold**
June 5, 2002. Printed by Walsall — 16.00
March 27, 2003. Printed by Walsall
Inscription 'The Real Network' under Royal Mail cruciform — 16.00
June 5, 2007. Printed by Walsall
Includes PiP information — 16.00

RETAIL, SELF-ADHESIVE BOOKLETS

■ 6 x E
July 4, 2002. Printed by Walsall 16.00
May 28, 2003. Printed by Walsall
Inscription 'The Real Network' under Royal Mail cruciform 16.00

■ 6 x 42p
July 4, 2002. Printed by Walsall 25.00
May 28, 2003. Printed by Walsall
Inscription 'The Real Network' under Royal Mail cruciform 25.00

■ 6 x 68p
July 4, 2002. Printed by Walsall 26.00
May 28, 2003. Printed by Walsall
Inscription 'The Real Network' under Royal Mail cruciform 26.00

■ 4 x Europe up to 20g
March 30, 2010. Printed by Walsall 10.50

■ 4 x Europe up to 40g
March 27, 2003. Printed by Walsall
Inscription 'The Real Network' under Royal Mail cruciform 11.00
June 15, 2004. Printed by Walsall
No 'The Real Network' inscription 11.00

■ 4 x Worldwide up to 20g
April 1, 2004. Printed by Walsall 10.50
March 30, 2010. Printed by Walsall 10.50

■ 4 x Worldwide up to 40g
March 27, 2003. Printed by Walsall
Inscription 'The Real Network' under Royal Mail cruciform 14.00
June 15, 2004. Printed by Walsall
No 'The Real Network' inscription 14.00

BOOKLETS OF SELF-ADHESIVE DEFINITIVES & COMMEMORATIVES, 2001–2008

Booklets with a cover design illustrating or alluding to the special stamps inside.

■ 2 x 1st orange-red, 10 x 1st Cats & Dogs
February 13, 2001. Printed by Walsall 25.00

■ 4 x 1st orange-red, 2 x 1st Submarines
April 17, 2001. Printed by Questa 67.50

■ 4 x 1st orange-red, 2 x 1st Punch & Judy
September 4, 2001. Printed by Questa 15.00

■ 4 x 1st orange-red, 2 x 1st Flags & Ensigns
October 22, 2001. Printed by Questa 15.00

■ 4 x 1st orange-red, 2 x 1st Airliners
May 2, 2002. Printed by Questa 8.00

■ 4 x 1st orange-red, 2 x 1st Football World Cup
May 21, 2002. Printed by Questa 8.00

■ 4 x 1st gold, 2 x 1st Bridges of London
September 10, 2002. Printed by Questa 8.00

■ 4 x 1st gold, 2 x 1st Hello!
March 4, 2003. Printed by Questa 8.00

■ 4 x 1st gold, 2 x 1st Extreme Endeavours
April 29, 2003. Printed by De La Rue 8.00

■ 4 x 1st gold, 2 x 1st British Journey: Scotland
July 15, 2003. Printed by De La Rue 8.00

■ 4 x 1st gold, 2 x 1st Toys
September 18, 2003. Printed by De La Rue 8.00

■ 4 x 1st gold, 2 x 1st British Journey: Northern Ireland
March 16, 2004. Printed by De La Rue 8.00

■ 4 x 1st gold, 2 x 1st Ocean Liners
April 13, 2004. Printed by De La Rue 8.00

BOOKLETS RETAIL, SELF-ADHESIVE

■ **4 x 1st gold, 2 x 1st British Journey: Wales**
June 15, 2004. Printed by De La Rue   8.00

■ **4 x 1st gold, 2 x 1st Beside The Seaside**
March 13, 2008. Printed by Walsall   8.00

BOOKLETS OF SELF-ADHESIVE SMILERS STAMPS, 2005–15

■ **6 x 1st Smilers stamps of October 4, 2005**
October 4, 2005. Printed by Walsall   10.00
July 17, 2006. Printed by Walsall. With PiP information.   10.50

■ **6 x 1st Smilers stamps of October 17, 2006**
October 17, 2006. Printed by Walsall   10.00

■ **1 x 1st 'Love', 5 x 1st gold**
January 16, 2007. Printed by Walsall   17.50

■ **2 x 1st 'Love', 4 x 1st gold**
January 15, 2008. Printed by Walsall   7.50

■ **6 x 1st Smilers stamps of 2005 and 2006**
February 28, 2008. Printed by Walsall   32.00

■ **12 x 1st Smilers stamps of 2015**
January 6, 2015. Printed by ISP   25.00

BOOKLETS OF SELF-ADHESIVE PRICING-IN-PROPORTION STAMPS, 2006–07

■ **12 x 2nd bright blue**
September 12, 2006. Printed by Walsall   13.00

■ **4 x 2nd Large bright blue**
August 15, 2006. Printed by Walsall   7.00

■ **6 x 1st gold**
September 12, 2006. Printed by Walsall   7.50
February 1, 2007. Printed by Walsall
With postcode advertisement inside front cover   8.00

■ **12 x 1st gold**
September 12, 2006. Printed by Walsall   16.00

■ **4 x 1st Large gold**
August 15, 2006. Printed by Walsall   11.00

BOOKLETS OF SELF-ADHESIVE SECURITY DEFINITIVES, 2009–16

■ **12 x 2nd blue**
March 31, 2009. Printed by Walsall
Back cover includes printer's name   13.00
August 19, 2010. Printed by Walsall
Back cover has printer's name removed   13.50
October 25, 2011. Printed by Walsall
Back cover includes FSC logo   13.00
2012 year code   18.00
2013 year code   17.50
2014 year code   14.00
2015 year code   17.50
2015. Printed by ISP. Security backing paper   80.00
2016. Printed by ISP. Security backing paper   25.00

■ **4 x 2nd Large blue**
March 31, 2009. Printed by Walsall
Back cover includes printer's name   8.00
March 22, 2011. Printed by Walsall
Back cover has printer's name removed   8.00
October 25, 2011. Printed by Walsall
Back cover includes FSC logo   8.00
2012 year code   10.50
2013 year code   15.00
2014 year code   10.00
2015 year code   27.50
2016. Printed by ISP Security backing paper   22.00

RETAIL, SELF-ADHESIVE BOOKLETS

■ 6 x 1st gold
March 31, 2009. Printed by Walsall
Inside front cover has web address 'Postcodes4free' — 15.00
December 15, 2009. Printed by Walsall
Back cover has printer's name removed — 8.00
January 26, 2010. Printed by Walsall
Inside front cover has web address 'postcodes4free' — 10.00
March 30, 2010. Printed by Walsall
Inside front cover has publicity for Festival of Stamps — 10.00
October 25, 2011. Printed by Walsall
Back cover includes FSC logo — 11.50

■ 12 x 1st gold
March 31, 2009. Printed by Walsall
Back cover includes printer's name — 16.00
December 15, 2009. Printed by Walsall
Back cover has printer's name removed — 16.00
October 25, 2011. Printed by Walsall
Back cover includes FSC logo — 16.00

■ 4 x 1st Large gold
March 31, 2009. Printed by Walsall
Back cover includes printer's name — 11.00
March 22, 2011. Printed by Walsall
Back cover has printer's name removed — 8.50
October 25, 2011. Printed by Walsall
Back cover includes FSC logo — 8.00

■ 6 x 1st diamond blue
October 1, 2012. Printed by Walsall — 8.00

■ 12 x 1st diamond blue
February 6, 2012. Printed by Walsall — 16.00

■ 4 x 1st Large diamond blue
April 25, 2012. Printed by Walsall — 8.00

■ 6 x 1st red
January 3, 2013. Printed by Walsall
2012 year code — 8.00
2013 year code — 11.00
2014 year code — 11.00
2015 year code — 15.00

■ 12 x 1st red
January 3, 2013. Printed by Walsall
2012 year code — 17.00
2013 year code — 17.00
2014 year code — 17.00
2015 year code — 40.00
2015. Printed by ISP. Security backing paper — £100
2015. Printed by ISP. Security backing paper — 22.00

■ 4 x 1st Large red
January 3, 2013. Printed by Walsall
2012 year code — 8.00
2013 year code — 24.00
2014 year code — 40.00
2015 year code — 11.00
2015. Printed by ISP. Security backing paper — 25.00

2016. Printed by ISP. Security backing paper — 15.00

■ 6 x 1st amethyst purple
September 9, 2015. Printed by ISP
Label portraying the Queen. Plain backing paper — 8.00
2015 year code. Printed by ISP
Label portraying the Queen. Security backing paper — £165
2016 year code. Printed by ISP
Label portraying the Queen. Security backing paper — 27.00

BOOKLETS OF SELF-ADHESIVE SECURITY DEFINITIVES & COMMEMORATIVES, 2009–2016

■ 6 x 1st. British Design Classics
4 x 1st gold, 1 x 1st Telephone Kiosk, 1 x 1st Routemaster
March 10, 2009. Printed by Walsall — 8.00
4 x 1st gold, 2 x 1st Mini
April 21, 2009. Printed by Walsall — 8.00
4 x 1st gold, 2 x 1st Concorde
August 18, 2009. Printed by Walsall — 8.00
4 x 1st gold, 2 x 1st Mini Skirt
September 17, 2009. Printed by Walsall — 8.00
4 x 1st gold, 2 x 1st Spitfire
September 15, 2010. Printed by Walsall — 8.00

■ 6 x 1st. National Association of Flower Arrangement Societies
4 x 1st, gold 1 x 1st Iris latifolia, 1 x 1st Tulipa
May 21, 2009. Printed by Walsall — 16.00

■ 6 x 1st. Olympic and Paralympic Games
4 x 1st gold, 1 x 1st Paralympic Archery, 1 x 1st Judo
January 7, 2010. Printed by Walsall — 8.00
4 x 1st gold, 1 x 1st Track Athletics, 1 x 1st Basketball
February 25, 2010. Printed by Walsall — 8.00
4 x 1st gold, 1 x 1st Paralympic Rowing, 1 x 1st Table Tennis
July 27, 2010. Printed by Walsall — 8.00
4 x 1st gold, 1 x 1st Football, 1 x 1st Cycling
October 12, 2010. Printed by Walsall — 8.00
4 x 1st gold, 1 x 1st Wheelchair Rugby, 1 x 1st Paralympic Sailing
July 27, 2011. Printed by Walsall — 8.00
4 x 1st gold, 1 x 1st Gymnastics, 1 x 1st Fencing
September 15, 2011. Printed by Walsall — 8.00

BOOKLETS RETAIL, SELF-ADHESIVE

■ **6 x 1st. Mammals**
4 x 1st gold, 1 x 1st Otter, 1 x 1st Hedgehog
June 15, 2010. Printed by Walsall — 12.00

■ **6 x 1st. Thunderbirds**
4 x 1st gold, 2 x 1st Thunderbirds
January 11, 2011. Printed by Walsall — 8.00

■ **6 x 1st. Medical Breakthroughs**
4 x 1st gold, 2 x 1st Beta-Blockers
February 24, 2011. Printed by Walsall — 8.00

■ **6 x 1st. Thomas the Tank Engine**
4 x 1st gold, 2 x 1st Goodbye Bertie
June 14, 2011. Printed by Walsall — 8.00

■ **6 x 1st. Classic Locomotives of England**
4 x 1st gold, 2 x 1st BR Dean Goods locomotive
August 23, 2011. Printed by Walsall — 8.00

■ **6 x 1st. Diamond Jubilee**
4 x 1st diamond blue, 2 x 1st Golden Jubilee 2002
May 31, 2012. Printed by Walsall — 8.00

■ **6 x 1st. Classic Locomotives of Scotland**
4 x 1st diamond blue, 2 x 1st Class D34 locomotive
September 27, 2012. Printed by Walsall — 8.00

■ **6 x 1st. London Underground**
4 x 1st red, 2 x 1st Boston Manor Station
January 9, 2013. Printed by Walsall — 8.00

■ **6 x 1st. Football Heroes (issue 1)**
4 x 1st red, 1 x 1st George Best, 1 x 1st Bobby Moore
May 9, 2013. Printed by Walsall — 15.00

■ **6 x 1st. Classic Locomotives of Northern Ireland**
4 x 1st red, 2 x 1st UTA W No.103 locomotive
June 18, 2013. Printed by Walsall — 8.00

■ **6 x 1st. Butterflies**
4 x 1st red, 1 x 1st Chalkhill Blue, 1 x 1st Comma
July 11, 2013. Printed by Walsall — 8.00

■ **6 x 1st. Royal Mail Transport**
4 x 1st red, 1 x 1st Morris Minor van, 1 x 1st RMS 'Britannia'
September 19, 2013. Printed by Walsall — 20.00

■ **6 x 1st. Football Heroes (issue 2)**
4 x 1st red, 1 x 1st John Charles, 1 x 1st Dave Mackay
February 20, 2014. Printed by Walsall — 11.00

■ **6 x 1st. Buckingham Palace**
4 x 1st red, 1 x 1st Grand Staircase, 1 x 1st Throne Room
April 15, 2014. Printed by Walsall — 8.00

■ **6 x 1st. Glasgow 2014 Commonwealth Games**
4 x 1st red, 2 x 1st Swimming
July 17, 2014. Printed by Walsall — 8.00

■ **6 x 1st. Sustainable Fish**
4 x 1st red, 1 x 1st Common Skate, 1 x 1st Cornish Herring
August 18, 2014. Printed by Walsall — 15.00

■ **6 x 1st. Classic Locomotives of Wales**
4 x 1st red, 2 x 1st LMS 2F No.7720 locomotive
September 18, 2014. Printed by Walsall — 8.00

■ **6 x 1st. Alice in Wonderland**
4 x 1st red, 1 x 1st Drink Me, 1 x 1st White Rabbit's House
January 6, 2015. Printed by ISP — 15.00

■ **6 x 1st. Comedy Greats**
4 x 1st red, 1 x 1st Norman Wisdom, 1 x 1st Morecambe & Wise
April 1, 2015. Printed by ISP — 15.00

■ **6 x 1st. Bees**
4 x 1st red, 2 x 1st Great Yellow Bumblebee
August 18, 2015. Printed by ISP — 8.00

■ **6 x 1st. Rugby World Cup**
4 x 1st amethyst, 1 x 1st Try, 1 x 1st Conversion
September 18, 2015. Printed by ISP — 12.00

■ **6 x 1st. The Queen's 90th Birthday (issue 1)**
4 x 1st amethyst, 1 x 1st Prince Charles, 1 x 1st Queen Elizabeth II
April 21, 2016. Printed by ISP — 15.00

■ **6 x 1st. The Queen's 90th Birthday (issue 2)**
4 x 1st amethyst, 1 x 1st Prince George, 1 x 1st Prince William
June 9, 2016. Printed by ISP — 8.00

■ **6 x 1st. Beatrix Potter**
4 x 1st amethyst, 1 x 1st Peter Rabbit, 1 x 1st Mrs Tiggy-Winkle
July 28, 2016. Printed by ISP — 20.00

■ **6 x 1st. Landscape Gardens**
4 x 1st amethyst, 1 x 1st Compton Verney, 1 x 1st Highclere Castle
August 16, 2016. Printed by ISP — 20.00

BOOKLETS OF SELF-ADHESIVE OLYMPIC GAMES DEFINITIVES, 2012

RETAIL, SELF-ADHESIVE **BOOKLETS**

■ **6 x 1st. Olympic and Paralympic Games**
3 x 1st Olympic Games logo, 3 x 1st Paralympic Games logo
Cover: Union flag. Inside front cover: quote from Lord Coe
January 5, 2012. Printed by Walsall   8.00

■ **6 x 1st. Olympic and Paralympic Games**
3 x 1st Olympic Games logo, 3 x 1st Paralympic Games logo
Cover: Union flag. Inside front cover: timetable of events
January 5, 2012. Printed by Walsall   8.00
(*The cover design and the arrangement of the stamps varies between these two booklets.)

BOOKLETS OF SELF-ADHESIVE COMMEMORATIVES, 2013-2016

■ **6 x 1st. Doctor Who**
4 x 1st Tardis, 1 x 1st Matt Smith, 1 x 1st William Hartnell
March 26, 2013. Printed by Walsall   15.00

■ **6 x 1st. 175th Anniversary of the Penny Black**
6 x 1st Penny Black
May 6, 2015. Printed by ISP   10.00

■ **6 x 1st. 175th Anniversary of the Penny Red**
6 x 1st Penny Red
February 18, 2016. Printed by ISP   10.00

BOOKLETS OF SELF-ADHESIVE SECURITY DEFINITIVES, 2016-21

Booklets with a cover design illustrating a padlock.

■ **6 x 1st red**
July 28, 2016. Printed by ISP.
Old typeface. Security backing paper   8.00

■ **6 x 1st deep red**
October 20, 2016. Printed by ISP.
New typeface. Security backing paper   10.00
2017 year code   19.00
2018 year code   11.00
2019 year code   12.00
2020 year code   12.00
2021 year code   22.00

Booklets with a cover matching the colour of the stamps.

■ **12 x 2nd blue**
October 20, 2016. Printed by ISP   18.00
2017 year code   23.00
2018 year code   18.00
2019 year code   18.00
2020 year code   18.00
2021 year code   18.00

■ **4 x 2nd Large blue**
October 20, 2016. Printed by ISP   12.00
2017 year code   30.00
2018 year code   25.00
2019 year code   11.00
2020 year code   11.00
2021 year code   11.00

■ **6 x 1st deep red**
June 5, 2017. Printed by ISP.
Inside front cover notes Machin Anniversary   8.00

■ **12 x 1st deep red**
October 20, 2016. Printed by ISP   19.00
2017 year code   19.00
2018 year code   18.00
2019 year code   19.00
2020 year code   19.00
2021 year code   19.00

■ **4 x 1st Large deep red**
October 20, 2016. Printed by ISP   33.00
2017 year code   18.00
2018 year code   11.00

BOOKLETS RETAIL, SELF-ADHESIVE

2019 year code	12.00
2020 year code	12.00
2021 year code	12.00

BOOKLETS OF SELF-ADHESIVE SECURITY DEFINITIVES & COMMEMORATIVES, 2016–21

■ **6 x 1st. Mr. Men and Little Miss**
4 x 1st deep red, 1 x 1st Mr. Happy, 1 x 1st Mr. Tickle
October 20, 2016. Printed by ISP — 9.00

■ **6 x 1st. Windsor Castle: St. George's Chapel**
4 x 1st deep red, 1 x 1st Bray roof boss, 1 x 1st Fan-vaulted roof
February 15, 2017. Printed by ISP — 8.00

■ **6 x 1st. David Bowie**
4 x 1st deep red, 1 x 1st Aladdin Sane, 1 x 1st Heroes
March 14, 2017. Printed by ISP — 8.00

■ **6 x 1st. Star Wars: Droids**
4 x 1st deep red, 1 x 1st BB-8, 1 x 1st R2-D2
October 12, 2017. Printed by ISP — 14.00

■ **6 x 1st. Star Wars: Aliens and Creatures**
4 x 1st deep red, 1 x 1st Maz Kanata, 1 x 1st Chewbacca
October 12, 2017. Printed by ISP — 12.00

■ **6 x 1st. RAF Centenary**
4 x 1st deep red, 1 x 1st Lightning F6, 1 x 1st Hurricane Mk1
March 20, 2018. Printed by ISP — 8.00

■ **6 x 1st. RAF Centenary: Red Arrows**
4 x 1st deep red, 1 x 1st Flypast, 1 x 1st Swan
May 11, 2018. Printed by ISP — 20.00

■ **6 x 1st. Dad's Army**
4 x 1st deep red, 1 x 1st Captain Mainwaring, 1 x 1st Lance Corporal Jones
June 26, 2018. Printed by ISP — 13.00

■ **6 x 1st. Hampton Court Palace**
4 x 1st deep red, 1 x 1st Great Hall, 1 x 1st King's Great Bedchamber
July 31, 2018. Printed by ISP — 26.00

■ **6 x 1st. First World War**
4 x 1st deep red, 1 x 1st Poppy by Fiona Strickland,
1 x 1st 100 Poppies by Zafer and Barbara Baran
September 13, 2018. Printed by ISP — 15.50

■ **6 x 1st. Harry Potter**
4 x 1st deep red, 1 x 1st Hermione Granger, 1 x 1st Harry Potter
October 16, 2018. Printed by ISP — 8.00

■ **6 x 1st. Marvel**
4 x 1st deep red, 1 x 1st Spider-Man, 1 x 1st Hulk
March 14, 2019. Printed by ISP — 10.00

■ **6 x 1st. Birds of Prey**
4 x 1st deep red, 1 x 1st Buzzard, 1 x 1st Hobby
April 4, 2019. Printed by ISP — 50.00

■ **6 x 1st. D-Day**
4 x 1st deep red, 1 x 1st Gold, 1 x 1st Sword
June 6, 2019. Printed by ISP — 10.00

■ **6 x 1st. Elton John**
4 x 1st deep red, 1 x 1st Goodbye Yellow Brick Road,
1 x 1st Captain Fantastic & The Brown Dirt Cowboy
September 3, 2019. Printed by ISP — 13.00

■ **6 x 1st. Royal Naval Ships**
4 x 1st deep red, 1 x 1st Mary Rose, 1 x 1st HMS Queen Elizabeth
September 19, 2019. Printed by ISP — 50.00

■ **6 x 1st. Star Wars (issue 3)**
4 x 1st deep red, 1 x 1st Poe Dameron, 1 x 1st Sith Trooper
November 26, 2019. Printed by ISP — 12.00

■ **6 x 1st. Tomb Raider**
4 x 1st deep red, 1 x 1st Tomb Raider 1996, 1 x 1st Tomb Raider 2013
January 21, 2020. Printed by ISP — 15.00

■ **6 x 1st. James Bond**
4 x 1st deep red, 1 x 1st Bell-Textron Jet Pack,
1 x 1st Aston Martin DB5
March 17, 2020. Printed by ISP — 15.00

■ **6 x 1st. Coronation Street**
4 x 1st deep red, 1 x 1st Vera and Jack Duckworth,
1 x 1st Deirdre and Ken Barlow
May 28, 2020. Printed by ISP — 8.00

■ **6 x 1st. Queen**
4 x 1st deep red, 1 x 1st Queen II, 1 x 1st A Night At The Opera
July 9, 2020. Printed by ISP — 15.00

■ **6 x 1st. Sherlock**
4 x 1st deep red, 1 x 1st The Adventure of the Speckled Band,
1 x 1st The Red-Headed League
August 18, 2020. Printed by ISP — 8.00

■ **6 x 1st. Star Trek**
4 x 1st deep red, 1 x 1st James T Kirk, 1 x 1st Jean-Luc Picard

RETAIL, SELF-ADHESIVE BOOKLETS

November 13, 2020. Printed by ISP — 8.00

■ **6 x 1st. National Parks**
4 x 1st deep red, 1 x 1st Peak District, 1 x 1st Snowdonia
January 14, 2021. Printed by ISP — 8.00

■ **6 x 1st. Only Fools and Horses**
4 x 1st deep red, 1 x 1st Del Boy, 1 x 1st Rodney
February 16, 2021. Printed by ISP — 8.00

■ **6 x 1st. Paul McCartney**
4 x 1st deep red, 1 x 1st McCartney, 1 x 1st Tug of War
May 28, 2021. Printed by ISP — 8.00

■ **6 x 1st. Dennis & Gnasher**
4 x 1st deep red, 1 x 1st Dennis, 1 x 1st Gnasher
July 1, 2021. Printed by ISP — 8.00

■ **6 x 1st. Wild Coasts**
4 x 1st deep red, 1 x 1st Orca, 1 x 1st Grey Seal
July 22, 2021. Printed by ISP — 8.00

■ **6 x 1st. DC Collection (Batman and Robin)**
4 x 1st deep red, 1 x 1st Batman, 1 x 1st Robin
September 17, 2021. Printed by ISP — 8.50

■ **6 x 1st. DC Collection (Wonder Woman)**
4 x 1st deep red, 2 x 1st Wonder Woman
September 17, 2021. Printed by ISP — 8.50

BOOKLETS OF SELF-ADHESIVE COMMEMORATIVES, 2016–21

■ **6 x 1st. Game of Thrones**
6 x 1st The Iron Throne
January 23, 2018. Printed by ISP — 8.50

■ **6 x 1st. London 2020 International Stamp Exhibition**
2 x 1st Penny Black, 2 x 1st Twopenny Blue, 2 x 1st Penny Red
March 10, 2020. Printed by ISP — 8.50
(*The exhibition itself was postponed until 2022.)

■ **6 x 1st. Queen**
6 x 1st Queen Studio Photograph
March 29, 2021. Printed by ISP — 8.50

BOOKLETS OF ELIZABETH II SELF-ADHESIVE SECURITY DEFINITIVES WITH DATA MATRIX CODES, 2022

■ **8 x 2nd holly green**
February 1, 2022. Printed by ISP — 9.00

■ **4 x 1st plum purple**
February 1, 2022. Printed by ISP — 6.50

■ **8 x 1st plum purple**
February 1, 2022. Printed by ISP — 11.00

■ **4 x 2nd Large dark pine green**
February 1, 2022. Printed by ISP — 8.00

■ **4 x 1st Large marine turquoise**
February 1, 2022. Printed by ISP — 10.00

BOOKLETS OF CHARLES III SELF-ADHESIVE SECURITY DEFINITIVES WITH DATA MATRIX CODES, 2023

■ **8 x 2nd holly green**
April 4, 2023. Printed by Cartor — 9.00

■ **4 x 1st plum purple**
April 4, 2023. Printed by Cartor — 6.50

■ **8 x 1st plum purple**
April 4, 2023. Printed by Cartor — 13.00

■ **4 x 2nd Large dark pine green**
April 4, 2023. Printed by Cartor — 7.00

■ **4 x 1st Large marine turquoise**
April 4, 2023. Printed by Cartor — 10.00

BOOKLETS CHRISTMAS

CHRISTMAS BOOKLETS

In this section, prices are quoted for mint condition only. These booklets may contain either definitive stamps or Christmas special issues, but are issued specifically for the holiday period.

COUNTER BOOKLETS, 1978–86

■ **1978, November 15**
£1.60 (10 x 7p, 10 x 9p definitives).
Cover shows decoration of holly and 'Christmas 1978'   3.00

■ **1979, November 14**
£1.80 (10 x 8p, 10 x 10p definitives).
Cover shows Christmas cracker and 'Christmas 1979'   3.50

■ **1980, November 12**
£2.20 (10 x 10p, 10 x 12p definitives).
Cover shows nativity scene and 'Christmas 1980'   3.50

■ **1981, November 11**
£2.55 (10 x 14p, 10 x 11½p definitives).
Cover shows skating scene and 'Christmas Greetings 1981'   4.50

■ **1982, November 10**
£2.50 (10 x 15½p, 10 x 12½p definitives).
Cover shows mummers and 'Christmas Special Offer'   5.50
(*Sold at a discount of 30p off face value; stamps have a blue star printed on the gummed side)

■ **1983, November 9**
£2.20 (20 x 12½p definitives).
Cover shows pantomime and 'Christmas Special Offer'   5.00
(*Sold at a discount of 30p off face value; stamps have a blue star printed on the gummed side.)

■ **1984, November 20**
£2.30 (20 x 13p Christmas stamps).
Cover shows manger scene and 'Christmas Special Offer'   5.50
(*Sold at a discount of 30p off face value; stamps have a blue star printed on the gummed side)

■ **1985, November 19**
£2.40 (20 x 12p Christmas stamps).
Cover shows Cinderella's slipper   5.00

■ **1986, December 2**
£1.20 (10 x 13p definitives, margin at left)   5.00
£1.20 (10 x 13p definitives, margin at right)   8.00
Cover shows Shetland yule cakes and 'Special Offer'
(*Sold at a discount of 10p off face value; stamps have a blue star printed on the gummed side.)

RETAIL BOOKLETS, 1990–2000

■ **1990, November 13**
20 x 17p Christmas stamps   6.00
Cover shows snowman

■ **1991, November 12**
20 x 18p Christmas stamps   6.00
Cover shows holly

■ **1992, November 10**
20 x 18p Christmas stamps   6.00
Cover shows Father Christmas and sleigh

■ **1993, November 9**
20 x 19p Christmas stamps   6.50
10 x 25p Christmas stamps   5.50
Covers show Father Christmas

CHRISTMAS BOOKLETS

■ **1994, November 1**
20 x 19p Christmas stamps	6.00
10 x 25p Christmas stamps	4.50

Covers show nativity play props

■ **1995, October 30**
20 x 19p Christmas stamps	6.50
10 x 25p Christmas stamps	10.00
4 x 60p Christmas stamps	9.00

Covers show robins

■ **1996, October 28**
20 x 2nd Christmas stamps	19.00
10 x 1st Christmas stamps	13.50

Covers show nativity scenes

■ **1997, October 27**
20 x 2nd Christmas stamps	19.00
10 x 1st Christmas stamps	13.00

Covers show Father Christmas and crackers

■ **1998, November 2**
20 x 20p Christmas stamps	6.50
10 x 26p Christmas stamps	4.50

Covers show angels

■ **1999, November 2**
20 x 19p The Christians' Tale stamps	7.00
10 x 26p The Christians' Tale stamps	5.00

Covers show part of stamp

■ **2000, November 7**
20 x 2nd Spirit and Faith stamps	19.00
10 x 1st Spirit and Faith stamps	13.00

Covers show part of stamp

SELF-ADHESIVE FOLDERS, 2001–05

■ **2001, November 6**
24 x 2nd Christmas stamps	23.00
12 x 1st Christmas stamps	15.00

■ **2002, November 5**
24 x 2nd Christmas stamps	23.00
12 x 1st Christmas stamps	15.00

■ **2003, November 4**
24 x 2nd Christmas stamps	23.00
12 x 1st Christmas stamps	15.00

■ **2004, November 2**
24 x 2nd Christmas stamps	23.00
12 x 1st Christmas stamps	15.00

■ **2005, November 1**
24 x 2nd Christmas stamps	23.00
12 x 1st Christmas stamps	15.00

SELF-ADHESIVE BOOKLETS, 2006–15

BOOKLETS CHRISTMAS

■ 2006, November 7
12 x 2nd Christmas stamps	12.50
12 x 1st Christmas stamps	15.00

■ 2007, November 6
12 x 2nd Christmas stamps	12.50
12 x 1st Christmas stamps	15.00

■ 2008, November 4
12 x 2nd Christmas stamps. Pane inscribed 'Oh yes it is'	12.50
12 x 2nd Christmas stamps. Pane inscribed 'Oh no it isn't'	12.50
12 x 1st Christmas stamps. Pane inscribed 'It's behind you'	15.00
12 x 2nd Christmas stamps. Pane inscribed 'Abracadabra'	15.00

■ 2009, November 3
12 x 2nd Christmas stamps	12.50
12 x 1st Christmas stamps	15.00

■ 2010, November 2
12 x 2nd Christmas stamps	12.50
12 x 1st Christmas stamps	15.00

Covers show Wallace and Gromit posting Christmas cards

■ 2011, November 8
12 x 2nd Christmas stamps	12.50
12 x 1st Christmas stamps	15.00

■ 2012, November 6
12 x 2nd Christmas stamps	12.50
12 x 1st Christmas stamps	15.00

■ 2013, November 5
12 x 2nd Christmas stamps	12.50
12 x 1st Christmas stamps	15.00

■ 2014, November 4
12 x 2nd Christmas stamps	12.50
12 x 1st Christmas stamps	15.50

■ 2015, November 3
12 x 2nd Christmas stamps	12.50
12 x 1st Christmas stamps	15.00

SELF–ADHESIVE BOOKLETS, 2016–21

■ 2016, November 8
12 x 2nd Christmas stamps	12.50
12 x 1st Christmas stamps	15.00

■ 2017, November 7
12 x 2nd Christmas stamps (Madonna and Child)	20.00
12 x 2nd Christmas stamps (six of each design)	12.50
12 x 1st Christmas stamps (Madonna and Child)	18.00
12 x 1st Christmas stamps (six of each design)	15.00

■ 2018, November 1
12 x 2nd Christmas stamps	16.00
12 x 1st Christmas stamps	19.00

■ 2019, November 5
12 x 2nd Christmas stamps	16.00
12 x 1st Christmas stamps	15.00

■ 2020, November 3
12 x 2nd Christmas stamps	12.00
12 x 1st Christmas stamps	15.00

■ 2021, November 2
12 x 2nd Christmas stamps (without data matrix code)	12.50
12 x 1st Christmas stamps (without data matrix code)	16.00

■ 2022, November 3
8 x 2nd Christmas stamps	9.00
8 x 1st Christmas stamps	13.00

GREETINGS BOOKLETS

In this section, prices are quoted for mint condition only. These booklets contain Greetings stamps, which are listed individually in the Queen Elizabeth II Decimal section. Normally the panes comprise one of each design, with additional greetings labels.

■ **1989, January 31. Greetings**
Two of each of the five 19p designs as January 31, 1989,
plus 12 labels. Cover designs differ — 25.00

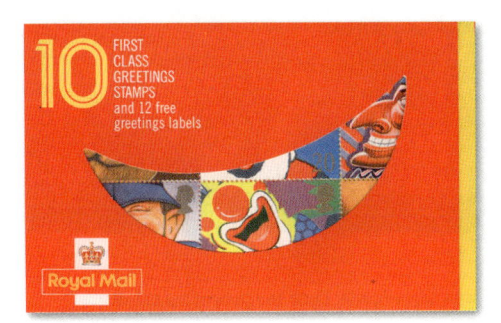

■ **1990, February 6. Smiles**
One each of ten 20p designs as February 6, 1990,
plus 12 labels. Cover shows smiling mouth — 14.00

■ **1991, February 5. Good Luck**
One each of ten 1st class designs as February 5, 1991,
plus 12 labels. Cover shows lucky charms — 13.00

■ **1991, March 26. Smiles**
One each of ten 1st class designs as March 26, 1991,
plus 12 labels. Cover shows laughing pillar box — 13.00

■ **1992, January 28. Memories**
One each of ten 1st class designs as January 28, 1992,
plus 12 labels. Cover shows label and pressed flowers — 13.00

■ **1993, February 2. Gift Giving**
One each of ten 1st class designs as February 2, 1993,
plus 20 labels. Cover shows Rupert and Wilfrid — 13.00

■ **1994, February 1. Messages**
One each of ten 1st class designs as February 1, 1994,
plus 20 labels. Cover shows Rupert and Paddington — 13.00

■ **1995, March 21. Art**
One each of ten 1st class designs as March 21, 1995,
plus 20 labels. Cover shows clown
Yellow strip has 'Pull Open' — 13.00
Yellow strip has no inscription — 14.00

■ **1996, February 26. Cartoons**
One each of ten 1st class designs as February 26, 1996,
plus 20 labels. Cover shows figure holding bowl
Inside cover has 1996 dates — 13.00

■ **1996, November 11. Cartoons**
One each of ten 1st class designs as November 11, 1996,
plus 20 labels. Figure holding bowl cover.
Inside cover omits 1996 dates — 25.00

■ **1997, January 6. Flower Paintings**
One each of ten 1st class designs as January 6, 1997,
plus 20 labels. Cover shows gentiana flower — 13.00

■ **1997, February 3. Flower Paintings**
One each of ten 1st class designs as January 6, 1997, plus
20 labels. Cover shows gentiana flower and 'Win a
beautiful bouquet instantly' — 14.00

■ **1998, January 5. Flower Paintings**
One each of ten 1st class designs as January 6, 1997, plus
20 labels. Cover shows box of chocolates — 14.00

■ **1998, August 3. Flower Paintings**
One each of ten 1st class designs as January 6, 1997, plus
20 labels. Cover shows Christmas cards — 14.00

PRESTIGE STAMP BOOKS

PRESTIGE STAMP BOOKS

In this section, prices are quoted for mint condition only.

Stamps for Cooks, 1969

■ **1969, December 1. £1.00 Stamps for Cooks**
Pane of six 1d, three 4d, three 4d, three 5d (recipe label)	6.00
Pane of fifteen 4d (label 'Stuffed Cucumber')	2.00
Pane of fifteen 4d (label 'Method')	2.00
Pane of fifteen 5d (recipe label)	2.00
Complete book	7.50

(*A stapled version of this stitched book exists that is much rarer. Price: £350.)

The Story of Wedgwood, 1972

■ **1972, May 24. £1.00 The Story of Wedgwood**
Pane of twelve 3p	3.00
Pane of six 2½p, six 3p	6.00
Pane of nine 2½p, one ½p	7.50
Pane of four ½p, two 2½p	40.00
Complete book	45.00

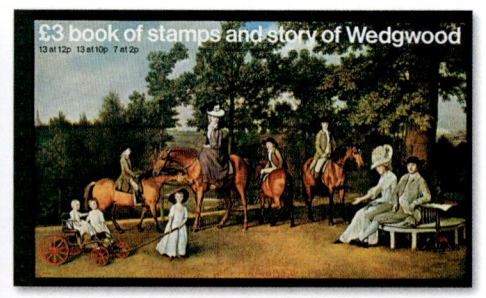

The Story of Wedgwood, 1980

■ **1980, April 16. £3.00 The Story of Wedgwood**
Pane of six 2p	0.50
Pane of nine 10p	2.00
Pane of nine 12p	2.00
Pane of one 2p, four 10p, four 12p	2.00
Complete book	5.00

■ **1982, May 19. £4.00 The Story of Stanley Gibbons**
Pane of six 12½p	1.75
Pane of six 15½p	1.75
Pane of nine 15½p	2.50
Pane of one 2p, one 3p, seven 12½p	3.00
Complete book	6.00

■ **1983, September 14. £4.00 The Story of the Royal Mint**
Pane of six 12½p (label 'The Royal Mint & America')	1.75
Pane of six 12½p (label 'Maundy Money')	1.75
Pane of nine 16p	2.50
Pane of one 3p, two 3½p, six 16p	3.00
Complete book	6.00

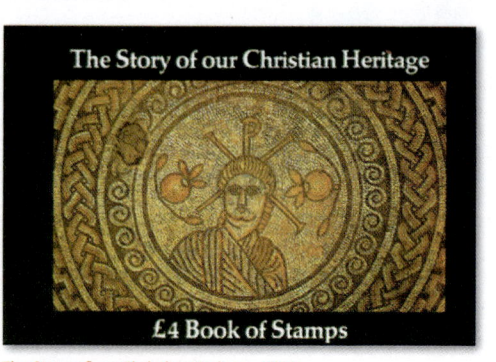

The Story of our Christian Heritage, 1984

■ **1984, September 4. £4.00 The Story of Our Christian Heritage**
Pane of six 17p	2.25
Pane of six 13p (label 'William Wilberforce')	2.00
Pane of six 13p (label 'Lillian Bayliss')	2.00
Pane of one 10p, one 13p, seven 17p	13.00
Complete book	15.00

■ **1985, January 8. £5.00 The Story of The Times**
Pane of six 17p	2.50
Pane of nine 13p	2.50
Pane of nine 17p	3.00
Pane of two 4p, four 13p, two 17p, one 34p	8.00
Complete book	10.00

■ **1986, March 18. £5.00 The Story of British Rail**
Pane of six 17p	2.50
Pane of nine 12p	3.00
Pane of nine 17p	3.00
Pane of six 12p, two 17p, one 31p	9.00
Complete book	11.00

PRESTIGE STAMP BOOKS

■ **1987, March 3. £5.00 The Story of P&O**
Pane of six 13p	2.25
Pane of nine 13p	2.75
Pane of nine 18p	3.00
Pane of one 1p, two 13p, five 18p, one 26p	8.00
Complete book	10.00

■ **1988, March 3. £5.00 FT100 (Financial Times)**
Pane of nine 18p	4.50
Pane of six 13p	2.50
Pane of six 13p, one 18p, one 22p, one 34p	14.00
Pane of six 18p	2.50
Complete book	17.50

■ **1989, March 21. £5.00 The Scots Connection**
Pane of nine 19p Scotland	2.75
Pane of six 14p Scotland	2.50
Pane of five 14p, two 19p, one 23p, all Scotland	10.00
Pane of six 19p Scotland	2.50
Complete book	11.00

■ **1990, March 20. £5.00 London Life**
Pane of four 20p Alexandra Palace	2.50
Pane of six 20p Penny Black Anniversary (label 'Eros')	2.50
Pane of six 20p Penny Black Anniversary (label 'Street Signs')	2.50
Pane of one 15p, one 20p, one 29p all Penny Black Anniversary, plus one 2nd, one 1st, one 15p, one 20p, one 50p	11.00
Complete book	14.00

■ **1991, March 19. £6.00 Alias Agatha Christie**
Pane of six 17p (label 'Styles')	2.25
Pane of six 17p (label 'Mousetrap')	2.25
Pane of nine 22p	4.50
Pane of six 22p, two 33p	5.50
Complete book	10.00

■ **1992, February 25. £6.00 Cymru Wales**
Pane of four 39p Wintertime	2.50
Pane of six 18p Wales	2.25
Pane of two 18p, two 24p, all Wales, plus one 2nd, one 1st, two 33p	7.50
Pane of six 24p Wales	2.25
Complete book	9.50

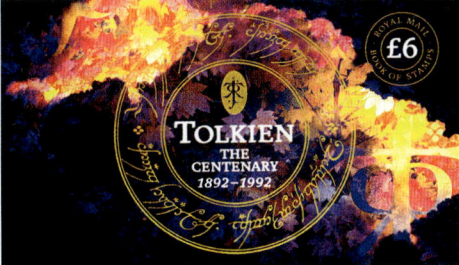

Tolkien: The Centenary, 1992

■ **1992, October 27. £6.00 Tolkien: The Centenary**
Pane of six 24p (label 'Runes')	2.50
Pane of six 24p (label 'Hobbit')	2.50
Pane of six 18p	2.00
Pane of one 2nd, one 1st, two 18p, two 24p, two 39p	7.50
Complete book	10.00

The Story of Beatrix Potter, 1992

■ **1993, August 10. £5.64 The Story of Beatrix Potter**
Pane of four 1st Beatrix Potter	3.00
Pane of one 24p of each of Scotland, Wales and Northern Ireland, one 18p of each of Scotland, Wales and Northern Ireland	7.50
Pane of three 1st, three 2nd	6.50
Pane of two 2nd, two 18p, two 33p, two 39p	7.50
Complete book	19.00

■ **1994, July 26. £6.04 Northern Ireland**
Pane of four 30p Prince of Wales Paintings	2.50
Pane of one 6p, one 19p, four 25p	7.50
Pane of two 19p, four 25p, one 30p, one 41p, all Northern Ireland	5.00
Pane of one 19p, one 25p, one 30p, one 41p, all Northern Ireland	5.00
Complete book	11.50

■ **1995, April 25. £6.00 The National Trust**
Pane of six 25p National Trust	2.00
Pane of two 19p, two 25p, one 10p, one 30p, one 35p, one 41p	9.00
Pane of one 19p of each of Scotland, Wales and Northern Ireland, plus one 25p of each of Scotland, Wales and Northern Ireland	5.50
Pane of six 19p	7.50
Complete book	11.00

■ **1996, May 14. £6.48 European Football Championships**
Pane of four 19p Football Legends	1.75
Pane of four 25p Football Legends	2.00
Pane of two 35p, two 41p, two 60p Football Legends	4.50
Pane of two 25p, two 25p Scotland, two 25p Wales, two 25p Northern Ireland	3.50
Complete book	9.00

BRITISH STAMP MARKET VALUES 2024   **295**

PRESTIGE STAMP BOOKS

■ 1997, September 23. £6.15 Celebrating 75 Years of the BBC
Pane of one 26p, one 37p Scotland, one 26p, one 37p Wales, one 26p, one 37p Northern Ireland	4.00
Pane of four 26p gold, four 1st gold	4.50
Pane of three 20p, three 26p	4.00
Pane of four 20p Children's Television	4.50
Complete book	11.00

■ 1998, March 10. £7.49 The Definitive Portrait
Pane of nine 26p Wilding	4.50
Pane of six 20p Wilding	3.00
Pane of four 20p, two 26p, two 37p Wilding	5.50
Pane of three 26p, three 37p Wilding	5.50
Complete book	12.00

Breaking Barriers, 1998

■ 1998, October 13. £6.16 Breaking Barriers
Pane of four 20p Land Speed Records	4.00
Pane of one 20p Scotland, one 20p Wales, one 20p Northern Ireland, three 43p	6.00
Pane of three 2nd, one 26p Scotland, one 26p Wales, one 26p Northern Ireland	5.00
Pane of three 43p, two 10p, three 2nd	6.50
Complete book	19.00

Profile on Print, 1999

■ 1999, February 16. £7.54 Profile on Print
Pane of eight 1st orange-red	7.00
Pane of four 1st Machin large format embossed	7.00
Pane of four Machin large format intaglio	7.00
Pane of four Machin large format typographed	7.00
Pane of nine 1st orange-red	9.00
Complete book	31.00

■ 1999, September 21. £6.99 World Changers
Pane of four 20p Millennium Jenner's vaccination	2.00
Pane of four 44p Millennium Faraday's electricity	6.00
Pane of four 26p Millennium Darwin's theory	6.50
Pane of four 63p Millennium Computers in brain	8.00
Pane of four 1p, three 19p, one 26p	3.00
Complete book	15.00

Special by Design, 2000

■ 2000, February 15. £7.50 Special by Design
Pane of eight 1st Millennium definitive	11.00
Pane of three 1st Scotland, three 1st Wales, three 1st Northern Ireland	11.00
Pane of four 19p, olive-green, two 38p	10.00
Pane of six 1st Penny Black Anniversary	10.00
Complete book	26.00

■ 2000, August 4. £7.03 HM Queen Elizabeth, The Queen Mother
Pane of six 2nd Scotland, two 65p Scotland	5.50
Pane of nine 1st olive brown	12.00
Queen Mother's Century miniature sheet	7.00
Pane of four 27p Queen Mother	6.00
Complete book	21.00

■ 2000, September 18. £7.00 A Treasury of Trees
Pane of two 65p Millennium Doire Dach forest	3.50
Pane of four 45p Millennium Sycamore seeds,	4.00
Pane of two 65p Millennium Bluebell wood	3.50
Pane of four 1st Millennium definitives, four 2nd Wales	8.00
Pane of four 2nd Millennium Roots of trees	2.50
Complete book	18.00

■ 2001, October 21. £6.76 Unseen and Unheard
Pane of two 1st, two 65p Submarines	8.00
Pane of two 2nd, two 45p Submarines	7.00
Pane of four Flags and Ensigns	6.00
Pane of four 1st Scotland, four E Scotland	6.00
Complete book	26.00

■ 2002, February 6. £7.29 A Gracious Accession
Pane of four 2nd, four E	14.00
Pane of one 2nd, one 1st, one E, one 45p Golden Jubilee	8.00
Pane of one 1st, one E, one 45p, one 65p Golden Jubilee	8.00
Pane of four 1st Wilding, five 2nd Wilding (one tilted)	9.00
Complete book	31.00

296 BRITISH STAMP MARKET VALUES 2024

PRESTIGE STAMP BOOKS

■ 2002, September 24. £6.83 Across the Universe
Pane of four 1st England, four 2nd England, one 1st Scotland	10.00
Pane of four 1st Millennium National Space Centre	8.50
Pane of four 1st gold, four E	15.00
Astronomy miniature sheet	6.00
Complete book	31.00

■ 2003, February 25. £6.99 Microcosmos
Pane of four 1st Northern Ireland, five 2nd Northern Ireland	9.00
Pane of four 1st gold, four E	15.00
Pane of two 1st and two 2nd Discovery of DNA	4.50
Pane of four E Discovery of DNA	10.00
Complete book	33.00

■ 2003, June 2. £7.46 A Perfect Coronation
Pane of four 1st gold, four 2nd	4.75
Pane of four 1st 50th Anniversary of Coronation	2.75
Pane of four (different) 1st 50th Anniversary of Coronation	2.75
Pane of two 47p Wilding, two 68p Wilding, one £1 Coronation	30.00
Complete book	35.00

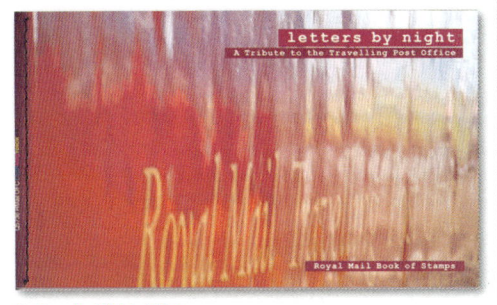

Letters by Night, 2004

■ 2004, March 16. £7.44 Letters by Night
Pane of three 2nd Scotland, three 68p Scotland	5.00
Pane of one 28p, one E, one 42p Classic Locomotives	6.00
Pane of four 1st Pub Signs	5.00
Pane of four 1st gold, four 37p	6.00
Complete book	20.00

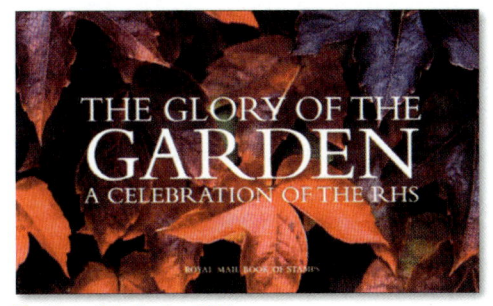

The Glory of the Garden, 2004

■ 2004, May 25. £7.23 The Glory of the Garden
Pane of four 1st gold, two 42p, two 47p	5.50
Pane of one 2nd, one E, one 68p, one 42p RHS	5.50
Pane of one 1st Iris latifolia, two 1st Tulipa, one 1st Gentiana acaulis	6.50
Pane of two 1st, two 47p RHS	6.50
Complete book	20.00

■ 2005, February 24. £7.43 The Brontë Sisters
Pane of four 2nd, two 39p, two 42p	4.50
Pane of two 2nd England, two 40p England	3.00
Pane of two 1st Brontë, two 1st Brontë	4.00
Pane of one 40p, one 57p, one 68p, one £1.12 Brontë	5.50
Complete book	15.00

■ 2005, October 4. £7.26 Bicentenary of the Battle of Trafalgar
Pane of four 1st, two 50p, two 68p	7.50
Pane of three 1st White Ensign	6.00
Pane of one 1st, one 42p, one 68p Trafalgar (first designs)	3.00
Pane of one 1st, one 42p, one 68p Trafalgar (second designs)	3.00
Complete book	16.50

■ 2006, February 23. £7.40 Brunel
Pane of one 40p, one 60p, one 47p all Brunel	3.50
Pane of one 1st, one 42p, one 68p all Brunel	3.00
Pane of four 1st, two 35p, two 40p	5.50
Pane of two 68p Ocean Liners, one 47p Brunel	10.00
Complete book	15.00

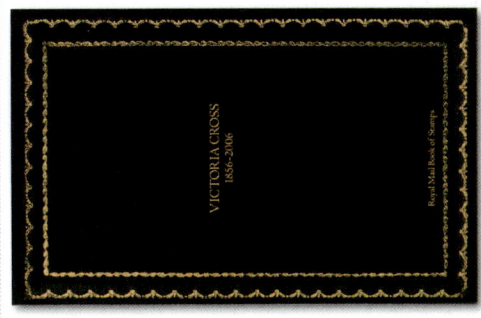

Victoria Cross, 2006

■ 2006, September 21. £7.41 Victoria Cross
Pane of first 1st, 64p and 72p Victoria Cross	3.50
Pane of second 1st, 64p and 72p Victoria Cross	3.50
Pane of four 20p Gallantry Awards	9.00
Pane of four 1st, four 50p	6.00
Complete book	15.00

■ 2007, March 1. £7.68 World of Invention
Pane of three 2nd Scotland and three 44p Wales	5.00
Pane of four 1st revised style and four 5p definitives	4.00
Pane of two 1st and two 64p World of Invention	6.50
Pane of two 1st and two 72p World of Invention	6.00
Complete book	18.50

BRITISH STAMP MARKET VALUES 2024 **297**

PRESTIGE STAMP BOOKS

■ **2007, June 5. £7.66 The Machin: The Making of a Masterpiece**
Pane of four 2p, two 46p, two 48p definitives	4.50
Pane of two £1 ruby definitives	5.00
Pane of two 1st Arnold Machin and two 1st 4d deep olive-sepia definitives	5.00
Pane of one 2nd and one 1st revised style, and two 2nd and two 1st Large definitives	6.00
Complete book	19.00

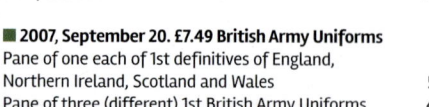

■ **2007, September 20. £7.49 British Army Uniforms**
Pane of one each of 1st definitives of England, Northern Ireland, Scotland and Wales	5.00
Pane of three (different) 1st British Army Uniforms	4.00
Pane of three (different) 78p British Army Uniforms	5.00
Pane of two 1p, four 46p and two 54p definitives	5.50
Complete book	15.00

Ian Fleming's James Bond, 2008

■ **2008, January 8. £7.40 Ian Fleming's James Bond**
Pane of one 1st Casino Royale, one 54p Goldfinger, one 78p For Your Eyes Only	3.75
Pane of one 1st Dr No, one 54p Diamonds Are Forever, one 78p From Russia With Love	3.75
Pane of eight 1st class gold	11.00
Pane of two 1st White Ensign and two 1st Union Jack, as of October 22, 2001	7.00
Complete book	20.00

■ **2008, September 18. £7.15 Pilot to Plane: RAF Uniforms**
Pane of three (different) 1st RAF Uniforms	4.00
Pane of three (different) 81p RAF Uniforms	4.50
Pane of four 1st gold and four 2nd definitives	6.00
Pane of two 1st Air Displays design of July 17, 2008, and two 20p Spitfire design of June 10, 1997	6.00
Complete book	17.50

■ **2008, September 29. £9.72 The Regional Definitives: Heraldry and Symbol**
Pane of the 1958 3d, 6d and 1s 3d designs of Northern Ireland, Scotland and Wales re-denominated as 1st	11.00
Pane of the 1958 3d, 6d and 1s 3d designs of Northern Ireland, re-denominated as 1st, and three 1st class Northern Ireland of October 14, 2003	6.00
Pane of the 1958 3d, 6d and 1s 3d designs of Scotland, re-denominated as 1st, and three 1st class Scotland of October 14, 2003	6.00
Pane of the 1958 3d, 6d and 1s 3d designs of Wales, re-denominated as 1st, and three 1st class Wales of October 14, 2003	6.00
Complete book	28.00

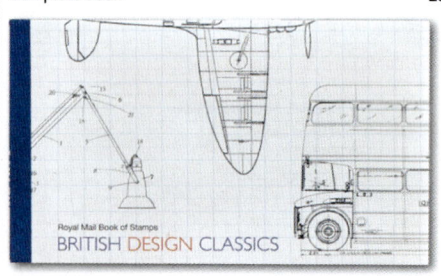

British Design Classics, 2009

■ **2009, January 13. £7.68 British Design Classics**
Pane of four 16p and four 50p definitives	5.50
Pane of one 1st Spitfire, two 1st Routemaster, one 1st Mini	4.50
Pane of one 1st London Underground Map, one 1st Telephone Kiosk, one 1st Penguin Books, one 1st Anglepoise Lamp, one 1st Polypropylene Chair, one 1st Mini Skirt	7.00
Pane of two 1st Concorde, and two 1st Concorde design of May 2, 2002	4.50
Complete book	21.00

■ **2009, February 12. £7.75 Charles Darwin**
Pane of the 48p, 50p and 56p Charles Darwin	11.00
Pane comprising the Charles Darwin miniature sheet	5.50
Pane of the 1st, 72p and 81p Charles Darwin	11.00
Pane of two 1st, two 5p, two 10p and two 48p definitives	6.00
Complete book	36.00

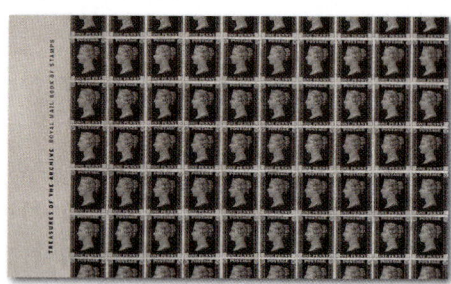

Treasures of the Archive, 2009

■ **2009, August 18. £8.18 Treasures of the Archive**
Pane of four 1st Penny Black Anniversary and four 20p Penny Black Anniversary	6.50
Pane of four 20p Royal Mail coach design of October 17, 1989	4.00
Pane of four (different) 1st Post Boxes	6.00
Pane of four 17p, two 22p and two 62p definitives	7.00
Complete book	15.00

PRESTIGE STAMP BOOKS

■ 2009, September 17. £7.93 Royal Navy Uniforms
Pane of the three (different) 90p Naval Uniforms	4.50
Pane of the three (different) 1st Naval Uniforms	4.00
Pane of two 1st White Ensign and two 1st Jolly Roger designs of October 22, 2001	6.00
Pane of two 1p, four 17p, and two 90p definitives	10.50
Complete book	16.50

■ 2010, January 7. £8.06 Classic Album Covers
Pane of four 20p, two 54p (wrong font), two 62p definitives	6.00
Pane of six (different) 1st Classic Album Covers	9.00
Pane of four (different) 1st Classic Album Covers	8.50
Pane of two 5p (wrong font), five 10p, two 22p definitives	6.00
Complete book	28.00

■ 2010, February 25. £7.72 The Royal Society
Pane of four (different) 1st Royal Society	5.00
Pane of four 22p and four 54p definitives (the 54p stamps with wrong font in error)	8.00
Pane of four (different) 1st Royal Society	5.00
Pane of four (different) 1st Royal Society	5.00
Complete book	19.00

■ 2010, May 8. £11.15 King George V
Pane of three 1st, three £1 Centenary of Accession	8.00
Pane of two (different) £1 Seahorses	6.00
Pane of four 1st British Empire Exhibition	6.00
Pane of four 1st, two 2nd, two 50p definitives, self-adhesive	8.00
Complete book	26.00

Britain Alone, 2010

■ 2010, May 13. £9.76 Britain Alone
Pane of four 5p, two 10p, two 60p definitives	4.00
Pane of four (different) Britain Alone	5.00
Pane of four (different) Britain Alone	5.50
Pane of four (different) Dunkirk	7.00
Complete book	16.00

■ 2011, March 22. £9.05 WWF
Pane of six (different) 1st WWF	8.00
Pane of four (different) 1st WWF	5.00
Pane of WWF miniature sheet	5.00
Pane of three 5p, three 10p, one 67p and one 97p definitives	9.00
Complete book	25.00

Morris & Co, 2011

■ 2011, May 5. £9.99 Morris & Co
Pane of two 1st, two £1.10 Morris & Co	6.00
Pane of one 1st, two 76p, one £1.10 Morris & Co	8.00
Pane of four 2nd Christmas designs of 2009	4.00
Pane of four 5p, two 10p, two 50p definitives, self-adhesive	6.00
Complete book	15.00

■ 2011, September 9. £9.97 First UK Aerial Post
Pane of one £1.10 Aerial Post and two 1st Aerial Post	8.00
Pane of one £1 Aerial Post and two 68p Aerial Post	6.50
Pane of four 50p Windsor Castle designs of 2005	11.00
Pane of four 5p, two 1st, two 76p definitives	20.00
Complete book	42.00

Roald Dahl, 2012

■ 2012, January 10. £11.47 Roald Dahl: Master Storyteller
Pane of two 2p, two 10p and four 68p definitives	8.00
Pane of 1st, 68p and 76p Roald Dahl	5.00
Pane of 66p, £1 and £1.10 Roald Dahl	6.50
Pane of 1st, 68p, 76p, £1 from Roald Dahl miniature sheet	10.00
Complete book	19.00

■ 2012, May 31. £12.77 Diamond Jubilee
Pane of four 1st Wilding, four 1st diamond blue definitives	10.00
Pane of 1st Trooping the Colour and 77p Royal Welsh	3.00
Pane of 1st Golden Jubilee, £1.26 United Nations Address, 87p Silver Jubilee and 87p Garter Ceremony	8.50
Pane of 77p First Christmas TV Broadcast and £1.28 Commonwealth Games	4.50
Complete book	20.00

BRITISH STAMP MARKET VALUES 2024

PRESTIGE STAMP BOOKS

■ **2012, July 27. £10.71 Keeping The Flame Alive**
Pane of three 1st Olympics, three 1st Paralympics, one Worldwide Olympics and one Worldwide Paralympics definitives	32.00
Pane of 1st Aquatics, 1st Field Athletics	3.00
Pane of 1st Paralympic Archery, 1st Equestrian	3.00
Pane of 1st Football, 1st Track athletics	3.00
Complete book	36.00

■ **2013, March 26. £13.77 50 Years of Doctor Who**
Pane of four 1st Tardis, one 5p, one 10p, one 20p and one 87p definitives	10.50
Pane of four (different) 1st Doctor Who	5.50
Pane of four (different) 1st Doctor Who	5.50
Pane of three (different) 1st Doctor Who	5.50
Pane of Doctor Who miniature sheet	5.50
Complete book	25.00

(*This book was designed with half the contents inverted, so it can be read from either end.)

Football Heroes, 2013

■ **2013, May 9. £11.85 Football Heroes**
Pane of five (different) 1st Football Heroes	13.00
Pane of six (different) 1st Football Heroes	14.00
Pane of two 2p, two 5p and two 10p definitives	2.50
Pane of two 1st red, two 1p definitives, one 1st England flag, one 1st Northern Ireland, one 1st Scotland flag and one 1st Wales flag	9.00
Complete book	26.00

(*This book was issued in a sealed plastic wrapper.)

■ **2013, September 19. £11.19 Merchant Navy**
Pane of three (different) 1st Merchant Navy	3.50
Pane of three (different) £1.28 Merchant Navy	5.00
Pane of four (different) 1st Atlantic and Arctic Convoys	5.00
Pane of four 5p, four 50p definitives	7.00
Complete book	17.00

■ **2014, February 20. £13.97 Locomotives of the United Kingdom**
Pane of two 1st and two 60p Classic Locos of England	7.00
Pane of two 1st and two 68p Classic Locos of Scotland	8.00
Pane of two 1st and two 78p Classic Locos of Northern Ireland	9.00
Pane of two 1st and two 78p Classic Locos of Wales	9.00
Pane of two 2p, two 5p, 1st Northern Ireland, 1st English flag, 1st Scottish flag and 1st Welsh flag	6.00
Complete book	34.00

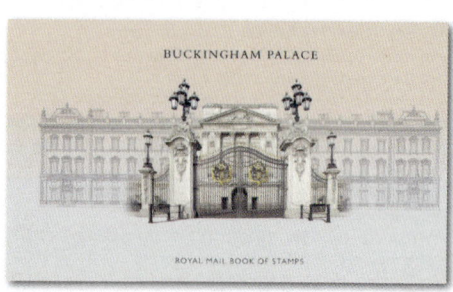

Buckingham Palace, 2014

■ **2014, April 15. £11.39 Buckingham Palace**
Pane of four 1st Buckingham Palace (exterior)	6.00
Pane of two 1st Buckingham Palace (exterior)	4.00
Pane of four 1st Buckingham Palace (interior)	6.00
Pane of two 10p, four 20p and two £1 definitives	7.00
Complete book	19.00

■ **2014, July 28. £11.30 The Great War, 1914**
Pane of three (different) 1st First World War	4.50
Pane of three (different) £1.47 First World War	10.00
Pane of two 10p, two 20p, 1st England, 1st Northern Ireland, 1st Scotland and 1st Wales	6.50
Pane of one £1 definitive	2.00
Complete book	19.00

■ **2015, February 19. £14.65 Inventive Britain**
Pane of two 1p, two 2p, one 81p and two 97p definitives	5.00
Pane of one 1st Station X, (2012) two 1st Bombe (2012) and one 1st Colossus	5.50
Pane of two (different) 81p, one £1.28 and one £1.47 Inventive Britain	8.00
Pane of two (different) 1st, one £1.28 and one £1.47 Inventive Britain	7.50
Complete book	22.00

■ **2015, May 14. £13.96 The Great War, 1915**
Pane of four 1st Observer Royal Field Artillery (2007)	5.00
Pane of three (different) 1st First World War 2015	4.00
Pane of three (different) £1.52 First World War 2015	7.50
Pane of two 1p, two 5p and two £1.33 definitives, and two 1st Poppies	6.00
Complete book	20.00

Battle of Waterloo, 2015

300 BRITISH STAMP MARKET VALUES 2024

PRESTIGE STAMP BOOKS

■ **2015, June 18. £14.47 Battle of Waterloo**
Pane of Battle of Waterloo miniature sheet	8.50
Pane of one 1st, two (different) £1.00, one £1.52 Battle of Waterloo	8.50
Pane of one 1st, one £1.52 Battle of Waterloo	6.50
Pane of two 5p, two 10p, two 50p, two £1 definitives	7.50
Complete book	28.00

The Making of Star Wars, 2015

■ **2015, December 17. £16.99 The Making of Star Wars**
Pane of six (different) 1st Star Wars	8.00
Pane of six (different) 1st Star Wars	8.00
Double pane of Star Wars miniature sheet. Self-adhesive	8.00
Pane of four 1st Union Flag, two 1st red, two 2nd blue definitives	8.00
Complete book	29.00

(*A limited edition of this book was produced with silver-foil printing, sold at £127.)

■ **2016, February 24. £16.36 Royal Mail 500**
Pane of two (different) 1st, one £1.52 Royal Mail 500	6.00
Pane of one 1st, two (different) £1.52 Royal Mail 500	6.00
Pane of two (different) 1st, two (different) £1.33 Classic GPO Posters	10.00
Pane of two 1st Penny Black, three 1st Twopenny Blue, three 1st Penny Red	14.50
Complete book	27.00

The Queen's 90th Birthday, 2016

■ **2016, April 21. £15.11 The Queen's 90th Birthday**
Pane of two (different) £1.52 Queen's Birthday	5.50
Pane of three (different) 1st, one £1.52 Queen's Birthday	6.00
Pane of Queen's Birthday miniature sheet	5.00
Pane of 1st England, 1st Northern Ireland, 1st Wales, 1st Scotland, two 1st red and two 1st amethyst definitives	7.50
Complete book	35.00

(*A limited edition of this book was produced with gold-foil printing, sold at £59.95.)

■ **2016, June 21. £16.49 The Great War, 1916**
Pane of three 1st First World War 2016	3.50
Pane of three £1.52 First World War 2016	7.00
Pane of two 1st, two £1.33 Post Office at War	6.00
Pane of four 1st Poppy, one 1st Northern Ireland, one 1st English flag, one 1st Scottish flag, one 1st Welsh flag	9.00
Complete book	25.00

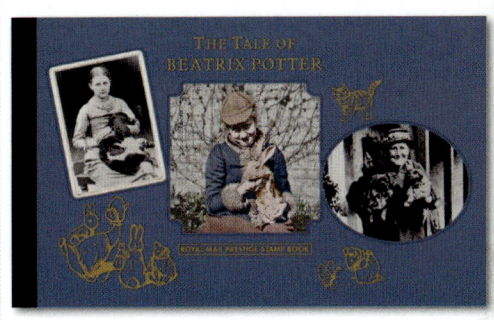

The Tale of Beatrix Potter, 2016

■ **2016, July 28. £15.37 The Tale of Beatrix Potter**
Pane of 1st, £1.33, £1.52 Beatrix Potter	5.50
Pane of 1st, £1.33, £1.52 Beatrix Potter (different)	5.50
Pane of two 1st, two £1.33 Tale of Peter Rabbit	6.50
Pane of three 5p, two 10p, three £1.05 definitives	6.00
Complete book	23.00

(*A limited edition of this book was produced with extra pages, sold at £59.99.)

■ **2017, February 15. £14.58 Windsor Castle**
Pane of two 1st, two £1.52 Windsor Castle	7.00
Pane of one 1st, one £1.52 Windsor Castle (different)	5.00
Pane of three 1st deep red, two 2p, two 10p and one £1.05 definitives	4.50
Pane of two 1st, two £1.33 St George's Chapel	6.50
Complete book	23.00

■ **2017, June 5. £15.59 The Machin Definitive: 50th Anniversary**
Pane of three 1st Machin Definitive Design Icon	4.50
Pane of three 1st Machin Definitive Design Icon	4.50
Pane of one 1p, one 2p, one 5p, one 10p, one 20p, one 50p, one 2nd, one £1 definitives	6.00
Pane of one 1st brownish black, two 20p Penny Black Anniversary, two 1st orange-red, one 1st gold, one 1st Millennium, one 1st PiP definitives	10.00
Pane of four £1 gold	14.00
Complete book	38.00

(*A limited edition of this book was produced wth silver-foil printing and a silver medallion, sold at £99.95.)

BRITISH STAMP MARKET VALUES 2024 301

PRESTIGE STAMP BOOKS

The Great War 1917, 2017

■ **2017, July 31. £15.41 The Great War, 1917**
Pane of four (different) 1st Poppies	6.00
Pane of three 1st First World War 1917	4.50
Pane of three £1.57 First World War 1917	7.00
Pane of eight 1st Poppies	10.00
Complete book	25.00

■ **2017, December 14. £15.99 Star Wars: The Making of the Droids, Aliens and Creatures**
Pane of four 1st deep red, two 2p, two £1.40 definitives	9.00
Pane of four (different) 1st Star Wars	6.00
Pane of four (different) 1st Star Wars	6.00
Pane of four (different) 1st Star Wars	6.00
Complete book	25.00

(*A limited edition of this book was produced, with silver-foil printing and an embossed metal case, sold at £75.)

■ **2018, January 23. £13.95 Game of Thrones**
Pane of six (different) 1st Game of Thrones	7.50
Pane of four (different) 1st Game of Thrones	6.00
Pane of four 1st Game of Thrones from miniature sheet	15.00
Pane of two 5p, one 20p, one £1.17 definitives, two 2nd Northern Ireland, two 1st Iron Throne	5.00
Complete book	25.00

(*A limited edition of this book was produced, with a leather folder, sold at £75.)

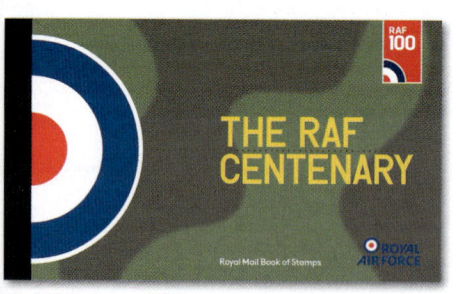

The RAF Centenary, 2018

■ **2018, March 20. £18.69 The RAF Centenary**
Pane of two 1st Lightning F6, two £1.40 Typhoon FGR4	7.00
Pane of 1st Hurricane Mk1, £1.40 Vulcan B2, £1.57 Sopwith Camel F1, £1.57 Nimrod MR2	7.00

Pane of four 1st 75th Anniversary of the Battle of Britain	6.00
Pane of two 1st, two £1.40 Red Arrows	6.00
Pane of three 2p, three 5p, two £1.17 definitives	4.50
Complete book	29.00

(*A limited edition of this book was produced, with an insert illustrating enlarged stamp artwork, sold at £45.)

■ **2018, September 13. £15.65 The Great War, 1918**
Pane of four 1st Poetry (First World War 2014–2017)	6.00
Pane of three 1st First World War 2018	4.50
Pane of three £1.55 First World War 2018	7.00
Pane of four 1st Poppies (2006), four 1st deep red definitives	10.00
Complete book	25.00

■ **2018, December 4. £15.50 Harry Potter**
Pane of five 1st (different) Harry Potter	5.50
Pane of five 1st (different) Harry Potter	5.50
Pane of two 1p, two 20p, two 50p, two £1.25 definitives	6.00
Double pane comprising Harry Potter miniature sheet	7.00
Complete book	25.00

(*A limited edition of this book was produced, with different covers and a card case, sold at £75.)

Leonardo da Vinci: 500 years, 2019

■ **2019, February 13. £13.10 Leonardo da Vinci: 500 Years**
Pane of four (different) 1st Leonardo da Vinci	4.50
Pane of four (different) 1st Leonardo da Vinci	4.50
Pane of four (different) 1st Leonardo da Vinci	4.50
Pane of two 5p, four 10p, two £1.55 definitives	6.00
Complete book	35.00

■ **2019, March 14. £17.45 Make Mine Marvel**
Pane of four (different) 1st Marvel	4.50
Pane of six (different) 1st Marvel	6.50
Panes comprising Marvel miniature sheet	8.00
Pane of two 1p, three 20p, two £1.25, one £1.45 definitives	8.00
Complete book	27.00

(*A limited edition of this book was produced with a retro-style cover and a tin presentation case, sold at £64.99. A second limited edition, with a 'cancellation' printed on each pane of stamps and the definitives year-coded '19' rather than '18', was issued on October 1, 2019, sold at £39.99.)

■ **2019, May 24. £17.20 Victoria: A Long and Glorious Reign**
Pane of two 1st and one £1.35 Queen Victoria Bicentenary	6.00
Pane of two 2p, two 50p definitives, two 1st Penny Black, one 1st Penny Red, one 1st Twopenny Blue	7.00

PRESTIGE STAMP BOOKS

Pane comprising Legacy of Prince Albert miniature sheet	31.00
Pane of one £1.35 and two £1.60 Queen Victoria Bicentenary	8.00
Complete book	50.00

■ 2019, November 26. £17.65 Star Wars: The Making of the Vehicles

Pane of four 2nd, two 5p, two £1.17, two 50p definitives	10.00
Double pane comprising Star Wars miniature sheet	9.00
Pane of four (different) 1st Star Wars	5.00
Pane of six (different) 1st Star Wars	7.00
Complete book	28.00

(*A limited edition of this book was produced, with a silver-foil cover and an embossed metal case, sold at £49.99.)

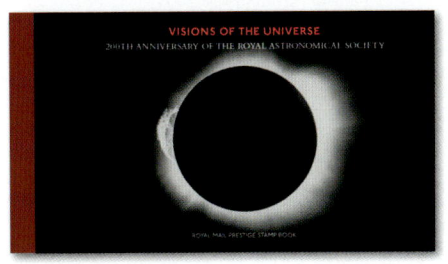

Visions of the Universe, 2020

■ 2020, February 11. £16.10 Visions of the Universe

Pane of one 2nd, one 1st, one £1.55 and one £1.60 Visions of the Universe	9.00
Pane of two 5p, two 10p, one 1st England, one 1st Northern Ireland, one 1st Scotland, one 1st Wales definitives	12.00
Pane of one 2nd, one 1st, one £1.55, one £1.60 Visions of the Universe (different)	9.00
Pane of two 1p, four 2p, two £1.35 definitives	9.00
Complete book	39.00

■ 2020, March 17. £16.99 Behind the Scenes of James Bond

Pane of two £1.60 James Bond	5.00
Pane of three 1st, one £1.60 James Bond	7.00
Pane of two 1st, two £1.55 from Q Branch miniature sheet	10.00
Pane of two 2nd definitives, four 2p definitives, two 2nd Scottish Flag, two 1st Union Flag	10.00
Complete book	39.00

(*A limited edition of this book was produced, with a silver-foil cover and an embossed metal case, sold at £64.99.)

End of the Second World War, 2020

■ 2020, May 8. £19.80 End of the Second World War

Pane of two 2nd, two 1st End of Second World War	7.00
Pane of four 5p, two 50p, two £1.63 definitives	14.00
Pane of two £1.42, two £1.63 End of Second World War	12.00
Pane of two 1st, two £1.63 from the End of Second World War miniature sheet	10.00
Complete book	41.00

■ 2020, July 9. £19.10 Queen

Pane of four 1st Queen	5.00
Pane of four £1.63 Queen	10.00
Pane of two 1st, two £1.63 from Queen: Live miniature sheet	8.00
Pane of four 1p definitives, four 1st Queen	6.00
Complete book	27.50

■ 2020, November 13. £18.35 Star Trek

Pane of six 1st Star Trek	7.00
Pane of six £1.65 Star Trek	7.00
Pane of six 1st from Star Trek: The Movies miniature sheet	9.00
Pane of three 2nd, two 2p, three 50p definitives	10.00
Complete book	27.00

(*A limited edition of this book was produced, with a silver-foil cover and a 3D-motion certificate, sold at £75.)

Only Fools & Horses, 2021

■ 2021, February 16. £21.70 Only Fools and Horses

Pane of four 1st Only Fools and Horses	6.00
Pane of three 2nd, two 1st, three 20p definitives	9.00
Pane of two 1st, two £1.70 from the Only Fools and Horses miniature sheet	9.00
Pane of four £1.70 Only Fools and Horses	11.00
Complete book	32.00

(*A limited edition of this book was produced, with a different cover and suitcase-style presentation box, sold at £54.99.)

■ 2021, May 28. £20.25 Paul McCartney

Pane of four 1st Paul McCartney	6.00
Pane of four £1.70 Paul McCartney	11.00
Pane of two 1st, two £1.70 from the Paul McCartney In The Studio miniature sheet	9.00
Pane of two 1st, two 2p, two 10p, two 50p definitives	9.00
Complete book	31.00

(*A limited edition of this book was produced, in a black folder with a silver foil signature, sold at £49.99.)

BRITISH STAMP MARKET VALUES 2024 **303**

PRESTIGE STAMP BOOKS

Industrial Revolutions, 2021

■ **2021, August 12. £18.03 Industrial Revolutions**
Pane of two 1st, two £1.70 Industrial Revolutions	10.00
Pane of two 2nd, two 1st (different) Industrial Revolutions	7.00
Pane of 2nd, 1st, £1.70 and £2.55 from the Electric Revolution miniature sheet	17.00
Pane of two 5p, two 10p, two 20p, two £1.70 definitives	20.00
Complete book	50.00

(*This book was designed with half the contents inverted, so it can be read from either end.)

■ **2021, September 17. £21.20 DC Collection**
Pane of six 1st DC Collections	8.00
Pane of six 1st DC Collections (different)	8.00
Double pane of six 1st from the Justice League miniature sheet	8.00
Pane of three 2nd, two 1st, two 20p definitives	9.00
Complete book	32.00

(*A limited edition of this book was produced, with a different cover design and silver-foil embossed box, sold at £49.99.)

■ **2022, January 20. £20.85 The Rolling Stones**
Pane of two 1st and two £1.70 Rolling Stones	8.00
Pane of two 1st and two £1.70 Rolling Stones (different)	8.00
Pane of two 10p, two 20p, two 50p, two £1.00 definitives	11.50
Pane of two 1st, two £1.70 from The Rolling Stones miniature sheet	8.00
Complete book	30.00

(*A limited edition of this book was produced, with a flight-case style presentation box, sold at £49.99.)

The Queen's Platinum Jubilee, 2022

■ **2022, February 4. £19.50 The Queen's Platinum Jubilee**
Pane of two 2p, two 10p, two 50p, two £1.50 definitives	18.00
Pane of two 1st, two £1.70 Platinum Jubilee	9.00
Pane of two 1st 90th Birthday and two 1st Diamond Jubilee	8.00
Pane of two 1st, two £1.70 Platinum Jubilee (different)	9.00
Complete book	29.00

(*A limited edition of this book was produced, in a foil-printed folder with a Royal Mail hologram, sold at £49.99.)

Unsung Heroes: Women of World War II, 2022

■ **2022, May 5. £20.75 Unsung Heroes: Women of World War II**
Pane of four 1st Women of World War II	6.00
Pane of two 1st, two £1.85 from the Spitfire Women miniature sheet	9.00
Pane of two 50p, three £1.00 definitives (self-adhesive)	9.00
Pane of six 1st Women of World War II (different)	9.00
Complete book	31.00

■ **2022, September 1. £21.25 Transformers**
Pane of four 1st Transformers	7.00
Pane of four £1.85 Transformers	12.00
Double pane of one 2nd, three 1st, one £1.85 from the Dinobots miniature sheet	10.00
Pane of two 50p, two £1 definitives (self-adhesive)	6.00
Complete book	32.00

(*A limited edition of this book was produced, with a different cover design and a bespoke slipcase, sold at £49.99.)

■ **2022, November 24. £21.55 Tutankamun: Finding a Pharaoh**
Pane of two 1st, two £1.85 Tutankamun	10.00
Pane of two 1st, two £1.85 from the Discovering Tutankamun's Tomb miniature sheet	11.00
Pane of two 10p, two 20p, one £1.85 definitives (self-adhesive)	5.00
Pane of two 2nd, two £2.55 Tutankamun	11.00
Complete book	33.00

■ **2023, February 16. £19.95 X-Men**
Pane of six 2nd X-Men	7.00
Pane of six 1st X-Men	10.00
Double pane of four 1st, one £1.85 from the X-Men miniature sheet	10.00
Pane of two 2nd, two £1.00 definitives (self-adhesive)	7.00
Complete book	28.00

(*A limited edition of this book was produced, with a silver-foil embossed cover and slipcase, sold at £49.99.)

■ **2023, March 9. £21.05 Flying Scotsman**
Pane of four 1st Flying Scotsman	7.00
Pane of four £1.85 Flying Scotsman	12.00
Pane of two 1st, two £1.85 from the Flying Scotsman miniature sheet	11.00
Pane three 20p, one £2.00 definitives (self-adhesive)	6.00
Complete book	32.00

(*A limited edition of this book was produced, with a different cover design and a presenation tin, sold at £64.99.)

magnet™
insurance

Looking to insure your collection?

- Stamps • Coins • Medals • Postcards • Model Railway + many more
We also offer Insurance for Clubs & Dealers

Contact us for a quote today!

Email: info@magnetinsurance.co.uk
Tel: 01636 858 249

Magnet Insurance Services Ltd.
Newark Beacon, Cafferata Way, Newark, NG24 2TN
Authorised & Regulated by the Financial Conduct Authority No.489228

BUSINESS SHEETS

BUSINESS SHEETS

Sheets comprising either 100 (1st class, 2nd class) or 50 (1st Large, 2nd Large, data matrix coded) self-adhesive stamps, intended as a convenient way for businesses to buy postage in bulk, are supplied folded in concertina style.

A year code identifying the date of printing has appeared within the stamps' security overlay since 2010, but separate dates are not listed here.

In this section, prices are given for what is typically collected: the top section of the sheet only, giving details of the contents and bearing four (1st class, 2nd class), five (1st Large, 2nd Large) or two (data matrix coded) stamps, mint on backing paper.

■ 1998–2000
Printed in gravure by Walsall. Matrix intact.
2nd bright blue (June 22, 1998)	75.00
1st orange-red (June 22, 1998)	80.00

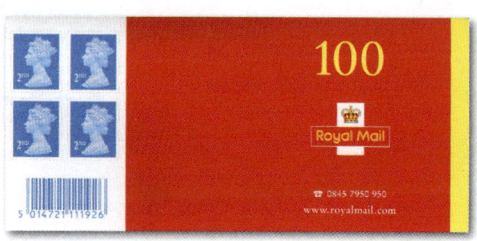

■ 2000–2002
Printed in gravure by Walsall (2nd) or Questa (1st). Matrix intact. Telephone number included.
2nd bright blue (September 4, 2000)	30.00
1st orange-red (September 4, 2000)	50.00

■ 2002
Printed in gravure by Enschedé. Matrix intact. Telephone number removed.
2nd bright blue (May 9, 2002)	25.00
1st orange-red (May 9, 2002)	25.00

■ 2002
Printed in gravure by Enschedé. Matrix intact.
2nd bright blue (July 4, 2002)	20.00
1st gold (July 4, 2002)	20.00

■ 2003–2007
Printed in gravure by Walsall or De La Rue. Matrix removed.
2nd bright blue
(March 18, 2003) 'The Real Network' added	17.00
(June 15, 2004) 'The Real Network' removed	15.00
(May 16, 2006) tariff change information added	15.00
(September 12, 2006) Pricing in Proportion stamps	15.00
(June 5, 2007) standard stamps with PiP information	15.00

2nd Large bright blue
(March 27, 2007) with PiP information	18.00

1st gold
(March 18, 2003) 'The Real Network' added	18.00
(June 15, 2004) 'The Real Network' removed	15.00
(May 16, 2006) tariff change information added	15.00
(September 12, 2006) Pricing in Proportion stamps	15.00
(June 5, 2007) standard stamps with PiP information	15.00

1st Large gold
(March 27, 2007) with PiP information	18.00

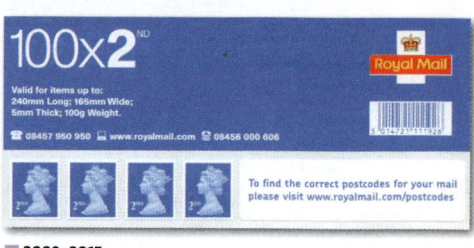

■ 2009–2015
Printed in gravure by Walsall except where stated. Matrix removed. Stamps with security overlay and U-shaped die-cut slits.

2nd bright blue
(March 31, 2009) 'To find the correct postcode...' added	15.00
(2013) FSC number added, fax number 08456 000606	10.00
(2014) FSC number added, fax number 03456 000606	10.00
(2015) backing paper with security overlay	10.00

2nd Large bright blue
(March 31, 2009)	14.00
(2013) FSC number added, fax number 08456 000606	17.00
(2014) FSC number added, fax number 03456 000606	17.00
(2016) backing paper with security overlay	17.00

1st gold
(March 31, 2009) 'To find the correct postcode...' added	15.00

1st Large gold
(March 31, 2009)	14.00

1st diamond blue
(February 6, 2012) FSC number C020244 (De La Rue)	35.00
(March 7, 2012) FSC number C023216	12.00

1st Large diamond blue
(March 19, 2012)	15.00

1st red
(2013) FSC number added, fax number 08456 000606	10.00
(2014) FSC number added, fax number 03456 000606	10.00
(2015) backing paper with security overlay	10.00

BUSINESS SHEETS

1st Large red
(2013) FSC number added, fax number 08456 000606   17.00
(2014) FSC number added, fax number 03456 000606   17.00
(2015) stamps and backing paper with security overlay   17.00

2016
Printed in gravure by ISP. Matrix removed. Revised font. Security backing paper, with text upright (SBP) or in alternate pairs of rows upright and inverted (SBP2).
2nd bright blue (October 20, 2016)   14.00
2nd Large bright blue (October 20, 2016)   16.00
1st dark red (October 20, 2016)   14.00
1st Large dark red (October 20, 2016)   19.00

2021
Printed in gravure by ISP. Matrix removed. Security backing paper (SBP2). Stamps with digital matrix codes.
2nd bright blue (March 23, 2021)   14.00

2022
Printed in gravure by ISP. Matrix removed. Security backing paper (SBP2). Stamps with digital matrix codes.
2nd holly green (February 1, 2022)   10.00
2nd Large dark pine green (February 1, 2022)   20.00
1st plum purple (February 1, 2022)   15.00
1st Large marine turquoise (February 1, 2022)   25.00

2023
Printed in gravure by Cartor. Matrix removed. Security backing paper (SBP2). Stamps with digital matrix codes.
2nd holly green   11.00
1st plum purple   16.00
2nd Large dark pine green   21.00

OFFICIALS

OFFICIAL STAMPS

During the reigns of Queen Victoria and King Edward VII stamps were overprinted for use by Government Departments. The prices in this section are quoted in two columns: mint (left) and fine used (right).

QUEEN VICTORIA, 1840–1901

■ Penny Black 'VR'
Printed by Perkins Bacon. Design as the standard stamp but with the stars in the top corners replaced by the letters 'V' and 'R'. Not officially issued.

1d black (1840 issue) with gum	£30,000	–
1d black (1840 issue) without gum	£16,000	–
1d black (1840 issue) with trial cancel	–	£40,000

■ Overprinted 'I.R. OFFICIAL' for use by the Inland Revenue
Printed by De La Rue.

½d green (1880 issue)	80.00	15.00
½d blue (1884 issue)	45.00	13.00
½d orange (1887 issue)	6.00	1.00
½d green (1900 issue)	8.00	3.50
1d lilac (1881 issue)	2.75	1.40
2½d lilac (1884 issue)	£350	50.00
2½d purple on blue paper (1887 issue)	£100	6.00
6d grey (1881 issue)	£350	50.00
6d purple on red paper (1887 issue)	£300	45.00
1/– green (1884 issue)	£6,000	£1,600
1/– green (1887 issue)	£900	95.00
1/– green, red (1900 issue)	£4,000	£1,100
5/– red (1884 issue)	£9,000	£2,000
10/– blue (1884 issue)	£10,000	£3,000
£1 brown (1884 issue)	£55,000	£24,000
£1 brown (1888 issue)	£75,000	£30,000
£1 green (1891 issue)	£10,000	£2,200

■ Overprinted 'O.W. OFFICIAL' for use by the Office of Works
Printed by De La Rue.

½d orange (1887 issue)	£200	£100
½d green (1900 issue)	£300	£150
1d lilac (1881 issue)	£350	£100
5d purple and blue (1887 issue)	£3,000	£900
10d purple and red (1887 issue)	£6,500	£2,000

■ Overprinted 'ARMY OFFICIAL'
Printed by De La Rue.

½d orange (1887 issue)	2.75	1.25
½d green (1900 issue)	3.00	5.00
1d lilac (1881 issue)	2.50	2.00
2½d purple on blue paper (1887 issue)	25.00	10.00
6d purple on red paper (1887 issue)	60.00	30.00

■ Overprinted 'GOVT PARCELS' for use by the Government
Printed by De La Rue.

1d lilac (1881 issue)	70.00	10.00
1½d lilac (1884 issue)	£300	40.00
1½d purple and green (1887 issue)	£100	4.00
2d green and red (1887 issue)	£150	14.00
4½d green and red (1887 issue)	£260	£110
6d green (1884 issue)	£2,400	£900
6d purple on red paper (1887 issue)	£200	40.00
9d green (1884 issue)	£2,000	£700
9d purple and blue (1887 issue)	£275	60.00
1/– brown (1881 issue)	£1,200	£200
1/– green (1887 issue)	£500	£110
1/– green, red (1887 issue)	£500	£125

OFFICIALS

■ **Overprinted 'BOARD OF EDUCATION'**
Printed by De La Rue.
5d purple and blue (1887 issue)	£4,500	£800
1/– green and red (1887 issue)	£10,000	£5,000

KING EDWARD VII, 1902–1904

■ **Overprinted 'I.R OFFICIAL' for use by the Inland Revenue**
Printed by De La Rue.
½d blue–green	20.00	2.00
1d red	15.00	1.25
2½d blue	£900	£200
6d purple	–	£300,000
1/– green and red	£3,500	£600
5/– red	£40,000	£9,000
10/– blue	£80,000	£40,000
£1 green	£50,000	£18,000

■ **Overprinted 'O.W. OFFICIAL' for use by the Office of Works**
Printed by De La Rue.
½d blue–green	£400	£110
1d red	£400	£100
2d green and red	£1,500	£400
2½d blue	£2,500	£500
10d purple and red	£35,000	£6,000

■ **Overprinted 'ARMY OFFICIAL'**
Printed by De La Rue.
½d blue–green	4.00	1.25
1d red	4.00	1.25
6d purple	£130	45.00

■ **Overprinted 'GOVT PARCELS' for use by the Government**
Printed by De La Rue.
1d red	30.00	10.00
2d green and red	£150	25.00
6d purple	£240	20.00
9d purple and blue	£550	85.00
1/– green and red	£1,200	£250

■ **Overprinted 'BOARD OF EDUCATION'**
Printed by De La Rue.
½d blue–green	£150	20.00
1d red	£150	20.00
2½d blue	£4,000	£275
5d purple and blue	£32,000	£9,000
1/– green and red	£150,000	–

■ **Overprinted 'R.H. OFFICIAL' for use by the Royal Household**
Printed by De La Rue.
½d blue–green	£300	£200
1d red	£275	£150

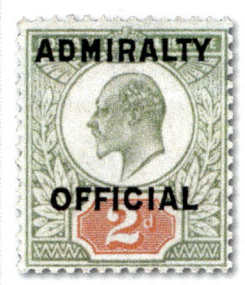

■ **Overprinted 'ADMIRALTY OFFICIAL' for use by the Royal Navy**
Printed by De La Rue.
½d blue–green	20.00	10.00
1d red	12.00	4.00
1½d purple and green	£275	70.00
2d green and red	£300	80.00
2½d blue	£425	75.00
3d purple on yellow paper	£375	70.00

BRITISH STAMP MARKET VALUES 2024

POSTAGE DUES

POSTAGE DUES

From 1914 until they were withdrawn from service in 2000, postage dues were affixed to covers by the postal service to denote postage unpaid or underpaid.

Up to 1936, prices are quoted in three columns: unmounted mint (left), mounted mint (centre) and used (right). After 1936, they are quoted for mint (left) and fine used (right).

PRE-DECIMAL ISSUES 1914–70

½d to 1/–

2/6 to £1

■ 1914–1923

Des: G. Eve. Printed in typography by Harrison (all values except 1/–) or Somerset House (½d, 1d, 5d, 1/–). Wmk: Simple Royal Cypher GVR. Perf 14x15.

Wmk sideways, with crown facing left when viewed from front

½d green	1.25	0.40	0.35
1d red on ordinary paper	1.25	0.50	0.25
1d red on chalky paper	7.50	4.00	4.00
1½d brown	95.00	35.00	13.00
2d black	1.25	0.80	0.30
3d violet	25.00	4.00	0.60
4d green	£300	£150	40.00
5d brown	11.00	4.00	2.00
1/– blue	90.00	19.00	3.00
Set	£400	95.00	22.00

Wmk inverted, with crown facing right

½d green	1.50	1.00	1.00
1d red	2.00	1.00	1.00
1½d brown	£120	50.00	15.00
2d black	3.00	1.00	1.00
3d violet	25.00	6.50	2.50
4d green	£110	35.00	5.00
5d brown	32.00	12.00	4.00
1/– blue	90.00	20.00	15.00

■ 1924–1935

Printed in typography by Waterlow and (from 1934) Harrison. Wmk: Multiple Crowns and Block GVR. Perf 14x15.

Wmk sideways, with crown facing left when viewed from front

½d green	1.25	0.50	0.30
1d red	1.25	0.50	0.10
1½d brown	90.00	27.00	9.00
2d black	6.00	1.25	0.20
3d violet	6.00	1.75	0.20
4d green	40.00	5.00	0.85
5d brown	110.00	35.00	17.00
1/– blue	25.00	4.00	0.25
2/6 purple (yellow paper)	190.00	50.00	0.80
Set	£450	£120	24.50

Wmk inverted, with crown facing right

½d green	4.50	2.00	1.50
1d red	–	–	8.50
1½d brown	–	–	25.00
2d black	–	–	8.50
3d violet	60.00	20.00	20.00
4d green	£125	40.00	40.00
1/– blue	–	–	–
2/6 purple (yellow paper)	–	–	–

■ 1936–1937

Printed in typography by Harrison. Wmk: Multiple Crowns and E8R, sideways. Perf 14x15.

½d green	7.00	6.50
1d red	1.00	1.50
2d black	6.00	6.00
3d violet	1.50	1.50
4d green	60.00	22.00
5d brown	40.00	18.00
1/– blue	20.00	6.50
2/6 purple on yellow paper	£300	10.00
Set	£425	65.00

■ 1937–1938

Printed in typography by Harrison. Wmk: Multiple Crowns and GVIR. Perf 14x15.

Wmk sideways, with crown facing left when viewed from front

½d green	8.50	4.50
1d red	2.00	0.20
2d black	1.25	0.30
3d violet	7.00	0.30
4d green	60.00	7.00
5d brown	7.00	0.80
1/– blue	45.00	0.90
2/6 purple on yellow paper	50.00	2.00
Set	£160	12.00

Wmk inverted, with crown facing right

1d red	£170	–
2d black	£170	–
3d violet	£170	–
4d green	£300	–
5d brown	£170	–
1/– blue	£170	–

■ 1951–1952

Printed in typography by Harrison. Wmk: Multiple Crowns and

POSTAGE DUES

GVIR. Perf 14x15.
Wmk sideways, with crown facing left when viewed from front

½d orange	3.50	3.50
1d blue	1.25	0.50
1½d green	1.25	1.50
4d blue	30.00	12.00
1/- brown	22.00	4.00
Set	45.00	18.00

Wmk inverted, with crown facing right

1d blue	–	–
1½d green	£110	–
1/- brown	£2,000	–

■ 1954–1955

Printed in typography by Harrison. Wmk: Tudor Crown and E2R. Perf 14x15.
Wmk sideways, with crown facing left when viewed from front

½d orange	8.00	8.50
2d black	25.00	16.00
3d violet	70.00	30.00
4d blue	20.00	16.00
5d brown	15.00	10.00
2/6 purple on yellow paper	£150	8.00
Set	£220	85.00

Wmk inverted, with crown facing right

½d orange	£150	–

■ 1955–1957

Printed in typography by Harrison. Wmk: St Edward's Crown and E2R. Perf 14x15.
Wmk sideways, with crown facing left when viewed from front

½d orange	4.00	4.00
1d blue	3.00	1.25
1½d green	7.00	4.50
2d black	25.00	5.25
3d violet	3.50	1.25
4d blue	16.00	2.00
5d brown	20.00	1.75
1/- brown	40.00	2.00
2/6 purple on yellow paper	£115	10.00
5/- red on yellow paper	60.00	18.00
Set	£240	40.00

Wmk inverted, with crown facing right

½d orange	60.00	–
1½d green	60.00	–
3d violet	90.00	–
4d blue	£125	–
1/- brown	–	–
2/6 purple on yellow paper	–	–
5/- red on yellow paper	–	£300

■ 1959–1963

Printed in typography by Harrison. Wmk: Multiple St Edward's Crown. Perf 14x15.
Wmk sideways, with crown facing left when viewed from front

½d orange	0.15	0.25
1d blue	0.15	0.10
1½d green	1.50	2.00
2d black	1.00	0.30
3d violet	0.35	0.15
4d blue	0.35	0.15
5d brown	0.35	0.30
6d purple	0.50	0.15
1/- brown	1.00	0.15
2/6 purple on yellow paper	1.50	0.20
5/- red on yellow paper	4.00	0.50
10/- blue on yellow paper	10.00	3.00
£1 black on yellow paper	30.00	4.50
Set	45.00	9.50

Wmk inverted, with crown facing right

½d orange	1.25	–
1d blue	90.00	–
2d black	£150	–
3d violet	60.00	–
4d blue	£225	–
5d brown	4.00	–
6d purple	£225	–
1/- brown	75.00	–
2/6 purple on yellow paper	15.00	–
5/- red on yellow paper	25.00	–
10/- blue on yellow paper	50.00	–

■ 1968–1969

Printed in typography by Harrison. No watermark. Perf 14x15. Chalky paper.
Gum Arabic

2d black	0.50	0.50
4d blue	0.40	0.20

PVA gum

2d black	1.50	1.00
3d violet	0.50	0.50
5d brown	5.00	5.00
6d purple	1.00	1.25
1/- brown	3.00	2.00

■ 1968–1969

Printed in gravure by Harrison. No watermark. Perf 14x15. Chalky paper. PVA gum.

4d blue	4.50	5.00
8d red	0.50	1.00

POSTAGE DUES

DECIMAL ISSUES 1970–2000

½p to 7p

10p to £5

1p to 5p

10p to £5

■ 1970–1975
Des: J. Matthews. Printed in gravure by Harrison. No watermark. Chalky paper. Perf: 14x15.

PVA gum. Original coated paper

½p turquoise	0.10	0.25
1p purple	0.50	0.10
2p green	0.25	0.10
3p blue	0.75	0.20
4p sepia	0.25	0.10
5p violet	1.00	0.30
10p carmine	0.80	0.30
20p deep green	1.10	0.50
50p blue	2.25	1.00
£1 black	4.00	0.25

PVA gum. Fluorescent coated paper

1p purple	0.50	–
3p blue	1.75	–
5p violet	2.25	–
10p carmine	45.00	–
20p deep green	45.00	–
£5 orange and black	15.00	1.00

PVAD gum, blue-tinged

1p purple	0.10	–
2p green	0.10	–
3p blue	0.15	–
4p sepia	0.15	–
5p violet	0.15	–
7p red-brown	0.25	0.25
10p carmine	0.25	–
11p green	0.40	0.35
20p deep green	0.50	–
50p blue	1.00	–
£1 black	2.00	–
£5 orange and black	18.00	1.00
Set (one of each value)	20.00	10.00

PVAD gum. Phosphor coated paper

10p carmine	0.70	0.50
20p deep green	1.00	0.75

■ 1982, June 9
Des: Sedley Place. Printed in gravure by Harrisons. No watermark. Perf: 14x15.

1p crimson	0.15	0.10
2p bright blue	0.15	0.10
3p purple	0.15	0.15
4p blue	0.15	0.10
5p brown	0.15	0.10
10p light brown	0.20	0.10
20p sage green	0.40	0.30
25p blue-grey	0.60	0.60
50p charcoal	1.00	1.50
£1 red	1.50	0.50
£2 turquoise	3.00	2.50
£5 dull orange	6.00	1.25
Set	11.00	5.00
Gutter pairs	30.00	–

1p to £5

■ 1994, February 15
Des: Sedley Place. Printed in lithography by Questa. No watermark. Perf: 15x14.

1p yellow, orange-red and black	0.15	0.30
2p magenta, purple and black	0.15	0.30
5p yellow, brown and black	0.20	0.30
10p yellow, green and black	0.30	0.40
20p violet, emerald-green and black	1.00	1.00
25p magenta, claret and black	1.50	1.50
£1 pink, violet and black	6.00	6.00
£1.20 green, blue and black	7.50	7.50
£5 green, charcoal and black	17.50	17.50
Set	27.00	28.00
First day cover	–	35.00

JOHN LAMONBY
FINE BRITISH ADHESIVES

MY EARLY GREAT BRITAIN TWICE MONTHLY LISTING...

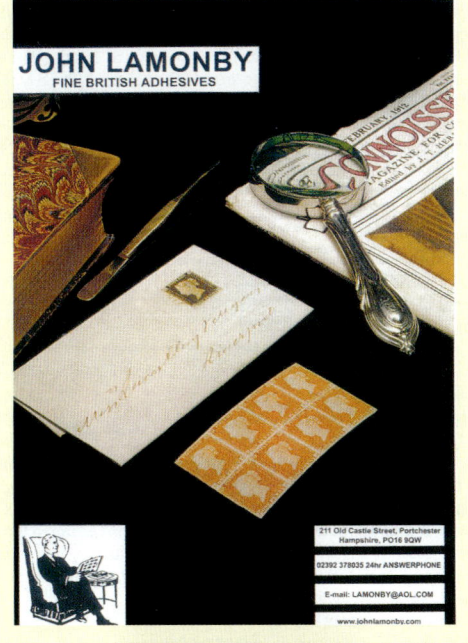

... IS FREE UPON REQUEST AND IS READY NOW

JOHN LAMONBY
FINE BRITISH ADHESIVES

SAME DAY DESPATCH

ALL ORDERS POST FREE

Callers by appointment
211 Old Castle Street, Portchester, Hampshire PO16 9QW, Great Britain,
Tel: 02392378035
E-mail: lamonby@aol.com   www.johnlamonby.com
ESTABLISHED IN PHILATELY FOR 45 YEARS

VENDING MACHINE STAMPS POST & GO

POST & GO STAMPS

In most of this section, prices are quoted in two columns: mint on backing paper (left) and fine used (right). Where there is only one column, this is for mint stamps on backing paper, except in the case of first day covers.

Post office machines

Since October 2008, self-service kiosks have been installed at an increasing number of post offices, vending self-adhesive stamps to order.

Besides a 'Post It Now' service with labels meeting a wide range of postage rates for immediate use (which are outside the scope of this publication), they offer a 'Buy A Stamp' service in which a pre-printed base design is overprinted at the time of the transaction with details of one of a limited selection of postage rates, along with a code which identifies the post office and machine number.

The machines installed in post offices from 2008 were manufactured by Wincor Nixdorf, and could print the stamps in strips of up to five. Between February 2014 and March 2015, these were gradually replaced by machines manufactured by NCR, which can print in strips of up to six.

Royal Mail machines

Since 2011, Royal Mail has also had its own range of machines, initially manufactured by Hytech and from 2014 by IAR. Overprints from these have a different typeface from the machines installed in post offices.

Royal Mail machines have been used to print the strips and packs which are available from the philatelic service. They have also been temporarily installed at events in Britain and abroad, in 'pop-up' post shops, and at a range of museums, in many cases dispensing stamps with an additional commemorative or location-identifying inscription. They have also been available at Royal Mail enquiry offices, initially with location-identifiers in 2014-15 although this practice was then discontinued.

Some machines, such as those at the Royal Mail Engineering Department at Wheatstone House, Swindon, and at RAF Northolt, were accessible only to people working there.

As the use of Post & Go has extended to other stamp-issuing countries, machines installed at Broad Street in Jersey, Envoy House in Guernsey and Gibraltar House in London have also dispensed stamps with UK postage rates and location-identifying overprints.

When machines are installed at exhibitions beyond Europe, strips with the same event inscription are also made available from Tallents House in Edinburgh.

Postage rates

From 2008, the five rates available were 1st class, 1st Large, Europe up to 20g, Worldwide up to 10g and Worldwide up to 20g. Towards the end of 2011, Worldwide up to 40g was added to offer a sixth option.

From 2011, vending machines have offered a 'collector's strip' comprising one of each of the six standard rates (although in the case of Wincor Nixdorf machines these were vended as two strips of three).

A 2nd class rate was introduced in 2013, although it was not made widely available until 2014 and is not included in standard collector's strips.

With tariff changes in 2014, the Worldwide up to 10g and Worldwide up to 20g rates were replaced by Europe up to 60g and Worldwide up to 60g, and after a short delay the Europe up to 20g rate was changed to Europe up to 20g/Worldwide up to 10g (expressed on the stamps as 'Euro 20g/World 10g'). In 2015, both 60g rates were uprated to 100g.

In September 2020, the six rates became 1st class up to 100g, 1st Large up to 100g, Euro 20g/World 10g, Euro 100g/World 20g, World 100g Zone 1–3 and World 100g Zone 2. To avoid confusion as to the meaning of Zone 1-3, the wording was quickly changed to World 100g Zone 1&3 (Royal Mail machines only).

In January 2021, the rates were altered again, to 1st class up to 100g, 1st Large up to 100g, Euro 100g/World 20g, Worldwide up to 100g, Europe Large 100g and Worldwide Large 100g.

In April 2023 the Euro 100g/World 20g from Royal Mail machines was changed to Europe up to 100g.

Although pictorial sets were regularly superseded by new designs until 2018, none has formally been withdrawn from use, with the result that new rates have been reported machine-printed on old designs. Examples have also been found of the 2nd class design printed with 1st class rates, and vice versa.

Printing

It is possible to distinguish the type of machine used to print a stamp from its typeface. In most cases the differences are slight, but two exceptions are '60g' and 'Euro 20g/World 10g', where there are clear differences between different machines.

Starting in September 2015, some rolls of stamps required in limited quantities were printed digitally. These have a shinier appearance than gravure printings.

Stamps printed in corrupted typefaces, with misplaced inscriptions and with incorrect values also exist, especially from the 2010–12 period, but they are are outside the scope of this publication.

Phosphor

All the stamps have two phosphor bands, except the 2nd class Machin, which has one phosphor band.

DEFINITIVE ISSUES

Machin portrait (1st, 1st L, E20g, W10g, W20g)

■ **2008, October 8. Machin Portrait**
Printed in gravure by Walsall. Self-adhesive. Olive-brown security overlay with no year code. Machine-printed in black.
Strip of five (one of each value) 35.00
Philatelic pack (one of each value) 90.00

POST & GO VENDING MACHINE STAMPS

Machin portrait (1st, 1st L and higher values)

■ **2010, September. Machin Portrait**
Printed in gravure by Walsall. Self-adhesive. Olive-brown security overlay with no year code, or year code from '13' onwards. Machine-printed in black, in a new typeface suitable for use with pictorial designs.

Basic collector's strips
1st, 1st L, E20, W10, W20, W40	20.00
1st, 1st L, E20, E60, W40, W60 (Wincor)	18.00
1st, 1st L, E20, E60, W40, W60 (NCR)	30.00
1st, 1st L, E20/W10, E60, W40, W60 (NCR)	18.00
1st, 1st L, E20/W10, E60, W40, W60 (RM)	25.00
1st, 1st L, E20/W10, E60, W20, W60 (Wincor)	45.00
1st, 1st L, E20/W10, E100, W20, W100 (NCR)	20.00
1st, 1st L, E20/W10, E100, W20, W100 (RM)	20.00
1st, 1st L, E20/W10, E100/W20, W100 Z1-3, W100 Z2	27.00
1st, 1st L, E100/W20, W100, EL, WL	22.00

Royal Mail offices collector's strips
'Crewe' (Royal Mail Enquiry Office), 2015	27.00
'Bradford N' (Royal Mail Enquiry Office), 2015	27.00
'Wheatstone House' (Royal Mail Engineering Dept), 2015	–
'Royal Mail HQ' (Unilever House), 2017	40.00

Postal Museum collector's strips
'The B.P.M.A.' (1st, 1st L, E20, W10, W20, W40)	25.00
'The B.P.M.A.' (1st, 1st L, E20/W10, E60, W40, W60)	25.00
'The B.P.M.A.' (1st, 1st L, E20/W10, E100, W20, W100)	25.00
'The Postal Museum', 2016	20.00
'The Postal Museum' with no logo, 2018	20.00
'The Postal Museum' (1st, 1st L, E20/W10, E100/W20, Z1&3, Z2)	20.00
'Mail Rail' (1st, 1st L, E20/W10, E100, W20, W100)	20.00
'Mail Rail' (1st, 1st L, E20/W10, E100/W20, Z1&3, Z2)	25.00
'Mail Rail' (1st, 1st L, E100/W20, W100, EL, WL)	20.00
'The Postal Museum' (1st, 1st L, E100/W20, W100, EL, WL)	22.00
'The Postal Museum' (1st, 1st L, E100, W100, EL, WL)	25.00
'Mail Rail' (1st, 1st L, E100, W100, EL, WL)	25.00

National Museum of the Royal Navy collector's strips
'The NMRN' (1st, 1st L, E20/W10, E60, W20, W60), 2014	25.00
'The NMRN' (1st, 1st L, E20/W10, E100, W20, W100), 2014	22.00
'Royal Navy', 2015	20.00
'Royal Navy' with logo, 2017	16.00
'Royal Navy' (1st, 1st L, E20/W10, E100/W20, Z1-3, Z2)	35.00
'Royal Navy' (1st, 1st L, E20/W10, E100/W20, Z1&3, Z2)	35.00
'Royal Navy' (1st, 1st L, E100/W20, W100, EL, WL)	20.00
'Royal Navy' (1st, 1st L, E100, W100, EL, WL)	25.00

Royal Marines Museum collector's strips
'The RMM' (1st, 1st L, E20/W10, E60, W20, W60), 2014	21.00
'The RMM' (1st, 1st L, E20/W10, E100, W20, W100), 2014	22.00
'Royal Marines', 2015	20.00

Fleet Air Arm Museum collector's strips
'The FAAM', 2015	21.00
'Fleet Air Arm', 2015	20.00
'Fleet Air Arm' (1st, 1st L, E20, W10, E100/W20, Z1-3, Z2)	35.00
'Fleet Air Arm' (1st, 1st L, E20, W10, E100/W20, Z1&3, Z2)	35.00
'Fleet Air Arm' (1st, 1st L, E100/W20, W100, EL, WL)	20.00
'Fleet Air Arm' (1st, 1st L, E100, W100, EL, WL)	25.00

Royal Navy Submarine Museum collector's strips
'The RNSM', 2015	21.00
'RN Submarine', 2015	20.00
'RN Submarine' (1st, 1st L, E20/W10, E100/W20, Z1-3, Z2)	35.00
'RN Submarine' (1st, 1st L, E20/W10, E100/W20, Z1&3, Z2)	35.00
'RN Submarine' (1st, 1st L, E100/W20, W100, EL, WL)	20.00
'RN Submarine' (1st, 1st L, E100, W100, EL, WL)	25.00

Royal Signals Museum collector's strips
'Royal Corps of Signals', 2016	23.00

HMS Trincomalee collector's strips
'HMS Trincomalee', 2017	20.00

Ministry of Defence collector's strips
'Ministry of Defence' (MOD Abbey Wood), 2017	20.00

Museum of the Great Western Railway collector's strips
'Steam GWR', 2015	22.00
'Steam GWR', 2017	20.00
'Steam' (1st, 1st L, E20/W10, E100/W20, Z1-3, Z2)	35.00
'Steam' (1st, 1st L, E20/W10, E100/W20, Z1&3, Z2)	35.00
'Steam' (1st, 1st L, E100/W20, W100, EL, WL)	20.00
'Steam' (1st, 1st L, E100, W100, EL, WL)	25.00

East Anglia Railway Museum collector's strips
'EARM', 2017	20.00

Shakespeare Birthplace Trust collector's strips
'Shakespeare Birthplace Trust', 2016	20.00
'Shakespeare Birthplace Trust' (1st, 1st L, E100/W20, W100, EL, WL)	20.00
'Shakespeare Birthplace Trust' (1st, 1st L, E100, W100, EL, WL)	25.00

Commemorative collector's strips
'Arnold Machin/1911-1999' (Autumn Stampex 2011)	20.00
'Diamond Jubilee/1952-2012' (Spring Stampex 2012)	20.00
'Perth 2012/19-22 October' (ABPS Exhibition 2012)	80.00
'The Coronation/60th Anniversary' (Spring Stampex 2013)	20.00
'84th Scottish/Congress 2013' (ASPS Congress 2013)	24.00
'Australia 2013/Stamp Expo' (Australia 2013)	30.00
'Australia 2013/World Stamp Expo' (Tallents House 2013)	20.00
'Stampex 2014/19-22 February' (Spring Stampex 2014)	24.00
'Stampex Spring/19-22 February' (Spring Stampex 2014)	30.00
'The B.P.M.A./Postage Due 1914' (BPMA 2014)	
(1st, 1st L, E20, W10, W20, W40)	32.00
(1st , 1st L, E20, E60, W40, W60)	26.00
'85th Scottish/Congress 2014' (ASPS Congress 2014)	30.00
'The B.P.M.A./Inland Airmail 1934' (BPMA 2014)	25.00
'PhilaKorea 2014/World Stamp Expo' (PhilaKorea 2014)	20.00
'The B.P.M.A./Trollope 200' (BPMA 2015)	
(1st, 1st L, E20/W10, E60, W20, W60)	22.00
(1st, 1st L, E20/W10, E100, W20, W100)	22.00
'86th Scottish Congress 2015' (ASPS Congress 2015)	25.00
'86th Scottish' (ASPS Congress 2015)	40.00
'Messe Essen/7-9 May 2015' (Essen Stamp Fair 2015)	27.00
'The B.P.M.A./Penny Black 175' (BPMA 2015)	20.00
'Europhilex London/Penny Black 175' (London 2015)	20.00
'Singpex 2015 World Stamp Expo' (Singpex 2015)	20.00
'Queen Elizabeth II Longest Reign' (Autumn Stampex 2015)	20.00
'Sindelfingen October 2015' (Sindelfingen Stamp Fair 2015)	20.00
'Paris November 2015' (Paris Autumn Stamp Fair 2015)	20.00
'500 Years of Royal Mail' (Spring Stampex 2016)	20.00
'500 Years of Royal Mail' (Guildhall June 2016)	20.00

VENDING MACHINE STAMPS POST & GO

'87th Scottish Congress' (ASPS Congress 2016)	25.00
'RN Submarine/Battle of Jutland' (RNSM 2016)	20.00
'Royal Navy/Battle of Jutland' (RMRN 2016)	20.00
'Royal Marines/Battle of Jutland' (RMM 2016)	20.00
'Fleet Air Arm/Battle of Jutland' (FAAM 2016)	20.00
'King Edward VIII 1936' (Postal Museum 2016)	20.00
'Liverpool 2016' (Labour Party Conference 2016)	45.00
'Glasgow 2016' (Scottish Nationalists Conference 2016)	35.00
'Birmingham 2016' (Conservative Party Conference 2016)	35.00
'Fleet Air Arm L2551/G 1st Jet Carrier Landing' (FAAM 2016)	20.00
'Season's Greetings from all at BFPO' (RAF Northolt 2016)	35.00
'Machin Anniversary 1967-2017' (Spring Stampex 2017)	20.00
'65th Anniversary of Accession' (Spring Stampex 2017)	20.00
'Steam GWR King George V 90th' (Museum of GWR 2017)	20.00
'Shakespeare Week' (Shakespeare Birthplace Trust 2017)	20.00
'88th Scottish Congress' (ASPS Congress 2017)	34.00
'Heligoland Big Bang 1947' (Explosion Museum 2017)	20.00
'HMS Alliance 14th May 1947' (Submarine Museum 2017)	20.00
'HMS Trincomalee 200 Years' (HMS Trincomalee 2017)	25.00
'Fleet Air Arm Sea King ZA298 Junglie' (FAAM 2017)	16.00
'Royal Navy Queen Elizabeth II Carrier' (NMRN 2017)	25.00
'Royal Navy Queen Elizabeth Carrier 2017' (NMRN 2017)	25.00
'Brighton 2017' (Labour Party Conference 2017)	30.00
'Glasgow 2017' (Scottish Nationalists Conference 2017)	30.00
'Manchester 2017' (Conservative Party Conference 2017)	30.00
'HMS Trincomalee 12th Oct 1817' (HMS Trincomalee 2017)	20.00
'HMS Trincomalee 19th Oct 1817' (HMS Trincomalee 2017)	20.00
'The Postal Museum/'F' box 50' (Postal Museum 2018)	20.00
'Fleet Air Arm Concorde 50' (FAAM 2019)	20.00
'Royal Navy Lest We Forget 100' (NMRN 2019)	20.00
'Shakespeare 1616' (Shakespeare Birthplace Trust 2019)	20.00
'Steam Celebrates 20 Years' (Museum of GWR 2020)	35.00
'NPM 50' (Postal Museum 2019)	20.00
'Virtual Stampex' (Postal Museum 2020)	25.00
'Wish You Were Here' (Postal Museum 2021)	20.00
'Royal Navy/Black Tot Day 31st July 1970' (NMRN 2021)	31.00
'RN Submarine/Black Tot Day 31st July 1970' (RNSM 2021)	31.00
'Fleet Air Arm/Black Tot Day 31st July 1970' (FAAM 2021)	31.00
'Royal Navy/Trafalgar Day' (NMRN 2021)	33.00
'Royal Navy/Lest We Forget' (NMRN 2021)	31.00
'The Postal Museum/London 2022' (Postal Museum 2022)	31.00
'The Postal Museum/Sorting Britain' (Postal Museum 2022)	22.00
'Mail Rail/Queen's Platinum Jubilee' (Postal Museum 2022)	25.00
'Royal Navy/Falklands 40th' (NMRN 2022)	31.00
'RN Submarine/Falklands 40th' (RNSM 2022)	31.00
'Fleet Air Arm/Falklands 40th' (FAAM 2022)	25.00
'Fleet Air Arm/The Queen's Platinum Jubilee' (FAAM 2022)	25.00
'Royal Navy/The Queen's Platinum Jubilee' (NMRN 2022)	25.00
'Steam/Queen's Platinum Jubilee' (Museum of GWR 2022)	25.00
'The Queen's Platinum Jubilee' (Shakespeare Trust 2022)	25.00
'Fleet Air Arm/Carrier Experience' (FAAM 2023)	25.00

Union flag (1st, 1st L and higher values)

■ **2012, May 21. Union Flag**
Des: Dick Davis, from illustration by Anton Morris. Printed in gravure by Walsall. Self-adhesive. Blue security overlay with no year code or year code '13'. Machine-printed in black.

Single (1st)	2.25
Philatelic pack (1st only)	3.25
First day cover	10.00
Basic collector's strips	
1st, 1st L, E20, W10, W20, W40	17.50
1st, 1st L, E20, E60, W40, W60 (Wincor)	20.00
1st, 1st L, E20/W10, E60, W40, W60 (RM)	30.00
1st, 1st L, E20/W10, E100, W20, W100 (RM)	25.00
1st, 1st L, E20/W10, E100, W20, W100 (NCR)	20.00
1st, 1st L, E20/W10, E100, W20, W100 Z1-3, W100 Z2	20.00
Postal Museum collector's strips	
'The B.P.M.A.' (1st, 1st L, E20, W10, W20, W40)	20.00
'The B.P.M.A.' (1st, 1st L, E20/W10, E60, W40, W60)	25.00
'The Postal Museum', 2016	20.00
'The Postal Museum' with no logo, 2018	20.00
'The Postal Museum' (1st, 1st L, E20/W10, E100/W20, Z1&3, Z2)	25.00
'The Postal Museum' (1st, 1st L, E100/W20, W100, EL, WL)	20.00
'The Postal Museum' (1st, 1st L, E100, W100, EL, WL)	25.00
National Museum of the Royal Navy collector's strips	
'The NMRN' (1st, 1st L, E20/W10, E60, W20, W60) 2014	22.00
'The NMRN' (1st, 1st L, E20/W10, E100, W20, W100) 2014	22.00
'Royal Navy', 2015	20.00
'Royal Navy' (1st, 1st L, E20/W10, E100/W20, Z1-3, Z2)	35.00
'Royal Navy' (1st, 1st L, E20/W10, E100/W20, Z1&3, Z2)	35.00
'Royal Navy' (1st, 1st L, E100/W20, W100, EL, WL)	20.00
'Royal Navy' (1st, 1st L, E100, W100, EL, WL)	25.00
Royal Marines Museum collector's strips	
'The RMM' (1st, 1st L, E20/W10, E60, W20, W60) 2014	22.00
'The RMM' (1st, 1st L, E20/W10, E100, W20, W100) 2014	22.00
'Royal Marines', 2015	20.00
Fleet Air Arm Museum collector's strips	
'The FAAM', 2015	22.00
'Fleet Air Arm', 2015	20.00
'Fleet Air Arm' (1st, 1st L, E20/W10, E100/W20, Z1-3, Z2)	35.00
'Fleet Air Arm' (1st, 1st L, E20/W10, E100/W20, Z1&3, Z2)	35.00
'Fleet Air Arm' (1st, 1st L, E100/W20, W100, EL, WL)	20.00
'Fleet Air Arm' (1st, 1st L, E100, W100, EL, WL)	25.00
Royal Navy Submarine Museum collector's strips	
'The RNSM', 2015	22.00
'RN Submarine', 2015	20.00
'RN Submarine' (1st, 1st L, E20/W10, E100/W20, Z1-3, Z2)	35.00
'RN Submarine' (1st, 1st L, E20/W10, E100/W20, Z1&3, Z2)	35.00
'RN Submarine' (1st, 1st L, E100/W20, W100, EL, WL)	20.00
'RN Submarine' (1st, 1st L, E100, W100, EL, WL)	25.00
Royal Signals Museum collector's strips	
'Royal Corps of Signals', 2016	20.00
Ministry of Defence collector's strips	
'Ministry of Defence' (MOD Abbey Wood) 2017	20.00
British Forces Post Office collector's strips	
'Headquarters BFPO' (RAF Northolt) 2016	35.00
Museum of the Great Western Railway collector's strips	
'Steam GWR', 2015	22.00
Shakespeare Birthplace Trust collector's strips	
'Shakespeare Birthplace Trust', 2016	20.00
'Shakespeare Birthplace Trust' (1st, 1st L, E100, W100, EL, WL)	25.00
Commemorative collector's strips	

POST & GO VENDING MACHINE STAMPS

'Diamond Jubilee/1952-2012' (Autumn Stampex 2012)	20.00
'Perth 2012/19-22 October' (ABPS Exhibition 2012)	80.00
'84th Scottish/Congress 2013' (ASPS Congress 2013)	22.00
"Australia 2013/Stamp Expo" (Australia 2013)	32.00
'Australia 2013/World Stamp Expo' (Tallents House 2013)	20.00
'The Coronation/60th Anniversary' (Autumn Stampex 2013)	17.00
'The B.P.M.A./Postage Due 1914' (BPMA 2014)	
(1st, 1st L, E20, W10, W20, W40)	25.00
(1st, 1st L, E20, E60, W40, W60)	27.00
'85th Scottish/Congress 2014' (ASPS Congress 2014)	30.00
'The NMRN/Trafalgar Day' (NMRN October 2014)	35.00
'The NMRN/V.E. Day 70' (NMRN May 2015)	22.00
'PhilaKorea 2014/World Stamp Expo' (Philakorea 2014)	22.00
'The RMM/V.E. Day 70' (RMM May 2015)	22.00
'Broad Street' (Jersey 2014)	27.00
'Spring Stampex/February 2015' (Spring Stampex 2015)	17.00
'The FAAM/V.E. Day 70' (FAAM May 2015)	22.00
'86th Scottish Congress' (ASPS Congress 2015)	40.00
'86th Scottish Congress 2015' (ASPS Congress 2015)	22.00
'Messe Essen/7-9 May 2015' (Essen Stamp Fair 2015)	27.00
'Gibraltar House' (Gibraltar Embassy, London 2015)	32.00
'Singpex 2015 World Stamp Expo' (Singpex 2015)	20.00
'Envoy House' (Guernsey 2015)	20.00
'Sindelfingen October 2015' (Sindelfingen Stamp Fair 2015)	20.00
'Hong Kong/November 2015' (Hong Kong 2015)	20.00
'Royal Navy/Trafalgar Day' (NMRN October 2015)	22.00
'Royal Marines/Trafalgar Day' (RMM October 2015)	22.00
'Steam GWR/Swindon 175' (GWR Museum 2016)	25.00
'87th Scottish Congress 2016' (ASPS Congress 2016)	22.00
'Royal Navy/Battle of Jutland' (NMRN June 2016)	21.00
'RN Submarine/Battle of Jutland' (RNSM June 2016)	21.00
'Royal Marines/Battle of Jutland' (RMM June 2016)	21.00
'Fleet Air Arm/Battle of Jutland' (FAAM June 2016)	21.00
'World Stamp Show NY2016' (New York 2016)	18.00
'Steam GWR Swindon 175' (Museum of GWR 2016)	20.00
'Fleet Air Arm L2551/G 03 Dec 45' (FAAM 2016)	20.00
'Shakespeare Week' (Shakespeare Birthplace Trust 2017)	20.00
'Heligoland Big Bang 1947' (Explosion Museum 2017)	20.00
'HMS Alliance 14th May 1947' (Submarine Museum 2017)	20.00
'Royal Signals White Helmets' (Royal Signals Museum 2017)	20.00
'HMS Trincomalee 200 Years' (HMS Trincomalee 2017)	20.00
'The Postal Museum Official Opening' (Postal Museum 2017)	20.00
'Fleet Air Arm GR9A Harrier ZD433' (FAAM 2017)	20.00
'Royal Navy QE II Carrier' (NMRN 2017)	20.00
'Royal Navy QE Carrier 2017' (NMRN 2017)	16.00
'HMS Trincomalee 12th Oct 1817' (HMS Trincomalee 2017)	20.00
'HMS Trincomalee' (HMS Trincomalee, January 2018)	20.00
'Fleet Air Arm Concorde 50' (FAAM 2019)	20.00
'Black Tot Day/31st July 1970' (NMRN 2021)	31.00
'Royal Navy/Trafalgar Day' (NMRN 2021)	33.00
'Royal Navy/Lest We Forget' (NMRN 2021)	31.00
'Fleet Air Arm/Lest We Forget' (FAAM 2021)	31.00
'Royal Navy/Falklands 40th' (NMRN 2022)	31.00
'RN Submarine/Falklands 40th' (RNSM 2022)	31.00
'Royal Navy/The Queen's Platinum Jubilee' (NMRN 2022)	31.00
'RN Submarine/The Queen's Platinum Jubilee' (RNSM 2022)	31.00
'Fleet Air Arm/The Queen's Platinum Jubilee' (FAAM 2022)	31.00
'Steam GWR/The Queen's Platinum Jubilee' (GWR 2021)	31.00
'The Queen's Platinum Jubilee' (Shakespeare Trust)	31.00
'Fleet Air Arm/Falklands 40th' (FAAM 2022)	25.00
'Royal Navy/Queen's Platinum Jubilee (MNRN 2022)	25.00
'Fleet Air Arm/Carrier Experience' (FAAM 2023)	25.00

Machin portrait (2nd, 2nd Large)

■ **2013, February 20. Machin Portrait**
Printed in gravure by Walsall. Self-adhesive. Blue security overlay with year code from '12' onwards. Machine-printed in black.

Pair (2nd, 2nd L)	5.00
Philatelic pack (2nd, 2nd L)	3.50
First day cover	4.00
Royal Mail offices collector's strips	
'Crewe' (Royal Mail enquiry office), 2015	14.00
'Bradford N' (Royal Mail enquiry office), 2015	14.00
'Wheatstone House' (Royal Mail Engineering Dept), 2015	–
'Royal Mail HQ' (Unilever House), 2017	12.00
Postal Museum collector's strips	
'The B.P.M.A.', 2013	7.50
'The Postal Museum', 2016	6.00
'The Postal Museum' with no logo, 2017	5.00
British Forces Post Office collector's strips	
statue motif (RAF Northolt), 2016	32.00
'Headquarters BFPO' (RAF Northolt), 2016	30.00
Commemorative collector's strips	
'The B.P.M.A./Inland Airmail 1934' (BPMA 2014)	12.00
'The B.P.M.A./Trollope 200' (BPMA 2015)	7.50
'The B.P.M.A./Penny Black 175' (BPMA 2015)	7.50
'King Edward VIII 1936' (Postal Museum 2016)	6.00
'The Postal Museum Official Opening' (Postal Museum 2017)	7.00
'Brighton 2017' (Labour Party Conference 2017)	10.00
'Glasgow 2017' (Scottish Nationalists Conference 2017)	10.00
'Manchester 2017' (Conservative Party Conference 2017)	10.00
'The Postal Museum/'F' box 50' (Postal Museum 2018)	7.00
'Wish You Were Here' (Postal Museum 2021)	5.00

Machin portrait (wide range of values on demand)

■ **2014, February 28. Machin Portrait. Open-value Faststamps**
Printed in gravure by Walsall. Self-adhesive. Olive-brown or blue security overlay with year code from '12' onwards. Machine-printed in black with new service indicia of NCR machines.

Collector's pack (2L, 1L, 2LG, 1LG, A)	30.00

(*The collector's pack was issued on July 7.)

VENDING MACHINE STAMPS POST & GO

PICTORIAL ISSUES

The values noted for each design are those which appertained when they were first issued, and should be expected in collector's strips. They may also exist with different values which were introduced later.

Blue tit (1st, 1st L, E20g, W10g, W20g)
Goldfinch (1st, 1st L, E20g, W10g, W20g)
House sparrow (1st, 1st L, E20g, W10g, W20g)
Robin (1st, 1st L, E20g, W10g, W20g)
Starling (1st, 1st L, E20g, W10g, W20g)
Wood pigeon (1st, 1st L, E20g, W10g, W20g)

■ **2010, September 17. Birds of Britain, series 1**
Des: Kate Stephens, from illustrations by Robert Gillmor. Printed in gravure by Walsall. Self-adhesive. Machine-printed in black.
Set of 6 (all 1st class)   20.00   –
Collector's strip (one of each value)   75.00   –
Philatelic pack (all 1st class)   20.00   –
First day cover   –   18.00

Blackbird (1st, 1st L, E20g, W10g, W20g)
Chaffinch (1st, 1st L, E20g, W10g, W20g)
Collared dove (1st, 1st L, E20g, W10g, W20g)
Greenfinch (1st, 1st L, E20g, W10g, W20g)
Long-tailed tit (1st, 1st L, E20g, W10g, W20g)
Magpie (1st, 1st L, E20g, W10g, W20g)

■ **2011, January 24. Birds of Britain, series 2**
Des: Kate Stephens, from illustrations by Robert Gillmor. Printed in gravure by Walsall. Self-adhesive. Machine-printed in black.
Set of 6 (all 1st class)   32.00   –
Collector's strip (one of each value)   40.00   –
Philatelic pack (all 1st class)   35.00   –
First day cover   –   20.00

Great crested grebe (1st, 1st L, E20g, W10g, W20g)
Greylag goose (1st, 1st L, E20g, W10g, W20g)
Kingfisher (1st, 1st L, E20g, W10g, W20g)
Mallard (1st, 1st L, E20g, W10g, W20g)
Moorhen (1st, 1st L, E20g, W10g, W20g)
Mute swan (1st, 1st L, E20g, W10g, W20g)

■ **2011, May 19. Birds of Britain, series 3**
Des: Kate Stephens, from illustrations by Robert Gillmor. Printed in gravure by Walsall. Self-adhesive. Machine-printed in black.
Set of 6 (all 1st class)   10.00   –
Collector's strip (one of each value)   20.00   –
Philatelic pack (all 1st class)   10.00   –
First day cover   –   8.00

Arctic tern (1st, 1st L, E20g, W10g, W20g, W40g)
Cormorant (1st, 1st L, E20g, W10g, W20g, W40g)
Gannet (1st, 1st L, E20g, W10g, W20g, W40g)
Oystercatcher (1st, 1st L, E20g, W10g, W20g, W40g)
Puffin (1st, 1st L, E20g, W10g, W20g, W40g)
Ringed plover (1st, 1st L, E20g, W10g, W20g, W40g)

■ **2011, September 16. Birds of Britain, series 4**
Des: Kate Stephens, from illustrations by Robert Gillmor. Printed in gravure by Walsall. Self-adhesive. Machine-printed in black.
Set of 6 (all 1st class)   10.00   –
Collector's strip (one of each value)   18.00   –
Philatelic pack (all 1st class)   10.00   –
First day cover   –   16.00

Dalesbred (1st, 1st L, E20g, W10g, W20g, W40g)
Jacob (1st, 1st L, E20g, W10g, W20g, W40g)
Leicester longwool (1st, 1st L, E20g, W10g, W20g, W40g)
Soay (1st, 1st L, E20g, W10g, W20g, W40g)
Suffolk (1st, 1st L, E20g, W10g, W20g, W40g)
Welsh mountain badger face (1st, 1st L, E20g, W10g, W20g, W40g)

■ **2012, February 24. British Farm Animals, series 1: Sheep**
Des: Kate Stephens, from illustrations by Robert Gillmor. Printed in gravure by Walsall. Self-adhesive. Machine-printed in black.
Set of 6 (all 1st class)   10.00   –
Collector's strip (one of each value)   20.00   –
Philatelic pack (all 1st class)   10.00   –
First day cover   –   7.50

POST & GO VENDING MACHINE STAMPS

Berkshire (1st, 1st L, E20g, W10g, W20g, W40g)
British saddleback (1st, 1st L, E20g, W10g, W20g, W40g)
Gloucestershire old spots (1st, 1st L, E20g, W10g, W20g, W40g)
Oxford sandy and black (1st, 1st L, E20g, W10g, W20g, W40g)
Tamworth (1st, 1st L, E20g, W10g, W20g, W40g)
Welsh (1st, 1st L, E20g, W10g, W20g, W40g)

■ **2012, April 24. British Farm Animals, series 2: Pigs**
Des: Kate Stephens, from illustrations by Robert Gillmor. Printed in gravure by Walsall. Self-adhesive. Machine-printed in black.

Set of 6 (all 1st class)	10.00	–
Collector's strip (one of each value)	20.00	–
Philatelic pack (all 1st class)	11.00	–
First day cover	–	12.50

Aberdeen Angus (1st, 1st L, E20g, W10g, W20g, W40g)
Highland (1st, 1st L, E20g, W10g, W20g, W40g)
Irish moiled (1st, 1st L, E20g, W10g, W20g, W40g)
Red poll (1st, 1st L, E20g, W10g, W20g, W40g)
Welsh black (1st, 1st L, E20g, W10g, W20g, W40g)
White park (1st, 1st L, E20g, W10g, W20g, W40g)

■ **2012, September 28. British Farm Animals, series 3: Cattle**
Des: Kate Stephens, from illustrations by Robert Gillmor. Printed in gravure by Walsall. Self-adhesive. Machine-printed in black.

Set of 6 (all 1st class)	10.00	–
Collector's strip (one of each value)	20.00	–
Philatelic pack (all 1st class)	10.00	–
First day cover	–	7.50

Robin (1st, 1st L, E20g, W10g, W20g, W40g)

■ **2012, November 6. Christmas Robin**
Des: Kate Stephens, from illustration by Robert Gillmor (as the Robin design from Birds of Britain series I, but with year code). Printed in gravure by Walsall. Self-adhesive. Year code '12' or '13' in security overlay. Machine-printed in black.

Single (1st)	2.50	–
Collector's strip (one of each value)	40.00	–
Collector's strip ('The B.P.M.A.')	20.00	–
First day cover	–	3.00

Emperor dragonfly (1st, 1st L, E20g, W10g, W20g, W40g)
Fairy shrimp (1st, 1st L, E20g, W10g, W20g, W40g)
Glutinous snail (1st, 1st L, E20g, W10g, W20g, W40g)
Lesser silver water beetle (1st, 1st L, E20g, W10g, W20g, W40g)
Smooth newt (1st, 1st L, E20g, W10g, W20g, W40g)
Three-spined stickleback (1st, 1st L, E20g, W10g, W20g, W40g)

■ **2013, February 22. Pond Life**
Des: Kate Stephens, from illustrations by Chris Wormell. Printed in gravure by Walsall. Self-adhesive. Machine-printed in black.

Set of 6 (all 1st class)	10.00	–
Collector's strip (one of each value)	20.00	–
Philatelic pack (all 1st class)	10.00	–
First day cover	–	7.50

Arctic char (1st, 1st L, E20g, W10g, W20g, W40g)
Caddis fly larvae (1st, 1st L, E20g, W10g, W20g, W40g)
Common toad (1st, 1st L, E20g, W10g, W20g, W40g)
Crucian carp (1st, 1st L, E20g, W10g, W20g, W40g)
European eel (1st, 1st L, E20g, W10g, W20g, W40g)
Perch (1st, 1st L, E20g, W10g, W20g, W40g)

■ **2013, June 25. Lake Life**
Des: Kate Stephens, from illustrations by Chris Wormell. Printed in gravure by Walsall. Self-adhesive. Machine-printed in black.

Set of 6 (all 1st class)	10.00	–
Collector's strip (one of each value)	22.00	–
Philatelic pack (all 1st class)	10.00	–
First day cover	–	21.00

BRITISH STAMP MARKET VALUES 2024   319

VENDING MACHINE STAMPS POST & GO

1st Class up to 100g

Atlantic salmon (1st, 1st L, E20g, W10g, W20,g W40g)
Blue-winged olive mayfly larva (1st, 1st L, E20g, W10g, W20g, W40g)
Brown trout (1st, 1st L, E20g, W10g, W20g, W40g)
Minnow (1st, 1st L, E20g, W10g, W20g, W40g)
River lamprey (1st, 1st L, E20g, W10g, W20g, W40g)
White-clawed crayfish (1st, 1st L, E20g, W10g, W20g, W40g)

■ **2013, September 20. River Life**
Des: Kate Stephens, from illustrations by Chris Wormell. Printed in gravure by Walsall. Self-adhesive. Machine-printed in black.

Set of 6 (all 1st class)	10.00	–
Collector's strip (one of each value)	20.00	–
Philatelic pack (all 1st class)	10.00	–
First day cover	–	7.50

1st Class up to 100g

Blackthorn (1st, 1st L, E20g, W10g, W20g, W40g)
Dog violet (1st, 1st L, E20g, W10g, W20g, W40g)
Lesser celandine (1st, 1st L, E20g, W10g, W20g, W40g)
Primrose (1st, 1st L, E20g, W10g, W20g, W40g)
Snowdrop (1st, 1st L, E20g, W10g, W20g, W40g)
Wild daffodil (1st, 1st L, E20g, W10g, W20g, W40g)

■ **2014, February, 19. Spring Blooms**
Des: Kate Stephens, from illustrations by Julia Trickey. Printed in gravure by ISP. Self-adhesive. Year code '14' in security overlay. Machine-printed in black.

Set of 6 (all 1st class)	10.00	–
Collector's strip (up to W40)	23.00	–
Philatelic pack (all 1st class)	11.00	–
First day cover	–	7.50

1st Class up to 100g

Forget-me-not (1st, 1st L, E20/W10, E60g, W20g, W60g)
Common poppy (1st, 1st L, E20/W10, E60g, W20g, W60g)
Dog rose (1st, 1st L, E20/W10, E60g, W20g, W60g)
Spear thistle (1st, 1st L, E20/W10, E60g, W20,g W60g)
Heather (1st, 1st L, E20/W10, E60g, W20g, W60g)
Cultivated flax (1st, 1st L, E20/W10, E60g, W20g, W60g)

■ **2014, September 17. Symbolic Flowers**
Des: Kate Stevens, from illustrations by Julia Trickey. Printed in gravure by ISP. Self-adhesive. Year code '14' in security overlay. Machine-printed in black.

Set of 6 (all 1st class)	10.00	–
Collector's strip (one of each value)	22.00	–
Collector's strip (Shakespeare Birthplace Trust)	20.00	–
Collector's strip (Shakespeare 1564)	20.00	–
Philatelic pack (all 1st class)	10.00	–
First day cover	–	11.00

Common Poppy collector's strips

1st, 1st L, E20/W10, E60, W20, W60 (2014)	30.00	–
1st, 1st L, E20/W10, E100, W20, W100 (2015)	20.00	–
'First World War/Centenary' (Sep 2014)	23.00	–
'The B.P.M.A.' (Oct 2014)	23.00	–
'The NMRM/Remembrance' (Oct 2014)	35.00	–
'The B.P.M.A.' (Oct 2015)	22.00	–
'Sindelfingen October 2015' (Oct 2015)	20.00	–
'Paris November 2015' (Nov 2015)	20.00	–
'RN Submarine' (Nov 2015)	21.00	–
'Royal Navy' (Nov 2015)	21.00	–
'Royal Marines' (Nov 2015)	21.00	–
'Fleet Air Arm' (Nov 2015)	21.00	–
'The Battle of the Somme' (Sep 2016)	20.00	–
'Royal Marines' (Oct 2016)	20.00	–
'Headquarters BFPO Lest We Forget' (Oct 2016)	35.00	–
'The Postal Museum' (Oct 2016)	20.00	–
'WWI Battle of Passchendaele' (Sep 2017)	20.00	–
'The Postal Museum' with no logo (Oct 2017)	20.00	–
'RN Submarine' (Oct 2017)	20.00	–
'HMS Trincomalee 12th Oct 1817' (Nov 2017)	35.00	–
'Postal Museum/WWI 1918–2018' (Oct 2018)	20.00	–
'Royal Navy Lest We Forget 100' (Nov 2019)	20.00	–
'RN Submarine Lest We Forget 100' (Nov 2019)	20.00	–
'Royal Navy/Lest We Forget' (Nov 2021)	31.00	–
'RN Submarine/Lest We Forget' (Nov 2021)	31.00	–
'Fleet Air Arm/Lest We Forget' (Nov 2021)	31.00	–
'Postal Museum Lest We Forget' (Nov 2022)	25.00	–

Spear Thistle collector's strips

'88th Scottish Congress' (Apr 2017)	20.00	–
'88th Scottish Congress 2017' (Apr 2017)	50.00	–

1st Large up to 100g

Common ivy (2nd, 2nd L)
Mistletoe (2nd, 2nd L)
Butcher's broom (1st, 1st L, E20/W10, E60g, W20g, W60g)
Holly (1st, 1st L, E20/W10, E60g, W20g, W60g)

■ **2014, November 13. Winter Greenery**
Des: Kate Stevens, from illustrations by Julia Trickey. Printed in gravure by ISP. Self-adhesive. One phosphor band (2nd), two

POST & GO VENDING MACHINE STAMPS

phosphor bands (1st). Year code '14', '17' or '21' in security overlay. Machine-printed in black.

Set of 4 (2nd, 2ndL, 1st, 1st L)	10.00	–
Collector's strip (2nd, 2nd L)	4.00	–
Collector's strip (1st values)	20.00	–
Collector's strip (2nd, 2nd L, BPMA)	5.00	–
Collector's strip (1st values, BPMA)	20.00	–
Collector's strip (2nd, 2nd L, Postal Museum)	5.00	–
Collector's strip (1st values, Postal Museum)	20.00	–
Collector's strip (Mail Rail)	20.00	–
Philatelic pack (2nd, 2nd,1st, 1st L)	10.00	–
First day cover	–	12.00

'Falcon' (1st, 1st L, E20/W10, E60g, W20g, W60g)
'Briar' (1st, 1st L, E20/W10, E60g, W20g, W60g)
'Harry' (1st, 1st L, E20/W10, E60g, W20g, W60g)
'Margaret' (1st, 1st L, E20/W10, E60g, W20g, W60g)
'Stag' (1st, 1st L, E20/W10, E60g, W20g, W60g)
'Nell Morgan' (1st, 1st L, E20/W10, E60g, W20g, W60g)

■ **2015, February 18. Working Sail**
Des: Osborne Ross. Printed in gravure by ISP. Self-adhesive. Year code '15' in security overlay. Machine-printed in black.

Set of 6 (all 1st class)	10.00	–
Collector's strip (one of each value)	20.00	–
Philatelic pack (all 1st class)	10.00	–
First day cover	–	7.50

Lion (1st, 1st L, E20/W10, E100g, W20g, W100g)
Unicorn (1st, 1st L, E20/W10, E100g, W20g, W100g)
Yale (1st, 1st L, E20/W10, E100g, W20g, W100g)
Dragon (1st, 1st L, E20/W10, E100g, W20g, W100g)
Falcon (1st, 1st L, E20/W10, E100g, W20g, W100g)
Griffin (1st, 1st L, E20/W10, E100g, W20g, W100g)

■ **2015, May 13. Heraldic Beasts**
Des: Osborne Ross. Printed in gravure by ISP. Self-adhesive. Year code '15' in security overlay. Machine-printed in black.

Set of 6 (all 1st class)	10.00	–
Collector's strip (one of each value)	20.00	–
Philatelic pack (all 1st class)	10.00	–
First day cover	–	10.00

Heraldic Lion collector's strips

'BPMA' (Sep 2015)	22.00	–
'Sindelfingen' (Oct 2015)	20.00	–
'Paris' (Nov2015)	20.00	–
'The Postal Museum' (Feb 2016)	13.00	–
'87th Scottish Congress' (Apr 2016)	22.00	–
'88th Scottish Congress' (Apr 2017)	20.00	–
'88th Scottish Congress 2017' (Apr 2017)	50.00	–

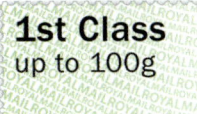

White Cliffs of Dover (1st, 1st L, E20/W10, E100g, W20g, W100g)
Hong Kong Harbour (1st, 1st L, E20/W10, E100g, W20g, W100g)
Sydney Opera House (1st, 1st L, E20/W10, E100g, W20g, W100g)
Ha Long Bay (1st, 1st L, E20/W10, E100g, W20g, W100g)
New York Harbour (1st, 1st L, E20/W10, E100g, W20g, W100g)
Venice (1st, 1st L, E20/W10, E100g, W20g, W100g)

■ **2015, September 16. Sea Travel**
Des: Osborne Ross, from illustrations by Andy Tuohy. Printed in gravure by ISP. Self-adhesive. Year code '15' in security overlay. Machine-printed in black.

Set of 6 (all 1st class)	15.00	–
Collector's strip (one of each value)	25.00	–
Philatelic pack (all 1st class)	15.00	–
First day cover	–	10.00

Hong Kong collector's strips

'Hong Kong November 2015' (Nov 2015)*	20.00	–
(*The Hong Kong strip was digitally printed.)		

New York collector's strips

'World Stamp Show NY 2016' (May 2016)	20.00	–

Mountain hare (2nd, 2nd L)
Redwing (2nd, 2nd L)
Red fox (1st, 1st L, E20/W10, E100g, W20g, W100g)
Red squirrel (1st, 1st L, E20/W10, E100g, W20g, W100g)

■ **2015, November 16. Winter Fur and Feathers**
Des: Osborne Ross, from illustrations by Robert Gillmor. Printed in gravure by ISP. Self-adhesive. One phosphor band (2nd), two

BRITISH STAMP MARKET VALUES 2024 321

VENDING MACHINE STAMPS POST & GO

phosphor bands (1st). Year code '15' in security overlay. Machine-printed in black.

Set of 4 (2nd, 2nd L, 1st, 1st L)	14.00	–
Collector's strip (2nd, 2nd L)	5.00	–
Collector's strip (1st values)	17.00	–
Collector's strip (2nd, 2nd L, BPMA)	6.00	–
Collector's strip (1st values, BPMA)	20.00	–
Collector's strip (2nd, 2nd L, Postal Museum)	6.00	–
Collector's strip (1st values, Postal Museum)	20.00	–
Philatelic pack (2nd, 2nd L, 1st, 1st L)	14.00	–
First day cover	–	7.00

Post boy 1640s (1st, 1st L, E20/W10, E100g, W20g, W100g)
Mail coach 1790s (1st, 1st L, E20/W10, E100g, W20g, W100g)
Falmouth packet ship 1820s (1st, 1st L, E20/W10, E100, W20, W100)
Travelling Post Office 1890s (1st, 1st L, E20/W10, E100, W20, W100)
Airmail 1930s (1st, 1st L, E20/W10, E100g, W20g, W100g)
Minivan 1970s (1st, 1st L, E20/W10, E100g, W20g, W100g)

■ **2016, February 17. Royal Mail Heritage: Transport**
Des: Howard Brown, from illustrations by Andrew Davidson. Printed in gravure by ISP. Self-adhesive. Year code '16' in security overlay. Machine-printed in black.

Set of 6 (all 1st class)	11.00	–
Collector's strip (one of each value)	20.00	–
Collector's strip (Postal Museum)	10.00	–
Collector's strip ('Liverpool 2016')	30.00	–
Collector's strip ('Glasgow 2016')	25.00	–
Collector's strip ('Birmingham 2016')	25.00	–
Philatelic pack (all 1st class)	11.00	–
First day cover	–	7.50

Mail Coach collector's strips

'The Postal Museum' (2016)	20.00
'The Postal Museum Official Opening' (2017)	20.00
'The Postal Museum' with no logo (Sep 2017)	20.00
'The Post Museum/NPM 50' (Feb 2019)	20.00
'New exhibit 2019' (Postal Museum, 2019)	20.00
'Postcards 150' (Postal Museum, 2020)	25.00
'Postcards 150' (Postal Museum, 2021)	20.00

Travelling Post Office collector's strips

'Spring Stampex 2016' (Feb 2016)	20.00
'Steam GWR Swindon 175' (Feb 2016)	25.00
'Steam GWR [logo] Swindon 175' (Sep 2016)	20.00
'Steam GWR' (Feb 2017)	20.00
'Steam GWR King George V 90th' (Mar 2017)	20.00
'EARM' (Mar 2017)	20.00
'Steam' (2019)	20.00

'Steam Celebrates 20 Years' (2019)	35.00
'The Postal Museum' (2019)	20.00
'Mail Rail' (2019)	20.00

Seven-spot ladybird (1st, 1st L, E20/W10, E100, W20, W100)
Fourteen-spot ladybird (1st, 1st L, E20/W10, E100, W20, W100)
Orange ladybird (1st, 1st L, E20/W10, E100, W20, W100)
Heather ladybird (1st, 1st L, E20/W10, E100, W20, W100)
Striped ladybird (1st, 1st L, E20/W10, E100, W20, W100)
Water ladybird (1st, 1st L, E20/W10, E100, W20, W100)

■ **2016, September 14. Ladybirds**
Des: Osborne Ross, from illustrations by Chris Wormell. Printed in gravure by ISP. Self-adhesive. Year code '16' in security overlay. Machine-printed in black.

Set of 6 (all 1st class)	16.00	–
Collector's strip (one of each value)	25.00	–
Philatelic pack (all 1st class)	16.00	–
First day cover	–	13.00

Hedgehog (2nd, 2nd L)
Grass snake (2nd, 2nd L)
Dormouse (1st, 1st L, E20/W10, E100, W20, W100)
Brown long-eared bat (1st, 1st L, E20/W10, E100, W20, W100)

■ **2016, November 14. Hibernating Animals**
Des: Osborne Ross from illustrations by Chris Wormell. Printed in gravure by ISP. Self-adhesive. One phosphor band (2nd) or two phosphor bands (1st). Year code '16' in security overlay. Machine-printed in black.

Set of 4 (2nd, 2nd L, 1st, 1st L)	14.00	–
Collector's strip (2nd, 2nd L)	4.50	–
Collector's strip (higher values)	20.00	–
Collector's strip (2nd, 2nd L, Postal Museum)	4.00	–
Collector's strip (high values, Postal Museum)	20.00	–
Philatelic pack (2nd, 2nd L, 1st, 1st L)	14.00	–
First day cover	–	12.00

POST & GO VENDING MACHINE STAMPS

TPO: bag exchange (1st, 1st L, E20/W10, E100, W20, W100)
Post Office Railway (1st, 1st L, E20/W10, E100, W20, W100)
Night Mail (1st, 1st L, E20/W10, E100, W20, W100)
TPO: loading (1st, 1st L, E20/W10, E100, W20, W100)
TPO: sorting (1st, 1st L, E20/W10, E100, W20, W100)
TPO: on the move (1st, 1st L, E20/W10, E100, W20, W100)

■ **2017, February 15. Royal Mail Heritage: Mail by Rail**
Des: Osborne Ross, from illustrations by Andrew Davidson.
Printed in gravure by ISP. Self-adhesive. Year code '17' in security overlay. Machine-printed in black.

Set of 6 (all 1st class)	10.00	–
Collector's strip (one of each value)	20.00	–
Collector's strip (Postal Museum)	10.00	–
Collector's strip (Steam GWR)	10.00	–
Collector's strip (New Exhibit 2019)*	25.00	–
Philatelic pack (all 1st class)	10.00	–
First day cover	–	10.00

(*This strip was available only in a presentation pack from the Postal Museum)

Post Office Railway collector's strips

'The Postal Museum' (Feb 2017)	20.00	–
'The Postal Museum Official Opening' (2017)	20.00	–
'The Postal Museum', no logo (Sep 2017)	20.00	–
'Mail Rail' (2021)	22.00	–
'Mail Rail/London 2022' (Feb 2022)	31.00	–

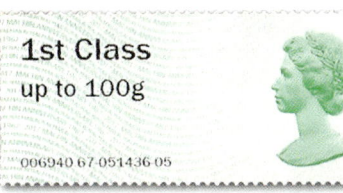

Commemorative head, orange (1st, 1st L, E20/W10, E100, W20, W100)
Commemorative head, gold (1st, 1st L, E20/W10, E100, W20, W100)
Commemorative head, violet (1st, 1st L, E20/W10, E100, W20, W100)
Commemorative head, olive (1st, 1st L, E20/W10, E100, W20, W100)
Commemorative head, green (1st, 1st L, E20/W10, E100, W20, W100)
Commemorative head, olive-brown (1st, 1st L, E20/W10, E100, W20, W100)

■ **2017, June 5. Machin Anniversary 1967–2017**
Des: Royal Mail Group. Printed in gravure by ISP. Self-adhesive. 'Machin Anniversary 1967–2017' security overlay. Machine-printed in black.

Set of 6 (all 1st class)	17.50	–
Collector's strip (one of each value)	20.00	–
Collector's strip (Postal Museum)	10.00	–
Collector's strip (Postal Museum Opening)	8.00	–

Collector's strip (Autumn Stampex 2017)	8.00	–
Collector's strip (Postal Museum)	8.00	–
Collector's strip (NPM 50, 2019)	7.00	–
Collector's strip (Platinum Jubilee, 2022)	11.00	–
Philatelic pack (all 1st class)	17.50	–
First day cover	–	20.00

(*A collector's strip comprising one stamp of each value, with the overprint '88th Scottish Congress 2017', was produced in error by the philatelic service, and sent out to subscribers in advance of the event in April. Price £150.)

First UK aerial mail, 1911 (1st, 1st L, E20/W10, E100, W20, W100)
Military mail flight, 1919 (1st, 1st L, E20/W10, E100, W20, W100)
International airmail, 1933 (1st, 1st L, E20/W10, E100, W20, W100)
Domestic airmail, 1934 (1st, 1st L, E20/W10, E100, W20, W100)
Flying boat airmail 1937 (1st, 1st L, E20/W10, E100, W20, W100)
Datapost service, 1980s (1st, 1st L, E20/W10, E100, W20, W100)

■ **2017, September 13. Royal Mail Heritage: Mail by Air**
Des: Osborne Ross, from illustrations by Andrew Davidson.
Printed in gravure by ISP. Self-adhesive. Year code '17' in security overlay. Machine-printed in black.

Set of 6 (all 1st class)	10.00	–
Collector's strip (one of each value)	20.00	–
Collector's strip (all 1st class, Postal Museum)	10.00	–
Collector's strip (2023 values, Postal Museum)	25.00	–
Collector's strip (Airmail 1919, Postal Museum)	15.00	–
Philatelic pack (all 1st class)	10.00	–
First day cover	–	10.00

The Iron Throne (2nd, 2nd L)
The Iron Throne (1st, 1st L, E20/W10, E100, W20, W100)

■ **2018, January 3. Game of Thrones**
Des: Robert Ball. Printed in gravure by ISP. Self-adhesive. Year code '18' in security overlay. Machine-printed in black.

Set of 2 (2nd, 1st)	6.00	–
Collector's strip (2nd, 2nd L)	5.00	–
Collector's strip (higher values)	20.00	–
Collector's strip (2nd, 2nd L, Postal Museum)	5.00	–
Collector's strip (higher values, Postal Museum)	20.00	–
Philatelic pack (2nd, 1st)	6.00	–
First day cover	–	7.00

VENDING MACHINE STAMPS POST & GO

Packet 'Antelope', 1780 (1st, 1st L, E20/W10, E100, W20, W100)
SS 'Great Western', 1838 (1st, 1st L, E20/W10, E100, W20, W100)
SS 'Britannia', 1887 (1st, 1st L, E20/W10, E100, W20, W100)
RMS 'Olympic', 1911 (1st, 1st L, E20/W10, E100, W20, W100)
RMS 'Queen Mary', 1936 (1st, 1st L, E20/W10, E100, W20, W100)
RMS 'St Helena', 1990 (1st, 1st L, E20/W10, E100, W20, W100)

■ 2018, February 14. Royal Mail Heritage: Mail by Sea
Des: Royal Mail Group Ltd, from illustrations by Andrew Davidson. Printed in gravure by ISP. Self-adhesive. Year code '18' in security overlay. Machine-printed in black.

Set of 6 (all 1st class)	10.00	–
Collector's strip (one of each value)	20.00	–
Collector's strip (Postal Museum)	10.00	–
Collector's strip (Voices from the Deep/TPM)	11.00	–
Philatelic pack (all 1st class)	10.00	–
First day cover	–	10.00

Pentacycle, 1882 (1st, 1st L, E20/W10, E100, W20, W100)
Motorcycle and trailer, 1902 (1st, 1st L, E20/W10, E100, W20, W100)
Tricycle and basket, 1920 (1st, 1st L, E20/W10, E100, W20, W100)
Bicycle, 1949 (1st, 1st L, E20/W10, E100, W20, W100)
Motorcycle, 1965 (1st, 1st L, E20/W10, E100, W20, W100)
Quad bike, 2002 (1st, 1st L, E20/W10, E100, W20, W100)

■ 2018, September 12. Royal Mail Heritage: Mail by Bike
Des: Royal Mail Group Ltd, from illustrations by Andrew Davidson. Printed in gravure by ISP. Self-adhesive. Year code '18' in security overlay. Machine-printed in black.

Set of 6 (all 1st class)	11.00	–
Collector's strip (one of each value)	20.00	–
Collector's strip (Postal Museum)	10.00	–
Philatelic pack (all 1st class)	11.00	–
First day cover	–	11.00

FRAMA VENDING MACHINE STAMPS

FRAMA LABELS

In this section, prices are quoted in two columns: mint (left) and fine used (right).

From May 1984 until April 1985, Frama machines were installed at five locations, printing labels to order for any value from ½p (until withdrawn in January 1985) to 16p (17p from August 28, 1984).

■ **1984, May 1**
Machine-printed in red on phosphor-coated security paper with a grey-green background pattern. Gummed and imperforate.

Set (½p to 17p)	12.50	15.00
Pack (all values from ½p to 16p)	25.00	–
Pack (16½p, 17p)	4.00	–
Pack (3½p, 12½p, 16p)	4.00	–
First day cover (3½p, 12½p, 16p)	–	2.50

Stamp Magazine is Britain's best for GB collectors

Every issue includes:
- Analysis of all Royal Mail issues
- Latest British and world news
- Regular features on GB themes
- Hard-hitting opinion columns
- Exhibition, auction and fair dates

Available from newsagents, or visit www.stampmagazine.co.uk

SMILERS & COLLECTOR'S SHEETS

SMILERS SHEETS & COLLECTOR'S SHEETS

In this section, prices are quoted for complete mint sheets only.

Smilers sheets were conceived as personalisable products, allowing customers to have a photograph or other supplied image printed on labels alongside postally valid stamps. Listed here are Royal Mail's generic sheets for each issue, which have decorative labels instead of customers' photographs.

No new personalisable sheets have been issued since October 2016, and the personalisation service was suspended in July 2018. Royal Mail has continued to offer generic sheets, but has renamed them collector's sheets.

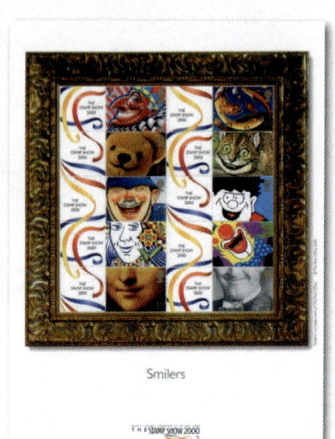

The Stamp Show, 2000

■ **2000, May 22. The Stamp Show 2000**
Sheet of 10 1st class Smiles as March 26, 1991 — 23.00

■ **2000, October 3. Christmas: Robin in Letterbox**
Sheet of 20 19p Christmas as October 30, 1995.
Inscribed copyright 'Post Office 2000' — £125

■ **2000, October 3. Christmas: Father Christmas**
Sheet of 10 1st class Christmas as October 27, 1997.
Inscribed copyright 'Post Office 2000' — £125

■ **2001, June 5. Occasions: Hallmarks**
Sheet of 20 1st class Occasions as February 6, 2001 — £120

■ **2001, July 3. Smiles**
Sheet of 10 1st class Smiles as March 26, 1991. As issue of May 22, 2000, but with revised labels and border — £170

■ **2001, October 9. Christmas: Robin in Letterbox**
Sheet of 20 19p Christmas as October 30, 1995.
Inscribed copyright 'Consignia 2001' — £600

■ **2001, October 9. Christmas: Father Christmas**
Sheet of 10 1st class Christmas as October 27, 1997.
Inscribed copyright 'Consignia 2001' — £600

■ **2001, December 18. Cartoons**
Sheet of 10 1st class Greetings as February 26, 1996 — 30.00

■ **2002, April 23. Occasions: Pictorial Messages**
Sheet of 20 1st class Occasions as March 5, 2002. — 60.00

■ **2002, May 21. Football World Cup**
Sheet of 20 1st class England Flag as May 21, 2002 — 25.00

■ **2002, October 1. Smiles**
Sheet of 20 1st class Teddy Bear and 1st class Dennis the Menace as March 26, 1991 — 27.00

■ **2002, October 1. Christmas: Father Christmas**
Sheet of 20 1st class Christmas as October 27, 1997 — 30.00

■ **2003, January 21. Flowers**
Sheet of 20 1st class Flower Paintings as January 6, 1997 — 30.00

Occasions, 2003

■ **2003, February 4. Occasions: Multiple Choice**
Sheet of 20 1st class Occasions as February 4, 2003 — 23.00

■ **2003, July 29. Cartoons Crossword**
Sheet of 20 1st class Greetings as February 26, 1996 — 23.00

■ **2003, September 30. Christmas: Winter Robins**
Sheet of 20 1st class Christmas as November 6, 2001.
Self-adhesive — 23.00

■ **2003, November 4. Christmas: Ice Sculptures**
Sheet of 20 2nd class Christmas as November 4, 2003.
Self-adhesive — 23.00
Sheet of 20 1st class Christmas as November 4, 2003.
Self-adhesive — 23.00

■ **2004, January 30. Hong Kong Stamp Exhibition**
Sheet of 20 1st class Hello as March 5, 2002 — 23.00

■ **2004, February 3. Occasions: Entertaining Envelopes**
Sheet of 20 1st class Occasions as February 3, 2004 — 23.00

■ **2004, May 25. Royal Horticultural Society**
Sheet of 20 1st class RHS as May 25, 2004 — 23.00

SMILERS & COLLECTOR'S SHEETS

Rule Britannia, 2004

■ **2004, July 27. Rule Britannia**
Sheet of 20 1st class Union Flag as October 22, 2001   23.00

■ **2004, November 2. Christmas: Father Christmas**
Sheet of 20 1st class and 2nd class Christmas. Self-adhesive   19.00

■ **2005, January 11. Farm Animals**
Sheet of 20 1st class Farm Animals as January 11, 2005   23.00

■ **2005, March 15. Magic**
Sheet of 20 1st class Magic Circle as March 15, 2005   23.00

■ **2005, April 21. Pacific Explorer Stamp Exhibition**
Sheet of 20 1st class Hello as March 5, 2002   23.00

■ **2005, June 21. White Ensign**
Sheet of 20 1st class White Ensign as October 22, 2001   23.00

■ **2005, September 15. Classic ITV**
Sheet of 20 1st class Classic ITV as September 15, 2005   23.00

■ **2005, November 1. Christmas: Winter Robins**
Sheet of 20 1st class and 2nd class Christmas as
November 6, 2001. Self-adhesive   19.00

A Bear Called Paddington, 2006

■ **2006, January 10. A Bear Called Paddington**
Sheet of 20 1st class Paddington Bear as January 10,
2006. Self-adhesive   23.00

■ **2006, March 7. Fun Fruit and Veg**
Sheet of 20 1st class Fun Fruit and Veg as March 7, 2006.
Self-adhesive   23.00

■ **2006, May 25. Washington Stamp Exhibition**
Sheet of 20 1st class Hello as March 5, 2002   23.00

■ **2006, June 6. World Cup Winners**
Sheet of 20 1st class World Cup Winners as June 6, 2006   23.00

■ **2006, July 4. For Life's Special Moments**
Sheet of 20 1st class Smilers as October 4, 2005.
Self-adhesive   23.00

■ **2006, October 17. For Life's Extra Special Moments**
Sheet of 20 1st class Smilers as October 17, 2006.
Self-adhesive   23.00

■ **2006, November 7. Christmas**
Sheet of 20 1st class and 2nd class Christmas as
November 7, 2006. Self-adhesive   19.00

■ **2006, November 9. We Will Remember Them, issue 1**
Sheet of 20 1st class Poppies as November 9, 2006   23.00

■ **2006, November 14. Belgica Stamp Exhibition**
Sheet of 20 1st class Hello as March 5, 2002   23.00

Glorious Wales, 2007

■ **2007, March 1. Glorious Wales**
Sheet of 20 1st class Wales as October 14, 2003.
Self-adhesive   23.00

■ **2007, April 23. Glorious England**
Sheet of 20 1st class England as October 14, 2003.
Self-adhesive   23.00

■ **2007, May 17. Wembley Stadium**
Sheet of 20 1st class Lion & Shield as May 17, 2007   23.00

■ **2007, June 5. 40th Anniversary of the Machin Definitive**
Sheet of 20 1st class Arnold Machin as June 5, 2007   23.00

SMILERS & COLLECTOR'S SHEETS

■ **2007, July 17. Harry Potter**
Sheet of 20 1st class Crest of Hogwarts School as
July 17, 2007. Self-adhesive　　　　　　　　　　23.00

Christmas, 2007

■ **2007, November 6. Christmas**
Sheet of 20 2nd class, 1st class and 78p Christmas as
November 6, 2007. Self-adhesive　　　　　　　22.00

■ **2007, November 8. We Will Remember Them, issue 2**
Sheet of 20 1st class Poppy as November 8, 2007　23.00

■ **2007, November 30. Glorious Scotland**
Sheet of 20 1st class Scotland as October 14, 2003.
Self-adhesive　　　　　　　　　　　　　　　　23.00

■ **2008, January 15. I Wrote To Say ...**
Sheet of 20 1st class Smilers as October 4, 2005.
Circular labels. Self-adhesive　　　　　　　　　23.00

■ **2008, March 11. Glorious Northern Ireland**
Sheet of 20 1st class Northern Ireland as October
14, 2003. Self-adhesive　　　　　　　　　　　23.00

■ **2008, July 17. 100 Years of Aviation**
Sheet of 20 1st class Air Displays as July 17, 2008　23.00

■ **2008, August 5. Beijing 2008 Olympic Expo**
Sheet of 20 1st class Hello as March 5, 2002　　23.00

■ **2008, September 29. Glorious United Kingdom**
Sheet of 20 1st class England, Northern Ireland, Scotland
and Wales as October 14, 2003. Self-adhesive　　23.00

■ **2008, November 4. Christmas**
Sheet of 20 2nd class, 1st class and 81p Christmas as
November 4, 2008. Self-adhesive　　　　　　　19.00

■ **2008, November 6. We Will Remember Them, issue 3**
Sheet of 20 1st class Poppy as November 6, 2008　23.00

■ **2009, January 13. The Mini**
Sheet of 20 1st class Mini as January 13, 2009　　23.00

Concorde, 2009

■ **2009, March 2. Concorde**
Sheet of 20 1st class Concorde as January 13, 2009　23.00

■ **2009, March 17. Castles of Northern Ireland**
Sheet of 20 1st class Northern Ireland as
October 14, 2003. Self-adhesive　　　　　　　23.00

■ **2009, April 23. Castles of England**
Sheet of 20 1st class English Flag as April 23, 2007.
Self-adhesive　　　　　　　　　　　　　　　23.00

■ **2009, August 3. Thaipex 2009 Exhibition**
Sheet of 20 1st class Hello as March 5, 2002　　23.00
(*Panes of 10 were sold separately at the exhibition.)

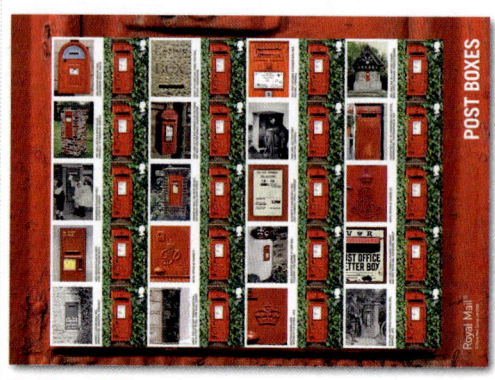

Post Boxes, 2009

■ **2009, August 18. Post Boxes**
Sheet of 20 1st class Post Boxes as August 18, 2009　23.00

■ **2009, October 21. Italia 2009 Exhibition**
Sheet of 20 1st class Hello as March 5, 2002　　23.00

■ **2009, November 3. Christmas**
Sheet of 20 2nd class, 1st class, 56p and 90p Christmas
as November 3, 2009. Self-adhesive　　　　　　20.00

SMILERS & COLLECTOR'S SHEETS

■ **2009, November 30. Castles of Scotland**
Sheet of 20 1st class Scotland as October 14, 2003.
Self-adhesive   23.00

■ **2009, December 4. MonacoPhil 2009 Exhibition**
Sheet of 20 1st class Hello as March 5, 2002   23.00

■ **2010, January 26. For All Occasions**
Sheet of 20 1st class, Europe and Worldwide Smilers
as January 26, 2010. Self-adhesive   32.00

■ **2010, March 1. Castles of Wales**
Sheet of 20 1st class Wales as October 14, 2003.
Self-adhesive   23.00

■ **2010, May 8. 10th Anniversary of Smilers**
Sheet of 20 1st class, Europe and Worldwide Smilers
as January 26, 2010. Self-adhesive   52.00

■ **2010, May 8. London 2010 Exhibition**
Sheet of 20 1st class Hello as October 4, 2005.
Self-adhesive   23.00

■ **2010, September 15. Battle of Britain**
Sheet of 20 1st class Spitfire as January 13, 2009   23.00

■ **2010, November 2. Christmas**
Sheet of 20 2nd class, 1st class, 60p and 97p Christmas
as November 2, 2010. Self-adhesive   20.00

Indipex, 2011

■ **2011, February 12. Indipex 2011 Exhibition**
Sheet of 20 1st class Union Flag as October 4, 2005.
Self-adhesive   23.00

■ **2011, July 28. Philanippon 2011 Exhibition**
Sheet of 20 1st class Union Flag as October 4, 2005.
Self-adhesive   23.00

■ **2011, September 15. 350 Years of Postmarks**
Sheet of 20 1st class Seal as January 26, 2010   23.00

■ **2011, November 8. Christmas**
Sheet of 20 1st class, 2nd class, 68p, £1.10 Christmas as
November 8, 2011. Self-adhesive   32.00

Year of the Dragon, 2012

■ **2012, January 20. Year of the Dragon**
Sheet of 20 1st class Firework as October 17, 2006.
Self-adhesive   23.00

■ **2012, June 18. Indonesia 2012 Exhibition**
Sheet of 20 1st class Hello as October 4, 2005.
Self-adhesive   23.00

■ **2012, June 27. Olympic and Paralympic Games Venues**
Sheet of 20 1st class and Worldwide Olympic Games and
Paralympic Games as January 5, 2012. Self-adhesive   95.00

■ **2012, November 6. Christmas**
Sheet of 20 1st class, 2nd class, 87p and £1.28 Christmas
as November 6, 2012. Self-adhesive   20.00

■ **2013, February 2. Year of the Snake**
Sheet of 20 1st class Firework as October 17, 2006.
Self-adhesive   23.00

Doctor Who, 2013

■ **2013, March 26. Doctor Who**
Sheet of 20 1st class Tardis as March 26, 2013.
Self-adhesive   23.00

■ **2013, May 10. Australia 2013 Exhibition**
Sheet of 20 1st class Hello as October 4, 2005.
Self-adhesive   23.00

SMILERS & COLLECTOR'S SHEETS

■ **2013, August 2. Thailand 2013 Exhibition**
Sheet of 20 1st class Hello as October 4, 2005.
Self-adhesive   23.00

■ **2013, November 5. Christmas**
Sheet of 20 1st class, 2nd class, 88p, £1.28 and £1.88
Christmas as November 5, 2013. Self-adhesive   40.00

■ **2013, December 10. Year of the Horse**
Sheet of 20 1st class Firework as October 17, 2006.
Self-adhesive   23.00

■ **2014, November 4. Christmas**
Sheet of 20 1st class, 2nd class, £1.28 and £1.47 Christmas
as November 4, 2014. Self-adhesive   25.00

■ **2014, November 19. Year of the Sheep**
Sheet of 20 1st class Firework as October 17, 2006.
Self-adhesive   23.00

■ **2014, December 1. Malaysia 2014 Exhibition**
Sheet of 20 1st class Hello as October 4, 2005.
Self-adhesive.   23.00

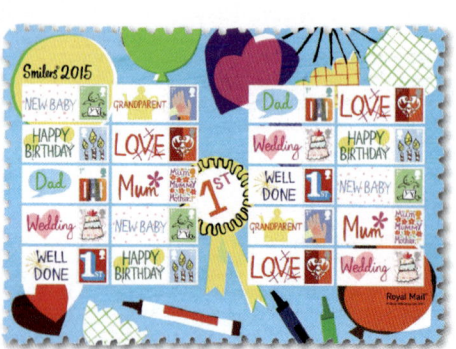

Smilers 2015

■ **2015, January 20. Smilers 2015**
Sheet of 20 1st class Smilers as January 20, 2015.
Self-adhesive   £200

■ **2015, May 6. 175th Anniversary of the Penny Black**
Sheet of 20 1st class Penny Black and 1st class
Twopenny Blue as May 6, 2015. Self-adhesive   65.00

■ **2015, May 13. London 2015 Exhibition**
Sheet of 20 1st class Hello as October 4, 2005.
Self-adhesive   23.00

■ **2015, October 20. Star Wars: Heroes and Villains**
Sheet of 10 1st class Yoda, Han Solo, Darth Vader and
Stormtrooper as October 20, 2015. Self-adhesive   16.00

■ **2015, November 3. Christmas**
Sheet of 20 1st class, 2nd class, £1, £1.33, £1.52 and £2.25
Christmas as November 3, 2015. Self-adhesive   30.00

■ **2015, November 9. Year of the Monkey**
Sheet of 20 1st class Firework as October 17, 2006.
Self-adhesive   23.00

175th Anniversary of the Penny Red, 2016

■ **2016, February 18. 175th Anniversary of the Penny Red**
Sheet of 20 1st class Penny Red as February 18, 2016.
Self-adhesive   23.00

■ **2016, May 26. New York 2016 Exhibition**
Sheet of 20 1st class Hello as October 4, 2005.
Self-adhesive   23.00

■ **2016, October 20. Mr. Men and Little Miss**
Sheet of 10 1st class Mr Men and Little Miss as
October 20, 2016. Self-adhesive   14.00

■ **2016, November 8. Christmas**
Sheet of 20 1st class, 2nd class, £1.05, £1.33, £1.52 and £2.25
Christmas as November 8, 2016. Self-adhesive   25.00

50 Years of Christmas Stamps, 2016

■ **2016, November 8. 50 Years of Christmas stamps**
Sheet of 20 1st class and 2nd class Christmas as
November 8, 2016. Self-adhesive   23.00

■ **2016, November 15. Year of the Rooster**
Sheet of 20 1st class Firework as October 17, 2006.
Self-adhesive   30.00

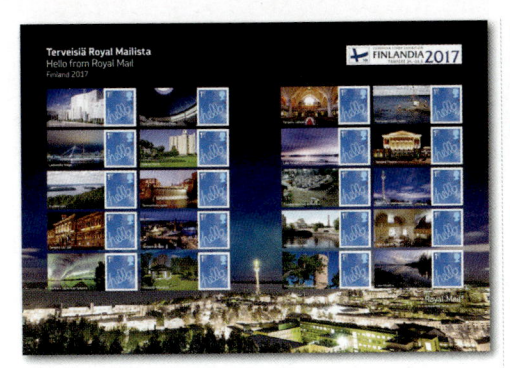

SMILERS & COLLECTOR'S SHEETS

Finlandia, 2017

■ **2017, May 24. Finlandia 2017 Exhibition**
Sheet of 20 1st class Hello as October 4, 2005.
Self-adhesive   23.00

■ **2017, October 12. Star Wars**
Sheet of 10 1st class Star Wars as October 12. 2017.
Self-adhesive   14.00

■ **2017, November 7. Christmas**
Sheet of 20 1st class, 2nd class, £1.17, £1.40, £1.57 and £2.27
Madonna and Child as November 7, 2017. Self-adhesive   55.00

■ **2017, November 7. Christmas**
Sheet of 20 1st class, 2nd class Children's Christmas as
November 7, 2017. Self-adhesive   27.00

■ **2017, November 16. The Year of the Dog**
Sheet of 20 1st class Firework as October 17, 2006.
Self-adhesive   23.00

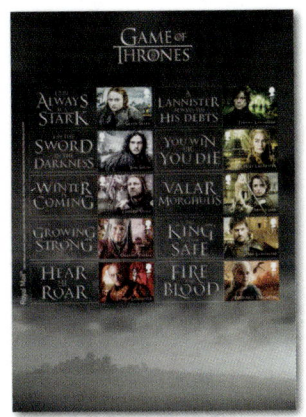

Game of Thrones, 2018

■ **2018, January 23. Game of Thrones**
Sheet of 10 1st class Game of Thrones as January 23, 2018.
Self-adhesive   14.00

■ **2018, June 26. Dad's Army**
Sheet of 10 1st class Dad's Army as June 26, 2018.
Self-adhesive   32.00

■ **2018, October 16. Harry Potter**
Sheet of 10 1st class Harry Potter as October 16, 2018.
Self-adhesive   36.00

■ **2018, November 1. Christmas**
Sheet of 20 1st class, 2nd class, £1.25, £1.45, £1.55, £2.25
Madonna and Child as November 7, 2017. Self-adhesive   25.00

■ **2018, November 15. The Year of the Pig**
Sheet of 20 1st class Firework as October 17, 2006.
Self-adhesive   23.00

■ **2019, March 14. Marvel**
Sheet of 10 1st class Marvel as March 14, 2019.
Self-adhesive   14.00

■ **2019, May 29. Stockholmia 2019 Exhibition**
Sheet of 20 1st class Hello as October 4, 2005.
Self-adhesive   23.00

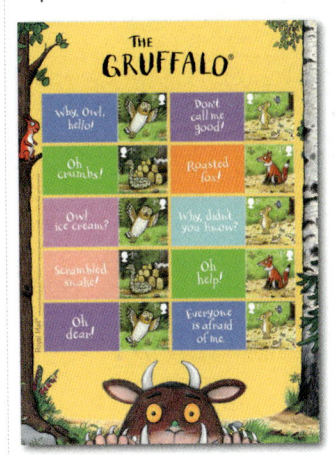

The Gruffalo, 2019

■ **2019, October 10. The Gruffalo**
Sheet of 10 1st class and £1.55 The Gruffalo as
October 10, 2019. Self-adhesive   25.00

■ **2019, November 5. Christmas**
Sheet of 20 1st class, 2nd class, £1.35, £1.55, £1.60 and £2.30
Christmas as November 5, 2019. Self-adhesive   37.00

■ **2019, November 18. The Year of the Rat**
Sheet of 20 1st class Firework as October 17. 2006.
Self-adhesive   23.00

■ **2019, November 26. Star Wars (issue 3)**
Sheet of 10 1st class Star Wars as November 26, 2019.
Self-adhesive   15.00

SMILERS & COLLECTOR'S SHEETS

■ **2020, January 21. Video Games: Tomb Raider**
Sheet of 10 1st class and £1.55 Tomb Raider as
January 21, 2020. Self-adhesive   25.00

■ **2020, March 17. James Bond**
Sheet of 10 1st class and £1.60 James Bond as
March 17, 2020. Self-adhesive   35.00

Coronation Street, 2020

■ **2020, May 28. Coronation Street**
Sheet of 10 1st class Coronation Street as May 28, 2020.
Self-adhesive   50.00

■ **2020, July 9. Queen, issue 1: Album Covers**
Sheet of 10 1st class and £1.63 Queen as July 9, 2020.
Self-adhesive   25.00

■ **2020, July 9. Queen, issue 2: Live**
Sheet of 10 1st class Queen as July 9, 2020.
Self-adhesive   12.00

■ **2020, August 18. Sherlock**
Sheet of 10 1st class, £1.42 and £1.68 Sherlock as
August 18, 2020. Self-adhesive   55.00

■ **2020, November 3. James Bond: No Time To Die**
Sheet of 10 1st class Aston Martin DB5 as March 17, 2020.
Self-adhesive   15.00

■ **2020, November 3. Christmas**
Sheet of 20 1st class, 2nd class, £1.45, £1.70, £2.50 and £2.55
Christmas as November 3, 2020. Self-adhesive   £150

■ **2020, November 13. Star Trek Captains**
Sheet of 10 1st class Kirk, Picard, Sisko, Janeway, Archer
and Lorca as November 13, 2020. Self-adhesive   15.00

■ **2020, December 8. The Year of the Ox**
Sheet of 20 1st class Firework as October 17. 2006.
Self-adhesive   25.00

Only Fools and Horses, 2021

■ **2021, February 16. Only Fools and Horses**
Sheet of 10 1st class Del Boy and Rodney as
February 16, 2021. Self-adhesive   15.00

■ **2021, May 28. Paul McCartney**
Sheet of 10 1st class and £1.70 Paul McCartney
as May 28, 2021. Self-adhesive   20.00

■ **2021, July 1. Dennis & Gnasher: Happy Birthday**
Sheet of 10 1st class Dennis and 1st class Gnasher
as July 1, 2021. Self-adhesive   20.00

■ **2021, July 22. Wild Coasts**
Sheet of 10 1st class Wild Coasts as July 22, 2021.
Self-adhesive   27.50

■ **2021, September 17. DC Collection**
Sheet of 12 1st class DC Collection as September 17, 2021.
Self-adhesive   18.00

■ **2021, November 2. Christmas**
Sheet of 20 1st class, 2nd class, £1.70 and £2.55
Christmas as November 2, 2021. Self-adhesive   30.00

■ **2021, December 8. The Year of the Tiger**
Sheet of 20 1st class Firework as October 17. 2006.
Self-adhesive   27.00

■ **2022, January 20. The Rolling Stones**
Sheet of 8 1st class and £1.70 The Rolling Stones as
January 20, 2022. Self-adhesive   17.50

SMILERS & COLLECTOR'S SHEETS

■ **2022, January 20. The Rolling Stones: Hyde Park 1969 and 2013**
Sheet of 8 1st class and £1.70 The Rolling Stones as
January 20, 2022. Self-adhesive   17.50

■ **2022, February 19. London 2022 International Stamp Exhibition**
Sheet of 20 1st class Hello as October 4, 2005.
Self-adhesive   27.00

■ **2022, June 9. Cats**
Sheet of 10 2nd class, 1st class, £1.70 and £2.55 Cats as
June 9, 2022. Self-adhesive   23.00

■ **2022, July 1. Pride**
Sheet of 8 1st class and £1.85 Pride as July 1, 2022.
Self-adhesive   18.00

■ **2022, September 1. Transformers**
Sheet of 8 1st class and £1.85 Transformers as
September 1, 2022. Self-adhesive   18.00

■ **2022, October 19. Aardman Classics**
Sheet of 8 2nd class, 1st class, £1.85 and £2.55 Aardman
Classics as October 19, 2022. Self-adhesive   20.00

■ **2022, November 3. Christmas**
Sheet of 20 1st class, 2nd class, £1.85 and £2.55
Christmas as November 3, 2022. Self-adhesive   32.00

■ **2022, December 8. The Year of the Rabbit**
Sheet of 20 1st class Firework as October 17, 2006.
Self-adhesive   30.00

■ **2023, January 12. Iron Maiden: Live Performances**
Sheet of 8 1st class and £1.85 Iron Maiden as January 12,
2023. Self-adhesive   18.00

■ **2023, January 12. Iron Maiden: Eddie**
Sheet of 8 1st class and £1.85 Iron Maiden as January 12,
2023. Self-adhesive   18.00

■ **2023, February 16. X-Men**
Sheet of 12 2nd class and 1st class X-Men as February 16,
2023. Self-adhesive   16.00

■ **2023, May 6. King Charles III: A New Reign**
Sheet of 8 1st class and £2.20 New Reign as May 6, 2023.
Self-adhesive   21.00

■ **2023, May 17. Blackadder**
Sheet of 10 2nd class, 1st class, £2.00 and £2.20 Blackadder
as May 17, 2023. Self-adhesive   23.00

■ **2023, June 8. Warhammer**
Sheet of 10 1st class, £2.00 and £2.20 Warhammer as
June 8, 2023. Self-adhesive   28.00

■ **2023, July 13. River Wildlife**
Sheet of 10 2nd class and 1st class River Wildlife as
July 13, 2023. Self-adhesive   15.00

SMILERS FOR KIDS

Peter Rabbit, 2008

■ **2008, October 28. Mr Happy**
Sheet of 20 1st class Balloons. Self-adhesive   £100
Sheet of 10 1st class Balloons, and writing pack   60.00

■ **2008, October 28. Almond Blossom**
Sheet of 20 1st class Flower. Self-adhesive   £100
Sheet of 10 1st class Flower, and writing pack   60.00

■ **2008, October 28. Peter Rabbit**
Sheet of 20 1st class New Baby. Self-adhesive   £100
Sheet of 10 1st class New Baby, and writing pack   60.00

■ **2008, October 28. Noddy**
Sheets of 20 1st class Balloons. Self-adhesive   £100
Sheets of 10 1st class Balloons, and writing pack   60.00

■ **2009, April 30. Little Miss Sunshine**
Sheet of 20 1st class Balloons. Self-adhesive   £100
Sheet of 10 1st class Balloons, and writing pack   60.00

■ **2009, April 30. Wild Cherry**
Sheet of 20 1st class Flower. Self-adhesive   £100
Sheet of 10 1st class Flower, and writing pack   60.00

■ **2009, April 30. Jeremy Fisher**
Sheet of 20 1st class Hello. Self-adhesive   £100
Sheet of 10 1st class Hello, and writing pack   60.00

■ **2009, April 30. Big Ears**
Sheets of 20 1st class Balloons. Self-adhesive   £100
Sheets of 10 1st class Balloons, and writing pack   60.00

COMMEMORATIVE SHEETS

In this section, prices are quoted for complete mint sheets only.

Commemorative sheets are an evolution of Smilers sheets. They are not personalisable but are customised as a souvenir product by Royal Mail, and sold at a premium, in a special folder.

Early issues had normal gum, but most subsequent issues have been self-adhesive.

GUMMED SHEETS

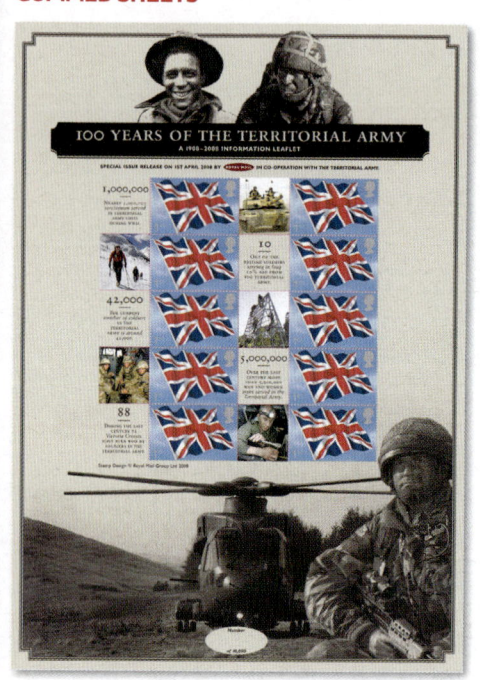

Centenary of the Territorial Army, 2008

■ **2008, April 1. Centenary of the Territorial Army**
Sheet of 10 1st class Union Flag as October 22, 2001   20.00

■ **2008, July 24. London 1908 Olympic Games**
Sheet of 10 1st class Union Flag as October 22, 2001   20.00

■ **2009, October 22. Olympic and Paralympic Games**
Sheet of 10 1st class as October 22, 2009   20.00

■ **2010, July 27. Olympic and Paralympic Games**
Sheet of 10 1st class as July 27, 2010   25.00

■ **2011, July 27. Olympic and Paralympic Games**
Sheet of 10 1st class as July 27, 2011   22.00

SELF-ADHESIVE SHEETS

■ **2008, November 14. 60th Birthday of Prince Charles**
Sheet of 10 1st class Wales   20.00

■ **2009, July 21. 40th Anniversary of the First Moon Landing**
Sheet of 10 1st class Union Flag as February 28, 2008   20.00

■ **2009, September 18. 150th Anniversary of Big Ben**
Sheet of 10 1st class Union Flag as February 28, 2008   20.00

■ **2009, October 7. 800th Anniversary of the University of Cambridge**
Sheet of 10 1st class Firework as February 28, 2008   20.00

■ **2010, May 18. Halley's Comet**
Sheet of 10 1st class Union Flag as February 28, 2008   20.00

■ **2010, July 8. British World Champion Grand Prix Drivers**
Sheet of 10 1st class Union Flag as February 28, 2008   20.00

■ **2010, August 10. 10th Anniversary of the London Eye**
Sheet of 10 1st class Union Flag as February 28, 2008   20.00

■ **2010, October 28. National Memorial Arboretum**
Sheet of 10 1st class Poppies as January 26, 2010   20.00

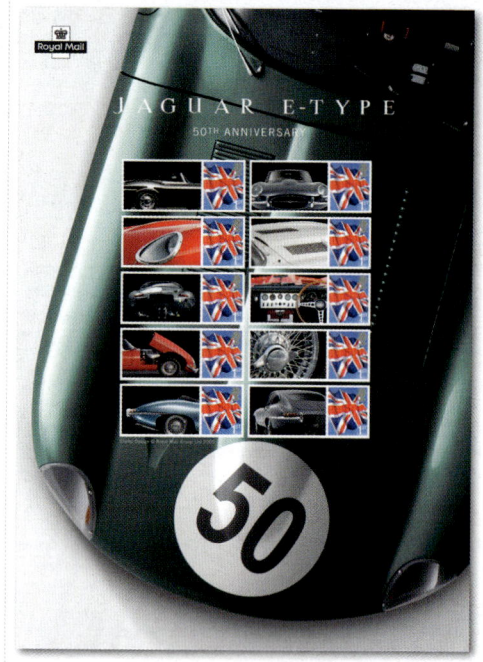

50th Anniversary of the Jaguar E-Type, 2011

■ **2011, March 30. 50th Anniversary of the Jaguar E-Type**
Sheet of 10 1st class Union Flag as February 28, 2008   20.00

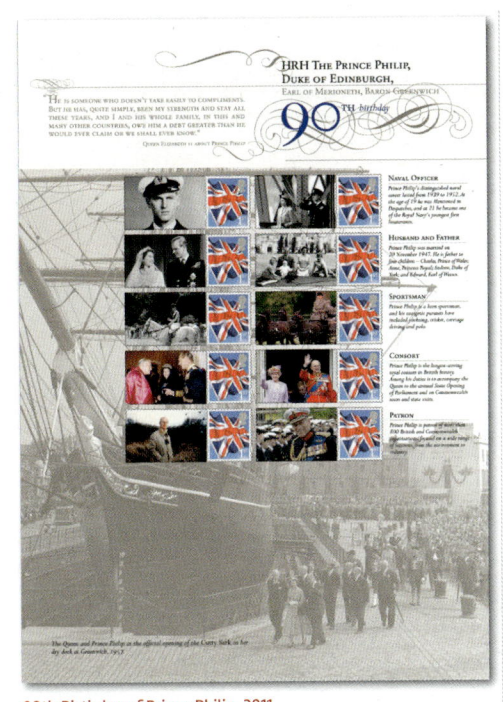

COMMEMORATIVE SHEETS

90th Birthday of Prince Philip, 2011

■ **2011, June 10. 90th Birthday of Prince Philip, Duke of Edinburgh**
Sheet of 10 1st class Union Flag as February 28, 2008   20.00

■ **2012, April 10. 100th Anniversary of the RMS Titanic**
Sheet of 10 1st class Seal as January 26, 2010   20.00

■ **2012, May 1. 50th Anniversary of James Bond**
Sheet of 10 1st class Union Flag as February 28, 2008   23.00

■ **2012, October 5. 40th Anniversary of the Last Goon Show**
Sheet of 10 1st class Union Flag as February 28, 2008   20.00

■ **2012, November 8. 150th Anniversary of Notts County Football Club**
Sheet of 10 1st class Firework as February 28, 2008   20.00

■ **2013, April 16. 60th Anniversary of the Launch of HMY Britannia**
Sheet of 10 1st class Union Flag as February 28, 2008   21.00

■ **2013, May 1. Bicentenary of the Birth of David Livingstone**
Sheet of 10 1st class Scottish Flag as November 30, 2006   20.00

■ **2013, September 19. 150th Anniversary of the Birth of Bertram Mackennel**
Sheet of 10 1st class Seal as January 26, 2010   22.00

■ **2014, February 25. 150th Anniversary of Middlesex County Cricket Club**
Sheet of 10 1st class Firework as February 28, 2008   22.00

■ **2014, March 26. 350th Anniversary of the Royal Marines**
Sheet of 10 1st class Union Flag as February 28, 2008   22.00

■ **2014, October 16. Donald Campbell**
Sheet of 10 1st class Union Flag as February 28, 2008   20.00

■ **2014, November 11. 100th Anniversary of the Christmas Truce**
Sheet of 10 1st class Poppies as January 26, 2010   20.00

■ **2015, March 18. The Post Office Rifles**
Sheet of 10 1st class Union Flag as February 28, 2008   20.00

■ **2015, April 24. Bicentenary of the Birth of Anthony Trollope**
Sheet of 10 1st class Union Flag as February 28, 2008   20.00

Bicentenary of the Gurkhas, 2015

■ **2015, August 20. Bicentenary of the Gurkhas' Service to the Crown**
Sheet of 10 1st class Union Flag as February 28, 2008   20.00

■ **2015, September 17. Animals of the First World War**
Sheet of 10 1st class Union Flag as February 28, 2008   20.00

BRITISH STAMP MARKET VALUES 2024   335

COMMEMORATIVE SHEETS

■ **2015, September 25. 30th Anniversary of Danger Mouse**
Sheet of 10 1st class Union Flag as February 28, 2008   26.00

■ **2016, January 12. 60th Anniversary of The Duke of Edinburgh's Award**
Sheet of 10 1st class Union Flag as February 28, 2008   20.00

■ **2016, March 8. 80th Anniversary of Oor Wullie**
Sheet of 10 1st class Scottish Flag as November 30, 2006   20.00

■ **2016, March 8. 80th Anniversary of The Broons**
Sheet of 10 1st class Scottish Flag as November 30, 2006   20.00

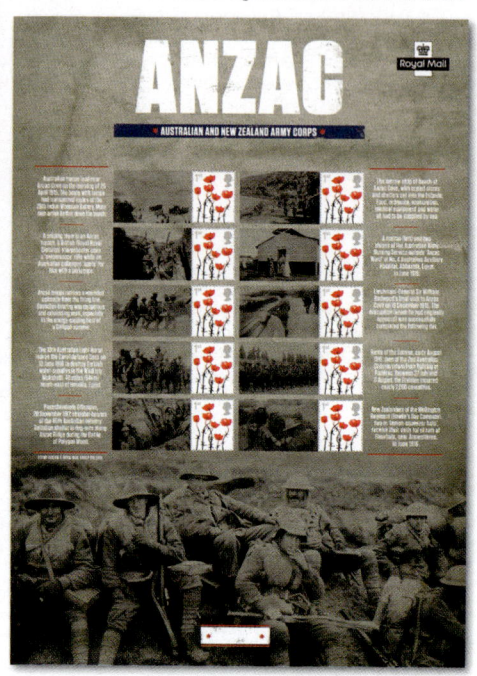

ANZAC, 2016

■ **2016, April 25. Australian and New Zealand Army Corps (ANZAC)**
Sheet of 10 1st class Poppies as January 26, 2010   20.00

■ **2016, May 18. Farewell Boleyn (West Ham United FC)**
Sheet of 10 1st class Union Flag as February 28, 2008   20.00

■ **2016, August 30. Eddie Stobart**
Sheet of 10 1st class Union Flag as October 22, 2001   26.00

■ **2016, October 14. 950th Anniversary of the Battle of Hastings**
Sheet of 10 1st class English Flag as April 23, 2007   20.00

■ **2017, May 25. 50th Anniversary of the Lisbon Lions**
Sheet of 10 1st class Scottish Flag as November 30, 2006   20.00

■ **2017, June 13. 30th Anniversary of The Princess Royal**
Sheet of 10 1st class Union Flag as October 22, 2001   20.00

■ **2017, June 30. Celebrating Canada**
Sheet of 10 1st class Firework as October 17, 2006   20.00

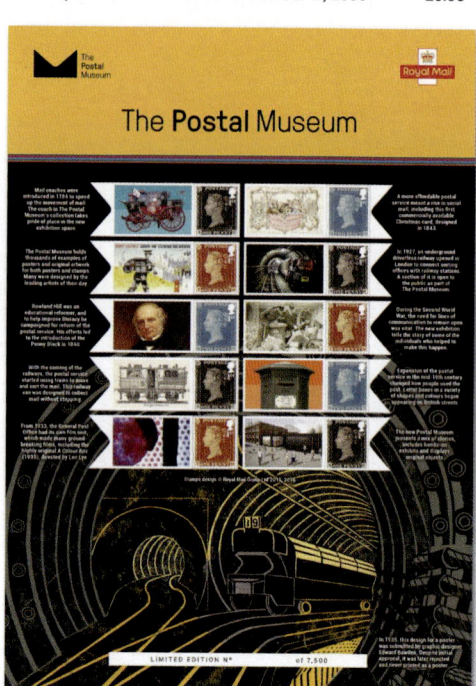

The Postal Museum, 2017

■ **2017, September 13. Opening of The Postal Museum**
Sheet of 10 1st class Penny Black, Penny Red and Twopenny Blue as May 6, 2015, and February 18, 2016   22.00

■ **2018, June 1. 150th Anniversary of the Trades Union Congress**
Sheet of 10 1st class Seal as January 26, 2010   22.00

■ **2018, October 10. United for Wildlife**
Sheet of 10 1st Seal as January 26, 2010   22.00

336   BRITISH STAMP MARKET VALUES 2024

STAMP POSTAL AUCTIONS

Held every few months with good selection of GB, Commonwealth and World, also Cigarette Cards. Suit both collectors and dealers. Keen estimates and no buyer premiums.

Free catalogue from:

G, Sharples, 5, The Knowle Bispham, Blackpool FY2 0RY

Tel: 01253 356267

email: sharples601@yahoo.co.uk

You won't regret it

PRESENTATION PACKS

PRESENTATION PACKS

In this section, prices are quoted for packs in mint condition only.

Presentation packs have been issued regularly for special stamp issues since 1964, and definitives since 1967, but many collectors regard the packs sold in 1960 (which were also marketed in the USA and therefore also found priced in US dollars) as the forerunners of these collectables.

Packs issued by Royal Mail in foreign language and other special versions are listed in this section, but those produced privately, commercially sponsored or not placed on general sale are outside the scope of this publication.

'FORERUNNERS'

Wilding definitives 'forerunner' pack, 1960

■ 1960

Wilding definitives (priced in Sterling)	£200
Wilding definitives (priced in Dollars)	£325
Phosphor-graphite definitives (priced in Sterling)	£200
Phosphor-graphite definitives (priced in Dollars)	£325
Regional definitives (priced in Sterling)	£200
Regional definitives (priced in Dollars)	£325
Castle high values (priced in Sterling)	£1,500
Castle high values (priced in Dollars)	£2,000
Castle high values (unpriced)	£1,750

SPECIAL ISSUES

Shakespeare Festival, 1964

■ 1964

Shakespeare Festival	17.00
Geographical Congress	£110
Botanical Congress	£125
Forth Road Bridge	£350

■ 1965

Churchill Commemoration	40.00
700th Anniversary of Parliament	65.00
Battle of Britain	45.00
Post Office Tower	13.00

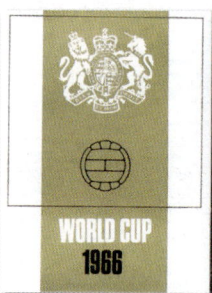

World Cup, 1966

■ 1966

Robert Burns	42.00
Westminster Abbey	40.00
World Cup	32.00
British Birds	16.00
British Technology	20.00
Battle of Hastings	12.00
Christmas	18.00

■ 1967

EFTA	50.00
British Wild Flowers	22.00
British Paintings	22.00
British Discovery and Invention	10.00

■ 1968

British Bridges	6.00
Anniversaries	5.50
British Paintings	5.00
British Paintings (German version)	30.00
Christmas	10.00
Christmas (German version)	30.00

■ 1969

British Ships	5.00
British Ships (German version)	40.00
British Ships (Cunard version)*	20.00
Concorde	8.00
Concorde (German version)	75.00
Anniversaries	4.50
Anniversaries (German version)	55.00
British Cathedrals	6.00
British Cathedrals (German version)	40.00

PRESENTATION PACKS

Investiture of the Prince of Wales	3.50
Investiture of the Prince of Wales (German version)	40.00
Investiture of the Prince of Wales (Welsh version)	25.00
Post Office Technology	5.00
Christmas	4.00

(*A version of the British Ships pack with slightly amended text was sold exclusively on the Cunard ocean liner QE2.)

General Anniversaries, 1970

■ 1970
Rural Architecture	3.50
General Anniversaries	4.50
Literary Anniversaries	5.00
Commonwealth Games	3.50
Philympia Exhibition	3.50
Christmas	5.00

■ 1971
Ulster Paintings	3.50
Literary Anniversaries	3.50
General Anniversaries	3.50
Modern University Buildings	5.50
Christmas	3.00

■ 1972
Polar Explorers	5.50
General Anniversaries	3.00
Village Churches	5.50
Village Churches (Belgica version)	7.00
BBC*	4.00
Christmas	3.00
Royal Silver Wedding	3.00
Royal Silver Wedding (Japanese version)	5.00

(*The BBC produced a souvenir pack in a similar format to the Royal Mail pack, titled '50th Anniversary of the BBC', as a gift to its staff; price £15.00)

■ 1973
European Communities	4.50
British Trees: Oak	2.00
British Explorers	3.00
County Cricket	4.00
British Painters	2.50
Inigo Jones	2.00
Parliamentary Conference	2.00

Royal Wedding	2.00
Christmas	2.50

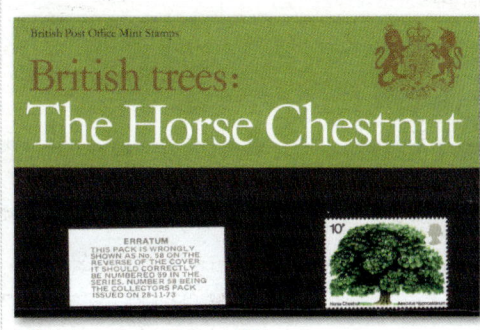

British Trees: Horse Chestnut, 1974

■ 1974
British Trees: Horse Chestnut	2.00
Fire Service	2.25
UPU	2.75
Medieval Warriorss	2.25
Winston Churchill	2.25
Christmas	2.25

■ 1975
J. M. W. Turner	2.25
Architectural Heritage Year	2.25
Sailing	2.00
Public Railways	3.00
Inter–Parliamentary Union Conference	1.50
Jane Austen	9.00
Christmas	2.00

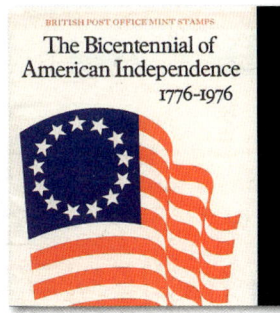

Bicentennial of American Independence, 1976

■ 1976
Telephones	2.00
Social Reformers	2.00
Bicentennial of American Independence	1.25
Royal National Rose Society	2.00
Cultural Traditions	2.00
British Printing	2.00
Christmas	2.00

BRITISH STAMP MARKET VALUES 2024   339

PRESENTATION PACKS

■ 1977
Racket Sports	2.00
Royal Institute of Chemistry	2.00
Silver Jubilee	2.00
Commonwealth Heads of Government	1.25
British Wildlife	2.50
Christmas	1.50

Energy Resources, 1978

■ 1978
Energy Resources	1.50
Historic Buildings	1.50
25th anniversary of Coronation	1.75
Horses	1.50
Cycling	1.50
Christmas	1.50

■ 1979
British Dogs	1.25
Spring Wild Flowers	1.00
Elections to European Assembly	1.25
Horse Racing Paintings	1.25
Year of the Child	3.75
Rowland Hill	1.00
Metropolitan Police	1.25
Christmas	1.50

■ 1980
Water Birds	2.25
Liverpool & Manchester Railway	1.25
London 1980 Exhibition	1.25
London Landmarks	1.00
Famous Authoresses	1.50
British Conductors	1.50
Sports Centenaries	1.00
Christmas	1.50

■ 1981
Folklore	1.50
Year of the Disabled	1.50
British Butterflies	1.75
British Landscapes	2.00
Royal Wedding	1.50
Duke of Edinburgh Awards	1.50
Fishing Industry	2.00
Christmas	1.50

Charles Darwin, 1982

■ 1982
Charles Darwin	2.00
Youth Organisations	2.00
British Theatre	1.50
Maritime Heritage	2.25
British Textiles	2.00
Information Technology Year	1.00
British Motor Cars	2.00
Christmas	2.00

■ 1983
British River Fish	2.00
Commonwealth Day	2.00
Engineering Achievements	1.50
British Army Uniforms	2.00
British Gardens	2.00
British Fairs	2.00
Christmas	2.00

■ 1984
College of Arms	2.00
British Cattle	2.00
Urban Renewal	2.00
CEPT/Elections to European Parliament	2.00
Greenwich Meridian	2.00
Mail Coaches	4.25
British Council	2.00
Christmas	2.50

■ 1985
Famous Trains	3.25
Insects	2.00
British Composers	2.50
Safety at Sea	2.00
350th Anniversary of Royal Mail	2.25
Arthurian Legend	2.25
British Film Year	2.50
Christmas	2.25

■ 1986
Industry Year	2.00
Halley's Comet	2.25
Queen's 60th Birthday	2.75
Nature Conservation	2.25

PRESENTATION PACKS

Domesday Book	2.25
Commonwealth Games/World Hockey Cup	2.25
Royal Wedding	1.00
Royal Air Force	3.25
Christmas	3.25

■ 1987
Flowers	2.25
Sir Isaac Newton	2.00
British Architects in Europe	2.00
St John Ambulance	2.00
Order of the Thistle	2.00
150th Anniversary of Accession of Queen Victoria	2.25
Studio Pottery	2.00
Christmas	2.25

■ 1988
Linnean Society	2.25
Welsh Bible	2.00
Sports Organisations	2.00
Transport and Mail Services	2.25
Bicentennary of Australian Settlement	2.25
Spanish Armada	2.00
Edward Lear	2.25
Christmas	2.25

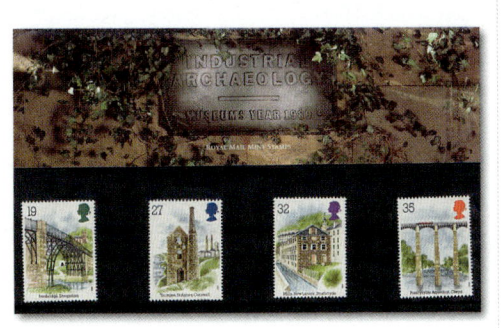

Industrial Archaeology, 1989

■ 1989
Royal Society for the Protection of Birds	2.25
Food and Farming Year	1.75
Anniversaries and Events	2.50
Games and Toys	2.00
Industrial Archaeology	2.00
Royal Microscopical Society	2.00
Lord Mayor's Show	2.00
Christmas	2.50

■ 1990
Penny Black Anniversary	3.50
RSPCA	2.50
Stamp World Exhibition and Glasgow	2.25
Queen's Awards for Export and Technology	2.25
Kew Gardens	2.00
Thomas Hardy	1.00
90th Birthday of the Queen Mother	3.50

Gallantry Awards	2.00
Astronomy	2.50
Christmas	3.25

■ 1991
Dog Paintings	2.50
Scientific Achievements	2.25
Europe in Space	2.50
World Student Games/Rugby World Cup	2.25
World Congress of Roses	2.50
Identification of Dinosaurs	3.25
Ordnance Survey	2.75
Christmas	3.25

Four Seasons: Wintertime, 1992

■ 1992
Four Seasons: Wintertime	2.40
40th Anniversary of Accession	3.50
Alfred, Lord Tennyson	2.50
International Events	2.75
Civil War	2.40
Gilbert and Sullivan Operas	2.50
Protection of the Environment	2.40
Single European Market	1.25
Christmas	2.75

■ 1993
Abbotsbury Swannery	5.25
John Harrison	2.50
World Orchid Conference	3.00
Contemporary Art	2.50
Roman Britain	2.40
Inland Waterways	2.50
Four Seasons: Autumn	2.75
Sherlock Holmes	5.25
Christmas	3.50

■ 1994
Age of Steam	3.50
25th Anniversary of Investiture of the Prince of Wales	3.00
Picture Postcards	3.00
Channel Tunnel	3.00
D-Day	4.00
Scottish Golf Courses	3.00
Four Seasons: Summertime	3.00
Medical Discoveries	3.00
Christmas	3.00

BRITISH STAMP MARKET VALUES 2024 341

PRESENTATION PACKS

Cats, 1995

1995
Cats	3.75
Four Seasons: Springtime	3.00
National Trust	3.00
Peace and Freedom	3.00
Novels of H. G. Wells	3.00
Shakespeare' Globe Theatre	3.00
Pioneers of Communications	3.00
Rugby League	3.00
Christmas	3.00

1996
Robert Burns	3.00
Wildfowl and Wetlands Trust	3.00
Cinema	3.00
European Football Championship	3.25
Olympic and Paralympic Games, Atlanta	3.00
Famous Women	3.00
Children's Television	3.00
Classic Sports Cars	3.50
Christmas	5.25

1997
King Henry VIII	6.00
Religious Anniversaries	4.00
Tales of Horror	3.50
British Aircraft Designers	4.00
All The Queen's Horses	3.50
Sub Post Offices	3.50
Enid Blyton	3.75
Christmas	5.25
Royal Golden Wedding Anniversary	5.25

Diana, Princess of Wales, 1998 (Welsh version)

1998
Endangered Species	4.75
Diana, Princess of Wales	8.50
Diana, Princess of Wales (Welsh version)	60.00
The Queen's Beasts	5.00
Lighthouses	4.00
Comedians	4.25
National Health Service	3.00
Children's Fantasy Novels	4.00
Notting Hill Carnival	3.00
British Land Speed Records	4.00
Christmas	4.00

(*A limited-edition Welsh language version of the Princess of Wales pack was available only at post offices in Wales.)

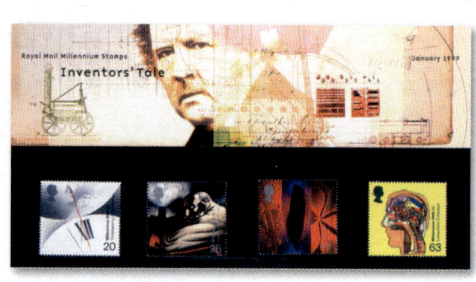

Inventors' Tale, 1999

1999
Inventors' Tale	3.50
Travellers' Tale	3.50
Patients' Tale	3.50
Settlers' Tale	3.50
Workers' Tale	3.50
Entertainers' Tale	3.50
Royal Wedding	2.50
Citizens' Tale	3.50
Scientists' Tale	3.50
Farmers' Tale	3.50
Soldiers' Tale	3.50
Christians' Tale	3.50
Artists' Tale	3.50
Millennium Timekeeper	12.00

2000
Above and Beyond	4.00
Fire and Light	4.00
Water and Coast	4.00
Life and Earth	4.00
Art and Craft	4.00
Her Majesty's Stamps	45.00
People and Places	4.00
Stone and Soil	4.00
Tree and Leaf	4.00
Queen Mother's 100th Birthday	12.00
Mind and Matter	4.00
Body and Bone	4.00
Spirit and Faith	4.00
Sound and Vision	4.00

PRESENTATION PACKS

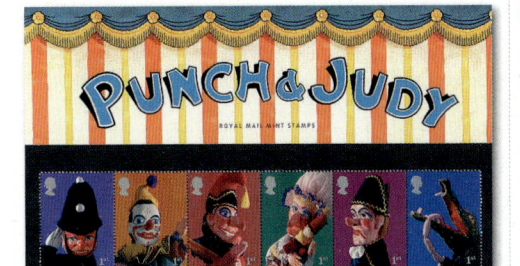

Punch and Judy, 2001

2001
Hopes for the Future	4.50
Occasions	10.00
Cats and Dogs	15.00
The Weather	10.00
Submarine Service	17.00
Double-Decker Buses	10.00
Fabulous Hats	4.50
Pond Life	5.50
Punch and Judy	8.50
Nobel Prizes	16.00
Flags and Ensigns	16.00
Christmas	8.00

2002
Just So Stories	15.00
Golden Jubilee	7.50
Occasions	10.00
British Coastlines	5.00
Circus	8.00
Queen Mother Memorial	6.00
Airliners	8.00
Football World Cup	7.00
Commonwealth Games	8.00
Peter Pan	7.50
Bridges of London	32.00
Astronomy	12.00
Pillar Boxes	8.00
Wilding Definitives, part I	27.00
Christmas	8.00

Rugby World Cup, 2003

2003
Birds of Prey	15.00
Occasions	11.00
Discovery of DNA	6.00
Fun Fruit and Veg	15.00
Extreme Endeavours	8.00
Wilding Definitives, part II	10.00
50th Anniversary of Coronation	15.50
21st Birthday of Prince William	8.50
British Journey: Scotland	8.00
Pub Signs	8.00
Classic Transport Toys	8.00
British Museum	8.00
Christmas	8.50
Rugby World Cup	22.00

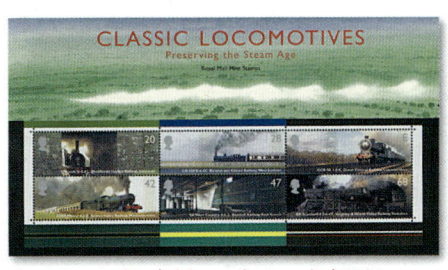

Classic Locomotives (miniature sheet version), 2004

2004
Classic Locomotives	11.00
Classic Locomotives (miniature sheet version)	12.00
Occasions	9.00
Lord of the Rings	15.50
British Journey: Northern Ireland	8.50
Entente Cordiale	9.00
Ocean Liners	7.50
Royal Horticultural Society	6.50
British Journey: Wales	5.00
Royal Society of Arts	6.50
Woodland Animals	15.50
Crimean War	7.00
Christmas	6.00

2005
Farm Animals	16.50
British Journey: South-West England	6.00
Jane Eyre	7.00
Magic Circle	9.00
50th Anniversary of the Castles Definitives	7.00
Royal Wedding	9.00
World Heritage Sites	8.00
Trooping the Colour	6.50
Motorcycles	6.00
London 2012 Host City	9.00
Changing Tastes in Britain	5.50
Classic ITV Programmes	5.50
The Ashes	4.75
Battle of Trafalgar	6.50
Christmas	6.50

BRITISH STAMP MARKET VALUES 2024 343

PRESENTATION PACKS

Modern Architecture, 2006

2006

Animal Tales	9.00
British Journey: England	15.50
Isambard Kingdom Brunel	6.50
Ice Age Animals	6.00
Queen's 80th Birthday	7.50
World Cup Winners	6.50
Modern Architecture	6.00
National Portrait Gallery	15.50
Victoria Cross	7.00
Sounds of Britain	6.50
Smilers	11.00
Christmas	10.00
Lest We Forget, issue I	8.00
Celebrating Scotland	6.00

Beside The Seaside, 2007

2007

The Beatles	12.00
Sea Life	14.50
The Sky at Night	7.50
World of Invention	7.00
Abolition of the Slave Trade	6.50
Celebrating England	5.50
Beside the Seaside	6.75
40th Anniversary of Machin Definitives	6.00
Grand Prix	6.50
Harry Potter	17.50
Scouting	6.50
Endangered Species: Birds	14.50
British Army Uniforms	7.50
Royal Diamond Wedding Anniversary	13.00
Christmas	10.50
Lest We Forget, issue II	7.00

2008

Ian Fleming's James Bond	15.50
Working Dogs	7.00
Houses of Lancaster and York	11.50
Celebrating Northern Ireland	5.50
Rescue at Sea	6.50
Endangered Species: Insects	14.50
Cathedrals	11.50
Classic Carry On & Hammer Films	7.00
Air Displays	7.00
Handover of Olympic Flag	32.00
RAF Uniforms	7.50
50th Anniversary of Country Definitives	14.00
Women of Distinction	6.50
Christmas	7.00
Lest We Forget, issue III	7.00

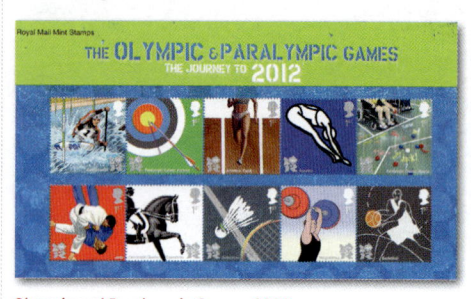

Olympic and Paralympic Games, 2009

2009

British Design Classics	16.00
Robert Burns	6.50
Charles Darwin	11.50
Celebrating Wales	5.50
Industrial Revolution	8.50
House of Tudor	13.50
Endangered Species: Plants	16.00
Mythical Creatures	8.00
Post Boxes	5.50
Fire and Rescue Services	7.50
Royal Navy Uniforms	8.00
Eminent Britons	16.00
Olympic and Paralympic Games, issue I	15.50
Christmas	10.00

2010

Classic Album Covers	20.00
Business Customised and Smilers Stamps	17.00
Girlguiding	7.00
Royal Society	16.00
Battersea Dogs & Cats Home	16.00
House of Stewart	15.00
Endangered Species: Mammals	14.50
Accession of George V/The King's Stamps	9.00
Britain Alone	14.00
House of Stuart	11.00
Olympic and Paralympic Games, issue II	15.50
Great British Railways	7.50

PRESENTATION PACKS

Medical Breakthroughs	8.00
Winnie-the-Pooh	12.50
Christmas	11.50

■ 2011

FAB. The Genius of Gerry Anderson	13.00
Classic Locomotives of England	7.50
Musicals	12.50
Magical Realms	10.50
WWF	17.00
Royal Shakespeare Company	14.00
Royal Wedding	14.00
Morris & Co	8.50
Thomas the Tank Engine	13.50
Olympic and Paralympic Games, issue III	15.00
Crown Jewels	10.50
First UK Aerial Post	5.75
House of Hanover	13.00
UK A–Z, part 1	15.00
Christmas	10.50

House of Windsor and Saxe-Coburg Gotha, 2012

■ 2012

Roald Dahl	21.00
House of Windsor and Saxe-Coburg Gotha	13.00
Diamond Jubilee (miniature sheet)	9.00
Britons of Distinction	15.50
Classic Locomotives of Scotland	7.75
Comics	15.50
UK A–Z, part 2	21.00
Great British Fashion	14.50
Diamond Jubilee (set)	18.00
Charles Dickens	15.00
Welcome to the Olympic Games	22.00
Welcome to the Paralympic Games	10.00
Memories of London 2012	20.00
Space Science	9.50
Christmas	13.00

■ 2013

London Underground	15.50
Jane Austen	10.50
Doctor Who	21.00
Great Britons	15.50
Football Heroes	18.00
Royal Portraits	13.50
Classic Locomotives of Northern Ireland	9.00
Butterflies	15.50
Andy Murray	7.00

British Auto Legends	16.50
Merchant Navy	14.00
Dinosaurs	15.50
Christmas	12.00
Children's Christmas	11.00

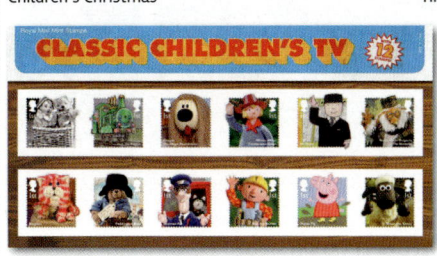

Classic Children's TV, 2014

■ 2014

Classic Children's TV	16.00
Working Horses	10.50
Classic Locomotives of Wales	8.50
Remarkable Lives	14.50
Buckingham Palace	14.00
Great British Film	14.50
Sustainable Fish	14.50
Commonwealth Games	12.50
First World War 1914	11.00
Seaside Architecture	16.50
Prime Ministers	13.00
Christmas	13.50

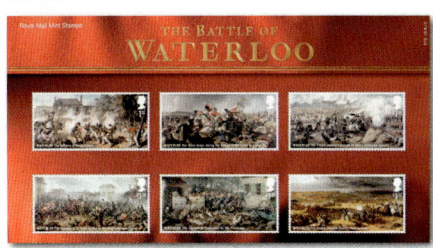

Battle of Waterloo, 2015

■ 2015

Alice's Adventures in Wonderland	26.00
Smilers	11.50
Inventive Britain	15.00
Bridges	15.50
Comedy Greats	13.50
175th anniversary of the Penny Black	11.50
First World War 1915	11.50
Magna Carta	13.50
Battle of Waterloo	18.00
Battle of Britain	12.50
Bees	20.00
Long To Reign Over Us	10.50
Rugby World Cup	13.00
Star Wars (issue 1)	20.00
Christmas	16.00

PRESENTATION PACKS

Royal Mail 500, 2016

■ 2016
Shackleton and the Endurance Expedition	18.00
Royal Mail 500	16.00
British Humanitarians	10.50
Shakespeare	18.00
The Queen's 90th Birthday	17.00
Animail	10.50
First World War 1916	18.00
Pink Floyd	25.00
Beatrix Potter	20.00
Landscape Gardens	13.50
The Great Fire of London	12.50
Agatha Christie	15.00
Mr. Men and Little Miss	20.00
Christmas	18.00

Racehorse Legends, 2017

■ 2017
Ancient Britain	16.00
Windsor Castle	18.00
David Bowie	19.00
Racehorse Legends	16.50
Songbirds	14.00
50th Anniversary of the Machin	23.00
Windmills and Watermills	12.50
Landmark Buildings	14.00
First World War 1917	11.50
Classic Toys	14.00
Ladybird Books	15.00
Star Wars (issue 2)	12.00
Christmas	21.00
Royal Wedding: Platinum Anniversary	14.00

■ 2018
Game of Thrones	18.00
Votes for Women	15.00
RAF Centenary	20.00
Reintroduced Species	13.00
Owls	18.00
Royal Wedding	8.50
Royal Academy of Arts	12.00
Dad's Army	23.00
Hampton Court Palace	18.50
Captain Cook and Endeavour Voyage	16.50
The Old Vic	17.00
First World War 1918	11.50
Harry Potter	18.00
Christmas	25.00
Prince of Wales' 70th Birthday	11.50

Leonardo da Vinci, 2019

■ 2019
Stamp Classics	11.50
Leonardo da Vinci	18.00
Marvel	20.00
Birds of Prey	15.00
British Engineering	21.00
Bicentenary of Queen Victoria	21.00
75th Anniversary of D-Day	19.00
Curious Customs	15.00
Forests	13.00
Elton John	23.00
Royal Navy Ships	17.50
Cricket World Cup Winners	16.00
The Gruffalo	20.00
Christmas	17.00
Star Wars (issue 3)	22.00

■ 2020
Video Games	23.00
Visions of the Universe	15.00
James Bond	20.00
The Romantic Poets	14.50
End of the Second World War	24.00
Coronation Street	24.00
Roman Britain	16.00
Queen	26.00
Palace of Westminster	21.00
Sherlock	22.00
Rupert Bear	16.00
Brilliant Bugs	14.00
Christmas	20.00
Star Trek	26.00

PRESENTATION PACKS

Paul McCartney 2021

■ 2021

National Parks	24.00
United Kingdom: A Celebration	9.00
Only Fools and Horses	26.00
Legend of King Arthur	31.00
Classic Science Fiction	18.00
The War of the Roses	20.00
Paul McCartney	27.00
Prince Philip	10.00
Dennis & Gnasher	22.00
Wild Coasts	23.00
Industrial Revolutions	21.00
British Army Vehicles	26.00
DC Collection	26.00
Rugby Union	20.00
Christmas	24.00

■ 2022

The Rolling Stones	27.00
The Queen's Platinum Jubilee	18.00
Stamp Designs of David Gentleman	11.00
The FA Cup	26.00
Heroes of the Covid Pandemic	12.00
Migratory Birds	16.00
Women of World War II	26.00
Cats	21.00
Pride	19.00
Commonwealth Games	19.00
Transformers	29.00
Royal Marines	30.00
Aardman Classics	31.00
Christmas	15.00
In Memoriam: Queen Elizabeth II	11.00
Tutankhamun	31.00

■ 2023

Iron Maiden	29.00
X-Men	26.00
Flying Scotsman	29.00
Flowers	19.00
The Legend of Robin Hood	19.00
King Charles III: A New Reign	12.00
Blackadder	32.00
Warhammer	30.00
Windrush: 75 Years	20.00
River Wildlife	15.00

LOW-VALUE DEFINITIVES

Low-value definitives, 1971

1967	½d to 1/9	7.50
1967	½d to 1/9 (German version)	£100
1971	½p to 9p	6.50
1971	½p to 9p (Scandinavia tour)	18.00
1971	½p to 10p	27.00
1977	½p to 50p	4.50
1981	2½p to 75p (pack No129a)	12.00
1983	½p to 75p (pack No1)	25.00
1984	½p to 75p	22.00
1987	1p to 75p	25.00
1988	14p to 35p	6.25
1989	15p to 37p	5.50
1990	Penny Black Anniversary issue	4.00
1990	10p to 33p	5.75
1991	1p to 75p	25.00
1991	6p to 39p	6.00
1993	self-adhesive booklet	20.00
1993	19p to 41p	5.00
1995	1p to £1	32.00
1996	20p to 63p	6.00
1997	2nd and 1st	4.00
1997	26p and 1st	4.50
1998	2nd, 1st, 1p to £1	14.00
1999	7p to 64p	10.00
2000	Millennium 1st	3.50
2000	Jeffery Matthews Colour Palette	80.00
2000	8p to 65p	7.00
2002	2nd, 1st, 1p to £1	15.00
2002	37p to 68p	4.25
2002	Wildings (issue 1)	27.00
2002	Definitives Collection folder, containing the low values pack (2002), high values pack (2002) and country packs (2001-02)	32.00
2003	Worldwide and Europe	5.50
2003	Wildings (issue 2)	10.00
2004	1st, Worldwide Postcard, 7p to 43p	10.00
2005	1p, 2p, 5p, 9p, 10p, 20p, 35p, 40p, 42p, 46p, 47p, 50p, 68p, £1, plus self-adhesive 2nd, 1st, Europe, Worldwide and postcard	50.00
2005	Definitives Collection folder, containing the low values pack (2005), high values pack (2003), country packs (2003) and country 42p values pack (2005)	32.00
2006	37p to 72p	10.00
2006	Pricing in Proportion	7.00
2007	16p to 78p	8.50

BRITISH STAMP MARKET VALUES 2024 **347**

PRESENTATION PACKS

2007	1p to £1 ruby	37.50
2008	15p to 81p	4.00
2009	2nd to £1	9.00
2009	17p to 90p	7.00
2010	Definitives Collection folder, containing 1p to £1.46, plus Europe, Worldwide, Worldwide Postcard and 'Recorded Signed For'	50.00
2010	Low values in current use	23.00
2010	Special Delivery	23.00
2011	1p to £1.65	14.00
2012	Olympic and Paralympic Games	12.00
2012	1st, 1st Large, 87p, £1.28, £1.90	11.00
2013	1p to £1 in new colour palette	8.00
2013	78p to £1.88 and 'Royal Mail Signed For'	13.00
2014	81p to £2.15	10.00
2015	£1.33 to £3.30	21.00
2016	£1.05	10.00
2017	£1.17 to £2.55	16.00
2018	£1.25 to £2.65	14.00
2019	£1.35 to £3.60	26.00
2020	£1.42 to £3.82	30.00
2020	£1.70 to £4.20	16.00
2022	2nd, 2nd Large, 1st, 1st Large	12.00
2022	1p to £1	11.00
2022	£1.85 to £4.20	20.00
2023	2nd, 2nd Large, 1st, 1st Large	12.50
2023	£2.20	6.00

HIGH-VALUE DEFINITIVES

£10 definitive, 1993

1969	2/6 to £1	15.00
1969	2/6 to £1 (German version)	60.00
1970	10p to 50p	7.00
1971	20p to £1	10.00
1977	£1 to £5 (pack no. 91)	13.50
1987	£1 to £5 (pack no. 13)	£125
1987	£1.60	19.00
1988	Castles £1 to £5	16.00
1992	Castles £1 to £5	16.00
1993	£10	30.00
1995	£3	14.00
1997	Castles £1.50 to £5	65.00
1999	£1.50 to £5 (Enschedé)	34.00
2000	£1.50 to £5 (De La Rue)	29.00
2003	£1.50 to £5 (gravure)	19.00
2009	£1.50 to £5 with security features	20.00
2017	£5 65th Anniversary of Accession	17.50
2022	£2 to £5	17.00

COUNTRY DEFINITIVES

Scotland definitives, 1983

■ Northern Ireland

1970	3d, 4d sepia, 4d red, 5d, 9d, 1/3, 1/6	3.50
1971	2½p, 3p, 5p, 7½p	2.50
1974	3p, 3½p, 5½p, 8p	3.00
1974	3p, 3½p, 4½p, 5½p, 8p	3.00
1976	6½p, 8½p, 10p, 11p	2.00
1981	7p, 9p, 10½p, 11½p, 12p, 13½p, 14p, 15p, 18p, 22p	6.00
1983	10p, 12½p, 16p, 20½p, 26p, 28p	13.00
1984	10p, 13p, 16p, 17p, 22p, 26p, 28p, 31p	10.00
1987	12p, 13p, 17p, 18p, 22p, 26p, 28p, 31p	14.00
1999	19p, 26p, 38p, 64p	14.00
2000	1st, 40p, 65p	12.50
2001	2nd, 1st, E, 65p	5.00
2003	2nd, 1st, E, 68p	5.50

■ Scotland

1970	3d, 4d sepia, 4d red, 5d, 6d, 9d, 1/3, 1/6	7.50
1971	2½p, 3p, 5p, 7½p	2.50
1974	3p, 3½p, 5½p, 8p	3.00
1974	3p, 3½p, 4½p, 5½p, 8p	3.00
1976	6½p, 8½p, 10p, 11p	2.00
1981	7p, 9p, 10½p, 11½p, 12p, 13½p, 14p, 15p, 18p, 22p	6.00
1983	10p, 12½p, 16p, 20½p, 26p, 28p	13.00
1984	10p, 13p, 16p, 17p, 22p, 26p, 28p, 31p	10.00
1987	12p, 13p, 17p, 18p, 22p, 26p, 28p, 31p	14.00
1999	2nd, 1st, E, 64p	8.50
2000	65p	9.00
2002	2nd, 1st, E, 65p	15.00
2003	2nd, 1st, E, 68p	5.00

■ Wales

1970	3d, 4d sepia, 4d red, 5d, 9d, 1/6	5.50
1971	2½p, 3p, 5p, 7½p	2.50
1974	3p, 3½p, 5½p, 8p	3.00
1974	3p, 3½p, 4½p, 5½p, 8p	3.00
1976	6½p, 8½p, 10p, 11p	2.00
1981	7p, 9p, 10½p, 11½p, 12p, 13½p, 14p, 15p, 18p, 22p	6.00
1983	10p, 12½p, 16p, 20½p, 26p, 28p	13.00
1984	10p, 13p, 16p, 17p, 22p, 26p, 28p, 31p	10.00
1987	12p, 13p, 17p, 18p, 22p,26p, 28p, 31p	12.00
1997	20p, 26p, 37p, 63p	10.50
1999	2nd, 1st, E, 64p	7.50
2000	65p	8.50
2002	2nd, 1st, E, 65p	14.00
2003	2nd, 1st, E, 68p	5.00

PRESENTATION PACKS

■ England

2001	2nd, 1st, E, 65p	5.00
2003	2nd, 1st, E, 68p	5.00

Country definitives, 2012

■ All Countries
(comprising the stamps of Northern Ireland, Scotland and Wales up to 1998, and additionally England from 2002)

1988	14p, 19p, 23p, 32p (three countries)	9.00
1989	15p, 20p, 24p, 34p (three countries)	9.00
1990	17p, 22p, 26p, 37p (three countries)	9.00
1991	18p, 24p, 28p, 39p (three countries)	9.00
1993	19p, 25p, 30p, 41p (three countries)	9.00
1996	20p, 26p, 37p, 63p (three countries)	14.00
1998	20p (centre band), 26p, 37p, 63p (three countries)	15.00
2002	68p (four countries)	5.00
2004	40p (four countries)	6.00
2005	42p (four countries)	6.00
2006	44p, 72p (four countries)	10.00
2007	48p, 78p (four countries)	8.50
2008	50p, 81p (four countries)	10.00
2008	2nd, 1st, 50p, 81p (four countries)	38.00
2009	56p, 90p (four countries)	11.00
2010	60p, 97p (four countries)	15.00
2011	68p, £1.10 (four countries)	12.00
2012	87p, £1.28 (four countries)	17.00
2013	88p (four countries)	7.00
2014	97p (four countries)	7.50
2015	£1, £1.33 (four countries)	22.00
2016	£1.05 (four countries)	16.50
2017	£1.17, £1.40 (four countries)	19.00
2018	2nd to £1.45 (four countries)	28.00
2019	£1.35, £1.55 (four countries)	20.00
2020	£1.42, £1.63 (four countries)	21.00
2020	£1.70 (four countries)	20.00
2022	2nd, 1st, £1.85 (four countries)	24.00

Isle of Man definitives, 1971

■ Isle of Man

1971	2½p, 3p, 5p, 7½p	2.50

POSTAGE DUES

Postage dues, 1977

1971	½p to 5p, 10p, 20p, 50p, £1	28.00
1977	½p to £1	10.00
1982	1p to £5	26.00
1994	1p to £5	34.00

CHRISTMAS ISSUES

Christmas, 1985

1985	Christmas stamps (50 x 12p)	25.00
1986	Christmas stamps (36 x 13p)	7.00
1987	Christmas stamps (36 x 13p)	6.00

GREETINGS ISSUES

Memories, 1992

1992	Memories	15.00
1993	Gift giving	15.00
1994	Messages	15.00
1995	Art	15.00
1996	Cartoons	15.00
1997	Flowers	15.00

PRESENTATION PACKS

SPECIAL PACKS

British Films, 1985

Year	Description	Price
1971	NABA Exhibition (definitives ½p to £1 and postage dues)	85.00
1972	Belgica Exhibition (1971 Christmas and 1972 Village Churches sets)	5.00
1972	Royal Silver Wedding	2.00
1973	County Cricket	4.00
1973	Palace of Westminster (Parliamentary Conference set)	4.00
1974	Winston Churchill	2.50
1975	Railways	2.50
1977	Silver Jubilee	2.00
1978	25th Anniversary of Coronation	2.00
1981	Royal Wedding	2.00
1982	Electronic Post (Information Technology set)	£175
1984	Royal Mail (Mail Coaches set)	4.00
1985	British Films	5.00
1986	The Queen's Birthday	5.00
1988	Australian Bicentennary	7.50
1990	Penny Black Anniversary (set of five stamps and miniature sheet)	10.50
1994	Channel Tunnel (joint issue with France)	35.00
1997	Royal Golden Wedding (Queen's Horses and Golden Wedding sets)	22.00
2000	Stamp Show 2000 (mint and cancelled miniature sheets)	70.00
2000	Stamp Show 2000 (The Definitive Portrait, Profile On Print and Special By Design prestige stamp books)	£100
2004	Entente Cordiale (joint issue with France)	12.00
2005	World Heritage (joint issue with Australia)	25.00
2008	Lest We Forget collection (2006, 2007 and 2008 miniature sheets)	35.00
2009	Brilliant Britain collection (2006 Celebrating Scotland, 2007 Celebrating England, 2008 Celebrating Northern Ireland and 2009 Celebrating Wales miniature sheets)	30.00
2009	Military Uniforms collection (2007, 2008, and 2009 miniature sheets)	30.00
2011	Harry Potter Heroes and Villains (Magical Realms block of 10)	20.00

FACSIMILE PACKS

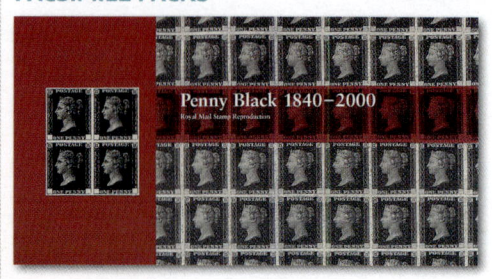

Penny Black, 2000

Year	Description	Price
2000	1840 Penny Black (Stamp Show 2000)	60.00
2010	1929 PUC £1 (London 2010)	17.50
2011	1841 Penny Red (170th anniversary)	9.00
2012	1948 Olympic Games set (London Olympics)	35.00
2013	1913 Seahorses set (100th anniversary)	15.00
2014	Festival of Britain 2½d	11.00

MINIATURE SHEET PACKS

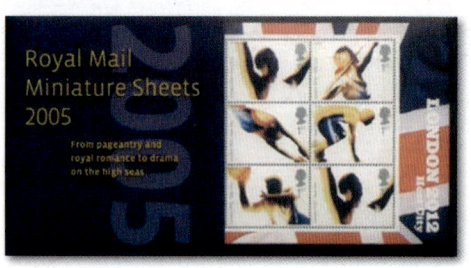

Miniature Sheets, 2005

Year	Description	Price
2005	Miniature Sheets collection	65.00
2006	Miniature Sheets collection	80.00
2007	Miniature Sheets collection	60.00
2008	Miniature Sheets collection	60.00
2009	Miniature Sheets collection	60.00
2010	Miniature Sheets collection	55.00
2011	Miniature Sheets collection	£130
2012	Miniature Sheets collection	60.00
2013	Miniature Sheets collection	70.00
2014	Miniature Sheets collection	40.00
2015	Miniature Sheets collection	70.00
2016	Miniature Sheets collection	70.00
2017	Miniature Sheets collection	85.00
2018	Miniature Sheets collection	85.00
2019	Miniature Sheets collection	90.00
2020	Miniature Sheets collection	85.00
2021	Miniature Sheets collection	90.00
2022	Miniature Sheets collection	90.00

YEAR PACKS & YEAR BOOKS

YEAR BOOKS & PACKS

In this section, prices are quoted for packs in mint condition only.

YEAR PACKS

Year Pack, 1967

1967 year pack	5.00
1968 year pack (blue cover)	3.50
1968 year pack (red cover)	3.50
1968 year pack (German version)	£100
1969 year pack	10.00
1970 year pack	15.00
1971 year pack	22.00
1972 year pack	14.00
1973 year pack	12.50
1974 year pack	6.00
1975 year pack	5.00
1976 year pack	7.50
1977 year pack	5.00
1978 year pack	4.50
1979 year pack	6.00
1980 year pack	7.00
1981 year pack	9.50
1982 year pack	12.50
1983 year pack	15.00
1984 year pack	17.00
1985 year pack	17.00
1986 year pack	17.00
1987 year pack	17.00
1988 year pack	17.00
1989 year pack	17.00
1990 year pack	19.00
1991 year pack	20.00
1992 year pack	20.00
1993 year pack	22.00
1994 year pack	29.00
1995 year pack	27.00
1996 year pack	32.00
1997 year pack	34.00
1998 year pack	42.00
1999 year pack	65.00
2000 year pack	65.00
2001 year pack	70.00
2002 year pack	68.00
2003 year pack	76.00
2004 year pack	70.00
2005 year pack	70.00
2006 year pack	70.00
2007 year pack	£125
2008 year pack	90.00

Year Pack, 2009

2009 year pack	£110
2010 year pack	£140
2011 year pack	£150
2012 year pack	£180
2013 year pack	£150
2014 year pack	£160
2015 year pack	£200
2016 year pack	£230
2017 year pack	£275
2018 year pack	£260
2019 year pack	£200
2020 year pack	£230
2021 year pack	£225
2022 year pack	£300

YEAR BOOKS

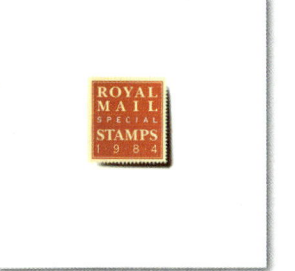

Year Book, 1984

1984 year book	45.00
1985 year book	30.00
1986 year book	25.00
1987 year book	14.00
1988 year book	14.00
1989 year book	15.00
1990 year book	18.00
1991 year book	18.50
1992 year book	19.00
1993 year book	22.00
1994 year book	23.00
1995 year book	23.00
1996 year book	22.00
1997 year book	27.00
1998 year book	37.00
1999 year book	50.00
2000 year book	50.00
2001 year book	50.00
2002 year book	50.00
2003 year book	55.00
2004 year book	60.00
2005 year book	60.00
2006 year book	75.00
2007 year book	90.00
2008 year book	£100

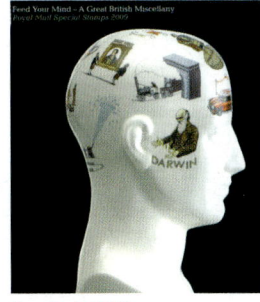

Year Book, 2009

2009 year book	£100
2010 year book	£120
2011 year book	£135
2012 year book	£250
2013 year book	£160
2014 year book	£165
2015 year book	£185
2016 year book	£300
2017 year book	£225
2018 year book	£200
2019 year book	£250
2020 year book	£250
2021 year book	£275
2022 year book	£350

Hawid Stamp Mounts

Size of stamp width x height	Ref. № black	Ref. № clear
Strips (pack of 25) £8.50		
217 x 21 mm	338554	326337
217 x 24 mm	335261	310224
217 x 25 mm	312198	316987
217 x 26 mm	323419	300986
217 x 27 mm	317187	333260
217 x 28 mm	366348	366342
217 x 29 mm	309167	328498
217 x 30 mm	324076	315369
217 x 31 mm	303713	310028
217 x 32 mm	340164	340165
217 x 33 mm	321470	303297
217 x 34 mm	300624	340166
217 x 35 mm	307169	321505
Strips (pack of 25) £9.95		
217 x 36 mm	336455	328328
217 x 37 mm	366349	366343
217 x 39 mm	302045	305002
217 x 40 mm	300452	303302
217 x 41 mm	337387	337353
217 x 42 mm	366350	x -
217 x 43 mm	320893	319764
217 x 44 mm	326937	300427
217 x 46 mm	366351	366345
217 x 48 mm	301752	302144
217 x 49 mm	308536	317809
217 x 51 mm	366352	366346
217 x 52 mm	337699	303174
217 x 53 mm	340168	340171
217 x 55 mm	302092	315368

Size of stamp width x height	Ref. № black	Ref. № clear
Strips (pack of 10) £8.50		
217 x 60 d mm	328987	311954
217 x 64 d mm	340169	340172
217 x 66 d mm	302426	309518
217 x 68 d mm	340170	340173
217 x 70 d mm	316852	334941
217 x 72 d mm	311100	336582
217 x 75 d mm	333277	316874
217 x 76 d mm	366354	366347
217 x 78 d mm	307779	302532
217 x 82 d mm	316488	303262
217 x 86 d mm	332423	328279

10% OFF HAWID ORDERS OVER £60

20% OFF HAWID ORDERS OVER £100

Assorted Strips	Ref. № black	Ref. № clear	Price Per pack
50 strips (217 mm long) 10x 30 mm, 10x 40 mm, 10x 52 mm, 10x 70 mm, 10x 86 mm	366369	366368	£15.95
100 strips (217 mm long) 10x 26 mm, 10x 30 mm, 10x 35 mm, 10x 40 mm, 10x 44 mm, 10x 52 mm, 10x 60 mm, 10x 70 mm, 10x 76 mm, 10x 86 mm	366371	366370	£27.95
200 strips (217 mm long) 20x 26 mm, 20x 30 mm, 20x 35 mm, 20x 40 mm, 20x 44 mm, 20x 52 mm, 20x 60 mm, 20x 70 mm, 10x 76 mm, 10x 86 mm, 10x 100 d mm, 10x 130 d mm	366373	366372	£54.95
500 strips (217 mm long) 40x 26 mm, 40x 30 mm, 50x 35 mm, 40x 40 mm, 50x 44 mm, 40x 52 mm, 40x 60 mm, 40x 70 mm, 30x 76 mm, 30x 86 mm, 30x 80 mm d, 30x 100 d mm, 20x 130 d mm, 20x 160 d mm	366379	366378	£109.95

Size of stamp width x height		Ref. № black	Ref. № clear
Small Block mounts £3.95			
122 x 90 mm	(p. of 10)	1280	2280
Block mounts £8.50			
130 x 85 d mm	(p. of 10)	330124	329381
148 x 105 d mm	(p. of 10)	319405	331350
160 x 120 d mm	(p. of 10)	302694	331828
162 x 115 s mm	(p. of 10)	327637	310328
165 x 95 s mm	(p. of 10)	312937	301081
Block mounts £14.95			
210 x 170 d mm	(p. of 10)	303792	303422
148 x 210 d mm	(p. of 10)	331731	327610
297 x 210 d mm	(p. of 5)	332741	327704

d = double seam / s = Schaufix

Ask for our FREE Stamp and Accessory price list
All mount orders are POST FREE!

DAUWALDERS *of Salisbury*
42 Fisherton Street, Salisbury, SP2 7RB
Telephone: 01722-412100
www.worldstamps.co.uk

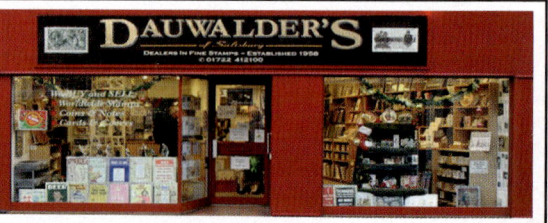

OUR SHOP is open 6 full days each week in centre of Salisbury

GB QUEEN VICTORIA ONLY

HOW TO ORDER

Payment accepted by:

Visa / Debit / Cheque Or Postal Order

Please add £2.50 to stamp orders

SHOP OPEN 6 full days each week

[5] WE HAVE AVAILABLE PART RECONSTRUCTIONS, PRICES UPON REQUEST.
WE ALSO SELL LARGE CARTRIDGE SHEETS TO ACCOMMODATE 240 LETTERINGS. Each £3.00

[2] 1847 EMBOSSED SERIES
SG54, 57 and 59,
6d 10d and 1/- all good used
Cut to shape SG cat £3500
OUR PRICE:
Each £85 (set of 3)

[3] SG 40 C10 from a very large stock we offer plated (mainly) examples (SG cat from £12 each)

100 stamps assorted plates sound used	£45
SG40 1d rose 100 stamps seconds	£24
SG40 1d rose 500 stamps seconds	£90

[6] SG8 1d reds used.
2-3 margins,
or plating copies
per 50: £35
per 100: £60

[6A] One Penny QV 1d Rose Red stamped envelopes
Good used per 10
Unsorted plates

£4.50 each - £40 per 10

[4] SG 43 1d Red plates.
The complete series 71-224, fine used, (less 77)
£250

Do. To include the very scarce Plate 225 (pl 71-225) fine used
£520

Do. Cheaper quality used stamps (will have perf trim or other small faults) (pl 71-225)
£250

[7] Penny Red Plates
SG43 1d plate numbers from an accumulation of over 100,000 unchecked for numbers or postmarks.
The quality of these is 50% good.

Per 100 £35

Per 500 £160

AS ABOVE
but all sound stamps, GU-FU, per 100 £55

[8] SG48
½ d rose,
plating copies

per 25 £24 - per 50 £45

[9] SG48
½d rose
plate PAIR

Good Used
£7.00

OUR BEST SELLER!
[10] 1858 2d Blue plate numbers
SG45 plates 7-15 (7 different)
good to fine used set
£60 (SG cat value £371)

[10A] 1870 ½d Rose plate
Numbers 1-20 (less plate 9)
in good used (14)
SG cat value totals £735!!!
£60

[11] SG 13-15
1841 2d Blue, plated examples.
Plate 3, 4 margin £30.00
Plate 3, 3 margin £9.50
Plate 4, 4 margin £27.00
Plate 4, 3 margin £9.00

[12] SG14 2d blue used,
plating copies, mainly 2-3 margins or better, with faults
Each: £4.00
per 10: £37 - per 25: £85

[13] SG45 2d blue plates,
second quality for plating.
per 25 £32.00
per 50 £60.00

[14] 1841 1d RED SHADES
The 1841 One Penny shades all four margins.
SG8 1d Red-Brown
SG8a very blued paper)
SG9 Pale red-brown
SG10 Deep red-brown.
All are Fine Used
and identified by plate.
(SG Cat £165)

OUR SPECIAL PRICE: £35.00

DAUWALDERS ORDER LINE   TEL: 01722 412100

ADVERTISING INDEX

AG Lajer	15
Arun Stamps	237
Alliance Auctions	4
BB Stamps	IFC
CDD	237
Dauwalders	352-353
Eric Paul	10
G.Sharples	337
Griffins Auctions	49
HW Wood	275
Jerwood Philatelics	281
John Lamonby	313
Magnet Insurance	305
Philatelink	233
Plumridge	255
Rowland Hill	237
Tony Lester	47
UPA	8-9, 78-79, 265, OBC
Warwick & Warwick	IBC